Clinical Psychology in Practice

To our team and all those trainees, service users, supervisors, colleagues and fellow trainers who have contributed both directly and indirectly to what we have learnt along our own professional journeys

Clinical Psychology in Practice

Edited by Helen Beinart, Paul Kennedy
and Susan Llewelyn

This edition first published 2009 by the British Psychological Society and Blackwell Publishing Ltd
© 2009 Blackwell Publishing Ltd

BPS Blackwell is an imprint of Blackwell Publishing, which was acquired by John Wiley & Sons in February 2007. Blackwell's publishing program has been merged with Wiley's global Scientific, Technical, and Medical business to form Wiley-Blackwell.

Registered Office
John Wiley & Sons Ltd, The Atrium, Southern Gate, Chichester, West Sussex, PO19 8SQ, UK

Editorial Offices
350 Main Street, Malden, MA 02148-5020, USA
9600 Garsington Road, Oxford, OX4 2DQ, UK
The Atrium, Southern Gate, Chichester, West Sussex, PO19 8SQ, UK

For details of our global editorial offices, for customer services, and for information about how to apply for permission to reuse the copyright material in this book please see our website at www.wiley.com/wiley-blackwell.

The right of Helen Beinart, Paul Kennedy and Susan Llewelyn to be identified as the author of the editorial material in this work has been asserted in accordance with the Copyright, Designs and Patents Act 1988.

Library of Congress Cataloging-in-Publication Data

Clinical psychology in practice / edited by Helen Beinart, Paul Kennedy, and Susan Llewelyn.
    p.   cm.
    Includes bibliographical references and index.
    ISBN 978-1-4051-6767-3 (pbk. : alk. paper) 1. Clinical psychology. I. Beinart, Helen. II. Kennedy, Paul, 1959– III. Llewelyn, Susan P.
    RC467.C58614 2009
    616.89–dc22

                                                         2009008320

A catalogue record for this book is available from the British Library.

Set in 10.5/13 pt Minion by SPi Publisher Services, Pondicherry, India
Printed and bound in Malaysia by KHL Printing Co Sdn Bhd

The British Psychological Society's free Research Digest e-mail service rounds up the latest research and relates it to your syllabus in a user-friendly way. To subscribe go to www.researchdigest.org.uk or send a blank e-mail to subscribe-rd@lists.bps.org.uk.

1   2009

Contents

About the Editors

Dr Helen Beinart is Clinical Director of the Oxford Doctoral Course in Clinical Psychology, where she has worked since 1994. Clinically, she works with children, young people and their families in a primary care setting. She trained in Cape Town and London and qualified as a Clinical Psychologist from the Institute of Psychiatry in 1979. She has worked in the NHS for the past 30 years as a clinician, service manager, consultant, supervisor, and trainer. She is Fellow of Harris Manchester College, University of Oxford. Over the past 15 years, she has been involved in clinical psychology training, supervisor training and research into the supervisory relationship. Prior to this she was Head of Child and Adolescent Health Clinical Psychology Services in Aylesbury and Kingston. Dr Beinart has chaired the Division of Clinical Psychology's Faculty for Children and Young People and was involved in providing psychological evidence to the Parliamentary Select Committee on Children's Mental Health. Professionally she has held several roles within the Division of Clinical Psychology and currently acts as National Assessor for senior appointments to the profession and as external adviser and teacher to a number of courses and services. She has a long-term interest in the development of professional competence and the contribution of clinical supervision and, in particular, supervisory relationships to the development of competent clinical psychologists.

Professor Paul Kennedy is Professor of Clinical Psychology at the University of Oxford, Academic Director on the Oxford Doctoral Course in Clinical Psychology, and Trust Head of Clinical Psychology based at the National Spinal Injuries Centre, Stoke Mandeville Hospital. He studied at the University of Ulster and Queens University, Belfast and has worked in clinical health psychology since graduating from his clinical training in 1984. Professor Kennedy is an active researcher with a broad portfolio of research on adjustment, coping and physical rehabilitation. He has published over 80 scientific papers for peer reviewed journals, been a chapter contributor to many books, and co-edited/edited a number of books on clinical health psychology and physical disability. He serves on the editorial board of the *Journal of Clinical Psychology in Medical Settings, Rehabilitation Psychology* and *Neurorehabilitation*. He was elected a Fellow of the British Psychological Society in 1999, served on the Committee of the Division of Health Psychology, and became a Fellow of Harris Manchester College, University of Oxford in 2001. He is founding Chair of both the Multidisciplinary Association of Spinal Cord Injury Professionals (MASCIP) and the European Spinal Psychologists Association (ESPA). In 2002 he was awarded the Distinguished Service Award by the American Association of Spinal Cord Injury Psychologists and Social Workers, and in 2005 he was awarded a visiting Fellowship to Australia by the New South Wales Government, Ministry of Science and Medical Research. He became Professor of Clinical Psychology in the University of Oxford in 2006 and is an enthusiastic scientist practitioner who enjoys the interplay between service provision, research and training.

Professor Susan Llewelyn has held the post of Director of the Oxford Doctoral Course in Clinical Psychology since 1997. She trained at Sheffield and Leeds University and has worked in both the NHS and University sectors in Nottingham, Sheffield, Dorset, Southampton and Edinburgh. She has a particular interest in the psychological therapies, and has published widely, particularly concerning process issues in psychotherapy. Her clinical work has concerned therapeutic interventions for adult survivors of childhood sexual abuse, and she has also trained in Cognitive Analytic Therapy. She is a Chartered Clinical Psychologist and Fellow of the British Psychological Society, past Chair of CTCP, Professor of Clinical Psychology at Oxford University, and Senior Research Fellow, Harris Manchester College, Oxford. She also has a particular interest in professional issues, leadership and teamwork, and was been awarded a postgraduate certificate in Higher Education leadership by Leicester University in 2006. She has written or co-authored six books and over one hundred academic and professional papers, and was an Associate Editor of *The Psychologist*. She also provides advice to the Oxford English Dictionary regarding psychological words and phrases, and has been a member of the Wiley-Blackwell strategy group for psychology.

List of Contributors

Dawn Bailham, Chartered Clinical Psychologist, Child and Adolescent and Mental Health Service, Clarendon House, 8–12 Station Road, Kettering, Northants NN15 7HH

Helen Beinart, Clinical Director, Oxford Doctoral Course in Clinical Psychology, University of Oxford, Isis Education Centre, Warneford Hospital, Oxford OX3 7JX

Sue Clohessy, Clinical Tutor and Supervisor Training Lead, Oxford Doctoral Course in Clinical Psychology, University of Oxford, Isis Education Centre, Warneford Hospital, Oxford OX3 7JX

Zoë Clyde, Consultant Clinical Psychologist, Chronic Fatigue Service, Cheviot House, Sutton Hospital, Cotswold Rd, Sutton SM2 5NF

Myra Cooper, Senior Research Tutor, Oxford Doctoral Course in Clinical Psychology, University of Oxford, Isis Education Centre, Warneford Hospital, Oxford OX3 7JX

Denise Cottrell, Macmillan Consultant Clinical Psychologist, Buckinghamshire Hospitals NHS Trust, Cancer Care and Haematology Unit, Stoke Mandeville Hospital, Mandeville Road, Aylesbury, Bucks HP21 8AL

Andrew Cuthbertson, Programme Director, Doctorate in Clinical Psychology, Parkside West Offices, University of Teeside, Middlesbrough TS1 3BA

Stephen Davies, Deputy Course Director, School of Psychology, University of Hertfordshire, College Lane Campus, Hatfield, Herts AL10 9AB

David Dean, Consultant Clinical Neuropsychologist, Heberden Unit, Amersham Hospital, Whielden Road, Amersham, Bucks HP7 0JD and Clinical and Admissions Tutor, Oxford Doctoral Course in Clinical Psychology, University of Oxford, Isis Education Centre, Warneford Hospital, Oxford OX3 7JX

Gráinne Fadden, Consultant Clinical Psychologist/Director, The Meriden West Midlands Family Programme, Birmingham and Solihull Mental Health NHS Foundation Trust, Tall Trees, The Uffculme Centre, Queensbridge Road, Moseley, Birmingham B13 8QY

Paul Flecknoe, Consultant Clinical Psychologist, Northamptonshire Service for the Treatment of Early Psychosis (N-STEP), Clarendon House, 8–12 Station Road, Kettering, Northants NN15 7HH

Kathryn Fordham, Clinical Psychologist, Child and Adolescent Mental Health Service, Clarendon House, 8–12 Station Road, Kettering, Northants NN15 7HH

Damian Gardner, Consultant Clinical Psychologist/Team Leader, St Mary's Hospital, London Road, Kettering, Northants NN15 7PW

Kim S. Golding, Consultant Clinical Psychologist, ISL, The Pines, Bilford Road, Worcester WR3 8PU

Cynthia A. Graham, Research Tutor, Oxford Doctoral Course in Clinical Psychology, University of Oxford, Isis Education Centre, Warneford Hospital, Oxford OX3 7JX

James Gray, Consultant Clinical Psychologist for Long Term Conditions, City and Hackney Teaching PCT, St Leonard's Primary Care Centre, Nuttall Street, London N1 5LZ

David S.J. Hawker, Clinical Psychologist, Psychological Health Services, InterHealth, 111 Westminster Bridge Road, London SE1 7HR

Antje Horsch, Academic Tutor, Oxford Doctoral Course in Clinical Psychology, University of Oxford, Isis Education Centre, Warneford Hospital, Oxford OX3 7JX and Clinical Psychologist, Berkshire Traumatic Stress Service, 25 Erleigh Road, Reading, Berks RG1 5LR

Paul Kennedy, Academic Director, Oxford Doctoral Course in Clinical Psychology, University of Oxford, Isis Education Centre, Warneford Hospital, Oxford OX3 7JX, Professor of Clinical Psychology, University of Oxford, and Trust Head of Clinical Psychology, Buckinghamshire Hospitals NHS Trust, Aylesbury, Bucks HP21 8AL

Nigel S. King, Consultant Clinical Neuropsychologist, Community Head Injury Service, The Camborne Centre, Jansel Square, Bedgrove, Aylesbury, Bucks HP21 7ET and Clinical Tutor, Oxford Doctoral Course in Clinical Psychology, University of Oxford, Isis Education Centre, Warneford Hospital, Oxford OX3 7JX

Adrienne Little, Consultant Clinical Psychologist/Head of Psychology and Psychological Therapy Services, Mental Health Older Adults, 1st Floor Administration, Maudsley Hospital, 115 Denmark Hill, London SE5 8AZ

Susan Llewelyn, Course Director, Oxford Doctoral Course in Clinical Psychology, University of Oxford, Isis Education Centre, Warneford Hospital, Oxford OX3 7JX and Professor of Clinical Psychology, University of Oxford

Claire Luthwood, Consultant Clinical Health Psychologist and Head of Clinical Health Psychology, Berkshire Healthcare NHS Foundation Trust, 25 Erleigh Road, Reading, Berks RG10 9QX

Annie Mitchell, Clinical Director, Doctorate in Clinical Psychology, School of Applied Psychosocial Studies, Faculty of Health and Social Work, University of Plymouth, Peninsula Allied Health Collaboration, College of St Mark and St John, Derriford Road, Plymouth, Devon PL6 8BH

Rachel Purtell, Folk.us Coordinator, Room 407, Noy Scott house, Royal Devon and Exeter Hospital, Barrack Road, Exeter EX2 5DW

Ann Rowland, Consultant Clinical Psychologist, Child and Adolescent Health Psychology Service, Buckinghamshire Primary Care Trust, Sue Nicholls Centre, Bierton Road, Aylesbury, Bucks HP20 1EG

Judith Samuel, Head of Psychology Services, Ridgeway Partnership (Oxfordshire Learning Disability NHS Trust), Slade House, Horspath Driftway, Headington, Oxford OX3 7JH

Stefan Schuller, Consultant Lead Psychologist for Psychosis, Oxon and Bucks Mental Health NHS Foundation Trust, May Davidson Building, Warneford Hospital, Oxford OX3 7JX

Rashmi Shankar, Consultant Clinical Psychologist, Berkshire Healthcare NHS Foundation Trust, Department of Clinical Psychology, Prospect Park Hospital, Honey End Lane, Reading, Berks RG30 4EJ

Selma Rikberg Smyly, Consultant Clinical Psychologist, Ridgeway Learning Disability NHS Trust, Abell house, Horspath Driftway, Headington, Oxford OX3 7JH

Penny Spinks, formerly Consultant Clinical Psychologist Paediatrics, Berkshire Healthcare NHS Trust

Paul Stallard, Consultant Clinical Psychologist/Professor of Clinical Psychology, University of Bath/Avon and Wiltshire Mental Health Partnership NHS Trust, Mental Health Research and Development Unit, 22–23 Eastwood, University of Bath, Bath BA2 7AY

Graham Turpin, Professor of Clinical Psychology/Unit Director, Department of Clinical Psychology, University of Sheffield, Western Bank, Sheffield S10 2TP

Kobus Van Rensburg, Consultant Clinical Psychologist, Transition and Liaison Team, St Mary's Hospital, London Road, Kettering, Northants NN15 7PW

Tim I. Williams, Consultant Clinical Psychologist, Berkshire Healthcare NHS Trust and Fellow, School of Psychology and Clinical Language Sciences, University of Reading, 3/5 Craven Road, Reading, Berks RG1 5LF

Rachel Woolrich, Clinical Psychologist, Oxford & Bucks Eating Disorder Services, Tindal Centre, Aylesbury, Bucks HP20 1HU

Preface

Knowing is not enough; we must apply.
Willing is not enough; we must do. (Goethe)

This book provides a clear, authoritative and lively introduction to the practice of clinical psychology. It outlines the unique characteristics of professional practice, which is to make use of empirically based, ethical and reflective interventions in order to reduce human distress, by working in partnership with clients, carers, families and systems. Evidence and theories about how difficulties develop and the best methods for ameliorating distress will be outlined within the context of psychological and biopsychosocial frameworks of emotional, health, relational, developmental, social and behavioural problems.

We wrote this book because we have a clear view of what a good and competent clinical psychologist is able to do, and what therefore comprise the essential elements of training. We hope it will provide an effective companion for all trainee practitioners to show how the profession works in practice, provide a good overview of competencies for the trained practitioner, and provide our colleagues, managers, and those who use and commission psychology services with a clear vision of what can be expected from a competent clinical psychologist. While we will make reference to academic and research evidence, this is not intended to be a reference text, but rather a helpful and authoritative source of approaches to the range of issues clinical psychologists are likely to face in practice.

Clinical psychology offers an alternative to other models in health care, such as the medical, psychiatric, forensic, moral or sociological. The rapid development of the profession out of an initial quasi-medical focus on psychiatry and child guidance has led to clinical psychologists progressively becoming able to identify their unique competencies and interventions, which call upon scientific as well as ethical practices. The book introduces and delineates those competencies and how they are applied in a range of clinical settings with a variety of client groups across the lifespan. The key issues that will recur throughout the book are likely to be awareness of the social context, the need for responsive and reflective practice, and respect for diversity and user perspectives. Examples and principles are provided which demonstrate the clinical psychologist in action, and explain why and how they work as they do.

Aimed at trainees as well as qualified psychologists and others in health and social care, the book aims not to oversimplify, but to explain succinctly the range of competencies which a psychologist is expected to possess, and how these can be applied in a variety of contexts. The book offers a unique partnership focus which reflects the nature of clinical psychology training, where academic, clinical and research aspects are offered in collaboration with clinical practitioners, who provide the clinical experience to foster the development of competencies in health and social care.

The structure and content of the book represent our belief that clinical psychology is an integration of academic theory, clinical practice and an evolving research base, delivered within an ethical and reflective framework. Contributors are drawn from both academic backgrounds and clinical practice, and most are involved in training tomorrow's practitioners. The range of topics covered in the short chapters cannot be comprehensive, because of the proposed size of this volume, but rather represent a demonstration of some significant innovations in practice as well as being clear examples of how competent clinical psychology is delivered in routine practice.

Helen Beinart, Paul Kennedy and Susan Llewelyn
Oxford 2008

Acknowledgements

The Editors would like to thank all the contributors for helping make this project such a positive experience. We are grateful for the quality of their contributions, as well as their responsiveness and support. We would also like to record our appreciation of Mrs Linda Hall who organised us well, attended to detail and efficiently administered this project. Her superb organisation made the editorial task a positive endeavour that ran exceptionally smoothly. Finally, we would all like to thank our families and close friends for being with us, tolerating our moments and making it all worthwhile.

Part I

Introduction

Philosophical, Practical and Ethical Underpinnings

1

The Key Elements of Clinical Psychology Practice

Susan Llewelyn, Helen Beinart and Paul Kennedy

Introduction

The profession of clinical psychology has grown exponentially over the past 50 years and, as this book will show, has demonstrated its value in a wide range of clinical contexts, thereby proving itself able to make a unique and important contribution to health and social care across the lifespan. It has developed from its origins in child guidance and the provision of psychological assessment in psychiatric settings to become an independent profession providing treatment and advice to clients, carers and services in a wide range of settings including primary care, social services, and secondary and tertiary care, as well as specialist services such as forensic units, palliative care and physical rehabilitation services.

This book presents an introduction to the essential features of the work of clinical psychology in practice, and demonstrates how clinical psychologists apply their knowledge and skills in a wide range of specialist settings. It is intended that this book will be of interest to both pre- and post-qualification clinical psychologists and also to a wider audience, and will remind all its readers of the value of the particular synthesis of theory, practice, a strong ethical base and commitment to the worth of people and evidence that the discipline represents. In line with social, political and academic developments, this book will also show how much further there is still to go in ensuring that the psychological is truly embedded in health and social care, particularly in the UK. Hence, the book raises questions about the future, and how important it is both that research continues to broaden and deepen the discipline theoretically and also that services continue to develop that enable users or carers in health and social care to have access to good quality psychological input, across the lifespan.

Clinical Psychology and How People Are Understood: Conceptual Models

Whilst medicine conceptualises the person primarily as a biological entity, albeit with emotions and thoughts, and the law thinks of people primarily as legal entities with rights and obligations, absolutely central to clinical psychology today is the notion of the person as a holistic, meaning-seeking body living within a particular social context. This approach, sometimes described as the biopsychosocial, indicates that each individual is best understood in terms of their psychological functioning and their physical and developmental history, but should also be understood in terms of the social context in which they live. The theoretical and empirical foundations of clinical psychology originated within empirical psychology, in academic centres and universities, where behavioural and subsequently cognitive models and approaches were dominant. When applied in the health context, these models fit reasonably well with an individualist medical approach, and have remained the dominant models. A more systemic approach has nevertheless been a consistent strand within the discipline, and community-based models have been developed which draw upon social conceptualisations of the person and their distress. Psychodynamic and interpersonal models have also played a significant part. Other important influences from psychology as an academic discipline include developmental psychology, personality psychology and neuropsychology. Nowadays most psychologists work in an integrated way, calling flexibly on a variety of models, all more or less subsumed within the biopsychosocial understanding of the person. Indeed, clinical training is deliberately generic, enabling the competent clinical psychologist to access and apply a variety of models as appropriate to the needs of the client or situation, in a range of settings, across the lifespan and with a range of presentations.

Although a multitude of approaches are used in clinical practice, the dominant models will now be examined in a little more detail. The behavioural model has historically played a highly significant role in the development of the discipline, and continues to be influential. Behavioural approaches focus primarily on changing current behaviour, and de-emphasise internal events and subjective experience. They are based on the premise that human behaviour, including various patterns of psychopathology, is learned and thus can be modified by new learning, or relearning of old patterns of behaviour. Both classical conditioning (Pavlov) and operant conditioning (Skinner) models have been applied to clinical practice (see Eysenck, 1976; Kanfer & Goldstein, 1980; O'Donohue & Krasner, 1994). Assessment and treatment aims to understand and manipulate the cues or antecedents that elicit behaviour, and the consequences or 'rewards' that follow it. Clinical psychologists were influential in the early application of behavioural theory and principles to a range of clinical problems. These included token economies (Allyon, 1999) for long-stay psychiatric patients, social skills training (Hollin & Trower, 1986), acquisition of speech, specific behaviours and skills in those with learning disabilities (Yule & Carr, 1980), and treatment of childhood conduct problems and parent training (Herbert, 1981). Behavioural models still flourish and are widely applied, particularly in work with children, parents, those with learning disabilities and in neuropsychological rehabilitation. Some of the core principles and strategies, for example those of reinforcement, role playing, extinction and modelling, have become embedded in everyday practice, even by those whose predominant orientation is not behavioural. Behavioural approaches continue to develop, and have recently been applied to eating disorders, psychosis, dementia care, and behavioural activation for depression, among other problems (Sturmey, 2007).

In response to behaviourism's lack of attention to internal, mental events, the cognitive model has become increasingly influential, and it is now the dominant model in clinical psychology in the UK. Cognitive models focus on thinking or cognition. Cognitive events (e.g. thoughts, images) are thought to be responsible for the maintenance of dysfunctional behaviour and mood disturbances. Cognitive assessment and therapy thus focuses on understanding and altering the cognitions that maintain disturbed mood and behaviour. Ellis devised rational emotive therapy (Ellis, 1961), while Beck (1976) simultaneously developed cognitive therapy. Beck's therapy has become particularly well known in the UK, where it is often referred to as cognitive behaviour therapy (CBT). Originally developed for depression, it has expanded to cover the range of clinical problems most typically seen by clinical psychologists, such as anxiety, trauma, obsessive-compulsive disorder (OCD) and eating disorders. It has also been adapted for use in healthcare settings, for work with children and for those with learning disabilities. While much of therapy is concerned with 'here and now' problems, schema-focused work has also been increasingly developed (e.g. Young, 1990) in order to treat those with chronic, severe and long-standing personality problems. Therapy is formulation driven, with the construction of an idiosyncratic formulation in collaboration with the client. A range of cognitive and behavioural strategies can then be used to challenge or modify cognitions, including verbal restructuring and behavioural experiments.

In recent years, a number of highly specific cognitive models have been developed for a range of adult psychological problems, including panic, social phobia, bulimia nervosa and OCD (see Wells, 1997, for an overview). Some of the models and treatments have been manualised and also published in the form of self-help guides. These have played a key role in the development of stepped care models of service provision, with minimal interventions (e.g. self-help) being offered before more intensive interventions (e.g. individual cognitive therapy). Cognitive behavioural interventions have been systematically evaluated for several disorders and shown to be highly effective (Roth & Fonagy, 2004), although, when thorough and even-handed comparisons have been made, cognitive therapy has not actually been shown to be more effective than other psychotherapies. Models for bipolar disorder, psychosis and also for personality disorders have been outlined, and preliminary treatment studies have produced encouraging results, although further development and evaluation are needed. Guidelines in the UK (e.g. National Institute for Health and Clinical Excellence (NICE)) and other countries strongly support the use of CBT, and a large programme to train new psychological therapists (Improving Access to Psychological Therapies (IAPT)) is under way in the UK, in order to make these therapies available to many more people.

A number of other therapies also focus on cognition, many of them developed in healthcare settings to facilitate adjustment to serious illness or chronic conditions, for example coping effectiveness training (Chesney & Folkman, 1994). Specific therapies to enhance motivation, for example in those with substance abuse (Marlatt *et al.*, 2002) or eating disorders (Geller, 2006), have been devised, with a focus on cognition. More recently, 'third wave' cognitive therapies have appeared, partly in response to criticisms of the proposed mechanisms of action in cognitive therapy, but also because a proportion of people do not improve significantly with cognitive therapy. These new developments focus on both control and acceptance, and typically aim to alter the person's relationship to their thoughts. They have been developed in a variety of formats, including mindfulness-based CBT (Segal *et al.*, 2001), metacognitive therapy (Wells, 2008) and acceptance and commitment therapy (Hayes & Strosahl, 2004).

Psychodynamic models have as their foundation a number of fundamental principles derived from psychoanalysis. These include the belief in unconscious material, the notion of intrapsychic conflict and mechanisms of defence to master anxiety, the presence of resistance and a developmental model which gives primacy to the oedipal conflict. As a developmental model, the psychodynamic perspective holds that infancy and childhood experience is formative for the adult personality. Initially, Freudian psychoanalytic theory was focused on unconscious desires based on the infant as primarily pleasure-seeking. However, following the advent of attachment theory (Bowlby, 1973) greater emphasis was placed on the infant's relational capacities. The psychodynamic infant is less pleasure-seeking than seeking the relational. This has informed the 'object relations' (Greenberg & Mitchell, 1983) school of contemporary psychodynamic practice which has given primacy to the therapeutic relationship in clinical practice with its notions of transference, counter-transference and defence mechanisms. For a contemporary account of the use of this in current clinical practice, see Coren (2001) and Stadter (1996). There are numerous theories which can be subsumed under the overarching psychodynamic label, but most share an emphasis on the use and analysis of the therapeutic relationship with the therapist to understand and work through the meaning of the symptom and its relation to the client's previous developmental, relational and family history. In this sense the symptom acts as a form of communication, and its relief, while desirable, is viewed as but one aspect of the treatment aims. Mutative change happens via the therapeutic relationship which, in the case of open-ended longer-term treatments, places considerable emphasis on therapist neutrality and relative passive therapeutic stance, whereby the client's difficulties are revealed via transference as if onto a 'blank screen'. For example, a young man presenting with social anxiety, who has experienced erratic or inconsistent parenting which may make him wary of successfully establishing relationships, may approach the clinician with the expectation that a similar response is likely from the therapist and utilise a number of defensive responses to deal with this expectation which would form the focus for the treatment. Other, more short-term, focal treatments work more collaboratively with clients using the therapeutic relationship more actively to address the current difficulty and its historical antecedents. Although it is sometimes claimed that this approach has less research evidence for effective outcome than CBT, for example, in fact there is good evidence particularly for brief time-limited therapies, such as interpersonal therapy (IPT) (Weissman & Markowitz, 1994) and psychodynamic interpersonal therapy (PIP) (Moorey & Guthrie 2003) and for the importance of the therapeutic relationship in all therapies (Lambert & Ogles, 2004).

Alternatively, the systemic model considers that people are best understood in a relational context and that any individual will be shaped and will develop in relation to their family and social context. Thus relationships, communication and interaction are central to the development of identity and experience and are the key to understanding problem development. Pathology is understood as resulting from interpersonal processes. General systems theory (von Bertalanffy, 1968) holds that any system is hierarchically organised and that change at any one point inevitably leads to disequilibrium which the system will resist in order to maintain stability. A system is understood as interacting parts structured by feedback that mutually communicate and influence one another. Fundamental to systemic family therapy are the patterns that develop which connect family members in a coherent and meaningful way (described as circularity). Within circular understandings of causality each person's behaviour is maintained by the actions of the other, thus problems are interpersonally maintained and may be shaped by broader contexts such as dominant gender or cultural roles. The epistemological basis of systemic family therapy has evolved from modernism, through postmodernism to constructionism (Dallos & Draper, 2000) and a large number of specific models have been derived from this overarching model and its evolution. These include structural family therapy (e.g. Minuchin, 1974) which focuses on boundaries and decision making between parental and child subsystems within the family. The more postmodern Milan approach (Palazzoli et al., 1980) uses hypothesising, circularity and positive connotation to help families shift their underlying beliefs, and sees the therapist as part of the system both being influenced by it and having influence upon it. Narrative therapy (e.g. White & Epston, 1990) and solution-focused therapy (e.g. Berg, 1991) are examples of therapies where experience and meaning are constructed in the stories that people tell about their lives, often influenced by multiple layers of context. Problems are understood as arising from personal idiosyncratic perceptions and meanings held by family members and the task of the therapist is to facilitate family members to explore their individual beliefs or narratives so that more positive, less problem-focused explanations can emerge. Therapy often utilises reflecting teams in order to generate many different perspectives, meanings or possible narratives. Therapy is seen as a collaborative process involving co-constructions of new ways of approaching a problem. Applications of systemic models include work with families, individuals, therapeutic letters, systemic consultation and in understanding organisations and teams. Dallos and Stedmon (2006) show how concepts such as power, influence and hierarchy are important in understanding the functioning of all organisations, no matter the size, and suggest that psychologists must factor this into both formulation and intervention.

A large number of other models and approaches are also used within clinical psychology (for example, Gestalt therapy, transactional analysis, cognitive analytic therapy), some of which will be mentioned later in this book. Many psychologists aim to work integratively across several models, and some may call upon concepts from developmental models and neuropsychology or spirituality in their work. But what most of the models noted above share in common to a lesser or greater degree is the assumption that people become who they are, and have the difficulties that they have, in part because of the context in which they develop, and in part because of what the individual brings and their ability to make unique sense of that context. In order to formulate or intervene, clinical psychologists therefore need to assess in some depth the origins of people's difficulties, their family context and their own particular psychological processing, as well as to understand the contribution of any developmental, medical, biological or physical factors to the difficulty (Johnstone & Dallos, 2006). Critical to the application of all these models is the ability to apply theory to practice, and vice versa, so that the psychologist's work is based on evidence but also contributes to the evidence base for the future. There are, of course, many similarities and much common ground between clinical psychology and other related professions, including psychiatry and psychotherapy. What particularly distinguishes the clinical psychologist, however, is this combination of the use of a range of psychological models, the scientific-practitioner stance, and an embedded emphasis on reflection and ethical awareness (see also Chapter 3).

In practice, this means that clinical psychologists need to take enough time and resources to assess people in some depth prior to reaching an adequate understanding of their difficulties, and in some cases may use detailed standardised measures to assist in the process. Their ability to conduct a thorough assessment means that the resulting formulation can be complex, and relatively time-consuming. Clinical psychologists will normally seek to address a wide range of issues, many of which may be ambiguous, and may need to call on a diverse range of theoretical understandings by which to make sense of what is presented, in order to contribute most effectively.

Clinical Examples

A good clinical example might be a man who is the survivor of a car accident in which he received a closed head injury, and who is finding it hard to readjust to work and family life post-injury. While the injury itself has physical consequences, with brain lesions linked to difficulties in memory and intellectual functioning, this will probably be compounded by a range of other factors which may well be more significant than the extent of the injury in determining the success of his recovery. These factors include the nature of his interpersonal relationships prior to the injury; the quality of support provided by his spouse and the attitude of his employers; the circumstances of the accident and whether or not the man has experienced any post-traumatic distress; the man's personality and history which will in part determine his own emotional reaction; and the man's own attitudes and appraisal of the significance and meaning of what has happened, that is, whether he sees it as a disaster with no opportunity for rehabilitation and growth, or whether he is able to build on personal and other resources to react as positively as possible to the circumstances. All these factors will vary from person to person, which means that although broad trends can be expected in how people react to such events, large differences also occur which need to be assessed and understood. The theoretical models which may need to be drawn upon in this work might include models of coping, post-traumatic stress disorder (PTSD), neuropsychological models and an understanding of brain–behaviour links, interpersonal relationship models and cognitive models which together can build an understanding of this man's situation and how best to intervene to help him.

Another example might be a 15-year-old girl presenting to services with depression and an eating disorder. Here it is necessary to understand both the nature of her depression and the eating disorder, what triggered and maintains them both and how they relate to each other, as well as understanding her developmental stage and relationships and her current physical condition. It is likely that an adequate formulation would also need to take account of early life experiences, family relationships and circumstances, sexual and emotional development, any cultural issues and any significant life events, as well as cognitive/emotional attitudes and appraisals. A full understanding would probably only develop over time, and would probably be modified as the intervention progressed. It is also likely that the psychologist would work together with other professionals, or the girl's family. Models or theories that might be relevant here include cognitive models of eating disorders and depression, risk assessment, adolescent developmental models, family systems, peer relationships, psychodynamic issues and cultural perspectives. Interventions might draw upon studies of effective treatments which relate to the chosen explanatory models, while the ability to work with and to appreciate the roles of other professionals such as psychiatrists, dieticians and family therapists would also be essential.

Key Qualities of Clinical Psychologists

It is possible to identify at least five equally important key qualities that characterise an effective clinical psychologist. First is an understanding of theory and research. The range of models and theories which may apply in the face of clinical complexity means that clinical psychologists need to have a good grasp of theory and evidence from within the base discipline of psychology. There is therefore a requirement that all clinical psychologists prior to training have a first degree in psychology, because the fundamental approach to people is psychological, that is, it concerns how people function in terms of making sense of and processing their experiences (cognition), as well as how they react to those experiences (emotion, motivation, personality) and what influences them (social, developmental, biological and environmental factors). The clinical psychologist applies those understandings to solve problems in practice, using evidence and theory. The point of theory is that it guides the practitioner, and tells the practitioner what is likely to be going on and what is likely to work. Clinical psychology has historically positioned itself as a science-based discipline, espousing the scientific-practitioner model in training (Hall *et al.*, 2002; and see also Chapter 3 of this book), which has meant that the aspiring clinical psychologist has had to possess a number of academic and research competencies. The current dominance in clinical practice of the therapeutic role for psychologists sometimes outweighs the scientific, research-based role; nevertheless the government's emphasis on evidence-based practice, clearly favours the scientific stance of the profession. Hence although sometimes somewhat obscured by the exigencies of immediate clinical practice, a key quality of clinical psychologists must be their ability to utilise a broad and evidence-based psychological understanding of how people function. Related to this is their competence in applied research methods: indeed, clinical psychology provides the highest level of pre-qualification clinical research training in the UK.

The second key quality for clinical psychologists is the ability to make positive working or therapeutic relationships with clients, carers or colleagues. Having emphasised the scientific and research-based competences of clinical psychologists, plenty of evidence also suggests that in addition to being able to draw on a range of conceptual models, and evidence about what works for whom, delivery of treatment relies very crucially on the ability of the psychologist to make good relationships with the recipients of services, since psychological techniques are delivered in large part through the personal qualities of the psychologist. It is now broadly accepted, for example, that although specific theoretically based techniques do play a significant role in bringing about change in psychological therapies with adults with mental health difficulties, a large part of the variance in outcome studies can be explained by the quality of the therapeutic relationship (Lambert & Ogles, 2004; Lambert, 2007). It is, of course, neither possible nor appropriate for psychologists to attempt to deliver therapeutic relationships without techniques, and indeed specific techniques have been demonstrated to be important factors when working with specific disorders; nonetheless, the quality of the relationship between psychologist and client is both the foundation and the medium for therapeutic work. As a further example, attention specifically paid to therapeutic relationship issues following a rupture or breakdown in therapy, however minimal, leads to substantially improved outcome (Bennett *et al.*, 2006), supporting the centrality of the personal interaction between psychologist and client in determining effectiveness.

The ability to make good professional relationships requires a number of personal qualities, including the ability to listen to another person, to attempt to understand them in their own terms, to respect diversity and difference, and to communicate clearly. The value base of the profession is critical here, since a commitment to the importance of each unique individual is needed if genuine and open communication is to take place. Arguably the key tool that psychologists use in their work is their ability to influence or facilitate people to think or behave differently.

Clearly linked with this is the third key quality, an ethical approach to professional work, whereby psychologists' ability to influence is used for the benefit of the client or colleague who seeks help or advice. All Chartered Clinical Psychologists are required to act according to the British Psychological Society's Code of Ethics and Conduct (2005a), which promotes high standards of conduct based on the notion of 'ethical thinking'. This document promotes an appreciation that ethical dilemmas are often complex and call for thoughtful judgements based on ethical standards, whilst also recognising that there are often contextual and cultural constraints and assumptions that influence what we do and believe. Nevertheless, it also enshrines a commitment to the importance of respect for persons and evidence, and to the need for psychologists to act with integrity, primarily in the interests of the recipients of their services (see Chapter 2 for more detailed discussion).

Most health and social care is delivered through teamwork and collaboration (Health Care Commission, 2006), hence the ability to understand and work constructively with groups and colleagues is critical. This can be seen as the fourth key quality. Since clinical psychology as a profession is very small in comparison with other professions such as medicine and nursing, one significant way of increasing the impact of clinical psychological knowledge and techniques is to work through other professional groups via teaching and consultancy and being involved in multidisciplinary teams. A number of writers, for example Ovretveit (1997) and West (2004), have described the factors which promote effective team working, including trust, positive leadership, organisation, having clear objectives and role clarity. Ideally psychologists should be able to work to enhance these factors. A critical understanding of the downside of group functioning, such as group think, stereotyping, conformity and inter-group conflict, can also be helpful, since these factors can impede good team working if not checked. Awareness of group dynamics can therefore be seen as crucial (see also Chapter 30).

The final key quality is that of a reflective practitioner, who is able to think carefully and creatively about his or her professional work. Lavender (2003), drawing on the work of Schön (1987), has distinguished four types of reflection: reflection in action (where, for example, the psychologist is able to respond flexibly to a client's particular needs); reflection on action (where, for example, the psychologist may reformulate a problem after discussing it in supervision); reflection on others (where, for example, the psychologist would consider the impact their particular gender or culture might have on a service user); and reflection on self (where, for instance, the psychologist might think carefully about how to mitigate the impact of working with sex offenders on their own sexual functioning). All these components of practice are needed for effective professional work and are implicated in ethical practice, besides contributing to the ongoing improvement of the psychologist's own professional work. A key component here is a commitment to ongoing supervision, and the willingness to subject one's own work to scrutiny and thought (see Chapter 28).

The Complexity of Clinical Problems

In essence, as shown in the two brief case examples above, clinical psychology is both multimodal and tailor-made in its approach to individual predicaments. Thus the practitioner has to attempt to understand and respond to the complexity of psychological problems, which often necessitates making use of a multiplicity of approaches when formulating and intervening. The psychologist is, however, also a practitioner operating in real time, and hence may often have to be pragmatic and act on incomplete evidence. Pisek and Greenhaigh (2001) suggest that most problems in health and social care are complex, where change at one level will inevitably affect another, and where coordinated skills and knowledge are almost always required. They argue, however, that we may spend too much time trying to apply complex solutions, and that sometimes we should just aim for 'good enough' solutions. Certainly many psychologists are aware that they do not always have a very sound evidence base for everything they do, and that many clinical problems do not fit neatly into textbook or research categories. It is here, however, that the creativity of the profession is needed, whereby the practitioner makes use of what evidence there is, applying it as a flexible scientist-practitioner to new and untried contexts or problems. An example might be applying a CBT model developed with adults to a child presenting with similar issues, but adapting the model for use in the new context. Overall there is a clear need to promote translational research and to engage in studies that refine laboratory-based work for clinical application.

One critical source of the complexity inherent in most clinical problems is the importance of context in determining and maintaining people's clinical difficulties. Appreciation of the crucial role of social and cultural issues is sometimes difficult to hold on to when focusing on individual clinical problems. Yet individuals do not live in a vacuum, and as the systemic model suggests, one of the major determinants of health problems is the social context in which people live. Smail (2005) suggests that we are often blind to macro-forces such as global economic interests and consumerism which have major and often destructive impacts on our lives, focusing instead on our own, or our clients', apparent inadequacies. Issues such as social class and comparative wealth, status and power are often overlooked in clinical formulations, where individuals are easily seen as living outwith social and economic structures. In fact some models risk encouraging such a focus. Cultural factors apply to everyone, although they are often most starkly observed when working with particularly disadvantaged groups such as some ethnic minorities or people with disability. Conversely, it is of course also likely to be the case that individuals vary widely in how they develop, and that biological factors play a significant part in both the genesis and maintenance of most health and psychological problems, and this again adds to the complexity of clinical work. Here again the value of generic training is demonstrated as it allows flexibility of response, and provides a broader evidence base on which to draw.

It seems that there is no shortage of distress in current society which needs to be addressed, and that a variety of models and interventions will always be needed as a response. These issues are discussed further in Chapter 30.

Clinical Psychology Training: The UK Example

Over the past 40 years, clinical psychology training in the UK has evolved from a fairly haphazard apprenticeship model to a carefully monitored and generic three-year post-graduate University-based doctoral training which is carried out in partnership with local services offered by the National Health Service (NHS). As described in Hall and Llewelyn (2006), the profession in the UK has sought to define itself by laying out its unique position in the professional marketplace, defining its intake via the British Psychological Society's training accreditation procedures. All clinical psychology training has thereby become formalised, overseen by relatively stringent external quality assurance processes, which define specified aims and competencies to be attained by all trainees. The ability of training programmes to meet these standards is regularly assessed, and only trainees who have completed accredited courses are eligible for Chartering. Additionally, in common with other NHS-funded training programmes, clinical psychology courses are subject to quality assurance assessment procedures. These apply standard criteria which evaluate the ability of training programmes to provide opportunities for students to fulfil specified educational and clinical outcomes. A regular quality assurance assessment process is now carried out by local NHS commissioners in collaboration with local NHS service providers. The content of training is broad and competency-based, that is, it is designed to allow trainees to demonstrate competence by attaining key learning outcomes. This is discussed in much greater depth in Chapter 2. Through training, trainees are encouraged to become aware of a variety of service models and to understand and apply different ways of working. They are encouraged always to work from the evidence base where that exists, and to feed back into the evidence base by both practice-based audit and research, and also through research into basic processes. The importance of working with users is also stressed, as is the need to work in collaboration with other professional groups.

Almost uniquely amongst NHS professions in the UK, all pre-qualification clinical psychologist trainees have been fully funded by the NHS since the 1980s. In the UK, health services are publicly resourced, and the precise arrangements whereby this is achieved are therefore subject to change, since political views about the best way to organise and distribute services and resources inevitably change. The current situation is for contractual agreements to exist between Strategic Health Authorities in England, or Health Boards or their equivalent elsewhere in the UK, and Universities, to deliver training in partnership with the local NHS, to agreed numbers, for trainees in each local area. Whilst academic teaching, research supervision, professional development support, appraisal and assessment, as well as some skills training, can be provided in academic settings, the bulk of training is provided via practical clinical work carried out under supervision in local NHS or social services settings.

A critical issue is therefore the quality of the relationship between the academic and the clinical sides of the training partnership. Most programmes provide additional training and support for clinical supervisors, and this helps to build and maintain positive relationships. Most programme staff also work part-time in local clinical services. The relationships between stakeholders, including commissioners or purchasers of training, are also important, and on the whole these have been reasonably good too, in part because, in contrast to many other NHS professional groups, the retention and eventual recruitment of clinical psychology trainees as NHS employees has been outstanding (British Psychological Society, 2005b). Finally, a crucial issue is the relationships within and between members of the programme itself (trainees and staff). Just as individuals learn relationship patterns and self-care strategies within their family of origin, so it seems likely that trainees learn much of their professional identity and standards within their training environment and clinical placements. Ideally this should include an expectation of a high standard of personal conduct and a commitment to both evidence and service user welfare, while at the same time fostering a tolerance of genuine mistakes and a willingness to learn.

In the UK, the training community (staff on all University programmes) works closely together, and although there is diversity between training providers, there is also a high degree of communication and mutual help between training programmes, which has helped to ensure a reasonably consistent standard of training across the UK. This has in turn helped to build and support the wider profession's identity and standards. It is notable, for instance, how prominent training programme staff have been in the professional leadership of UK clinical psychology as a whole, and how many initiatives for innovative services are often led by NHS and University training staff working together. These issues are discussed further in Chapter 29.

Clinical Psychology Services

Clinical psychology training covers a wide range of issues across the lifespan because clinical psychology services operate in a wide range of settings, including adult, child and family, people with learning disabilities, older people and specialist services. Clinical psychologists also work across social and health care, and need to work collaboratively with management and commissioners in order to meet the needs of both service users and carers, and of other service providers, as far as is possible within existing resources. Unlike training, however, there are no accepted patterns or standards of service organisation, and so a huge variety of types of provision exist across the health and social care sector. Limitations in resources mean that many service users do not in fact have good access to clinical psychology, and one constant problem remains inequality of provision, especially for hard-to-reach groups. An important principle here is recognition that services should be provided to all populations in need. For example, learning disabled and older people have poorer access than other client groups to evidence-based psychological therapies for emotional distress, despite evidence that they may benefit from such interventions. Clinical psychologists therefore have an important function in developing such services in areas where there are none. All the qualities and competencies noted in this chapter will be needed for such service development, including the establishment of good working relationships, the ability to assess and formulate problems, the competence to communicate effectively and to establish what form of intervention will be most appropriate, and the ability to implement and evaluate change. Since areas which are well researched are those most likely to receive funding, and hence better services, one important role for psychologists may well be to conduct research with under-served populations and thereby to encourage extension of good practice. In all circumstances the ability to evaluate the services provided will be critical. One further important issue is the dissemination of effective practices, so, for example, effective techniques in parenting can be passed on to health visitors and to families, leaving psychologists to work with more complex cases or in areas of work which have yet to be explored.

Within the UK, a recent government initiative has been to finance a large expansion of evidence-based therapy in primary care, the Increasing Access to Psychological Therapy (IAPT) programme designed to address the substantial amount of untreated level of emotional distress (depression and anxiety) which is reported in the community. Much of this work will be provided by therapists with less training than clinical psychologists, so an important future role is likely to be the provision of supervision and training for others. This ties in closely with recent proposals to revise how psychologists should work, to include a greater emphasis on teamwork, leadership and collaboration (New Ways of Working, 2007); see Chapter 29 for further discussion of this initiative.

This Book: Brief Overview

This book is structured to show how clinical psychologists think and work, and hence it comprises a series of chapters which present the key elements of practice, competency approaches and the conceptual base. Included is discussion of models, ethical issues and values, and the need to work in partnership with others who also provide or receive services. These discussions recognise the need for clinical psychologists to take both a reflective and a scientific stance to psychological practice, and hence to ground the discipline securely on sound empirical evidence as well as on clear ethical foundations. Examples of services across the lifespan will be presented in a series of short chapters by specialists in their fields, most of whom have roles as providers of services and also as educators for tomorrow's practitioners. The breadth of clinical psychology services now available means that this cannot be comprehensive, and it is inevitable that some important innovations and areas of work will have been omitted. Nevertheless, it is hoped that a reasonably wide range of areas of practice will be covered. The final section of the book discusses contextual questions, skills-sharing and the centrality of user involvement, and also raises questions about the future of the discipline. It is hoped that this volume will thereby provide a stimulating and illuminating coverage of the practice of clinical psychology as it exists in the first part of the 21st century.

References

Allyon, T. (1999). *How to use token economy and points systems.* Austin, TX: Pro-Ed.

Beck, A.T. (1976). *Cognitive therapy and the emotional disorders.* New York: International Universities Press.

Bennett, D., Parry, G. & Ryle, A. (2006). Resolving threats to the therapeutic alliance in cognitive analytic therapy of borderline personality disorder: A task analysis. *Psychology and Psychotherapy, 79,* 395–418.

Berg, I.M. (1991). *Family preservation: A brief therapy workbook.* London: B.T. Press.

Bertalanffy, von, L. (1968*). General systems theory: Foundation, development, applications.* New York: Brazillier.

Bowlby, J. (1973). *Attachment and loss*. London: Hogarth Press.

British Psychological Society (2005a). *Code of ethics and conduct*. Leicester: British Psychological Society.

British Psychological Society (2005b). *English survey of applied psychologists in health & social care and in the Probation & Prison Service*. Leicester: British Psychological Society.

Chesney, M.A. & Folkman, S. (1994). Psychological impact of HIV disease and implications for intervention. *Psychiatric Clinics of North America, 17,* 163–182.

Coren, A. (2001). *Short-term therapy: A psychodynamic approach*. London: Palgrave.

Dallos, R. & Draper, R. (2000). *An introduction to family therapy: Systemic theory and practice*. Buckingham: Open University Press.

Dallos, R. & Stedmon, J. (2006). Systemic formulation: Mapping the family dance. In L. Johnstone and R. Dallos (Eds.) *Formulation in psychology and psychotherapy* (pp. 72–97). London: Routledge.

Ellis, A. (1961). *A guide to rational living*. Englewood Cliffs, NJ: Prentice Hall.

Eysenck, H.J. (1976). The learning theory model of neurosis – a new approach. *Behaviour Research and Therapy, 14,* 251–267.

Geller, J. (2006). Mechanisms of action in the process of change: Helping eating disorder clients make meaningful shifts in their lives. *Clinical Child Psychology and Psychiatry, 11,* 225–237.

Greenberg, J.R & Mitchell, S.A. (1983). *Object relations in psychoanalytic theory*. Cambridge, MA: Harvard University Press.

Hall, J., Lavender, A. & Llewelyn, S. (2002). A history of clinical psychology in Britain: Some impressions and reflections. *History and Philosophy of Psychology, 4,* 32–48.

Hall, J. & Llewelyn, S. (2006). *What is clinical psychology?* (4th edn). Oxford: OUP.

Hayes, S.C. & Strosahl, K.D. (2004). *A practical guide to acceptance and commitment therapy*. New York: Springer.

Health Care Commission (2006). *National survey of NHS staff*. London: Commission for Healthcare Audit and Inspection.

Herbert, M. (1981). *Behavioural treatment of problem children*. London: Academic Press.

Hollin, C.R. & Trower, P. (1986). *Handbook of social skills training*. Oxford: Pergamon.

Johnstone, L. & Dallos, R. (2006). *Formulation in clinical psychology and psychotherapy*. London: Routledge.

Kanfer, F.H. & Goldstein, A.P. (1980). *Helping people change: A textbook of methods*. Oxford: Pergamon.

Lambert, M, (2007). What we have learned from a decade of research aimed at improving outcome in routine care. *Psychotherapy Research, 17,* 1–14.

Lambert, M. & Ogles, B. (2004). The efficacy and effectiveness of psychotherapy. In M. Lambert (Ed.) *Bergin & Garfield's handbook of psychotherapy and behavior change* (5th edn, pp. 139–193). New York: Wiley.

Lavender, T. (2003). Redressing the balance: The place, history and future of reflective practice in clinical training. *Clinical Psychology, 27,* 11–15.

Marlatt, G.A., Monti, P.M., Kadden, R.M. & Rohsenow, D.J. (2002). *Treating alcohol dependence: A coping skills guide*. New York: Guilford Press.

Minuchin, S. (1974). *Families and family therapy*. Cambridge, MA: Harvard University Press.

Moorey, J. & Guthrie, E. (2003). Persons and experience: Essential aspects of psychodynamic interpersonal therapy. *Psychodynamic Practice, 9*(4), 547–564.

New Ways of Working in Mental Health (2007). *Mental health: New ways of working for everyone*. London: Department of Health.

O'Donohue, W.T. & Krasner, L. (Eds.) (1994). *Handbook of psychological skills training*. Boston: Allyn & Bacon.

Ovretveit, J. (1997). Leadership in multidisciplinary teams. *Health and Social Care in the Community*, 5, 276–283.

Palazzoli, M., Boscolo, L., Cecchin, G. & Prata, G. (1980). Hypothesising–circularity–neutrality: Three guidelines for the conductor of the session. *Family Process*, 19, 3–12.

Pisek, P. & Greenhaigh, T. (2001). The challenge of complexity in healthcare. *British Medical Journal*, 323, 625–628.

Roth, A. & Fonagy, P. (2004). *What works for whom? A critical review of psychotherapy research* (2nd edn). New York: Guilford Press.

Schön, D. (1987). *Educating the reflective practitioner*. Oxford: Jossey-Bass.

Segal, Z.V., Williams, J.M.G. & Teasdale, J.D. (2001). *Mindfulness-based cognitive therapy for depression*. New York: Guilford Press.

Smail, D.J. (2005). *Power, interest and psychology*. Glasgow: Bell & Bain.

Stadter, M. (1996). *Object relations brief therapy: The therapeutic relationship in short-term work*. Northvale, NJ: Aronson.

Sturmey, P. (Ed.) (2007). *Functional analysis in clinical treatment*. London: Elsevier.

Weissman, M.M. & Markowitz, J. (1994). Interpersonal therapy: Current status. *Archives of General Psychiatry*, 51, 599–606.

Wells, A. (1997). *Cognitive therapy of anxiety disorders: A practice manual and conceptual guide*. Chichester: John Wiley.

Wells, A. (2008). *Metacognitive therapy for anxiety and depression*. New York: Guilford Press.

West, M. (2004). *Effective teamwork: Practical lessons from organizational research* (2nd edn). Oxford: Blackwell.

White, M. & Epston, D. (1990). *Narrative means to therapeutic ends*. New York: W.W. Norton.

Young, J.E. (1990). *Cognitive therapy for personality disorders: A schema-focussed approach*. Sarasota, FL: Professional Resource Exchange.

Yule, W. & Carr, J. (1980). *Behaviour modification for the mentally handicapped*. London: Croom Helm.

2

Competency Approaches, Ethics and Partnership in Clinical Psychology

Helen Beinart, Susan Llewelyn and Paul Kennedy

Clinical psychologists have been grappling with how to describe effectively and to define what they do since the 1930s (Woodworth, 1937). There has been much debate about how to capture clearly the particular mix of theory, science, practice and person that embodies our profession. Some applied psychologists do not believe that the use of the language of competency does justice to the sophistication or complexity of their contribution, and that much is lost by defining the parts rather than the whole. However, the authors of this chapter are convinced by the argument that in the current context of practice, applied psychologists must be able to clearly define their professional activities and that this must be understood in the light of a value base as well as a social and political context. Rather than reject competency approaches as a reductionist narrative, we argue here that it is possible to capture professional contributions through careful and detailed discussion of competence.

Competency is a much used and difficult to define construct, although widely used in the world of professional training. Up until 2002, the British Psychological Society (BPS) used an experiential model as the basis for training; for example, those learning to become clinical psychologists were expected to undergo a particular range of clinical experiences during their training. These included work with a range of clinical populations, ages, complexity, service settings and contexts. However, the profession questioned whether simply gaining experience was sufficient since new practitioners need to be competent and to be able to demonstrate competence, not just experience, at the end of their training. Hence the BPS thought it important to articulate the competencies required for the expected roles and responsibilities of a newly qualified clinical psychologist. These were documented as learning outcomes and placed in the context of knowledge, skills and values in the accreditation criteria for clinical psychology doctoral programmes (British Psychological Society, 2002, 2007).

A similar movement has taken place in the USA and Canada where accreditation of professional education programmes in psychology is now based largely on the programme's ability to demonstrate the competencies developed in their graduates (Kaslow, 2004). In the USA, for example, the American Psychological Association (APA) has developed a Task Force on the Assessment of Competence in Professional Psychology (Kaslow *et al.*, 2006), based on a multinational competencies conference held in 2002. Much of this work has been recently published and gives a detailed overview of the findings of the working groups, covering a broad range of competencies such as ethical and legal, individual and cultural diversity, scientific foundations and research, psychological assessment, intervention, consultation and inter-professional collaboration, supervision and professional development (see *Professional Psychology: Research and Practice*, October, 2007, for detailed reports).

This chapter will define competence, and place the development of the centrality of competence within a professional and ethical context. It will then discuss models of competence, articulate the competences required for clinical psychology in the UK, and raise some of the complex issues in the development, training and assessment of professional competence.

What Is Competence?

Competence is defined by the *Concise Oxford English Dictionary* (1995) as 'ability or skill', while competent is defined as 'adequately qualified, capable or effective'. Clearly the literal definition is not particularly helpful in understanding professional training since it assumes an end-state, whereas professional learning and development are continuous and ongoing throughout a professional career. Competence is variously defined in professional writings, and in the context of applied psychology, it involves the complex interaction of four major components: knowledge, skills, judgement and diligence (for example, New Zealand Psychologists Board, 2006). Knowledge involves having absorbed and comprehended a body of information sufficient to understand and conceptualise a range of professional issues. It is a necessary, but not sufficient, foundation for competence. Skill is the ability to apply knowledge effectively in actual practice. Judgement involves knowing when to apply which skills under what circumstances. It also includes a self-reflective element, including awareness of personal values, attitudes and context, and to know how these may influence actions. Diligence suggests a consistent application of knowledge, skills and judgement in professional activities, giving careful priority to client needs, and aiming to provide the highest quality of care.

Epstein and Hundert (2002) in their discussion of medical education have developed a broadly accepted definition of professional competence:

Professional competence is the habitual and judicious use of communication, knowledge, technical skills, clinical reasoning, emotions, values and reflection in daily practice for the benefit of the individual and community being served. Competence builds on a foundation of basic clinical skills, scientific knowledge and moral development. It includes a cognitive function – acquiring and using knowledge to solve real life problems; an integrative function – using biomedical and psychosocial data in clinical reasoning; a relational function – communicating effectively with patients and colleagues; and an effective moral function – the willingness, patient and emotional awareness to use these skills judicially and humanely. Competence depends on habits of mind, including attentiveness, critical curiosity, self-awareness, and presence. Professional competence is developmental, impermanent and context dependent. (p. 227)

Professional competence as thus defined by Epstein and Hundert is clearly applicable to clinical psychology. It suggests the capability of critical thinking and analysis, the use of professional judgement based on applied knowledge to make assessments and decisions and, through reflective practice, to evaluate and change decisions as needed. It clearly identifies competence as a developmental construct which is context-dependent, and which changes as the psychologist continues to develop over their professional lifetime. It also places competence within the context of moral decision making, which links closely with ethical values, as exemplified by the BPS Code of Ethics and Conduct (British Psychological Society, 2006).

The BPS's Code of Ethics and Conduct is based on four core ethical principles of respect, competence, responsibility and integrity. Each ethical principle includes a statement of values which describes a fundamental set of beliefs guiding ethical reasoning, decision making and behaviour, and a set of standards which clarify the ethical conduct expected from members of the Society. Interestingly, competence is seen as a core ethical principle within clinical psychology, both in the UK and USA, and is embedded within both the BPS and APA ethical codes. The BPS statement of values associated with competence is described as follows: 'Psychologists value the continuing development and maintenance of high standards of competence in their professional work, and the importance of preserving their ability of functioning optimally within the recognised limits of their knowledge, skill, training, education and experience' (British Psychological Society, 2006, p. 14). This value sits alongside respect for the dignity and worth of all people, responsibility to clients, the general public, the profession and commitment to promoting integrity in all professional interactions. The other overarching and widely accepted professional stance of clinical psychology is that of working collaboratively. This is an attitude and approach which encourages the individual psychologist to work with the client, be they individual, group, team, wider organisation or community, in partnership. Hence, our understanding of competence needs to be placed within ethical frameworks and a collaborative stance.

It is probably clear from the discussion thus far that although there are many competencies required by a clinical psychologist (for example, relationship formation, assessment, formulation, intervention, research and evaluation, consultation and education, management and supervision), these individual areas form only part of the building blocks of professional competence. Nonetheless, professional competence is a much broader term which cuts across the various competency areas listed above, and reflects the integration of knowledge, skills and attitudes with professional practice and the science of psychology. Professional competence also involves meta-knowledge, knowledge about knowledge: knowing what you know and what you don't know. Hence, meta-knowledge includes being aware of the range and limits of what you know: knowing your own strengths and weaknesses, how to apply available skills and knowledge to a variety of tasks, how to acquire new or missing skills, or being able to judge when not to intervene due to lack of knowledge or competence. The development of meta-knowledge and meta-competencies therefore depends on self-awareness, self-reflection and self-assessment (Weinert, 2001). Schön (1983) has contributed to our understanding of this discussion by suggesting that, in addition to 'technical rationality' (understanding of basic science, its application and the skills and attitudes required), competence develops through 'reflection on action' and develops in a mature professional to 'reflection in action'. This is understood as moment-to-moment self-supervision which involves the practitioner reflecting during practice in order to make decisions about how best to proceed in each individual context. Reflective practice thus involves meta-cognitive and self-awareness as well as interpersonal awareness.

A final consideration in thinking about what we mean when we are discussing competence must include some clarification of the terms used in this area. In general, competencies usually refer to an area or domain such as assessment or intervention, both of which are components of competence. Normally, competencies are observable and measurable and can be evaluated against accepted standards (Kaslow, 2004). 'Competence' usually refers to a level of attainment or minimum threshold an individual has acquired such as the development of basic competence in, for example, assessment, while 'competent' is a description of a particular level of skill. However, a 'competency-based approach' can also refer to a more aspirational striving towards excellence and in this context all competence is developmental in nature. Perhaps it is most helpful to use the minimum threshold understanding in a professional training context and the more aspirational interpretation in an ongoing professional development context. However, Erault (2008) stresses that competence should be understood in terms of the context, prevailing conditions and situation. He also distinguishes the term capability which emphasises personal knowledge and lifelong learning rather than expected standards or qualifications.

Models of Competence

Several authors have attempted to develop models to account for the development of professional competence. For example, Roe (2002) developed the Competence Architecture Model (Figure 2.1) where he depicts competence as a building which has, as its foundation layers, abilities and personal attributes that are supported by pillars of acquired learning, such as knowledge, skills and attitudes. The roof of the model is made up of the competencies essential to practice, such as assessment and intervention skills, which are thought to be learnt largely through the integration of practical learning through supervised practice and knowledge, skills and attributes.

One of the most widely used schemes for describing the development of competence is that of Dreyfus and Dreyfus (1986), who define five stages: Novice, Advanced Beginner, Competent, Proficient and Expert. Their main thesis suggests that as the learner becomes more familiar with the analytic and practical tasks required of the profession, performance becomes more integrated, flexible, efficient and skilled. Patterns and actions that have to be carefully considered or supervised become internalized and increasingly automatic. Stoltenberg *et al.* (1998) in their Integrated Developmental Model of Supervision (see Chapter 28 for a detailed discussion) describe the journey of development from a novice to competent professional which they

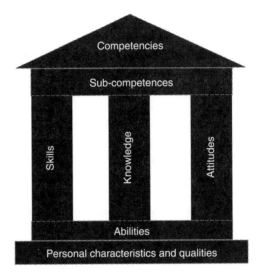

Figure 2.1   Competence Architecture Model.
Source: Adapted from Roe (2002).

suggest involves the development of competence, professional identity and maturity. The main developmental tasks involved are self-awareness and awareness of others, motivation and autonomy. The model identifies eight domains reflecting professional competence: intervention skills, assessment techniques, interpersonal assessment, client conceptualisation, individual differences (including impact of difference and diversity), theoretical orientation, treatment plans and goals, and professional ethics.

Skovholt and Ronnestad (1992) interviewed and qualitatively analysed interviews with a range of therapists and counsellors across the professional lifespan. They developed a model which suggests that the evolving professional self follows a series of stages in development which include: untrained/intuitive and common sense (prior to training), transition to professional training, imitation of experts and conditional autonomy (towards the end of training), exploration (as a newly qualified professional), integration and individuation (as a mature professional).

Rodolfa *et al.* (2005) developed a competencies cube model (Figure 2.2) to describe the development of competencies throughout a professional career. The model is seen as developmental and interactional, and will vary according to clinical context and setting, such as the populations and problems served and the theoretical models used. The foundation competencies, or building blocks, are conceptualised as reflective practice and self-assessment, scientific knowledge and methods, relationships, ethical and legal standards, individual and cultural diversity and interdisciplinary systems. The functional competencies are seen as the knowledge, skills and values to perform the work of a psychologist, and these areas of professional functioning include: assessment, diagnosis, conceptualisation (formulation), intervention, consultation, research/evaluation, supervision/teaching and management/administration. The cube model assumes that the relationship between the functional and foundation competency domains is orthogonal, that is, each of the foundation domains has implications for the functional competencies. Additionally, stages of professional development are also represented in the

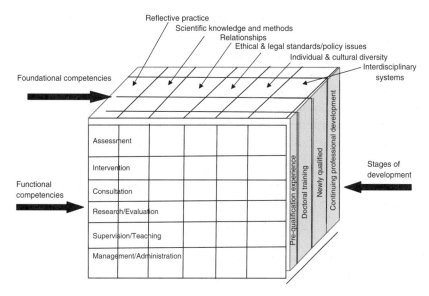

Figure 2.2   Cube model describing competency development in professional psychology. *Source*: Adapted for the UK from Rodolfa *et al.* (2005).

model such as doctoral training, post-doctoral supervision and continuing professional development, suggesting that psychologists gain and enhance competencies throughout their professional careers. Rodolfa *et al.* (2005) suggest that functional competencies will develop according to the speciality or context within which the psychologist works and that this further specialisation will usually take place post-qualification.

Core Competencies, Ethics and Partnership in Clinical Psychology

One of the challenges in dissecting professional competence into its component competencies is that they inevitably become reductive since they lose the overall purpose and integration, ethical stance and value of partnership which is central to good practice. Hence it is perhaps worth restating the overall aims of UK professional clinical psychology here:

> Clinical psychologists aim to reduce psychological distress and to enhance and promote psychological well-being by the systematic application of knowledge derived from psychological theory and research. Clinical psychology services aim to enable service users to have the necessary skills and abilities to cope with their emotional needs and daily lives in order to maximise psychological and physical well-being; to develop and use their capacity to make informed choices in order to enhance and maximise independence and autonomy; to have a sense of self-understanding, self-respect and self-worth … (British Psychological Society, 2007, p. 8)

Additionally, clinical psychologists work with colleagues, teams and services to enhance and promote psychological understanding of human distress. This latter point is particularly important in certain clinical settings where more medically focused models of care may pathologise rather than empower service users. Psychologists have an important role to support their colleagues and teams to use normative lifespan developmental and psychological models to work in partnership to understand and enhance people's psychological well-being (see Chapter 30 for further discussion of teamwork).

The training accreditation criteria for UK clinical psychology courses (British Psychological Society, 2007) couch competencies in the language of skills, knowledge and values, and emphasise the capability to combine knowledge and competencies to achieve a set of learning outcomes by the end of training. The summary learning outcomes are noted below:

> The skills, knowledge and values to develop working alliances with clients, including individuals, carers and/or services, in order to carry out psychological assessment, develop a formulation based on psychological theories and knowledge, carry out psychological interventions, evaluate their work and communicate effectively with clients, referrers and others, orally, electronically and in writing;

> The skills, knowledge and values to work effectively with clients from a diverse range of backgrounds, understanding and respecting the impact of difference and diversity upon their lives;

> The skills, knowledge and values to work effectively with systems relevant to clients, including for example statutory and voluntary services, self-help and advocacy groups, user-led systems and other elements of the wider community;

> The skills, knowledge and values to work in a range of indirect ways to improve psychological aspects of health and healthcare;

> The skills, knowledge and values to conduct research that enables the profession to develop its knowledge base and to monitor and improve the effectiveness of its work;

> and

> High level skills in managing a personal learning agenda and self-care, and in critical reflection and self-awareness that enable transfer of knowledge and skills new settings and problems. (British Psychological Society, 2007, p. 9)

The Health Professions Council which now regulates the profession in the UK uses the format of statements of proficiency to highlight required competencies. These proficiency statements can be mapped onto the learning outcomes noted here, although they are less specifically clinical, since they apply to all branches of psychology eligible for regulation. In a similar vein the APA has also developed a Competency Benchmarks Document (2007) applicable to all health service providers in professional psychology. The common competencies are listed as follows:

> Reflective practice self-assessment, which includes practicing within the boundaries of competence, being committed to lifelong learning and scholarship, engaging in critical thinking, and being dedicated to the development of the profession;

> Scientific knowledge and methods, including a respect for scientifically derived knowledge, the ability to understand research methods, data collection and analyses, and the capacity to appropriately evaluate and judge the quality of research. This area also includes specific knowledge of psychological models of behavior, as well as lifespan development;

The capacity to have meaningful and productive professional relationships with individuals, groups, and communities including core relationship skills such as empathy, warmth and genuineness.

Individual-cultural diversity, which includes awareness of self within the cultural context and sensitivity when working with individuals, groups and communities with diverse cultural backgrounds and unique personal characteristics;

Ethical-legal standards-policy, which involves the appropriate application of ethical standards as well as an awareness of legal issues associated with professional activities and advocacy for the profession; and

Interdisciplinary systems, including teamwork and appropriate professional involvement with colleagues and the ability to interact knowledgeably with professionals in related fields.

The working group of the APA tasked with developing basic clinical competencies in intervention (Spruill *et al.*, 2004) built on the foundation competencies above, and divided intervention into intervention planning (including assessment and formulation), implementation (building the relationship, choice and timing of intervention, endings and communication) and evaluation competencies (monitoring client progress and therapist reactions). Additionally, they suggested that competent clinicians must be able to deal with the unexpected or with clinical emergencies or crises (for example, abuse, risk or self-harm issues) without rupturing the therapeutic relationship. The role of supervision and consultation is seen as essential in this context both to enhance learning and competence and also to allow for scrutiny and clinical governance.

For more specific detail, the core competencies for clinical psychologists outlined by the BPS (2007) can be seen in Box 2.1 (overleaf).

The Training, Development and Assessment of Competence

Competency-based education is challenging in that it needs to straddle the training of competence and capabilities alongside facilitating the learning of specific competencies. In other words, specific, clearly articulated competencies such as specific assessment techniques need to be learnt together with the ability to adapt to change, be flexible, and show sound judgement and decision making in complex and changing environments. It is essential therefore that competency-based education is developmentally informed and incorporates progressively more complex and sophisticated content (Kaslow, 2004). It could be argued that training should begin with foundation competencies and develop to training core competencies, and then move to more specific speciality-related competencies. However, many of the foundation competencies are more complex to learn, and also somewhat more difficult to teach. For example, teaching of ethics, reflective practice or cultural diversity is perhaps not as straightforward or indeed measurable as teaching interviewing skills. Many of the models of competence development suggest a linear developmental pathway, but experienced trainers will be aware of competence fluctuating depending on many factors such as familiarity with the clinical context, client group and complexity of the work, as well as personal factors such as confidence and life stresses. Thus an interactional, developmental model, such as the Competency Cube Model (Rodolfa *et al.*, 2005) introduced above, may be most helpful in this area.

Additionally, adult learning models, such as that proposed by Kolb (1984), may be helpful in supporting adult learners who will start their professional careers with an

---

Box 2.1   Summary of learning outcomes for UK clinical psychology training (BPS, 2007)

Psychological assessment includes the ability to:

- develop and maintain effective working alliances with clients
- choose, use and interpret a broad range of appropriate assessment methods (standardised psychometric measures, clinical interviews, structured observation)
- assess social context and organisations
- conduct appropriate risk assessment and using this to guide practice.

Psychological formulation includes the ability to:

- develop formulations of presenting problems or situations
- integrate information from assessments using psychological theory and evidence, incorporating interpersonal, societal, cultural and biological factors
- use formulation to facilitate clients' understanding of their experience
- collaboratively plan appropriate interventions
- revise as necessary as understanding deepens
- assist inter-professional communication and understanding.

Psychological intervention includes the ability to:

- implement psychological therapy or interventions appropriate to the presenting problem and to the psychological and social circumstances of the client(s)
- collaborate with the client (individual, couple, family, group, team, service)
- be proficient in at least two evidence-based models, one of which is cognitive behaviour therapy
- work with and through others
- recognise when intervention is unlikely to be helpful
- manage caseload and handle endings sensitively and effectively.

Evaluation includes the ability to:

- select and implement appropriate methods to evaluate the effectiveness, acceptability and impact of interventions
- devise innovative procedures and audit clinical effectiveness.

(Continued)

Box 2.1   (Cont'd)

Psychological research includes the ability to:

- identify, review and critically appraise the research evidence
- understand techniques for clinical research, including quantitative and quali-tative approaches
- collaborate in small-scale and service-related research
- conceptualise, design and conduct independent, original research
- identify research questions
- demonstrate an understanding of ethical issues
- choose appropriate research methods and analysis
- report outcomes and disseminate findings.

Personal and professional skills and values include the ability to:

- understand ethical issues and apply in complex contexts
- appreciate the inherent power imbalance between practitioners and clients and the impact of difference, diversity and social inequalities on people's lives
- be aware of the impact of one's own value base
- work effectively at an appropriate level of autonomy
- work within the limits of one's own competence, and accept accountability
- use supervision and manage learning needs
- reflect on practice and the emotional impact of the work
- maintain the health, safety and security of self and others.

Communication and teaching include the ability to:

- communicate psychological information effectively
- adapt the style of communication to people with a range of cognitive ability, sensory acuity and modes of communication
- take into account the needs and goals of the participants
- attend to the supervision process for both supervisee and supervisor roles
- provide psychological advice and consultation.

Service delivery includes the ability to:

- adapt practice to a range of different organisational contexts
- provide supervision, consultancy and leadership
- work effectively with formal service systems, procedures, legislative and national planning contexts
- work with users and carers to facilitate their involvement in service planning and delivery
- work effectively in multidisciplinary teams and understand how to support change
- understand quality assurance, management roles and organisational policies.

existing wealth of previous personal and professional experience as well as preferred styles of learning. Training is clearly most effective when it occurs in a respectful, supportive and facilitative learning environment where adult learners are encouraged to hold or at least share responsibility for their learning. In the UK, clinical training includes parallel streams of academic teaching (usually a mix of didactic and experiential learning), research training (learnt through a combination of teaching, mentoring or supervision and application), clinical placements where the focus is on competence development in a range of contexts supported by clinical supervision, and personal, professional development and reflective, ethical practice which are developed across all spheres. Following its successful development in medical education, problem-based learning has been recently introduced into clinical training and appears to be a promising strategy for the development of competencies (Stedmon *et al.*, 2005).

In the UK, each clinical training course has a slightly different emphasis, although through the rigorous BPS accreditation systems as well as NHS quality control mechanisms most newly qualified psychologists have roughly comparable competencies after taking into account individual differences. To our knowledge, we do not yet know which elements of training are most effective in the development of competent and capable professionals, so most courses have developed their own preferred method of competence development. In Oxford, for example, following a competencies conference with supervisors, trainees and tutors, we produced a *developmental guide to the assessment of clinical competence* to help supervisors to make informed judgements about the development of clinical competence over the three years of training, and this is outlined here as an illustration. We emphasise needs-led supervision which takes into account individual learning needs and goals, since all trainees join the programme with a range of different experiences and abilities. Additionally, case complexity, level of risk, familiarity with the client group and service context all influence the development of competence. These general guidelines therefore need to be interpreted and applied in the light of individual trainee needs and experience, and specific service issues such as complexity. The specific competencies we assess are: use of supervision, therapeutic relationships, assessment, formulation, intervention, communication, teaching, research and evaluation, multidisciplinary working, services, contexts and organisation, personal/professional practice and cultural competence.

As a general framework we would expect the following:

- In year 1, trainees will show basic knowledge and skills, emergent competencies and awareness of learning needs. They will show flexibility and capacity to learn from feedback. They are likely to require structured and detailed guidance from their supervisors.
- In year 2, trainees will show basic applied skills and knowledge and a greater level of maturity in their competence development. General engagement and relationship skills are in place and formulation and intervention skills are developing but will still require some structured guidance from supervisors, particularly in new, complex or high-risk situations. A more collaborative approach will facilitate supervision.
- In year 3, trainees will show the majority of competencies with the exception of highly specialist or complex issues. Trainees will show appropriate strategies to

manage high complexity/risk. They will show clear application of theory, ongoing development of knowledge and an ability to explain and teach others. They will show an increasing integration of ideas and approaches as they consolidate their clinical skills and develop an autonomous professional style. They will show a commitment to ongoing professional development post-qualification. A collaborative style will facilitate supervision. (Oxford Doctoral Course in Clinical Psychology, 2006)

Assessment of competence needs to take into account developmental factors, and will usually include both formative (feedback aimed at developmental needs) and summative (evaluation based on whether expected level of competence is reached, and gate keeping) feedback. Kaslow, Bebeau *et al.* (2007) argue that in keeping with the common *Zeitgeist*, psychologists have embraced competency-based training but still have much work to do to develop competency-based assessment. They have therefore developed some guiding principles for the assessment of competence and suggest that: assessment of competence requires a major cultural shift towards the assessment throughout professional life, and also that competencies should be conceptualised as generic, holistic and developmental. Assessment of competence should reflect fidelity to practice and incorporate reliable, valid and practical methods. Self-reflection and self-assessment are seen as key components in the assessment of competence, and a comprehensive assessment should include a focus on interpersonal functioning and professional development, highlight the importance of individual and cultural diversity and the development and maintenance of ethical practice. Additionally, it is suggested that it is important to assess capability as well as competence, where capability refers to the extent to which competent individuals can adapt their skills to new contexts, generate new knowledge and continue to improve their competence through lifelong learning.

Leigh *et al.* (2007) argue that the multidimensional nature of competence requires a multifaceted approach to assessment. Assessment should be viewed as a continuum from early stages of professional training through continued learning and professional development in practice (Bashook, 2005). A variety of models of assessment may be used which include measures of knowledge (e.g. multiple choice questionnaires), measures of professional decision making (e.g. case-based oral examinations), measures of performance (e.g. portfolios) and integrated assessment of practice-based skills and tasks (e.g. through observation or simulation of practice). Leigh *et al.* conclude that good assessment is expensive to develop and maintain and that psychology lags behind many other healthcare professions in the development of reliable and valid methods to assess competence. Bashook (2005) recommends that best practice in the assessment of competence should be grounded in a conceptual model and include multiple assessment methods tailored to the competencies to be measured which take into account credibility, feasibility and career stage of the practitioner.

Barber *et al.* (2007) distinguish global competence from limited-domain competence and argue that most empirical investigations of competence have assessed limited-domain competence, for example in randomised control trials investigating the outcome of specific therapies. They report that the majority of therapy outcome studies show a small but positive correlation between competence and outcome in several limited domains. In the UK, much new financial investment has occurred on the basis of these studies and limited-domain competencies in, for example, cognitive behaviour therapy have been developed (Roth & Pilling, 2007). Barber *et al.* (2007) argue that while it is conceivable that therapy outcome may result from competence demonstrated within a single domain, it is likely that global competence, in particular the ability to deal with the unexpected, is more likely to predict therapy outcome, but that this requires further empirical study.

Problems in the Development of Professional Competence

When problems with competence are identified, it is important to have strategies in place for their remediation and management. Professional psychology has struggled with how and when to intervene when behaviour or performance does not meet expected levels of competence (Elman & Forrest, 2007). This is a challenging area and trainers, supervisors and managers need to be trained in effective methods for ongoing assessment of competence and how to manage poor performance. Identifying learning needs, feedback and constructive challenge are normally the first steps in supporting learning and managing difficulties (Scaife, 2001). Additionally, training programmes need to foster an ethos of openness and acceptance of feedback so that any problems are brought to light early. If one accepts a developmental model of competence development, then much work can be done preventatively by clearly identifying what needs to change. However, it is also essential that training programmes have clear written and transparent policies and procedures regarding remediation, failure and, if necessary, dismissal. These are best couched in a terminology which clearly describes the competencies and standards required and hence emphasises the ongoing need for definition, assessment and ethical practices. Kaslow, Rubin *et al.* (2007) propose several methods for recognising, assessing and intervening with problems of professional competence. These include clear definitions of the competence required, preparing the system to ensure that policies and procedures for assessment are in place, encouraging self-assessment and learning from feedback, considering cultural diversity and the impact of beliefs and values in the identification, assessment and resolution of problems, and maintaining clear communication at all times (including transparent discussions of confidentiality and limitations to the individual's rights to privacy bearing in mind ethical and regulatory principles).

Conclusion

This chapter has focused on understanding the competency approach in clinical psychology by discussing the meaning of competence and competencies, exploring models of competency development, articulating the competencies required in the training of clinical psychologists both in the UK and USA and raising issues concerning the training and assessment of professional competence. It is evident that defining and assessing competence in clinical psychology is a challenging task and psychology has lagged behind other professions in defining what professional psychologists know and can contribute, resulting in a possible failure to communicate the nature of their competence to the public and policy makers (Kaslow, 2004). This is not entirely surprising in an area where the meaning of competence can range from an ethical principle to a specific definition of a technical skill. In the current *Zeitgeist* of evidence-based, competency approaches, there is a danger of defining competencies as a collection of specific skills which may lead to a focus on training technicians rather than competent and capable professionals who have the capacity to think critically, evaluate and develop new and innovative methods. Despite these challenges, there is an opportunity for the profession to develop a developmentally informed competency-based model and methods of training and assessment that reflect the diversity, creativity and flexibility of the profession across the professional lifespan.

References

American Psychological Association (2007). Assessment of competency benchmarks workgroup. A developmental model for the defining and measuring competence in professional psychology. June 2007. Retrieved 9 January 2008 from www.apa.org/ed/graduate/comp_benchmark.pdf

Barber, J., Sharpless, B., Klostermann, S. & McCarthy, K. (2007). Assessing intervention competence and its relation to therapy outcome: A selected review derived from the outcome literature. *Professional Psychology: Research and Practice, 38*, 493–500.

Bashook, P. (2005). Best practices for assessment of competence and performance of the behavioural health workforce. *Administration and Policy in Mental Health, 32*, 563–592.

British Psychological Society (2006). *Code of ethics and conduct.* Leicester: Author.

British Psychological Society (2002 & 2007). *Criteria for the accreditation of post-graduate training programmes in clinical psychology.* Leicester: Author.

Dreyfus, H.L. & Dreyfus, S.E. (1986). *Mind over machine: The power of human intuition and expertise in the era of the computer.* New York: The Free Press.

Elman, N. & Forrest, L. (2007). From trainee impairment to professional competence problems. *Professional Psychology: Research and practice, 38*, 501–509.

Epstein, R. & Hundert, E. (2002). Defining and assessing professional competence. *Journal of the American Medical Association, 287*, 226–235.

Erault, M. (2008). *Towards an epistemology of practice.* Inaugural lecture, Kellogg's Centre for Professional Learning, Oxford University.

Kaslow, N. (2004). Competencies in professional psychology. *American Psychologist, 59*, 774–781.

Kaslow, N., Bebeau, M., Lichtenberg, J., Portnoy, S., Rubin, N., Leigh, I. *et al.* (2007). Guiding principles and recommendations for the assessment of competence. *Professional Psychology: Research and Practice, 38*, 441–451.

Kaslow, N., Rubin, N., Forrest, L., Elman, N., Van Horne, B., Jacobs, S. *et al.* (2007). Recognizing, assessing and intervening with problems of professional competence. *Professional Psychology: Research and Practice, 38*, 479–492.

Kaslow, N., Rubin, N., Leigh, I., Portnoy, S., Lichtenberg, J. & Smith, I. (2006). *Task Force on the assessment of competence in professional psychology*. Washington, DC: American Psychological Association.

Kolb, D. (1984). *Experiential learning – experience as the source of learning and development.* Englewood Cliffs, NJ: Prentice Hall.

Leigh, I., Smith, I., Bebeau, M., Lichtenberg, J., Nelson, P., Portnoy, S. *et al.* (2007). Competency assessment models. *Professional Psychology: Research and Practice, 38,* 463–473.

New Zealand Psychologists Board (2006). *Core competencies for the practice of psychologists.* Retrieved 3 January 2008 from www.psychologistsboard.org.nz

Oxford Doctoral Course in Clinical Psychology (2006). *A developmental guide to the assessment of clinical competence.* Retrieved 4 January 2008 from Course Handbook at www.hmc.ox.ac.uk/clinicalpsychology/COURSEHANDBOOK2007.pdf

Oxford English Dictionary (1995). Ninth Edition edited by Della Thompson. Oxford: Clarendon Press.

Rodolfa, E., Bent, R., Eisman, E., Nelson, P., Rehm, L., & Ritchie, P. (2005). A cube model for competency development: Implications for psychology educators and regulators. *Professional Psychology: Research and Practice, 36,* 347–354.

Roe, R.A. (2002). What makes a competent psychologist? *European Psychologist, 7*(3), 192–202.

Roth, A.D. & Pilling, S. (2007). *The competences required to deliver effective cognitive and behavioural therapy for people with depression and with anxiety disorders.* London: Department of Health.

Scaife, J. (2001). *Supervision in the mental health professions: A practitioner's guide.* Hove: Brunner-Routledge.

Schön, D. (1983). *The reflective practitioner: How professionals think in practice.* New York: Basic Books.

Skovholt, T.M. & Ronnestad, M.H. (1992). *The evolving professional self: Stages and themes in therapist and counselor development.* New York: John Wiley.

Spruill, J., Rozensky, R., Stigall, T., Vasquez, M., Bingham, R., & Olvey, C. (2004). Becoming a competent clinician: Basic competencies in intervention. *Journal of Clinical Psychology, 60,* 741–754.

Stedmon, J., Wood, J. Curle, C. & Haslam, C. (2005). Development of PBL in the training of clinical psychologists. *Psychology Learning and Teaching, 5,* 52–60.

Stoltenberg, C., McNeill, B. & Delworth, U. (1998). *IDM supervision: An integrated developmental model for supervising counsellors and therapists.* San Francisco: Jossey-Bass.

Weinert, F.E. (2001). Concept of competence: A conceptual clarification. In D.S. Rychen & L.H. Salganik (Eds.) *Defining and selecting key competencies* (pp.45–66). Seattle, WA: Hogrefe & Huber.

Woodworth, R.S. (1937). The future of clinical psychology. *Journal of Consulting Psychology, 1,* 4–5.

3

The Conceptual Base

Paul Kennedy, Susan Llewelyn and Helen Beinart

To introduce this discussion of the conceptual base of clinical psychology, we will start by briefly outlining some of the historical context. Lightner Witmer established the first psychological clinic in the USA, coining the term 'Clinical Psychologist' as long ago as 1896 (Strickland, 1988). Following this, professional development for the next fifty years or so was variable, being particularly slow in the UK although a little more focused in Germany and the USA (Hall & Llewelyn, 2006). Yet despite this unpromising start, the expansion of the profession in the subsequent fifty years or so has largely confirmed Woodworth's (1937) prediction that 'the number of Clinical Psychologists would be very great'. So how and why did this happen?

This chapter aims to suggest some answers to these questions and explores the scientist-practitioner model underpinning the profession. In it we include an examination of pre- and post-Second World War developments, which highlight the links between research and professional practice, and examination of some of the risks, biases, constraints and contradictions associated with this model, particularly as practice and research has developed into the 21st century. Finally, we discuss the integration of reflective practice, as well as the need and strategies for managing the potentially uncomfortable disconnect between practice and research.

Historical Perspectives

In the early days of the profession in the USA, the US Public Health Service (USPHS) and the Veterans Administration (VA) appropriated funds to support University training programmes to deliver accredited training of graduate psychologists in clinical psychology. Part of the impetus behind this was the US government's wish to avoid a repeat of blunders following the First World War that led to significant dissatisfaction amongst veterans with the then available mental health care. The federal Government wanted to take proactive measures to ensure that the mental health needs of the veterans would be better addressed following the Second World War. Some graduate (academic) psychology departments, however, feared the expansion within their programmes, and were concerned about the possible domination of clinical psychology within their departments. Doubts were also expressed (see Benjamin & Baker, 2000) about whether a psychologist could be both a practitioner and a researcher.

The Boulder Conference of 1949 (reported by Raimy in 1950) was arguably a defining event for the status of the profession; its legacy included the rapid expansion of US government-funded training places in clinical psychology (the UK was to follow a decade later), the adoption of the scientist-practitioner model of training in professional psychology, and a strong endorsement of the belief that the professional psychologist could and should be both researcher and practitioner. Despite the anxiety of the Universities noted above, the decision of the Boulder Conference was to recommend the training of clinical psychologists for research and practice, with equal emphasis placed on both, and to suggest that this synthesis should chart major policies in training institutions for some time to come (Raimy, 1950, p. 79). The Boulder Conference also delivered the most comprehensive statement of training for clinical psychology ever written, detailing recommendations on achieving competence and diagnosis, therapy and research. It thereby brought together opinion from practitioners, researchers, federal funders and professional bodies, and was successful in achieving a level of consensus that was considered way beyond the dreams of many of those in attendance (Benjamin & Baker, 2000).

The successful advance of clinical psychology today and its cognate practitioners (specialists, counsellors, etc.) owes much to the early vision and pragmatism of the architects at Boulder. The widespread endorsement of the scientist-practitioner model confirmed it as the core conceptual base for clinical training in the USA, while in the UK the creation of the National Health Service in 1948 provided a framework for the expansion of clinical psychology as a scientific profession, since many of the early clinical psychologists were appointed and paid as scientists, primarily concerned with the provision of assessment and research advice. Courses based loosely on this notion were set up in a few institutions in the fifties, namely the Maudsley, Tavistock and Creighton Royal, while the National Health Service began to formally approve training for clinical psychologists, leading to significant expansion in the sixties.

Also at around this time, Raimy (1950) suggested that the basic needs of our society for the services of clinical psychology could be understood using two dimensions:

a)   Provision of professional services to
   i.   individuals through corrective and remedial work, as well as diagnostic and therapeutic services;
   ii. groups and social institutions needing positive mental hygiene programmes in the interest of better community health;
   iii. students in training, members of other professions and the public through systematic education and general dissemination of information.

and

b) Research contributions designed to
    i.   develop better understanding of human behaviour;
    ii. improve the accuracy and reliability of diagnostic procedures;
    iii. develop more efficient methods of treatment;
    iv. develop methods of promoting mental hygiene and preventing maladjustment.

In these early days, and notwithstanding Boulder, many doubted the sustainability of maintaining both dimensions of this model. Indeed, Eysenck, rather than emphasising the need to combine research and clinical intervention, proposed a British scientist-practitioner model that diminished the role of therapeutic practice. Eysenck (1949) believed that the profession should concern itself solely with research and diagnosis, and should be removed from the social needs that could interfere with scientific requirements. Despite Eysenck's opinion, however, Shapiro in the Maudsley (Institute of Psychiatry, London) applied the methods of experimental psychology and learning theory to the clinical management of individual cases, which Hall (2007) has argued provided the effective basis for clinical psychology in the UK as it is today.

While the architects at Boulder established a formal template for scientist-practitioner programmes, in fact North American clinical psychology training programmes established prior to Boulder had already included many of the elements that later became identified with the Boulder model (Routh, 2000). If science and practice were the bride and groom, was it a marriage of convenience, a shotgun wedding or a joint partnership based on mutual respect, love and admiration? Despite the affirmation of scientific values at Boulder, it is impossible not to consider the historical context within which Boulder occurred. The pressure applied to address the mental health needs of a nation in the post-war atmosphere at the time created a cultural expectation that compelled the various stakeholders at Boulder to agree on a model of training and practice, more or less in line with the profession's aspirations. If the quality of the science and practice *at the time* were scrutinised using *current* standards of evidence, one could reasonably raise questions about generalisability, reliability and validity. Nevertheless, the aspirations at the time created conditions which, we wish to argue, have enabled the profession's continued enhancement, credible scientific advancement and recognition to the present day, despite any reservations we may currently have.

The Nature of Scientific Enquiry

To explore these issues further, it is helpful to review the scientific basis of clinical psychology today. O'Donohue *et al.* (2007) believe that science (which they describe as an applied epistemology or approach to knowledge) features specialised ways of forming beliefs, and is the safest way to minimise error in our methods. They suggest that science is the best safeguard we have at our disposal against commonplace biases and lapses in reasoning to which we all are prone. It thereby provides the most trustworthy basis for solving the myriad of problems we confront in psychological phenomena related to what causes disorders, and how we can measure and treat them.

The struggle for developing the science of the mind is, of course, not new. While ancient Greeks may have made many profound statements which appear to set the context of our current understanding of the functioning of the human mind, it was 18th-century empiricists who began to understand the importance of doing this in a systematic way, using emerging scientific methodologies. The 18th-century empiricist Thomas Reid, in his enquiry into the human mind on the principles of common sense, commented that 'all the knowledge we have in agriculture, gardening, chemistry and medicine is built upon the same foundation and if ever our philosophy concerning the human mind is carried so far as to deserve the name of science, which ought never to be despaired of, it must be by observing facts, reducing them to general rules and drawing just conclusions from them' (1764, p. 113).

Scientific method involves a) *observation:* a constant feature of scientific inquiry; b) *description*: information must be reliable, i.e. replicable (repeatable) as well as valid (relevant to the inquiry); c) *prediction*: information must be valid for observations, past, present and in the future of a given phenomenon; d) *control:* to sample fairly the range of possible occurrences wherever possible, as opposed to the passive acceptance of opportunistic data (control being the best way to control or counterbalance of risk of empirical biases); and e) *falsification:* this is a gradual process which requires repeated experiments by multiple researchers who must be able to replicate results in order to corroborate them. As a body of knowledge grows and a particular hypothesis or theory repeatedly brings predictable results, confidence in the hypothesis or theory increases.

This framework has provided the basis of the scientific revolution that underpins much of 21st-century life. The reason why this method is necessary when investigating humans is because we all have firmly held beliefs about functioning that are mistaken. Meehl (1993) emphasises that this tendency is not limited to practising clinicians, since academic researchers are just as prone to such errors as everyone else. O'Donohue *et al.* (2007) further emphasise that confounding this is the fact that most people are unaware of their own cognitive biases. They describe the three most important ways in which human cognition is subject to error: confirmation bias, illusory correlation and hindsight bias. Confirmation bias refers to the tendency to selectively seek out and recall information consistent with one's hypotheses and to neglect information inconsistent with them. Illusory correlations are likely to arise when individuals hold powerful *a priori* expectations regarding the co-variation between certain events or stimuli, thereby leading to our propensity to detect meaningful patterns in random data. The final bias is described by O'Donohue *et al.* as hindsight bias whereby individuals tend to over-estimate the likelihood that they would have predicted an outcome once they had become aware of it, known as the 'I knew it all along' effect.

The scientific method effectively challenges such erroneous belief formations and instead proposes beliefs more likely to be true. O'Donohue *et al.* suggest that randomised double-blind control trials are partial control against confirmation bias because they minimise the probability that investigators will influence participants. Systematic correlational designs minimise illusory correlation because they ensure the accurate computation of co-variation among variables, while carefully controlled longitudinal designs militate against hindsight bias because they collect data at multiple time points. They conclude that science is an essential safeguard against error, albeit not a foolproof one, and that scientific method can be creatively utilised to subject theories to scrutiny, and to ensure that replacements do not contain falsehoods.

Popper (1962) characterises the growth of scientific knowledge as the repeated overthrow of scientific theories and their replacement by better and more satisfactory ones. Popper, using the concept of truth likeness, recognises that the final truth is never obtained and that the better scientists attempt to maximise constructive criticism, feedback and the identification of errors. Progress is made by being proved wrong. McFall (1991) suggests that scientific clinical psychology is the only legitimate and acceptable form, arguing that no one would tolerate unscientific clinical psychology. He believes that clinical psychology's 'split personality', as manifested in the Boulder model, has allowed the notion of equity between science and practice, although he also believes in the primacy of science over practice.

This issue still divides the discipline today. Scientists argue that controlled research will be the final arbiter of truth in clinical psychology whereas many practitioners believe that their own clinical experience should be privileged. Some practitioners dismiss the relevance of research findings on psychotherapy and assessment for their everyday practice, maintaining that these findings should be disregarded when they conflict with clinical intuition or clinical experience. This divide has been exacerbated further by scientists sometimes adopting condescending attitudes towards clinicians and the validity of their experience.

The Nature of Clinical Psychology in Practice

In addition to suggesting that the cardinal principles of science should provide the only legitimate form of clinical psychology, McFall (1991) also proposed two important corollaries. The first suggests that psychological services should not be administered to the public until:

1. the exact nature of the service is described clearly;
2. the claimed benefits of the service are stated explicitly;
3. the claimed benefits are validated scientifically;
4. possible negative side effects that might out weigh any benefits are ruled out empirically.

The second corollary suggests that the primary and overriding objective of doctoral training programmes in clinical psychology must be to produce the most competent clinical scientists possible. Consequently he argues that the Boulder model, with its stated goal of training scientist-practitioners, is confusing and misleading, proposing instead that all students should be trained to think and function as a scientist in every aspect and setting of their professional lives, rather than completing particular clinical requirements.

These issues are currently being debated. Touyz (1995), for example, raises concerns about clinical psychology abandoning the scientist-practitioner approach and suggests that a clinical psychologist without a scientific background would become a counsellor indistinguishable from a social worker, counsellor or nurse consultant. Professional competencies could eventually become devoid of a scientific basis and would become focused on reified professional guild issues. Beutler *et al.* (1995), however, point out that in virtually every discipline in which the usual access to knowledge is through the scientific method, scientists lament that practitioners are inadequately trained, are insensitive to the value of scientific findings and fail to read the right journals. Conversely, practitioners are dismayed because scientists are consumed by irrelevant questions and fail to appreciate the knowledge that arises from practice.

Kennedy and Llewelyn (2001), with the backdrop of rapid growth of clinical psychology training in the late 20th century and the apparent variability in the acceptance of the principles of Boulder, reviewed the current approach to clinical psychology training in the UK, using a Delphi methodology to explore the likely future components of clinical training courses, key professional strategic developments and the model that underpins training. They compared and contrasted these questions in a group of clinical psychology trainers, clinical psychology trainees and practitioner clinical psychologists. Their research confirmed the centrality of the evidence-based scientist-practitioner model, but also suggested the need to include a high degree of responsiveness to the cultural and institutional context of practice. They concluded that the scientist-practitioner model primarily reflected an attitude to practice rather than a commitment to participation in the academic community requiring the submission of research papers to refereed journals. Results also showed that trainers were strongly committed to the model, although practitioners were significantly more likely to emphasise socio-cultural, social care and diversity issues. Kennedy and Llewelyn (2001) suggested that there may be a need to reformulate the scientist-practitioner model to incorporate the more complex understanding of the practice of science, as well as to integrate a more social perspective.

This last point raises the question of the profession's responsiveness to social need. In the USA, the Vail Conference of 1973 (reported by Korman, 1974) de-emphasised the scientist-practitioner model in favour of a practitioner-oriented approach, proposing that doctoral dissertations should be relevant to the delivery of social welfare. Extensive focus on the production of empirical work was considered unnecessary, since trainees principally needed to develop an awareness of research and to acquire the ability to evaluate its implications for practice. So while the development of professional training in clinical psychology as distinct from academic training validated the claim for professional status, are we at risk of simply wanting the best of both worlds? There is no doubt that from a professional perspective we have benefited from the status of doctoral programmes and have promoted our research competencies as unique selling points when compared to other healthcare professionals. So perhaps we have acted at least partially in self-interest. Another related issue is that of the social construction of the discipline. Lane and Corrie (2006), for example, have argued that our professional practice happens in specific social contexts, and that our self-identity is based on relational discourses, whereby we create our identities out of the conversations we have within our practice. The implication of this is that our scientific practice is not pure or objective, but is socially embedded within the contextual relations we happen to have. Further, these are normally organised to act at least as much in our own interests as in the interests of the recipients of our services.

The Nature of our Discipline

The debates reported above raise the question of how all these different imperatives and issues are to be understood and integrated satisfactorily. There is no doubt that from a professional perspective we have benefited from the status of doctoral programmes and have effectively promoted our research competencies as unique selling points when compared to other healthcare professionals. Yet if we are to pursue the ideal suggested by McFall (1991), that we should hold our theories and practice up to the utmost scientific scrutiny, then we probably need to broaden the base of our inquiry. In support of this point, the British Psychological Society's report on the future of psychological science (1991) has recognised both the impact on minority professionals of the dominant academic rhetoric and the impact on marginal groups of the imposition of primarily white, male and colonial theories of deviant behaviour. From this perspective, Lane and Corrie (2006) suggest that we should actively confront the priority given to certain forms of knowledge over others. Indeed, as an illustration of the way in which permitted narratives determine what is legitimate and true, we have shown above how the Boulder report was heavily influenced by the social economic objectives of post-war North America, being convened by a grouping of stakeholders that included the Federal Government, the Veterans Administration Hospitals, the American Psychological Association and the Universities, in order to endorse a model that would result in rapid expansion of professional services. Another example is the acceptance in the USA by psychologists of the use of the medically constructed *Diagnostic and Statistical Manual* (DSM) in diagnosing and describing human problems, which is fully embedded within the funding system, such that clinical psychologists must code according to the manual if they are to deliver funded services to clients.

There are now, however, significant calls for us to draw upon a wider range of evidence and theory to inform current practice. For example, in the USA there has been some recent debate and challenge to the use of the DSM, and the possible abuses of it in practice. Lane and Corrie (2006) claim that by failing to legitimise clients' stories (or rather by requiring clients to conform to our way of telling them) we have come to favour technical solutions which do not challenge those in authority. They argue that the lay public is expert in other ways to which we have often failed to give sufficient credence. In this way, we are failing to recognise how we contribute to the problem rather than the solution.

As our world of knowledge and practice expands, perhaps we also need to redefine, re-explore and reappraise the type of bridge we require between these various perspectives. To do this, it is important to consider the nature of the problem. For instance, Beutler *et al.* (1995) challenge the belief held by many researchers that clinicians are not interested in research. In a survey of 365 scientists and practitioners, they found that clinicians report finding research writings to be useful and that they regularly incorporate results into their daily work. Conversely, however, academics often fail to acknowledge the value of clinical practice, and report reading clinical accounts less often than scientific writings are read by clinicians. Moreover, academic researchers often suggest unrealistic ways in which clinicians may correspond with them in order to establish collaboration, i.e. by writing research articles (Beutler *et al.*, 1995). These findings suggest that to bridge the gap between scientists and practitioners, communication needs to be increased in both directions, but perhaps particularly by exposing researchers to clinical issues in practice.

Interestingly, Beutler *et al.* (1995) report that both psychological scientists and psychological practitioners believe that they alone are concerned with 'reality'. To resolve this discrepancy, they suggest: the building of links between scientific research groups; and that scientists should initiate and maintain relationships with practitioners. They also suggest that practitioners should reconsider the role of science; and research should be relevant to clinicians, developing vehicles for translating science to practice. There is therefore a growing recognition of the need for greater integration, and more recent attention may provide a stronger foundation and clearer strategies for resolving this divide. We also propose that both perspectives need to incorporate service user views (see Chapter 29) to comprehensively address this divide.

Hofmann and Weinberger (2007), who come from opposing 'camps', believe that differences between scientist and practice are indeed complementary and not incompatible. Westen (2007) proposes three forces that have strained relationships between clinician and researchers in the USA. The first is managed care, which has reduced resources for mental health. The second is described as a 'capitalisation of academia' which creates incentives for Universities to select faculty with strong grant records. In the UK the RAE exercise has contributed to similar strains. Westen (2007) identifies the evidence-based practice (EBP) movement in medicine as the third force. He believes that this is largely due to EBP being operationalised in psychology as the utilisation of brief manualised therapies, tested in randomised clinical trials. Westen indicates that the convergence of these forces has resulted in many researchers not only devaluing clinicians and clinical practice but also attempting to prescribe and proscribe how clinicians should practise. He adds that most practitioners would like to be partners with researchers in a bi-directional exchange of ideas to learn what could be most helpful to service users.

To resolve this, Westen and Morrison (2001) suggest a strategy that could be viewed as a bridge, proposing that scientists should observe the therapeutic strategies used by experienced clinicians, in a wide range of patients with broadly defined symptom patterns, who may or may not have substantial comorbidities, in order to examine the relationship between specific intervention strategies and outcome. This is conceived as a way of utilising scientific methods to evaluate clinical outcomes, and the associated efficacy of a constellation of treatment strategies. This would also enable these empirically derived treatments to be subject to community scrutiny and to identify what works in practice. For example, Morrison *et al.* (2003) carried out a naturalistic study of successful treatments in clinical practice. Participants were 242 experienced doctoral-level clinicians (from a wide range of orientations) who reported on their last successfully treated patients for significant depression, panic or anxiety. Most patients were treated for longer than the 8–16 sessions characteristic of efficacy trials and most presented with significant comorbidity. The authors concluded that such effectiveness studies could bridge the gap between research and practice by examining ecologically valid samples and using such data to generate prototypic treatments. As another example, Thompson-Brenner and Westen (2005) examined 145 completed treatments of people with bulimic symptoms. The mean length of cognitive behavioural therapy was 69 sessions and even longer for eclectic and psychodynamic therapies. Over 40 per cent of this sample would have been excluded from randomised controlled trials using four common exclusion criteria. These patients showed higher pre-treatment severity and required longer treatment to achieve positive outcomes relative to patients who did not meet the exclusion criteria. Thompson-Brenner and Weston concluded that such research confirms the validity of genuinely collaborative endeavours, with clinicians doing what they do best by treating patients, and researchers doing what they do best, i.e. testing hypotheses, especially those generated by senior clinicians.

Reflective Practice

Many clinical psychology training programmes (Scott *et al.*, 2004), especially in the UK, now highlight the importance of reflective practice as an important way of making sense of the interface between science and practice. Stedmon *et al.* (2003) propose that a reflective approach recognises the importance of giving equal amounts of attention to different sources of knowledge in clinical practice. Reflection requires an individual to take a critical and evaluative position in relation to their understanding of practice, often by going beyond models to explore their wider cultural and socio-political background. Reflection begins with the individuals developing self-awareness about their own histories, and how their own personal experiences and values contribute to their professional development. This self-awareness is then extended to understanding the importance of diversity, the social and cultural context of work, working within an ethical framework and the need for continuing professional and personal development. The British Psychological Society (2004) recommends that reflective practice is incorporated into personal development plans, which enable psychologists to identify needs and reflect upon learning and application to practice. Lane and Corrie (2006) also believe that reflective practice is an appropriate adjunct to counter the Western slant of most models and case conceptualisations. They argue that psychotherapy is primarily about overcoming problems located within an individual, whereas Eastern philosophies are more systemically oriented and contextually aware.

Lavender (2003), drawing on the ideas of Schön (1983), summarises the four main processes involved in reflective practice. The first concerns reflection in action whereby the individual reflects cognitively and emotionally about what is happening at a given point and what should happen in the future. This involves rapid analysis of the specifics of the context using immediately available theories and constructions. It parallels the notion of meta-cognition or 'supervisor within'. The second process is reflection on action. This occurs after an event and can happen by reviewing therapy tapes, writings, etc. or with supervision. The third process comprises reflection on the impact of self on others, whereby the individual seeks feedback from a variety of sources such as clients, peers and members of the team. The fourth process concerns reflection about the self which includes having an awareness of our background histories and contexts as well as our vulnerabilities and social experiences. A final process has been added by Smail (2006), amongst others, who points to the need both to be aware of, and to attempt to tackle, aspects of the sometimes invisible but dysfunctional context of our work, including the operation of discrimination, inequalities, covert interest groups, and power.

New Proposals

An attempt to resolve some of the conceptual ambiguities of the profession has been made by Snyder and Elliott (2005). They consider that although clinical psychology has prospered in the sixty years following Boulder, the Boulder model does not prepare graduates to meet the diverse demands of likely mental and physical health issues in the 21st century and that its emphasis on mental illness rather than mental health renders it outdated. Instead, they propose a four-quadrant matrix model, derived from the ideas of Wright (1991), in which there are two dimensions. The first is *Valence*, the degree to which any given diagnostic focus is either positive or negative, that is, on the person's strengths or weaknesses. The second dimension is *Source*, which locates significant factors within the person or within the person's environment. Snyder and Elliott argue that previous clinical training has emphasised the individual, with lesser attention being given to the interpersonal level, or larger institutional and societal community contexts. The matrix model is also embedded within four levels, i.e. the individual, interpersonal, institutional and the societal-community levels. At the individual level, research, diagnosis and therapeutic activities are normally aimed towards an identified person and delivered by a single clinical psychologist, usually in a therapeutic context. The overall curriculum for educating at this level focuses on weaknesses. Snyder and Elliott, however, consider that positive dimensions are needed to validate personal strengths, hope, optimism and self-efficacy, as a counterpoint to the traditional widely used pathology-oriented DSM approach (American Psychiatric Association, 1994). The matrix model instead fosters a thorough search of the total person, recognising weaknesses and strengths.

Next, they suggest that the interpersonal level has been given too little attention. Humans live within a social context, and almost everything that is done across the lifespan is based on interpersonal issues. They argue that greater focus should be placed on these issues. Third, the institutional level involves research, consultation, administration and liaison roles, conducted in schools, hospitals and employment settings. Psychological expertise at this level should promote coordinated provision of psychological research and practitioner services across institutions. Snyder and Elliott believe we still operate out of 20th-century models when we ignore the behavioural and social mechanisms which are known to have profound impact on the physical health and psychological well-being of persons with chronic conditions (Israel *et al.*, 1998).

The final level can be described as societal-community, and addresses the major issues and challenges facing all delivery systems, including those providing mental and physical health care. Future trainers need to know how to conduct research in large settings using archival data, how to allocate resources and how to influence the formation of healthcare policies. While current clinical psychology services focus on delivery to a single client, Snyder and Elliott argue that we would have more impact with a top-down approach. Future clinical psychologists should be much more involved in commissioning, accrediting and validating service provision. Finally, they argue that there is no intrinsic loss of kudos or effectiveness in promoting less costly forms of psychological treatment possibly delivered by less intensively trained staff, as long as such individuals are appropriately monitored, supervised and evaluated. This is an argument which is currently finding much favour in the UK, which is introducing the widespread delivery of evidence-based psychological therapies by relatively junior therapists under the supervision of trained clinical psychologists. In conjunction with the New Ways of Working initiative, this project (Improving Access to Psychological Therapies, see also Chapter 29) aims to significantly increase the influence of psychology in healthcare contexts (British Psychological Society, 2007).

Finally, Stricker (2007) presents the Local Clinical Scientist (LCS) model as another potential bridge between science and practice. The LCS model operates from the assumption that science is not defined by activities or generalisations, but by attitudes. Activities vary, generalisations decay, but attitudes cut across disciplines and findings. All scientists should aim to be keen observers, characterised by disciplined inquiry, critical thinking, imagination, rigour, scepticism, and openness to change in the face of evidence. The LCS carries these attitudes into the practice setting, raising hypotheses in the consulting room and seeking confirmatory or disconfirmatory evidence in the immediate response to the patient. This scientific attitude towards clinical phenomena is crucial since it is the systematic study of clinical work that reduces distortions and refines effective clinical decision making. The model recognises the salience of idiographic aspects of practice, but also accommodates knowledge of data and the balance of evidence. Stricker (2002) calls for more research to be based on naturalistic phenomena which are more likely to be of value to the clinician and be incorporated within daily practice.

A Way Forward

Many advocates of practice-focused research now consider that the gap between the scientist and practitioner aspects of the profession could be bridged by bringing more science into the practice. Reflective practice also plays a significant part in articulating this junction. The methodological pluralism that is necessary to achieve this would create an alliance that is likely to be increasingly effective in managing psychological problems, if only because it calls on a much broader understanding of clinical phenomena.

The bi-directional integrated approach also necessitates a more active patient participant and a more flexible therapist or experimenter. Patients or clients would therefore no longer be passive participants who are studied and manipulated by researchers to produce findings which have limited generalisability. Snyder and Elliott (2005) believe that it should not be beyond the scholarship of the 21st century to manage the 'disconnect' between academic research and applied clinical areas. They further suggest that our research expertise should be used to triage persons who require the services of high-cost doctoral-level providers, as compared to those who may fare well with low-cost providers. Research should examine existing clinical practice, which could be uplifted by newer applied research methodologies and more sophisticated forms of clinical data analysis. Such joint scholarship may help move away from the simplistic, reductionist perspective of linear causality, and may help to build a model to promote clinical psychology in the 21st century, just as constructively as the Boulder model did for the 20th.

References

American Psychiatric Association (1994). *Diagnostic and Statistical Manual of Mental Disorders* (4th edn). Washington, DC: Author.

Benjamin, L.T., Jr. & Baker, D.B. (Eds.) (2000). Special section: Boulder at 50. *American Psychologist, 55,* 233–254.

Beutler, L.E., Williams, R.E., Wakefield, P.J. & Entwistle, S.R. (1995). Bridging scientist and practitioner perspectives in clinical psychology. *American Psychologist, 50,* 984–994.

British Psychological Society (1991). *The future of psychological science.* Leicester, UK: Author.

British Psychological Society (2004). *Continuing professional development.* Leicester: Author. Retrieved 25 February 2009 from www.bps.org.uk/cpd. Also available from: the British Psychological Society, St Andrews House, 48 Princess Road East, Leicester LE1 7DR; Tel: 0116 252 9568.

British Psychological Society (2007). *New ways of working for applied psychologists in health and social care.* Leicester: Author.

Eysenck, H.J. (1949). Training in clinical psychology: An English point of view. *American Psychologist, 4,* 173–176.

Hall, J. (2007). The emergence of clinical psychology in Britain from 1943–1958. *History and Philosophy of Psychology, 92,* 1–33.

Hall, J. & Llewelyn, S. (2006). What is clinical psychology? In J. Hall & S. Llewelyn (Eds.) *What is clinical psychology?* (pp. 1–30). Oxford: Oxford University Press.

Hofmann, S.G. & Weinberger, J. (2007). The art and science of psychotherapy: An introduction. In S.G. Hofmann & J. Weinberger (Eds.) *The art and science of psychotherapy* (xvii–2). New York: Routledge.

Israel, B.A., Schulz, A.J., Parker, E.A. & Becker, A.B. (1998). Review of community-based research: Assessing partnership approaches to improve public health. *Annual Review of Public Health, 19,* 173–202.

Kennedy, P. & Llewelyn, S. (2001). Does the future belong to the scientist practitioner? *The Psychologist, 14*(2), 74–78.

Korman, M. (1974). National conference on levels and patterns of professional training in psychology: The major themes. *American Psychologist, 29,* 441–449.

Lane, D.A. & Corrie, S. (2006). What does it mean to be a scientist-practitioner? Working towards a new vision. In *The modern scientist practitioner: A guide to practice in psychology* (pp. 9–22). London: Routledge.

Lavender, T. (2003). Redressing the balance: The place, history and future of reflective practice in training. *Clinical Psychology, 27,* 11–15.

McFall, R.M. (1991). Manifesto for a science in clinical psychology. *Clinical Psychologist, 44,* 75–78.

Meehl, P.E. (1993). Philosophy of science: Help or hindrance? *Psychological Reports, 72*(3), 707–733.

Morrison, C., Bradley, R. & Westen, D. (2003). The external validity of efficacy trials for depression and anxiety: A naturalistic study. *Psychology and Psychotherapy: Theory Research and Practice, 76,* 109–132.

O'Donohue, W., Lilienfeld, S. & Fowler, L. (Eds.) (2007). *Sage handbook of personality disorders.* Thousand Oaks, CA: Sage.

Popper, K. (1962). *Conjectures and refutations.* New York: Basic Books.

Raimy, V. (1950). *Training in clinical psychology.* New York: Prentice Hall.

Reid, T. (1764). *An inquiry into the human mind on the principles of common sense* (p.113).

Routh, D.K. (2000). Clinical psychology training: A history of ideas and practices prior to 1946. *American Psychologist, 55,* 236–241.

Schön, D. (1983). *The reflective practitioner: How professionals think in action.* New York: Basic Books.

Scott, D., Brown, A.J., Lunt, I. & Thorne, L. (2004). *Professional doctorates: Integrating academic and professional knowledge.* Buckingham, UK: Open University Press.

Smail, D.J. (2006). *Power, interest and psychology.* Bath, UK: Bath Press.

Snyder, C.R. & Elliott, T.R. (2005). Twenty-first century graduate education in clinical psychology: A four level matrix model. *Journal of Clinical Psychology, 61,* 1033–1054.

Stedmon, J., Mitchell, A., Johnstone, L. & Staite, S. (2003). Making reflective practice real: Problems and solutions in the South West. *Clinical Psychology, 27,* 30–33.

Stricker, G. (2002). What is a scientist-practitioner anyway? *Journal of Clinical Psychology, 58* (10), 1277–1283.

Stricker, G. (2007). The local clinical scientist. In S.G. Hofmann & J. Weinberger (Eds.) *The art and science of psychotherapy* (pp. 85–99). New York: Routledge.

Strickland, B.R. (1988). Clinical psychology comes of age. *American Psychologist, 43,* 104–107.

Thompson-Brenner, H. & Westen, D. (2005). Personality subtypes in eating disorders: Validation of a classification in a naturalistic sample. *British Journal of Psychiatry, 186,* 516–524.

Touyz, S.W. (1995). Clinical psychology in disarray: The challenge ahead. *Australian Psychologist, 30,* 191–195.

Westen, D. (2007). Discovering what works in the community: Toward a genuine partnership of clinicians and researchers. In S.G. Hofmann & J. Weinberger (Eds.) *The art and science of psychotherapy* (pp. 3–29). New York: Routledge.

Westen, D. & Morrison, K. (2001). A multidimensional meta-analysis of treatments for depression, panic, and generalized anxiety disorder: An empirical examination of the status of empirically supported therapies. *Journal of Consulting and Clinical Psychology, 69,* 875–899.

Woodworth, R.S. (1937). The future of clinical psychology. *Journal of Consulting Psychology, 1,* 4–5.

Wright, B.A. (1991). Labeling: The need for greater person-environment individuation. In C.R. Snyder & D.R. Forsyth (Eds.) *Handbook of social and clinical psychology: The health perspective* (pp. 469–487). Elmsford, NY: Pergamon.

4

Research and Evaluation

Myra Cooper and Cynthia Graham

Overview

This chapter will outline the importance and significance of psychological research and evaluation in modern health care. It will highlight the unique contribution that clinical psychologists can make, and introduce our idea of 'research' as a state of mind characteristic of much of the work conducted by a competent clinical psychologist. We will consider why relatively few clinical psychologists undertake formal research, despite growing interest in psychological aspects of health care. The key skills, qualities and support we have observed to be commonly used and required by the researcher are identified, with suggestions for how to obtain this support. Ability to consume, teach and supervise research and its application to clinical and organisational practice and change will be emphasised. The methods currently used in psychological research will then be briefly summarised. We will make explicit some of the processes we have observed to be involved in successful research, and emphasise that these are not mysterious, but can be readily learnt and taught. Finally, we will consider differences between research and audit, evaluation, service and quality improvement, and discuss ethical approval and research governance.

Research Is a State of Mind

The development of qualitative methodologies, with their emphasis on socially constructed, multiple realities, has made definitions of research that refer only to use of the scientific method problematic. In the absence of an agreed technical definition of 'research', one definition that we find useful is 'careful search or inquiry after or for or into' (Sykes, 1982). This epitomises not only what we consider to be an essential characteristic of a good researcher, but is also a vital and highly desirable characteristic of a good clinical psychologist, including the times when they are engaged in clinical work.

One aspect of research is nevertheless 'formal research', by which we mean research activity that is distinct from day-to-day clinical work, although we acknowledge that research activity and clinical work are invariably complementary and often overlap significantly.

Research, both formal, and as defined above by Sykes, is a skill that should, and can, be a core competency for all clinical psychologists (Kennedy & Llewelyn, 2001). Importantly, research is not simply 'what' you know but it also involves 'knowing how', i.e. what questions should be asked, what strategy or process should be adopted. Knowing how is essential; and our belief is that clinical psychologists who succeed in clinically focused work also have the potential to succeed in research. Both components will be covered here; indeed a particular aim of this chapter is to demystify 'knowing how', drawing on our own experience of many years of teaching and supervising the research work of trainee clinical psychologists and others.

Importance of Psychological Research and Evaluation

Psychological research has produced a large amount of evidence relevant to clinical practice, particularly in the past 20–25 years. It has had a major role in influencing important clinical guidelines, not only in mental health, but also in general medicine, and in practice related to children, the elderly and those with learning disabilities. In the UK the National Institute for Health and Clinical Excellence has produced many of these guidelines. This research has provided an evidence base for a range of psychological therapies, and has also helped to support carer and service user engagement and involvement, service and delivery and organisational development in the National Health Service (NHS). While many clinicians are familiar with the guidelines, it is important to remember that they are the outcome of basic exploratory and experimental study, as well as theory and treatment development work. Psychologists have conducted a considerable amount of this work.

The publication of 'Best Research for Best Health' (Department of Health, 2006) recognises the need for the NHS to encourage research excellence, to attract the best research professionals to conduct people-based research, and to continue to invest in the basic formal research that underpins everyday clinical practice. Clinical psychologists are extremely well placed to participate in all aspects of research excellence, not least because they are the only healthcare professionals to receive extensive training in research design and methodology as part of their core professional training. They also have the unique advantage of a solid grounding in normal psychological processes from undergraduate study. This is invaluable in completing basic and clinical research and also in both theory and treatment development.

Psychological issues are increasingly being identified as important in fields that have not traditionally attracted or employed many clinical psychologists. For example, although their role is not yet well understood, medical, biological and neuroscience investigators are recognising the importance of psychological aspects of disease and disorder in their work. Interestingly, while the 1990s was termed the decade of the brain, the start of the new millennium has been termed the decade of behaviour (e.g. Wagemans *et al.*, 2001).

Political and policy shifts have also emphasised the value of psychological research in health care. There has been a shift in service attitudes to patients as consumers, and an emphasis on patient choice. Patients now insist on greater accountability and monitoring, and expect certain standards. Many of these can be monitored and evaluated with appropriate research and audit to demonstrate that standards are in place and operating effectively. There has also been a call for greater attention to be paid to the 'person', to the patient experience, and to quality of treatment and quality of life. Changing demographics, cost and efficiency concerns, the increased burden of an ageing population and improvements in medical science, increasing the range of new treatments, must all be factored into these developments, and all need monitoring and evaluation (Department of Health, 2005a). Clinical psychologists are well placed to contribute to these agendas.

Secondary research skills (see below) have become particularly important in recent years. At a national level this includes sifting and evaluating research evidence to create guidelines. Psychologists have an important role to play here with their sophisticated ability to assess and evaluate others' research work. At the individual patient level, the trend for clinical psychologists to see complex cases also makes these skills crucial. Many patients do not fit national guidelines and treating them effectively involves skills in assessing and evaluating a huge body of research knowledge in order to decide on the best or optimal care. Indeed, the study of 'what works for whom' is one of the big challenges facing clinicians on a day-to-day basis, as well as in identifying and pursuing new research topics. Even processes once thought to be purely biologically driven, such as neuronal development, are increasingly found to be affected by psychological factors, opening up new research and ultimately novel treatment options.

Interestingly, a survey conducted in 2001 (Kennedy & Llewelyn, 2001) indicated that clinical psychology trainers, practitioners and those in training predicted that research would remain a cornerstone of the profession, although the authors of this survey caution that it is not clear that, despite the rhetoric in the UK at least, where clinical psychology is closely aligned to the NHS, sufficient resources are in place to ensure that this continues in the future, in terms of both quantity and quality of research conducted.

Research Activity by Clinical Psychologists

Despite the potential, evident skills, and fact that clinical psychologists do contribute important research relevant to health care, the lack of formal research, particularly that which involves collecting new data, amongst the majority of practising clinical psychologists has been of great concern for some time (Salkovskis, 1984; Milne *et al.*, 1990). Relatively few clinical psychologists do any formal research, either small or large scale, once they are qualified (Milne *et al.*, 1990, 2000). There do not appear to be any published data on clinical psychology involvement in audit in the NHS. While we have noticed that audit is likely to be conducted more often than research (at least in the UK), our impression is that the proportion of clinical psychologists who carry out audit or service evaluation projects is still fairly small.

Factors Affecting Research Activity

The reasons for lack of formal research activity have not been systematically investigated (Milne & Paxton, 1998). One study has, however, investigated the factors that affect clinical psychology trainee publication of their research projects (primarily their large-scale projects) in peer reviewed journals (Cooper & Turpin, 2007). Themes that were perceived to be associated with publication included supervisor factors, trainee factors, general course factors, study characteristics and the demands of a new job following qualification. Other related issues will now be described.

Anxiety and lack of confidence

One factor we have observed to affect research activity is anxiety and lack of confidence, amongst both trainees and qualified psychologists. The reasons for this are not completely clear. In the UK many trainees are academic high achievers, who are well motivated and able. In our experience, even though many have the potential to achieve in research, trainees are often highly anxious about it. Anxiety also extends to service-related or audit projects, even though one might suppose that these are more straightforward to conduct. Despite this, our experience is that these projects are often of high quality, are valued by services, and can play an important role in local policy and service development.

Training courses have a role in decreasing anxiety and increasing confidence, and in promoting a sense of research 'self-efficacy', but the support and help of colleagues and the wider profession, as well as the systems and structures of healthcare organisations, become important once psychologists qualify. Just as mentoring and supervision are important for clinical work, the same is needed for research work. Sadly, the latter is not often provided routinely, and even those who begin their careers with confidence and significant research 'self-efficacy' may find it hard to stay motivated and actively engaged in research. Our observation is that those who do continue with research typically organise their own personal support systems and supervision, even if it means some travel or long-distance telephone or email contact. This can be invaluable in managing the inevitable ups and downs of research, providing peer support, mentoring, feedback and a forum for discussion of issues and progress of projects.

Negative experiences

Anecdotally, some psychologists report feeling 'traumatised' by their experience of research. Sometimes this is attributed to the associated bureaucracy involved in research ethics or research and development (R&D) applications, e.g. lengthy forms, scrutiny, approval, checks with delays at each stage, and 'unhelpful' feedback, including from those with little or no research experience. Procedures frequently change or break down, so it is hard to keep up to date with local requirements, all of which are different across trusts and organisations. This often results in frustration, but it is important to consider how clinical psychologists might make such processes easier and more flexible, including at the organisational level. An important part of a psychologist's role in the NHS should be to assist with these processes and with their management and implementation.

Benefits of Conducting Research

Much is written about the drawbacks of research, but there are also many benefits. These need to be highlighted and encouraged, and promoted more widely during and after training. Some of the benefits we have observed and enjoy personally include variety, flexibility, the excitement of being at the cutting edge, and of discovery, opportunities for national and international contact and networking, making a difference to large numbers of people versus treating an individual patient, positive feedback on findings, and the excitement and status of becoming an expert in a particular area.

Redefining What Is Meant by Research

Trainees, and also some qualified psychologists, may, in our experience, have an overly narrow perception of what research is and what would constitute good, clinically relevant research (e.g. only research involving clients, or only research evaluating treatment). This excludes a great deal of useful research that can be conducted on sub-clinical samples, analogue groups and healthy volunteers as well as valuable work that can be done with existing data sets (either secondary analysis of previous data or retrospective analysis of routinely collected data). It also excludes important basic work, including the development and validation of psychological theory.

Much good research is collaborative, and others can be enrolled to assist with a range of tasks, from ideas, planning and data collection to analysis. This, however, can be particularly difficult for clinical psychology trainees, when much of the research conducted in training must be one's own work, and relatively little collaboration may take place, partly to meet the criterion for 'own work' required for qualification. However, successful research increasingly involves collaboration with others, particularly with colleagues from other disciplines.

Consuming Research

Application of skills to consume research for a variety of purposes has been noted above. Perhaps one of the most important skills that psychologists can bring to this is the capacity to critically evaluate research done by others, and to place it in the context of other relevant knowledge. The quality of published work varies tremendously, and invariably contains limitations, not always acknowledged by the authors, but identifiable to those with the relevant training. This is an important skill, not least in light of sometimes misleading claims that X is the best or only acceptable treatment for Y, etc.

Teaching and Supervising

One of the challenges faced by clinical psychologists is to disseminate knowledge and skills about research. Providing education and demonstrating the value of research and audit in practice is one aspect of this task. The skills of teamwork, and managing systems, which will all be acquired on clinical placements, are invaluable here. Although in reality we have observed that this does not often seem to feature in many psychologists' current work, teaching others about research and audit skills, and supervising project work, just as they supervise and teach clinical skills, is an area in which clinical psychologists can make an important contribution.

Research Design and Methodology

Some of the research designs and methodologies most commonly used by clinical psychologists are shown in Box 4.1.

Box 4.1   Research designs and methodologies commonly used by clinical psychologists

Case study and case series designs
Experimental and quasi-experimental studies
Cross-sectional studies
Survey methods
Naturalistic observational studies
Correlational studies
Audit and service evaluations
Quality improvement studies
Grounded theory
Interpretative phenomenological analysis (IPA)
Focus groups
Discourse analysis
Randomised controlled trials
Clinical trials
Longitudinal studies

This list is neither exhaustive nor definitive but demonstrates the range of approaches/methods that clinical psychologists use. In the past decade or so, the use of qualitative methodologies among psychologists has increased; in particular, in the UK the qualitative approach known as Interpretative Phenomenological Analysis (IPA) (Smith & Osborn, 2003) has become increasingly popular. While IPA is a valuable research method, as researchers involved in training clinical psychologists we believe that it is important to be aware of, and consider use of, alternative qualitative methodologies, e.g. discourse analysis, which may be better suited to particular research questions. Another trend in recent years has been the growing use of mixed methods research, where both quantitative and qualitative data are collected and analysed in a single study (Creswell, 2003). In our view this is a welcome move away from the traditional divide between quantitative and qualitative research paradigms (Onwuegbuzie & Leech, 2005).

Demystifying the Research Process

Steps in carrying out a research project

Successful research, in our experience, can be characterised by a series of well-defined steps; indeed, this perspective can demystify the research process and make it seem more manageable. The process of preparing to do a research project is very much an iterative one, where each consideration feeds back into previous ideas, shaping up the project.

There are a number of useful websites containing information relevant to the various stages of the research process. These include the Web Center for Social Research Methods (www.socialresearchmethods.net/), a comprehensive web-based textbook on social research methods, and Research Design Explained (spsp.clarion.edu/RDE3/start/), which contains helpful guidance on how to generate a research hypothesis, how to select a measure, etc. Other useful web-based resources include the US National Institute of Mental Health (NIMH) website (www.nimh.nih.gov/), which includes fact sheets, publications, and statistics on specific psychological disorders, and the website of the American Psychological Association (APA) (www.apa.org/) which has links to scientific and media articles, policy documents and fact sheets on more than fifty psychological topics. With a more European focus, Psychology Press run a site that provides opportunities for online questions, links to other researchers, and blogs (www.researchmethodsarena.com/), while for those seeking research related information in European (and other) non-English languages a good starting point is the international list of psychology societies provided by the University of Waterloo (www.scholarly-societies.org/psychol_soc.html). Many of these produce fact sheets or other publications in languages other than English that can be useful for the researcher.

In the next section we provide a brief overview of each of these stages of this process, as we have observed it, and identify some common problems/obstacles and tips that we have found useful for overcoming them:

1.   Formulating a research problem and research objective(s). You may be starting from a broad topic or from a very specific question that you would like to answer. In either case an essential part of this stage is to find out what previous research has been done in the area and what gaps/unanswered questions remain. Selecting a theoretical model/framework for your project should also be done at this stage. Identifying the key journals and texts in an area, carrying out a focused literature search and making contact with other researchers, e.g. about possible ongoing studies, may be helpful. It might also be useful to discuss your preliminary ideas with colleagues, who can provide feedback/suggestions. Lastly, particularly if this project is being conducted in the NHS, it is important to consider the clinical and service implications of the project (this will be important in 'selling' the project to managers/ funding bodies/clinicians).

In our experience the most common difficulty experienced at this stage is in narrowing down a topic. It might be helpful here to consider what your priorities are in carrying out this piece of research. This may enable you to prioritise certain elements of the project, e.g. a key research question, the timeframe you have, the scope of the project, whom to involve, etc.

2.   Developing research questions and (if applicable) hypotheses. All studies contain one or more research questions, although these are not always explicitly stated in research papers. However, we would encourage researchers to focus on making their research questions explicit as these will provide the specificity needed to guide later steps of the research process, e.g. data analysis. Explicit hypotheses, however, may not be needed for more exploratory studies.

Common problems at this stage are that research questions lack precision/specificity and/or that there are too many (or too ambitious) questions. A fundamental point to bear in mind is that research questions and hypotheses should provide information that is of clear relevance to the research objective(s).

3.   Selecting a research design/methodology. As discussed above, this is a critical step in planning a research project and should be done only once the preceding steps have been completed. Selecting an appropriate research design and methodology to answer your research questions can be relatively straightforward or it can be a daunting task. Whether the research objective is exploratory or confirmatory will also influence the choice of design and methodology. Consulting the literature to look at previous examples and discussion with colleagues who have experience of certain methods can be helpful. If you decide on a specific methodology that you have little experience of, it is worth finding out about training courses or workshops offered.

4.   Data collection. Two primary issues that relate to data collection are decisions about sampling (and sample size) and choice of measures. Although probability (i.e. random) sampling is usually regarded as optimal, these types of designs are not always feasible and, moreover, may not be appropriate if the study is an exploratory one. Regarding sample size, it is important to consider conducting a formal power calculation. Although there are no clear guidelines for determining sample sizes in qualitative studies (Guest *et al.*, 2006), previous studies can be helpful to ascertain the range of typical sample sizes. The selection of assessment measures that are reliable

and valid, and that will provide the necessary information to answer your research questions, is another important task. Here it might be necessary to contact the authors of a measure to obtain permission to use the instrument, or to obtain information about scoring; in our experience most researchers are very responsive to such requests. One common problem encountered at this stage occurs when there are no validated questionnaires to measure a construct of interest. In these cases it might be necessary to develop a measure for your particular study aims, in which case it is worth considering how you might incorporate some method(s) to assess the reliability/validity of the new measure.

5.   Data analysis and interpretation. Once again, the type of data analysis undertaken should be determined by the research objective(s). In some exploratory quantitative studies, and in most audits, descriptive statistics might be all that is required, while other studies will involve use of sophisticated data analytic methods. Regarding qualitative research, there are also a number of analysis techniques to choose from and published guidelines for these techniques exist (e.g. Hsieh & Shannon, 2005; Ritchie & Spencer, 1994). In qualitative studies, data analysis is often done alongside data collection rather than in a separate phase. Qualitative studies can produce vast amounts of data; systematic analysis of these data can be very time-consuming. It is therefore important to build in sufficient time for data analysis when mapping out a timeline.

6.   Communicate findings. Communicating findings from research is not only accomplished by publishing in scientific journals; dissemination can also take place through presentations at departmental/service meetings and conferences, feeding back results to study participants, publishing a summary of the results in newsletters, on websites, etc. Although most psychologists would agree that publication of research findings is important, as noted above in relation to trainees, much psychological research is not published. In our view one of the reasons for this is that this step, unlike the other stages in the research process, is often not planned. Specific goal setting and timetables, plans to access support (e.g. statistical help), obtaining feedback on drafts and support from colleagues, and identifying potential obstacles and ways to deal with them can all be helpful strategies, as can selecting a target journal and writing an outline of the paper early on.

Differentiating audit, service evaluation, quality improvement and research

Although the above steps apply to both small-scale service-related projects, such as audits, and large-scale research studies, such as epidemiological surveys, there are some important differences between these types of project that are worth highlighting. Firstly, ideally service-related research should be linked to local audit plans and service needs/priorities. Service-related research is also more likely to involve dealing with NHS staff and managers. It is important to think carefully about how you can best communicate your findings to ensure that managers and any staff involved clearly see the outcome and impact of the project. Unlike research, projects defined as audit or service evaluation do not require approval by an NHS Research Ethics Committee (REC); generally, audit is considered by the relevant local Audit or Clinical Effectiveness Committee. A third type of project that psychologists often carry out is service or quality improvement/evaluation projects, which do not fit easily into either the audit or research categories (Cooper *et al.*, 2005).

Defining research and how it differs from audit and service evaluation has been far from straightforward. Some projects seem to occupy a grey area and this may cause confusion about whether REC review for a given project is necessary or not. The Good Practice Guidelines for the Conduct of Research within the NHS (Cooper *et al.*, 2005) include a helpful decision tree to decide whether or not a project is audit or research. The National Research Ethics Committee (NRES) website has published a leaflet on differentiating audit, service evaluation, and research (National Research Ethics Service, 2008), which makes it clear that service evaluation and audit projects do not require NHS REC review.

Ethical approval and research governance

Ethical practice in research is guided by three core principles: justice, respect for persons, and beneficence (the expectation that researchers will protect participants from possible harm and maximise possible benefits for both the participant and society at large). In our view it is unfortunate that because NHS research ethics procedures have often been perceived as complex and onerous, these fundamental and important principles may be obscured.

The British Psychological Society's 'Guidelines for Minimum Standards of Ethical Approval in Psychological Research' (British Psychological Society, 2004) makes it clear that *all* research requires some form of ethical approval, whether by a departmental or institutional committee or, if necessary, by an external ethics committee such as an NHS REC. Since 2004, any research involving NHS patients, staff, premises or equipment requires approval by an NHS REC. In addition to REC approval, investigators must also seek permission to carry out their research from the R&D directorate of the trust(s) from which they wish to recruit. Other countries operate different systems and criteria for scrutinising the ethical aspects of psychological research projects, although projects based in the UK and conducted overseas will usually also require some form of scrutiny in the UK, often by the NHS review system.

The system of NHS research and ethics governance has undergone major changes in recent years. Many psychologists (and other health professionals) have been very critical of the procedures (e.g. Wald, 2004). However, some of the changes have simplified the procedure, e.g. the creation of a standardised national R&D application, which has been merged with the REC application form. In 2007, the Central Office for REC (COREC) was re-launched as the National Research Ethics Service (NRES), with one of its tasks to develop a more integrated application system for NHS-based research. Further developments are likely, following on from the Department of Health's 'Report of the Ad Hoc Advisory Group on the Operation of NHS Research Committees' (Department of Health, 2005b). Pilot work of a new triage system is currently under way, whereby a group of independent 'National Research Ethics Advisors' will screen applications at an early stage to identify those that present no material ethical issues. Studies in this category would not require scrutiny by a REC committee but would undergo a streamlined process of review by small sub-committees. As many psychological studies are likely fall into this category, this initiative has important implications for clinical psychologists.

The BPS 'Good Practice Guidelines for the Conduct of Research within the NHS' (Cooper *et al.*, 2005) put forward a number of useful recommendations for psychologists (and students) conducting NHS research. We also offer the following additional practical tips based on our experience:

1. As changes in REC procedures and required paperwork are commonplace, it is essential that researchers check the NRES website (www.nres.npsa.nhs.uk/) so that they are aware of recent developments. This website also contains detailed guidelines for researchers on preparing study information sheets and consent forms.
2. You should consider the specific ethical issues most likely to be raised by your study and make sure that you have considered all possible risks and protection for participants. A good rule of thumb is to consider risk from the perspective of the research participant. One way to do this is to obtain input on study information sheets, consent forms, etc. from service user groups or patient advisory panels.
3. The ethical issues most likely to arise in psychological research involve possible distress/discomfort experienced by participants as a result of their participation, informed consent, confidentiality of data, and the identification and recruitment of participants. You should ensure that due attention is paid to all of these issues in your application.
4. In our experience every effort should be made to attend the REC meeting at which your application will be considered, where queries/concerns about your research can be discussed with the committee.
5. If you have questions about REC procedures, you can always contact the coordinator of the relevant REC committee to which your application is being submitted.

Finally, it is often worth someone in your research team or group of colleagues becoming a member of the relevant local bodies that are responsible for promoting and monitoring research. These include not only Local Research Ethics Committees, but also Research and Development Committees and Audit/Clinical Effectiveness Committees. Some of the advantages of this include keeping up to date with policies and procedures and networking, all of which can be invaluable in assisting with one's own projects, as well as those of one's colleagues, trainees, etc.

Conclusions

Research and evaluation are core skills of an effective clinical psychologist and, in our view, are characteristic of much of the work conducted by clinical psychologists. Formal research activity is one very important aspect of this, and both the contribution from psychologists historically and the potential for further work are immense. Research activity, although often regarded as a rather mysterious process by those not already engaged in it, can be of many different types. In providing an overview of psychological research and evaluation in modern health care, we have summarised some of the key skills, qualities, support and methods we have observed to be commonly used and required. We have also made explicit some of the skills and processes involved that we consider are not always well explained or taught, and provided information that may assist researchers, particularly those who have less experience, to complete research projects. Clinical psychologists, by virtue of their extensive research training, are uniquely well placed in health care to conduct successful research. The contributions from psychologists to date have been huge, but unfortunately only a relatively small number have made significant contributions. While the reasons behind this need more study, and at a national and international level the necessary resources need to be made available, our belief is that broadening the concept of research, demystification of the processes involved, and ensuring that research is viewed as one aspect of a broader competency possessed by all effective clinical psychologists may go some way towards redressing this.

References

British Psychological Society (2004). *Guidelines for minimum standards of ethical approval in psychological research*. Leicester: Author.

Cooper, M.J. & Turpin, G. (2007). Clinical psychology trainees' research productivity and publications: An initial survey and contributing factors. *Clinical Psychology and Psychotherapy, 14*, 54–62.

Cooper, M.J., Turpin, G., Bucks, R. & Kent, G. (2005). *Good practice guidelines for the conduct of psychological research in the NHS*. Leicester: Author.

Creswell, J.W. (2003). *Research design: Qualitative, quantitative, and mixed approaches*. Thousand Oaks, CA: Sage.

Department of Health (2005a). *Research governance framework for health and social care*. London: Author.

Department of Health (2005b). *Report of the ad hoc advisory group on the operation of NHS research ethics committees*. London: Author.

Department of Health (2006). *Best research for best health*. London: Author.

Guest, G., Bunce, A. & Johnson, L. (2006). How many interviews are enough? An experiment with data saturation and variability. *Field Methods, 18*, 59–82.

Hsieh, H. & Shannon, S.E. (2005). Three approaches to qualitative content analysis. *Qualitative Health Research, 15*, 1277–1288.

Kennedy, P. & Llewelyn, S. (2001). Does the future belong to the scientist practitioner? *The Psychologist, 14*, 74–78.

Milne, D., Keegan, D., Paxton, R. & Seth, K. (2000). Is the practice of psychological therapists evidence-based? *International Journal of Health Care Quality Assurance, 13*, 8–14.

Milne, D. & Paxton, R. (1998). A psychological reanalysis of the scientist-practitioner model. *Clinical Psychology and Psychotherapy, 5*, 216–230.

Milne, D.L., Britton, P.G. & Wilkinson, I. (1990). The scientist-practitioner in practice. *Clinical Psychology Forum, 30,* 27–30.

National Research Ethics Committee (2008). *Defining research.* London: National Patient Safety Agency.

Onwuegbuzie, A.J. & Leech, N.L. (2005). Taking the 'Q' out of research: Teaching research methodology courses without the divide between quantitative and qualitative paradigms. *Quality and Quantity, 39,* 267–296.

Ritchie, J. & Spencer, L. (1994). Qualitative data analysis for applied policy research. In A. Bryman & R. Burgess (Eds.) *Analysing qualitative data* (pp. 173–194). London: Routledge.

Salkovskis, P.M. (1984). Psychological research by NHS clinical psychologists: An analysis and some suggestions. *Bulletin of the British Psychological Society, 37,* 375–377.

Smith, J.A. & Osborn, M. (2003). Interpretative phenomenological analysis. In J.A. Smith (Ed.) *Qualitative psychology: A practical guide to methods* (pp. 51–80). London: Sage.

Sykes, J.B. (1982). *The concise Oxford dictionary.* Oxford: Oxford University Press.

Wagemans, J., Verstraten, F.A.J. & He, S. (2001). Beyond the decade of the brain: Towards a functional neuroanatomy of the mind. *Acta Psychologica, 107,* 1–7.

Wald, D.S. (2004). Bureaucracy of ethics applications. *British Medical Journal, 329,* 282–284.

Part II

Areas of Clinical Practice

1

Working with Children
and Young People

5

Clinical Psychology Services for Children in Primary Care

Ann Rowland and Helen Beinart

Introduction

There is significantly more psychological distress in the general child population than ever gets identified, let alone referred to specialist Child and Adolescent Mental Health Services (CAMHS). Most distressed or unhappy children will initially present to their general practitioner (GP), or health visitor (HV), depending on their age, and often through parental distress/concern or with physical health complaints (Appleton & Hammond-Rowley, 2000; Garralda, 2004). Primary care services are possibly the only true lifespan service within health care where service users can be seen from cradle to grave. Additionally, it is often the case that members of the same family are registered with the same GP or practice, which results in the practitioner developing an understanding of the familial and broader social and economic context. It could be argued that due to the rapid rate of developmental change in early childhood and the contextual nature of childhood problems, primary care is the most appropriate context in which to work psychologically with the majority of children and young people. Primary care in the UK is a universal service to which all children have access, and which normally provides the first contact to health care. It includes a preventive, longitudinal and family-centred service in a familiar environment. Primary care services in the National Health Service (NHS) usually provide access to comprehensive specialist services (Appleton, 2000) and are central to the coordination of individual care.

Clinical psychologists have a long history of working with adults in primary health care (e.g. Robson & France, 1997). Stevenson (1990) reviewed the work of child clinical psychologists, with health visitors also suggesting an early and effective involvement in primary care. After a brief overview of children's needs, this chapter aims to discuss the role of child clinical psychology in primary care, review the policy and evidence for different types of work and provide detailed service examples demonstrating how services can be delivered in this context.

Overview of Children's Psychological Needs

The Mental Health Foundation (2005) defines a mentally healthy child or young person as one who has the ability to develop psychologically, emotionally, socially, intellectually and spiritually; initiate, develop and sustain mutually satisfying relationships; use and enjoy solitude; become aware of others and empathise with them; play and learn; develop a sense of right and wrong; and face problems and setbacks satisfactorily, and learn from them. There is clearly a continuum between emotional well-being, emotional distress and having a mental disorder. The Office for National Statistics (2000), using ICD-10 criteria, identified that 10 per cent of children had some significant mental health disorder (5 per cent conduct disorder, 4 per cent emotional disorder, <1 per cent hyperactivity, 0.5 per cent other disorders). However, comparatively few children receive intervention from CAMHS; for example, Ford *et al.* (2003) report that more than half of children with emotional disorders have no contact with mental health services. Kramer and Garralda (2000) found that one in four children aged 7–12 and four in ten of 13–16-year-olds attending GP surgeries had mental health problems, suggesting greater need than the prevalence figures suggest.

A number of risk factors are associated with increased prevalence rates for child and adolescent mental health problems. Risk factors can be described as being within child, such as having physical illness or special educational needs, or within family, including being part of a single parent or step family, maternal mental health problems, poor parental educational achievement and low socioeconomic status (Care Services Improvement Partnership, 2006).

The social and economic impact of childhood mental health difficulties can be high, and can have a significant impact on school attendance and educational achievement (Care Services Improvement Partnership, 2006). In financial terms, studies suggest that children with mental health difficulties cost ten times more to society than other children, in terms of education, mental health services, and judicial and penal systems (Hutchings & Webster-Stratton, 2004). Mental health disorders in childhood have been found to increase the risk of a mental health problem in adulthood, and impact negatively on qualifications, employment and relationship formation in adulthood (Mental Health Foundation and Office of Health Economics, 2005). The high prevalence rates, number of children presenting in primary care, and social and economic impact, both in the short and long term, if difficulties are not resolved, suggest that alternative models of increasing access to CAMHS need to be considered.

Policy and Contextual Background to Service Delivery in Primary Care

In recent years, in the UK, there has been an increasing emphasis on developing policies and guidance to support children's well-being and mental health. The National Service Framework for Children, Young People and Maternity services (Department of Health,

2004) aims to build services that are designed and delivered around the needs of children and families who use the service. This document emphasises the importance of developing these services at a primary care level. The Every Child Matters: Change for Children (2005) outcomes framework clearly identifies that children's needs include being emotionally and mentally healthy within the 'Be Healthy' outcome. This paper suggests that services should focus on: better prevention, better support to parents and families, earlier intervention, and school- and neighbourhood-based services. The consultation document Commissioning Framework for Health and Wellbeing (Department of Health, 2007) states its key aims as improving the delivery of integrated and coordinated services to individuals and improving the health and well-being of individuals.

A further aspect of recent guidance has been the emphasis on involving service users, including children, in the planning of services (Audit Commission, 1999). This was echoed by the Department of Health (2002) and the Children's Commissioner for England in 2005. Young Minds has launched a guide to involving young people in service planning (Street & Herts, 2005). The research available in this area shows that young people want accessible services staffed by those they are able to trust and who demonstrate an ability to listen; most importantly, young people also want to be involved in the decisions made about them (Dogra, 2005). Referrers want quick, easy access to CAMHS, better communication with CAMHS and to be able to share their anxieties (Potter *et al.*, 2005).

In terms of current services, CAMHS are structured according to the Health Advisory Service (HAS) Together We Stand (1995) conceptual framework for ensuring that a comprehensive range of services is commissioned and available to meet all the mental health needs of children and young people in an area. The HAS model describes services as arranged within tiers and argues for clear referral pathways between tiers. Tier 1 comprises frontline primary care professionals, providing initial contact for children in a range of community settings. Tier 2 consists of specialist mental health workers supporting Tier 1 work and providing brief interventions. Tier 3, typically known as specialist CAMHS, provides multidisciplinary and specialist support for more complex difficulties. The importance of the interface between primary care and more specialist services is emphasised both within the model and in subsequent national reports. The provision of CAMHS in primary care is a model supported by national UK guidance on developing integrated, local, neighbourhood services, which are easily accessible and acceptable to users.

Having established the clinical need and policy guidance to support work in this area, we now review previous work which has been published in this field.

Evidence Base for Psychological Services in Primary Care

Child clinical psychologists have now taken on several roles within primary care services. These include education and training of the primary care team (much early work was done on training health visitors and school nurses to use behavioural methods), supervision, consultation and liaison, joint work with a member of the primary care team, running drop-in clinics, group work, parent training, psychoeducation and direct clinical work. Direct psychological case management by specialists in primary care has been referred to as 'shifted outpatients' (Gask *et al.*, 1997) or Tier 2 work (Health Advisory Service, 1995; Appleton, 2000) and it is this area which has the strongest evidence base. In a review of CAMHS in primary care, Bradley *et al.* (2003) surveyed NHS trusts in the UK and found that a third had developed primary mental health worker posts (PMHW), 21 per cent provided shifted outpatients, 33 per cent consultation, 19 per cent joint case work and 66 per cent education and training. To our knowledge, there is no national overview specifically of child clinical psychology services in primary care; however, many use a combination of educational, consultation and direct clinical interventions.

In a recent systematic review, Bower *et al.* (2001) found a paucity of evidence to support consultation-liaison methods, although some studies (e.g. Davis *et al.*, 1997) showed support for increasing the skills and confidence of primary care staff.

Few studies have reported actual changes in professional behaviour or clinical outcomes using these methods. Indeed, Cockburn and Bernard (2004) surveyed GPs and found that the majority rated their own skills and competence in child and adolescent mental health as less than satisfactory. Wiener and Rodwell (2006), in a recent evaluation of a PMHW service, found that informal consultation-liaison was valued but that the service resulted in an increase of referrals to specialist CAMHS. These findings would suggest that the majority of primary care staff do not have the necessary skills to manage children's psychological needs and that consultation and liaison, although valued, are probably not sufficient without significant training input.

However, there is some evidence that direct training/educational interventions by psychologists working in primary care (Tier 2 services) are effective. For example, Davis and Spurr (1998) found that trained parent advisers were effective in supporting parents in managing their children's behaviour compared with those in a waiting list control group.

Most of the literature in this area relates to shifted outpatients or Tier 2 work that is often, but not always, delivered by psychologists. Early studies show that services with child clinical psychologists using behavioural techniques resulted in significant reductions in child behaviour problems, as well as reduced consultation rates and increased parental satisfaction compared to treatment-as-usual service (e.g. Finney *et al.*, 1991; Blakey, 1986). Cooper and Murray (1997) found that specialist psychotherapeutic interventions (compared with routine primary health care) decreased maternal reports of infant relationship problems in a group of mothers with postnatal depression.

Boyle *et al.* (1997) describe a primary care child psychology service with high levels of referrer and client satisfaction and a large increase of appropriate referrals compared with previous referrals to the CAMHS hospital-based team. They report reduced waiting time for the initial appointment (4 weeks), low non-attendance rates (11 per cent) and good clinical outcomes. Clydesdale (1998) compared non-attendance and outcome ratings of children seeing the same psychologist in primary care with a similar client group referred to a hospital-based CAMHS. She found that non-attendance rates were significantly lower in primary care and that half the children seen in primary care were discharged with no symptoms, compared with less than a third in CAMHS. A full range of emotional and behavioural problems was seen in both settings; however, problem severity and complexity were found to be higher in the hospital-based group. In a similar study, Abrahams and Udwin (2002) compared a primary care-based clinical psychology service with CAMHS in the same inner London area in terms of characteristics of the referrals and clinical outcomes. The two groups were remarkably similar in terms of nature, complexity and duration of presenting problems and demographic variables. The practice-based service had more adolescents referred, however, and waiting time was lower. Children were seen for significantly more sessions in the specialist clinic but there was no difference in clinical outcomes or numbers completing treatment. Overall, referrer satisfaction was high and the authors argue that CAMHS delivery by psychologists in primary care are effective and cost efficient.

Day and Davis (1999, 2006) describe a tiered approach to delivering CAMHS in inner London where specialist mental health workers, based in primary health care, deliver Tier 2 services direct to children and families referred by general practitioners or health visitors. A comparison control group was recruited from a CAMHS waiting list in a neighbouring area. Findings suggest significant reductions in children's problem severity, distress and impairment, particularly for behavioural difficulties (the most common reason for referral), and high levels of satisfaction with the service. Changes were maintained over a 12-month period.

Salmon and Jim (2007) designed a study to explore whether Tier 2 services were meeting their key targets, which include early assessment and intervention, client population presenting earlier with less defined/entrenched symptoms, improved ease of access, shorter waiting times and shorter treatment duration. They did this by comparing CAMHS mapping data for Tier 2 and Tier 3 services within a large inner London area. They found that the children seen in Tier 2 were considerably younger and had less well-defined psychological difficulties. Waiting times and duration of treatment were shorter and more referrals were received from primary care, consistent with enhanced accessibility. Unfortunately, outcome data was not available in this study. However, a study in the same area (Day & Davis, 2006), reported above, found significant clinical benefits.

Appleton (2000) argues that there is a further function for Tier 2 workers to act as gatekeepers for access to Tiers 3 and 4, and to 'hold' complex cases waiting for specialist work. Currently there is little evidence to support this, with some contraindications such as increased rates of referral to CAMHS (Wiener & Rodwell 2006). However, Bradley et al. (2003) found that the interface between CAMHS and primary care improved where there was direct clinical work provided in primary care.

In summary, there is limited evidence for consultation/liaison methods alone, some evidence for training primary care staff, specifically in behavioural methods, and quite promising evidence for psychological delivery of Tier 2 CAMHS within primary care. These services are cost effective, liked by users and referrers, possibly more acceptable to some groups such as adolescents, and may reduce stigma and increase accessibility for both families and primary care staff. In the next section we describe two further examples of service developments within primary care.

Primary Care Initiatives for Preschool Children

Aylesbury Vale serves a population of approximately 166,000, with 44,000 being aged 18 or under (26.5 per cent of the population), and of these, 1000 (6.6 per cent) are aged under 5. It is a mixed rural and urban community. Behaviour problems are common in preschool children and problems are not transient (Richman *et al.*, 1975, 1982). A prevalence study carried out locally in 1993, using the Preschool Behaviour Checklist (McGuire & Richman, 1988), suggests similar figures for the prevalence of preschool difficulties as those ascertained in a national study (Stallard, 1993).

The Child and Adolescent Health Psychology Service in Buckinghamshire Primary Care Trust is a Tier 2 service, with dedicated time (0.2wte (whole time equivalent) child clinical psychologist) working in primary care with preschool children in Aylesbury. Given the impact of continuing behaviour problems, the service considered it important to provide accessible and acceptable services for parents to try to address these issues when they first arise. The primary care service for preschool children has now been established for 15 years, and at its core are joint working practices between clinical psychologists and health visitors. These include:

- training and supervision workshops and problem solving groups for health visitors and others;
- consultation via a telephone consultation service;
- direct clinic work via community drop-in clinics and joint health visitor clinics.

Training and supervision: The initial training programme aims is to equip health visitors and community nursery nurses with the key behavioural principles to help them support parents in managing a range of behaviours, and to provide knowledge of normal adjustment reactions to loss and change. Many other training interventions supply information and skills, but leave participants unsupported in the application of their training within the workplace. This is addressed in Aylesbury via monthly problem-solving groups, facilitated by a child clinical psychologist, to which health visitors bring cases for discussion. These are at times open forums, and on other occasions focus on specific preschool behavioural or developmental problems. Participant evaluations have been extremely positive and inform the development of the content.

Telephone consultation: The consultation aspects of the service are based on the work of Stallard (1991) who reported that a consultation service increased health visitor competency and enabled them to offer the appropriate services to families, without the need for families to see a clinical psychologist. A child clinical psychologist is available for telephone consultation each morning for half an hour. The service was audited over a three-month period and users of the service were asked to complete a satisfaction survey. Respondents rated their satisfaction with the usefulness of the clinically related advice they received, with an average of 8 out of 10.

Drop-in clinics: These clinics developed from local surveys of health visitor clinic attendances, which revealed that a large proportion of parents were attending for advice about behavioural concerns. The clinics are based on a model developed by Portnoy (1990) and consist of a psychologist joining the 'well-baby' health visitor clinic as an early intervention access point for families. The clinics aim to provide focused behavioural advice for families during a 20-minute session with the psychologist, supported by leaflets on behaviour management, toileting, sleep and feeding. This project then evolved such that the drop-in clinics are now offered in a number of community settings across Aylesbury. Families are informed about the clinics by their health visitor. An audit of the initial pilot service suggested high levels of parental satisfaction with location and accessibility. An audit focusing on health visitors' views of the service highlighted that the main reasons for attendance at the drop-ins were general behavioural concerns, sleeping difficulties and separation anxiety. Health visitors positively rated, as 7 out of 10, the usefulness of the consultation and the impact of the advice on child difficulties. The audit also asked about changes in the frequency of health visitor contact following attendance at the drop-in clinic. Health visitors reported that following attendance, over 50 per cent of families required less support from the health visitor, indicating that a brief intervention by a psychologist can have a direct and significant positive benefit to the workload of another group of primary care professionals.

Joint health visitor clinics: This service is offered to all referred children under the age of 5, except those with developmental difficulties, who follow the child development team pathway. Parents attend the child psychology clinic with their health visitor for a one-hour appointment. The aim of the clinic is to offer families strategies to help with the difficulties that they are experiencing. Since the health visitor attends these sessions they are also involved in the discussions and are able to help the family to implement the ideas. At the end of the session the family, health visitor and GP are sent a brief resumé of the difficulties discussed and the strategies suggested together with appropriate departmental leaflets. A recent audit of this service highlighted that families were most commonly referred for behaviour and sleep problems. In 67 per cent of cases, one appointment was sufficient and children required no further support from the Tier 2 clinical psychology service (Smiton, 2004).

This primary care initiative for preschool children was developed to provide brief, easily accessible (in relation to both referral and location) advice in a community setting, as well as health visitor training, supervision and a consultation service offering advice and support to the health visitors directly involved with families, hence increasing their skills and sense of competency. The audits suggest that the health visitors feel that all aspects of the service are supportive and that the drop-in clinic has an impact on their workload. The service is a highly efficient use of child clinical psychology time. Annual audits suggest a 0.2wte psychologist, in addition to providing training and supervision, offered appointments to 118 children in primary care settings, and offered formal consultation to a further 108 children aged under 5. There is also a significant impact of the primary care initiatives on the workload of the Tier 2 child clinical psychology service, with only one-third of families requiring further specialist input. The service has recently expanded this model to working with 5–7-year-olds using specialist seconded health visitors.

Delivering a Child Clinical Psychology Service in Primary Care

The child psychology service described here is similar to some of the service initiatives outlined above (e.g. Clydesdale, 1998; Abrahams & Udwin, 2002). It was initially developed in response to a request from a GP fund-holding practice in Thame, UK and is provided via a contract with a provider mental health trust. Geographically, it is quite a large area and the mixed urban and rural population is spread across several primary care and specialist Trusts. The population served is approximately 10,000, of whom 25 per cent are children and young people (under 18). The psychological input is half a day per week (0.1wte).

Research and training: The initial psychological involvement was to support research and train the primary care team. An initial needs assessment using the Rutter Screening Questionnaire for parents revealed a prevalence rate of 19 per cent for children scoring above the cut-off for emotional and behavioural disorder, which is consistent with other non-inner-city populations (Davis *et al.*, 2000). Additionally, practice records were consulted for risk factors (Health Advisory Service, 1995) and consultation rates. User views were sought by holding focus groups facilitated by the practice manager. A consultation/liaison role was developed by the clinical psychologist attending monthly practice meetings and holding termly consultation sessions with the health visitors and the local secondary school counsellor. In addition to the training and support to Tier 1 services, a Tier 2 service that comprised direct referrals from the GPs and health visitors was developed (described in more detail below).

Tier 2 service: A direct referral-based clinical service was provided at one of the practice sites. Initial assessments took one hour with half-hour follow-up appointments. The characteristics of the first 100 referrals and the nature of the service offered were systematically examined by exploring the pattern of referral problems, the length of wait, number of sessions, non-attendance, basic outcomes and pattern of risk factors using the Association of Child Psychology and Psychiatry (ACPP) core-data set (Berger *et al.*, 1993). The referral profile showed that slightly more boys than girls were referred. The average age at referral was 8.7 years with a range of 1 to 16 years; the girls were somewhat older than the boys. The most common reason for referral (just over a third) was for behaviour problems, with boys in the majority. The service profile showed an initial no-show rate of 13 per cent. Average wait time for appointments was 4 weeks, and treatment lasted for an average of 4 to 5 sessions (range 24). Outcomes were generally positive, with 67 per cent of referral problems rated as resolved or partially resolved at the end of treatment. Slightly under half of the children had previously been referred to other services, including a quarter to child psychology or psychiatry. An examination of risk factors showed a high rate of child physical illness (38 per cent); similarly, there was a high rate of family breakdown (42 per cent) and parental mental and physical illness (43 per cent). This is consistent with previous studies of child and adolescent mental health (Health Advisory Service, 1995). The social class of the sample reflected the relative affluence of the area. Most referrals were contained within primary care, with only 4 per cent referred on to specialist CAMHS. Overall high rates of satisfaction, particularly from referrers, were reported.

This service therefore shows similar advantages to some of the reports mentioned above, with low waiting times and drop-out rates, good outcomes, and similar patterns of referrals. An additional benefit for this service is the clear ownership and commitment of the primary care team, including excellent administrative and practical support as well as good communication and liaison.

Conclusion

Research and clinical evidence suggests that child clinical psychology services provided within primary care are an accessible and efficient method of service delivery which is acceptable to children, families and referrers and yields positive outcomes for children, families, primary care professionals and specialist CAMHS. The major service implication is that skilled delivery of psychological care in a primary care context is an economical service alternative to specialist CAMHS that may prove attractive to purchasers of health care. This raises a dilemma for the profession, which is increasingly required to deliver specialist services at Tiers 3 and 4. Existing research, and examples such as those included in this chapter, provide promising evidence that services can be effectively delivered in primary care to a range of children and families presenting with problems which reflect a range of complexity and severity. Future research is needed with more sophisticated outcome measures to ascertain more definitively whether a primary care service is preventative and reduces the load on Tier 3 CAMHS and, indeed, on Adult Mental Health Services. The recent report in the UK from the New Ways of Working for Applied Psychologists group (Lavender & Hope, 2007) makes a strong case for increasing access to psychological therapies and services for adults in a community setting. The service examples above also make a strong case for child clinical psychologists being in a good position to support a raft of services through research, training, support and supervision, and to provide high-quality clinical input for children and families in community settings.

References

Abrahams, S. & Udwin, O. (2002). An evaluation of a primary care-based child clinical psychology service. *Child and Adolescent Mental Health, 7,* 107–113.

Appleton, P. (2000). Tier 2 CAMHS and its interface with primary care. *Advances in Psychiatric Treatment, 6,* 388–396.

Appleton, P. & Hammond-Rowley, S. (2000). Addressing the population burden of child and adolescent mental health problems: A primary care model. *Child Psychology and Psychiatry Review, 5,* 9–16.

Audit Commission (1999). *Children in mind: Child and adolescent mental health services.* London: Author.

Berger, M., Hill, P., Sein, E., Thompson, M. & Verduyn, C. (1993). *A proposed core data set for child and adolescent psychology and psychiatry services.* London: Association for Child Psychology and Psychiatry.

Blakey, R. (1986). Psychological treatment in general practice: Its effect on patients and their families. *Journal of Royal College of General Practice, 36,* 209–211.

Bower, P., Garralda, E., Kramer, T., Harrington, R. & Sibbald, B. (2001). The treatment of child and adolescent mental health problems in primary care: A systematic review. *Family Practice, 18,* 373–382.

Boyle, F.M., Lindsay, W.R. & McPherson, F.M. (1997). A primary-care based clinical child psychology service. *Clinical Psychology Forum, 106,* 22–24.

Bradley, S., Kramer, T., Garralda, E., Bower, P., Macdonald, W., Sibbald, B. *et al.* (2003). Child and adolescent mental health interface work with primary services: A survey of NHS provider trusts. *Child and Adolescent Mental Health, 8,* 170–176.

Care Services Improvement Partnership (2006). *Mental health and well-being in the south east.* London: Department of Health.

Clydesdale, J.K. (1998). A primary-care based clinical psychology service: A reply to Boyle, Lindsay and McPherson. *Clinical Psychology Forum, 113,* 16–18.

Cockburn, K. & Bernard, P. (2004). Child and adolescent health within primary care: A study of general practitioners' perceptions. *Child and Adolescent Mental Health, 9,* 21–24.

Cooper, P. & Murray, L. (1997). The impact of psychological treatments of post-partum depression on maternal mood and infant development. In L. Murray & P. Cooper (Eds.) *Postpartum depression in child development* (pp.201–220). New York: Guilford Press.

Davis, H., Day, C., Cox, A. & Cutler, L. (2000). Child and adolescent mental health needs assessment and service implications in an inner city area. *Clinical Child Psychology and Psychiatry, 5,* 169–188.

Davis, H. & Spurr, P. (1998). Parent counselling: An evaluation of a community child mental health service. *Journal of Child Psychology and Psychiatry, 39,* 365–376.

Davis, H., Spurr, P., Cox, A., Lynch, A., von Roenne, A. & Hahn, K. (1997). A description and evaluation of a community child mental health service. *Clinical Child Psychology and Psychiatry, 2,* 221–238.

Day, C. & Davis, H. (1999). Community child mental health services: A framework for the development of parenting initiatives. *Clinical Child Psychology and Psychiatry, 4,* 475–482.

Day, C. & Davis, H. (2006). The effectiveness and quality of routine child and adolescent mental health care outreach clinics. *British Journal of Clinical Psychology, 45,* 439–452.

Department of Health (2002). *Improvement, expansion and reform: The next 3 years. Priorities and planning framework 2003–2006.* London: Author.

Department of Health. (2004). *National Service Framework for children, young people and maternity services.* London: Author.

Department of Health (2007). *Commissioning framework for health and well-being.* London: Author.

Dogra, N. (2005). What do children and young people want from mental health services? *Current Opinion in Psychiatry, 18*(4), 370–373.

Every Child Matters: Change for Children (2005). London: HM Government.

Ford, T., Goodman, R. & Meltzer, H. (2003). Service over 18 months among a nationally representative sample of British Children with psychiatric disorder. *Clinical Child Psychology and Psychiatry, 8,* 37–51.

Finney, J., Riley, A. & Cataldo, M. (1991). Psychology in primary health care: Effects of brief targeted therapy on children's medical care utilisation. *Journal of Paediatric Psychology, 16,* 447–461.

Garralda, M.E. (2004). The interface between physical and mental health problem and medical health seeking behaviour in children and adolescents. *Child and Adolescent Mental Health, 9,* 146–155.

Gask, L., Sibbald, B. & Creed, F. (1997). Evaluating models of working at the interface between mental health services and primary care. *British Journal of Psychiatry, 170,* 6–11.

Health Advisory Service (1995). *Child and Adolescent Mental Health Services: Together we stand. The commissioning role and management of Child and Adolescent Mental Health Services.* London: HMSO.

Hutchings, J. & Webster-Stratton, C. (2004). Community-based support for parents. In M. Hoghughi & N. Long (Eds.) *Handbook of parenting: Theory and research practice* (pp. 334–351). London: Sage.

Kramer, T. & Garralda, E. (2000). Child and adolescent mental health problems in primary care. *Advances in Psychiatric Treatment, 6,* 287–294.

Lavender, A. & Hope, R. (2007). *New ways of working for applied psychologists in health and social care: The end of the beginning.* Leicester: British Psychological Society.

McGuire, J. & Richman, N. (1988). *Pre-school behaviour checklist.* Windsor: NFER-Nelson.

Mental Health Foundation (2005). *Childhood and adolescent mental health: Understanding the lifetime impact.* London: Author.

Mental Health Foundation and Office of Health Economics (2005). *Childhood and adolescent mental health; Understanding the lifetime impacts.* London: Mental Health Foundation.

Office for National Statistics (2000). *The mental health of children and adolescents in Great Britain.* London: The Stationery Office.

Portnoy, S. (1990). A drop-in clinic for under fives. *Clinical Psychology Forum, 29,* 6–8.

Potter, R., Langley, K. & Sakhuja, D. (2005). All things to all people: What referrers want from their child and adolescent mental health service. *Psychiatric Bulletin, 29,* 262–265.

Richman, N., Stevenson, J. & Graham, P. (1975). Prevalence of behaviour problems in 3-year-old children: An epidemiological study in a London borough. *Journal of Child Psychology and Psychiatry, 16,* 277–287.

Richman, N., Stevenson, J. & Graham, P. (1982). *Preshool to school: A behavioural study.* London: Academic Press.

Robson, M. & France, R. (1997). *Cognitive behaviour therapy in primary care.* London: Jessica Kingsley.

Salmon, C. & Jim, J. (2007). A characterisation of Tier 2 services in child and adolescent mental health. *Child and Adolescent Mental Health, 12,* 87–93.

Smiton, M. (2004). *Evaluation of a joint clinical psychology and health visitor clinic.* Unpublished small-scale research project, Oxford Doctoral Course in Clinical Psychology.

Stallard, P. (1991). The development and evaluation of a health visitor consultation service. *Clinical Psychology Forum, 35,* 10–12.

Stallard, P. (1993). The behaviour of 3 year old children: Prevalence and parental perception of problem behaviour: A research note. *Journal of child Psychology and Psychiatry, 34,* 413–421.

Stevenson, J. (Ed.) (1990). Health visitor based services for pre-school children with behaviour problems. Association of Child Psychology and Psychiatry Occasional Paper, No 2. Bournemouth: Bourne Press.

Street, C. & Herts, B. (2005). *Putting participation into practice: A guide for practitioners working in services to promote the mental health and well being of child and young people.* London: Young Minds.

Wiener, A. & Rodwell, H. (2006). Evaluation of a CAMHS in primary care service for general practice. *Child and Adolescent Mental Health, 11,* 150–155.

6

Self-Harm in Young People

Kathryn Fordham and Dawn Bailham

Introduction

Self-harm is a common phenomenon in Child and Adolescent Mental Health Services (CAMHS), encompassing a wide range of behaviours including self-starvation, anorexia and substance misuse, to name a few. Evidence suggests that 7–14 per cent of adolescents will self-harm at some time in their lives, and that 20–45 per cent of older adolescents report the presence of suicidal thoughts (Hawton & James, 2005). In CAMHS self-harm most commonly manifests as cutting, self-poisoning, ingestion of substances, or self-strangulation. Self-cutting is common amongst adolescents and in most cases serves the function of dealing with difficult/overwhelming emotions, or relieving tension. Cutting often remains private and may never come to the attention of professionals. In contrast, self-poisoning is more likely to result in admission to Accident and Emergency departments and the involvement of medical and mental health professionals.

Self-harm is not a diagnostic criteria in either DSM or ICD classification systems, although it is often present in young people with depression, anxiety disorders, post-traumatic stress disorder (PTSD), or those who have experienced sexual or emotional abuse (Fox & Hawton, 2004). From clinical experience, some young people with developmental disorders may also present with self-harm. For the purpose of this chapter we will refer to self-harm as defined by the UK's National Institute for Health and Clinical Excellence (NICE) guidelines as 'self-poisoning or injury, irrespective of the apparent purpose of the act'. The guidelines state further that 'self-harm is an expression of personal distress not an illness, and there are many varied reasons for a person wishing to harm him or herself' (NICE, 2004, p. 7).

The NICE guidelines stipulate that when a young person is admitted to hospital following self-harm a member of CAMHS should conduct a risk assessment and provide consultation to the young person, family, paediatric team and other agencies. Young people often give varied reasons for their self-harm behaviour, including:

- to die;
- to escape from a situation, unbearable anguish or gain relief from tension;
- to change others' behaviour, get back at them or make them feel guilty;
- to show desperation to others or seek help. (Hawton & James, 2005, p. 891)

Risk assessment is a priority as there is a strong link between suicide and self-harm, with 25–50 per cent of those committing suicide having previously carried out a non-fatal act of self-harm (Hawton & James, 2005). However, evidence suggests that there is a gender division both in self-harm behaviour and in the link between self-harm and suicidal behaviour (Fox & Hawton, 2004). Non-lethal self-harm is approximately three times more common amongst young females (Coleman, 2004). In contrast, males are more likely to commit suicide, with the rates for 15–25-year-olds rising substantially during the 1980s and 1990s (Hawton & James, 2005). In addition, when they self-harm, males are likely to use more lethal methods (e.g. jumping, strangulation or hanging) and their behaviour tends to be more impulsive than that of females (Shaffer & Pfeffer, 2001). These gender differences highlight the importance of not underestimating the level of risk associated with self-harm in young males. For a discussion on possible reasons for these gender differences, see Coleman (2004) and Griffin and Tyrrell (2003).

Despite the fact that many young people who commit suicide will have previously self-harmed, it is also true that many young people who self-harm will not go on to kill themselves. They may experience episodes of suicidal ideation, but when questioned further would not act on these thoughts and can rationalise why suicide would not be a preferable option to cope with their distress (Welch, 2001). In addition, studies have found that the level of intent to do harm or kill oneself can be predictive of suicide in the future (Harriss *et al.*, 2005). Therefore, we feel it is useful to view self-harm on a continuum of intent, as shown below.

High intent – → Low intent
(Strong suicidal   (Behaviour intended
intent & wish   to help person stay
to die)   alive, or manage
                                                                      difficult or over-
                                                                      whelming emotions)

While much has been written about suicide and suicidal ideation, less is known about self-harm amongst young people. The focus of this chapter will therefore be young people with low intent who self-harm. This chapter aims to provide an overview of self-harm as it presents in child and adolescent services, and will present clinical approaches to assessment and intervention, as well as discuss some of the challenges that can arise for clinicians working in this area.

Models of Self-Harm

The reasons young people engage in self-harm behaviour are many and varied. These behaviours can be meaningfully dichotomised into those with an interpersonal function and those with an intrapsychic function. Interpersonal models view self-harm as a form of communication or 'cry for help'. For example, this may involve the individual showing others their pain and desperation, or attempting to change other people's behaviour. Historically self-harm has been construed as a strategy for gaining attention. However, evidence suggests that this has been overstated and probably only occurs when young people feel they have no other means of getting their needs met, as most self-harm is conducted in isolation and hidden from others (Fox & Hawton, 2004; National Inquiry into Self-Harm, 2006).

Intrapsychic models include those that view self-harm as 'reactive'. As such it may be an attempt to relieve emotional tension and distress, punish oneself, or redirect intense anger and hatred felt towards someone who has inflicted pain. This could include actions that elicit a stronger sense of reality or control for the individual. Williams' (1997) 'Cry of pain' model is an example, and postulates that self-harm occurs when an individual feels defeated by external factors (e.g. relationship stress, internal turmoil). Whereas with suicide the individual cannot envisage any alternative means of escaping from their situation, non-lethal self-harm is viewed as a way of managing pain and re-establishing escape routes.

In support of Williams' model, research conducted by the UK's National Children's Home (NCH) discovered that self-injury not intended to be life threatening was usually employed as a coping mechanism to relieve emotional pain and distress. This pain was often linked to broken and/or conflictual relationships (e.g. parental divorce, entering local authority care) or distressing events (e.g. bullying, abuse, unwanted pregnancy). In addition to gaining relief from pent-up emotions, some individuals highlighted factors such as wanting to punish themselves or regain control of their lives. Others reported feeling addicted to the act itself or to the 'high' that follows some self-harm (especially cutting). In summarising this research, Bywaters and Rolfe (2002, p. 1) state that, 'their perspective was that self-injury can be seen as a means of preventing suicide'. This further adds support to the notion that suicidal acts and self-harm are distinct behaviours (Welch, 2001).

From a risk and resilience perspective, there is general agreement that self-harm, in common with many clinical presentations, arises not due to a single stressor but to 'complex and confounding vulnerabilities' (Fox & Hawton, 2004, p. 26). Research by the World Health Organisation (1989–1992, cited in Welch, 2001) found that the most important risk factors for self-harm were being young and female (i.e. 15–24 years old). Psychological post-mortem studies have consistently revealed that primary risk factors for suicide include mental health disorders (especially depressive or anxiety-related disorders), a previous suicide attempt, and substance or alcohol misuse (Bridge et al., 2006; Hawton & James, 2005). In addition to these, risk factors for non-fatal self-harm in young people include abuse, anxiety, low self-esteem and relationship difficulties (Coleman, 2004). There is evidence that the media can influence self-harm behaviour in young adults. For example, data suggests that media coverage may prompt some young people to self-harm, while encouzraging others to seek help (Zahl & Hawton, 2004). For a more complete list of suicide and self-harm risk factors see Box 6.1.

Box 6.1   Risk factors for suicide and self-harm amongst young people

Risk factors for suicide

Primary:

- Psychiatric disorder (especially depression, panic and anxiety disorders, conduct disorder)
- Previous suicide attempt
- Drug or alcohol misuse
- Sense of hopelessness about the future

Secondary:

- Family history of suicide
- Someone close committing suicide
- A recent loss
- A significant blow to self-esteem, resulting in shame or guilt

Risk factors for self-harm

Personal characteristics:

- Being female
- Impulsivity
- Hopelessness about the future
- Anger and hostility
- Problem-solving deficits
- Very low self-esteem
- Physical ill-health

Mental health disorders:

- Depression
- Panic and anxiety disorders
- Conduct disorder
- Substance misuse

Family factors:

- Parental problems (e.g. parental criminality, reliance on benefits)
- Disrupted upbringing (such as local authority care, separation, divorce, death of parent, lone parent family)

Relationship factors:

- Physical or sexual abuse
- Interpersonal crisis (e.g. relationship problems with family members or peers; bullying)
- Knowing others who self-harm

Media:

- Dramatic reporting of self-harm in newspapers, TV and books; specifying methods and involving celebrities (Hawton & Williams, 2001)

Source: adapted from Coleman, 2004; Fox & Hawton, 2004

Competencies

Working with young people that self-harm is emotionally demanding work. This arises partly from the intense, conflicting, and sometimes unacknowledged emotions surrounding the young people and their families; and partly from the fact that, regardless of intent, self-harm carries a risk of fatality or significant health repercussions. Clinicians therefore need excellent communication skills, the ability to engage young people and families who are experiencing high levels of distress and/or turmoil, tolerance, and a non-judgemental approach. They also need to be able to think clearly in the presence of these challenges, while coping with the emotional impact of the work on themselves and colleagues (NICE, 2004). This requires a reflective, and reflexive, approach to enable the clinician to separate out their own emotional responses from those of the young person and family. To meet the challenges of this work, it is important for clinicians to have regular supervision and access to consultation with experienced colleagues, and for these to be used effectively to process this impact and guarantee a thorough risk assessment and appropriate follow-up care.

Engagement and Assessment

In the UK, the NICE guidelines (2004) state that, following self-harm, individuals should be given a comprehensive psychosocial assessment covering the areas of needs and risk (see Box 6.2). Crucially, this is considered part of a therapeutic process aimed at understanding and building rapport with clients, with engagement as an essential prerequisite. The guideline's emphasis on respect and compassion for the client is powerfully backed up by reports from service users who self-harm (Bywaters & Rolfe, 2002; National Inquiry into Self-Harm among Young People, 2006; YoungMinds, 2003).

Assessment of needs: an evaluation of the psychological, social and motivational factors pertaining to the episode of self-harm, including current suicidal intent, whether the young person informed someone after the self-harm attempt, mental health and feelings of hopelessness. Assessing social needs involves considering the family and social situation, including exploring the young person's experience of school and peer relationships, their ability to cope with work and exams, and any child protection issues.

Risk assessment: focuses on the likelihood of further self-harm or suicide, including identifying clinical, demographic and psychological factors known to be associated with this, and ongoing suicidal intent.

In terms of suicidal risk, evidence has demonstrated the value of measuring suicidal intent, especially in the short term (Harriss et al., 2005), as some self-harm behaviour may represent a serious attempt to die while other self-harm may be a coping strategy young people adopt to enable them to stay alive (Bywaters & Rolfe,

---

Box 6.2   Areas to consider in a self-harm assessment

Components of an assessment of needs:

- Social situation (e.g. living arrangement, school or work)
- Personal relationships
- Recent life events
- Current difficulties
- Psychiatric history and mental state assessment, including previous self-harm attempts and drug or alcohol use
- Enduring psychological characteristics associated with self-harm (e.g. low self-esteem, hopelessness)
- Motivation for the self-harm

Components for the risk assessment:

- Characteristics related to self-harm, including intent, medical seriousness, violence of methods used, evidence of planning and precautions to prevent rescue
- Is this the first attempt at self-harm or have there been others? Is the nature of the self-harm behaviour becoming more severe?
- Personal characteristics, such as forensic history, ongoing suicidal intent and hopelessness
- Current circumstances, including consideration of social isolation, physical illnesses, recent bereavement and social class

---

2002). In addition, the lethality of the method used doesn't necessarily reflect motive (Bridge *et al.*, 2006). Thus, a teenager may intend to die but not have the understanding of, or access to, the types of methods this would require, while another young person may wish to express their level of distress and misjudge the seriousness of their actions. This is especially true with over-the-counter analgesics such as paracetamol, with young people often unaware that as few as six tablets could cause significant brain damage or even death. It is therefore crucial that clinicians check out what the young person expected, and hoped, would happen as a result of their actions and do not rely on inferred intent (Pierce, 1984). As some suicidal young people deny suicidal intent, clinicians are advised to compare the detailed circumstances surrounding the self-harm with factors associated with high intent (Hawton & James, 2005). In addition, escalation in self-harm behaviour or increased severity must always be taken seriously, which is why it is important to ask the young person about their history of self-harm behaviour (Carter *et al.*, 2005). For a list of the factors associated with high suicidal intent see Box 6.3.

Standardised scales, such as PATHOS (Kingsbury, 1996) and the Suicide Intent Scale (Beck *et al.*, 1974), can help identify individuals at high risk of suicide or repetition

---

Box 6.3   Factors associated with high suicidal intent

- Conducted in isolation
- Timed to make intervention unlikely and precautions taken to avoid discovery
- Preparations made in anticipation of death (e.g. how possessions are to be distributed)
- Communicated suicidal thoughts to someone beforehand
- Planned the act for hours or days
- Left a note or message
- Did not alert others during or after

Source: from Hawton & James, 2005

---

of self-harm. As part of a semi-structured assessment tool they provide a helpful memory aid for what can be emotionally charged work. However, it is crucial that these tools supplement clinical judgement based on a good understanding of the *meaning* the young person ascribes to the act, instead of replacing this judgement. Moreover, as a young person's life experiences and psychological state can change rapidly, and the reason behind an initial self-harm act may be different from subsequent ones, it is important to check out an individual's reasons for each episode of self-harming behaviour.

Interventions

The first rule of planning any intervention is to be guided by formulation. Assessment of risk is paramount in self-harm and interventions should aim both to reduce risk and to address underlying factors that predisposed the young person to self-harm. The formulation will also guide the level that intervention occurs – for example, the multi-agency or systemic level if there are child protection concerns, referring the young person to, or working collaboratively with, colleagues in social care and health or child protection units.

While reducing risk is an important aspect of intervention, it is often unrealistic to expect the young person to stop all self-harm behaviour straightaway. Self-harm behaviour may have become a coping strategy, although not an adaptive one. It can be useful to negotiate a written or verbal contract to reduce and eventually cease self-harming. However, caution should be taken in the use of contracts or safety plans. They should never be used in a coercive or prescriptive way that could hamper engagement or distract attention from the true risk of suicidal intent. While they are used frequently in clinical practice, there is currently insufficient evidence for their effectiveness

---

Box 6.4   Alternatives to self-cutting

Drawing on arm with red pen
Applying ice cubes to arms/body
Using elastic bands for sensory stimulation similar to cutting
Punching a pillow or punchbag
Listening to music
Going for a walk/run
Texting a friend
Distraction
Writing/poetry/music
Meditation

(Shaffer & Pfeffer, 2001). In parallel with self-harm reduction, the therapist should aim to help the young person develop more adaptive coping strategies than self-harm for dealing with overwhelming emotions and crisis (Box 6.4).

The 'Protective Behaviours' (PBs) model (Margetts, 2002) is a useful intervention aid in guiding individual work with self-harm behaviour. The PBs model originates from child protection work but can be applied to a number of psychological difficulties in children and adults. It evolved primarily from clinical experience and draws on principles from theoretical frameworks such as Gestalt, transactional analysis, and social learning theory.

The principles of PBs that can be applied in self-harm include:

- teaching young people to identify 'early warning signs' that difficult feelings are building up;
- identifying the link between feelings, thoughts and behaviour involved in self-harm in a way that is not dissimilar to cognitive behavioural models;
- identifying sources of support in their environment, especially for times of crisis or when they feel vulnerable;
- 'risking on purpose' – i.e. trying a strategy or a way of being that may feel uncomfortable but could bring substantial benefits, such as instigating new peer relationships or starting a new activity;
- 'one step removed' – this can help the young person to see a situation from another perspective. For example, discussing a scenario where the young person imagines their best friend is experiencing a problem and asks them for advice. By encouraging the young person to separate the problem from the emotion underpinning it, this strategy facilitates more effective problem solving.

Many young people self-harm in an attempt to cope with a difficult family life, for example in families that are 'chaotic', where family members have rigid values or difficult communication styles, or where there are child protection concerns. Where entrenched or difficult family dynamics underlie a young person's self-harming behaviour, Selekman and King (2001) suggest that solution-oriented brief family therapy is valuable. They recommend a number of tasks, including:

- externalising the problem;
- imaginary feelings x-ray machine;
- visualising movies of success.

The NICE guidelines (2004) recommend that young people who have self-harmed several times should be offered 'developmental group psychotherapy'. However, our clinical experience indicates that 'experiential' group work with young people who self-harm could encourage some group members to experiment with new forms of self-harm discussed in the group. In contrast, groups focusing on problem-solving or skills-based training may be more beneficial. While there is some evidence that problem-solving approaches may be of use to young people who self-harm, the overall effectiveness of these interventions has yet to be proven with adolescents (Fox & Hawton, 2004).

For young people where self-harm behaviour is a manifestation of more complex difficulties in emotional regulation, or where the young person displays interpersonal difficulties not unlike emerging borderline personality disorder, the use of strategies from dialectical behaviour therapy (DBT) may be appropriate. Learning mindfulness techniques and skills training using strategies such as behavioural chain analysis to reconstruct the events, feelings, thoughts and behaviour underlying an episode of self-harm are useful. For further details of DBT techniques see Miller *et al.* (2007).

Challenging Issues

Some common challenges arising from this work have already been mentioned, including managing the emotional impact of the work reflexively, assessing risk comprehensively, making decisions about ongoing treatment within a context of uncertainty, and using supervision and consultation appropriately. In addition, clinicians who work frequently with self-harm may experience heightened anxiety, or become desensitised and numb. It can therefore be helpful for professionals to apply the PB principles of one step removed, early warning signs and a support network, to themselves. It is crucial that clear boundaries are maintained with clients and colleagues, especially when working with individuals exhibiting borderline personality behaviour, to help avoid splitting amongst professionals and agencies.

An additional challenge is that young people who come to the attention of mental health services usually exhibit complex needs, which may include depression, PTSD or a history of abuse. In planning interventions the young person's safety is paramount. It is crucial that they first learn how to reduce symptoms of hyperarousal, then develop and implement alternative coping strategies to self-harm, before tackling issues which may uncover further emotional distress. As self-harm can elicit strong reactions, it is perhaps particularly important that clinicians are aware of their own cultural and moral views, and adopt a stance that seeks to understand the function and meaning of the self-harm for the individual concerned and actively avoids reliance on inappropriate personal or cultural assumptions.

A further challenge arises from the fact that treatment non-compliance is common amongst individuals who self-harm, especially those who are suicidal, and this has been found to be linked to the likelihood of future self-harm (Fox & Hawton, 2004). Clinicians therefore need to maximise the opportunities for engagement, monitor ongoing risks and make sound clinical judgements about how best to manage non-attendance and disengagement. To this end, evidence suggests that interventions targeting specific difficulties, such as poor problem solving, negative cognitions or dysfunctional family communication, are linked with increased treatment compliance and reduced suicidal ideation (Fox & Hawton, 2004). In addition, establishing strong links with other agencies such as school, with the young person's consent, can help counteract non-compliance and monitor risk.

Further complications arise from the fact that self-harm is often impulsive, and young people may provide discrepant information to different adults involved in their care (Brent *et al.*, 1988). As part of an ongoing risk assessment clinicians must decide when and what information to share, and with whom. In most cases where there is a risk of suicide it is particularly important that attempts are made to engage with the young person's family or guardians, both to understand the context around the episode of self-harm from their perspective and to enlist their assistance in securing the young person's ongoing safety. However, young people should be made aware of their rights and the bounds of confidentiality, and should a young person not wish their parents/guardians to be involved in the assessment or ongoing treatment, then consideration of their wishes, age and Gillick competence must be balanced against their welfare and the level of risk. Usually it is advisable that such ethical decisions are not made in isolation but discussed with experienced colleagues and/or a supervisor. Despite these challenges, it can be helpful to remember that while we have a professional responsibility *to* our clients, to discharge our professional duties competently, we cannot ultimately be responsible *for* our clients or their actions.

Broader Issues and Future Directions

As the evidence base for effective interventions with adolescents is scarce, future research should prioritise outcome studies, particularly those that examine the effectiveness of group work interventions with adolescents. In addition, investigations into the experiences of young people with a history of self-harm have highlighted other gaps. For example, a UK National Inquiry into Self-Harm among Young People (2006) identified the need to increase awareness of self-harm and provide guidance on its management amongst the various professionals that come into contact with young people, especially in primary care and schools. Such input should help to allay anxieties, as well as clarifying appropriate pathways for professionals to access on the behalf of young people presenting with self-harm. At present, such multi-agency care pathways are being developed in Northamptonshire and are in place in areas such as South West Staffordshire (Roberts, 2006). Consideration of service users' views is also beginning to provide useful information to help shape services and clinical interventions, ranging from highlighting the unhelpful use of language such as the word 'deliberate' as a prefix to 'self-harm' (Harriss *et al.*, 2005) to furthering our understanding of the reasons individuals engage in self-harm. Readers are directed to websites listed in the references for more information on these matters.

As professionals working with self-harm often find their clinical expertise and emotional boundaries stretched, it is hoped that this chapter will help to increase the 'toolbox' of clinicians, alleviate anxieties, and 'demystify' the challenge of self-harm behaviour in adolescents.

References

Beck, A., Schuyler, D. & Herman, J. (1974). Development of suicidal intent scales. In A. Beck, H. Resnick & D.J. Lettieri (Eds.) *The prediction of suicide* (pp. 45–56). Bowie, MD: Charles.

Brent, D.A., Perper, J.A., Goldstein, C.E., Kolko, D.J., Allan, M.J., Allman, C.J. *et al.* (1988). Risk factors for adolescent suicide. A comparison of adolescent suicide victims with suicidal inpatients. *Archives of General Psychiatry, 45,* 581–588.

Bridge, J.A., Goldstein, T.R. & Brent, D.A. (2006). Adolescent suicide and suicidal behaviour. *Journal of Child Psychology and Psychiatry, 47,* 327–394.

Bywaters, P. & Rolfe, A. (2002). *Look beyond the scars: Understanding and responding to self-injury and self-harm.* London: National Children's Home.

Carter, G., Reith, D.M., Whyte, I.M. & McPherson, M. (2005). Non-suicidal deaths following hospital-treated self-poisoning. *Australian and New Zealand Journal of Psychiatry, 39*(1–2), 101–107.

Coleman, J. (2004). *Teenage suicide and self-harm: A training pack for professionals.* Brighton: Trust for the Study of Adolescents.

Fox, C. & Hawton, F. (2004). *Deliberate self-harm in adolescence.* London: Jessica Kingsley.

Griffin, J. & Tyrrell, I. (2003). *Human givens: A new approach to emotional health and clear thinking.* Chalvington: Human Givens Publishing Ltd.

Harriss, L., Hawton, K. & Zahl, D. (2005). Value of measuring suicidal intent in the assessment of people attending hospital following self-poisoning or self-injury. *British Journal of Psychiatry, 186,* 60–66.

Hawton, K. & James, A. (2005). Suicide and deliberate self-harm in young people. ABC of adolescence. *British Medical Journal, 330,* 891–894.

Hawton, K. & Williams, J. (2001). The connection between media and suicidal behaviour warrants serious attention. *Crisis, 22,* 137–140.

Kingsbury, S. (1996). PATHOS: A screening instrument for adolescent overdose: A research note. *Journal of Child Psychology and Psychiatry, 37,* 609–611.

Margetts, D. (2002). *Protective behaviours.* Retrieved July 2007 from www.protectivebehaviours. co.uk

Miller, A.L., Rathus, J.H. & Linehan, M. (2007). *Dialectical behavior therapy with suicidal adolescents.* London: Guilford Press.

National Inquiry into Self-Harm among Young People (2006). *Truth hurts: The truth about self-harm for young people and their friends and families.* The Mental Health Foundation & Camelot Foundation. Retrieved 26 February 2009 from www.thesite.org/healthandwellbeing/mentalhealth/selfharm

National Institute for Health and Clinical Excellence (NICE) (2004). *Self-harm. The short-term physical and psychological management and secondary prevention of self-harm in primary and secondary care.* Clinical Guideline 16, July. Retrieved 26 February 2009 from www.nice.org./Guidance/CG16

Pierce, D. (1984). Suicidal intent and repeated self-harm. *Psychological Medicine, 14,* 655–659.

Roberts, B. (2006). Development of a school nurse care pathway for self-harm. *British Journal of School Nursing, 1,* 32–37.

Selekman, M. & King, S. (2001). 'It's my drug'. Solution orientated brief family therapy with self-harming adolescents. *Journal of Systemic Therapies, 20,* 88–105.

Shaffer, D. & Pfeffer, C. (2001). Practice parameter for the assessment and treatment of children and adolescents with suicidal behavior. *Journal of the American Academy of Child and Adolescent Psychiatry, 40*(7), 24S–52S.

Welch, S.S. (2001). A review of the literature on the epidemiology of parasuicide in the general population. *Psychiatric Services, 52*(3), 368–375.

Williams, J. (1997). *Cry of pain. Understanding suicide and self-harm.* Harmondsworth: Penguin.

YoungMinds (2003). *Worried about self-injury?* London: Author. Retrieved July 2007 from www.youngminds.org.uk

Zahl, D.L. & Hawton, K. (2004). Media influences on suicidal behaviour: An interview study of young people. *Behavioural and Cognitive Psychotherapy, 32*(2), 189–198.

7

Supporting Children and Young People Growing up in Care

Kim S. Golding

This chapter will explore the contribution of clinical psychology practice to children, like Paul described below, who are growing up outside of their family of origin. These children so often have a disadvantaged life path ahead of them, with increased likelihood of school failure, unemployment, homelessness, prison and unsatisfactory relationships (Warren, 1999). Risk for mental health problems, learning difficulties and under-achievement is high (Meltzer *et al.*, 2003). Government statistics (Department for Children, Schools and Families (DCSF), 2007) provide a stark list of difficulties that increase the risk of such poor outcomes including:

- 45% of children in care are assessed as having a mental health disorder;
- 50% of a sample of children in care reported having difficulties in accessing positive activities;
- 9.6% of over 10-year-olds in care had received a caution or conviction for an offence in the past year;
- 30% of care leavers aged 19 were not in education, training or employment.

The increased risk and poor outcomes for this population will be as a consequence of a range of factors. These children have typically had negative early experiences that increase their risk of developmental difficulties, especially affecting social and emotional well-being and capacity for relationships, but also impacting on cognitive development and their capacity for learning. Additionally they have had to cope with the emotional and practical implications of separation from, and loss of, their birth family. Disrupted family and educational life as a consequence of placement moves within the care system add to these early risks, further contributing to poor outcomes.

With such a catalogue of poor outcomes it is apparent that clinical psychology in isolation has little to offer these young people. I will argue, however, that, working in collaboration with children's services, schools and carers, clinical psychology can be a useful partner in changing the life path along which the children and young people walk. Health and education professionals need to work closely with social work colleagues to ensure that children and young people get appropriate and sufficient help provided in a timely fashion. These children cannot afford to wait, while their emotional, relationship and educational difficulties place intolerable pressure on carers and teachers, leading to further instability of placement and education. Early intervention is a priority. The following clinical example raises some of the dilemmas for clinical psychologists working in this field.

Paul, an appealing 8-year-old child, comes into Jackie's office happily. He is pleased to see Jackie, the clinical psychologist, and keen to start drawing straightaway. Jane, his foster carer, follows behind looking tired and defeated. She reports yet another difficult week with Paul. He continues to wake early, refuse breakfast, and become angry and aggressive when he can't have what he wants. His oppositional behaviour means that she struggles to get him to school on time. The teacher has had another quiet word about the 'importance of punctuality'. The last straw was when the contact session with his birth mother was cancelled because she did not turn up. Paul's anger seems to have been directed at his younger sister; her favourite doll now bears the marks of Paul's artistic efforts.

Jackie finds it difficult to square the description she is hearing with the child in front of her. He comes across to her and gives her a hug. 'You're my best friend,' he whispers. She smiles at him and then whispers 'How about a hug like that for Jane?' Paul turns to Jane. As he approaches her Jackie notices Jane tense slightly. Paul is still holding one of the crayoning pencils; he throws it forcefully towards her head and turns away.

Jackie recalls an earlier phone call from the fostering social worker. 'You have to do something with him or this placement will break down. He has already had four placements since he was removed from home three years ago. We are running out of options.'

What are the options for a psychologist like Jackie in working with a child like Paul? She is under pressure to work with Paul, to help him to adjust to his foster family and to cope with the stress of school and contact with his birth family. She is not sure that this work is appropriate or could give results quickly enough. The environment also needs to adjust to accommodate Paul's needs. She wonders about parenting advice to Jane, but is concerned that she is too worn out at the moment to put different ideas into practice. There is a statutory review next week. Jackie will attend but is unclear, at this stage, what she can contribute.

Children in Care

Under the Children Act 1989 a child is 'looked after' by a local authority if provided with accommodation for more than 24 hours. The child can be placed into care by a court, with the local authority sharing parental responsibility, or voluntarily accommodated in agreement with parents who retain parental responsibility.

In the UK, The Department for Children, Schools and Families records that 60,300 children were being looked after on 31 March 2006, including 3200 unaccompanied asylum-seeking children. Seventy per cent of these children lived in foster care.

During 2006 the statistics record that 55 per cent of adolescents stayed in care until they were 18. Additionally, 3700 children were adopted, a legal procedure in which all parental responsibility is transferred to the adopters. An adopted child has no legal tie to his birth parents, becoming a full member of the new adopting family. Most of these children will have spent some time in the looked after system prior to the adoption.

'Looked after children' is the generic term used to describe children growing up in foster, residential or kinship placements rather than with their birth families. The recent White Paper, 'Care Matters', uses the term 'Children in Care' (DCSF, 2007), a welcome return to a phrase which reminds us that these are children first – children who have generally experienced an early history of poor parenting and traumatic life experiences, as well as the separation and loss that always accompanies being brought into care (see Golding *et al.*, 2004; Sinclair, 2005). Risk factors are high and protective factors low for this group. Both early and later experiences contribute to reduced resilience and a challenging path through life.

Models of Working

In the UK there has been a large increase in the number of clinical psychologists having specific responsibilities for working with, or on behalf of, children and young people in care (see www.CPLAAC.org.uk).

These psychologists draw upon the full range of knowledge and skills underpinning the profession. However, the special needs of this group provide a challenge to traditional ways of working with children and families. For example, cognitive-behavioural interventions are often less successful until the children are beginning to achieve some coherence in their mental representations of self and others, and have gained some understanding and ability to reflect on their emotional life (Howe, 2005). Parenting interventions need to take into account the special needs of children who have experienced abuse, neglect and loss, drawing upon developmental and attachment theory as well as social learning theory (Golding, 2007b).

There are a range of considerations when designing and implementing psychological interventions for this group of children and young people:

- The complex networks around the children mean that multi-agency working is an imperative rather than a luxury (Stott, 2006).
- Additionally, there are child protection frameworks in the UK that have to be understood, including a range of court orders to ensure that children are adequately cared for and safeguarded. This affects parental responsibility and has implications for gaining consent to intervention, for confidentiality and for information sharing (see Golding *et al.*, 2004). Psychologists should expect to spend time in liaison activities, attending network meetings and gaining advice from legal departments. In the United Kingdom local safeguarding boards can be an important source of advice and guidance.

- The experience of inadequate parenting, loss and separation means that attachment difficulties are prevalent, resulting in children and young people who find it difficult to trust carers and who cannot elicit care and comfort in straightforward ways. All interventions need to be mindful of this context, with a higher emphasis on working with the environment around the child (school and home) than is typical in much child and family work (Golding, 2006a, 2007a).
- The neurodevelopmental impact of their experience leaves the children 'out of synch' with their environments; developmentally traumatised (van der Kolk, 2005). This provides the context for 'bottom-up' interventions, addressing the core difficulties of emotional and physiological regulation (see Perry, 2006).
- There needs to be a strong emphasis on collaborative working. Therapists work with carers to enter into, and support the child with, intersubjective experience. Such experience, or the lack of it, has been frightening in the past, but is necessary for attachment security. It provides the safety children need to grow, develop and explore within their ever-expanding world (Hughes, 2007; Trevarthen, 2001).

Assessment and Engagement

Children living in care can often present with complex needs for assessment. The clinical psychologist might be:

- Involved with the court process and the complex decisions around where a child should live, and what level of ongoing contact with the birth family should be available (see Stevenson & Hamilton-Giachritsis, 2006).
- Asked to comment on the suitability of alternative placements and the needs of the child, or carers within these placements.
- Asked to consider sibling relationships and the viability of placement together (see Rushton et al., 2001; Lord & Borthwick, 2001; Whelan, 2003).
- Asked to comment on the current functioning of the child. Such assessment needs to be holistic, considering obvious and subtler learning and emotional difficulties.
- Involved in thinking about the reasons for highly challenging behaviour at home, school and in the community, to inform ways of working with the young person and the environments to reduce such behaviours.

Using assessment to guide choice of intervention can be complex. In particular, recommendations need to be made in a way that helps the whole network to reach a shared understanding of the way forward. This can be particularly difficult when different parts of the network may have very different ideas of what is needed. For example, it is not uncommon for the social worker to want individual intervention for the child, while the carers need increased support for themselves and the teacher is hopeful that referral to a psychiatrist, and medication, will help the child to manage school.

Assessment and intervention with the children or young people presents challenging issues of engagement. Traditional services, which are often clinic based, have a brief focus and require attendance to keep the case open, are not easy for this group to engage with. In particular, these children have a high level of mistrust in adults and need to feel in control of relationships in order to feel safe. Providing choices of location for sessions and time to build trust and a relationship are essential prerequisites for any therapeutic work.

In addition, external factors such as changes to contact arrangements with birth parents, a period of exclusion from school, or changes to day-to-day care arrangements will often throw interventions off track. Opportunities to stop and start work, and helping the child to trust in a dependable and continuous relationship are important backdrops to the intervention. It is also important to grapple with the issue of stability; refusing to intervene because of lack of stability is not helpful, but finding creative ways to facilitate stability through well-placed interventions with carers, school and sometimes the child can be an important role of the psychologist, in collaboration with the network around the child (Golding, 2006a).

Evidence-Base for Interventions with Children in Care

There is as yet no clear evidence base specifically tailored to helping children in care. Obviously the clinical psychologist has access to the evidence base for working with children and families (see British Psychological Society, 2006); but most of the research informing the development of this base has not been carried out with children in care. Psychologists have to be creative and innovative in working with this population.

Adapting traditional approaches is an important part of this work. For example, the Treatment Foster Care Project has explored the adaptation of a successful intervention for children experiencing youth custody (Chamberlain & Smith, 2005; Gulliford, 2005).

Many psychologists, however, look towards the trauma and attachment literature to guide interventions (see Golding, 2007a). It is important that these interventions are well grounded in theory, and are continuously evaluated. Some interventions, such as holding therapy, have been developed in the name of attachment theory, where links to this theory are spurious at best. Such interventions have been linked to damaging outcomes and even child death (O'Connor & Zeanah, 2003; Barth et al., 2005; BAAF, 2006). Good supervision, monitoring of outcome and a solid understanding of the theoretical underpinnings of the approach being used are essential to safe practice.

There are a number of promising approaches that focus on working dyadically with child and carer that aim to improve security of attachment. For example, dyadic developmental psychotherapy has been developed based upon theories of attachment and intersubjectivity. The therapist works with the child together with his or her carer to facilitate positive relationship experience within which the child learns to trust and rely on the carer for comfort and security. This fosters security of attachment with a positive impact on developmental outcomes (Hughes, 2004, 2006, 2007).

Theraplay capitalizes on the therapeutic value of play, working with parents and carers to play with their children in ways that enhance attachment, self-esteem, trust in others and joyful engagement (Jernberg & Booth, 2001). Additionally, Lacher and colleagues, using a narrative approach, involve parents in generating stories with their children with the aim of altering the child's negative, self-destructive, internal working model of relationships. Parent narratives communicate to the child that he or she will be cared for and protected by available and responsive parents (Lacher *et al.*, 2005). Dallos (2006) suggests a psychotherapeutic approach that brings together attachment, narrative and systemic approaches. This focuses on using therapy as a secure base from which narratives can be explored and revised, leading to positive change for the child and family.

In addition, the developmental trauma literature is guiding programmes aimed at building resilience and competency in the children, beginning with developing feelings of safety, capacity for regulation, and security of attachment (see van der Kolk, 2005; Perry, 2006).

So How Does This Look for Paul?

Let us return to Paul. I would like to imagine that Jackie refers Paul to a multi-agency service set up to provide specialised support to looked after children and their carers. The referral leads to an initial assessment with Paul's social worker. This collects information about Paul's current circumstances and background experience and explores who is currently involved in his care.

A consultation is offered. The aim of this consultation is to increase understanding of Paul's emotional and learning needs, to improve working together in the network and to provide further support to the foster family. Jane, the foster mother, her fostering social worker, Paul's social worker, the designated teacher for looked after children at Paul's school, the contact supervisor and Jackie, representing the Child and Adolescent Mental Health Services (CAMHS) team, attend. A social worker and the clinical psychologist from the multi-agency service run this consultation. The social worker guides everyone through the two-hour meeting, ensuring that everyone is heard and Paul's story is told. The psychologist supports the network to further explore this story, deepening understanding. Drawing upon attachment and trauma theories she helps the network consider the impact of the early experience of neglect, domestic violence and multiple carers on Paul's development. She explains his need to remain in control through oppositional and seductive behaviours. Paul has learnt to be non-compliant and to be charming as a way of controlling the responses he gets from adults. This provides him with some sense of predictability, increasing his feeling of safety in a world where he expects that adults will not keep him safe. In addition, thought is given to Paul's tendency to be hyper-aware and angry in response to signs of emotional withdrawal or rejection from Jane. This is linked to his core fear of abandonment, stemming from early neglect and the subsequent loss of his birth parents. This leads to a discussion about the difficulty Paul has regulating his increasing levels of arousal and his understandable anger when he feels let down by his mum.

This psychological formulation and discussion helps the network to consider:

1. *Paul's need for therapy*. The social workers are keen for therapy to begin immediately; Jane is less sure, recognising the impact this will have on her, both in getting Paul to his sessions and dealing with the aftermath. Jackie expresses concern that therapy could increase Paul's distress at least in the short term. The teacher, who wonders whether Paul might be suffering from attention deficit hyperactivity disorder (ADHD), learns that his poor attention and high activity levels are more likely to be related to the trauma he has experienced. The network begins to understand that neither therapy nor medication is likely to help Paul to settle into the placement.

2. *Paul's need for increased stability and highly responsive, sensitive parenting*. Jane begins to see how she might change her approach to Paul, parenting him as a younger child and being more responsive to his need for her attention, rather than expecting the independence of a typical 8-year-old. The fostering social worker raises concerns about the emotional impact this might have, and Jane acknowledges that she does find aspects of Paul's behaviour particularly difficult as he reminds her of her own son who had a particularly turbulent adolescence. The psychologist offers to work further with her on this, and to help her think through some of the parenting ideas that have been discussed. She also recommends that Jane attend the next Fostering Attachments Group (Golding, 2006b, 2008). Mindful that Jane's husband is not at the consultation, she offers to talk through the discussions with him and recommends that he might attend one-day workshops on child development and attachment so that he can support Jane in making changes.

3. *Paul's need for additional support in school*. The teacher reflects on how hard Paul finds the transitions during the school day. The psychologist mentions some success another school has had with using music and movement activities to help children regulate their arousal around transition times. Support is offered to the teacher to help her explore these and other ideas for helping Paul. Some further reading is recommended (Cairns & Stanway, 2004; Geddes, 2006; Bombèr, 2007).

4. *Contact arrangements*. The erratic appearance of his birth mother is unsettling for Paul, reminding him of the instability and rejection of his early childhood. Those at the meeting are concerned that monthly contact is too high for both Paul and his mum. They wonder if reduced frequency and a bit more support will help his mother to be more reliable. The social worker agrees to take this issue forward for discussion at the next looked after children's review.

This case example illustrates how multi-agency working can provide a platform for shared understanding and closer working together, leading to increased support for the foster carer, Paul and his school.

Issues, Tensions and the Way Forward

The Laming report, following the tragic death of Victoria Climbié, highlighted the importance of holistic, joined-up services for children who have experienced abuse, neglect and fear within their families of origin (Laming, 2003). Children living within the care system are amongst the most vulnerable of these vulnerable children. Psychologists working within services for children in care need a good understanding of the impact of traumatic abuse, neglect and disrupted attachments on a child's development. They need to be able to apply this understanding to collaborative interventions aimed at working with the whole network, providing good parenting and school experience and building emotional health and resilience. This means moving away from single-agency services, clinic-based therapies and direct interventions with children.

New ways of working do, however, bring their own challenges – issues of confidentiality balanced with information sharing, tensions of balancing the needs of the child with the needs of the network, and the complexity of liaison and collaborative working around children who can push carers and schools to their limits. The psychologist needs to listen to the multiple perspectives of carers, children and networks, be aware of the complex legal and cultural contexts surrounding the child, and find creative, innovative ways of applying new and more traditional interventions based on good theory, while contributing to the developing research and evidence base.

Working with children and young people in care is challenging, complex and creative. These children are experiencing the state at its most intrusive. Psychologists need to dig deep into their personal resources as they search the limits of collaborative, holistic, multi-agency working. The children will accept and adapt to their life experience, but we do not have to accept on their behalf.

> Often and often afterwards, the beloved Aunt would ask me why I had never told anyone how I was being treated. Children tell little more than animals, for what comes to them they accept as eternally established. (Rudyard Kipling 1865–1936)

References

BAAF (2006). *Attachment disorders, their assessment and intervention/treatment*. BAAF position statement 4. London: British Association for Adoption and Fostering.

Barth, R.P., Crea, T.M., John, K., Thoburn, J. & Quinton, D. (2005). Beyond attachment theory and therapy: Towards sensitive and evidence-based interventions with foster and adoptive families in distress. *Child and Family Social Work, 10,* 257–268.

Bombèr, L.M. (2007). *Inside I'm hurting. Practical strategies for supporting children with attachment difficulties in schools*. London: Worth.

British Psychological Society (2006). *Drawing on the Evidence*. Published by the Faculty for Children and Young People (CYP), Division of Clinical Psychology, The British Psychological Society in collaboration with the National Institute of Mental Health (England), the BPS Centre for Outcomes Research and Evaluation (CORE) and the CAMHS Evidence Based Practice Unit at UCL.

Cairns, K. & Stanway, C. (2004). *Learn the child. Helping looked after children to learn. A good practice guide for social workers, carers and teachers*. London: BAAF.

Chamberlain, P. & Smith, D.K. (2005). Multidimensional treatment foster care: A community solution for boys and girls referred from juvenile justice. In E.D. Hibbs & P.S. Jensen (Eds.)

Pyschosocial treatments for child and adolescent disorders. Empirically based strategies for clinical practice (2nd edn, pp. 557–573). Washington, DC: American Psychological Association.

Dallos, R. (2006). *Attachment narrative therapy. Integrating narrative, systemic and attachment therapies.* Maidenhead: Open University Press.

DCSF (2007). *Care Matters. Time for Change.* London: Author.

Geddes, H. (2006). *Attachment in the classroom. The links between children's early experience, emotional well-being and performance in school.* London: Worth.

Golding, K.S. (2006a). Opening the door. How can therapy help the child and young person living in foster or adoptive homes? In K.S. Golding, H.R. Dent, R. Nissim & E. Stott (Eds.) *Thinking psychologically about children who are looked after and adopted. Space for reflection* (ch. 11). Chichester: John Wiley & Sons.

Golding, K., Taylor, J., Thorp, D., Berger, M. & Stevenson, J. (2004). *Briefing paper: Looked after children: Improving the psychological well-being of children in the care of the looked after system. A guide for clinical psychologists working with or considering the development of psychological services for looked after children and their carers.* London: Faculty for Children and Young People of the Division of Clinical Psychology, British Psychological Society, January.

Golding, K.S. (2006b). *Fostering attachments with children who are looked after and adopted. A group for foster carers and adoptive parents. Training manual.* Unpublished document.

Golding, K.S. (Ed.) (2007a). *Briefing paper: Attachment theory into practice.* London: The Faculty for Children & Young People of the Division of Clinical Psychology, The British Psychological Society.

Golding, K.S. (2007b). Developing group-based parent training for foster and adoptive parents. *Adoption and Fostering, 31*(3), 39–48.

Golding, K.S. (2008). *Nurturing attachments. Supporting children who are fostered or adopted.* London: Jessica Kingsley.

Gulliford, F. (2005). Multi-dimensional treatment foster care in England: What contribution can psychologists make? *Service and Practice Update, 4*(1), March 23–26.

Howe, D. (2005). *Child abuse and neglect. Attachment, development and intervention.* Basingstoke: Palgrave.

Hughes, D.A. (2004). An attachment-based treatment of maltreated children and young people. *Attachment and Human Development, 6*(3), 263–278.

Hughes, D.A (2006). *Building the bonds of attachment. Awakening love in deeply troubled children* (2nd edn; 1st edn 1998). London: Jason Aronson.

Hughes, D.A. (2007). *Attachment-focused family therapy.* New York: W.W. Norton.

Jernberg, A. & Booth, P.B. (2001). *Theraplay: Helping parents and children build better relationships through attachment-based play* (2nd edn). San Francisco: Jossey-Bass.

Lacher, D.B, Nichols, T. & May, J.C. (2005). *Connecting with kids through stories. Using narratives to facilitate attachment in adopted children.* London: Jessica Kingsley.

Laming, Lord (2003). *The Victoria Climbié Enquiry.* London: The Stationery Office.

Lord, J. & Borthwick, S. (2001). *Together or apart? Assessing brothers and sisters for permanent placement.* London: BAAF.

O'Connor, T.G. & Zeanah, C. (2003). Attachment disorders: Assessment strategies and treatment approaches. *Attachment and Human Development, 5*(3), 223–244.

Meltzer, H., Gatward, R., Corbin, T., Goodman, R. & Ford, T. (2003). *The mental health of young people looked after by local authorities in England.* London: The Stationery Office.

Perry, B.D. (2006). Applying principles of neurodevelopment to clinical work with maltreated and traumatized children. The neurosequential model of therapeutics. In N.B. Webb (Ed.) *Working with traumatized youth in child welfare* (ch. 3, pp. 27–52). New York: Guilford Press.

Rushton, A., Dance, C., Quinton, D. & Mayes, D. (2001). *Siblings in late permanent placements.* London: BAAF.

Sinclair, I. (2005). *Fostering now: Messages from research.* London: Jessica Kingsley.

Stevenson, J. & Hamilton-Giachritsis, C. (2006). A snapshot in time. The role of psychological assessment of children and young people in the court system. In K.S. Golding, H.R. Dent, R. Nissim & E. Stott (Eds.) *Thinking psychologically about children who are looked after and adopted: Space for reflection.* Chichester: John Wiley & Sons.

Stott, L. (2006). Holding it all together: Creating thinking networks. In K.S. Golding, H.R. Dent, R. Nissim & E. Stott (Eds.) *Thinking psychologically about children who are looked after and adopted: Space for reflection* (pp.37–67). Chichester: John Wiley & Sons.

Trevarthen, C. (2001). Intrinsic motives for companionship in understanding: Their origin, development, and significance for infant mental health. *Infant Mental Health Journal, 22,* 95–131.

van der Kolk, B.A. (2005). Child abuse and victimisation (editorial). *Psychiatric Annals, 35*(5), 374–378.

Warren, D. (1999). Setting new national standards for foster care. *Adoption and Fostering, 23*(2), 48–56.

Whelan, D.J. (2003). Using attachment theory when placing siblings in foster care. *Child and Adolescent Social Work Journal, 20*(1), 21–36.

8

Intensive Approaches for Childhood Fears

Tim I. Williams

Fears are common in childhood (Ollendick *et al.*, 2002). In general, preschool children report more fears than school-age children (Gullone, 2000). Furthermore, there is a characteristic pattern of development of fears. Fears of separation and of strangers are common from around 8 months, followed by fears of animals, the dark, blood-injection fears and finally, in adolescence, fears of failure, panic and performance (Marks, 1987).

A phobia is a fear that is marked, persistent, out of proportion, beyond voluntary control and interferes with everyday life. The interference may result from avoidance of situations or extreme reactions to the feared situation such as running away, freezing or having temper tantrums. Phobias are a subgroup of the anxiety disorders in both international systems of classification of mental health (DSM-IV, ICD-10). The prevalence of anxiety disorders in pre-adolescent children varies widely between studies (range 2.6 to 41 per cent – see Cartwright-Hatton *et al.*, 2006). Unsurprisingly, the prevalence of specific phobias also shows a huge range (<1 to >20 per cent). Ollendick *et al.* (2002) in their review concluded that about 5 per cent of young people have specific phobias sufficient to cause major interference in their everyday lives, e.g. failure to attend school. In the UK, a recent epidemiological study has found figures of about 4 per cent being affected by anxiety disorders and 1 per cent by specific phobias over the school age range (Ford *et al.*, 2003). Somers *et al.* (2006) point out that the number of adults suffering from anxiety disorders is constant across the lifespan at around 10 per cent of the population, and around 3 per cent for specific phobias. While some phobias might not seem worthy of treatment, their effects can be quite devastating for the affected child. For example, a child whose fear of dogs makes it difficult for them to play with friends in neighbourhood parks or walk to school.

The ætiology of specific phobias has been the subject of a recent review. Armfield (2006) proposes a model in which vulnerability schemata about uncontrollability, unpredictability, dangerousness or disgustingness of stimuli can be heightened by specific traumatic experiences and successive exposure to the fear stimulus. The vulnerability schemata are themselves based on personality factors and possibly vicarious learning experiences (e.g. modelling by significant others).

A systematic review of interventions for anxiety disorders (Cartwright-Hatton *et al.*, 2004) found that cognitive behaviour therapy (CBT) met criteria for an effective intervention (see also King *et al.*, 2005; James *et al.*, 2007), although James *et al.* (2007) cautioned that only about 50 per cent of children who received CBT recovered. The CBT interventions encompassed psychoeducation about the nature of anxiety (physiological and behavioural), information about the role of cognitions and activities, including exposure to feared situations, and learning how to manage the resultant emotions, and largely used group formats with multiple sessions. In the adult field there has been a move towards treatments for anxiety disorders which require less therapeutic time by, for instance, by using fewer sessions (Clark *et al.*, 1999; Öst, 1989). In this chapter, an intensive approach to the treatment of specific phobias is described. Although the approach is primarily used with specific phobias, our experience suggests that it may have wider applicability and therefore should be part of the 'toolkit' for clinical psychologists working with young people. In the context of this chapter 'intensive' is used to describe a method of delivering a particular treatment over a longer single session. Overall it requires less therapist time than the traditional multi-session approach. In contrast, for externalising disorders, such as conduct or behaviour problems, there has been considerable interest in developing intensive interventions that are characterised by more therapy time being provided, such as in multi-systemic therapy (see Kazdin & Weisz, 2003, for a review).

Evidence Base for Brief Interventions

A few studies have demonstrated the feasibility of brief interventions for children with phobias (Muris *et al.*, 1997, 1998; Öst *et al.*, 2001). Both the Muris studies involved children with spider phobia. Muris *et al.* (1997) used a cross-over design with 22 girls (aged 9–14 years) in the comparison of single 90-minute sessions of both exposure and eye movement desensitisation and reprocessing (EMDR). This is rather less than the length of session often used in adult work which is of the order of three hours in length (Öst *et al.*, 2001). The results showed that exposure reduced avoidance more than EMDR, although the groups were equal on self-rated anxiety. Muris *et al.* (1998) compared EMDR, exposure *in vivo*, and computerised exposure for 26 girls (aged 8–17 years). Exposure *in vivo* was found to be more effective than both EMDR and computerised exposure. Öst *et al.* (2001) extended these results by comparing three conditions (exposure alone, exposure with a parent present and a four-week wait list control group) to which a total of 60 children were randomly allocated. They included 37 girls and 23 boys with a variety of specific phobias. Both forms of single session treatment were effective and did not differ.

In the next section a brief intensive treatment method for phobias is described in terms of the models of practice and the competencies required.

Models and Competencies Used

Over the years a number of theories have been proposed to account for the development and maintenance of anxiety disorders. Broadly these have concentrated on biological and psychological factors. There is some evidence of a genetic component, with one estimate of the genetic component as high as 58 per cent (Lichtenstein & Annas, 2000). A large number of surveys have reported that more girls than boys report phobias (Ollendick *et al.*, 2002). From the point of view of psychological treatment, the biological factors provide some level of explanation about causes but do not help in the development of psychological treatment approaches. Most theoretical accounts of phobia aetiology, however, incorporate an important learned component. For instance, work by Field (e.g. Field & Lawson, 2008) has demonstrated that providing frightening information about animals leads to a fearful reaction to them, which is strengthened by the personal characteristic of behavioural inhibition. A likely source of this information is parents or other caregivers. Indeed, a recent study found that anxious children often have anxious parents and that in the case of specific phobias, the rate of maternal-specific phobias approaches 50 per cent (Cooper *et al.*, 2006). However, a meta-analysis has suggested that the influence of parenting is quite small (McLeod *et al.*, 2007), and suggests that instead more attention should be given to the child's history of traumatic events.

Armfield's (2006) review describes several competing accounts but concludes that the data is best fitted by a model which incorporates individual vulnerabilities (such as fear sensitivity which might be part of the inherited component), cognitive schemata and experience of frightening situations. Important components of the model are that the phobia is seen to result from a perception of vulnerability arising from perceptions of the feared object being uncontrollable, unpredictable, dangerous and/or disgusting. The maintenance of the fear is then seen as being a consequence of a failure to find evidence that the feared object is not uncontrollable, unpredictable, dangerous and/or disgusting. The failure to find evidence may be due to avoidance of the object itself or due to avoidance of information about the object. Cognitive behaviour therapy aims to address both the cognitive schemata and the failure to find evidence by re-educating the child about their symptoms, changing the meaning (appraisal) of those symptoms, improving knowledge of the feared object, and providing exposure to the feared object in such a way that the association of fear and the phobic response is reduced. At the same time the intensive model also encourages a degree of response prevention (i.e. encouraging the child to remain close to the feared object) so that the learned associations between a fearful appraisal and the behavioural, physiological and emotional responses can reduce. A broad outline of the formulation is shown in Figure 8.1 together with the intended targets of the psychoeducation and exposure and response prevention components of treatment.

The use of CBT for the treatment of phobias presupposes a number of generic clinical skills as well as those specific to CBT itself (see Chapter 10). Broadly, the basis of the treatment is a model which states that phobias are maintained by both cognitive processes

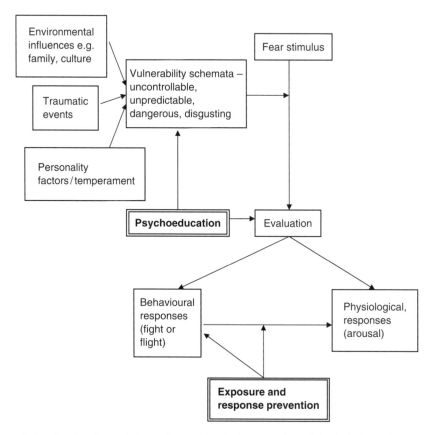

Figure 8.1 Outline formulation of cognitive behavioural model of phobia, showing the components of treatment in bold text and double-bordered boxes.

such as appraisals of the object as being dangerous and avoidance of the feared object. One example would be the child with injection phobia who believed that injections might cause significant scarring. For young people, another significant issue is the behaviour of adults (especially parents) and peers that may also serve to maintain the problem. This can be exemplified by a young boy who needed repeat injections to treat a congenital disease whose mother was also afraid of injections. She was therefore unable to help her son manage the injections since she had very similar fears. The development of the phobia in childhood is not a primary concern of the intensive treatment approaches, although it can form part of the psychoeducational component of treatment.

In order to be successful in the implementation of intensive approaches the psychologist needs to be empathic towards the child and able to maintain a perspective which includes the treatment goal at the same time as managing the immediate situation. The latter will often be complicated by the presence of a caregiver. The psychologist needs to be organised and to have all the required materials available. In the case of injection and needle phobias this will mean that they have arranged to work with a nurse, usually in a clinical setting. When dealing with phobias of flying insects, access to a beekeeper may prove helpful in ensuring the availability of flying insects, or the psychologist may have had to collect spiders of various sizes. Psychologists working with phobias need to be aware of their own fears. For instance, if the psychologist is truly phobic of spiders, they are unlikely to be able to model handling them, which is a task that will almost certainly be part of the treatment hierarchy.

Engagement and Assessment

The assessment gives the psychologist the opportunity to engage with the young person and their family. It is helpful to start the interview with a family and developmental history, which can lead to the initial stages of formulation and psychoeducation. The use of a standardised interview (e.g. DAWBA – Goodman et al., 2000; ADIS-C – Silverman & Nelles, 1988) is best practice as it ensures that the psychologist is aware of all areas that may be important in planning the intervention. Additionally, the psychologist should try to get detailed information about the thoughts and behaviour associated with the feared object. Where there are suitable standardised measures these can be used to measure level of fear, type of response (disgust, fear) and cognitive aspects (see appendix for examples). The Fear Survey Schedule for Children and Adolescents (FSSC-II: Gullone & King, 1992) comprises 78 items, including socially significant items, such as AIDS and nuclear war, frequently excluded from other fear survey schedules. Its factor structure suggests that five factors describe the pattern of children's fears: Fear of Failure and Criticism (e.g. 'Being teased', 'Failing a test'), Fear of the Unknown (e.g. 'Closed places', 'Dark rooms or closets'), Fear of Injury or Small Animals (e.g. 'Lizards', 'Guns'), Fear of Danger and Death (e.g. 'Earthquakes', 'Not being able to breathe'), and Medical Fears (e.g. 'Getting a shot from the doctor', 'Going to the dentist'). However, standardised measures should always be used alongside careful clinical interviewing.

The psychologist can then build up an initial formulation, taking into account both individual and systemic factors such as family interactions and school or peer issues. Finally, the assessment should end with the development of a hierarchy of the feared situation. The whole assessment takes up to two hours depending on how many other problems are revealed and on how loquacious the child and parent are. Thus the aim of the assessment is to identify the maintaining factors, including those in the environment, such as avoidance enabled by caregivers or reassurance seeking from caregivers.

Examples of Specific Interventions

The brief exposure-based treatment condenses graded exposure, modelling, cognitive restructuring and education about the phobic object into a single three-hour session. The treatment was based on that described by Öst et al. (2001). The treatment is explained as cognitive behavioural, with a clear expectation during the assessment that the child will expose themselves to frightening stimuli during the treatment session. A large part of the cognitive intervention addresses the beliefs that the child has about the feared situation, as well as ensuring that the child and the parents understand the nature of anxiety and its treatment. During the session, the child is helped to carry out exposure tasks and helped to discover that anxiety declines naturally, without the need for avoidance or escape behaviours.

During the intensive treatment session a great deal of information is provided for the child and their parents on anxiety and phobia. As we were aware of evidence about how little is recalled from medical and psychological consultations we decided to improve the child's and parent's memory of the treatment by writing a personalised booklet using simple language, which is specially edited for each child and their phobia.

Before using the booklet itself, the misconceptions that the child has about the feared object may need addressing. For instance, one child who was afraid of dogs believed that if a dog looked at you, it was going to attack you. He also thought that tail wagging in dogs was a sign of aggression. In his case we borrowed a dog training book from the public library, so that he could learn how to understand the behaviour of dogs better. We have used similar books for dental- and injection-phobic children because their appraisals of the threat posed by a needle or the dentist's procedures are far greater than the actual threat, and they often imagine catastrophic events.

The booklet describes, in words and colour pictures, the fight or flight response to fear and the body's preparation for this response. One 10-year-old boy with a dog phobia felt that he should attack and kill or maim the dog before it attacked him. This reaction was written into the booklet so that he could refer to it. The booklet explains that anxiety symptoms are sometimes unpleasant but that they are natural and can reduce quite quickly if the child remains in the vicinity of the feared object. We list good and bad things about anxiety in a table, including things the children are unable to do because of their phobia, such as visiting the dentist. The symptoms of panic attacks can also be included here if relevant. Next a description of phobias is given and the link between thoughts and feelings is shown. Then we explain why avoidance does not work in the long term. Finally, a variety of coping strategies such as relaxation exercises are described. We try to keep the relaxation exercises as simple as possible so we concentrate on teaching measured patterns of breathing, for instance by counting, so that the out breath takes twice as long as the in breath. If a child has a blood, injection or injury phobia that leads them to faint, we suggest using applied tension following the recommendations of Öst et al. (1989) in order to maintain the child's blood pressure rather than reducing muscle tension which could exacerbate the fainting response.

During the treatment session the child reads the booklet out to their parent and psychologist, allowing them to become actively involved with the explanation of anxiety, their phobia and possible coping strategies. Graded exposure to the anxiety-provoking stimuli then takes place. To avoid overwhelming the children, we proceed slowly through the fear hierarchy constructed during the assessment, making sure the children are happy to continue to the next step. During this time we take the opportunity to practise safety tips given on the subject of their fear. In the case of dogs, we instruct the child to ask the animal's owner if the pet is friendly before approaching a strange dog or stand sideways avoiding eye contact if a loose dog approaches. At the same time we make a note of any coping strategies the child is using, e.g. slow breathing (for relaxation), fist clenching (to combat the faintness of blood phobia) and helpful thoughts that help maintain their exposure. For example, 'I'm remembering my anxious feelings will pass if I am brave and stay calm'. These are written up after the session and sent on to the child to include in their booklet under the 'How I coped' heading.

The single session is framed as a big first step rather than as a cure. Parents are encouraged to assist their children to continue to face their fears. To promote continued exposure a reward chart is introduced. Parent and child put together a fear hierarchy; a list of anxiety-provoking situations from least to worst that can be carried out in the home setting. In this way children are motivated to continue exposure by the rewards and parents are reminded of the importance of continued exposure.

When giving the child the booklet to take home we encourage the child to read it again to an absent parent or caregiver. This allows the absent parent to become involved with assisting in the treatment and the child the opportunity to rehearse what they have learnt in the single session. At the three-month follow-up appointment, children and their parents report that the booklet has proved very helpful and serves to remind them of the treatment session and the strategies that overcome phobias.

Our initial evaluation of this approach is promising. From a consecutive series of 22 referrals of children aged between 7 and 18 years, 16 entered the treatment phase. The drop-outs included two with obsessive compulsive disorder as the primary problem, two who refused treatment and two who were found to have multiple problems and so were referred to local Child and Adolescent Mental Health Services (CAMHS). Six of the 16 treated cases were found on assessment to have other anxiety disorders such as generalised anxiety disorder and separation anxiety disorder. At follow-up three months after treatment, 12 of the 16 no longer met criteria for a phobia, although some were still a little fearful.

Challenging Issues

Three to three and a half hours is a long time for a child to be interacting with a psychologist. Psychologists need to work hard to keep the child's cooperation over that period and it is often necessary to have breaks for a drink and a snack. Children who have externalising disorders present particular difficulties. In general, these are of two kinds: an unwillingness to engage with the therapist, which will be clear in the assessment session; or argumentativeness in the treatment session. If the child is argumentative, the therapist may be able to use this to check out the cognitions that underlie the fear, although the psychologist has to be careful not to become confrontational in return. Because the treatment can be quite fast moving, even children with attention deficit hyperactivity disorder (ADHD) can be treated, particularly if the psychologist uses lots of movement during the session, rather than expecting the child to sit still in a chair.

More subtle difficulties may arise from the nature of the work. Many mental health settings expect psychological treatment to take place in one-hour sessions. In addition, the workplace may have difficulties with allowing animals on to the premises, so the psychologist may have to work in a variety of different sites.

User and Carer Perspectives

Intensive interventions with children remain under-researched and the perspective of the caregiver and child has not been investigated. Informal feedback suggests, however, that young people appreciate not having to take so much time off school or other activities. From their point of view it is much better to miss only one or two episodes of their favourite TV soap rather than the whole series that is required by group anxiety treatments such as Coping Cat (Kendall, 1990). Our experience suggests too that caregivers like to minimise the number of appointments and the very rapid progress seen in session. The psychologist may be rewarded by the smile of triumph on a child's face as they take a dog for a walk round the local park in front of their parents, saying that they do not need any help.

Research and Future Directions

A number of areas require further work. As yet the UK has not hosted a trial of single-session intensive treatment for phobias, and internationally there are no economic evaluations to guide commissioners in determining which form of phobia treatment they should purchase on behalf of their populations.

In the National Health Service the use of intensive interventions to reduce phobias to a level at which they no longer interfere with the child's life is valuable. Treatment is sufficiently clearly defined to allow delivery by less qualified practitioners, such as assistant psychologists working under the supervision of clinical psychologists, which may improve the economics of service delivery and access to psychological therapies for children.

From the point of view of the theory of interventions it would be helpful to find out which component of the treatment is doing the most work. For instance, there is some evidence that the cognitive component (psychoeducation, reappraisal of intrusive thoughts) of CBT for obsessive compulsive disorder (OCD) has a more powerful effect than the behavioural component (exposure and response prevention) in adults (Salkovskis, pers. comm.). On the other hand, the literature on panic disorder and depression in adults is moving in the direction of more behavioural techniques (exposure/response prevention for panic and activation for depression).

From a more clinical point of view the scope of this type of intervention needs investigation. As yet it is not clear what the limitations on the efficacy of the intervention are. Would it be useful for young people with wider-ranging anxiety conditions such as social phobia? To what extent is it possible to engage parents in delivering the treatment and is there an interaction with the parent's own fears and anxieties? Equally the age range over which the intervention is effective remains unknown. In principle, children as young as 4 or 5 years of age should be able to participate, but below that age their developmental understanding of thinking and emotion may make the approach less accessible.

Conclusion

Brief intensive interventions offer more economical use of scarce professional time, disrupt children's lives less than multiple clinic attendances and appear to be effective, at least for phobias. Further work to gauge whether they can be used for a wider range of psychological difficulties is warranted. However, the way in which psychologists deliver the treatments may require some adjustment to current practice.

References

Armfield, J.M. (2006). Cognitive vulnerability: A model of the etiology of fear. *Clinical Psychology Review, 26,* 746–768.

Cartwright-Hatton, S., McNicol, K. & Doubleday, E. (2006). Anxiety in a neglected population: Prevalence of anxiety disorders in pre-adolescent children. *Clinical Psychology Review, 26,* 817–833.

Cartwright-Hatton, S., Roberts, C., Chitsabean, P., Fothergill, C. & Harrington, R. (2004). Systematic review of the efficacy of cognitive behaviour therapies for childhood and adolescent anxiety disorders. *British Journal of Clinical Psychology, 43,* 421–436.

Clark, D.M., Salkovskis, P.M., Hackmann, A., Wells, A., Ludgate, J. & Gelder, M. (1999). Brief cognitive therapy for panic disorder: A randomized controlled trial. *Journal of Consulting and Clinical Psychology, 67*(4), 583–589.

Cooper, P.J., Fearn, V., Willetts, L., Seabrook, H. & Parkinson, M. (2006). Affective disorder in the parents of a clinic sample of children with anxiety disorders. *Journal of Affective Disorders, 93,* 205–212.

Field, A.P. & Lawson, J. (2008). The verbal information pathway to fear and subsequent causal learning in children. *Cognition and Emotion, 22*(3), 459–479.

Ford, T., Goodman, R. & Meltzer, H. (2003). The British child and adolescent mental health survey: The prevalence of DSM-IV Disorders. *Journal of the American Academy of Child and Adolescent Psychiatry, 42*(10), 1203–1211.

Goodman, R., Ford, T., Richards, H., Gatward, R. & Meltzer, H. (2000). The Development and Well-Being Assessment: Description and initial validation of an integrated assessment of child and adolescent psychopathology. *Journal of Child Psychology and Psychiatry, 41,* 645–655.

Gullone, E. (2000). The development of normal fear: A century of research. *Clinical Psychology Review, 20*(4), 429–451.

Gullone, E. & King, N.J. (1992). Psychometric evaluation of a revised fear survey schedule for children and adolescents. *Journal of Psychology and Psychiatry, 33*(6), 987–998.

James, A., Soler, A. & Weatherall, R. (2007). Cochrane review: Cognitive behavioural therapy for anxiety disorders in children and adolescents. *Evidence-Based Child Health: A Cochrane Review Journal, 2*(4), 1248–1275.

Kazdin, A.E. & Weisz, J.R. (2003). *Evidence based psychotherapies for children and adolescents.* New York: Guilford Press.

Kendall, P.C. (1990). *Coping Cat manual.* Ardmore, PA: Workbook Publishing.

King, N., Muris, P. & Ollendick, D.G. (2005). Childhood fears and phobias: Assessment and treatment. *Child and Adolescent Mental Health, 10,* 50–56.

Lichtenstein, P. & Annas, P. (2000). Heritability and prevalence of specific fears and phobias in childhood. *Journal of Child Psychology and Psychiatry, 41*(7), 927–937.

Marks, I. (1987). The development of normal fear: A review. *Journal of Child Psychology and Psychiatry, 28*(5), 667–697.

McLeod, B.D., Wood, J.J. & Weisz, J.R. (2007). Examining the association between parenting and childhood anxiety: A meta-analysis. *Clinical Psychology Review, 27,* 155–172.

Muris, P., Merckelbach, H., Holdrinet, I. & Sijsenaar, M. (1998). Treating phobic children: Effects of EMDR versus exposure. *Journal of Consulting and Clinical Psychology, 66*(1), 193–198.

Muris, P., Merckelbach, H., VanHaaften, H. & Mayer, B. (1997). Eye movement desensitisation and reprocessing versus exposure *in vivo* – a single-session crossover study of spider-phobic children. *British Journal of Psychiatry, 171,* 82–86.

Ollendick, T.H., King, N. & Muris, P. (2002). Fears and phobias in children: Phenomenology, epidemiology and aetiology. *Child and Adolescent Mental Health, 7*(3), 98–106.

Öst, L.G. (1989). One session treatment for specific phobias. *Behaviour Research and Therapy, 27,* 1–7.

Öst, L.G., Sterner, U. & Fellenius, J. (1989). Applied tension, applied relaxation, and the combination in the treatment of blood phobia. *Behaviour Research and Therapy, 27,* 109–121.

Öst, L.G., Svensson, L., Hellstrom, K. & Lindwall, R. (2001). One-session treatment of specific phobias in youths: A randomized clinical trial. *Journal of Consulting and Clinical Psychology, 69*(5), 814–824.

Silverman, W.K. & Nelles, W.B. (1988). The Anxiety Disorders Interview Schedule for Children. *Journal of the American Academy of Child and Adolescent Psychiatry, 27*(6), 772–778.

Somers, J.M., Goldner, E.M., Waraich, P. & Hsu, L. (2006). Prevalence and incidence studies of anxiety disorders: A systematic review of the literature. *Canadian Journal of Psychiatry, 51*(2), 100.

Appendix: Measures of specific fears

Spider Phobia Questionnaire for Children (Kindt, Brosschot & Muris, 1996)
Dental anxiety scale for young children (Humphris *et al.*, 2002)
Dental Anxiety Inventory – Short form (Aartman, 1998)
Acrophobia questionnaire (Cohen, 1977) – height phobia – not specifically for children
Blood Injection Symptom Scale (Page *et al.*, 1997)
Claustrophobia General Cognitions Questionnaire (Febbraro & Clum, 1995)
Claustrophobia Situations Questionnaire (Febbraro & Clum, 1995)
Claustrophobia Questionnaire (Radomsky *et al.*, 2001)
References for Phobia Scales
Aartman, I.H.A. (1998). Reliability and validity of the short version of the Dental Anxiety Inventory. *Community Dentistry and Oral Epidemiology, 26*(5), 350–354.

Cohen, D.C. (1977). Comparison of self-report and overt-behavioral measures for assessing acrophobia. *Behavior Therapy, 8,* 17–23.

Febbraro, G.A.R. & Clum, G.A. (1995). A dimensional analysis of claustrophobia. *Journal of Psychopathology and Behavioral Assessment, 17,* 335–351.

Kindt, M., Brosschot, J.F. & Muris, P. (1996). Spider phobia questionnaire for children (SPQ-C): A psychometric study and normative data. *Behaviour Research and Therapy, 34*(3), 277–282.

Page, A.C., Bennett, K.S., Carter, O., Smith, J. & Woodmore, K. (1997). The Blood-Injection Symptom Scale (BISS). Assessing a structure of phobic symptoms elicited by blood and injections. *Behaviour Research and Therapy, 35,* 457–464.

Radomsky, A.S., Rachman, S., Thordarson, D.S., McIsaac, H.K. & Teachman, B.A. (2001). The Claustrophobia Questionnaire. *Journal of Anxiety Disorders, 15*(4), 287–297.

Wenzel, A. & Holt, C.S. (2003). Validation of the Multidimensional Blood/Injury Phobia Inventory: Evidence for a Unitary Construct. *Journal of Psychopathology and Behavioral Assessment, 25*(3), 203–211.

9

Paediatric Services

Penny Spinks

This chapter provides an overview of the work of paediatric psychologists, initially providing a definition and background information. Communication with children with physical health problems will then be discussed. The main focus will be on two important topics, reducing the psychological impact of chronic illness on the child and family and facilitating good adjustment, and supporting children in managing pain and adherence to medical treatment regimes. Paediatric psychology practice is well developed in these areas and there is an evidence base of research for this practice. Somatisation is then discussed briefly and the final section examines methods of service delivery. For a wider review of the field of paediatric psychology, see Roberts and Walker (2003) and Spirito and Kazak (2006).

Paediatric psychology is a relatively new branch of child clinical psychology, with the Paediatric Psychology Network only becoming established as a subgroup of the British Psychological Society in 2006. In the United States paediatric psychology was recognised earlier and the first issue of the *Journal of Paediatric Psychology* was published in 1976. Roberts *et al.* (1984) described paediatric psychology as an area of practice concerned with the relationship between the psychological and physical well-being of children, including behavioural and emotional aspects of illness, the role of psychology in paediatrics, and health promotion and prevention in healthy children. This broad understanding of paediatric psychology is still apposite today.

The National Service Framework (NSF) for Children in the UK acknowledges the psychosocial needs of children by specifying that child-centred hospital services should consider the 'whole child', not simply the illness being treated (Department of Health, 2004). The importance of children having access to mental health professionals is also stated. However, paediatric psychology provision is still patchy across the UK both in terms of geographical area and within hospitals, where children with one illness may receive a psychology service and others do not. Also, funding for some posts is dependent on charitable resources.

More generally, there are disparities in access to health care for people from black and ethnic minority groups, including many conditions such as asthma, cancer, HIV/ Aids, diabetes and mental health conditions where there is a significant paediatric population (Institute of Medicine, 2002). McQuaid (2008) draws attention to the lack of attention to cultural diversity in research in paediatric psychology.

Communication

The NSF for Children (Department of Health, 2004) states that children should be given appropriate information about their health care and that staff should have training in 'how to listen to and communicate with children ...'. Clinical psychologists' knowledge of cognitive development ensures that they can play an important part in this process, both working directly with children and also through staff training and ongoing consultation.

Bibace and Walsh (1980) used stage theory based on Piagetian concepts to provide a framework for the development of children's understanding of illness and bodily functions. Stage theory postulates that the misconceptions of younger children result inevitably from their age-limited level of understanding. However, this does not account for the individual experience of the child, and Rushforth (1999) presents a model based on the work of Vygotsky and Bruner which proposes that given certain limitations of their conceptual framework, children's understanding can be enhanced by knowledge and teaching.

In practice, most information giving and preparation for medical procedures is undertaken by medical, nursing or play therapy staff. However, clinical psychologists may be involved in providing support to these professionals and in some cases they work directly with children and their families. It is important as a first step to assess the child's and family's knowledge of the illness and the procedure before giving information at an appropriate level. Dolls and drawings may be used and leaflets or written notes provided. Generally analogies should be avoided to prevent unforeseen misunderstandings, for example a young child hearing a scanner compared to a washing machine could fear drowning. The child's understanding should be checked at the end of the session to ensure that the information has been comprehended.

Chronic Health Conditions

There are considerable discrepancies in the definition of chronic health conditions in children which, together with widely varying methods of data collection, result in reported prevalence rates ranging from 0.22 per cent to 44 per cent (van der Lee *et al.*, 2007). The most widely cited study of prevalence in Great Britain (Pless & Douglas, 1971), based on the National Child Development Study, defines chronic illness as 'a physical, usually non-fatal condition that has lasted longer than 3 months in a given year or necessitated a period of continuous hospitalization of more than 1 month; of sufficient severity to interfere with the child's ordinary activities to some degree'. The prevalence rate quoted in the study is 11 per cent of children under 16, but this may be an underestimate of current levels, given the improvements in neonatal and paediatric medical care since this study was published. Chronic health conditions include cystic fibrosis, epilepsy, diabetes, asthma, sickle cell disease, leukaemia and other childhood cancers.

Children with chronic health conditions are at greater risk for behavioural and emotional adjustment problems. Lavigne and Faier-Routman (1992) report twice the level found in healthy controls and similar results are reported by Hysing *et al.* (2007) in their study of a Norwegian primary school sample. Family members are also at risk, not only parents (Eiser, 1990) but also siblings (Stallard *et al.*, 1997). Recent research has also identified the risk of post-traumatic stress symptoms following injury or diagnosis of a severe illness in both children and their parents (Landolt *et al.*, 2003).

Despite the increased risk of adjustment difficulties in children with a chronic illness, the majority of such children and their families cope well. Current practice aims to understand children with chronic illness and their families as ordinary people coping with specific stressors (Kazak, 1989). Wallander and Varni (1998) propose a disability-stress-coping model of adjustment to paediatric chronic physical disorders in which the disorder is conceptualised as an ongoing chronic strain for both the child and their family. Modifiable risk and resistance factors are identified to provide a focus for interventions.

For children, risk factors are:

- disease-related factors such as diagnosis, severity, visibility, pain and neurological functioning;
- functional dependence, including mobility, self-care and school attendance, particularly in adolescence;
- psychosocial stress: specifically the child's appraisal of stressors such as fear associated with the disorder (for example cancer), adversity of treatment, violation of the body and loss of privacy.

Child-related resistance factors include:

- intrapersonal factors such as locus of control, psychosocial development and pre-morbid psychological well-being;
- socio-ecological factors, most importantly family patterns of functioning which are socially cohesive and expressive, as well as teacher, parent, friend and classmate support;
- stress processing, the child's appraisal of circumstances and events together with the cognitive and behavioural strategies used to manage these.

Wallander *et al.* (1990) have found that level of adjustment in mothers does not differ in relation to different disease-specific factors such as level of daily care, severity of illness, diagnosis, visibility of disorder, etc. However, psychosocial stress is a risk

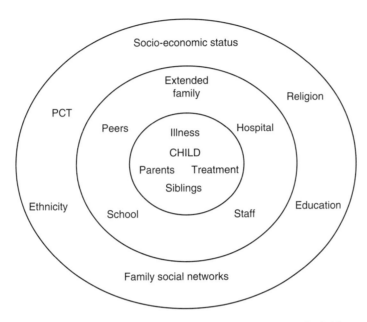

Figure 9.1   Example of socio-ecological systems in relation to a sick child.

factor; maternal reports of adjustment difficulties are associated with frequency of perception of problems, particularly those concerning school and family life.

Stress processing is a factor in resilience to adjustment difficulties in parents. For example, parents with an adaptive problem-solving approach to coping with their child's illness and related stress have fewer adjustment problems than those who adopt emotion-focused palliative coping strategies (Thompson *et al.*, 1994). Intrapersonal factors are also significant, particularly coping ability and perceptions of hope and of adequate social support (Wallander & Venters, 1995).

Resilience in parents is also mediated by socio-ecological factors such as family support, marital satisfaction and wider social and practical support. Kazak (1989) provides a framework which defines spheres of social influence relative to children within the paediatric healthcare system and their families. See Figure 9.1 for an example. Most direct involvement for paediatric teams is working with the child and their immediate family, but wider social factors also impact directly.

Implications for intervention

For those children and/or families who are identified as requiring psychological intervention, the models outlined above demonstrate the need for a comprehensive assessment, not only of the child and their illness but the also the family and the wider social context. The child's physical health needs, demands on parents and the necessity of coordinating with the rest of the team often dictate that the assessment is carried out less formally than in other settings, perhaps over several shorter sessions.

It is important to bear in mind that the majority of children and families will cope and may need only minimal psychological intervention, for example psychoeducation.

This may be delivered by non-psychologist members of the paediatric team with support from a clinical psychologist. Interventions such as groups for peers of children with diabetes (Greco *et al.*, 2001) and social skills training (Varni *et al.*, 1993) to facilitate peer relationships and reintegration into school have also been reported, as well as group family interventions such as the Surviving Cancer Competently Intervention Program (SCCIP; Spirito & Kazak, 2006).

There is a need to identify those children who may be at risk for adjustment problems and the Strengths and Difficulties Questionnaire (Goodman, 1997) has been suggested as a possible screening instrument (Hysing *et al.*, 2007). However, the PedsQL (Varni *et al.*, 2005) has been developed specifically for the paediatric population, and measures health-related quality of life. There are alternative modules for different diseases providing sensitive measures of well-being.

Pain and Adherence

For many children with chronic health problems, pain is an inevitable element of the illness and/or the treatment process. Often the child is required to adhere to a complex treatment regime which may be unpleasant and interfere with daily life. These issues are addressed in the following section.

Assessment of pain

Assessment of pain is important if clinical pain interventions are to be implemented and evaluated. McGrath (1995) stresses the importance of self-report because of the subjective nature of pain. From the age of 3, most children can give some gross indication of the intensity of pain such as 'a little' or 'a lot' and from 5 years, abstract instruments such as face scales depicting a graded set of facial expressions can be introduced. Visual analogue scales, straight lines with fixed points at each end for 'no pain' and 'worst pain possible', can be used for children of 7 and over; numerical or verbal gradations (no pain, slight pain, etc.) may be included in such scales. Another useful instrument for this age group, the Varni and Thompson Pain Questionnaire (Varni & Thompson, 1987), employs outline drawings of a child's body. The child is invited to use different colours to represent levels of pain severity and to colour the body in accordance with the location and severity of their own pain.

For younger children and those who cannot communicate, observational methods are necessary. Stallard *et al.* (2002) identified a core of six specific pain cues reported by caregivers to identify definite or severe pain in children with significant cognitive impairment. These included crying, screaming, distressed facial expression, inability to be comforted, flinching from contact and tense appearance. However, there is evidence to suggest that judgements of infant pain vary according to type of caregiver and age of infant (Pillai Riddell & Craig, 2007). In their study of caregivers' ratings of pain in infants from 2 to 18 months, parents attributed higher levels of pain than paediatricians, and older infants were rated as experiencing higher levels of pain than younger babies, suggesting that there is a need for research to provide more objective observational measures of pain.

Interventions

Procedural pain

There have been considerable advances in paediatric pharmacological interventions to reduce the painful effects of invasive medical procedures with more effective sedation and analgesia, including the use of topical anaesthetic creams for injections and blood tests, and more frequent use of general anaesthetics. For children requiring frequent intravenous medications and blood tests, as in chemotherapy for leukaemia, surgically implanted venous access devices preclude the need for frequent needle pricks.

Psychological procedures also have an important role in reducing procedural distress for those children for whom pharmacological procedures are either impractical or ineffective or who have high levels of anxiety. There is evidence to suggest that a combination of pharmacological and psychological interventions may be more effective in reducing procedural related pain in children with cancer (Spirito & Kazak, 2006).

Distraction has been shown to be effective in reducing procedural distress particularly for preschool children (Carr, 2000). Distracters such as interactive toys or books which require both cognitive processing and motor skills seem to hold the attention of children more effectively than passive tasks such as watching cartoons. Blowing bubbles may also be helpful both as a distracter and as an aid to relaxation. Hypnotic-induced distraction techniques have also been shown to reduce distress (Kuttner *et al.*, 1988, cited in Carr, 2000).

Cognitive behavioural programmes for procedural pain have been shown to be helpful for school-age children (Powers, 1999). These often comprise several components, including psychoeducation, giving children detailed information about the procedure, particularly duration, as younger children often do not realise that pain from needle procedures will be over quickly (McGrath, 1995). Coping skills training may include watching a film of a coping model undergoing the procedure, relaxation, using distracting mental images or engaging in comforting self-talk. Protocols for use with both preschool and school-age children are given in Spirito and Kazak (2006). Some children experience high levels of anxiety in relation to procedures, most commonly injections, and may require desensitisation. Dahlquist and Pendley (2005) report that parental anxiety is an important mediator of such anxiety, suggesting that parents should also be included in desensitisation interventions.

Chronic pain

Headaches and recurrent abdominal pain are the most frequently presenting problems. For headache, several cognitive behavioural therapy (CBT) interventions have been shown to be effective in pain management, including self-hypnosis, guided imagery and other relaxation techniques. There is also some evidence for the efficacy of biofeedback both in isolation and in combination with other CBT techniques (Powers *et al.*, 2005).

Sanders *et al.* (1994) demonstrated the effectiveness of a cognitive behavioural family intervention in adolescents with recurrent abdominal pain. Chronic pain often occurs in the absence of any identifiable organic aetiology but cognitive behavioural interventions are still helpful in work with the child and family. This will also be discussed in the section on somatisation.

There is less evidence to support psychological interventions for disease-related pain, for example in sickle cell disease or juvenile rheumatoid arthritis, and close cooperation with the paediatric team is a priority. Relaxation and distraction techniques may need to be introduced when pain is less severe and monitoring of pain levels is important to assess the efficacy of intervention (Spirito & Kazak, 2006).

Adherence

Many chronic physical disorders require the child or young person to adhere to a strict medical regime in terms of oral or injected medication, diet, physiotherapy, exercise, etc. This can be difficult when the regime involves painful procedures or impinges on lifestyle, particularly during adolescence when non-adherence and conflict between young person and parents are part of a normal developmental pattern. As the young person becomes more independent they need to assume more responsibility for their treatment regime, which may be difficult for some parents to accept. Paediatric teams may need to support families in this transition. There is also a need for awareness that cultural influences may impact on illness management behaviour, for example Mansour *et al.* (2000) reported that many African-American and Latino parents were reluctant to give their children regular prescribed medication for asthma because of concerns about addiction or dependency.

There is evidence to support the efficacy of behavioural family systems therapy in reducing family conflict and improving adherence and metabolic control in adolescents with diabetes (Wysocki *et al.*, 2006) and cystic fibrosis (Quittner *et al.*, 2004, cited in Spirito & Kazak, 2006). Kazak (2006) has also developed a group family-based intervention to reduce post-traumatic stress symptoms in adolescent cancer survivors and their families.

Motivational interviewing is a client-centred treatment which aims to explore the individual's own issues, interests and concerns as a basis for effecting change. This intervention has been effective in improving adherence in adolescents with diabetes, asthma, cystic fibrosis and juvenile rheumatoid arthritis (Channon *et al.*, 2005; Erikson *et al.*, 2005). There have also been promising results in terms of decrease in body mass index of obese young children following motivational interviewing with parents (Schwartz *et al.*, 2007).

Somatisation

There are many children seen within both in- and out-patient paediatric settings with symptoms for which there is no clear medical aetiology. Somatisation is described as persistent, severe and distressing symptoms that cannot fully be explained by medical knowledge or investigation (Husain *et al.*, 2007). Recurrent abdominal pain and headaches are the most common problems but children may also present with a range of other symptoms, including limb pains, dizziness, seizures, fainting, nausea and fatigue. Eminson *et al.* (1996) report a higher incidence of somatisation symptoms among girls than boys aged 11–16 years, with 9.5 per cent of girls compared with 7.1 per cent of boys reporting a lifetime prevalence of 13 or more symptoms. However, these differences were significant only in those above the age of 13 years 6 months and were associated with more distress about illness. Although the majority of children with somatisation disorders do not report associated psychological problems, there is an increased risk of internalising disorders such as anxiety or depression.

Social learning may contribute to somatisation, with children modelling illness behaviour of other family members. For some children symptoms may persist following recovery from an injury or illness. Such experiences can underlie strongly held beliefs in a medical causality among the children and their families. There is also evidence of psychosocial difficulties, particularly with siblings or at school, but not with parents who may provide a protective relationship (Garralda, 2004).

Cognitive behavioural interventions for chronic pain are described above and can be used irrespective of the causality of the physical symptoms. This is particularly helpful in engaging children and families who persist in seeking a medical diagnosis. However, it is important to assess the wider social system, including immediate and extended family beliefs, relationships and social circumstances, school, and the network of professionals working with the family. Intervention can then be directed to the relevant part of the system. In the case of children with severe disability, a rehabilitation model can improve functioning and reduce the need for paediatric treatment (Lock & Giammona, 1999).

Models of Service Delivery

There are three principal ways of delivering clinical psychology services to paediatrics:

- dedicated paediatric posts;
- child clinical psychologists with dedicated paediatric time;
- psychology posts with no dedicated paediatric time but where some paediatric referrals are accepted (British Psychological Society, 2003).

Psychologists working in dedicated paediatric posts are usually based within children's hospitals or paediatric teams which may be in general hospitals, child development centres or community based. This type of service delivery is based on a psychosocial model which aims to address the child's health needs holistically. Psychologists with dedicated paediatric time may also work to this model. For those psychologists who have no time dedicated to paediatric work, the model adopted is more likely to be based on a paediatric liaison model where staff are based in Child and Adolescent Mental Health Services (CAMHS) and deal predominantly with mental health problems which present to paediatrics. Emergency mental health referrals are a focus of this type of service, especially deliberate self-harm and acute psychosis, but somatisation and habit disorders are also prevalent.

The focus of this chapter has been on a limited range of direct work with children and families. However, it should be emphasised that the role can be much broader, covering such problems as habit disorders (sleep, feeding and elimination difficulties) or issues relating to the transition to adult services for young people with chronic health problems. In addition to direct work, psychologists may provide supervision and consultation to members of paediatric teams, formal teaching and staff support which may comprise a regular group for neonatal or paediatric ward staff, or an ad hoc debrief for the network of staff who are working with a child and family who present particularly difficult issues. Psychologists based within paediatric services are also asked to contribute to organisational work such as service protocols and planning, developments in psychosocial services and clinical governance. Increasing awareness of the importance of the mediating role of psychosocial factors in many areas of child health and improvements in medical science, resulting in increasing survival rates for children with chronic health problems, should ensure that the role of the paediatric psychologist continues to be challenging and highly valued.

References

Bibace, R. & Walsh, M. (1980). Development of children's concepts of illness. *Pediatrics*, *66*, 912–917.

British Psychological Society, Division of Clinical Psychology, Faculty for Children and Young People (2003). *Briefing paper: Child clinical psychologists working with children with medical conditions*. Leicester: Author.

Carr, A. (2000). *What works with children and adolescents?* London: Routledge.

Channon, S., Huws-Thomes, M.V., Gregory, J.W. & Rollnick, S. (2005). Motivational interviewing with teenagers with diabetes. *Clinical Child Psychology and Psychiatry*, *10*(1), 43–52.

Dahlquist, L.N. & Pendley, J.S. (2005). When distraction fails: Parental anxiety and children's responses to distraction during cancer procedures. *Journal of Pediatric Psychology*, *30*(7), 623–628.

Department of Health (2004). *National Service Framework for Children – standard for hospital services*. London: HMSO.

Eiser, C. (1990). Psychological effects of chronic disease. *Journal of Child Psychology and Psychiatry*, *31*(1), 85–98.

Eminson, M., Benjamin, S., Shortall, A., Woods, T. & Faragher, B. (1996). Physical symptoms and illness attitudes in adolescents: An epidemiological study. *Journal of Child Psychology and Psychiatry*, *37*(5), 519–528.

Garralda, M.E. (2004). The interface between medical and mental health problems and medical help seeking in children and adolescents: A research perspective. *Child and Adolescent Mental Health*, *9*(4), 146–155.

Goodman, R. (1997). The Strengths and Difficulties Questionnaire: A research note. *Journal of Child Psychology and Psychiatry*, *38*(5), 581–586.

Greco, P., Pendley, J.S., McDonell, K. & Reeves, G. (2001). A peer group intervention for adolescents with type 1 diabetes and their best friends. *Journal of Pediatric Psychology*, *26*(8), 485–490.

Husain, K., Browne, T. & Chalder, T. (2007). A review of psychological models and interventions for medically unexplained somatic symptoms in children. *Child and Adolescent Mental Health*, *12*(1), 2–7.

Hysing, M., Elgen, I., Gillberg, C., Lie, S.A. & Lundervold, J.A. (2007). Chronic physical illness and mental health in children. Results from a large-scale population study. *Journal of Child Psychology and Psychiatry*, *48*(8), 785–792.

Institute of Medicine (2002). *Unequal treatment: Confronting racial and ethnic disparities in healthcare*. Washington, DC: Author.

Kazak, A.E. (1989). Families of chronically ill children: A systems and social ecological model of adaptation and challenge. *Journal of Consulting and Clinical Psychology*, *57*, 25–30.

Kazak, A.E. (2006). *Evidence based assessment and intervention in pediatric oncology*. Workshop presentation at Paediatric Psychology Network UK Annual Study Days, Oxford.

Kuttner, L., Bowman, M. & Teasdale, M. (1988). Psychological treatment of distress, pain and anxiety for young children with cancer. *Journal of Developmental and Behavioural Pediatrics*, *9*, 374–81. Cited in Carr, A. (2000). *What works with children and adolescents?* London: Routledge.

Landolt, M.A., Vollrath, M., Ribi, K., Gnehm, H.E. & Sennhauser, F.H. (2003). Incidence and associations of parental and child posttraumatic stress symptoms in pediatric patients. *Journal of Child Psychology and Psychiatry*, *44*(8), 1199–1207.

Lavigne, J.V. & Faier-Routman, J. (1992). Psychological adjustment to pediatric physical disorders: A meta-analytic review. *Journal of Pediatric Psychology*, *17*(2), 133–157.

Lock, J. & Giammona, A. (1999). Severe somatoform disorder in adolescence; a case series using a rehabilitation model for intervention. *Clinical Child Psychology and Psychiatry*, *4*(3), 341–351.

Mansour, M.E., Lanphear, B.P. & DeWitt, T.G. (2000). Barriers to asthma care in urban children: Parent perspectives. *Pediatrics*, *106*(3), 512–519.

McGrath, P.J. (1995). Annotation: Aspects of pain in children and adolescents. *Journal of Child Psychology and Psychiatry*, *36*(5), 717–730.

McQuaid, E.L. (2008). Introduction to Special Issue: *Journal of Pediatric Psychology* statement of purpose – special section on diversity and health care disparities. *Journal of Pediatric Psychology*, *33*(1), 22–25.

Pillai Riddell, R.R. & Craig, K.D. (2007). Judgements of infant pain: The impact of caregiver identity and infant age. *Journal of Pediatric Psychology*, *32*(5), 501–511.

Pless, I.B. & Douglas, J.W. (1971). Issues involved in the definition and classification of chronic health conditions. *Pediatrics*, *47*, 405–414.

Powers, S.W. (1999). Empirically supported treatments in pediatric psychology: Procedure-related pain. *Journal of Pediatric Psychology*, *24*(2), 131–145.

Powers, S.W., Jones, J.S. & Jones, B.A. (2005). Behavioral and cognitive-behavioral interventions with pediatric populations. *Clinical Child Psychology and Psychiatry*, *10*(1), 65–77.

Quittner, A.L., Drotar, D. & Ievers-Landis, C. (2004). *Improving adherence in adolescents with cystic fibrosis: Comparisons of family therapy and psychoeducation*. Paper presented at the National Conference on Child Health Psychology, Charleston, SC. Cited in Spirito, A. & Kazak, A.E. (2006). *Effective and emerging treatments in pediatric psychology*. New York: Oxford University Press.

Roberts, M.C., Maddux, J. & Wright, L. (1984). The developmental perspective in behavioural health. In J.D. Matarazzo *et al.* (Eds.) *Behavioural health; A handbook of health enhancement and disease prevention.* New York: Wiley-Interscience. Cited in Houghton, J. (2005). Paediatric psychology in the twenty-first century. *Clinical Child Psychology and Psychiatry, 10*(1), 112–117.

Roberts, M.C. & Walker, E.C. (Eds.) (2003). *Handbook of pediatric psychology* (3rd edn). New York: Guilford Press.

Rushforth, H. (1999). Practitioner review: Communicating with hospitalised children: review and application of research pertaining to children's understanding of health and illness. *Journal of Child Psychology and Psychiatry, 40*(5), 683–691.

Sanders, M., Shepherd, R., Cleghorn, G. & Woolford, H. (1994). The treatment of recurrent abdominal pain in children: A controlled comparison of cognitive-behavioral family intervention and standard pediatric care. *Journal of Consulting and Clinical Psychology, 62*(2), 306–314.

Schwartz, R.P., Hamre, R., Dietz, W.H., Wasserman, R.C., Slora, E.J., Myers, E.F. *et al.* (2007). Office-based motivational interviewing to prevent childhood obesity – a feasibility study. *Archives of Pediatrics and Adolescent Medicine, 161*(5), 495–501.

Spirito, A. & Kazak, A.E. (2006). *Effective and emerging treatment in pediatric psychology.* New York: Oxford University Press.

Stallard, P., Mastroyannopoulou, K., Lewis, M. & Lenton, S. (1997). The siblings of children with life-threatening conditions. *Child and Adolescent Mental Health, 2*(1), 26–33.

Stallard, P., Williams, L., Velleman, R., Lenton, S. & McGrath, P.J. (2002). Brief report: Behaviors identified by caregivers to detect pain in noncommmunicating children. *Journal of Pediatric Psychology, 27*(2), 209–214.

Thompson, R.J., Gil, K.M., Gustafson, K.E., George, L.K., Keith, B.R., Spock, A. *et al.* (1994). Stability and change in the psychological adjustment of mothers of children and adolescents with cystic fibrosis and sickle cell disease. *Journal of Pediatric Psychology, 19*(2), 171–188.

van der Lee, J.H., Mokkink, L.B., Grootenhuis, M.A., Heymans, H.S. & Offringa, M. (2007). Definitions and measurement of chronic health conditions in childhood: A systematic review. *Journal of the American Medical Association, 297*(24), 241–251.

Varni, J.W., Burwinkle, T.M. & Seid, M. (2005). The PedQL as a pediatric patient-reported outcome: Reliability and validity of the PedsQL measurement model in 25,000 children. *Future Drugs, 5*(6), 705–719.

Varni, J.S., Katz, E.R., Colegrove, R. & Dolgin, M. (1993). The impact of social skills training on the adjustment of children with newly diagnosed cancer. *Journal of Pediatric Psychology, 18*(6), 751–767.

Varni, J.S. & Thompson, R.J. (1987). *The paediatric pain questionnaire.* Child Psychology Portfolio. London: NFER Nelson.

Wallander, J.L., Pitt, L.C. & Mellins, C.A. (1990). Child functional independence and maternal psychosocial stress as risk factors threatening adaptation in mothers of physically or sensorially handicapped children. *Journal of Consulting and Clinical Psychology, 58*(6), 818–824.

Wallander, J.L. & Varni, J.W. (1998). Effects of pediatric chronic physical disorders on child and family adjustment. *Journal of Child Psychology and Psychiatry, 39*(1), 29–46.

Wallander, J.L. & Venters, (1995). Perceived role restriction and adjustment of others of children with chronic physical disability. *Journal of Pediatric Psychology, 20*(5), 619–632.

Wysocki, T., Harris, M.S., Buckloh, L.M., Mertlich, D., Lochrie, A.S., Taylor, A. *et al.* (2006). *Journal of Pediatric Psychology, 31*(9), 928–938.

10

Cognitive Behaviour Therapy with Children and Young People

Paul Stallard

Introduction

The application of cognitive behaviour therapy (CBT) to children and young people is a comparatively recent development. It was early in the 1990s that the first randomised controlled trials of CBT for the treatment of depression and anxiety were published (Kendall, 1994; Lewinsohn *et al.*, 1990). Randomised controlled trails (RCTs) have now been undertaken for children and young people with many conditions, including post-traumatic stress disorder (PTSD) (Cohen *et al.*, 2004), obsessive compulsive disorder (Barrett *et al.*, 2004), phobias (Silverman *et al.*, 1999), social phobia (Spence *et al.*, 2000), school refusal (King *et al.*, 1998) and chronic fatigue (Stulemeijer *et al.*, 2005). Most of this research has been undertaken in America or Australia, with comparatively few UK-based RCTs being reported (Wood *et al.*, 1996; Smith *et al.*, 2007; Goodyer *et al.* 2007). The purpose of this chapter is to review the evidence base for child-focused CBT, to discuss the clinical practice of CBT with children and young people and to consider key issues and future directions.

The majority of CBT trials have highlighted significant improvements following therapy, leading Graham (2005) to conclude that, at present, CBT is the best-evidenced child therapy. These positive conclusions have been reflected in systematic reviews of depression (Compton *et al.*, 2004), anxiety (Cartwright-Hatton *et al.*, 2004) and PTSD (Stallard, 2006). Further support for the use of CBT with children and young people has come from reviews undertaken by the National Institute for Health and Clinical Excellence, who have recommended CBT in the treatment of depression, obsessive compulsive disorder (OCD), eating disorders and PTSD (National Institute for Health and Clinical Excellence, 2005a, 2006, 2004, 2005b). However, recent studies, particularly in the area of depression, have begun to question the additional value of CBT over other interventions, particularly when compared against medication (March *et al.*, 2006; Goodyer *et al.*, 2007).

Positive results from methodologically sound studies, the growth in evidence-based practice and increased practitioner awareness have fuelled the interest in the practice of child-focused CBT, particularly since the start of the millennium. Practitioners have reflected upon how this adult-derived model can be creatively adapted to work with children, young people and their families. The use of more visual materials, simpler concepts, concrete examples, everyday metaphors, quizzes, games, puppetry and attractive worksheets has provided child-friendly ways in which CBT can be made more accessible for children. This has resulted in a number of books and manuals where worksheets and creative ideas have been shared and become widely available for clinicians to adapt and use (see Stallard, 2002; Friedberg & McClure, 2002).

In addition to the issue of presentation and appropriately tailoring CBT to the interests of the child, the clinician also needs to ensure that the intervention is pitched at the right level for them to access. CBT with children and young people needs to be adapted so that it is cognisant with the cognitive ability, developmental level and verbal and memory skills of the child. Thought bubbles have been used as a way of helping the child to identify and communicate their cognitions; cartoons as a method of eliciting automatic thoughts; 'if/then' quizzes to identify predictions and attributions; visual prompt cards to aid memory recall; and the use of simple, structured worksheets for undertaking complex tasks such as cognitive restructuring and problem solving.

Once the clinician has tailored the techniques and strategies of CBT to the child's developmental level, they need to attend to the process of undertaking CBT. The process of therapy will be unfamiliar and may feel uncomfortable to many children. There is therefore a need to explicitly clarify the nature and expectations of the therapeutic process and to ensure that therapy is a positive and engaging experience. The clinician may need to adopt a more active role than they would when working with adults. Therapy may be less didactic and there may be times when self-reflection and discovery is not possible, resulting in the therapist offering the child options and suggestions. With reticent or unforthcoming children a rhetorical approach may be helpful in which the therapist may muse aloud about a range of possibilities from which the child may select or reject. Finally, the pacing of therapy needs careful attention and the length of sessions may need to be shortened so that they do not exceed the child's attention span.

The therapeutic process of child-focused CBT is built upon a number of key principles such as collaboration, guided discovery and self-reflection. These principles will be largely unfamiliar to children and young people who may expect the therapist to take an active and directive role. The expectations of CBT therefore need to be made explicit, with Stallard (2004) summarising the important elements of the therapeutic process using the acronym PRECISE: Partnership working, pitched at the Right developmental level; provided in an Emphatic and Creative manner; encouraging Investigation; facilitating Self-efficacy but above all is Enjoyable.

Given the rapid expansion in research and interest in the use of child-focused CBT, it would appear timely to review three of the key issues that continue to be the subject of debate.

How Good Is the Evidence Base?

Although there is considerable data from individual studies detailing the positive benefits of CBT, the evidence base is nonetheless limited. At present there are only a few published RCTs of CBT for the treatment of conditions such as chronic fatigue, social anxiety and phobias and none involving eating disorders or psychosis. The sample sizes of many of the earlier RCTs were comparatively small, raising questions about whether they were appropriately powered to detect small but important changes and the wider applicability of their findings. A more important issue relates to the comparison groups against which CBT has been assessed. Many of the early studies compared CBT to waiting list control groups, and found significant post-intervention improvements. For example, in one of the earliest and best-evaluated CBT programmes for the treatment of anxiety disorders, the Coping Cat programme, significant post-treatment improvements were found at one-year follow-up (Kendall, 1994; Kendall *et al.*, 1997). While these results clearly highlight the positive benefits of providing CBT rather than doing nothing, they do not demonstrate the additional gains of CBT over other active interventions. Indeed, where CBT is compared with other active interventions the results are more modest. Weisz *et al.* (2006), for example, found in a recent meta-analysis of psychotherapy for the treatment of childhood depression that CBT fared no better than non-cognitive approaches.

The uncertainty about the comparative efficacy of CBT is highlighted by the results of two recent, large, methodologically robust studies exploring the treatment of depression. The Treatment for Adolescents with Depression Study (TADS) recruited 439 children aged 12–17 with mild to severe depression (March *et al.*, 2006). CBT on its own was less effective at 12-week follow-up compared with either medication on its own or medication combined with CBT. Similar findings have been reported in the recent UK Adolescent Depression Anti-depression and Psychotherapy Trial (ADAPT; Goodyer *et al.*, 2007). A total of 208 adolescents aged 11–17 with moderate to severe major depression received either medication or medication and CBT. The addition of CBT did not result in any additional improvements over and above medication on its own when assessed at 28 weeks. These studies highlight that while CBT does result in positive gains, its superiority over other forms of therapy for depression has not been consistently proven.

Does CBT Work with Children of All Ages?

The age at which children are able to participate in CBT has been the subject of debate. Scrutiny of the eligibility criteria for the published clinical trials highlights that the inclusion age is wide. For example, the anxiety programmes, Coping Cat and its Australian derivative Coping Koala, have been used with children and young people aged 9–17; the trauma-focused CBT programme for the treatment of sexual abuse, developed by Cohen and colleagues, with children aged 8–14 and the OCD family

FOCUS programme (Barrett *et al.*, 2004) have been used with children aged 7–17. However, although many report a wide age range for inclusion, few actually involve children under the age of 7 (Cartwright-Hatton *et al.*, 2004; Stallard, 2006). In terms of the age effect of CBT, some reviewers have concluded that young children benefit less from CBT and that it is only over the age of 12 that the optimum benefits become apparent (Durlak *et al.*, 2001, 1991). Whether this is due to younger children not having sufficiently developed cognitive skills to engage in CBT or whether CBT has not been adapted in a developmentally appropriate way for the child to access has been a source of debate (Shirk, 2001; Friedberg *et al.*, 2000; Ronen, 1997; Stallard, 2002).

The widespread view amongst practitioners is that with appropriate modification and adaptation, some form of CBT can be used with children aged 7 and over. Some of the core tasks of CBT, such as identifying different emotions, accessing thoughts and differentiating between thoughts, feelings and behaviours, can be achieved by simple and practical worksheets and games. Feeling worksheets can help the child to notice and attend to important non-verbal cues such as facial expression, body posture and behaviour. Awareness of emotional states can be encouraged by emotional dictionaries created from newspaper photographs or by the use of games such as emotional charades. Thought bubbles provide a familiar medium for children to convey their thoughts, and, with training, children as young as 3 can understand that thought bubbles represent what a person may think (Wellman *et al.*, 1996). The ability to recognise self-talk or inner speech is present before the age of 6 (Flavell *et al.*, 2001). Similarly, children under the age of 7 can distinguish between thoughts, feelings and actions, can acknowledge that thoughts are subjective and that two people can have different thoughts about the same event (Quakley *et al.*, 2004; Wellman *et al.*, 1996). These studies suggest that young children do have the ability to engage in many of the tasks required in CBT, although whether CBT is the optimum method for working with this age group is unclear.

What Is the Cognitive Aspect of Child-Focused CBT?

CBT is based upon the premise that biases in cognitions and processes underlie psychological problems. Identifying, challenging and reappraising these dysfunctional cognitions is a key aspect of CBT. With adults, robust cognitive theories have been developed to explain disorders, including OCD and PTSD (Salkovskis, 1999; Ehlers & Clark, 2000). These theories clearly identify cognitions which are specifically targeted during interventions. With children, underlying theories are less developed and the cognitive component of many CBT interventions can appear quite limited. Indeed, the primary cognitive intervention used by a number of programmes is to generally teach children to identify their negative self-talk and to replace this with more helpful, coping self-talk. In the best-known programme for the treatment of OCD, 'How I ran OCD off my land' (March & Mulle, 1998), children are taught to boss back their OCD. The direct focus upon particular cognitions, e.g. threat appraisals or attributions relating to responsibility or processes, e.g. selective attention, that are assumed to underlie specific disorders, is limited. Indeed, a significant proportion of CBT with children and young people tends to focus primarily upon the emotional and behavioural, not the cognitive, domain. In many respects this is developmentally appropriate since the cognitive capacity of many younger children will be limited, thereby restricting their ability to engage in more complex or abstract cognitive strategies. Similarly, it is undoubtedly the case that learning through doing, i.e. exposure and behavioural experiments, will produce cognitive change. The issue is whether the effectiveness of CBT may or may not be enhanced by paying greater attention to specific underlying cognitions and processes or indeed whether such direct attention is not necessary for children.

A second, more theoretical issue is the distinction between CBT and behaviour therapy (BT). How much of a cognitive focus is required before BT becomes CBT? This issue is important since there is considerable variation in the content of interventions described under the generic term of CBT. For example, the programme described by King *et al.* (2000) for the treatment of trauma is primarily behavioural, with 70 per cent of the sessions being devoted to graded exposure. In contrast, the programme described by Celano *et al.* (1996) has a predominantly cognitive focus and addresses important cognitions associated with sexual abuse. Both are described as CBT, although their content and emphasis are very different.

Future Directions and Issues

This brief review has highlighted some of the key issues surrounding the practice of child-focused CBT. The limitations of the evidence base have been noted, although it should be emphasised that, in addition to randomised trials, there are numerous published studies that have reported positive outcomes from CBT for a variety of childhood problems. CBT does have the strongest evidence base but this does not imply that other forms of child psychotherapy are not effective. Within a developing and evolving area such conclusions would be premature and unwise.

In terms of the future there are a number of research and practice issues that require attention.

Developmentally appropriate CBT models

At present, there is an absence of good theoretical models which explain common child problems within a CBT framework. Recent studies exploring the applicability of adult-derived models to children have suggested that similar cognitions and processes may be present in children. Stallard and Smith (2007) investigated the Ehlers and Clark model of PTSD and found that core elements of the model, including cognitions of trauma severity, sequelae appraisals and cognitive coping involving distraction and rumination, were evident in children. Similarly, there is emerging evidence that some of the specific attributions about responsibility and thought action fusion that underpin the Salkovskis adult OCD model are also evident in children (Barrett & Healy, 2003: Libby *et al.*, 2004). However, these models need to be developmentally appropriate and need to include important family and systemic influences, including parental cognitions that contribute to the development and maintenance of problems in the child.

Effective elements of CBT

Robust, developmentally appropriate models are testable and should inform the specific focus and content of child-focused CBT. At present, CBT is a generic term that refers to a variety of interventions that differ in terms of their content, length and primary focus. There are also differences in the degree to which parents are involved in the intervention. The view amongst clinicians is that parental involvement offers many benefits in terms of helping the generalisation, practice and maintenance of newly acquired skills. However, the results from research studies are equivocal and it is unclear under what circumstances the involvement of parents results in additional benefits (Creswell & Cartwright-Hatton, 2007). Further studies are required to differentiate more clearly the role of parents in child-focused CBT and those factors which indicate when their involvement is beneficial. In addition, the issue of the balance between the different components and the relative contribution of the different strategies that constitute the intervention needs to be addressed. Finally, in order to ensure sound clinical practice CBT needs to be delivered in a flexible and sensitive way that responds to diversity and context and is specifically tailored to the developmental level of the child.

Real-world applicability

A criticism levelled at many of the standardised CBT programmes that have been evaluated through clinical trials is their applicability to everyday clinical practice. Many of the subjects recruited into the earlier trials were volunteers who presented with less severe problems than those referred for treatment to clinics. Exclusion criteria in most RCTs are strict, resulting in a lot of children who are seen within traditional services with comorbid conditions or highly complex situations being excluded. Similarly, the manualised interventions that have been evaluated are highly structured, typically delivered by researchers, often involve a large number of sessions and are singularly focused upon a particular disorder. These do not necessarily fit with the workload demands of a busy clinic and may not be appropriate for children with multiple problems. There is therefore a need for pragmatic clinical trials in which CBT interventions are delivered by clinicians and evaluated in actual clinical settings under everyday conditions.

Increasing accessibility and use of new technology

Although CBT appears to be an effective intervention for many child mental health disorders, the fact remains that comparatively few children in need access CBT. The UK National Mental Health Survey found that over an 18-month period only 22 per cent of those with significant mental health disorders received treatment from specialist child and adolescent mental health services (Ford et al., 2003). The availability of CBT skills within specialist Child and Adolescent Mental Health Services (CAMHS) is extremely limited, with only 20 per cent of practitioners reporting CBT to be their dominant therapeutic approach (Stallard *et al.*, 2007). These figures highlight the need to develop and evaluate alternative ways of providing CBT for those in need. Recent developments include the use of self-help materials such as the Feeling Good Guide for adolescents with depression (Dummett & Williams, 2007) and the development of interactive computer programs such as Stressbusters (Robinson, 2007) and Think Feel Do (TFD; Stallard, 2007). Computerised programs such as TFD have the potential to substantially increase the availability of CBT. TFD can be delivered by non-mental-health specialists with limited expertise in CBT, such as school nurses and teachers, in non-clinical settings, such as schools, to children with mild and moderate disorders. These examples highlight the need to ensure that CBT adapts to utilise technologies that are familiar to young people. Computer records and video diaries as methods of self-monitoring, emailing as way of downloading 'hot cognitions' and the use of text messages as real-life prompting and feedback are possible future developments.

Preventive CBT

An alternative approach that has received recent interest is that of prevention, and in particular whether school-based CBT programmes are effective in improving the mental health of children. A number of interventions have been reported. The FRIENDS programme for the prevention of anxiety (Barrett *et al.*, 2006) and the Resourceful Adolescent Programme (RAP) for depression (Shochet *et al.*, 2001) appear particularly promising. However, the best way of delivering these interventions, that is, universally to whole classes of children versus more selective approaches targeting high-risk groups or children beginning to display moderate problems, is not clear (Merry *et al.*, 2004; Spence & Shortt, 2007). Similarly, whether these programmes transfer to a UK educational context and their immediate and longer-term preventive benefits need to be assessed.

Conclusion

Child-focused CBT has rapidly established itself as an effective intervention for the treatment of many emotional disorders. CBT is a practical and time-limited approach with a here-and-now focus. It is appealing and has high face validity for many children and young people. However, CBT was developed for use with adults and the predominant verbal emphasis needs to be adapted. Abstract and complex concepts and processes need to be simplified, made more concrete and greater use made of more visual materials. Developmentally appropriate theoretical models need to be generated and used to inform the content, focus and balance of CBT interventions. Future studies need to substantiate the evidence base for child-focused CBT as both a treatment and a preventive intervention under real-world conditions. These would help to understand the key question: what specific CBT strategies, used in which combinations, delivered in which settings, are effective with which populations in alleviating which symptoms?

References

Barrett, P., Healy-Farrell, L. & March, J.S. (2004). Cognitive behavioural treatment of childhood obsessive compulsive disorder: A controlled trial. *Journal of the American Academy of Child and Adolescent Psychiatry, 43*(1), 46–62.

Barrett, P.M., Farrell, L.J., Ollendick, T.H. & Dadds, M. (2006). Long-term outcomes of an Australian universal prevention trial of anxiety and depression symptoms in children and youth: An evaluation of the FRIENDS programme. *Journal of Clinical Child and Adolescent Psychology, 35*(3), 403–411.

Barrett, P.M. & Healy, L.J. (2003). An examination of the cognitive processes involved in childhood obsessive-compulsive disorder. *Behaviour Research and Therapy, 41*(3), 285–299.

Cartwright-Hatton, S., Roberts, C., Chitsabesan, P., Fothergill, C. & Harrington, R. (2004). Systematic review of the efficacy of cognitive behaviour therapies for childhood and adolescent anxiety disorders. *British Journal of Clinical Psychology, 43,* 421–436.

Celano, M., Hazzard, A., Webb, C. & McCall, C. (1996). Treatment of traumagenic beliefs among sexually abused girls and their mothers: An evaluation study. *Journal of Abnormal Child Psychology, 24,* 1–16.

Cohen, J.A., Mannarino, A.P. & Knudsen, K. (2004). Treating childhood traumatic grief: A pilot study. *Journal of the American Academy of Child and Adolescent Psychiatry, 43*(10), 1225–1233.

Compton, S.N., March, J.S., Brent, D., Albano, A.M., Weersing, V.R. & Curry, J. (2004). Cognitive-behavioural psychotherapy for anxiety and depressive disorders in children and adolescents: An evidence based medicine review. *Journal of the American Academy of Child and Adolescent Psychiatry, 43*(8), 930–959.

Creswell, C. & Cartwright-Hatton, S. (2007). Family treatment of child anxiety: Outcomes, limitations and future directions. *Clinical Child and Family Psychology Review, 10*(3), 232–252.

Dummett, N. & Williams, C. (2007). *The feeling good guide: A five areas approach.* London: Arnold.

Durlak, J.A., Furnham, T. & Lampman, C. (1991). Effectiveness of cognitive-behaviour therapy for maladapting children: A meta-analysis. *Psychological Bulletin, 110*(2), 204–214.

Durlak, J.A., Rubin, L.A. & Kahng, R.D. (2001). Cognitive behaviour therapy for children and adolescents with externalizing problems. *Journal of Cognitive Psychotherapy, 15*(3), 183–194.

Ehlers, A. & Clark, D.M. (2000). A cognitive model of post-traumatic stress disorder. *Behaviour Research and Therapy, 38,* 319–345.

Flavell, J.H., Flavell, E.R. & Green, F.L. (2001). Development of children's understanding of connections between thinking and feeling. *Psychological Science, 12,* 430–432.

Ford, T., Goodman, R. & Meltzer, M. (2003). Service use over 18 months among a nationally representative sample of British children with psychiatric disorder. *Clinical Child Psychology and Psychiatry, 8*(1), 37–51.

Friedberg, R.D., Crosby, L.E., Friedberg, B.A., Rutter, J.G. & Knight, K.R. (2000). Making cognitive behavioural therapy user-friendly to children. *Cognitive and Behavioural Practice, 6,* 189–200.

Friedberg, R.D. & McClure, J.M. (2002). *Clinical practice of cognitive therapy with children and adolescents: The nuts and bolts.* New York: Guilford Press.

Goodyer, I., Dubicka, B., Wilkinson, P., Kelvin, R., Roberts, C., Byford, S. *et al.* (2007). Selective serotonin reuptake inhibitors (SSRIs) and routine specialist care with and without cognitive behaviour therapy in adolescents with major depression: A randomized controlled trial. *British Medical Journal, 335,* 142–149.

Graham, P. (2005). Jack Tizard lecture: Cognitive behaviour therapy for children: Passing fashion or here to stay? *Child and Adolescent Mental Health, 10*(2), 57–62.

Kendall, P.C. (1994). Treating anxiety disorders in children: Results of a randomized clinical trial. *Journal of Consulting and Clinical Psychology, 62,* 100–110.

Kendall, P.C., Flannery-Schroeder, E., Panichelli-Mindel, S.M., Southam-Gerow, M., Henin, A. & Warman, M. (1997). Therapy for youths with anxiety disorders: A second randomized clinical trial. *Journal of Consulting and Clinical Psychology, 65*(3), 366–380.

King, N.J., Tonge, B.J., Heyne, D., Pritchard, M., Rollings, S., Young, D. *et al.* (1998). Cognitive behavioural treatment of school-refusing children: A controlled evaluation. *Journal of American Academy of Child and Adolescent Psychiatry, 37*(4), 395–403.

King, N.J., Tonge, B.J., Mullen. P., Myerson, N., Heyne, D., Rollings, S. *et al.* (2000). Treating sexually abused children with post-traumatic stress symptoms: A randomised clinical trial. *Journal of the American Academy of Child and Adolescent Psychiatry, 39*(11), 1347–1355.

Lewinsohn, P.M., Clarke, G.N., Hops, H. & Andrews, J. (1990). Cognitive behavioural treatment for depressed adolescents. *Behaviour Therapy, 21,* 385–401.

Libby, S., Reynolds, S., Derisley, J. & Clark, S. (2004). Cognitive appraisals in young people with obsessive-compulsive disorder. *Journal of Child Psychology and Psychiatry, 45*(6), 1076–1084.

March, J., Silva, S., Vitiello, B. & the TADS team (2006). The Treatment for Adolescents with Depression Study (TADS): Methods and message at 12 weeks. *Journal of the American Academy of Child and Adolescent Psychiatry, 45*(12), 1393–1403.

March, J.S. & Mulle, K. (1998). Obsessive-compulsive disorder in children and adolescents: A cognitive-behavioural treatment manual. New York: Guilford Press.

Merry, S., McDowell, H.M., Hetrick, S. & Muller, N. (2004). Psychological and/or educational interventions for the prevention of depression in children and adolescents. *The Cochrane Database of Systematic Reviews, 2.*

National Institute for Health and Clinical Excellence (2004). *Eating disorders: Core interventions in the treatment and management of anorexia nervosa, bulimia nervosa and related eating disorders.* National Clinical Practice Guideline 9. Leicester: British Psychological Society.

National Institute for Health and Clinical Excellence (2005a). *Depression in children and young people: Identification and management in primary, community and secondary care.* National Clinical Practice Guideline 28. Leicester: British Psychological Society.

National Institute for Health and Clinical Excellence (2005b). *Post-traumatic stress disorder: The management of PTSD in adults and children in primary and secondary care.* National Clinical Practice Guideline 26. Leicester: British Psychological Society.

National Institute for Health and Clinical Excellence (2006). *Obsessive compulsive disorder: Core interventions in the treatment of obsessive compulsive disorder and body dysmorphic disorder.* National Clinical Practice Guideline 31. Leicester: British Psychological Society and the Royal College of Psychiatrists.

Quakley, S., Reynolds, S. & Coker, S. (2004). The effects of cues on young children's abilities to discriminate among thoughts, feelings and behaviours. *Behaviour Research and Therapy, 42,* 343–356.

Robinson, A. (2007). *Stressbusters: The development and evaluation of a computerized cognitive behavioural therapy (CBT) package for the treatment of depression in adolescents.* Paper presented at the World Congress of Behavioural and Cognitive Therapies. Barcelona, July.

Ronen, T. (1997). *Cognitive developmental therapy with children.* Chichester: Wiley.

Salkovskis, P.M. (1999). Understanding and treating obsessive-compulsive disorder. *Behaviour research and Therapy*, *37*(1), S29–S52.

Shirk, S.R. (2001). Development and cognitive therapy. *Journal of Cognitive Psychotherapy*, *15*(3), 155– 163.

Shochet, I.M., Dadds, M.R., Holland, D., Whitefield, K., Harnett, P.H. & Osgarby, S.M. (2001). The efficacy of a school-based program to prevent adolescent depression. *Journal of Clinical Child Psychology*, *30*, 303–315.

Silverman, W.K., Kurtines, W.M., Ginsburg, G.S., Weems, C.F., Rabian, B. & Serafini, L.T. (1999). Contingency management, self-control and educational support in the treatment of childhood phobic disorders: A randomized clinical trial. *Journal of Consulting and Clinical Psychology*, *67*(5), 675–687.

Smith, P., Yule, W., Perrin, S., Tranah, T., Dalgleish, T. & Clark, D. (2007). Cognitive-behavioural therapy for PTSD in children and adolescents: A preliminary randomized controlled trial. *Journal of the American Academy of Child and Adolescent Psychiatry*, *46*(8), 1051–1061.

Spence, S.H., Donovan, C. & Brechman-Toussaint, M. (2000). The treatment of childhood social phobia: The effectiveness of a social, skills training based, cognitive-behavioural intervention, with and without parental involvement. *Journal of Child Psychology and Psychiatry*, *41*(6), 713–726.

Spence, S.H. & Shortt, A.L. (2007). Research review: Can we justify the widespread dissemination of universal, school based interventions for the prevention of depression amongst children and adolescents? *Journal of Child Psychology and Psychiatry*, *48*(6), 526–542.

Stallard, P. (2002). *Think good feel good. A cognitive behaviour therapy workbook for children and young people*. Chichester: Wiley.

Stallard, P. (2004). Cognitive behaviour therapy with prepubertal children. In P. Graham (Ed.) *Cognitive behaviour therapy for children and families* (2nd edn, pp. 121–135). Cambridge: Cambridge University Press.

Stallard, P. (2006). Psychological interventions for post-traumatic reactions in children and young people: A review of randomised controlled trials. *Clinical Psychology Review*, *26*, 895–911.

Stallard, P. (2007). *Child focused CBT: A spectrum of interventions*. Paper presented at the Association of Child and Adolescent Mental Health and the British Association of Behavioural and Cognitive Psychotherapy conference: Cognitive Behaviour Therapy with Children and Families; current practice, innovations, future developments. Oxford, March.

Stallard, P. & Smith, E. (2007). Appraisals and cognitive coping styles associated with chronic posttraumatic symptoms in child road traffic accident survivors. *Journal of Child Psychology and Psychiatry*, *48*(2), 194–201.

Stallard, P., Udwin, O., Goddard, M. & Hibbert, S. (2007). The availability of cognitive behaviour therapy within specialist Child and Adolescent Mental Health Services (CAMHS): A national survey. *Behaviour and Cognitive Psychotherapy*, *35*(4), 501–506.

Stulemeijer, M., de Jong, L.W.A.M., Fiselier, T.J.W., Hoogveld, S.W.B. & Bleijenberg, G. (2005). Cognitive behaviour therapy for adolescents with chronic fatigue syndrome: Randomised controlled trial. *British Medical Journal*, *330*, 14–17.

Weisz, J.R., McCarty, C.A. & Valeri, S.M. (2006). Effects of psychotherapy for depression in children and adolescents: A meta-analysis. *Psychological Bulletin*, *132*(1), 132–149.

Wellman, H.M., Hollander, M. & Schult, C.A. (1996). Young children's understanding of thought bubbles and thoughts. *Child Development*, *67*, 768–788.

Wood, A., Harrington, R. & Moore, A. (1996). Controlled trial of a brief cognitive-behavioural intervention in adolescent patients with depressive disorders. *Journal of Child Psychology and Psychiatry*, *37*, 737–746.

2

Working with Chronic Ill-health and Disability

11

Oncology

Denise Cottrell and Claire Luthwood

Introduction

In recent years there have been significant strides in the detection and treatment of cancer and there is increasing confidence that this trend will continue. Many cancers are now curable, and many others are viewed as a chronic condition that can be managed. As survival rates improve, the number of people living with cancer continues to rise. This chapter will explore the contribution clinical psychologists can make to this rapidly expanding area. It highlights the complexity of a person's experience of cancer, including their medical, psychological, social and spiritual needs. It also argues that psychologists can play a useful role in the organisational and economic context of health care and that comprehensive and methodically rigorous audit and research are needed for the continued development of appropriate interventions.

A diagnosis of cancer can generate uncertainty and fear, and in many instances it creates a greater sense of dread than for other illnesses with a similar or worse prognosis (Mishel, 1984). For the individual facing the diagnosis of cancer, and their loved ones, it is often a traumatic and life-changing event. Differences in the way individuals respond may reflect different social contexts such as social and cultural background, age, gender and spirituality. Naturally, understanding of self, the world and others, and individual coping styles also play a part.

There have been many studies that reveal a high prevalence of emotional distress, with most studies detecting significant distress in 35–45 per cent of cancer patients (Carlson & Bultz, 2003). A large study of over 3000 cancer patients attending a large tertiary cancer centre in Canada over a 4-week period found that 37 per cent met criteria for significant distress on the Brief Symptom Inventory (Carlson & Bultz, 2004; Derogatis & Melisaratos, 1983).

Macmillan Cancer Support (2006) examined the impact of cancer on the everyday life of patients in the UK and those close to them; 45 per cent of cancer patients reported that the emotional aspects of cancer are the most difficult to cope with, and that these continue after treatment has been completed. The structure and provision of high-quality cancer care in the UK is governed by a number of government initiatives, such as the National Cancer Plan (Department of Health, 2000) and the Cancer Reform Strategy (Department of Health, 2007). A number of National Service Frameworks have made a commitment to providing not only excellent medical and nursing care but also psychosocial and spiritual care. The National Institute for Health and Clinical Excellence guidelines on improving Supportive and Palliative Care for Adults with Cancer (National Institute for Health and Clinical Excellence, 2004) addresses broader concerns of emotional, social, psychological and spiritual well-being and states that 'individual patients have different needs at different phases of their illness, and services should be responsive to patients' needs' (p. 5).

Understanding the Patient's Experience

The cancer journey, from first symptoms, diagnosis and treatments to living with cancer and end of life, may present the individual with many challenges. Psychologists strive to understand how the individual adapts to, and sometimes grows through, these experiences. The processes involved in adjustment are complex and dynamic, and psychologists can play a role in helping the patient to gain an understanding of them and manage the distress associated with them. Brennan (2001) describes adjustment as '… the processes of adaptation that occur over time as the individual manages, learns from and accommodates the multitude of changes which have been precipitated by changed circumstances in their lives' (p. 2).

This perspective allows us to consider the illness experience within the context of a person's life and can incorporate psychological, social and spiritual factors. It serves as a reminder that it is unrealistic for psychologists to expect clients to reach an 'end point' in their adjustment, as illnesses and life circumstances, as well as internal processes, are always subject to change. Psychologists working in the field of cancer have drawn on various theoretical models from the coping literature to understand the nature of adjustment to this potentially life-threatening illness and to develop appropriate clinical interventions in an area where many patients' concerns are realistic.

Some theorists, such as Bowlby (1980) and Parkes (1996, 1998), have explored the processes associated with the different stages and transitions of the human life cycle. These theories accommodate the personal growth which is often described by the individual as they adapt to these transitions and find new meaning and purpose from their experiences.

The literature on stress and coping has also had a significant impact on the clinical approaches adopted by psychologists working in oncology. Lazarus and Folkman's Transactional Model (Lazarus & Folkman, 1984; Lazarus, 1993) and Leventhal's Self Regulation Model (Leventhal et al., 1992) contribute to our understanding of the individual's appraisal of the demands of their illness, treatment and changed circumstances and their perception of the internal and external resources available to cope with these demands. In their cognitive model of adjustment Moorey and Greer (2002) maintain that it is not the symptoms of the disease or the effects of treatment *per se* which produce the emotional response, but the meanings they hold for the person involved: 'Adjustment involves the interpretation of the type of stress cancer imposes, evaluation of how well the stresses can be managed and the mobilization of coping behaviours'. They conceptualise the threat of cancer along two dimensions: threat to survival and threat to self-image (mental and physical abilities, personal and social roles, and physical appearance).

The Social-Cognitive Transition (SCT) model of adjustment (Brennan, 2001) draws on both cognitive and lifespan theories to account for the acquisition and continuous revision of a complex matrix of assumptions about the self and how the world functions. The SCT model acknowledges the challenges that the experience of illness and treatment present to an individual's mental model of the world, including the key assumptions they hold about themselves, their world and their future. Brennan argues that there are three primary factors accounting for the individual differences in the way people respond to these life-changing events:

1. different underlying cognitive models of the world, constructed through different life experiences;
2. differences in the social environments within which people live and learn (e.g. race, gender, social deprivation, etc.);
3. differences in the way people typically respond to information that does not conform to their core assumptions. If the core assumptions are rigidly held, then new information cannot be easily assimilated, e.g. 'bad things shouldn't happen to good people.'

These factors may influence the development of psychological disorders or provide a foundation for personal growth.

Coping is a process that changes over time due to cognitive changes in the perceived threat, the meaning assigned to it, attention given to it and the demands of the threat itself. Coping efforts may be *problem-focused*, e.g. problem solving or planning health-promoting behaviour, or *emotion-focused* by seeking emotional support, distraction or religion.

There is debate in the coping literature about whether people use consistent coping styles or whether their cognitive, behavioural and emotional responses to stressors are situation specific. Whatever one's theoretical standpoint, the literature on coping style has been fertile ground for the development of psychological interventions in cancer care.

Watson *et al.* (1988) identified five key coping styles in cancer patients in their study: fighting spirit, denial/avoidance, fatalism, helplessness/hopelessness and anxious preoccupation. These styles are explained by variation in underlying schemas. Adjuvant Psychological Therapy (Moorey & Greer, 1989), based on cognitive behavioural therapy, was developed as an approach to address unhelpful beliefs and assumptions and to promote fighting spirit.

Whether people wish to be given information or not, talk about their feelings or focus on practical issues, the psychologist must be mindful of the patient's preferences and consider them when deciding on a therapeutic approach. For example, where a patient uses denial as a strategy for coping with overwhelming distress, it might be considered appropriate to avoid challenging this unless absolutely necessary.

Case example 1

The multidisciplinary team in a palliative care unit requested a psychological assessment for an inpatient, Patsy, with a view to offering advice on communication.

Patsy always presented immaculately dressed, wearing make-up, and had managed to maintain a fairly normal lifestyle, despite her rapidly advancing breast cancer, which had now broken through her skin. She was very calm and articulate about the prospect of dying but acknowledged her distress at the sight of the tumour. Despite several conversations with the medical team, Patsy minimised her concerns by continuing to believe that her cancer was on the outside of her skin and that it was being managed (and might even be cured) by the nurses who were dressing her wound. It was very apparent to the multidisciplinary team that Patsy was extremely anxious. They respected her need to minimise the implications of her illness by not continuously challenging comments as she persisted in reframing medical information she was given to maintain her construct of the illness. There was also concern that Patsy might experience a psychological crisis if she came to acknowledge the reality of her situation.

The psychologist reassured the team that Patsy's strategy was effective in protecting her from the distress of her situation. Very occasionally, Patsy would ask a direct question and would be given the answers she sought, but she would then revert to her preferred coping style of denial. Patsy died peacefully and never addressed her distress at her tumour.

Respecting coping styles can be even more challenging for the psychologist when working with couples who have different styles. It may be that one partner wants information and the other does not, or one wants to talk about feelings while the other is unwilling to do so. In these cases, the therapist needs to negotiate with the couple about the best way to accommodate these differences.

Managing Distress

As we have shown, adjusting to new and challenging situations can be associated with high levels of emotional distress. Multiple concerns can lead to emotional exhaustion. The National Comprehensive Cancer Network (2008) in Canada defines psychological distress as:

> ... a multi-determined, unpleasant emotional experience of a psychological (cognitive, behavioural, emotional), social, and/or spiritual nature that may interfere with the ability to cope effectively with cancer, its physical symptoms and its treatment. Distress extends along a continuum, ranging from common normal feelings of vulnerability, sadness and fears to problems that can become disabling, such as depression, anxiety, panic, social isolation and spiritual crisis. (DIS2)

Brennan (2007) urges caution when using the language of mental illness around cancer-related distress. He uses the example of adjustment disorder, defined in DSM-IV as an emotional response to a stressor in excess of 'what would be expected'. He questions how one might judge an appropriate level of distress and points out the complex and pervasive losses that may be associated with a cancer diagnosis. Indeed, psychological processes may also allow the individual and their family to find positive meaning in their experiences and to develop skills to improve their ability to cope with new situations, treatments and uncertainty. Psychologists can help people understand what is happening to them through the mutual development of a formulation which may or may not include predisposing, precipitating and maintaining factors. Frequently people express enormous relief once they are able to understand their distress and its context.

Case example 2

Parveen was receiving chemotherapy. Her husband reported a 'change in her personality' and described her as being withdrawn and excessively fatigued. She felt that she would be unable to complete the course of treatment, fearing that she had no physical or emotional resources left. As a previously active and busy person, she had coped with previous stresses in her life by 'getting on and doing things', which gave her a sense of control. She described the distress she experienced following the tragic death of her teenage son, when her husband had turned to alcohol and this had threatened the future of their relationship. Fearful that this could happen again, she was troubled with thoughts of abandonment. Understanding the context of her distress and developing a formulation with the psychologist enabled Parveen to identify appropriate coping strategies, including seeking practical and emotional support from family and friends, discussing her fears with her husband and negotiating mutually supportive ways to cope with stress. She also recognised that she needed to allow time for rest.

Achieving an understanding of her difficulties was sufficient for Parveen to generate strategies for change. However, there are specific challenges for a patient with cancer and their therapist when the context is one of a potentially life-threatening illness that may require more direct intervention. Although many of the patient's concerns may be based on realistic threat, unhelpful thinking patterns may be apparent. Moorey (1996) suggested a number of strategies for working with realistic negative automatic thoughts:

1. Identify the personal meaning of the thoughts.
2. Challenge underlying distortions.
3. Identify and solve problems.
4. Encourage appropriate emotional expression.
5. Examine the usefulness of the negative automatic thoughts.
6. Teach distraction strategies.
7. Use activity scheduling to enhance personal control.
8. Plan for the future.
9. Schedule worry/grief.

Behavioural techniques such as goal setting, planning and pacing can supplement cognitive therapy, providing evidence for the patient that change is possible and distracting from pain or ruminative thoughts.

Case example 3

Stephen, an inpatient in a cancer unit, was referred for depression and low self-esteem. He remained in bed all day, saying he felt too weak to walk. He said he had no pleasure in life and wanted to die. This was distressing for staff who perceived that he could do more for himself but had 'given up.'

During his first appointment Stephen revealed his passion for wood turning and he was distraught at planning to sell his lifetime's collection of tools. The subject of wood-turning was the only thing that produced any kind of positive emotional response and the psychologist wondered whether he might be motivated to try to return to woodturning.

Stephen agreed to work with the physiotherapist to improve his walking with the goal of walking to his shed on a day trip home. This trip was a success and the psychologist negotiated a programme for increasing his ability to work with wood. After two more visits home the programme was abandoned as Stephen was once again turning wood. His depression lifted and he eventually resumed a more active role.

Patients, professionals and healthcare commissioners need to know whether psychological interventions are effective, both clinically and economically, and there is ongoing discussion in the research literature about what constitutes a successful outcome.

In a review chapter, Kilbourne and Durning (2006) summarise a number of areas in which psychological interventions may be used to promote a range of target outcomes. These include reducing psychological distress and promoting adjustment, managing symptoms such as nausea, pain and fatigue and perhaps promoting positive health behaviours. While much of the literature supports the effectiveness of psychosocial interventions, Lepore and Coyne (2006) argue that published reviews may be subject to positive reporting bias and argue for greater methodological rigour in future studies and meta-analyses.

Another question for debate is whether psychological interventions can directly effect physiological functioning and thus prolong life expectancy. The evidence on the effect of psychological interventions on survival rates is equivocal at best (Coyne *et al.*, 2007) and the review literature is plagued by methodological problems (Coyne *et al.*, 2006; Anderson, 2002). More research is needed in this area before firm conclusions may be drawn.

With regard to the economic efficacy of psychological interventions in oncology, there is a paucity of studies upon which to base arguments for the expansion of access to psychological services. One small-scale, but promising, study by Simpson *et al.* (2001) demonstrated significant medical cost savings through providing a coping skills group intervention for women diagnosed with breast cancer. Researchers, clinicians and managers need to work with health economists to provide meaningful evidence of cost-offset if commissioners are to be convinced to provide financial backing for service development.

Working within an Organisation

In the UK, NICE (2004) proposed a four-level model (Table 11.1) to provide a framework for psychological assessment and intervention.

The model encompasses a range of psychological therapies on which patients may draw. In order for it to operate effectively, all healthcare professionals need to be clear about their own level of expertise and know when and how to access further support. Clinical supervision and support should be provided throughout the service to facilitate clinical governance. It is within this framework that psychological services in the UK are striving to develop.

There are significant demands on staff at each of the four levels. Oncology and palliative care settings are inherently emotionally demanding areas of health care. Working with distressed patients and their families who are facing uncertainty and possible life-threatening conditions has been recognised as a source of stress. Confronting our own fears and beliefs on issues of mortality and illness highlights our vulnerabilities, which can be a daily challenge. People who work in cancer care show high levels of stress, absenteeism and burnout (Escot et al., 2001). Having an opportunity to reflect on the emotional impact of the clinical role and the way we allow ourselves to be touched by

Table 11.1   NICE four-level model for psychological assessment and intervention

Level	Group	Assessment	Intervention
1	All health and social care professionals	Recognition of psychological needs	Effective information giving, compassionate communication and general psychological support
2	Health and social care professionals with additional expertise	Screening for psychological distress	Psychological techniques such as problem solving
3	Trained and accredited professionals	Assessed for psychological distress and diagnosis of some psychopathology	Counselling and specific psychological interventions such as anxiety management and solution-focused therapy, delivered according to an explicit theoretical framework
4	Mental health specialists	Diagnosis of psychopathology	Specialist psychological and psychiatric interventions such as psychotherapy, including cognitive behavioural therapy (CBT)

our patients' experiences is vitally important if we are to be able to continue to be effective in our work.

In order to develop the confidence and skills to detect and manage emotional distress in others, all staff require training and ongoing support. Staff are not good at recognising even severe levels of distress amongst their patients (Söllner *et al.*, 2001). It is all too easy to avoid addressing a patient's or family's distress to protect ourselves by leaving it to the patient to raise any concerns they have or by blocking patients' attempts to communicate their concerns (Detmar *et al.*, 2000; Maguire, 1992).

Linzer *et al.* (2002) looked at physician stress and identified three factors predicting the amount of distress reported. They were:

- the demands of the work;
- the degree of control they have over it;
- the amount of support they feel they receive in their personal and professional lives.

Staff stress can be addressed through looking at the organisational structure, relationships at work, opportunities for personal development, debriefing and individual supervision and appraisal. Learning how to manage and reduce stress and avoid burnout has clear individual and organisational benefits.

Future Directions

Perhaps the biggest challenge facing those working in oncology and palliative care services is to establish a truly bio-psychosocial model of care in which the patient's changing perceptions of their illness and its implications are understood and accepted, and that appropriate and timely support is made available to them throughout their cancer journey.

Psychologists can influence the evolution of service provision in a variety of ways. They can help design consistent patient pathways and develop strategies with other professional groups for assessing emotional and practical concerns. They have a role in equipping others to use assessment tools and identify resources needed to address patient concerns. Psychologists need to take a lead in raising psychological care provision at all levels of a healthcare network and work with other professions to identify competencies and training needs. Clinically, further well-designed research is needed before we can more accurately tailor psychological interventions to the individual. Finally, it is essential for psychologists to collaborate with further research and audit into the economic benefits of improving psychological provision for people with cancer (Chiles *et al.*, 1999). Demonstrating cost-savings would encourage those commissioning services to consider alternative models of care delivery.

Supporting people living with cancer and the teams that care for them requires sensitivity and flexibility in the application of psychological theory and practice. The clinician may be faced with clinical, ethical and existential challenges and, in return, will be rewarded with the opportunity to learn from the wisdom of their patients.

References

Anderson, B.L. (2002). *Journal of Consulting and Clinical Psychology, 20*(3), 590–610.

Bowlby, J. (1980). *Attachment and loss: Vol. 3. Loss: Sadness and depression.* London: Hogarth Press.

Brennan, J. (2001). Adjustment to cancer – coping or personal transition? *Psycho-oncology, 10,* 1–18.

Brennan, J. (2007). *Is cancer distress a mental illness or an expression of emotion?* Paper presented at the World Congress of Psycho-Oncology, London, September.

Carlson, L.E. & Bultz, B.D. (2003). Cancer distress screening: Needs, methods and models. *Journal of Psychosomatic Research, 55,* 403–409.

Carlson, L.E. & Bultz, B.D. (2004). Efficacy and medical cost offset of psychological interventions in cancer care: Making the case for economic analyses. *Psycho-oncology, 13,* 837–849.

Chiles, J.A., Lambert, M. & Hatch, A. (1999). The impact of psychological interventions on medical cost offset: A meta-analytic review. *Clinical Psychology: Science and Practice, 6*(2), 204–219.

Coyne, J.C., Lepore, S.J.M. & Palmer, S.C. (2006). Efficacy of psychosocial interventions in cancer care: Evidence is weaker than it first looks. *Annals of Behavioral Medicine, 32*(2), 104–110.

Coyne, J.C., Stefanek, M. & Palmer, S.C. (2007). Psychotherapy and survival in cancer: The conflict between hope and evidence. *Psychological Bulletin, 133,* 367–394.

Derogatis, L.R. & Melisaratos, N. (1983). The Brief Symptom Inventory: An introductory report. *Psychological Medicine, 13*(3), 595–605.

Department of Health (2000). *The NHS cancer plan.* London: HMSO.

Department of Health (2007). *Cancer reform strategy.* London: HMSO.

Detmar, S.B., Aaronson, N.K., Wever, L.D.V., Muller, M. & Schornagel, J.H. (2000). How are you feeling? Who wants to know? Patients' and oncologists' preferences for discussing health-related quality of life issues. *Journal of Clinical Oncology, 18,* 3295–3301.

Escot, C., Artero, S., Boulenger, J.P. & Ritchie, K. (2001). Stress levels in nursing staff working in oncology. *Stress and Health, 17,* 273–9.

Kilbourne, K.M. & Durning, P.E. (2006). Oncology and psycho-oncology. In P. Kennedy & S. Llewelyn (Eds.) *The essentials of clinical health psychology* (pp. 79–110). Chichester: John Wiley & Sons.

Lazarus, R.S. (1993). Coping theory and research: Past, present and future. *Psychosomatic Medicine, 55,* 234–247.

Lazarus, R.S. & Folkman, S. (1984). *Stress, appraisal and coping.* New York: Springer.

Lepore, S.J. & Coyne, J.C. (2006). Psychological interventions for distress in cancer patients: A review of reviews. *Annals of Behavioural Medicine, 32,* 85–92.

Leventhal, H., Diefenbach, M. & Leventhal, E.A. (1992). Illness cognition: Using common sense to understand treatment adherence and affect cognition interventions. *Cognitive Therapy Research, 16,* 143–163.

Linzer, M., Gerrity, M., Douglas, J.A., McMurray, J.E., Williams, ES. & Konrad, T.R. (2002). Physician stress: Results from the physician worklife study. *Stress and Health, 18*(1), 37–42.

Macmillan Cancer Support (2006). Worried sick: The emotional impact of cancer. Oxford: Oxford Medical Publications.

Maguire, P. (1992). Improving the recognition and treatment of affective disorders in cancer patients. *Recent Advances in Clinical Psychiatry, 7,* 15–30.

Mishel, M.H. (1984). Perceived uncertainty and stress and illness. *Research in Nursing and Health*, 7(3), 163–171.

Moorey, S. (1996). When bad things happen to rational people: Cognitive therapy in adverse life circumstances. In P. Salkovskis (Ed.) *Frontiers of cognitive therapy* (pp. 450–469). New York: Guilford Press.

Moorey, S. & Greer, S. (1989). *Psychological therapy for people with cancer: A new approach*. Oxford: Heinemann Medical Books.

Moorey, S. & Greer, S. (2002). *Cognitive behaviour therapy for people with cancer*. Oxford: Oxford University Press.

National Comprehensive Cancer Network, I (2008). *Practice guidelines in oncology – v.1.2008: Distress management*. Ford Washington, PA: Author.

National Institute for Health and Clinical Excellence (2004). *Guidance on cancer services. Improving supportive and palliative care for adults*. London: Author.

Parkes, C.M. (1996). *Bereavement* (3rd edn). London: Routledge.

Parkes, C.M. (1998). Bereavement as a psychosocial transition: Process of adaptation to change. *Journal of Social Issues*, 44, 53–65.

Simpson, J.S.A., Carlson, L.E. & Trew, M. (2001). Impact of a group psychosocial intervention on health care utilization by breast cancer patients. *Cancer Practice*, 9, 19–26.

Söllner, W., DeVries, A., Steixner, E., Lukas, P., Sprinzi, G., Rumpold, G. & Maislinger, S. (2001). How successful are oncologists in identifying patient distress, perceived social support, and need for psychosocial counselling? *British Journal of Cancer*, 84, 179–185.

Watson, M., Greer, S., Young, J., Inayat, C., Burgess, C. & Robertson, B. (1988). Development of a questionnaire measurement of adjustment to cancer: The MAC Scale. *Psychological Medicine*, 18, 203–209.

Recommended Further Reading

Brennan, J. & Moynihan, C. (2004). *Cancer in context: A practical guide to supportive care*. Oxford: Oxford Medical Publications.

12

Chronic (Persistent) Pain

Zoë Clyde

Overview of Clinical Problems

Introduction

Chronic (or persistent), non-malignant pain is a complex phenomenon currently best understood using a biopsychosocial framework that integrates biomedical understanding with psychological and social factors (Waddell, 1992). Psychological factors play a key role in the development and maintenance of chronic pain (Linton, 1999; Pincus et al., 2001), and this, together with the significant impact of chronic pain on individuals' lives, merits the inclusion of clinical psychologists as core members of multidisciplinary pain management teams (Royal College of Anaesthetists/The Pain Society, 2003). Working in this area presents opportunities for clinical psychologists to use the whole range of their competencies. In addition, clinical psychologists working in health need to develop competencies in understanding the biological basis of the condition and the medical aspects of care.

Pain management services exist for individuals across the lifespan and clinical psychologists may contribute particular competencies in working with those who have multiple physical and psychological needs, and with issues such as capacity, neurological and intellectual impairments. Treatment involves both physical and psychological interventions and needs to follow careful assessment of the individual's experience. The main focus of intervention, for reasons that will be described below, is on management rather than cure of the pain.

This chapter will emphasise the role of clinical health psychologists who are employed as part of a pain management service; however, the issues raised are relevant to clinical psychologists working in any setting who may encounter chronic pain.

Acute vs. chronic pain

Acute pain is familiar to all but a very few of the world's population. It is usually preceded by an assault to the body and nocioceptor stimulation which is relayed to the central nervous system, which in turn responds to protect the body. We learn quickly what to do and what not to do in situations which incur the pain response; indeed, without this process we would not survive for long. Response to acute pain includes rest, immobilisation of the specific area, seeking medical attention and medication, e.g. painkillers. Chronic pain is defined as that which has persisted beyond the timeframe for normal healing of an injury, which is normally upwards of three months. Therefore, although the signal remains, it is not indicative of underlying pathology. The definition of chronic pain (International Association for the Study of Pain (IASP), 1979) refers to the experience having both sensory and affective components, due to actual or potential tissue damage. Problems develop when individuals respond to chronic pain as if it were acute, often because it is the only way they know to cope with pain. Providing information about the difference between acute and chronic pain, and reinforcing this message, are key in the assessment and treatment of chronic pain and are part of the role of a clinical psychologist, highlighting the need to understand the physical and psychological aspects of the condition and the need for management rather than cure.

The physical, psychological and social impact of chronic pain

Individuals may report widespread chronic pain (e.g. fibromyalgia), pain in a single site (e.g. back pain, headache, repetitive strain injury, complex regional pain disorder) or pain in multiple sites.

The cause may be sudden and 'known' to the individual, or the onset might be more insidious. The constant presence of pain can relatively quickly result in an individual limiting their everyday activities, including work, leisure, social and household tasks in an attempt either to reduce the pain or to prevent further exacerbation or harm. Over time decreased activity, or bursts of over activity followed by under-activity contingent on pain levels (activity cycling), can lead to decreased fitness, increased pain, deconditioning and compensatory strategies (e.g. limping, use of aids). These are classed as secondary effects. Consequently, individual lives often become very restricted and dominated by the pain as it becomes a guide for activity. Chronic pain impacts on interpersonal relationships and can be difficult for others to comprehend, especially if the sufferer themselves finds it hard to understand, and its invisibility can further compound the difficulties, leaving individuals feeling isolated, misunderstood and often helpless. Morley and Eccleston (2004) describe a 'psychological cascade', whereby initially the pain interrupts activity by its capture of attention, goes on to interfere with tasks due to the actual pain, anticipated pain, fatigue or distress, and finally affects identity through the fundamental challenge to an individual's roles and future goals.

As a result of the multiple physical and psychological losses, emotional responses such as frustration, anger, anxiety and low mood are common and understandable, although not inevitable. The extent of disability resulting from pain is not directly linked to the duration of the pain, but mediated by psychological variables.

Frustration

Frustration is the most commonly reported emotional response (Price, 1999) and can be related to blocked goals and unrealistic expectations of self, others, and often the healthcare system. Seeking help can be a frustrating process as diagnosis is commonly made once other possibilities have been excluded, and even once chronic pain is diagnosed, medical treatments may be offered with varying success. In the meantime the individual suffering can increase and this journey can further compound the problem. Frustration may lead to anger, and referral to a clinical psychologist may be perceived as disbelief, or that the problem is being seen as all in the mind, resulting in potential issues for engagement and assessment.

Depression

High levels of depression are commonly reported in chronic pain groups (Romano & Turner, 1985) and are thought to be even higher than in other chronic illness groups (Sprangers *et al.*, 2000). This may be partly understood by a diathesis-stress model of depression (Banks & Kerns, 1996), highlighting the particular characteristics of pain as a stressor. These include the multiple losses incurred, the unrelenting nature of the pain, frustration, lack of control and hopelessness induced by failed attempts to 'cure' the pain. Estimates of prevalence vary widely (Banks & Kerns, 1996), partly due to difficulty measuring depression in pain populations because of symptom overlap. Self-report measures of mood rely on questionnaires standardised for use in mental health settings and so care needs to be taken in interpreting scores (Pincus & Williams, 1999). In the absence of a more valid measure of mood for use in chronic pain populations, careful assessment needs to be made, paying particular attention to individual attribution of symptoms and to their self-beliefs. Do they describe general negative beliefs about the self, world and future, or are their beliefs more specific to the pain? For example, 'I am a worthless person' compared to 'I feel worthless because of the pain'. Clinical psychologists possess competencies in multi-modal assessment and drawing on different theoretical models to inform understanding of the individual. Suicidal ideation needs to be discussed and clinical psychologists have skills and experience in risk assessment and management which may be a unique contribution to a service. Consideration of the impact that symptoms of depression might have on motivation for treatment and engagement with a self-management approach (Turk & Monarch, 2003) are further examples of the contribution of clinical psychologists.

Anxiety

Anxiety is an understandable response in the context of uncertainty which dominates many individuals' pain experience. (Acute) pain is a signal of damage and one which should not be ignored. Attempts to try to find causal explanations for the pain may be unsuccessful, yet individuals continue to be alarmed by its presence. A diagnosis of exclusion is often not reassuring as it leaves the question unanswered as to what it is that is wrong. Misinterpretations of bodily sensations can cause further anxiety, and therefore thorough assessment of beliefs and cognitions about pain, activity and bodily sensations is needed. Higher rates of health anxiety have been found in chronic pain populations compared control groups (Rode *et al.*, 2006), which may contribute to evidence suggesting the need to match intervention to specific psychological profiles within chronic pain populations in order to improve treatment efficacy (Tang *et al.*, 2007).

As in other clinical settings, anxieties can be multiple, widespread, or specific. Responses by others, real or predicted, and lack of understanding of the 'invisible' condition can result in individuals feeling socially anxious, as can decreased opportunity to go out, fear of embarrassment or decreased self-confidence. The object of fear can be unique and range from specific fear of movement to more abstract and difficult to describe fears (Morley & Eccleston, 2004), such as losses of identity and purpose. Clinical psychologists have a clear role in drawing on psychological models of anxiety, in addition to more specific pain-related models and using different modes of assessment, including interview, observation and self-report, to try to make sense of the individual circumstances.

A specific model of pain-related fear (Vlaeyen *et al.*, 1995) has enhanced understanding in cases where anxiety plays a key role in the development and maintenance of chronic pain through catastrophising and fear of pain or re-injury. This often applies to those who have experienced a sudden onset to their pain, maybe through an everyday activity such as bending over, lifting or carrying. Given the ordinariness of the activity it can be hard to understand what happened, resulting in fear of movement, leading to further problems. The fear may unwittingly be fuelled by health professionals' advice and beliefs such as increased rest, and descriptive explanations such as a 'slipped disc' or 'trapped nerve'. It can be hard to differentiate between coping and safety behaviours and careful examination of beliefs can help clarify this (Thwaites & Freeston, 2005). For example, making small increments in activity quota might be considered pacing, but could also be an attempt to avoid sudden increases in activity which may be perceived as harmful. A detailed formulation and assessment would highlight the use of gradual activity as an intervention in the first instance, and graded exposure in the second.

Social impact

Chronic pain poses a considerable cost to the individual, significant others, health services and society. Pain problems are common in the population, though it is hard to accurately measure prevalence due to diagnostic issues and variation in presentation to services, but it is estimated that around 20 per cent of Europeans experience a chronic pain problem (Breivik *et al.*, 2006). Pain is also the second biggest reason for absence from work and about a quarter of those with persistent pain become unemployed (Kemler & Furnee, 2002). Pain-related disability is associated with higher use of healthcare services (Blyth *et al.*, 2004).

Models and Competencies

Seminal work by Melzack and Wall (1965) describing the gate control theory significantly enhanced understanding of pain by highlighting the interaction of physical and psychological factors, as opposed to previous debate over unidimensional physical or psychological theories (Turk & Monarch, 2003). In contrast to a straightforward stimulus–response model, the perception of pain was described by Melzack and Wall (1965) as a sequence of events involving both peripheral and cortical factors. The gate control theory emphasised that not only were pain signals sent from the body to the brain, but that signals descending from the brain could impact on the ascending signals, thereby influencing the message sent. The idea that pain is not a straightforward stimulus response, but can be moderated by psychological, social and environmental factors, underpins the biopsychosocial understanding and treatment approach currently taken.

Since that time, models of chronic pain have evolved from behavioural theories focusing on pain behaviour and classical conditioning (Fordyce, 1976) to the subsequent inclusion of cognitive factors (e.g. catastrophising) and the development of more specific models, e.g. pain-related fear. Cognitive behavioural approaches to pain management are currently favoured due to their demonstrated efficacy (Morley *et al.*, 1999), although further investigation is needed to explore more specifically what works for whom. As a result, pain management programmes tend to offer a generic package to address understanding and misperceptions of chronic pain and the secondary effects of deconditioning, through graded exercise and activity pacing, exploration of beliefs, effect on mood and relationships, addressing fear of pain, medication use, goal setting and return to valued activities, and setback management.

Third-wave cognitive therapies incorporating acceptance and commitment therapy, and mindfulness approaches, are currently receiving increased attention both in chronic pain (Dahl & Lundren, 2006; McCracken *et al.*, 2004) and general clinical psychology practice. These therapies are an exciting addition to the toolbox of clinical health psychologists, offering an alternative to challenging unhelpful thoughts and a way of assisting sufferers to 'accept' and learn to 'live with, rather than fight the pain'. Acceptance of the pain has been suggested to be more helpful in managing chronic pain than coping strategies (McCracken & Eccleston, 2006), as it allows greater psychological flexibility than the goal of gaining more control over pain, by allowing individuals to reconnect and move towards their values (Dahl & Lundren, 2006).

Although the context of pain is often acknowledged and was significant in early behavioural theories of chronic pain, systemic ideas and the social aspects remain relatively neglected. Exceptions include the relational approach to pain management (Mason, 2004), which emphasises the primacy of the relationship between the individual and their pain, compared to their relationship with significant others, and the communal coping model of pain (Sullivan *et al.*, 2004) which views catastrophising as a strategy to gain social support. This is of interest because catastrophising is widely associated with the tendency to report more intense pain and pain-related distress, and has received much attention as an individual coping process and important predictor of the pain experience. Sullivan *et al.* (2001) suggest a framework to conceptualise the relationship between catastrophising and pain at both the individual (proximal) level and social-behavioural (distal) level. This accounts for the role of catastrophising as a basic cognitive process as well as potentially a strategy to solicit help, which may explain why catastrophising persists despite its adverse consequences in increasing the pain experience.

Competencies – direct work

Clinical psychologists have core competencies in engaging individuals by listening and understanding their unique situation while containing distress and uncertainty, retaining a curious stance, gathering information and using it collaboratively to build a working formulation of the current difficulties

Formulation

A central competency of clinical psychologists is the ability to construct a formulation that makes sense of a multitude of problems, draws on applicable theoretical approaches and is flexible to new information. This is invaluable to both the individual and other health professionals involved. Clinical health psychologists need to apply and often adapt models developed in mental health services and may be the only mental health professional an individual sees. A core competency of clinical psychologists in a multidisciplinary team is the ability to recognise, understand and manage comorbid problems such as depression, anxiety and post-traumatic stress disorder (PTSD). Individuals presenting with chronic pain may have a complex history or have had little or no contact with health services prior to the onset of the pain. The ability to develop an individual formulation and to aid understanding of the relationship between problems is central to planning treatment. For example, an individual presenting with chronic pain who has used activity as a way of managing an eating disorder is faced with a threat to their coping skills when unable to participate in vigorous exercise due to the pain. Another individual, who has developed chronic pain following injuries sustained in a road accident and on assessment is reporting symptoms of PTSD, may benefit from understanding how the symptoms of one may affect the other, as well as requiring treatment for both problems. In the case of comorbid depression, good assessment is required to establish whether the individual is suffering from clinical depression which may require treatment before they can engage in pain management, or whether the individual's mood is a result of the limitations posed by the pain and may therefore improve with return to valued activities. Clinical psychologists are able to work with different levels of formulation, for example generic cognitive behavioural therapy (CBT) formulations; more specific pain-related models, e.g. pain-related fear; and more complex cognitive behavioural models which may incorporate psychological issues in addition to the chronic pain (Clyde & Williams, 2006; White, 2001).

Treatment approaches

Pain management refers to a broad range of physical and psychological treatments that may be delivered by a single professional, or may be interdisciplinary (Main & Spanswick, 2000). The aim of treatment is to empower individuals in their ability to manage their pain through education, reframing and behavioural change to enable them to improve their quality of life despite the pain. As a result of this process some individuals report pain reduction; for others, acceptance of the pain reduces the task of fighting it and the suffering incurred, and allows progress.

Therefore, the key focus of pain management is change, and more recently acceptance. This involves individuals changing the relationship with the pain, by changing their behaviour, their understanding and beliefs, and their acceptance and interaction with others. Clinical psychologists can contribute to understanding the process of change and the stages (Prochaska & Diclemente, 1992; Jensen *et al.*, 2003) that individuals might experience, and techniques such as motivational interviewing (Miller & Rollnick, 1991) that can enhance this.

Traditionally psychological management has been offered as 'last resort' treatment once other biomedical approaches have failed (Hadjistavropoulos & Williams, 2004). Given the increased evidence of the role of psychological factors in the transition from acute to chronic pain, it is being recognised that psychological intervention should be integrated earlier to minimise chronicity by preventing secondary effects and reducing the impact of decreased levels of activity.

Competencies – indirect work

The role of the clinical health psychologist in chronic pain extends beyond individual case work, often to group work, joint working, supervision, consultation, teamwork and management, research, teaching and training. In addition to the supervision of other psychologists, clinical psychologists may be involved in the supervision of other professionals. Differing from profession-specific supervision, the role of supervision in this context includes application of psychological models to clinical practice, as well as the opportunity to reflect on the personal impact of the work, the effect of individual values and beliefs, boundaries, ethics and supporting others to maintain fitness to practise. Good communication skills are essential competencies, particularly when dealing with complex cases and in deciding what information is relevant to share within the multidisciplinary team and in liaising with other healthcare providers. Clinical psychologists may be involved in teaching and training within the profession and with multidisciplinary groups both in the service and externally.

Clinical psychologists possess skills and competencies in audit and evaluation which are a key part of professional and ethical practice and vital in terms of developing and justifying services.

Engagement and Assessment

Engagement can be a complex and challenging task given the journey many patients have taken to reach appropriate services. Being able to elicit, hear and understand the individual's unique presentation in terms of their medical, psychological and social history, and convey a sense of hope for the future, are core aims. Clinicians need to be flexible in their approach to doing this.

The purpose of assessment may vary depending on the setting and treatment offered. In a pain clinic setting, the clinical psychologist may be involved in assessing individuals for surgical interventions such as spinal cord stimulation, as well as pain management programmes.

Assessment needs to cover multiple domains, including the experience of the pain and related symptoms, other physical symptoms, treatment history, impact of the pain on the individual and significant others, triggers and coping strategies, psychological history, concerns and expectations. The potential impact of ongoing legal cases on treatment should also be carefully discussed with individuals.

Assessment usually involves a combination of approaches, including the use of self-report questionnaires, pain diaries, physical measures, observation and interview. Eliciting and understanding an individual's beliefs about their pain, its cause, and meaning are central to developing a formulation and providing a credible rationale for treatment. More detailed descriptions of assessment, including specific measures, can be found elsewhere (Turk & Monarch, 2003; Williams, 2002; White, 2001).

Evidence Base

Cognitive behavioural therapy is the only systematically evaluated psychological treatment and has been shown to be effective in improving self-efficacy to manage pain, reducing distress and increasing activity (Morley et al., 1999). While there is evidence for the more specific model of pain-related fear (Vlaeyen et al., 2001, 2002) this does not apply to all and further work is necessary to refine treatment and understand more about what works for whom. Pain management programmes based on CBT provided primarily by clinical psychologists and physiotherapists as part of an interdisciplinary team are recommended treatment for chronic pain (RCA/BPS, 2003). Such programmes are based on a generic CBT model of chronic pain and comprise a number of components as previously described. A particular role for clinical psychologists is in ensuring adherence to the model and also in adapting CBT techniques for use in the management of chronic pain. There is a wealth of evidence to support the efficacy of CBT for many other clinical problems and particular components may be applicable to chronic pain. For example, there has been little investigation into the use of imagery (aside from relaxation) in chronic pain, despite the vivid descriptions of pain often used, and the burgeoning literature on imagery (e.g. Winterowd et al., 2003).

Clinical case study (this is a composite case to ensure confidentiality)

Jane, 32 years old, described her 'back snapping' following a sneeze two years previously. She could not move for several hours afterwards and was petrified that she was paralysed. She reported not making any sudden movements since that time. She described her spine as precarious and recounted a vivid image of her spine as a 'rigid, cracking tree trunk'. She had not returned to work since that day and reported carrying out tasks in a planned and carefully executed way. Her biggest fear was sneezing and the pain or further damage it might cause, and she tried hard to avoid catching a cold or other triggers to sneezing. She could not understand how 'a sneeze' could have resulted in such damage to her back or why the damage could not been seen on a scan. She had previously been referred for physiotherapy and felt that this had made her much worse and consequently she reported being wary of any treatment that required activity. She also felt frustrated that she had now been referred to a clinical psychologist because the problem was obviously in her back.

She felt that people doubted that anything was wrong. Her relationship with her husband was strained as he had had taken over a majority of the household tasks and their plans to start a family had been put on hold. She felt that her friends were fed up with her and she felt resigned to living such a restricted life.

Initial engagement with Jane was vital to the treatment process. Listening to her experience and conveying a sense of belief and understanding, in addition to eliciting and providing information, was key. Jane had high levels of pain-related fear, beliefs about activity causing further damage to her back and clear images about the physical state of her back. In this case, Vlaeyen and Linton's (2000) model of pain-related fear was used to inform the formulation and shared with Jane to help explain her current predicament. Individual treatment followed establishing a hierarchy of feared scenarios, and graded exposure in the form of behavioural experiments was used to test out the strongly held beliefs 'A sudden movement will cause further damage to my back' and 'I can only do things in a planned or measured way otherwise I will cause more pain'. Education and information about the physiological processes and sensations were very important in the intervention and consequently sessions were held jointly with a physiotherapist. Repeated exposure to feared scenarios, including unplanned movement, travelling over uneven surfaces, bending down and eventually coughing, gradually led to a reduction in the belief that sudden, jerky movements would cause further damage and a revision of the image of the back to a strong and supple support. As a result she participated in an increased range of daily activities, including household tasks and leisure activities, and underwent a graded return to part-time work. She reported feeling more involved in life again, less subsumed by the pain, and although still she experienced significant pain she felt that life had more purpose and potential to it.

Challenging Issues

The settings in which chronic pain services are offered vary greatly. Services can be found both in the NHS and in the private sector, and in departments including Anaesthetics, Rheumatology, Clinical Health Psychology or primary care. There are several different models of clinical health psychology service provision and so those working in chronic pain may find themselves part of a larger department managed by a clinical psychology lead, working within a chronic pain service with other clinical psychologists, or working as a lone psychologist albeit within a multidisciplinary team, but expected to be a highly specialised resource to the team. This can be particularly demanding for newly qualified clinical psychologists who will require the provision of good professional support. It is important to stress the transferability of skills, the value of taking a psychological perspective and contributing this to a team approach. The clinical psychologist might be the only health professional in the team with mental health experience, which is important given the comorbidity issues raised earlier. Demand for pain management services is often high and careful thought needs to be given to the use of clinical psychology resources within a team regarding direct and indirect work. The specific expectations of a clinical psychologist may differ depending on the setting and team makeup, as there can be overlap in competencies.

Changing NHS

Improving access to psychological therapies is now recognised as an issue in mental health settings and hopefully increased awareness will follow in health settings.

Ensuring equal access to pain management services across the country is a challenge as different service models exist and some areas are under-resourced. Chronic pain services situated in acute hospital trusts can struggle to be understood and fit within waiting list pressures. Some services are now provided in the private sector. Managing, responding to and being prepared for change are emerging competencies in the NHS and ones to which clinical psychologists can contribute.

The need for earlier intervention in pain management is increasingly being recognised in order to prevent long-term chronicity. Possible ways to achieve this includes increased availability of services in primary care, educational interventions and models of stepped care in which services are offered in a graded way according to need (Von Korff, 1999; Von Korff & Moore, 2001).

User and carer perspectives, diversity and values

Pain is influenced by cultural and societal values as well as personal beliefs and attitudes. Pain is a universal experience, though its meaning and management may vary. The challenge for health professionals working in the UK with diverse populations is to improve accessibility of treatment and meet the differing needs of individuals. Good practice guidelines for Pain Management Services (RCA/BPS, 2003) clearly state that provision should be made for 'vulnerable and potentially disadvantaged groups such as the elderly, children, non-verbal, and disabled, intellectually handicapped and non-English speakers'. Access to appropriate services needs to be available for those in forensic settings, with substance abuse problems, victims of torture (Amris & Williams, 2007), pain resulting from spinal injury and other traumatic experiences. Clinical psychologists may aid service development for such groups whose needs are not currently being recognised or met. Patient involvement in the planning and delivery of services varies greatly and is an area where there is recognition of the need for improvement. Expert patient programmes exist throughout the country offering a generic self-management approach for those with a variety of chronic conditions, though the efficacy of these approaches is unknown.

Although the predominance of the biopyschosocial model has been highlighted, so has the observation that the social aspects are less developed than the biomedical and psychological. The impact on carers is an under-researched area, and, in particular, the impact on young carers of adults with chronic disability. In order to address many of these issues, increased collaboration between patients, carers, health professionals, employers and support groups is being advocated by the Chronic Pain Policy Coalition.

Research and Future Directions

As previously highlighted, although there is evidence for the efficacy of CBT-based interventions in chronic pain (Morley *et al.*, 1999), there are still noticeable variations in individual response to treatment and very little is known about the process of change (Morley & Williams, 2006). Exploration of mediators of treatment response in CBT is in its early stages and warrants further attention (Morley & Keefe, 2007). Recognising heterogeneity within the chronic pain population based on psychological variables may led to targeting treatment based on factors such as pain-related fear (e.g. Woods & Asmundson, 2008), depression or health anxiety (Tang *et al.*, 2007) in a bid to improve efficacy. This may increase the scope for the application of cognitive techniques such as behavioural experiments and imagery modification to target specific cognitive processes.

In addition, third-wave cognitive therapies, including mindfulness and acceptance and commitment therapy (ACT), are still in their infancy in terms of the evidence base for chronic pain. Other theoretical approaches to managing chronic pain are under-investigated and therefore not included here due to lack of evidence, though their efficacy remains untested. Addressing the diverse needs of those who experience chronic pain and present to a variety of services is clearly needed, as is a change in patient pathways to include biopsychosocial intervention earlier in the process.

Chronic pain is a rapidly evolving speciality and one in which clinical (health) psychologists have made significant contributions in recent years and can continue to play a central role in both treatment and research. Working in chronic pain management offers a great deal of variety, usually involving interdisciplinary team working, integrating physical, psychological and social information, and requires therapists to be adaptable and flexible in their approach, aware of their own beliefs regarding pain and injury and have the continued capacity to reflect and learn from the experience of the individuals whom they work alongside.

Acknowledgements

Thank you to Nicole Jamani, Hilary Rankin and Janine Watts for their comments on earlier drafts of this chapter.

References

Amris, K. & Williams, A. (2007). *Chronic pain in survivors of torture. Pain: Clinical update.* Seattle, WA: IASP.

Banks, S.M. & Kerns, R.D. (1996). Explaining high rates of depression in chronic pain: A diathesis-stress framework. *Psychological Bulletin, 199,* 95–110.

Blyth, F.M., March, L.M., Brnabic, A.J.M. & Cousins, M.J. (2004). Chronic pain and frequent use of healthcare. *Pain, 111,* 51–58.

Breivik, H., Collett, B., Ventafridda, V., Cohen, R. & Gallacher, D. (2006). Survey of chronic pain in Europe: Prevalence, impact on daily life, and treatment. *European Journal of Pain*, *10*, 287–333.

Clyde, Z. & Williams, A. (2006). The psychological management of persistent (chronic pain). In P. Kennedy (Ed.) *Psychological management of physical disabilities* (pp. 80–103). London: Routledge.

Dahl, J. & Lundren, T. (2006). Acceptance and commitment therapy (ACT) in the treatment of chronic pain. In R.A. Baer (Ed.) *Mindfulness-based treatment approaches* (pp. 285–306). Amsterdam: Elsevier.

Fordyce, W.E. (1976). *Behavioural methods for chronic pain and illness*. St. Louis, MO: Mosby.

Hadjistavropoulos, H. & Williams, A. CdeC. (2004). Psychological interventions and chronic pain. In T. Hadjistavropoulos & K.D. Craig (Eds.) *Pain: Psychological perspectives* (pp. 271–301). Mahwah, NJ: Lawrence Erlbaum Associates.

International Association for the Study of Pain (1979). Pain terms: A list with definitions and notes on usage. *Pain*, *6*, 249–252.

Jensen, M., Nielson, W.R. & Kerns, R.D. (2003). Toward the development of a motivational model of pain self-management. *The Journal of Pain*, *4*(9), 477–492.

Kemler, M.A. & Furnee, C.A. (2002). The impact of chronic pain on life in the household. *Journal of Pain Symptom Management*, *23*(5), 433–441.

Linton, S.J. (1999). Prevention with special reference to chronic musculo-skeletal disorders. In R.J. Gatchel & D.C. Turk (Eds.) *Psychosocial factors in pain: Critical perspectives* (Vol. 1, pp. 374–389). New York: Guilford Press.

Main, C.J. & Spanswick, C.C. (2000). *Pain management: An interdisciplinary approach*. Edinburgh: Churchill-Livingstone.

Mason, B. (2004). A relational approach to the management of chronic pain. *Clinical Psychology Forum*, *35*, 17–24.

McCracken, L., Carson, J.W., Eccleston, C. & Keefe, F.J. (2004). Acceptance and change in the context of chronic pain. *Pain*, *109*, 4–7.

McCracken, L.M. & Eccleston, C. (2006). A comparison of the relative utility of coping and acceptance-based measures in a sample of chronic pain sufferers. *European Journal of Pain*, *10*(1), 23–29.

Melzack, R. & Wall, P. (1965). Pain mechanisms: A new theory. *Science*, *150*, 971–979.

Miller, W.R. & Rollnick, S. (1991). *Motivational interviewing. Preparing people to change addictive behaviour*. London: Guilford Press.

Morley, S. & Eccleston, C. (2004). The object of fear in pain. In G.J.G. Asmundson, J.W.S. Vlaeyen & G. Crombez (Eds.) *Understanding and treating fear of pain* (pp. 163–188). New York: Oxford University Press.

Morley, S., Eccleston, C. & Williams, A. (1999). Systematic review and meta-analysis of randomized controlled trials of cognitive behaviour therapy and behaviour therapy for chronic pain in adults, excluding headache. *Pain*, *80*(1–2), 1–13.

Morley, S. & Keefe, F.J. (2007). Getting a handle on process and change in CBT for chronic pain. *Pain*, *127*, 197–198.

Morley, S. & Williams, A. CdeC. (2006). RCTs of psychological treatments for chronic pain: Progress and challenges. *Pain*, *121*, 171–2.

Pincus, T., Burton, A.K., Vogel, S. & Field, A.P. (2001). A systematic review of psychological factors as predictors of disability in prospective cohorts of low back pain. *Spine*, *27*, 109–120.

Pincus, T. & Williams, A. (1999). Models and measurements of depression in chronic pain. *Journal of Psychosomatic Research, 47*, 211–219.

Price, D.D. (1999). *Psychological mechanisms of pain and analgesia.* Seattle, WA: IASP Press.

Prochaska, J. & Diclemente, C. (1992). Stages of change in the modification of problem behaviours. In M. Hersen, R. Eisler & P. Miller (Eds.) *Progress in behavior modification* (Vol. 28, pp. 183–218). Sycamore, IL: Sycamore Publishing.

Rode, S., Salkovskis, P.M., Dowd, H. & Hanna, M. (2006). Health anxiety levels in chronic pain clinic attenders. *Journal of Psychosomatic Research, 60,* 155–161.

Romano, J.M. & Turner, J.A. (1985). Chronic pain and depression: Does the evidence support a relationship? *Psychological Bulletin, 97,* 18–34.

Royal College of Anaesthetists and The British Pain Society (RCA/BPS). (2003). *Pain Management Services: Good practice.* London: Author.

Sprangers, M.A., de Regt, E.B., Andries, F., van Agt, H.M., Bijl, R.V., de Boer, J.B. *et al.* (2000). Which chronic conditions are associated with better or poorer quality of life? *Journal of Clinical Epidemiology, 53*(9), 895–907.

Sullivan, M.J.L., Adams, H. & Sullivan, M.E. (2004). Communicative dimensions of pain catastrophising: Social cueing effects on pain behaviour and coping. *Pain, 107,* 230–236.

Sullivan, M.J.L., Thorn, B., Haythornthwaite, J.A., Keefe, F., Martin, M., Bradley, L. *et al.* (2001). Theoretical perspectives on the relation between catastrophizing and pain. *The Clinical Journal of Pain, 17*(1), 52–64.

Tang, N.K.Y, Salkovskis, P.M, Poplavskaya, E., Wright, K.J., Hanna, M. & Hester, J. (2007). Increased use of safety-seeking behaviours in chronic back pain patients with high health anxiety. *Behaviour Research and Therapy, 45,* 2821–2835.

Thwaites, R. & Freeston, M. (2005). Safety-seeking behaviours: Fact or fiction? How can we clinically differentiate between safety behaviours and adaptive coping strategies across anxiety disorders? *Behavioural and Cognitive Psychotherapy, 33,* 177–188.

Turk, D.C. & Monarch, E.S. (2003). Chronic pain. In S. Llewelyn & P. Kennedy (Eds.) *Handbook of clinical health psychology* (pp. 131–154). Chichester: Wiley.

Vlaeyen, J.W., de Jong, J., Geilen, M., Heuts, P.H. & van Breukelen, G. (2001). Graded exposure in vivo in the treatment of pain-related fear: A replicated single case experimental design in four patients with chronic low back pain. *Behavioural Research and Therapy, 39,* 151–166.

Vlaeyen, J.W., de Jong, J., Geilen, M., Heuts, P.H. & van Breukelen, G. (2002). The treatment of fear of movement/(re)injury in chronic low back pain: Further evidence on the effectiveness of exposure in vivo. *Clinical Journal of Pain, 18,* 251–261.

Vlaeyen, J.W., Kole-Snijders, A.M., Boeren, R.G. & van Eek, H. (1995). Fear of movement/(re) injury in chronic low back pain and its relation to behavioural performance. *Pain, 62*(3), 363–372.

Vlaeyen, J.W. & Linton, S.J. (2000). Fear-avoidance and its consequences in chronic musculoskeletal pain: A state of the art. *Pain, 85,* 317–332.

Von Korff, M. (1999). Pain management in primary care: An individualised stepped-care approach. In R.J Gatchel & D.C. Turk (Eds.) *Psychosocial factors in pain* (pp. 360–373). New York: Guilford Press.

Von Korff, M. & Moore, J. (2001). Stepped care for back pain: Activating approaches for primary care. *Annuals of Internal Medicine, 121,* 187–195.

Waddell, G. (1992). Biopsychosocial analysis of low back pain. *Baillieres Clinical Rheumatology, 6*(3), 523–557.

White, C.A (2001). *Cognitive behaviour therapy for chronic medical problems.* Chichester: Wiley.

Williams, A. CdeC. (2002). Selecting and applying pain measures. In H. Breivik, W. Campbell & C. Eccleston (Eds.) *Clinical pain management: Practical applications and procedures* (pp. 3–14). London: Arnold Publications.

Winterowd, C., Beck, A.T. & Gruener, D. (2003). Eliciting and modifying imagery. In *Cognitive therapy with chronic pain patients*. New York: Springer.

Woods, M.P. & Asmundson, G.J.G (2008). Evaluating the effects of graded in vivo exposure for the treatment of fear in patients with chronic back pain: A randomised controlled trial. *Pain*, *136*(3), 271–280.

13

Neuropsychological Rehabilitation following Acquired Brain Injury

Nigel S. King and David Dean

Introduction

The term 'acquired brain injury' (ABI) is used to describe a range of injuries to the brain which occur after birth. These include head injury, stroke, anoxic brain injury, encephalitis and brain tumour. They are often characterised by a relatively sudden onset followed by a period of organic recovery before improvements level off and plateau. Other conditions, where injury to the brain is progressive (such as dementia and later stages of multiple sclerosis), are not usually included within a definition of ABI. The focus of this chapter will be on head injury and stroke as these are the two most common causes of ABI. Common cognitive, emotional and social problems experienced by adults following ABI will be described and how these may be addressed through neuropsychological rehabilitation. Many elements of this chapter can also be found in King and Tyerman (2003).

Clinical neuropsychologists play an essential role in assessment and rehabilitation after ABI. Drawing upon both specialist neuropsychological knowledge and their general training, clinical neuropsychologists provide a number of key functions: assessing the nature and degree of cognitive impairment; assessing mood, behaviour and adjustment; devising and implementing appropriate interventions; liaising with educational agencies/employers to advise on the resumption of educational/vocational life; providing and advising about long-term care; facilitating personal, family and social adjustment; dissemination of psychological skills and knowledge to others; and contribution to research and service development (British Psychological Society, 1989, 2002). As such, clinical neuropsychologists contribute at all stages following acquired brain injury, from acute care to long-term follow-up, and in a range of settings including acute hospitals, rehabilitation units and the community (see also The National Service Framework for Long-term Conditions, Department of Health, 2005).

In the acute setting clinical neuropsychologists are often based in regional neurosciences centres and in dedicated stroke units, working closely with hospital consultants, nursing staff and other members of the acute team during the patient's admission. Once patients are medically stable, they will often be seen for more detailed assessment in post-acute rehabilitation units or as outpatients. At this point, the attention has shifted more to cognitive and other psychological changes (King & Tyerman, 2003). Historically, clinical neuropsychologists working in rehabilitation in the UK were based primarily within regional inpatient neurological rehabilitation centres or in specialist units in the independent sector for the management of severe behavioural difficulties. However, more recently there has been a growth in clinical neuropsychology posts in a range of services, including: generic physical disability teams, stroke units, specialist community brain injury rehabilitation teams and specialist centres for cognitive and vocational rehabilitation after brain injury.

Acquired Brain Injury

Pathophysiology

Head injury or 'traumatic brain injury' has been defined as 'brain injury caused by trauma to the head including the effects of direct complications of trauma notably hypoxaemia, hypotension, intracranial haemorrhage and raised intracranial pressure' (British Society of Rehabilitation Medicine, 1998). The annual incidence of hospital admission after head injury is estimated to be 229 per 100,000 in England. While 75–85 per cent of such injuries are mild in nature, the incidence of moderate or severe head injury is estimated to be 25 per 100,000. Outcome ranges from complete recovery to persistent coma or death. Prevalence of disability from head injury is estimated to affect 100–150 per 100,000, thereby affecting one family in 300.

There are two main types of head injury – open and closed: open head injury occurs when the skull and protective linings of the brain are damaged and the brain is exposed; closed head injury occurs when the skull and protective linings of the brain are not penetrated. In the UK head injury is predominantly of a closed, blunt impact nature arising from sudden changes in velocity (e.g. acceleration/deceleration injuries from road traffic accidents), assaults or falls. Open, penetrating injuries (e.g. arising from gun-shot wounds or bomb blasts) are uncommon in the UK but common in war zones (King & Tyerman, 2008).

Primary brain damage occurs due to haemorrhagic contusions (areas of bruising) and diffuse axonal injury (widespread damage to axons). Contusions are more common after falls and direct blows; axonal injury after acceleration/deceleration injuries such as road traffic accidents. Haemorrhagic contusions on the crests of the gyri of the cortex can occur under the point of impact (especially after depressed skull fractures) or directly opposite it ('contrecoup' injury), but are seen most often on the under surfaces of the frontal lobes and around the pole of the temporal lobes, where the brain impacts on the sharpest and most confined parts of skull. Diffuse axonal injury refers to widespread tearing or shearing of axons in the white matter due to violent movement of the largely unrestrained brain, causing stretching and compressing of axons (i.e. the part of the neuron which conveys impulses from the cell body to the next neuron in the chain). Diffuse axonal injury is considered to be the more important mechanism of primary brain damage.

Further damage may arise due to secondary complications, including respiratory failure, hypoxia (insufficient oxygen), hypotension (loss of blood flow), haemorrhage (bleeding), haematomas (collections of blood following haemorrhage), cerebral oedema (brain swelling), infection (after open wounds) and hydrocephalus (build up of cerebrospinal fluid) (see King & Tyerman, 2008).

A cerebrovascular accident (cva) and 'stroke' are terms used to describe the sudden disruption of blood supply to the brain, resulting in a disturbance of neurological function which lasts more than 24 hours. There are two main types of stroke: ischaemic stroke where blood vessels are blocked or obstructed to a degree that blood is not able to reach the brain, and haemorrhagic stroke, where a blood vessel bursts leading to blood leaking into the brain (intercerebral haemorrhage) or into the subarachnoid space (subarachnoid haemorrhage). It is estimated that approximately 110,000 people in England and Wales have a first stroke each year and 30,000 go on to have further strokes (National Service Framework for Older People, Department of Health, 2001). Cognitive changes following stroke depend on the location and degree of damage and the previous health of the person. Approximately 80 per cent of strokes are due to ischaemia caused by narrowing or blockage of a blood vessel (thrombosis and embolism) (Beaumont *et al.*, 1996). Incidence of stroke increases with age; however, each year approximately 10,000 people under the age of 55 will have a stroke. About 65 per cent of stroke survivors are able to live independently following a stroke. The remainder require significant support often due to resulting physical disability.

Clinical presentation and natural course

For the majority of severely injured patients, improvement takes place slowly over months and years. It is usually best to use the word 'improvement' rather than 'recovery' after more severe injuries, since recovery implies complete restoration of function which may well not occur. Permanent cognitive impairments are probable with severe injuries, although for some they will be quite subtle and only evident under stress, in busy environments or on formal testing. Cognitive impairments are rarely absent after very and extremely severe injuries.

The rate and extent of recovery is impossible to predict early on, and the process is not fully understood. It may involve the following: i) disrupted neurotransmitters regaining some of their original efficiency; ii) damaged neurones repairing themselves/ axonal sprouting; iii) resolution of brain swelling and contusion, leading to restoration of neuronal efficiency; and possibly iv) some degree of neural plasticity for very widely distributed functions (e.g. language). For head injured patients the majority of recovery typically occurs in the first two years such that significant difficulties evident at two years rarely resolve completely thereafter. However, further small amounts of natural recovery can occur up to and beyond five years for extremely severe injuries. Recovery following stroke usually occurs over a shorter timescale, with most recovery often occurring within the first 6 months. However, there may be smaller improvements beyond this, particularly in areas such as motor functioning. The prognosis in stroke is complicated by the increased risk of a further stroke and in older patients the possibility of dementia. There is evidence that early intervention improves outcome. However, adaptation to long-term disability is an ongoing process and improvements in function may occur many years post-injury, even when early rehabilitation has been limited.

Neuropsychological impairments

When physical disability (such as paresis, ataxia, dysarthria, dyspraxia or reduced motor speed) is present, it is often the main concern for the patient during the first months after injury. Cognitive impairments, however, tend to have greater impact on long-term disability and handicap. In head injury these occur predominantly in the areas of attention, speed of information processing, explicit memory and executive functioning. They reflect the most common areas of damage in the frontal and temporal cortical areas and with diffuse axonal shearing. The pattern of impairments in stroke will depend on the area where blood supply has been interrupted. Middle cerebral artery (MCA) strokes are most common and often result in weakness, sensory loss and hemianopia on the opposite side of the body to the stroke itself. Left MCA strokes can lead to language impairments, whilst right MCA strokes are more likely to give way to visuospatial deficits, including neglect. Memory problems are also common, but can be difficult to assess in aphasic patients and patients with visuospatial deficits. Strokes also occur in the anterior and posterior arteries. Strokes that occur in smaller arteries that have branched off larger arteries can result in focal deficits and in some cases these may escape detection.

Rehabilitation

The focus of neuropsychological rehabilitation varies according to the nature and severity of injury, the patient's psychosocial context, the clinical setting (e.g. acute, specialist inpatient or community) and time since injury. Early rehabilitation optimises outcome, but rehabilitation at a later stage in recovery can also improve function significantly.

Two key principles, however, underpin all types of rehabilitation:

i)   engaging and maintaining patient (and family) involvement with rehabilitation services by the provision of an emotionally supportive environment and relationships within which empathic expert help can be easily accessed.

ii) increasing patient's (and their family's) understanding of acquired brain injury, their strengths and weaknesses and the means by which impairments may be best managed.

These principles become increasingly important as the patient moves beyond acute settings to post-acute and community settings where engagement with services may be impeded by poor insight, lack of understanding, psychological denial, emotional disorder, physical disability or challenging behaviour.

A goal-oriented approach is an important aspect of early rehabilitation and includes: i) engaging the patient (and their family) in the rehabilitation process; ii)setting realistic goals for rehabilitation; iii) facilitating the achievement of goals via coordinated interventions; and iv) evaluating, reviewing and modifying targets goals over time.

Successful engagement of a patient (and their family) is often linked intrinsically to the collaborative development of goals that are meaningful to the patient. It is common for the patient (and their family), initially, to have unrealistic expectations about the extent and pace of targets that are achievable (e.g. complete cognitive recovery or return to full-time work within weeks of injury). Goals need to be discussed carefully with the patient (and their family) and where necessary, agreement reached to extend the time period for achieving them (Tyerman & King, 2004). Long-term goals will need to be broken down into smaller steps that can be achieved in a shorter period of time and, in some cases, additional forms of support to facilitate achievement of goals will be included. Formal goal-planning procedures may help this process, although there is no consistent evidence as yet that they affect outcomes (Levack et al., 2006).

The principles which should guide neuropsychological rehabilitation include the following: i) appropriate pacing of activity/treatment post-injury to take into account likely increases in fatigue (particularly in the early stages); ii) maintenance and development of appropriate levels of cognitive stimulation while avoiding cognitive overloading; iii) education and minimisation of the vicious cycle of cognitive impairments leading to reduced coping, leading to distress, leading to exacerbated cognitive impairments, etc.; iv) the emphasis of cognitive rehabilitation through compensatory strategies and prostheses rather than through cognitive restoration and 'brain function therapy'(i.e. de-emphasising the analogy that the brain operates like a muscle and discouraging inappropriate attempts to train unaffected brain areas to take over damaged areas); v) the provision of emotional support and specific psychological interventions for the emotional sequelae associated with acquired brain injury for both the patient and their family; vi) facilitating patient's and family's adjustment to changes in personality, identity and psychosocial functioning; and vii) liaison with education and vocational systems where appropriate (King & Tyerman, 2003). Coordination and review of interventions is essential so that there is continuous feedback between professionals, patient and family. This helps interventions to remain focused on mutually agreed goals, and targets and goals to be refined and modified as the patient progresses and circumstances change.

The use of groups for cognitive rehabilitation, education and emotional support should not be underestimated. These allow peer support, sharing of cognitive and emotional coping responses and an opportunity to provide formal education in an efficient way. They can be a very powerful and supportive means for developing insight into impairments and for exploring ways of minimising disability. Local groups in the community (e.g. Headway, Different Strokes) can also provide support, advice and models of successful adjustment to an acquired brain injury.

Cognitive rehabilitation strategies which benefit patients with severe brain injury are usually pragmatic in nature. Neuropsychological assessment, however, provides vital information for knowing what strategies should be attempted, what modifications might be beneficial, what might cause strategies to be unsuccessful, how to develop new strategies and what kind of advice and education is appropriate. The following section highlights frequent examples of management strategies for common areas of difficulty such as attention and visuospatial skills, memory, executive function, communication skills, fatigue and emotional and behavioural difficulties (King & Tyerman, 2003). There is, of course, significant overlap between these areas.

General strategies
- *Developing habits, routines and over-learnt procedures* to: i) maximise the use of implicit and procedural memory functions; ii) provide structure; and iii) minimise cognitive load.
  Developing a tidy living and working environment where belongings are kept in the same, intuitively obvious, places and can easily be found. This helps to minimise demand on memory and problem-solving skills and make maximum use of spared implicit memory.
  Taking many small breaks when impairments become apparent rather than 'pushing on' until forced to take a break due to 'cognitive overload'.
- *Rearranging working environments* to minimise background noise, 'busyness', unexpected events and time pressures. This helps to reduce restrictions arising from attentional deficits, slow speed of information processing and cognitive inflexibility.
- *Graduated return to pre-morbid activities and minimisation of non-essential activity* to reduce cognitive overload and fatigue. This maximises the chances of successful completion of activities.
- *Training the patient to allow extra time* for tasks where temporal judgement or speed of information processing is reduced.
- *Emphasising the positive effects of maintaining/enhancing physical and mental health.* Getting a good night's sleep, healthy eating, avoiding excessive alcohol use and dealing effectively with stress can all help in optimising cognitive performance.

Strategies for improving attention and managing visuospatial difficulties
- *A difficulty with sustained attention* (i.e. the ability to remain on task) can be addressed by encouraging/training the patient to plan regular breaks, alternating high- and low-interest tasks and carrying out the latter when most alert, adopting a method of self-cueing (e.g. an alarm reminder to stay on task) or cueing by others, and using reinforcement/rewards to encourage on-task behaviour.
- *A difficulty with focused attention* (i.e. the ability to focus on relevant information and ignore irrelevant information) is best managed by advising the patient on ways to avoid distractions.
- *A difficulty with divided attention* (i.e. the ability to ability to pay attention to more than one thing at a time) is best managed by advising the patient to avoid carrying out multiple tasks simultaneously.
- *Hemispatial inattention or unilateral spatial neglect* is a phenomenon common in stroke but less so in head injury. It refers to a lack of awareness of one side of space and can include both the outside world and the patient's own body. It is important

to differentiate neglect from simpler visual field deficits such as *hemianopia*. The latter can be managed by providing information about the deficits and teaching patients simple scanning and cueing techniques. Neglect, on the other hand, may require a more robust approach and the provision of convincing evidence that the problem exists. There is also evidence of poor generalisation of skills learnt to compensate for neglect. Limb activation training (e.g. Robertson & North, 1992) has also been demonstrated as an effective strategy in reducing neglect.

Strategies for managing memory
Strategies for managing memory can broadly be divided into external (use of practical aids) and internal (cognitive) strategies. Both can be effective; however, the degree of cognitive effort required for internal memory strategies often exceeds their utility for patients with memory and executive impairments. Internal strategies can be useful for specific tasks like remembering names of people or studying for an exam where external strategies are inappropriate.

- *External memory strategies include getting more organised by*: keeping things in the same place (e.g. keys, loose change); using a filing system (e.g. for paying bills); making lists (starring priorities, crossing things off when item completed etc.); using diaries, calendars, wall planners and electronic devices to plan ahead; carrying a notebook around to write down important information; keeping a notepad by the phone for recording messages and phone numbers; using a dosset box for tablets; getting into a routine; and setting an alarm as a reminder to do important things.
- *Other external memory strategies include* using journals, diaries, photograph albums, videos, etc. to record events and compensate for difficulties in episodic memory.
- *Internal memory strategies include* rehearsal/repetition of information, finding ways of making information more meaningful to the patient, using techniques to process information at a deeper level, associating new information with existing knowledge, chunking and grouping, visualisation of verbal material, verbalisation of visual material and use of other mnemonics such as acronyms.

NB: There is evidence to suggest that amnesic patients learn better through errorless learning techniques (i.e. prompting and cueing in such a way that no errors are made during a training process) than trial and error (e.g. Wilson *et al.*, 1994).

Strategies for executive difficulties
- Providing problem-solving skills training to help develop an explicit and systematic approach to solving difficulties e.g.: i) defining the problem to be overcome; ii) generating different strategies to overcome problem; iii) highlighting the pros and cons of each strategy; iv) deciding the best strategy based on the pros and cons; v) implementing the strategy; and vi) evaluating the outcome.
- Using an alarmed stopwatch to help patients monitor the amount of time taken on given tasks to help planning and temporal judgement impairments.

- *Using self-talk and self-instruction (verbal mediation)* to help overcome initiation problems and to remind the patient of self-statements for aiding social regulation.
- *Breaking tasks down into their component steps with written instructions* to reduce disabilities from planning deficits.
- *Introducing repeating routine/cycles* to reduce unnecessary decision-making (e.g. weekly menus; shopping lists, set times for visiting church, etc.).

Strategies for communication skills
- *Using alternative means of communication (e.g. writing, drawing and other communication aids)*. These are often facilitated through the involvement of speech and language therapy.
- *Teaching conversation skills* for slowing, pacing and allowing 'thinking time' during interactions to help minimise word finding, sentence construction and concentration difficulties in conversation.
- *Teaching social skills* so that the patient is comfortable asking for things to be repeated during conversation when attention, memory or language deficits have caused them to lose track.
- *Encouraging others to modify their use of language to take into account the patient's cognitive deficit*. Examples of this include using shorter sentences and slower speech to aid understanding and providing choices rather than asking open-ended questions, where decision making and initiation of ideas are impaired.

Strategies for behavioural management
Behavioural problems following ABI can arise at different stages of recovery and result from a range of causes. The aetiology may include organic and psychosocial factors and be related to pre-morbid personality and behaviour (e.g. Alderman, 2004). In some cases a pharmacological approach may be indicated in addition to psychological management. Following careful assessment, psychological approaches may include:

- *Specialist inpatient rehabilitation, which may comprise a structured approach adopted by a multidisciplinary team based on principles of applied behaviour analysis*. These principles may be extended to community-based rehabilitation where appropriate.
- *Increasing the patient's awareness of inappropriate behaviour which can be achieved by setting up a carefully selected group of close friends/relatives to provide behavioural feedback, providing video feedback of inappropriate behaviour and by encouraging the use of self-monitoring (e.g. using a hand-held counter)*. These techniques should be employed with careful and sensitive collaboration between the patient and any others involved, as patients may be surprised, upset or embarrassed by being confronted with inappropriate behaviours.

Strategies for emotional disorders
There is a higher incidence of emotional disorders in people who have had an ABI than in the general population. For any individual patient, these may be related to the ABI to

a greater or lesser extent. It is often the case that emotional disorders following an ABI represent the combination of organic, psychosocial and pre-morbid factors. It is therefore essential that careful assessment is carried out. Psychological interventions for emotional disorders following acquired brain injury have largely been developed from the adult mental health field of clinical psychology and have been adapted to the specific challenges of this population (Tyerman & King, 2004). Interventions have been carried out both within an individual and a group format, often within a cognitive behavioural therapy (CBT) model.

Depressive disorders   Depression needs to be differentiated from an understandable reaction to the losses associated with ABI. Grief models have been applied to understand the adjustment process. Awareness and adjustment to loss may be an ongoing process, and the reaction to the initial losses associated with the injury may give way to awareness of the longer-term impacts on areas such as work and hobbies. Equally, other causes of symptoms associated with depression need to be considered, for example the lack of initiation associated with frontal lobe damage and tearfulness associated with 'emotionalism' in some patients following stroke. Where depression is indicated, CBT approaches may be helpful. However, there is currently limited evidence for the efficacy of CBT following ABI. In addition, the effective use of goal planning (as described earlier) may be helpful in addressing problems of low mood by increasing self-efficacy and reducing notions of learned helplessness (e.g. Williams, 2003).

Anxiety disorders   Anxiety is also common following ABI and in some cases (e.g. stroke) may be linked to fears of further injury or illness. As in the general population, anxiety may coexist with depression, and different types of anxiety such as generalised anxiety disorder, phobia and panic may be present. Some anxiety symptoms can best be understood and treated using a model of post-traumatic stress disorder. Modified versions of CBT either in a group or individual setting can be used to address these symptoms. For both anxiety and depression an indirect approach may be necessary where cognitive impairment is more severe.

Adjustment and coping   Many persons with acquired brain injury face major challenges of adjustment as they seek to come to terms with the effects of an ABI (Tyerman, 2008; Barton, 2006). An ABI can result in physical, cognitive, emotional and behavioural problems; and these problems may mean that the person is unable to resume their former work, family and social roles. The process of psychological adjustment may be compounded by executive difficulties, especially lack of insight and reduced capacity for self-appraisal and problem solving, often combined with lack of emotional and behavioural control. Without specialist help many struggle to make the necessary adjustments to their residual disability and continue to strive for an unrealistic degree of recovery. Others make decisions which do not take due account of restrictions arising from their injury, leading to repeated failure and loss of confidence and self-belief.

Common approaches in neuropsychological rehabilitation to facilitate the adjustment process include: clarifying the long-term effects of the injury; reviewing strengths and weaknesses; making sense of and reconciling changes in the person and their lives; identifying, clarifying and prioritising unresolved issues; and supported problem solving in finding a new direction through which to start to rebuild the patient's lives (Tyerman, 1991). Interventions based on the transactional model of stress have also been demonstrated to be effective in helping people to cope effectively with chronic conditions such as spinal cord injury (e.g. Kennedy *et al.*, 2003). In ABI this approach may help adjustment by exploring both primary (threat) and secondary (coping) appraisals and teaching problem-solving skills.

Return to education or employment represents for many a major decision, which can either facilitate positive adjustment or provoke a downward spiral of failure. For those unable to return to previous employment, a programme of specialist vocational rehabilitation may be required to highlight vocational restrictions, prepare the person for a graded return to employment and guide and support them in their vocational adjustment to a position more suited to their residual disability.

It is vital to include the family as fully as possible in the process of rehabilitation. Close liaison with the family is essential both to obtain feedback about difficulties and progress in the home and to explain rehabilitation strategies, which can then be reinforced by family members. The needs of families warrant attention in their own right as family members may themselves need specialist advice and support in understanding and coping with the impact of severe acquired brain injury both upon themselves and the family as a whole. A range of family services is required to facilitate family adjustment, including family education; individual family support; and specialist marital and family counselling.

While the above list outlines some of the most commonly used interventions, it is in no way exhaustive. Also, it is essential that emotional disorders after acquired brain injury are addressed within the overall context of the acquired brain injury and patients' aspirations, hopes, social network and overall psychosocial circumstances. 'Atomising' their emotional experiences to a series of disorders or symptoms will not adequately address the complexity of emotional needs. Indeed, this principle must underpin all forms of rehabilitation for head injured patients.

Effectiveness

Studies evaluating the effectiveness of neuropsychological rehabilitation for patients with acquired brain injury are relatively sparse and frequently suffer from significant methodological constraints. There is some modest evidence that restorative techniques involving repeated practice of specific tasks in laboratory settings can be effective for improving some specific attention and language-based functions. There is insufficient evidence, however, that any gains are generalised to everyday activities. Restorative strategies for other impairments have virtually no empirical support. In contrast, the current evidence suggests that compensatory strategies are effective in reducing everyday memory failures, minimising anxiety and increasing self-concept and quality of interpersonal relationships. Behavioural approaches aimed at maximising skill acquisition and monitoring, including performance feedback and reinforcement, have also demonstrated their efficacy. It is these types of rehabilitation that generalise best to everyday life situations (Halligan & Wade, 2005; Carney *et al.*, 1999).

Neuropsychological rehabilitation programmes which have the strongest outcomes tend to be those combining early intervention, compensatory strategies and supported employment for patients of working age. There is also evidence that services provided by specialist multidisciplinary teams working in a coordinated way result in improved outcomes for patients, reducing emotional distress and speeding up the course of recovery (e.g. Wade, 2003).

The continued evaluation of neuropsychological rehabilitation through both evidence-based practice and practice-based evidence is therefore of paramount importance in this complex field of clinical endeavour.

References

Alderman, N. (2004). Disorders of behavior. In J. Ponsford (Ed.) *Cognitive and behavioural rehabilitation* (pp.269–298). London: Guilford Press.

Barton, J. (2006). Psychological aspects of stroke. In P. Kennedy (Ed.) *Psychological management of physical disabilities: A practitioner's guide* (pp. 61–79). London: Routledge.

Beaumont, J.G., Kenealy, P.M. & Rogers, M.J.C. (1996). *The Blackwell dictionary of neuropsychology*. Oxford: Blackwell.

British Psychological Society (1989). *Services for adult patients with acquired brain injury*. Leicester: Author.

British Psychological Society (2002). *Psychological services for stroke survivors and their families*. Leicester: Author.

British Society of Rehabilitation Medicine (1998). *Rehabilitation after traumatic brain injury*. A working party report. London: Author.

Carney, N., Chestnut, R.M., Maynard, H., Mann, N.C., Patterson, P. & Helfund, M. (1999). Effect of cognitive rehabilitation on outcomes for persons with traumatic brain injury: A systematic review. *Journal of Head Trauma Rehabilitation, 14*, 271–307.

Department of Health (2001). *The national service framework for older people*. London: Author.

Department of Health (2005). *The national service framework for long-term conditions*. London: Author.

Halligan, P.W. & Wade, D.T. (Eds.) (2005). *Effectiveness of rehabilitation for cognitive deficits*. Oxford: Oxford University Press.

Kennedy, P., Duff, J., Evans, M. & Beedie, A. (2003). Coping effectiveness training reduces depression and anxiety following traumatic spinal cord injuries. *British Journal of Clinical Psychology, 42*, 41–52.

King, N.S. & Tyerman, A. (2003). Neuropsychological presentation and treatment of head injury and traumatic brain damage. In P.W. Halligan, U. Kischau & J. Marshall (Eds.) *Handbook of clinical neuropsychology* (pp. 487–505). Oxford: Oxford University Press.

King, N.S. & Tyerman, A. (2008). Introduction to traumatic brain injury. In A. Tyerman & N.S. King (Eds.) *Psychological approaches to rehabilitation following traumatic brain injury* (pp. 1–14). Oxford: Blackwell.

Levack, W.M.M., Taylor, K., Siegert, R.J., Dean, S.G., McPherson, K.M. & Wetherall, M. (2006). Is goal planning in rehabilitation effective? A systematic review. *Clinical Rehabilitation*, *20*(9), 739–755.

Robertson, I. & North, N. (1992). Spatio-motor cueing in unilateral neglect: The role of hemispace, hand and motor activation. *Neuropsychologica*, *30*, 553–563.

Tyerman, A. (1991). Counselling in head injury. In H. Davis & L. Fallowfield (Eds.) *Counselling and communication in healthcare* (pp. 115–128). Chichester: John Wiley & Sons.

Tyerman, A. (2008). Facilitating psychological adjustment. In A. Tyerman & N.S. King (Eds.) *Psychological approaches to rehabilitation following traumatic brain injury* (pp. 320–348). Oxford: Blackwell.

Tyerman, A. & King, N.S. (2004). Interventions for psychological problems after brain injury. In L.H. Goldstein & J. McNeil (Eds.) *Clinical neuropsychology. A practical guide to assessment and management for clinicians* (pp. 385–404). Chichester: Wiley.

Wade, D.T. (2003). Stroke rehabilitation: The evidence. In R.J. Greenwood, M.P. Barnes, T.M. McMillan & C.D. Ward (Eds.) *Handbook of neurological rehabilitation* (2nd edn, pp. 487–504). Hove: Psychology Press.

Williams, W.H. (2003). Rehabilitation of emotional disorders following acquired brain injury. In B.A. Wilson (Ed.) *Neuropsychological rehabilitation: Theory and practice* (pp. 115–136). London: Taylor & Francis.

Wilson, B., Baddeley, A.D., Evans, J.J. & Shiel, A. (1994). Errorless learning in the rehabilitation of memory impaired people. *Neuropsychological Rehabilitation*, *4*, 307–326.

14

Working Systemically with People with Learning Disabilities

Selma Rikberg Smyly

Overview of Presenting Problems and Clinical Psychology Approaches and Services for This Client Group

Historically, services for people with learning disabilities have evolved from hospital-based to more inclusive community-based models of social and health care, where individual choice, options for different lifestyles and voice of the client is gradually gaining predominance (Department of Health and Social Security, 1971; Department of Health, 2001, 2002). There has been a corresponding increase in diversity of thera-peutic orientations available to this client group. Starting with mainly behavioural ori-entations, these have expanded to include psychodynamic (Sinason, 1992; Beail, 1995) and psychotherapeutic (Waitman & Conboy-Hill, 1992) as well as cognitive behav-ioural approaches (Stenfert Kroeze *et al.*, 1997). Family therapy and systemic approaches have developed most recently (Vetere, 1996; Baum & Lynggaard, 2006).

Even though the ethos of current service provision (Valuing People, Department of Health, 2001) has become more focused on integration, the reality of living in the com-munity can still be an isolating experience for many people with a learning disability (PLD), where their main relationships evolve around people from a variety of different agencies who provide for their everyday care. Living with a permanent disability within a cultural context which admires and promotes as desirable images of youth, beauty and independence means that the reality for our clients can feel very alienating, frus-trating and disempowering. Being disabled, as Sinason (1992) pointed out, still remains one of the taboo subjects both culturally and within services.

The fact that people tend to be referred by others is another important consideration for psychologists working within a learning disability service. A profession trained on interviewing techniques and relying on verbal communication as its main source of activity can find it challenging when working with people who are often unable to tell us what is wrong, and whose use of language may be idiosyncratic, non-conventional or difficult to understand. Typically, clients often lead lives told, explained and interpreted by a variety of others. Their very life stories may or may not be known by people around them, often mainly paid carers. Depending on whom we ask, these stories may vary. Hearing the 'voice' of the client can be a truly challenging task. An important part of therapy becomes therefore the finding of the voice of the client and in so doing changing some of the predominant problem-saturated descriptions which still can surround and shape client lives (Rikberg Smyly, 2006; Scior & Lynggaard, 2006).

For example, a glance at 'reasons for referral' for psychology (Rose et al., 2001) still provides a relatively high proportion of 'challenging behaviour' as one of the main referral categories. The frequency of this referral category must be unique for learning disability services, particularly in an adult service context. It is a generic short hand, which covers an infinite variety of possible presenting problems. However, too often within the learning disability service context this label is seen as inherent to the disability (e.g. 'She has always been difficult', 'It's because he has a learning disability that he shouts', etc.) rather than a possible expression of human distress in relation to particular situations and events in one's life. Enabling carers to develop different understandings of the distress the client might be experiencing and creating more helpful alternative meanings around such problems is seen as an important part of a systemic approach.

People with a learning disability and their families often experience problems at times of significant changes such as changes in life-cycle stages and transitions (Goldberg et al., 1995). Such themes can present as important contexts for 'challenging behaviour' referrals. For example, loss of key people in one's life, either through bereavement or often, equally painfully, through staff moving on, as well as transition periods of moving from home to community-based services are examples of the kind of life events often associated with 'challenging behaviour' referrals. Systemic approaches offer a specifically helpful contribution in looking at presenting problems in the context of wider life experiences. Problems are primarily perceived as residing within particular relationships at particular times and places (Carr, 2000). Because of this a systemic approach avoids the pitfalls of pathologising further a client group who potentially already carry so many negative labels. Another important emphasis in systemic approaches is the focus on finding the voice of the client and locating it within the context of other voices, other stories held by the network of concern. Offering new and alternative ways of bringing the client's voice into the therapeutic context is seen as another central contribution of a systemic approach (Baum & Lynggaard, 2006).

What Do We Mean by Systemic and What Does This Model Offer?

The focus of this chapter will be on two predominant systemic models currently used within adult learning disability services in the UK, namely social constructionist and narrative therapy models. A historical overview of other family therapy models can be found in Baum (2006). An account of the social constructionist theory can be found in an excellent handbook compiled by Ekdawi et al. (2000) as well as a collection of papers in McNamee and Gergen (1992) and, for narrative therapy, White and Epstein (1990) and Morgan (2000).

A central concept in social constructionist thinking is the emphasis on the meanings and beliefs attributed to behaviours and the assumption that the therapeutic focus is primarily, but not exclusively, on change at the level of beliefs (Carr, 2000). Fredman (2006) in writing about systemic ideas within the learning disability context emphasises, apart from viewing symptoms as residing within the interactional patterns of specific relationships, the importance of exploration of the context, including meanings and beliefs, within which problems emerge and are constructed. For example, by asking the referrer (assuming they are not the client) a few typical systemic questions at the beginning of therapy, relating to the context of the referral, can help define the relationship to the problem of the existing network of people involved (Reder & Fredman, 1996). This can include questions relating to who is involved with the client and the different views (meanings and beliefs) that network members might have about the problem, e.g. 'who is most/least concerned about the problem?', 'what triggered the referral being made now?', i.e. what life-cycle stages might be involved and/or relevant life events. In addition, exploring the current expectations of the referrer and network of people involved, e.g. 'what has been helpful in the past?', 'what expectations might the team/referrer have about the psychology input they have asked for?', may be a useful way of exploring beliefs surrounding help-seeking (Reder & Fredman, 1996). Establishing what efforts have been made to find out 'what the client views might be', as well as recognising areas of strengths, resources and positive functioning, 'what aspects of her/his life might be going well at the moment', both for the client and the referrer are all part of defining the context of the referral as well as the potential resources and alternative stories in the client's life. Being mindful of the way in which the disability context might determine how problems are perceived, considering 'what/who would be of most concern/most concerned about the current presenting problem if the client did not have a learning disability' are ways of exploring the cultural context of the referral issues. All the above questions can be helpful initial ways of broadening the context of the referral and beginning to recognise and explore the different beliefs about specific relationships, times, places, life events and cultural context which may contribute to the understanding about how the problem has emerged and been constructed.

Another important contribution in thinking in this field comes from the post-modern social constructionist model (Anderson & Goolishian, 1992) of questioning the position of the therapist as the outside expert and introducing the concept of the participant observer who influences and is in turn influenced by the therapeutic conversation. The therapist works from a position of respect and curiosity (Cecchin, 1987; Cecchin *et al.*, 1994), which opens up the possibility of hearing new stories or alternative meanings to old stories. The therapist models a position of multiple perspectives where 'both/and' explanations are preferred to 'either/or' (Carr, 2000). This involves the co-creation of alternative narratives in the context of the client and/or relevant networks engaging in conversations where ideas, meanings and situations can be explored in a way which sees difference as valued and where presenting problems have multiple meanings and hence also multiple solutions. Finding the 'fit' involves identifying many possible narratives as potentially helpful explanations in different contexts, e.g. personal, family stories and/or cultural and societal narratives, and co-creating with the client/relevant network the stories which are seen to be most helpful at a particular point in time in a particular context. In systemic practice a particularly helpful way of doing this is the inclusion of some form of reflecting team/process into the therapeutic conversation (Andersen, 1987, 1992).

Using Reflecting Teams with People with a Learning Disability

The method of using reflecting teams in the therapeutic session is an important part of social constructionist practice where a non-expert position, multiple perspectives and the co-creation of alternative stories can be modelled. A typical session involves a lead therapist interviewing the client, carers and/or family members. In addition there is another therapist present, or preferably two (the reflecting team), listening to the lead therapist's interview. The reflecting team never speaks directly to the clients. Andersen (1987, 1991) suggests some parameters for reflecting teams. Reflections should be tentatively offered, be respectful of all views expressed, be situated in the preceding conversation, and not differ too much from the current views expressed. If possible they should also be as transparent as possible in terms of where the ideas come from and why the reflecting therapist is expressing these views. Andersen (1987) talks about how both the therapist and clients are given the opportunity to offer inner conversations as outer conversations. The reflecting-team process allows each person the space to listen and to have an inner conversation with what they hear. Following the reflecting team conversation the clients are invited to comment on what they have heard (outer conversation) and what thoughts it generated. The process can be repeated a number of times in each session. Reflecting teams are seen as a way of introducing alternative or new understandings as well as multiple perspectives into the room, in a tentative and transparent way, which the client can either accept or reject.

Halliday and Robbins (2006) comment on the potential helpfulness of the reflecting team in offering positive feedback to client stories as well as alternative ways of seeing a problem. In particular, they comment on how discussions with care staff changed from discourses about the disability to discourses about more universal themes such as belonging and separation, protection and risk, etc. Cardone and Hilton (2006) suggest adapting aspects of the reflecting process in work with PLD by, for example, always asking the person with a learning disability first about their views following a reflection as well as the reflecting team offering just one idea to each person being interviewed.

Andersen (1995) describes how he encourages clients to explore the 'inside of a word' to evoke more specific and representative images and meanings of words used. Working with an individual client together with a reflecting therapist can be a particularly helpful way of exploring alternative meanings to common words and expressions used by PLD. Exploring what terms such as 'feeling upset' or 'being important' might mean for the client can be done through wondering about possible explanations in the reflecting conversation (Rikberg Smyly, 2006). Asking the client to choose from possible alternatives, which the reflecting person has tentatively suggested, can be a way of offering options to clients which they might otherwise have found difficult to express (Booth & Booth, 1996).

Using reflecting conversations when working with staff teams can help to broaden perspectives about perceived problems, and can offer people a structured and safe space to hear and reflect on alternative stories. By focusing on different beliefs and assumptions held by carers one can facilitate the understanding of the different views and hence actions taken by different staff members (Rikberg Smyly, 2006).

For example, a 45-year-old man was referred by his staff team manager for bereavement work following what was felt as 'incessant and inappropriate' conversations about a funeral of one of the co-residents in his house. During the systemic consultation meeting with the staff team, they were encouraged to explore their ideas and beliefs about grief. The team held many varied views about the extent to which one should talk about what had happened, how long one grieved for, different cultural norms and acceptable ways of expressing grief, etc. It transpired that in this particular case some staff members had found the client's conversations particularly distressing and felt that the client was singularly and on purpose picking them out for these conversations, whereas other staff members had not perceived his behaviour as so problematic. The exploration of these ideas with the staff team enabled the referral problem to be seen in the context of these different beliefs. This enabled alternative explanations for the client's behaviour to be voiced as well as highlighting the different expectations the staff members had about the client and hence their varied response to his perceived 'problem'. In this case his possible need to talk about the funeral was recognised as legitimate and those staff members who where not themselves distressed by the content of these conversations agreed to offer him time to do so. The staff members particularly distressed about these conversations were supported to explain to the client the reasons for their unwillingness to discuss the funeral further and to direct the client to other staff members.

Using Narrative Ideas with People with a Learning Disability

'Thinly/thickly' described narratives

A central idea according to a narrative perspective is that we live our lives according to the stories we tell ourselves and the stories that are told about us (White & Epstein, 1990). White (1997) uses the term 'thinly' described narratives as limited narrow understandings of a situation where the preferred perspectives of the client are often excluded. In their paper on narrative discourses in learning disability service settings, Wilcox and Whittington (2003) point out how these concepts fit into the lives of people with learning disabilities. For example, carers may only be aware of a client's life in relation to one context such as the residential home (with little contact with other service providers in day services or the client's family), which may result in alternative stories of the client or alternative explanations for current behaviours being lost. In this sense a life becomes single storied rather than multi-storied, hence the idea for the need to thicken existing descriptions of a client's life. Drawing on narrative techniques when working with an individual client, Scior and Lynggaard (2006) describe how they enabled the inclusion of other submerged stories of 'competence and strength' to be added to the predominant client views of 'weakness and failure' and how through exploring the meaning of unique outcomes in different contexts these new alternative narratives could be thickened.

Externalising

Another key aspect of narrative therapy sees people as separate from the problem for which they have been referred. In other words, 'the person is not the problem, the problem is the problem' (Morgan, 2000). An important aspect of the therapeutic conversation becomes its emphasis on *externalising conversations* (White & Epstein, 1990). For a client group who is used to being seen as 'the problem' and where the dominant psychological and medical models have combined to reinforce this view, beginning to see oneself as separate from the problem can be liberating (Scior & Lynggaard, 2006). This is helped by the way in which externalising conversations invite the client to characterise the problem; in other words, finding a way of describing 'the worry' or 'the sadness' or 'the confusion', etc. in a way which makes it separate from the person.

Recently a clinical psychology trainee working with a client was able to explore some difficult issues in a client's life in this way. The client had been referred for anger management due to aggression shown towards the staff team members and co-residents. Previous lack of engagement in therapeutic sessions had been an issue and attempts at discussing 'her anger' had resulted in the client walking out. However, by engaging in externalising conversations and finding a meaningful way of describing the anger, the trainee was able to explore the influence of the problem in the client's life. In this case the client chose 'the hyper' as a way to describe the problem. Questions about 'what happens when "the hyper" comes along?' 'How does "the hyper" help or hinder something from happening?' helped to further examine the influence of the problem in her life. Questions exploring if 'there are times when you can avoid the "the hyper" doing this in your life? How did you manage that?' create further space between the person and the problem in a way which helps the problem to be seen from different perspectives. Once the therapist found a way of externalising the client's experience of what was happening in her life, in a meaningful way, she was able to explore what influenced 'the hyper' and when and how it affected the client's life. New stories were beginning to emerge for the client of managing 'the hyper' by walking out of difficult meetings and seeing these as constructive and positive steps in coping with 'the hyper'. In this way, once a relationship to the problem has been created the person can be seen as separate from the problem and a way of talking about the difficulties can be created without the person being blamed for the problem.

Engaging clients in conversation

How we engage clients in therapeutic conversation can be very challenging. Sometimes this can only happen by others representing the client view. Thinking about how this is done and who could be a representative voice needs to be considered at each meeting. Cardone and Hilton (2006) outline different ways of engaging clients in conversations. They point out that giving clients enough time and pacing the conversation appropriately is important, as well as avoiding the temptation to interpret too soon what a client might be trying to say. As Fidell (1996) points out, many PLD are not used to having their voices heard and being able to express ideas and experiencing them as being respected and heard can often be a novel experience. Clinicians need to be mindful that meaning is created in particular contexts and thus when interviewing any client with a learning disability one needs to be very careful about how meanings are attributed to words. Systemic therapists are inherently curious about how language creates meaning and how experiences and cultural contexts might influence language use and hence what meanings are attributed to experiences. Cardone and Hilton (2006) describe how the use of systemic ideas such as circular questions, genogrammes and metaphor can be helpful tools to aid the process of meaning making.

Different Service Models and Contexts for Applying Systemic Approaches

Clinical psychologists working in multidisciplinary teams (MDTs) within the NHS have varied roles which may, in addition to psychological therapies, encompass service development, developing performance standards, evaluating outcomes, individual psychometric assessments, etc. Establishing a systemic practice may seem both difficult and contradictory to expectations. Around the country different models have developed. Halliday and Robbins (2006) describe a lifespan family therapy service, developed in Leeds, where referrals to the family therapy service could come from any speciality, including learning disability services. This way of providing a service makes it more possible to emphasise themes common to everyone's lives, locating difficulties in the context of a lifespan approach rather than the context of disability. Clegg and King (2006) discuss the relevance and helpfulness of using systemic ideas within a transition service from children's to adult teams in Nottingham. They demonstrate how using systemic conversations with families in transition enabled new themes to develop which, while taking into consideration the concerns families may have about, for example, autonomy/independence, also enable multiple views to emerge. Baum and Walden (2006) have described setting up a family therapy service in Newham in London within a community team for people with learning disabilities. In Wales, Jenkins and Parry (2006) describe how systemic ideas have influenced their work with the wider network. Work in Oxford has focused on working with staff teams using reflecting processes (Rikberg Smyly, 2006). More recently a systemic consultation model for new referrals to psychology within the community team for people with learning disabilities has been developed (Rikberg et al., 2009).

Many of the above authors have commented on the fact that systemic ideas seem particularly helpful for more complex referrals where therapists or MDTs are feeling stuck about their work with a system and/or client (Jenkins & Parry, 2006). Offering consultations to colleagues as well as using systemic ideas in supervision/case discussions with MDT members have been mentioned as helpful (Donati *et al.*, 2000; Lynggaard *et al.*, 2001; Dixon & Matthews 1992; Clegg & King, 2006.)

Evaluation and Future Direction

The introduction of systemic ideas in the context of a service for people with learning disabilities is relatively new. As outlined above, some very encouraging examples of practice exist; however, outcome research in this area has been limited (Pote, 2006). A number of therapists have engaged in pilot or small-scale evaluation of outcome as part of their practice. For example, Halliday and Robbins (2006) described how they asked some of their carers and service users who had attended sessions of their views. Apparently both the clients and carers had perceived the reflecting team initially as strange but had found this way of talking very helpful. The clients involved had commented that they actually liked having more people present who were interested in them. Baum and Walden (2006) described a pilot project in Newham where they interviewed nine families who attended family therapy sessions and found that out of those who completed, all had achieved the goals identified at the initial meeting. Arkless (2005) interviewed 10 family members attending systemic consultation sessions and found a mixture of responses from clients and other family members. Rikberg Smyly *et al.* (2009) interviewed 64 participants of initial systemic consultations, mostly carers and colleagues, and found mainly positive feedback. People particularly commented on how helpful they had found the contributions of the reflecting team and how this had broadened their perspectives on the presenting problems. On a different note, Pote (2006) describes her research into some common dilemmas experienced by therapists who engage in using systemic models. She comments on issues such as therapist neutrality as well as difficulties in discharging clients, i.e. when is someone 'cured' in the context of a permanent disability, and suggests the possible need to redefine the way the beginnings and endings of therapy are conceptualised.

There is a clear need for more outcome research; however, this poses its own dilemma when working within this particular model. Change is seen as a direct consequence of new information being co-constructed and co-created by those (usually more than one) participating in sessions. There are also multiple accounts of change from the different members of the relevant network who took part in the therapeutic process. There is considerable wealth of research into the efficacy of systemic therapy from a wide range of child- and adult-focused work (Asen, 2002; Stratton, 2005). Most of this research has been qualitative, emphasising, for example, the development of dominant themes. In the context of people with a learning disability one would have to be very careful about how one obtained or interpreted client views (Booth & Booth, 1996).

Despite these problems it is important that we can demonstrate the helpfulness of any approach used. Evidence-based practice within the NHS is here to stay and clinical psychologists as a profession are encouraged to demonstrate their scientist-practitioner role (British Psychological Society, 2007). Thinking about service development within the learning disability context, we need to look at when applying a systemic approach might be most helpful. The onus is on the current practitioners within leaning disability services to collect data on their systemic practice to enable us to look more closely at what aspects of systemic models might be most helpfully applied for what kind of referrals and in what kind of context.

The enthusiasm for using systemic ideas is evident, and as the model becomes more familiar to a wider audience of practitioners its inclusion in practice will no doubt increase. Working with people who do not always refer themselves, where the voice of the client can be difficult to hear and where multiple views about the perceived problem are commonplace, systemic ways of working offer an important shift in emphasis. By focusing on context and the relational nature of problems it avoids pathologising clients and instead promotes and encourages stories of ability, together with stories of hope and change. Intrinsic to this model is respecting existing knowledge and expertise by inviting the client and important people in the client's life to use their own knowledge and resourcefulness to co-create alternative ways of seeing a problem and new and potentially more helpful ways of being together. This can be an empowering, respectful and positive way of working with a client group whose lives are still often characterised by being marginalised and ignored.

References

Andersen, T. (1987). The reflecting team: Dialogue and meta-dialogue in clinical work. *Family Process, 26*, 415–428.

Andersen, T. (1991). *The reflecting team: Dialogues and dialogues about dialogues.* New York: Norton.

Andersen, T. (1992). Reflections on reflecting with families. In S. McNamee & K. Gergen (Eds.) *Therapy as social construction* (pp. 54–68). London: Sage.

Andersen, T. (1995). Reflecting processes: Acts of informing and forming. You can borrow my eyes, but you must not take them away from me! In S. Friedman (Ed.) *The reflecting team in action* (pp. 11–37). New York: Guilford Press.

Anderson, H. & Goolishian, H. (1992). The client is the expert: A not-knowing approach to therapy. In S. McNamee & K. Gergen (Eds.) *Therapy as social construction* (pp. 25–39). London: Sage.

Arkless, L. (2005). *Talking to people with learning disabilities and their families about the experience of systemic therapy.* Unpublished doctoral dissertation, University College London.

Asen, E. (2002). Outcome research in family therapy. *Advances in Psychiatric Treatment, 8*, 230–238.

Baum, S. (2006). The use of the systemic approaches to adults with intellectual disabilities and their families: Historical overview and current research. In S. Baum & H. Lynggaard (Eds.) *Intellectual disabilities: A systemic approach* (pp. 21–41). London: Karnac.

Baum, S. & Lynggaard, H. (Eds.) (2006). *Intellectual disabilities: A systemic approach*. London: Karnac.

Baum, S. & Walden, S. (2006). Setting up and evaluating a family therapy service in a community team for people with intellectual disabilities. In S. Baum & H. Lynggaard (Eds.) *Intellectual disabilities: A systemic approach* (pp. 64–82). London: Karnac.

Beail, N. (1995). Outcome of psychoanalysis, psychoanalytic psychodynamic psychotherapy with people with intellectual disabilities: A review. *Changes, 13,* 186–191.

Booth, T. & Booth, W. (1996). Sounds of silence: Narrative research with inarticulate subjects. *Disability and Society, 11*(1), 55–69.

British Psychological Society (2007). *Leading psychological services: A report by the Division of Clinical Psychology, The British Psychological Society*. Leicester: Author.

Cardone, D. & Hilton, A. (2006). Engaging people with intellectual disabilities in systemic therapy. In S. Baum & H. Lynggaard (Eds.) *Intellectual disabilities: A systemic approach* (pp. 83–99). London: Karnac.

Carr, A. (2000). *Family therapy: Concepts, process and practice*. Chichester: Wiley.

Cecchin, G. (1987). Hypothesizing, circularity and neutrality revisited: An invitation to curiosity. *Family Process, 26,* 405–413.

Cecchin, G., Lane, G. & Ray, W. (1994). *Irreverence: A strategy for therapist survival*. London: Karnac.

Clegg, J. & King, S. (2006). Supporting transitions. In S. Baum & H. Lynggaard (Eds.) *Intellectual disabilities: A systemic approach* (pp. 120–141). London: Karnac.

Department of Health (2001). *Valuing people: A new strategy for learning disability for the 21st century*. London: HMSO.

Department of Health (2002). *Valuing people: Towards person centred approaches*. London: HMSO.

Department of Health and Social Security (1971). *Better services for the mentally handicapped*. Cmnd 4683. London: HMSO.

Dixon, M. & Matthews, S. (1992). Learning difficulty in the family: Making systemic approaches relevant. *Clinical Psychology Forum, 39,* 17–21.

Donati, S., Glynn, B., Lynggaard, H. & Pearce, P. (2000). Systemic interventions in a learning disability service: An invitation to join. *Clinical Psychology Forum, 144,* 24–27.

Ekdawi, I., Gibbons, S., Bennett, E. & Hughes, G. (2000). *Whose reality is it anyway? Putting social constructionist philosophy into everyday clinical practice*. Brighton: Pavilion Publishing.

Fidell, B. (1996). Making family therapy user-friendly for learning disabled clients. *Context, 26,* 11–13.

Fredman, G. (2006). Working systemically with intellectual disability: Why not? In S. Baum & H. Lynggaard (Eds.) *Intellectual disabilities: A systemic approach* (pp. 1–20). London: Karnac.

Goldberg, D., Magrill, L., Hale., Damaskindou, K., Paul, J. & Tham, S. (1995). Protection and loss: Working with learning disabled adults and their families. *Journal of Family Therapy, 17,* 263–280.

Halliday, S. & Robbins, L. (2006). Lifespan family therapy services. In S. Baum & H. Lynggard (Eds.) *Intellectual disabilities: A systemic approach* (pp. 42–63). London: Karnac.

Jenkins, R. & Parry, R. (2006). Working with the support network: Applying systemic practice in learning disabilities services. *British Journal of Learning Disabilities, 34*(2), 77–81.

Lynggaard, H., Donati, S., Pearce, P. & Sklavounos, D. (2001). A difference that made a difference: Introducing systemic ideas and practices into a multidisciplinary learning disability service. *Clinical Psychology, 3,* 12–15.

McNamee, S. & Gergen, K. (1992). *Therapy as social construction*. Newbury Park, CA: Sage.

Morgan, A. (2000). *What is narrative therapy? An easy-to-read introduction*. Adelaide: Dulwich Centre Publications.

Pote, H. (2006). The practitioner's position in relation to systemic work in intellectual disability contexts. In S. Baum & H. Lynggaard (Eds.) *Intellectual disabilities: A systemic approach* (pp. 164–184). London: Karnac.

Reder, P. & Fredman, G. (1996). The relationship to help: Interacting beliefs about the treatment process. *Clinical Child Psychology and Psychiatry*, *1*(3), 457–467.

Rikberg Smyly, S. (2006). Who needs to change? Using systemic ideas when working in group homes. In S. Baum & H. Lynggaard (Eds.) *Intellectual disabilities: A systemic approach* (pp. 142–163). London: Karnac.

Rikberg Smyly, S., Elsworth, J., Mann, J. & Coates, E. (2009). *Working systemically in a learning disability service: What do colleagues and carers think?* Manuscript in preparation.

Rose, J., Simmons, S., Hughes, K. & Smith, M. (2001). Establishment and function of clinical psychology services for people with learning disabilities. *Clinical Psychology*, *5*, 9–12.

Scior, K. & Lynggaard, H. (2006). New stories of intellectual disabilities: A narrative approach. In S. Baum & H. Lynggaard (Eds.) *Intellectual disabilities: A systemic approach* (pp. 100–119). Karnac.

Sinason, V. (1992). *Mental handicap and the human condition: New approaches from the Tavistock*. London: Free Association Books.

Stenfert Kroese, B., Dagnan, D. & Loumidis, K. (Eds.) (1997). *Cognitive-behaviour therapy for people with learning disabilities*. London: Routledge.

Stratton, P. (2005). *Report on the evidence base of systemic family therapy* (pp. 1–25). Warrington: Association of Family Therapy.

Vetere, A. (1996). Soapbox: The neglect of family systems ideas in services for children and young people with learning difficulties. *Clinical Child Psychology and Psychiatry*, *1*, 485–488.

Waitman, A. & Conboy-Hill, S. (1992). *Psychotherapy and mental handicap*. London: Sage.

White, M. (1997). *Narratives of therapists' lives*. Adelaide: Dulwich Centre.

White, M. & Epstein, D. (1990). *Narrative means to therapeutic ends*. New York: W.W. Norton.

Wilcox, E. & Whittington, A. (2003). Discovering the use of narrative metaphors in work with people with learning disabilities. *Clinical Psychology*, *21*, 31–35.

15

Intensive Interaction for People with Profound and Complex Learning Disabilities

Judith Samuel

In this chapter intensive interaction is described within the historical context of interventions for people with profound and complex learning disabilities (PCLD). The evidence base is briefly outlined, current practice in one county in the UK is described and research and further directions are proposed.

Overview of Clinical Psychology Approaches for People with PCLD within an Historical Context

Within a British historical framework, support for people with PCLD may be viewed as underpinned by differing theoretical traditions based on models of early human development (biological, behavioural, cognitive and contextual) and on the principle of normalisation. In the early 20th century, the biological model prevailed. Instinctive behaviour patterns were seen as unfolding in a biologically determined age-related sequence, IQ was construed as a measure of fixed potential and support for people with PCLD comprised hospitalisation for containment rather than education or treatment.

The behavioural model views development primarily as response to events (cf. Pavlov, Watson, Skinner and Bandura). These approaches, initially exploring learning experimentally with animals in laboratories, were found to be effective with people with PCLD. By the 1950s the use of behavioural approaches transferred to more naturalistic settings and proliferated. Using functional analysis they have been applied both to skill acquisition and to the reduction of challenging behaviour.

The cognitive model views humans as active agents of their own development, occurring in qualitative stages in a non-random order that cannot be reduced to the passage of time (cf. Piaget). This model suggests that in learning disability any cognitive deficits are similar to those found within normal limits for a child, being present or absent in the usual sequence but developing much more slowly. This model has influenced assessment tools and curricula for people with PCLD.

The contextual model acknowledges innate maturational factors, uses reinforcement and contingency-awareness and construes the person as an active participant. Much psychological research has explored the micro-system of carer–infant interaction. In the dynamic mutually enjoyable social context of early life, both carer and infant initiate, maintain and respond contingently to each other's behaviour (i.e. vocalisation, facial expression, body proximity, gesture and physical contact) with imitation, turn-taking and joint attention. Initially carers impute intentionality and accept a wide range of actions and vocalisations as meaningful. Over time this acceptance narrows, thus offering experiences that provide a balance between the familiar and new to promote learning. In attachment terms, features of carers that provide this experience become internalised for the infant and serve as a secure base from which to explore and operate in the world.

A tenet of UK services from the 1970s based on Wolfensberger's principle of normalisation/social role valorisation (SRV) was that people with learning disability should be treated 'age appropriately'. This refers to 'social expectations, opportunities and experiences' typical for a particular chronological age within a specific culture (O'Brien & Tyne, 1981, p. 15). Albeit well-intentioned in terms of improving the social image of people with learning disability as well as upholding their legal and civil rights and especially contributing to de-institutionalisation, age appropriateness has sometimes led to neglect of their developmental/emotional needs (Nind & Hewett, 1996). Talking to someone as if they had the comprehension of a typically developed adult, and inferring from non-response that they have understood, has been reinforced by concern that to behave otherwise would be patronising. Carers have not always been aware of a developmental model and while SRV addresses the damaging effect of under-expectation and disadvantage, over-expectation also increases communication failure and exacerbates social withdrawal (Bartlett & Bunning, 1997). Furthermore, although social inclusion is promoted in general, it may in fact be considered better that the person with PCLD does not form close attachment with staff, who work shifts and are likely to eventually leave, resulting in grief to the person with PCLD and discomfort/guilt in the staff.

People with PCLD are often perceived as undemanding of emotional support albeit in receipt of a high degree of functional care (Samuel & Pritchard, 2001). Many can appear to be 'done to' without apparent complaint and otherwise left alone 'relaxing/watching TV'. They rarely present with behaviours that are a danger to others and by definition cannot benefit from talking therapies. Nonetheless, reasons for referral to clinical psychologists of people with PCLD have traditionally included self-injurious behaviour, face slapping or eye poking, etc., screaming or other noises that disturb others, sleep difficulties or public masturbation. Stereotypy (e.g. hand flapping or repeated manipulation of objects) may be a reason for referral because it adversely affects a person's social image and so became the target of behavioural reduction programmes. People with PCLD may also be viewed as socially withdrawn, tactile defensive and unmotivated, although as noted these problems would be unlikely to trigger a clinical psychology or psychiatry referral.

What is Intensive Interaction?

Intensive interaction (Nind & Hewett, 1988, 2005) is a transactional approach aimed at enhancing the responsiveness of carers, thus improving the communication and relationship skills of people with PCLD and thereby aiming to increase their social inclusion (Department of Health, 2001). It was developed from Ephraim's (1986) idea of 'augmented mothering' in an institutional school context where practitioners found the prevailing behavioural approaches inadequate to teach fundamental communication and social abilities (Nind & Hewett, 2005). Intensive interaction sensitively and respectfully applies a (Western) contextual model of early human development to people with PCLD whatever their age. Features that intensive interaction borrows from carer–infant interaction include (Nind, 1996):

- fostering mutual pleasure and interactive games;
- altering interpersonal behaviour to become more engaging and meaningful;
- making micro-adjustments to the flow of interactions with pauses, repetitions and blended rhythms;
- imputing intentionality to pre-communicative behaviours;
- using contingent responding.

It involves learning through the process rather than being goal-oriented.

Depending on aetiology, a person with PCLD may have an uneven profile of cognitive deficits exacerbated by neural dormancy or delayed maturation, sensory and physical impairments and emotional difficulties. Nevertheless, abilities in any given sub-domain are considered likely to follow the sequence of ordinary human development (Coupe O'Kane & Goldbart, 1998). People with PCLD have also had much longer than typically developing infants to embed repeated patterns of unusual behaviours (e.g. stereotypy or self-injury) as ways to reduce stress and shut out an unsafe external world as a consequence of unpredictability, trauma, pain or sensory hypersensitivity, or to provide interest in an otherwise under-stimulating environment. The person with PCLD may, for example, vocalise, frown, blow bubbles, rock, flick their fingers in front of their eyes, sigh, shake their head or tap an object against their leg. The interactive partner carefully observes this personal repertoire of behaviours and responsively mirrors an aspect of it (for example, taps in the same rhythm, imitates a sigh, leans towards, etc.). If the person with PCLD recognises what the interactive partner is doing as familiar, this is calming and enables them to shift attention from their inner world to the source outside themselves (Caldwell with Horwood, 2007). A genuine emotional connection is therefore made. Contingent elaboration, turning taking and joint attention follow in a non-verbal conversation (Caldwell & Stevens, 2005; Barber, 2007). McIntosh and Whittaker (2000, p. 20) quote a mother as saying 'I used to have a child who I had to care for, now I have a person I can chat to all the time'. As rapport builds, the opportunity for increased learning and engagement in other areas of life occurs (Nind & Hewett, 1988, 2005). Intensive interaction differs from intuitive early parenting, however, in the attention given to teamwork, planning, monitoring and reflection. Nevertheless, it is possible that early childhood circumstances were detrimental for some people with PCLD. There is much literature on the stress of caring for a child with disabilities, where minimal or unusual social signalling and slow progress may be unrewarding. The negative impact of (early) institutionalisation is also well known.

Who is Intensive Interaction for?

Intensive interaction is used with people with PCLD who do not seem to appreciate human company and/or who spend much time 'relaxing/watching TV' or where a formulation about challenging behaviour indicates the presence of extensive communication difficulties. Intensive interaction is also used with people with severe learning disability compounded by autistic spectrum disorder (ASD) (Nind, 1999; Caldwell, 2002). People with ASD find it hard to engage socially, but may have a range of more highly developed competencies in other domains (such as self-care, mobility, functional academic skill, etc.). They may also have problems with sensory integration or sensory hypersensitivities and emotional regulation. It has been suggested that if one incoming modality, for example, speech, is reduced this may leave space for the individual to attend to another: i.e. emotional connection (Caldwell with Horwood, 2007). Intensive interaction is also useful for people with profound physical disability who may have relatively better functional communication (e.g. by eye-pointing) but have no opportunity for spontaneous playful conversation (Caldwell & Stephens, 2005).

Evidence Base

Evidence for the efficacy of intensive interaction is accumulating, although the heterogeneity of people with PCLD weakens any claim to generalisation, and studies are context bound. Studies vary in the robustness of their design, participant and setting characteristics, practitioner characteristics and expertise, intervention duration, frequency and content. The larger studies have also used a quasi-experimental design which, although ethically more sound, is empirically less rigorous.

Using a multiple-baseline across participants interrupted time-series, Nind (1996) evaluated intensive interaction with three men and three women, aged 27–36 years, who were institutionalised. The skilled practitioners (teachers who knew the participants well) conducted twice-daily sessions for 12–18 months. Participants showed new behaviours that effectively encouraged others to be with them and a trend towards a reduction in stereotypy; time spent in interactive social behaviour also increased.

Lovell *et al.*'s (1998) short-term single-case study used an external skilled practitioner with a 53-year-old institutionalised man in a context where intensive interaction was unfamiliar. The alternating treatment design (five-minute intensive interaction sessions and five minutes of 'proximity' over three days in a single week) found increased frequency of initiating physical contact, looking at people, joint attention, smiling/laughing and vocalising in both conditions, but greater for intensive interaction. Initial success was, however, not subsequently transferred to novice staff. Elgie and Maguire's (2001) single-case study with a 39-year-old blind woman with self-injurious behaviour in a community residential setting showed an increase in spontaneous hand contact and vocalisation during 16 weekly sessions, but no change in self-injurious behaviour.

In Oxfordshire where intensive interaction was emerging practice, Samuel and colleagues (Samuel & Maggs, 1998; Samuel, 2001a & b; Samuel, 2003; Samuel et al., 2008) carried out an intervention study in the community homes of four people with PCLD. It was hypothesised that 12 support staff who were novice practitioners could learn the principles of intensive interaction sufficiently to have a positive impact on the participants' abilities (during five sessions per week over 20 weeks) and that they would also experience a better relationship. Based on Nind's (1993) design, data were collected via video observations, assessment schedules and staff questionnaires. Although fewer sessions were recorded and practitioner reflection did not occur as formally as requested, practitioners learned to use mirroring and contingent responding, and participants' abilities developed to look at faces and become engaged in interaction and joint focus. Improved quality of relationships was noted, although the evidence for this was not robust.

Leaning and Watson's (2006) study of five people with PCLD found that a number of interactive behaviours increased from baseline during an eight-week day service 'intensive interaction group' and then reduced at follow-up.

Research with children includes Watson's (1994; Watson & Knight, 1991) study of six staff–pupil pairs aged 10–19 throughout a school year, which found enhanced development, and Kellett's (2001; Kellett & Nind, 2003) replication of Nind (1993). Kellett studied six children aged 4–11 years interacting with novice practitioners (three teachers and three learning support assistants) who knew the participants. All the participants developed their communication and social abilities, highlighting features of the service context required for sustaining effective practice.

Service Delivery

Availability of intensive interaction

Published resources now include a Practical Guide (Nind & Hewett, 2001) and training DVDs (Caldwell, 2002; Caldwell & Stevens 2005; Hewett, 2006); consequently, carers and support staff are able to try using intensive interaction principles in a range of settings whether or not they have access to formal training, supervision and support. Nevertheless, it can be useful to have external clinical input from a learning disability team or an experienced peer facilitator. This practitioner then works in partnership with carers who have volunteered to use the principles too, and who are able to sustain practice. Of course, the decision for a person with PCLD to see a clinician, and any subsequent assessment, intervention and monitoring (e.g. video recording), would need to be made in their best interests. The reason for referral might be challenging behaviour or, where resources permit, for proactive input (Samuel & Pritchard, 2001).

Training, reflection and supervision

Ideally, all carers supporting someone for whom intensive interaction is deemed appropriate should have access to training. Within Oxfordshire from 1996, there was over a decade of one-day introductory training workshops facilitated by Melanie Nind. These were targeted at those care staff whose manager had also had the training. Some follow-up training was also given and some training has been accessed by family carers. Subsequently, to aid sustainability, a group of 11 support staff from different agencies have been trained by Cath Irvine as peer facilitators (trainers and mentors) and have been given dedicated time to fulfil this role. This is based on a model she introduced in Somerset and replicated in Oldham and Brighton (www.intensiveinteraction.co.uk). Together with service managers and local clinicians the facilitators have developed a self-learning training pack for new starters, a one-day introductory training course for carers and an advanced practitioner course. These learning opportunities are in line with competencies required for UK qualifications for support staff.

It is also essential that practitioners have time to reflect and to receive adequate supervision that focuses on process, attachment issues and endings. Some Oxfordshire practitioners have met regularly for peer support (Nind & Hewett, 2001 p. 90). Attendance fluctuated and finding a mutually convenient time presented challenges. A more action-learning focus linked to in-service qualifications is now being tested. Elsewhere innovative forms of peer support with or without services users present have been tried. For example, an interactive café in Leeds (*Intensive Interaction Newsletter*, Winter 2005/6 Issue 14, p. 5) and a special interest group in Nottingham (www.intensiveinteraction.co.uk).

Sessions versus everyday interactions

Carers sometimes suggest that the use of intensive interaction principles during everyday encounters is preferable to sessions or indeed claim 'we do it all the time'. While, if true, this is the ideal, nevertheless, having planned sessions enables both interactive partners to have dedicated learning time. The practitioner also needs time to reflect. If the principles are only used informally without planning or monitoring there is a risk of inadequate practitioner skill, challenge about appropriateness, subtle progress may go unnoticed or use may diminish due to competing demands.

Where sessions are used there has been no prescribed number, frequency or duration. Indeed, rapport may be enhanced immediately with the reintroduction of historically preferred rhymes or games, which is not indicative of new learning but rather of a more responsive social environment. However, this is not always the case, and patience is likely to be required over many (brief) sessions.

Monitoring

Video recording is an essential tool for reflective practice. The person's response to filming is noted and discontinued if they object. For someone who has sight, Hewett

(2006) suggests trying filming with the camera connected to the TV or turning around the viewfinder so that they can see themselves. For some carers, being filmed can be extremely daunting at first. A reflective compassionate approach is essential as any practitioner is a learner too. An edited video or DVD is an extremely useful teaching resource and the finished product can become part of someone's person-centred plan, enabling new carers to learn more quickly how to interact.

Determining a way of describing session content both to record what occurs and to prompt new ideas for the team is necessary. For carers overburdened by paperwork, new styles of monitoring may be initially greeted with enthusiasm and then completion wanes (Samuel, 2003). Nind and Hewett (2001, pp. 104–108) offer two styles of session forms containing reflective prompts to the practitioner such as 'How did it feel (my response and performance)?' A checklist of possible content is also a useful reminder of both the principles and preferred games or sequences.

How many practitioners?

Where person-centred support teams are created, all members can be employed, trained and supported to use intensive interaction where appropriate. However, in existing and larger teams, intensive interaction may be better introduced via a volunteer sub-team of three or four carers who are willing to experiment with using the principles, together with an external practitioner/facilitator, thus aiding sustainability.

Assessing the appropriateness for intensive interaction

When the use of intensive interaction is being considered it is important to gather information from carers and notes about history and previous best developmental levels (for example, for an adult this might have been at school, if subsequent support has been minimal). Useful assessment tools of present functioning include Kiernan and Reid (1987); Sparrow *et al.* (1984); The Physical Sociability Scale (Kellett, 2001 after Nind, 1996) and of practitioner behaviour: Clark and Seifer (1983). A functional analysis of any challenging behaviour should be completed. It is essential to know how the individual expresses a range of emotions and pain and especially how they show they might want contact to stop (Coupe O'Kane & Goldbart, 1998). Spending time observing the person in the most appropriate context (e.g. home, education, health/social care setting) includes assessment of the environment and what circumstances: location, ambience, time of day, position, sensory modalities, etc., are preferred. The interaction of familiar carers with the person should also be observed, and only then should intensive interaction principles be tentatively tried and reflections shared.

Touch

Intensive interaction usually involves some degree of physical touch. This raises ethical concerns as any touch may be misconstrued for cultural or other reasons as abuse or there may be anxiety that it might provoke sexual arousal. Hewett (2007) cites seminal ethnological research about the crucial role of touch in primate development. Functional touch is an inevitable everyday experience of people with PCLD for intimate and personal care yet otherwise they can seem 'untouched'. They are often strapped into wheelchairs or other equipment which creates a physical barrier to proximity. They may be unable to cuddle up next to someone on a sofa, may be construed as too fragile or their unyielding stiffness experienced by carers as unrewarding. It is essential that services develop guidelines about the use of touch. Hewett (2007, p. 121) outlines eight safeguards:

- Know why you do it.
- Have consent from the person.
- Be prepared to discuss and explain your practices.
- Document – have it acknowledged in the school curriculum or workplace brochure.
- Document – have it acknowledged in any individual programme for the person.
- Have good teamwork, both organisational and emotional.
- Use of physical contact should be discussed openly and regularly.
- Have other people present where possible.

Sustainability

Service management endorsement is essential for intensive interaction. In Oxfordshire, practice guidelines have been written. Where over-stretched carers are employed to attend to basic care needs, sitting next to someone waiting patiently for them to initiate a sound or movement which you then mirror may not be perceived as 'work' by yourself or colleagues. Where an external practitioner involvement is time-limited it is essential that attention is paid to generalisation. For children, intensive interaction is described as 'a therapeutic treatment' by the Qualifications and Curriculum Authority (www.qca.org.uk/qca_1833.aspx, accessed 26 September 2007). For adults, the use of intensive interaction needs to be written into an individual's care plan as commissioned by a local authority care manager. Its use within services for people with PCLD should also be subject to external scrutiny by quality-monitoring officers and Commission for Social Care inspectors.

Research and Future Directions

The transactional nature of intensive interaction presents challenges for empirical investigation. The use of insufficiently skilled practitioners has reduced intervention fidelity. There needs to be improvement in the quality of training and supervision. Accreditation for facilitators/coordinators now exists via The Intensive Interaction Institute (www.intensiveinteraction.co.uk). Longitudinal follow-up and evaluation of any generalisation to other carers and wider social contacts would be timely. Research that compares intensive interaction across settings and with other interventions is important, though it presents significant implementation difficulties. Sustainability in services is an emerging theme both in terms of research (e.g. Firth *et al.*, 2007) and policy (e.g. Kellett & Nind, 2003; Hewett, 2007). Use with other client groups is also occurring. For example, intensive interaction principles are being applied with people with dementia (Astell & Ellis, 2006), and Caldwell with Horwood (2007, p. 138) poignantly describes their use when visiting a friend with dementia:

> She no longer recognised me. Her fingers were scratching her bedclothes. When I scratched the same rhythm on her sheet, she paused and attended. It may not sound much but for us even though her cognitive faculties had perished, we were able to rejoin each other in affect, through an imitative act that was meaningful to both of us … fleetingly it brought us together again, meeting for the last time.

Pioneering neuropsychological research is also exploring the possibility of dysfunctional mirror neuron systems affecting the ability of people with ASD to imitate, and suggests that such people have missing or disorganised connections between the limbic system and the rest of the brain, leading to extreme emotional responses (Ramachandran & Oberman, 2006). It will be interesting to see whether intensive interaction can be found to activate dormant neural systems or alter neural connections in a functionally useful way for all the client groups mentioned here.

Acknowledgements

Thanks to the service users from whom I have learnt so much. Thanks to the Oxfordshire support staff, families, assistant psychologists and trainee clinical psychologists who have contributed to service development, audit and research. Thanks especially to Melanie Nind for her inspiration, teaching and supervision and to Cath Irvine for her significant contribution to enhancing sustainability within the county.

References

Astell, A.J. & Ellis, M.P. (2006). The social functioning of imitation in severe dementia. *Infant and Child Development, 15,* 211–319.

Barber, M. (2007). Imitation interaction and dialogue using intensive interaction: Tea party rules. *Support for Learning, 22*(3), 124–130.

Bartlett, C. & Bunning, K. (1997). The importance of communication partnerships: A study to investigate the communicative exchanges between staff and adults with learning disabilities. *British Journal of Learning Disability, 25,* 148–152.

Caldwell, P. (2002). *Learning the language.* Brighton: Pavilion Publishing [DVD].

Caldwell, P. & Stevens, P. (2005). *Creative conversations.* Brighton: Pavilion Publishing [DVD].

Caldwell, P. with Horwood, J. (2007). From isolation to intimacy: Making friends without words. London: Jessica Kingsley.

Clark, G.N. & Seifer, R. (1983). Facilitating mother–infant communication: A treatment model for high-risk and developmentally delayed infants. *Infant Mental Health Journal, 4*(2), 67–82.

Coupe O'Kane, J. & Goldbart, J. (1998). *Communication before speech: Development and assessment* (2nd edn). London: David Fulton.

Department of Health (2001). *Valuing people: A new strategy for learning disability in the 21st century.* London: The Stationery Office.

Elgie, S. & Maguire, N. (2001). Intensive interaction with a woman with multiple and profound disabilities: A case study. *Tizard Learning Disability Review, 6*(3), 18–24.

Ephraim, G.W. (1986). *A brief introduction to augmented mothering.* Playtrac Pamphlet, Harperbury Hospital, Radlett, Herts.

Firth, G., Elford, H., Leeming, C. & Crabbe, M. (2007). Intensive interaction as a novel approach in social care: Care staff's views on the practice change process. *Journal of Applied Research in Intellectual Disabilities* (online published article 30 June 2007).

Hewett, D. (2006). Intensive interaction. DVD available from www.davehewett.com/dvd.php, retrieved 24 February 2009.

Hewett, D. (2007). Do touch. Physical contact and people who have severe profound and multiple learning difficulties. *Support for Learning, 22*(3), 116–122.

Kellett, M.C. (2001). *Implementing intensive interaction: An evaluation of its efficacy and of factors influencing its implementation in community special schools with young children who have severe learning difficulties.* Unpublished PhD thesis, Oxford Brookes University.

Kellett, M. & Nind, M. (2003). Implementing intensive interaction in schools: Guidance for practitioners, managers and coordinators. London: David Fulton.

Kiernan, C. & Reid, B. (1987). *Pre-Verbal Communication Schedule.* Windsor: NFER Nelson.

Leaning, B. & Watson, T. (2006). From the inside looking out – an intensive interaction group for people with profound and multiple learning disabilities. *British Journal of Learning Disabilities, 24,* 103–109.

Lovell, D.M., Jones, S.P. & Ephraim, G. (1998). The effect of intensive interaction on the sociability of a man with severe intellectual disabilities. *International Journal of Practical approaches to Disability, 22*(2/3), 3–9.

McIntosh, B. & Whittaker, A. (2000). *Unlocking the future.* London: King's Fund.

Nind, M. (1993). *Access to communication: Efficacy of intensive interaction teaching for people with severe developmental disabilities who demonstrate ritualistic behaviours.* Unpublished PhD Thesis, Institute of Education, Cambridge.

Nind, M. (1996). Efficacy of intensive interaction. *European Journal of Special Needs Education, 11,* 48–66.

Nind, M. (1999). Intensive interaction and autism, is it a useful approach? *British Journal of Special Education, 26*(2), 96–102.

Nind, M. & Hewett, D. (1988). Interaction as curriculum. *British Journal of Special Education, 15*(2), 55–57.

Nind, M. & Hewett, D. (1996). When age-appropriateness isn't appropriate. In J. Coupe O'Kane & J. Goldbart (Eds.) *Whose choice? Contentious issues for those working with people with learning difficulties* (pp. 48–57). London: David Fulton.

Nind, M. & Hewett, D. (2001). *A practical guide to intensive interaction.* Kidderminster: British Institute of Learning Disabilities.

Nind, M. & Hewett, D. (2005). *Access to communication: Developing the basics of communication in people with severe learning difficulties through intensive interaction* (2nd edn). London: David Fulton.

O'Brien, J. & Tyne, A. (1981). *The principle of normalisation: A foundation for effective services.* London: The Campaign for Mentally Handicapped People.

Ramachandran, V.S. & Oberman, L.M. (2006). Broken mirrors, a theory of autism. *Scientific American*, 295(5), 39–45.

Samuel, J. (2001a). Intensive interaction. *Clinical Psychology Forum, 148*, 22–25.

Samuel, J. (2001b). Intensive interaction in context. *Tizard Learning Disability Review, 6(3)*, 25–30.

Samuel, J. (2003). *Intensive interaction in community living settings for adults with profound learning disability*. Dissertation submitted in part fulfilment of the Open University Validation Service/British Psychological Society Doctorate in Clinical Psychology (admission with academic credit).

Samuel, J. & Maggs, J. (1998). Introducing intensive interaction for people with profound learning disabilities living in small staffed houses in the community. In D. Hewett & M. Nind (Eds.) *Interaction in action: Reflections on the use of intensive interaction* (pp. 119–148). London: David Fulton.

Samuel, J., Nind, M., Volans, A. & Scriven, I. (2008). An evaluation of intensive interaction in community living settings for adults with profound intellectual disabilities. *Journal of Intellectual Disability, 12(2)*, 111–126.

Samuel, J. & Pritchard, M. (2001). The ignored minority: Meeting the needs of people with profound learning disability. *Tizard Learning Disability Review, 6(2)*, 34–44.

Sparrow, S.S., Balla, D.A. & Cicchetti, D.V. (1984). *Vineland Adaptive Behaviour Scales* (expanded version). Circle Pines, MN: American Guidance Service.

Watson, J. (1994). Using intensive interaction in the education of pupils with profound multiple learning difficulties: Two case studies. In J. Ware (Ed.) *Educating children with profound and multiple learning difficulties* (pp. 115–159). London: David Fulton.

Watson, J. & Knight, C. (1991). An evaluation of intensive interaction teaching with pupils with very severe learning difficulties. *Child Language Teaching and Therapy, 7(3)*, 310–325.

3

Working with Adults with Mental Health Problems through the Lifespan

16

Early Intervention in Psychosis

Paul Flecknoe and Stefan Schuller

Overview and Scope of Chapter

Early intervention (EI) in psychosis is an approach which emphasises early detection of psychosis, leading to treatment using intensive biopsychosocial interventions, during the first 3–5 years following a client first experiencing distressing symptoms. This is considered to be a critical period during which there is a unique opportunity to prevent longer-term deterioration for the client and their family, and thereby to improve long-term outcomes.

This new paradigm is in contrast to the more traditional, pessimistic view of psychosis as a gradually deteriorating brain disease, expected to lead to a long-term pattern of disability and distress. The new approach was pioneered initially in Australia (McGorry et al., 1995, 1996) and then in the UK (Birchwood, 1995; Birchwood & Wells, 1992) during the 1990s. Currently, the National Service Framework Policy Implementation Guide in the UK recommends that EI services should be available to all young people (aged 14 to 35) who experience psychosis for the first time, and dedicated teams have rapidly been set up to implement this policy across the UK.

EI is an approach which requires collaboration from a wide range of professionals, and is widely agreed to include the following key elements:

- early detection and intervention for psychotic symptoms;
- a focus on sustained and meaningful therapeutic engagement;
- therapeutic optimism and the promotion of a hopeful attitude;
- the offer of a range of interventions, including psychological, medical, social and vocational;
- low-dose pharmacological treatment based on best practice guidelines;
- a family-focused approach, with active engagement, support and involvement for families and other members of the person's social network;

- a focus on recovery and meaningful goals for the client and their family beyond the remission of psychotic symptoms;
- support to work on difficulties as well as psychosis, such as low self-esteem, trauma, depression, etc.;
- assisting the client to seek meaningful activity and supporting them in returning to a valued vocational role.

The main focus of this chapter will be to consider the role of the clinical psychologist in providing the EI approach. In many areas this takes place within dedicated EI teams, but in some cases intervention is provided from within existing community mental health teams, perhaps with some dedicated workers. Clients are usually discharged from the dedicated teams after 2–3 years, and a significant proportion of these may need further support from other mental health providers. This chapter will therefore consider the role of the clinical psychologist working both within specialist EI teams and also as part of a more generalist role.

Clinical Psychologists Working in Early Intervention Teams

Psychological interventions are recognised as a key component of the early intervention paradigm, and as such almost all dedicated EI teams include a clinical psychologist. The British Psychological Society Briefing Paper on the role of the clinical psychologist in EI teams (British Psychological Society/Division of Clinical Psychology, 2005) states that '… a clinical psychologist is an essential part of the core team', and makes a number of recommendations about their role, summarised in Box 16.1.

In practice, the role can vary considerably, from being the clinical lead for the whole service to being employed as a single, part-time member of the team. Ideally, the structure of the team will mean that the psychologist has significant input into the overall leadership and management of the team as well as providing specialised clinical input. However, this is not the case in every service, and in some instances recently qualified clinical psychologists are working as single, part-time members of a team, without a clear mandate to participate in broader strategic developments. As noted, it is important for clinical psychologists working in EI teams to retain their professional links with other psychologists. This helps them to maintain a sense of professional identity, as well as providing opportunities for continued CPD and cross-fertilisation with those working in other specialities.

Key Issues

The nature of psychosis

A crucial dilemma is how EI psychologists conceptualise psychosis and how this might relate to beliefs in the broader team environment. Clinical psychologists are increasingly

Box 16.1

- EI services are based on a biopsychosocial model, and the use of a formulation-driven approach. This increase in emphasis on psychological approaches over more traditional approaches makes a clinical psychologist an essential part of the core team. The role should include supporting the team in maintaining a more engaging and accessible ethos and identity than in traditional services.
- For clinical psychologists to make the maximum contribution to the service, they need to be based within the core team, but arrangements must be in place to ensure they retain their professional links with psychologists in other parts of the wider service.
- Clinical psychologists bring a unique breadth and depth of theory-based knowledge about psychological interventions to EI services. Other team members trained specifically in psychosocial interventions should complement, not replace, clinical psychologists. The potential range and complexity of the clinical psychologist's role suggests that an experienced and autonomous practitioner (consultant) should be recruited, especially where they are the only psychologist.
- EI is an evolving area and clinical psychologists have a key role and the necessary skills to contribute to both research and service development.

seeing psychosis as existing on a continuum with normal experience, and therefore conceptualising it as an exaggeration or extension of normal psychological processes (British Psychological Society, 2000). In addition, most psychological approaches to psychosis are based on the underlying assumption that the experiences are meaningful and can be made sense of when the client is understood in the context of their life experiences and current circumstances. Currently, many psychologists base their research, theoretical models and treatment approaches on the study of individual 'symptoms' such as hearing voices or holding so-called delusional beliefs, arguing that more specific diagnoses such as 'schizophrenia' are of limited utility, and that the concept of psychosis itself is a fairly crude umbrella term for a wide range of different experiences (Bentall, 1990, 2003).

These conceptual approaches to psychosis are in stark contrast to the more conventional medical view of psychosis as an illness or brain disease. While the EI paradigm emphasises the importance of a range of treatment approaches, and acknowledges that psychosis can be triggered off or worsened by stress, and that it can be ameliorated through psychological and social interventions as well as medical ones, the underlying understanding of psychosis is nevertheless primarily medical. As such, the initial diagnosis of psychosis is seen as a temporary state of affairs, until the underlying 'disease' such as schizophrenia or schizo-affective disorder can be correctly diagnosed. Since the experiences of the client are viewed as symptoms of an underlying illness, the idiosyncratic meaning of these experiences can be overlooked and the client encouraged to externalise their experiences as an illness, rather than try to make sense of them and integrate them. While team members often welcome psychological interventions as another treatment avenue to help clients recover, sharing psychological formulations or developing shared treatment strategies can sometimes prove to be a challenge.

The assertive outreach model

Another key issue for clinical psychologists working in EI teams is the interface between the role of the psychologist and the assertive outreach model of engagement often utilised by teams. This assertive outreach model encourages workers to engage flexibly with clients, so that team members will gently persist in delivering a service even to clients who initially may be very reluctant to engage. Strategies include meeting the person in an informal setting where they feel comfortable and engaging with them on the issues that are most important to them, even if these are not directly related to their mental health issues.

This raises some important issues for clinical psychologists working in this setting in terms of how much the psychologist directly adopts this style of working. The benefits of working flexibly and being prepared to meet clients in a range of settings need to be balanced with the need to maintain appropriate therapeutic boundaries and to maintain a distinctive role in the wider team. In practice it can be helpful to offer to meet clients for a period of 'pre-therapy' during which some assertive outreach principles can be employed to engage the client and to offer information about psychological interventions. However, this should be considered as part of a process that enables the client to make an informed choice about whether or not to engage in a more formal psychological intervention. While some flexibility can still be employed at this stage, in terms of the venue and timing of sessions, it is important the psychological interventions are offered as a discrete intervention, and that appropriate therapeutic boundaries are maintained.

Competencies for clinical psychologists in EI teams

The core skills provided by clinical psychology training will go a long way towards equipping most clinical psychologists to work in EI teams, with appropriate support and supervision. Working with clients during their adolescence and early adulthood is assisted by clinical psychologists having undertaken training placements with children and adolescents as well as in adult mental health. Additionally, the breadth of training can be as asset where presentations are often complex, since many clients have difficulties in addition to psychosis. Clinical psychologists are trained in a range of therapeutic approaches, many of which are applicable to this population. While these require some adaptation for work with clients experiencing psychosis, psychologists who are unfamiliar with working with psychosis often find that their core skills are more applicable that they might have imagined.

In terms of more specialist skills, some psychologists may have acquired significant experience in working with people experiencing psychosis during their training, since working with psychosis is increasingly being seen as a core component of adult mental health practice rather than purely a specialised area. It is important to have knowledge of the theoretical ideas and research relevant to psychotic experiences, as well as some ideas about how existing intervention skills may need adapting for this client population. In EI, family interventions are far more commonplace than in adult mental health settings, and therefore family intervention skills are also a key specialist competency (see also Chapter 17). Some psychologists may choose to develop their skills by undertaking specialised further training in cognitive therapy for psychosis, behavioural family therapy training, or systemic training.

Interventions Offered in EI Teams

Engagement

Considerable emphasis is placed on engaging the client and their family in EI teams, which aim to work creatively to try and achieve this. Disengagement is not normally seen as a reason to discharge clients, and teams endeavour to actively engage clients who would often be discharged in other service settings. Clinical psychologists working in EI teams also need to attend carefully to engaging clients in therapeutic work, and be prepared to take a very patient, persistent and flexible approach. As mentioned previously, a period of 'pre-therapy' can also be helpful. Where clients or families are reluctant to engage, psychologists may be able to assist the team to conceptualise engagement patterns and reflect from a psychological point of view on the possible meanings of disengagement. Offering psychological frameworks for understanding psychosis can also help with engaging clients who are alienated by the medical account of psychosis.

Assessment

EI teams encourage referrals that reflect some diagnostic uncertainty where the referrer may be unsure whether or not the client's difficulties are best described by the term psychosis. As such, all EI teams need an operational definition and clear assessment protocols to help guide their decision about which clients to accept into the team. Clinical psychologists may assist the EI team to systematise assessment protocols, and may support other team members to make use of structured assessments to guide clinical decision making. In cases where the clinical presentation is complex or confusing, the clinical psychologist can often help with making sense of the presentation by drawing on a broad knowledge of different kinds of clinical presentations (e.g. autistic spectrum difficulties, personality difficulties). Sometimes using psychometric tests, such as the WAIS-III (Wechsler, 1997) or MMPI-2 (Butcher et al., 1989), that relate to personality or cognitive functioning can also help clarify the presenting picture.

When working in a therapeutic role, assessment often involves helping the person work through and describe their own experiences of psychosis and psychiatric care and relate this to their own life story. There are a range of idiosyncratic measures that relate to specific psychotic experiences (e.g. Beliefs about Voices Questionnaire; Chadwick *et al.*, 2000) that can also be clinically useful when undertaking therapeutic assessments.

Formulation and making sense of psychotic experiences

Developing psychological formulations and helping the client, team, and families make psychological sense of psychotic experiences is arguably one of the most important and distinctive contributions. While this draws on the generic formulation skills of clinical psychologists, it is also important to have specialist knowledge of the increasing array of theories and psychological models of the development and maintenance of distressing psychotic experiences. Examples of relevant models include adapted cognitive models of psychosis as a whole (e.g. Fowler, 2002; Garety *et al.*, 2001), theories about the links between trauma and psychosis (e.g. Morrison *et al.*, 2003; Read *et al.*, 2005), and cognitive-interpersonal approaches to preventing relapse (Gumley & Schwannauer, 2006).

In working individually with people who experience psychosis, formulation can function as an important intervention in itself, as it can offer an alternative way to understand unusual and frightening experiences. Developmental formulations can also help the client integrate their experience of psychosis into their wider life story and to develop a more coherent narrative about the experience. Psychological formulations offer a different explanation for psychosis for clients who do not readily engage with a more medical model and can assist with promoting a more flexible approach to engagement.

Interventions

While there are a range of different psychological interventions recommended for working with this client group, it is important to emphasise the importance of establishing a sound therapeutic relationship and the 'common factors' in undertaking individual therapy. Clients often report that not many people find it easy to tolerate listening to the experiences and beliefs associated with psychosis without becoming distressed or trying to reassure them or disprove their beliefs. Often clients feel ashamed about discussing some of their psychotic experiences retrospectively and doubtful about whether or not others will be able to understand or empathise with their experiences. Taking time to develop a trusting relationship where the person feels their experiences will be taken seriously can be a powerful intervention in itself.

In terms of more formalised interventions, both the Policy Implementation Guide (Department of Health, 2001a) and the NICE Guidelines for Schizophrenia (National Institute for Health and Clinical Excellence, 2002) recommend that both cognitive therapy and family interventions should be made routinely available for EI clients and their families. Cognitive therapy interventions can be offered both for distressing psychotic symptoms and for comorbid or secondary difficulties such as depression, social anxiety, low self-esteem, and trauma. The NICE guidelines particularly recommend that cognitive behavioural therapy (CBT) is considered when the client has not fully responded to a range of anti-psychotic drug treatments, and this is reflected in some services where cognitive therapy is routinely offered to patients who have ongoing residual psychotic symptoms. Family interventions are not prescribed too precisely by the existing guidelines, and services are increasingly recognising the need to offer a range of approaches. Currently there are examples of services offering behavioural family therapy, systemic family therapy, and approaches which blend aspects of both (e.g. Burbach & Stanbridge, 1998). Clinical psychologists in teams are often referred complex family situations to work with, where there may be difficulties which pre-date the family member's experience of psychosis. It is important that psychologists working in this setting have the experience and skills to work therapeutically with families as this is a significant clinical demand in this area, possibly in contrast to more traditional adult mental health psychology roles.

It is also important to consider the developmental context when undertaking psychological interventions with EI clients. Many of the people seen in EI began to experience psychosis during adolescence, and significant developmental tasks may have been interrupted by the experience of psychosis. In many cases, the negotiation of developmental tasks proved stressful for the client and may have contributed to the onset of psychosis. Clinical work thus often takes place against a backdrop of developmental issues such as separation, the development of identity and the negotiation of peer relationships. These are often then complicated by the experience of psychosis, and introduce issues such as stigma and dilemmas about how to reintegrate with peers following an episode of psychosis.

Group interventions can also be extremely useful with this client group, and provide a powerful opportunity to connect with other people who have had similar experiences. This can be especially effective in reducing the sense of shame, stigma and isolation that people often carry following an episode of psychosis. Group interventions can also provide an opportunity to share ideas about coping with psychotic experiences, and help people consider ways to approach some of the issues associated with social reintegration following a psychotic episode.

While formal guidelines tend to prescribe particular therapeutic approaches, the complex nature of many EI cases means that the clinical psychologist's distinctive contribution can be the ability to develop idiosyncratic formulations and intervention plans based on a broad practical and theoretical knowledge of different therapeutic models. In practice, many EI clinical psychologists draw on a range of models, and work flexibly to tailor their interventions to the needs of the client of family that they are working with.

Consultation, supervision and teaching

The clinical psychologist in EI teams also has a vital role as a core team member in ensuring that the team includes a psychological perspective in its overall philosophy and interventions. If there is only one psychologist in the team, it is helpful if the post is at a senior grade and that this person is able to exert some influence on overall team development. In practice, this indirect work may be undertaken in a wide variety of ways. In terms of consultation, the clinical psychologist can perform a valuable role in helping other team members conceptualise difficult clinical dilemmas and presentations that guide their care planning and approach as a care coordinator. For some team members, this may take the form of regular clinical supervision individually or in groups. For teams where there are other team members trained in specific therapies, the clinical psychologist will often be asked to provide supervision and support for that person to develop their skills.

In many teams, psychologists can contribute usefully in a teaching role. Sharing information about psychological models and research evidence that is relevant to the client group can be useful, as well as providing direct training on intervention packages which the whole team can deliver, such as relapse prevention.

It can also be useful to offer consultation specifically around family and systemic dilemmas, and where the clinical psychologist has some systemic training this can be offered as an internal consultation service. Team members often find this helpful in terms of having a chance to reflect and make sense of family dynamics, as well as being able to consider their own position as a worker in the wider system.

Research and evaluation

Like other services, EI services are increasingly under scrutiny to demonstrate their effectiveness and superiority over a more generic approach. Clinical psychologists are often approached to assist the team with evaluation and research initiatives. If the EI team is participating in a national evaluation project (such as the First Episode Research Network, FERN) then clinical psychologists may take a lead role in helping teams implement the research protocols.

Working in an EI team also can provide the opportunity to expand the research base of this relatively new intervention paradigm. There are numerous opportunities to initiate or supervise research projects which explore more specific aspects of the experience of first-episode psychosis and the developing approaches to its treatment.

Clinical Psychologists Working outside EI Teams

Services with no specific EI provision

In services where there is not (yet) any dedicated EI provision, there is not normally a mandate to address the needs of people who present with recent onset psychotic symptoms, let alone the needs of people who appear to be at high risk of developing such symptoms. However, psychologists working in more generic services should keep themselves up to date if only for their own professional development, and whenever possible, carry out work with 'at risk' young people or with recent-onset service users who would arguably benefit from EI provision. This includes indirect work via promotion of awareness of these issues during multidisciplinary care planning and primary care liaison meetings, as well as direct work which can include co-constructing and sharing psychological problem formulations with the service user and the wider care network where appropriate. This can include recovery formulations, stating concrete, positive therapy targets and specifying, for example, how vicious cycles may be replaced with more virtuous cycles. Opportunities regularly crop up when talking to colleagues, service users, their friends and carers, siblings, teachers, etc. to correct misconceptions and to portray positive images of people who have achieved a good level of recovery following the experience of distressing psychotic symptoms.

As noted above, clinical psychologists are well placed to initiate and carry out relevant audits, identifying strengths and weaknesses in local service provision for people with recent-onset psychosis. They can then lobby for the improvements in such provision, and can make a positive contribution to subsequent service development. As ever, this benefits from good working relationships with other colleagues in statutory and non-statutory services as well as with local service users and carers. Inviting speakers who have experience of EI work, or arranging local clinician and service user visits to EI services where provision is in keeping with national guidelines, can enthuse people and helps to sustain the momentum when the pace of local change is frustratingly slow.

It has been argued that a high-fidelity EI approach, in terms of its value base and recovery orientation, stands a better chance of being maintained in a dedicated EI service rather than within a 'hub and spoke' model or having a small dedicated EI resource attached to mainstream mental health teams (British Psychological Society/Division of Clinical Psychology, 2005). While this may make pragmatic sense, mainstream mental health services must also face the challenge of re-examining their value base, improving partnership working and maximising access to evidence-based talking treatments, delivered in a timely manner. The latter can be conceptualised as tertiary prevention, i.e. a range of interventions aimed at maximising functioning while preventing or delaying relapse in people who may no longer be deemed to be in the 'critical period' but who arguably are no less deserving of a quality service.

Working in mainstream services when dedicated EI provision also exists

Given that some EI service users require longer-term support beyond the critical period, clinical psychologists in mainstream mental health services should maintain close links with the local EI service and can play a key role in helping people to 'step down' from time-limited EI input, and to use the transition as an opportunity to embrace a life with less intensive input from services, while still drawing on all the 'staying well skills' acquired. Most psychologists working across the lifespan in mainstream mental health services in fact share a similar value base to those within dedicated EI services, although they may be operating in service contexts probably limited by greater resource constraints. This creates an opportunity to state a positive choice to keep working in mainstream services and to do the best job possible, while keeping the EI service in mind and remaining on the lookout for appropriate referrals. Work which is broadly preventative in orientation should still be prioritised, but the emphasis is again on preventing or delaying *recurrence* of distressing symptoms through *timely* (rather than early) intervention, while maximising functioning and the principles of social inclusion.

As noted, EI psychologists require professional management links, beyond operational links with EI team managers, for safe and reflective practice, and this is commonly provided by senior, experienced clinical psychologists who may work in a different but overlapping specialty. EI psychologists can further benefit from specialist supervision and/or peer supervision with other clinical psychologists, and from working in another specialty on a time-limited basis, in order to maintain a range of clinical skills. Time-limited secondments between EI and mainstream services can provide powerful learning opportunities.

Psychologists working in mainstream services are also well placed to promote a balanced discourse about EI teams, if real-life outcomes don't reach the level aspired to by policy makers. Values that are shared across the entire organisation, i.e. therapeutic optimism and working towards individuals' best possible recovery, should be emphasised. In this context, it is important to value the holistic outcomes achieved by EI services, in terms of engaging service users in working towards increasing self-esteem and self-management, as well as increasing confidence to re-enter education and employment, since the impact of this goes well beyond mere symptom reduction.

Final Considerations

The health needs of populations, particularly in relatively affluent nations, have changed considerably since the Second World War. Infectious diseases are no longer the biggest causes of death or disability; instead these have been replaced by chronic conditions, powerfully maintained by psychosocial factors (Llewelyn & Kennedy, 2003). In part because of financial constraints and in part because of changing beliefs and values, the role of the patient as a passive recipient of simply pharmaceutical interventions will likely change in coming decades to that of the 'expert patient' who is offered *timely* – hence the emphasis on EI – cost-effective, evidence-based biopsychosocial interventions of appropriate complexity, promoting self-management (Department of Health, 2001b). Clinical psychologists bring a highly relevant set of skills and knowledge to this area. They are well placed to continue to develop, lead and evaluate such services.

In this context it may be worth noting that the EI paradigm is increasingly being applied to mental health problems other than psychosis, such as eating disorders which, if not addressed in a timely manner, can also cause disability on an enormous scale (McGorry, 2007). For once, happily, economical and moral considerations appear to point in the same direction. It is to be hoped that such approaches will flourish in the future and will continue to attract funding, enthusiastic staff, and good research output.

References

Bentall, R. (1990). *Reconstructing schizophrenia*. London: Routledge.

Bentall, R. (2003). *Madness explained*. Harmondsworth: Allen Lane, Penguin.

Birchwood, M. (1995). Early intervention in psychotic relapse: Cognitive approaches to detection and management. *Behaviour Change, 12*(1), 2–19.

Birchwood, M. & Wells A. (1992). *Innovations in the psychological management of schizophrenia*. Chichester: Wiley.

British Psychological Society/Division of Clinical Psychology (2005). *Early intervention in psychosis services – the role clinical psychologists can play*. Briefing paper No. 20. Leicester: Author.

British Psychological Society (2000). *Understanding mental illness: Recent advances in understanding mental illness and psychotic experience*. Leicester: Author.

Burbach, F. & Stanbridge, R. (1998). A family intervention in psychosis service integrating the systemic and family management approaches. *Journal of Family Therapy, 20*, 311–325.

Butcher, J., Dahlstrom, W., Graham, J., Tellegen, A. & Kaemmer, B. (1989). *The Minnesota Multiphasic Personality Inventory-2 (MMPI-2): Manual for administration and scoring*. Minneapolis: University of Minnesota Press.

Chadwick, P., Lees, S. & Birchwood, M. (2000). The Revised Beliefs about Voices Questionnaire. *British Journal of Psychiatry, 177*, 229–232.

Department of Health (2001a). *The mental health policy implementation guide*. London: Author.

Department of Health (2001b). *The expert patient: A new approach to disease management for the 21st century*. London: Author.

Fowler, D.G. (2002). Psychological formulation of early psychosis: A cognitive model. In M. Birchwood, D. Fowler & C. Jackson (Eds.) *Early intervention in psychosis: A guide to concepts, evidence and interventions* (pp. 331–347). John Wiley & Sons.

Garety, P., Kuipers, E., Fowler, D., Freeman, D. & Bebbington, P. (2001). A cognitive model of the positive symptoms of psychosis. *Psychological Medicine, 31*, 189–195.

Gumley, A. & Schwannauer, M. (2006). *Staying well after psychosis: A cognitive interpersonal approach to recovery and relapse prevention*. Chichester: Wiley.

Llewelyn, S.P. & Kennedy, P. (2003). *Handbook of clinical health psychology*. Chichester: Wiley.

McGorry, P., McFarlane, C., Patton, G.C., Bell, R., Hibbert, M.E., Jackson, H.J. *et al.* (1995). The prevalence of prodromal features of schizophrenia in adolescence: A preliminary survey. *Acta Psychiatrica Scandinavica, 92*, 241–249.

McGorry, P., Edwards, J., Mihalopoulos, C., Harrigan, S. & Jackson, H. (1996). The Early Psychosis Prevention and Intervention Centre (EPPIC): An evolving system of early detection and optimal management. *Schizophrenia Bulletin, 22*(2), 305–326.

McGorry, P. (2007). Editorial: Welcome to early intervention in psychiatry. *Early Intervention in Psychiatry, 1*, 1–2.

Morrison, A.P., Frame, L. & Larkin, W. (2003). Relationships between trauma and psychosis: A review and integration. *British Journal of Clinical Psychology, 42*, 331–352.

National Institute for Health and Clinical Excellence (2002). *Schizophrenia: Core interventions in the treatment and management of schizophrenia in primary and secondary care*. London: Author.

Read, J., van Os, J., Morrison, A. & Ross, C. (2005). Childhood trauma, psychosis and schizophrenia: A literature review with theoretical and clinical implications. *Acta Psychiatrica Scandinavia, 112*(5), 330–350.

Wechsler, D. (1997). *WAIS-III administration and scoring manual*. San Antonio, TX: The Psychological Corporation.

17

Family Interventions and Psychosis

Gráinne Fadden

Overview

In the past the contribution of clinical psychology to adult mental health services has focused on the management of anxiety disorders and mild to moderate depression. More recently, however, psychologists have made significant contributions to the management of psychosis and other serious mental health problems both in terms of challenging conventional models of disorder (Bentall, 2003) and in developing effective treatments, most notably cognitive approaches to psychosis (Haddock & Slade, 1996) as well as the development of family approaches and their dissemination in practice (Barrowclough & Tarrier, 1992; Fadden & Birchwood, 2002; Burbach & Stanbridge, 2006).

Awareness of the needs of families caring for those experiencing episodes of severe disorder has been recognised in the UK via recent government policies, including Standard 6 of the National Service Framework for Mental Health (Department of Health, 1999), which describes the rights of carers to have their own assessment and care plan, and the government white paper, Our Health, Our Care, Our Say (Department of Health, 2006). These documents outline plans for an 'Expert Carers' Programme in addition to other support structures such as respite care and telephone helplines. Additional policies such as those relating to social inclusion highlight the importance of a person's broader social network.

The rationale for involving families is straightforward and intuitive: we live in social contexts; when one person in a family or other social network is unwell, this impacts on those around them in terms of the reciprocity of role functions, kinship obligations, and the emotional impact in terms of concern, empathy and a broad range of emotions triggered by the situation. Dealing with troubling and unfamiliar behaviours such as those that are common in psychosis is difficult, and in the absence of information and advice, family and friends struggle to know how best to help.

In epidemiological terms, psychosis usually first presents in adolescents or young adults, with males having an earlier age of onset than females (Hafner et al., 1995).

Between 60 and 70 per cent of young people will still be living with or in very close contact with parents and family (Addington & Burnett, 2004). Because of this, there are often complicating adolescent issues such as separation and individuation factors, and family disruption. Any therapeutic interventions therefore must be flexible, developmentally informed, and cater for both the individual's and the family's needs (Power & McGorry, 1999).

This chapter will summarise the nature of family interventions, the evidence base supporting family work, current issues, and the role that clinical psychologists can play in relation to their widespread dissemination in clinical practice.

Models

In terms of explaining aetiology, most family approaches to schizophrenia are predicated on a diathesis-stress model, acknowledging both biological and other vulnerabilities, as well as increased sensitivity to stress (Zubin & Spring, 1977; Nuechterlein & Dawson, 1984). This biopsychosocial approach allows for the acknowledgement of a range of factors, biological, psychological and social, that can contribute both to the initial development of disorder and to subsequent recurrences of difficulties. In clinical experience, this model is one that families find extremely helpful as it enables them to make sense of their experiences, to alleviate feelings of blame and guilt in that there is no single cause, and also to look positively at what contributory factors can be modified to decrease the likelihood of relapse.

The approaches that have been found to be most effective come under the broad heading of psychosocial or psychoeducational models of intervention. The core components of these have been described in various texts (Fadden, 1998a), but in summary include a combination of information-sharing and the development of a range of skills, including more effective communication and strategies for dealing with day-to-day problems as they arise. They are based on a skills-deficit rather than a pathological model, with clear underlying principles (Falloon et al., 2004). These include the idea that the family is doing its best to cope with a traumatic and difficult situation, but lacks certain skills to do this in the most effective manner. The positive focus inherent in these models is the assumption that these skills can be acquired in the context of a collaborative working relationship with the professionals delivering the support.

There is debate about whether different modes of delivery of family work produce the same outcomes, for example individual compared to group approaches. Readers who wish to explore this further can refer to various texts (Fadden, 1998b; Johnson, 2007). In summary, family support or educational groups that do not include the person with the disorder can benefit family members in terms of increased understanding and reductions in stress, but do not produce reductions in relapse or hospitalisations. Family group approaches that include the service user, known as multi-family groups (McFarlane, 2002), are effective in reducing relapse, but individual family intervention where the approach is tailored for the needs of the particular family appears to be the most effective (Pilling et al., 2002).

In mental health, the recovery model has increasingly been adopted in recent years (Jacobson & Greenley, 2001; Frese *et al.*, 2001). In this model, the service user is an equal and active member of the care team rather than a passive recipient of care. The concept of a 'whole person' with preferences, needs and goals and with a unique history, family circumstances and culture, is core. The service user determines treatment goals which emphasise functioning and social integration rather than symptom management (Ralph, 2000). Glynn *et al.* (2006) highlight how consistent these family approaches are with the recovery model because of their focus on consumer knowledge, empowerment, hope and optimism.

Evidence Base

The evidence base in this area falls into two domains, first relating to the impact on relatives when someone in the family develops a mental health problem, and second the evidence for the efficacy of family approaches. The literature on impact commonly refers to family burden or caregiver stress. The term burden is used less commonly now as it implies unidirectionality and fails to reflect the complexity of reciprocal relationships. Terms such as impact or stress are now therefore more commonly used. The varied reactions of loved ones when a family member develops a serious mental health problem such as psychosis have been documented for the past twenty years (Fadden *et al.*, 1987), and are very consistent. There are practical impacts such as disruption to household activities, effects on the relatives' social activities, impact on work, employment and education. Allied to these are a whole range of emotional reactions such as anger, guilt, self-blame and grief and loss reactions.

Families consistently cite the lack of information and support from services as contributing to their difficulties. Of concern in this area is the fact that the stress of caregiving for families does not appear to have lessened, with recent studies continuing to highlight the same issues (Caqueo-Urizar & Gutierrez-Maldonado, 2006; Perlick *et al.*, 2006; Rose *et al.*, 2006; Corcoran *et al.*, 2007). In Western countries this may be linked to the preponderance of community models of care, while in developing countries, most caregiving activities fall to families (Shankar *et al.*, 2007).

The evidence for the effectiveness of psychoeducational family approaches is amongst the most robust in mental health. The earliest studies in the 1980s showed dramatic reductions in relapse and hospitalisation rates for those who received family work in addition to medication and standard care. These findings have been replicated in numerous randomised controlled trials since then, and several reviews and meta-analyses confirm the efficacy of these approaches (Pharoah *et al.*, 2006; Pfammatter *et al.*, 2006). Other outcomes include improvement in social functioning of service users, better adherence to medication regimes and net savings in direct and indirect costs. Pitschel-Walz *et al.* (2001), Bustilla *et al.* (2001) and Pilling *et al.* (2002) all conclude that psychoeducational family interventions are essential and should be offered to people with schizophrenia who are in contact with family members.

Because of the strong evidence base, national guidelines such as the PORT guidelines in the USA (Lehman *et al.*, 2004) and the NICE guidelines for schizophrenia in the UK (National Institute for Health and Clinical Excellence, 2002) recommend that services to families are provided, with the NICE Guidelines recommending that they should be available to 100 per cent of families.

However, the availability of family work in practice is very limited. In a study of implementation in five European countries, Magliano *et al.* (1998) reported that between 0 and 14 per cent of families were in receipt of this approach. Similar results were found in a recent study where only 2 per cent of families had received this type of help, with psychoeducation being offered for one in every 50th service user (Rummel-Kluge *et al.*, 2006). In a recent UK study, evidence of any family intervention was recorded in only 5 per cent of case files (Krupnik *et al.*, 2005). The reasons for this will be discussed further when covering challenges in this area.

Competencies

The skills and attitudes required for family work have been described in detail in other texts (Burbach & Stanbridge, 2006; Fadden, 2006a, 2007; Stanbridge & Burbach, 2007), and are central to the success of family work. In the past, families met with hostility, criticism, and frequently felt labelled or blamed. If family work is to be successful, the starting point is a positive attitude to the family, coupled with an acknowledgement of their strengths and the contribution they can make to their relative's recovery. The development of a collaborative working relationship where different types of expertise are recognised is core: the service user is considered to be the expert on the experience of psychosis, the family are the most knowledgeable about their own circumstances and what is effective for them, and the professional has expertise about the disorder and general principles about what is helpful. Through sharing these different types of expertise, the best outcomes can be achieved.

One of the skills that is crucial is the ability to work with a group, because a family is, in essence, a group. In our extensive experience in the Meriden Programme in Birmingham over the past 10 years where we have trained 2500 therapists in family work skills, lack of confidence in group work is one of the biggest obstacles. The training of most professionals is based on individual therapeutic models, and they lack basic necessary skills of ensuring that everyone has a say, knowing how to manage over-talkative and quiet members, and managing conflicts and intense emotions. Other essential elements include knowledge of family life cycles, the ability to deal with issues of grief and loss, good communication skills, an awareness of political, social and cultural contexts, and the ability to sustain relationships over time. To work effectively with families, therefore, therapists need a broad repertoire of skills. Another additional but significant issue is that clinical staff frequently do not receive any training in family work, with surveys showing that 70–80 per cent of clinicians do not have training to work with families prior to undertaking in-service training post-qualification (Fadden & Birchwood, 2002), usually resulting in them not having the specific skills needed to work with families (Stanbridge & Burbach, 2007).

Engagement and Assessment

By definition, engaging families in therapy is crucial, but is the element that therapists report as being most challenging, primarily due to their lack of confidence. From the family's point of view, there can be a range of factors that can influence their readiness to engage in this process. Previous experiences with mental health services where they felt unsupported can make them wary of what is being offered. Anxiety that they may be blamed for contributing to their relative's difficulties can interact with their sense of guilt. They will also be aware that they are in contact with a service whose prime concern is with the individual who is unwell, and therefore feel that they are not entitled to help. For these reasons, the family worker must assertively try to engage with the family, and be explicit about adopting a non-blaming and normalising approach (Burbach & Stanbridge, 2006; Fadden, 2007). The idea that the family members are doing their best in difficult circumstances must be emphasised, and it is important to remember that the therapist is offering something that families have repeatedly said that they want – information and the acquisition of skills that will enable them to cope better (Cleary *et al.*, 2005).

The skills required for engagement have already been touched on above. James *et al.* (2006) expand on these further, emphasising therapist qualities of humanity, flexibility, seeing the family as like self or equal, and willingness to reflect on one's own practice. The concept of flexibility is central. Those who are unfamiliar with psychoeducational approaches often assume that because they are described in detail in manuals, these approaches are rigidly applied, as if clinicians were technicians. In fact these approaches are structured but not packaged. They are formulation based, and what is offered is tailored for the needs of the individual family. Those who are successful in engaging with families integrate family work skills into their existing repertoire of clinical skills in a seamless fashion.

In terms of when is the best time to engage with families, offering help as early as possible is recommended, and families are particularly willing to engage in times of crisis such as during acute episodes or during hospital admissions (Fadden, 1998a; Hardcastle *et al.*, 2007). Engagement is a process that can take time, especially in different cultural groups.

Assessment within these models generally involves assessment of individual family members as well as the family unit, and a plan for how to proceed is drawn up in collaboration with the family group.

Carer and Service User Involvement

Carer and service user involvement in a range of capacities in services is crucial if we are to make the transition to family-sensitive care. This involvement is extremely effective at changing staff attitudes. For example, having someone with psychosis speak about the benefits of family work to them challenges the views of some professionals that service users do not want their families involved. Similarly, having family members speak about what they gained from family work is an excellent motivator for hesitant staff.

Organisations that have attempted to involve families more at a systemic level in services, emphasise the need to have comprehensive strategies (Stanbridge & Burbach, 2004) and describe the preparation needed for staff to adapt to initiatives such as this (Cleary *et al.*, 2006).

The involvement of carers and service users in professional training can also help to ensure that positive attitudes develop from the start. In 2005, the Royal College of Psychiatrists was the first professional body in the UK to make it mandatory that trainees receive training from carers and service users (Fadden *et al.*, 2005). This is being explored in clinical psychology training and a guidance paper has recently been published (Division of Clinical Psychology of the British Psychological Society, 2008).

The concept of carer consultants is to date most common in Australia and the UK, and the variety of ways in which experts by experience can contribute to the development of better services has been described by Woodhams (2007).

Challenges

Some of the challenges in relation to the availability of family work have already been articulated in previous sections. The limited availability of family interventions in spite of the extensive evidence base, policy and guidelines remains one of the biggest challenges to be addressed. The influence of traditional healthcare systems with their inherent focus on individual rights is difficult to change. The consequence, however, is needless suffering by family members at a time when they are most vulnerable, and a process whereby they have to learn by trial and error when there are effective approaches that would help them. In spite of pockets of good practice, little progress has been made at a global level, although this issue was identified over ten years ago (Fadden, 1997).

Unless the issue of training in family and group work skills is addressed, it is unlikely that implementation rates will improve. Those charged with clinical psychology training need to reflect on their responsibility in this regard in that training in psychoeducational family work is not available on many clinical psychology courses in spite of the robust evidence base. Apart from training to deliver therapy at an individual family level, psychological skills could be applied to bring about the change in service systems, given that many of the impediments to implementation occur at an organisational level (Burbach & Stanbridge, 2007; Fadden, 2006b).

Family work by its nature gives rise to ethical dilemmas, and has sometimes come under criticism because of a lack of consideration for the rights of the individual in a theoretical paradigm that focuses on systems (Walker & Akister, 2004). On the other hand, existing systems that value individual autonomy over family interdependence may be insensitive to the needs of many families, and in particular in relation to diverse cultural groups where there is often a different perception of kinship ties from that in

Western cultures. Therapists need to reflect on their own values and offer what is proven to be effective and meets the needs of the family in question. This dilemma is played out in relation to confidentiality dilemmas where clinicians often struggle to reconcile the individual's right to confidentiality with the family's right to information (Allison et al., 2004; Slade et al., 2007). This has become more pronounced since government policy in the UK stipulates that health professionals have obligations to both the individual and their key relatives (Department of Health, 1999, 2002).

A final area that is gaining attention recently is in relation to children taking on age-inappropriate caring roles when their parents develop mental health difficulties (Becker, 2007).

Future Directions

The field of family work has been subject to much research and evaluation, yet certain areas have been neglected. Traditionally, the outcomes that have been measured relate to benefits to service users, with, ironically, little attention being paid to issues and outcomes for family members (Brooker & Brabban, 2004). In a similar vein, interventions have often focused on the needs of key relatives, usually parents or spouses, with little attention being paid, for example, to the needs of those with mental health problems who are in parental roles (Craig & Bromet, 2004), or to the needs of siblings (Smith et al., 2009). There is a need for more specificity in relation to the needs of individual family members.

Another area that needs attention is phase-of-life issues, for example the differing needs of adolescents or older people with mental health problems (Palmer et al., 1999). The notion of phase-specific treatments is being articulated in early psychosis services (Addington & Burnett, 2004). Glynn et al. (2006) comment on the lack of integration of developmental life tasks into family interventions.

Services need to become more aware of social context issues, and more research that focuses on implementation rather than efficacy of treatments is required. The differing needs of multicultural groups should also be addressed. Finally, the transition from psychoeducational approaches being linked with the medical model to a transformed conceptualisation, allying them with a recovery model, should be more clearly articulated.

References

Addington, J. & Burnett, P. (2004). Working with families in the early stages of psychosis. In P. McGorry & John Gleeson (Eds.) Psychological interventions in early psychosis: A practical treatment handbook (pp. 99–116). Chichester: John Wiley & Sons.

Allison, S., Fadden, G., Hart, D., Launer, M. & Siddle, J. (2004). Carers and confidentiality in mental health. Issues involved in information sharing. London: Royal College of Psychiatrists, Partners in Care Campaign. Retrieved 23 February 2009 from(www.partnersincare.co.uk).

Barrowclough, C. & Tarrier, N. (1992). Families of schizophrenic patients: Cognitive behavioural intervention. London: Chapman & Hall.

Becker, S. (2007). Global perspectives on children's unpaid caregiving in the family: Research and policy on 'Young Carers' in the UK, Australia, the USA and Sub-Saharan Africa. *Global Social Policy*, 7(1), 25–50.

Bentall, R.P. (2003). *Madness explained: Psychosis and human nature*. London: Penguin.

Brooker, C. & Brabban, A. (2004). *Measured success: A scoping review of evaluated psychosocial interventions training for work with people with serious mental health problems*. NIMHE/Trent WDC.

Burbach, F.R. & Stanbridge, R.I. (2006). Somerset's family interventions in psychosis service: An update. *Journal of Family Therapy*, 20, 311–325.

Burbach, F.R. & Stanbridge, R.I. (2007). Developing family-inclusive mainstream mental health services. *Journal of Family Therapy*, 29, 21–43.

Bustilla, J.R., Lauriello, J., Horan, W.P. & Keith, S.J. (2001). The psychological treatment of schizophrenia: An update. *American Journal of Psychiatry*, 158(2), 163–175.

Caqueo-Urizar, A. & Gutierrez-Maldonado, J. (2006). Burden of care in families of patients with schizophrenia. *Quality of Life Research*, 15, 719–724.

Cleary, M., Freeman, A., Hunt, G.E. & Walter, G. (2005). What patients and carers want to know: An exploration of information and resource needs in adult mental health services. *Australian and New Zealand Journal of Psychiatry*, 39, 507–513.

Cleary, M., Freeman, A. & Walter, G. (2006). Carer participation in mental health service delivery. *International Journal of Mental Health Nursing*, 15, 189–194.

Corcoran, C., Gerson, R., Sills-Shahar, R., Nickou, C., McGlashan, T., Malaspina, D. *et al.* (2007). Trajectory to a first episode of psychosis: A qualitative research study with families. *Early Intervention in Psychiatry*, 1, 308–315.

Craig, T. & Bromet, E.J. (2004). Parents with psychosis. *Annals of Clinical Psychiatry*, 16, 35–39.

Department of Health (1999). *National service framework for mental health*. London: HMSO.

Department of Health (2002). *Developing services for carers and families of people with mental illness*. London: HMSO.

Department of Health (2006). *Our health, our care, our say: A new direction for community health services*. London: Department of Health.

Division of Clinical Psychology of the British Psychological Society (2008). *Good practice guide: Service user and carer involvement within clinical psychology training*. Leicester: British Psychological Society.

Fadden, G. (1997). Implementation of family interventions in routine clinical practice: A major cause for concern. *Journal of Mental Health*, 6, 599–612.

Fadden, G. (1998a). Family intervention. In C. Brooker & J. Repper (Eds.) *Serious mental health problems in the community* (pp. 159–183). London: Balliere Tindall.

Fadden, G. (1998b). Research update: Psychoeducational family interventions. *Journal of Family Therapy*, 20, 293–309.

Fadden, G. (2006a). Family interventions. In G. Roberts, S. Davenport, F. Holloway & T. Tattan (Eds.) *Enabling recovery: The principles and practice of rehabilitation psychiatry* (pp. 158–169). London: Gaskell.

Fadden, G. (2006b). Training and disseminating family interventions for schizophrenia: Developing family intervention skills with multi-disciplinary groups. *Journal of Family Therapy*, 28, 23–38.

Fadden, G. (2007). Involving and training professionals in family work. In D. Froggatt, G. Fadden, D.L. Johnson, M. Leggatt & R. Shankar (Eds.) *Families as partners in care:*

A guidebook for implementing family work (pp. 38–49). Toronto: World Fellowship for Schizophrenia and Allied Disorders.

Fadden, G., Bebbington, P. & Kuipers, L. (1987). The burden of care – the impact of functional psychiatric illness on the patient's family. *British Journal of Psychiatry, 150*, 285–292.

Fadden, G. & Birchwood, M. (2002). British models for expanding family psychoeducation in routine practice. In H.P. Lefley & D.L. Johnson (Eds.) *Family interventions in mental illness: International perspectives* (pp. 25–41). Westport, CT: Praeger.

Fadden, G., Shooter, M. & Holsgrove, G. (2005). Involving carers and service users in the training of psychiatrists. *Psychiatric Bulletin, 29*, 270–274.

Falloon, I.R.H., Fadden, G., Mueser, K., Gingerich, S., Rappaport, S., McGill, C. et al. (2004). *Family work manual*. Birmingham: Meriden Family Programme.

Frese, F.J., Stanley, J., Kress, K. & Vogel-Scibilia, S. (2001).Integrating evidence-based practices and the recovery model. *Psychiatric Services, 52*, 1462–1468.

Glynn, S.M., Cohen, A.N., Dixon, L.B. & Niv, N. (2006). The potential impact of the recovery movement on family interventions for schizophrenia: Opportunities and obstacles. *Schizophrenia Bulletin, 32*(3), 451–463.

Haddock, G. & Slade, P.D. (1996). *Cognitive-behavioural interventions with psychotic disorders*. London: Routledge.

Hafner, H. Maurer, K., Loffler, W., Bustamante, S., an der Heiden, W., Riecher-Rossler, A. & Notworthy, B. (1995). Onset and early course of schizophrenia. In H. Hafner & W.F. Gattaz (Eds.) *Search for the causes of schizophrenia* (Vol. III, pp. 43–66). New York: Springer-Verlag.

Hardcastle, M., Kennard, D., Grandison, S. & Fagin, L. (Eds.) (2007). *Experiences of mental health in-patient care: Narratives from service users, carers and professionals*. London: Routledge.

Jacobson, N. & Greenley, D. (2001). What is recovery? A conceptual model and explanation. *Psychiatric Services, 52*, 482–485.

James, C., Cushway, D. & Fadden, G. (2006). What works in engagement of families in behavioural family therapy? A positive model for the therapist perspective. *Journal of Mental Health, 28*, 23–38.

Johnson, D.L. (2007). Models of family intervention. In D. Froggatt, G. Fadden, D.L. Johnson, M. Leggatt & R. Shankar (Eds.) *Families as partners in care: A guidebook for implementing family work* (pp. 10–21). Toronto: World Fellowship for Schizophrenia and Allied Disorders.

Krupnik, Y., Pilling, S., Killaspy, H. & Dalton, J. (2005). A study of family contact with clients and staff of community mental health teams. *Psychiatric Bulletin, 29*, 174–176.

Lehman, A.F., Kreyenbuhl, J., Buchanan, R.W., Dickerson, F.B., Dixon, L.B., Goldberg, R. et al. (2004). The Schizophrenia Patient Outcomes Research Team (PORT): Updated treatment recommendations, 2003. *Schizophrenia Bulletin, 30*(2), 193–217.

Magliano, L., Fadden, G., Madianos, M., Caldas de Almeida, J-M., Held, T., Guarneri, M. et al. (1998). Burden on the families of patients with schizophrenia: Results of the BIOMED 1 study. *Social Psychiatry and Psychiatric Epidemiology, 33*, 405–412.

McFarlane, W.R. (2002). *Multifamily groups in the treatment of severe psychiatric disorders*. New York: Guilford Press.

National Institute for Health and Clinical Excellence (2002). *Schizophrenia: Core interventions in the treatment and management of schizophrenia in primary and secondary care*. London: National Collaborating Centre for Mental Health.

Nuechterlein, K.H. & Dawson, M.E. (1984). A heuristic vulnerability/stress model of schizophrenic episodes. *Schizophrenia Bulletin, 10*, 300–312.

Palmer, B.W., Heaton, S.C. & Jeste, D.V. (1999). Older patients with schizophrenia: Challenges in the coming decades. *Psychiatric Services, 50,* 1178–1183.

Perlick, D.A., Rosenheck, R.A., Kaczynski, R., Swartz, M.S., Canive, J.M. & Lieberman, J.A. (2006). Components and correlates of family burden in schizophrenia. *Psychiatric Services, 57,* 1117–1125.

Pfammatter, M., Junghan, U.M. & Brenner, H.D. (2006). Efficacy of psychological therapy in schizophrenia: Conclusions from meta-analyses. *Schizophrenia Bulletin, 32,* S64–S80.

Pharoah, F., Mari, J., Rathbone, J. & Wong, W. (2006). Family interventions for schizophrenia. *Cochrane Database of Systematic Reviews, 4.*

Pilling, S., Bebbington, P., Kuipers, E., Garety, P., Geddes, J., Orbach, G. & Morgan, C. (2002). Psychological treatments in schizophrenia. I: Meta-analysis of family intervention and cognitive behaviour therapy. *Psychological Medicine, 32,* 763–782.

Pitschel-Walz, G., Leucht, S., Bäuml, J., Kissling, W. & Engel, R.R. (2001). The effect of family interventions on relapse and rehospitalisation in schizophrenia – a meta-analysis. *Schizophrenia Bulletin, 27,* 73–92.

Power, P. & McGorry, P. (1999). Initial assessment of first-episode psychosis. In P.D. McGorry & H.J. Jackson (Eds.) *The recognition and management of early psychosis* (pp. 155–183). Cambridge: Cambridge University Press.

Ralph, R.O. (2000). *Review of recovery literature: A synthesis of a sample of recovery literature.* Alexandria, VA: National Technical Assistance Centre for State Mental Health Planning. Retrieved 28 February 2009 from http://www.nasmhpd.org/nasmhpd_collections/collection5/publications/ntac_pubs/reports/ralphrecovweb.pdf

Rose, L.E., Mallinson, K. & Gerson, L.D. (2006). Mastery, burden and areas of concern among family caregivers of mentally ill persons. *Archives of Psychiatric Nursing, 20,* 41–51.

Rummel-Kluge, C., Pitschel-Walz, G., Bauml, J. & Kissling, W. (2006). Psychoeducation in schizophrenia – results of a survey of all psychiatric institutions in Germany, Austria, and Switzerland. *Schizophrenia Bulletin, 32,* 765–775.

Shankar, R., Vartak, A. & Goswami, M. (2007). Voluntary initiatives in low-income countries – the potential for partnership. In D. Froggatt, G. Fadden, D.L. Johnson, M. Leggatt & R. Shankar (Eds.) *Families as partners in care: A guidebook for implementing family work* (pp. 115–124). Toronto: World Fellowship for Schizophrenia and Allied Disorders.

Slade, M., Pinfold, V., Rapaport, J., Bellringer, S., Banerjee, S., Kuipers, E. & Huxley, P. (2007). Best practice when service users do not consent to sharing information with carers. *British Journal of Psychiatry, 190,* 148–155.

Smith, J., Fadden, G. & O'Shea, M. (2009, in press). Interventions with siblings. In F. Lobban & C. Barrowclough (Eds.) *A casebook of family interventions for psychosis.* Chichester: Wiley & Sons.

Stanbridge, R.I. & Burbach, F.R. (2004). Enhancing working partnerships with carers and families in mainstream practice: A strategy and associated staff training programme. *The Mental Health Review, 9*(4), 32–37.

Stanbridge, R.I. & Burbach, F.R. (2007). Developing family inclusive mainstream mental health services. *Journal of Family Therapy, 29,* 21–43.

Walker, S. & Akister, J. (2004). *Applying family therapy: A guide for caring professionals in the community.* Lyme Regis: Russell House Publishing.

Woodhams, P. (2007). Involving and training carers: Part 2. In D. Froggatt, G. Fadden, D.L. Johnson, M. Leggatt & R. Shankar (Eds.) *Families as partners in care: A guidebook for implementing family work.* (pp. 65–75). Toronto: World Fellowship for Schizophrenia and Allied Disorders.

Zubin, J. & Spring, B. (1977). Vulnerability – a new view of schizophrenia. *Journal of Abnormal Psychology, 86,* 103–126.

18

Bibliotherapy and Self-Help

David S.J. Hawker

Bibliotherapy and Self-Help

Why bother seeing a professional when you can treat yourself from a book? Unevaluated self-help books, or bibliotherapy, crowd the psychology sections of non-academic bookshops and libraries. The potential benefits of bibliotherapy include better access, empowerment, preventive value and privacy, and reduced stigma, labelling and cost (Papworth, 2006). Does bibliotherapy make psychologists redundant?

Far from it: in fact psychologists have a responsibility to develop and evaluate evidence-based self-help therapeutic and psychoeducational interventions (Rosen, 1976). In this chapter I present an overview of the evidence for the effectiveness of bibliotherapy, including self-help materials using media such as books, booklets, videotapes, audiotapes, television programmes, computer programs and websites. Self-help group approaches, which have been less well researched (National Institute for Mental Health in England, 2003), are not reviewed here.

What Is Bibliotherapy and Self-Help?

Bibliotherapy aims to deliver the contents of therapy to its users. One of the best-selling evidence-based self-help books is *Feeling Good* (Burns, 2000). Burns offers readers from adolescence to older adulthood a systematic and engaging course of cognitive behaviour therapy (CBT) for depression, from self-assessment and formulation through to relapse prevention. Chapters with titles like 'Verbal judo: Learn to talk back when you're under the fire of criticism' are filled with practical examples of homework tasks, ways to challenge thoughts, therapist–client dialogues and other techniques.

Here are some more examples of bibliotherapy. Parents can read a book to coach themselves in behavioural treatment of their children's anxiety (Rapee *et al.*, 2000), or watch videotapes of a televised course for managing their children's behaviour problems

(Sanders *et al.*, 2000). Children as young as infant school age can be taken through workbooks on grief (Heegaard, 1991) or storybooks to help overcome phobias (Santacruz *et al.*, 2006). Aiming to fulfil a psychoeducational function, 'Your Good Health' (British Institute of Learning Disabilities, 2005) is a range of illustrated health information books designed for people with a learning disability. Computerised bibliotherapy can offer an interactive response to users' input of self-ratings, homework tasks and so on. Computerised CBT for depression and anxiety is available free online (e.g. www.livinglifetothefull.com/), or with therapist phone support, if purchased by a healthcare provider (see Marks *et al.*, 2007).

Does Bibliotherapy Work?

No fewer than nine meta-analyses have looked at the effects of bibliotherapy. Averaged post-treatment effects for bibliotherapy, compared to waiting-list or no-treatment controls, have been comparable to those for psychotherapy in general. Specifically, mean effects[1] due to bibliotherapy have ranged from 0.31 for reducing alcohol use in self-referred problem drinkers (Apodaca & Miller, 2003), to 0.57 (Gould & Clum, 1993), 0.86 (Marrs, 1995) and 0.96 (Scogin *et al.*, 1990) in three meta-analyses encompassing a range of problems. Specifically for depression, an early meta-analysis reported a bibliotherapy effect size of 0.82 (Cuijpers, 1997), with more recent meta-analyses reporting 0.77 (Gregory *et al.*, 2004) and 1.36 (Anderson *et al.*, 2005). Gregory *et al.* (2004) noted that 0.77 compared well with an effect size of 0.83 reported in a comprehensive review of individual cognitive therapy for depression. Meta-analyses combining depression and anxiety have reported effect sizes of 0.41 (Bower *et al.*, 2001) and 0.84 (den Boer *et al.*, 2004, including in that instance one study of self-help group treatment).

There are limitations to the strength of the evidence across these meta-analyses. Many of the studies included in them are methodologically flawed (Kaltenthaler *et al.*, 2002; Anderson *et al.*, 2005), and there is a shortage of long-term follow-up data. The large variation in average effect sizes reflects not only the variable impact of bibliotherapy on different problems, but also inclusion criteria which vary between meta-analyses. Nevertheless, they offer promising evidence in favour of bibliotherapy. The two most comprehensive meta-analyses (Gould & Clum, 1993; Marrs, 1995) have shown that bibliotherapy remains more effective than no treatment at such follow-up intervals as have been assessed. In those meta-analyses, bibliotherapy was most effective for assertion training, skills deficits and anxiety. It was also effective for depression, headache, sleep disturbance, parent training and sexual dysfunction. Bibliotherapy was least effective for habit control, including weight control, smoking, drinking and study problems.

Does Computer-Based Bibliotherapy Work?

Studies of bibliotherapy delivered via computer packages or the internet have been reviewed qualitatively. Computerised CBT for adults' anxiety and depression appeared generally to be more effective than standard treatment, and much less costly in therapist time (Kaltenhaler *et al.*, 2002). Marks *et al.* (2007) identified effective computer-aided psychotherapy for a range of problems, including anxiety and emotional problems, eating problems, alcohol and smoking problems, and childhood asthma. Some of the asthma treatments were computer games, a self-help format which the authors noted would be of great value in engaging young users. In at least some versions, bibliotherapy delivered through websites was effective for depression, anxiety, stress, headaches, insomnia, encopresis and subclinical eating problems (Griffiths & Christensen, 2006).

Does Bibliotherapy Work Across the Age Span?

Several recent reviews have looked at bibliotherapy for children and their parents. Bibliotherapy for parents, in some instances using videotapes, is generally more effective than no intervention in treating children's conduct and sleep problems (Montgomery *et al.*, 2006). A review of interventions for nocturnal enuresis, however, concluded that small trials and equivocal results gave insufficient evidence to evaluate whether written information given to parents or children was effective (Glazener *et al.*, 2004). Bibliotherapy used directly by children or adolescents themselves has been effective for headaches, aggression and depression (Elgar & McGrath, 2003). Computerised bibliotherapy has been effective in treating children's anxiety, headaches, encopresis, behavioural management after head injury, and teaching children with autism to recognise emotions (Marks *et al.*, 2007).

Feeling Good (Burns, 2000) compares favourably in effectiveness with individual psychotherapy in the treatment of depression among adults, adolescents and older adults (Ackerson *et al.*, 1998; Burns, 2000; Floyd *et al.*, 2006). Across studies and different self-help materials, Gregory *et al.* (2004) found effect sizes of bibliotherapy for depression to be moderate (0.57) among older adults, compared to high among adults (1.18) and adolescents (1.32). The authors argued that the lesser effect was due to a lower pre-intervention level of depression among older adult participants than among the younger participants.

Does Bibliotherapy Work as Well as Standard Therapy?

Not only is bibliotherapy more effective than no therapy, but in many instances it appears to be as effective as standard psychotherapy with an active therapist. Meta-analyses have repeatedly found no significant overall difference between the effects of bibliotherapy and face-to-face psychotherapy (Gould & Clum, 1993; Marrs, 1995; Apodaca & Miller, 2003; den Boer *et al.*, 2004), though this is by no means true of every individual comparison. For example, some studies show that parents have learnt to manage children's behaviour better from self-help materials than from therapists (Heifetz, 1977; O'Dell *et al.*, 1979), while others suggest that therapists are better than self-help materials (Montgomery *et al.*, 2006).

Limitations to the quality of bibliotherapy research, as mentioned earlier, rightly lead to caution about the relative benefits of bibliotherapy (Kaltenhaler *et al.*, 2002). One concern which has been raised is that a minority of users' problems worsen after using bibliotherapy (Papworth, 2006). Scogin *et al.* (1996) investigated this concern in relation to bibliotherapy for depression, and showed that the rate of negative outcome was similar to that for gold-standard individual psychotherapy. Marks *et al.* (2007) found that computerised bibliotherapy was disproportionately used by well-educated women, a bias perhaps shared by face-to-face psychotherapy. However, when computerised psychotherapy was offered via GP referral and accessible from patients' homes, 64 per cent of referrals came from the three lowest socioeconomic groups, and initial computer literacy was unrelated to outcome (Marks *et al.*, 2003).

Does Bibliotherapy Work for Clinical Problems?

Many of the problems treated in studies included in meta-analyses of bibliotherapy were mild or subclinical. But at least one meta-analysis has shown bibliotherapy to be more effective than control treatment, and no less effective than face-to-face psychotherapy, for diagnosable depressive and anxiety disorders at both post-treatment and follow-up (den Boer *et al.*, 2004). Even when only studies of the most severe and chronic conditions were included in the analysis, the effect size for self-help was 0.88, with an even greater effect size of 1.4 for six studies which used objective observer-rated outcome measures.

Less voluminous evidence supports the efficacy of bibliotherapy for adults with bulimia and binge-eating disorder (Stefano *et al.*, 2006) and obsessive-compulsive disorder (Mataix-Cols & Marks, 2006). Computerised bibliotherapy is more effective in at least some instances than control treatments for phobias, panic disorder, depression, obesity, problem drinking, childhood anxiety and encopresis (Marks *et al.*, 2007).

Are Therapists Needed to Make Bibliotherapy Work?

The authors of bibliotherapy often caution that it should only be used to support active psychotherapy with a qualified therapist. In fact many studies have shown that bibliotherapy is more effective than no treatment, even if its users have no contact with a therapist (Gould & Clum, 1993; Marrs, 1995). Thus it is not surprising that bibliotherapy has featured prominently as a low-intensity component of stepped care models (e.g. Richards & Suckling, 2008), for example in the UK's Improving Access to Psychological Therapy (IAPT) programme. Bibliotherapy overcomes numerous barriers to psychotherapy, such as unavailability of therapists, long waiting times, difficulty attending appointments, reluctance to seek help or to self-disclose, and not knowing that help is available. It is as accessible as picking up a book.

Books can, however, be put down easily, too. In many instances, at least some minimal contact with a therapist seems to enhance the effectiveness of bibliotherapy, perhaps partly because therapists encourage compliance and provide some accountability. Thus Gould and Clum (1993) found that effects were much greater in studies which reported higher compliance with bibliotherapy. In a qualitative review of bibliotherapy for anxiety disorders, Newman *et al.* (2003) concluded that unassisted bibliotherapy was sufficient for motivated clients to overcome simple phobias, but that there were greater benefits for phobias and other anxiety disorders with therapist assistance.

In computerised bibliotherapy too, some minimal therapist contact may be necessary for encouraging completion of treatment (Marks *et al.*, 2007). Marks and others have argued that only a basic level of therapeutic training is needed to fulfil such a function, which in one IAPT demonstration site was carried out by 'case managers' (Richards & Suckling, 2008). But offering completely unsupported bibliotherapy as part of an IAPT package will not, in most instances, provide more accessible therapy.

The way in which therapist assistance is offered can be important. For example, scheduled telephone conversations with a therapist were more effective in helping parents use bibliotherapy for their children's anxiety than scheduled emails or unlimited therapist contacts initiated by the parents (Lyneham & Rapee, 2006). In contrast, bibliotherapy has worked for children without any therapist assistance for a range of problems in at least four comparison trials (Rakos *et al.*, 1985; Winett *et al.*, 1992; Ackerson *et al.*, 1998; Felder-Puig *et al.*, 2003). Where it is assisted by therapists, bibliotherapy generally uses less therapist time and is less expensive than conventional therapy (Cuijpers, 1997; Kaltenhaler *et al.*, 2002). For example, computerised cognitive behaviour therapy for anxiety and depression in adults needed an average of 64 minutes' therapist support per patient, compared to an estimated eight hours when delivered by a therapist (Marks *et al.*, 2003).

Limitations and Further Needs in Development of Bibliotherapy

There is a clear need to develop more bibliotherapy materials suitable for children and adolescents, rather than using those developed for adults (Ackerson *et al.*, 1998), particularly in child-friendly formats such as storybooks (Santacruz *et al.*, 2006) or computer games (Marks *et al.*, 2007), and building on a long tradition of unevaluated inspirational bibliotherapy (Cohen, 1987; Elgar & McGrath, 2003). More research on the use of bibliotherapy with older adults for conditions other than depression would be valuable, as well as the development of targeted computerised applications for older adults (Marks *et al.*, 2007) and people with disabilities. Although some early studies (e.g. Heifetz, 1977; see Montgomery *et al.*, 2006 for further examples) were targeted at the parents of children with learning disabilities, more research on bibliotherapy for adults with intellectual disabilities is needed.

Papworth (2006) noted that little attention has been paid to ethnic minorities, and speculated that bibliotherapy might not cross cultures well, even after good linguistic and cultural translation. An alternative view is that bibliotherapy could be even more valued by some cultures than individual psychotherapy. For example, members of some cultures may consider it odd to talk to a stranger outside the family about their problems, while they may have been educated to respect material published by a recognised authority.

Rosen *et al.* (2007) warned that not all self-help materials are equally effective, and that too few are evaluated. They noted that good psychotherapy does not automatically translate to good bibliotherapy, and even small changes in the format or delivery of bibliotherapy can have large and counterintuitive effects on outcome. Careful research is needed on the efficacy of individual bibliotherapy materials, and also other matters: cost-effectiveness relative to standard treatment (especially given the expense of developing computerised psychotherapy; Marks *et al.*, 2003); the level of expertise needed to support different forms of bibliotherapy on offer; the extent to which bibliotherapy is genuinely more accessible than other forms of treatment (Papworth, 2006); predicting who will benefit from bibliotherapy rather than more intensive treatment (Baillie & Rapee, 2004); and the use of bibliotherapy as an intervention for service users waiting for conventional treatment.

Summary

The evidence across all these studies shows that bibliotherapy is generally more effective than no treatment and can be as effective as or, occasionally, more effective than therapist-assisted treatment. It is efficacious for both mild and more severe problems. Bibliotherapy may be effective even without any support from a therapist, but there is some evidence that its effectiveness is enhanced with minimal support, at least for some problems. There is strong evidence for its effectiveness for treating adults' and some older adults' problems, growing evidence for its use in training parents to manage their children's problems, and some limited evidence that children can benefit from using bibliotherapy themselves. More bibliotherapy is needed for older adults, children and parents, people with disabilities and people from ethnic minorities. Especially given its potentially prominent role in IAPT, more research that pays careful attention to the factors affecting the effectiveness of bibliotherapy in comparison to higher-intensity interventions is needed.

Acknowledgements

I am grateful to Paul Montgomery, Anne Stewart and colleagues in Oxfordshire Child and Adolescent Mental Health Services for their comments on earlier drafts of this chapter.

Note

1   An effect size of 1.0 is equivalent to one standard deviation's difference. By convention, an effect size of 0.20 is denoted small, 0.50 is medium, and 0.80 is large (Cohen, 1988).

References

Ackerson, J., Scogin, F., McKendree-Smith, N. & Lyman, R.D. (1998). Cognitive bibliotherapy for mild and moderate adolescent depressive symptomatology. *Journal of Consulting and Clinical Psychology, 66,* 685–690.

Anderson, L., Lewis, G., Araya, R., Elgie, R., Harrison, G., Proudfoot, J. *et al.* (2005). Self-help books for depression: How can practitioners and patients make the right choice? *British Journal of General Practice, 55,* 387–392.

Apodaca, T.R. & Miller, W.R. (2003). A meta-analysis of the effectiveness of bibliotherapy for alcohol problems. *Journal of Clinical Psychology, 59,* 289–304.

Baillie, A.J. & Rapee, R.M. (2004). Predicting who benefits from psychoeducation and self help for panic attacks. *Behaviour Research and Therapy, 42,* 513–527.

Bower, P., Richards, D. & Lovell, K. (2001). The clinical and cost-effectiveness of self-help treatments for anxiety and depressive disorders in primary care: A systematic review. *British Journal of General Practice, 51,* 838–845.

British Institute of Learning Disabilities (2005). *Your good health: Complete set.* Kidderminster: British Institute of Learning Disabilities.

Burns, D.D. (2000). *Feeling good: The new mood therapy* (2nd edn). New York: Avon.

Cohen, L.J. (1987). Bibliotherapy: Using literature to help children deal with difficult problems. *Journal of Psychosocial Nursing, 25,* 20–24.

Cohen, J.W. (1988). *Statistical power analysis for the behavioral sciences* (2nd edn). New York: Academic Press.

Cuijpers, P. (1997). Bibliotherapy in unipolar depression: A meta-analysis. *Journal of Behavior Therapy and Experimental Psychiatry, 28,* 139–147.

den Boer, P.C.A.M., Wiersma, D. & van den Bosch, R.J. (2004). Why is self-help neglected in the treatment of emotional disorders? A meta-analysis. *Psychological Medicine, 34,* 959–971.

Elgar, F.J. & McGrath, P.J. (2003). Self-administered psychosocial treatments for children and families. *Journal of Clinical Psychology, 59,* 321–339.

Felder-Puig, R., Maksys, A., Noestlinger, C., Gadner, H., Stark, H., Pfluegler, A. *et al.* (2003). Using a children's book to prepare children and parents for elective ENT surgery: Results of a randomized clinical trial. *International Journal of Pediatric Otorhinolaryngology, 67,* 35–41.

Floyd, M., Rohen, N., Shackelford, J.A.M., Hubbard, K.L., Parnell, M.B., Scogin, F. & Coates, A. (2006). Two-year follow-up of bibliotherapy and individual cognitive therapy for depressed older adults. *Behavior Modification, 30,* 281–294.

Glazener, C.M.A., Evans, J.H.C. & Peto, R.E. (2004). Complex behavioural and educational interventions for nocturnal enuresis in children. *Cochrane Database of Systematic Reviews, 1.* Art. No.: CD004668. DOI: 10.1002/14651858.CD004668.

Gould, R.A. & Clum, G.A. (1993). A meta-analysis of self-help treatment approaches. *Clinical Psychology Review, 13,* 169–186.

Gregory, R.J., Schwer Canning, S., Lee, T.W. & Wise, J.C. (2004). Cognitive bibliotherapy for depression: A meta-analysis. *Professional Psychology: Research and Practice, 35,* 275–280.

Griffiths, K.M. & Christensen, H. (2006). Review of randomised controlled trials of internet interventions for mental disorders and related conditions. *Clinical Psychologist, 10,* 16–29.

Heegaard, M. (1991). *When someone very special dies: Children can learn to cope with grief (drawing out feelings).* Minneapolis: Woodland Press.

Heifetz, L. (1977). Behavioral training for parents of retarded children: Formats based on instructional manuals. *American Journal of Mental Deficiency, 82,* 194–203.

Kaltenthaler, E., Shackley, P., Stevens, K., Beverley, C., Parry, G. & Chilcott, J. (2002). A systematic review and economic evaluation of computerised cognitive behaviour therapy for depression and anxiety. *Health Technology Assessment, 6*(22).

Lyneham, H.J. & Rapee, R.M. (2006). Evaluation of therapist-supported parent-implemented CBT for anxiety disorders in rural children. *Behaviour Research and Therapy, 44,* 1287–1300.

Marks, I.M., Cavanagh, K. & Gega, L. (2007). *Hands-on help: Computer-aided psychotherapy.* Maudsley Monographs 49. Hove: Psychology Press.

Marks, I.M., Mataix-Cols, D., Kenwright, M., Cameron, R., Hirsch, S. & Gega, L. (2003). Pragmatic evaluation of computer-aided self-help for anxiety and depression. *British Journal of Psychiatry, 183,* 57–65.

Marrs, R.W. (1995). A meta-analysis of bibliotherapy studies. *American Journal of Community Psychology, 23,* 843–870.

Mataix-Cols, D. & Marks, I.M. (2006). Self-help with minimal therapist contact for obsessive-compulsive disorder: A review. *European Psychiatry, 21,* 75–80.

Montgomery, P., Bjornstad, G. & Dennis, J. (2006). Media-based behavioural treatments for behavioural problems in children. *The Cochrane Database of Systematic Reviews, 1.* Art. No.: CD002206.pub3. DOI: 10.1002/14651858.CD002206.pub3.

National Institute for Mental Health in England (2003). Self-help interventions for mental health problems. Retrieved 24 October 2007 from www.nimhe.csip.org.uk/silo/files/selfhelppdf.pdf on

Newman, M.G., Erikson, T., Przeworski, A. & Dzus, E. (2003). Self-help and minimal-contact therapies for anxiety disorders: Is human contact necessary for therapeutic efficacy? *Journal of Clinical Psychology, 59,* 251–274.

O'Dell, S.L., Mahoney, N.D., Horton, W.G. & Turner, P.E. (1979). Media-assisted parent training: Alternative models. *Behavior Therapy, 10,* 103–110.

Papworth, M. (2006). Issues and outcomes associated with adult mental health self-help materials: A 'second order' review or 'qualitative meta-review'. *Journal of Mental Health, 15,* 387–409.

Rakos, R.F., Grodek, M.V. & Mack, K.K. (1985). The impact of a self-administered behavioral intervention program on pediatric asthma. *Journal of Psychosomatic Research, 29,* 101–108.

Rapee, R.M., Spence, S.H., Cobham, V. & Wignall, A. (2000). *Helping your anxious child: A step-by-step guide for parents.* Oakland, CA: New Harbinger.

Richards, D.A. & Suckling, R. (2008). Improving access to psychological therapy: The Doncaster demonstration site organisational model. *Clinical Psychology Forum, 181,* 9–16.

Rosen, G.M. (1976). The development and use of nonprescription behavior therapies. *American Psychologist, 39,* 139–141.

Rosen, G.M., Glasgow, R.E. & Barrera, M., Jr. (2007). Good intentions are not enough: Reflections on past and future efforts to advance self-help. In P.L. Watkins & G.A. Clum (Eds.) *Handbook of self-help therapies* (pp. 25–39). New York: Routledge.

Sanders, M.R., Montgomery, D.T. & Brechman-Toussaint, M.L. (2000). The mass media and the prevention of child behavior problems: The evaluation of a television series to promote positive outcomes for parents and their children. *Journal of Child Psychology and Psychiatry, 41,* 939–948.

Santacruz, I., Mendez, F.J. & Sanchez-Meca, J. (2006). Play therapy applied by parents for children with darkness phobia: Comparison of two programmes. *Child and Family Behavior Therapy, 28,* 19–35.

Scogin, F., Bynum, J., Stephens, G. & Calhoun, S. (1990). Efficacy of self-administered programs: Meta-analytic review. *Professional Psychology: Research and Practice, 21,* 42–47.

Scogin, F., Floyd, M., Jamison, C., Ackerson, J., Landreville, P. & Bissonnette, L. (1996). Negative outcomes: What is the evidence on self-administered treatments? *Journal of Consulting and Clinical Psychology, 64,* 1086–1089.

Stefano, S.C., Bacaltchuk, J., Blay, S.L. & Hay, P. (2006). Self-help treatments for disorders of recurrent binge eating: A systematic review. *Acta Psychiatrica Scandinavica, 113,* 452–459.

Winett, R.A., Anderson, E.S., Moore, J.F., Sikkema, K.J., Hook, R.J., Webster, D.A. *et al.* (1992). Family/media approach to HIV prevention: Results with a home-based, parent-teen video program. *Health Psychology, 11,* 203–206.

19

Clinical Psychology in Primary Care

James Gray

Introduction

It is over thirty years since the first published report of a clinical psychologist working in primary care in the UK (described in Day & Wren, 1994). Primary care psychology has continued to expand from a conference and newsletter in the early 90s, leading in 2007 to the establishment of a Primary Care Special Interest Group within the British Psychological Society (BPS) Division of Clinical Psychology.

Within this chapter there is insufficient scope for comprehensive coverage of all factors pertaining to clinical psychology in primary health care (see e.g. Bor & McCann, 1999; Cape & Miller, 2006; Haas, 2004). The focus is therefore on what is different about primary care, and what specific competencies such work entails. The rise of stepped care will also be covered, and there is an outline of some of the innovations associated with the UK's expanding Improving Access to Psychological Therapies programme.

Defining Primary Care

First there is a need to define primary health care. This refers to services accessed directly by patients, as opposed to secondary care services which require a referral. While there are a range of the former services, this chapter will focus on family doctors/ general practitioners (GPs) and the other staff working within the typical clinic: practice nurses, health visitors, receptionists, administrators, counsellors, etc.

Background and Context

Sixty years ago, GPs in the UK needed strong inducement and encouragement to join the new National Health Service (NHS) and today remain a highly regarded, popular and powerful professional group. So far they have avoided the fate of other primary care services, as Kat (1994) points out: 'Three of the four primary health care services brought into the NHS in 1946 – pharmacy, dentistry and opticians – have already become privatized [sic] or available to the majority of the working population only at substantial cost at the time of use' (p. 23).

GPs are frequently self-employed, contracting their services to the NHS. As a concrete example, the clinic building is frequently owned by the practice partners, not the NHS. GPs are robust, independent professionals with strongly held beliefs about how best to help their patients. This includes a vast range of attitudes to the provision of psychological therapy within their practices, from highly supportive to sceptical.

In an attempt to improve quality and reduce this variability, the Department of Health has paid increasing attention to mental health and primary care. In the 1999 National Service Framework for Mental Health, two of the seven standards are the direct responsibility of primary care providers, and they are partners in the other five (Cohen, 2000). Within the new GP contracts there is an explicit emphasis on managing psychological distress. For example, depression correctly identified and appropriately treated is specifically rewarded within the Quality and Outcomes Framework – and this means direct financial reward. With the introduction of the National Institute for Health and Clinical Excellence (NICE) guidelines for treatment of psychological disorders, there is also a strong emphasis on management within primary care. Practice-based commissioning is likely to further place primary care at the heart of mental health financing and decision making.

High Levels of Psychological Distress in Primary Care

It is estimated that between 40 and 60 per cent of GP consultations are primarily psychological in nature (e.g. Newman & Rozensky, 2005) and up to 70 per cent have a strong psychological component (Shiers, 2001). Meanwhile 90 per cent of common mental health problems are treated wholly in primary care (Foster, 2005). Despite this, almost all mental health resources are targeted at people with severe difficulties. Cohen (2000) estimated that 80 per cent of all NHS monies spent on mental health go to in-patient services, although these are used by less than one in twenty-five of those with psychological difficulties.

Additionally, some people with very high levels of psychological need are managed by GPs, primarily or exclusively. About 30 per cent of people with severe mental illness are managed wholly in primary care. They may have disengaged from secondary care, for example. These are not the 'worried well' but the 'worried unwell.'

Clinical Psychologists in Primary Care

During the 1970s, UK clinical psychologists began moving out of traditional psychiatric hospital settings, spurred by concerns about patient access and stigma. Such moves were encouraged by the 1977 Trethowan sub-committee report on NHS workforce planning, with specific recommendations made for clinical psychologists to develop work directly with GPs. Simply moving location and yet providing the same service as in secondary care was never really an option. From the start there were concerns about potential overwhelming demand and the need to have a broader remit than simply providing individual therapy (Griffiths, 1984).

Perhaps the cardinal feature of primary care work is *breadth* and therefore the need to develop a *generalist* approach. Just like the medically trained family doctor who is a *general* practitioner, the psychologist needs, perhaps, to be a general psychological practitioner (*a GPsyP?*). This means that assessment skills are paramount, both for developing a formulation of 'the problem', but also as to whether primary care is the right place for any treatment, and what can realistically be achieved in the current episode of care.

Clinical Psychology Approaches and Services

Breadth can also be a feature of the roles a psychologist can adopt. While usually centring on provision of individual psychological therapy (occasionally couple, family or group), psychologists can encompass broader remits. These can include supervision or consultation to the wider team; providing training and education; and developing services through management and leadership roles, research and audit. Finally there are roles for health promotion, prevention of ill health being a major feature of primary care work. The most cost-effective of all health interventions is simply a GP mentioning to a patient to stop smoking; only a tiny percentage will successfully stop but, given the miniscule 'outlay', this proportion still makes a significant difference. Papworth (2000) sees prevention work as one of the core competencies for a clinical psychologist in primary care; both individual prevention and community approaches to improving the wider population-based mental or physical health. Clinical psychologists working in primary care should be cognisant of the health psychology literature and may benefit from a placement in this field during training.

Lifespan Perspective

Given the generalist approach of clinical psychologists in primary care, some will see patients from across the full lifespan. This could include preschool children with sleeping or toileting difficulties through to people in their 70s or 80s experiencing mood difficulties or concern about memory problems. It is here that the initial professional training, with its emphasis of working across the lifespan, can make clinical psychologists stand out from other mental health workers. In the UK, however, it is more usual that psychologists work only with adults of 'working age', and that the other groups are seen within specialist services. Nevertheless, the full age range may be 'brought' into the consulting room, as it is common for advice to be sought about children or elderly parents.

Particular Competencies Required

Given the pace of primary care work, the ability to rapidly make a good enough *engagement* with patients is a core competence, and there are also some particular features of working in primary care. The patient has often developed a specific 'transference' to the GP and clinic and this can include the psychologist. Asking early on in assessment 'How do you feel about being here?' can help to elucidate such relationships. Similarly, the way that the referral has been made sets up certain expectancies for the patient, both helpful and unhelpful. Patients who view their problems as 'physical' rather than 'psychological' may need careful engagement towards a '*both-and*' position.

Assessment needs to be broad-reaching but also efficient, requiring a trade-off between extensive psychotherapy intake assessment and more focused explorations. One major role of primary care is to help patients make sense of their multiple 'symptoms' – to help them to organise them into a coherent experience. Often in primary care there will be a mixture of psychological, physical and social issues interacting to form a complex picture. Psychologists with both *formulation* skills and a knowledge of diagnostic frameworks (and their limitations) will be able both to help patients structure their experience of distress and to communicate with medical colleagues.

One outcome of assessment may be that the patient's needs are best met elsewhere; either in specialist secondary care services or in the voluntary sector. An important role for psychologists is either making these onward referrals or *signposting* the patient to such services. Much GP frustration is often expressed about the difficulty in accessing secondary care services, especially when patients are deemed unsuitable for secondary care and are sent back without much explanation or any alternative suggestions. Given that GPs see patients on average for only nine minutes (up from six minutes in the 1960s), referral letters or form-filling can take much longer than the consultation. Any help with expediting referrals is welcomed. Similarly, communicating and liaising with services to encourage acceptance of patients is a key skill. Many GPs do not hold a particularly bio-medical view of psychological distress (at least for the common mental health difficulties) and there is often no 'battle' to get a psychosocial view recognised. GPs, being close to the community and seeing people over the lifespan and in the family context, are often well able to see the broad picture.

Where patients are accepted for psychological therapy in primary care, this is usually brief (or even ultra-brief) and structured. Competence in such approaches is required. However, just as with a GP, there is the option of intermittent but prolonged contact.

Mr P was originally seen for agoraphobia and panic attacks. He had not been able to attend the secondary care psychotherapy service due to his anxiety but was just able to attend the medical centre as it was in his 'safe zone.' Psycho-education and exposure over four sessions resulted in a rapid improvement and he became much more active. Six months later Mr P was again seen, this time for low mood and poor self-esteem. He had been dwelling on the 'wasted years' when house-bound, and comparing his situation with those around him. He also felt hopeless regarding getting back to work or into a relationship. This time six sessions helped him to 'mourn' the wasted time and to develop ways of facing his fears and improving his self-confidence. Eighteen months later two top-up sessions helped him deal with a relationship breakdown and get back on track.

Challenging Issues – Customers vs. Window Shopper

As a psychologist with expertise in psychological therapy, there is a need to think carefully about the person's relationship to the 'help' offered – does the person want what the psychologist thinks they are 'selling' and are they likely to benefit from it? If you only have a hammer it is tempting to view all problems as nails. It is important to recall that people may be attending to help other people's anxieties, or to show they are addressing problems when they have little intention to do so.

GPs are powerful allies in the battle to obtain housing, benefits and asylum entitlement. Working in surgeries, psychologists may often be asked for letters to support such applications. This can provoke strong emotional reactions as therapists can feel misled into providing therapy when what was really wanted was a letter. This needs to be taken to supervision, explored and addressed in order to prevent cynicism or other negative emotional responses.

Service and Contextual Issues

Being a sessional worker in a number of surgeries, it is important to try to become viewed as a core team member rather than an infrequent visitor. Public relations skills are required in abundance, while at the same time earning respect as a professional colleague. It is easy to become isolated and feel unsupported from one's professional peers. Regular meetings, supervision within one's own professional family and peer support are essential.

Noticing and participating in the culture, e.g. around lunch and festivities, is highly valued. Surgeries are hierarchical, to a greater or lesser degree, and not all the power relations are immediately obvious. Where the psychologist fits in the hierarchy is variable, depending on their own behaviour and handling of the situation. There can be competition or cooperation between counsellors, mental health nurses, graduate mental health workers and clinical psychologists as to who is best placed to provide what to whom. There is often an undercurrent of 'better than/not as good as' and strong interpersonal dynamics of envy. Indeed, simply having 'Dr' as a title creates a particular context for working within a GP surgery. Handling such issues skilfully is crucial to being able to contribute effectively as a psychologist.

Requesting special treatment (which the psychologist may view as in no way special or demanding) can trigger hostility. For example, having control over appointments marks psychologists as unusual (usually receptionists or patients book into open diary slots). However, handing over control can make planning follow-up/ongoing appointments impossible. Similarly, wanting the same room, or even comfortable 'therapy' chairs and an absence of medical equipment, can come across as requiring VIP handling. Explaining the rationale, negotiating demands and compromise can all minimise these issues.

Ethics

Perhaps the most pertinent ethical issues affecting work in primary care concern maintaining boundaries and preserving confidentiality. It is a relatively frequent occurrence that there are invitations to breach boundaries (e.g. requests for help for colleagues or even GPs' family or friends). Similarly, confidentiality can be viewed as different in a GP clinic where care is shared more directly within the team. For an in-depth discussion of this issue see Waskett (1999) and Pembroke (1999), who provide helpful chapters on confidentiality and boundaries, respectively.

Models Used in Primary Care

Psychologists have usually struggled with meeting the high levels of demand for their services. In secondary care this has been managed by long waiting lists, opt-ins, etc. In primary care various innovations have been adopted. Rather than traditional weekly, hour-long therapy, there have been moves to shorten the appointment length, or reduce the frequency. For example, Carey and Mullan (2007), working in Scotland, advocate completely relinquishing control over referral criteria and the psychologist's diary. They describe how giving GPs full power over the referral decision-making process, and letting patients decide the frequency and duration of appointments (potentially being able to be seen more than weekly and by two psychologists simultaneously), led to a situation of increased access, satisfaction and no waiting list in their primary care practices. Robson and France (1997) had also found this a decade earlier and in a West London (as opposed to Scottish) context.

Advice clinics (White, 1998) or self-help resource centres (Moore, 2007) have also been used in primary care to manage demand. These can be viewed as providing a consultation model or 'low intensity' service according to the principles of stepped care (see Bower & Gilbody, 2005). Stepped care means providing the 'least restrictive' interventions first (e.g. guided self-help or group psychoeducation), but if these are unsuitable, ineffective or unacceptable to the patient they are 'stepped up' to more traditional 'high intensity' therapy.

Ms H was referred by her GP for long-standing issues including chronic depression, debt, poor health and relationship difficulties. Despite the complexity of the problems she chose to begin with guided self-help targeting her low mood. This entailed a weekly phone call from an assistant psychologist with assignment of various workbooks (behavioural activation, challenging extreme thinking and assertiveness). She was motivated and did well with the low-intensity work, becoming more active and feeling more in control of her life. She was eventually seen by a clinical psychologist for a further 12 sessions over eight months, targeting a deeply held sense of worthlessness and self-disgust, stemming from difficult childhood experiences.

Improving Access to Psychological Therapies (IAPT)

In the UK the IAPT project, launched in 2007, is bringing big changes to clinical psychology in primary care. In two national demonstration sites, Doncaster and Newham, the government invested large sums of money in making access to evidence-based therapy much more widely available. Many more sites are now also up and running with a planned rollout throughout the UK. This initiative stemmed from economist Lord Layard's big idea that government should focus on Gross National Happiness rather than the Gross National Product, a purely monetary measure, since evidence suggests that, beyond a certain limit, increasing wealth does not increase well-being (Layard, 2005). Layard argued that one of the best ways of increasing happiness is by reducing the distress inherent in common mental health difficulties. There is good evidence that talking therapy, particularly cognitive behavioural therapy (CBT), can alleviate this, but there is insufficient current provision to meet the demand.

In both national demonstration sites there has been implementation of a stepped care model with use of trained low-intensity workers conducting mainly telephone-based guided self-help or computerised CBT. In Newham, in addition to far greater use of telephone delivery, other innovations included opt-out rather than opt-in for clients (the latter can reduce access for some groups); evening and weekend work; community languages spoken; and partnership with employment coaches. Clinical governance is maintained within a supervision structure of both regular, weekly and duty supervision. The latter ensures that assistants conducting low-intensity and telephone assessment have immediate access to a senior member of the team to assist in decision making and to provide containment/support. There is currently a telephone brief assessment within three days of GP or self-referral and an immediate start of low-intensity work if appropriate. How this will impact clinical psychologists in primary care is currently unclear but it is envisaged that supervision of IAPT work may be a key role. Analysis of the outcomes of both projects is ongoing, although initial reports have been positive and more resources have been allocated for the expansion of IAPT nationwide.

Conclusion

Primary care is viewed as increasingly pivotal within the NHS and this will continue as practice-based commissioning develops over the next decade. As a result of their broad based training, clinical psychologists are well placed for these developments. Having knowledge, skills and competencies in direct clinical work, supervision and consultation, and in planning, managing and evaluating, psychologists have much to offer in this setting, as well as in more traditional secondary care settings.

References

Bor, R. & McCann, D. (Eds.) (1999). *The practice of counselling in primary care*. London: Sage.

Bower, P. & Gilbody, S. (2005). Stepped care in psychological therapies: Access, effectiveness and efficiency; narrative literature review. *British Journal of Psychiatry, 186,* 11–17.

Cape, J. & Miller, Y. (2006). Working in primary health care. In J. Hall & S. Llewelyn (Eds.) *What is clinical psychology?* (4th edn, ch. 2). Oxford: Oxford University Press.

Carey, T.A. & Mullan, R.J. (2007). GP referral guidelines: Is there another side to the coin? *Clinical Psychology Forum, 170,* 29–32.

Cohen, A. (2000). *Primary care mental health*. HSJ monographs no. 2. London: Emap public sector management.

Day, C. & Wren, B. (1994). Journey to the centre of primary care: Primary care psychology in perspective. *Clinical Psychology Forum, 65,* 3–6.

Foster, J. (2005). Commissioning psychological therapies: A brave new world? *Primary Care Mental Health, 3,* 279–282.

Griffiths, T.A. (1984). Clinical psychology in primary health care. In F.N. Watts (Ed.) *New developments in clinical psychology* (pp. 221–233). BPS/Wiley: Chichester.

Haas, L.J. (2004). *Handbook of primary care psychology*. Oxford: Oxford University Press.

Kat, B. (1994). The contribution of psychological knowledge to primary health care: Taking a step back to go forward. *Clinical Psychology Forum, 65,* 23–26.

Layard, R. (2005). *Happiness: Lessons from a new science*. London: Penguin.

Moore, P. (2007). The resource centre: An innovative stepped-care approach to common mental health problems in primary care. *Clinical Psychology Forum, 170,* 11–15.

Newman, R. & Rozensky, R. (2005). Psychology and primary care: Evolving traditions. *Journal of Clinical Psychology in Medical Settings, 2*(1), 3–6.

Papworth, M. (2000). Primary care psychology: Towards a model of service delivery. *Clinical Psychology Forum, 142,* 22–25.

Pembroke, G. (1999). Deeper issues in collaboration: Avoiding pitfalls and managing internal boundaries. In R. Bor & D. McCann (Eds.) *The practice of counselling in primary care* (pp. 62–76). London: Sage.

Robson, M. & France, R. (1997). *Cognitive behavioural therapy in primary care*. London: Jessica Kingsley.

Shiers, D. (2001). Preface. In R. Chambers, E. Boath & G. Wakley (Eds.) *Mental healthcare matters in primary care* (pp. vi–x). Oxford: Radcliffe Medical Press.

Waskett, C. (1999). Confidentiality in a team setting. In R. Bor & D. McCann (Eds.) *The practice of counselling in primary care* (pp. 118–139). London: Sage.

White, J. (1998). An advice clinic in primary care. *Clinical Psychology Forum, 113,* 9–12.

20

Developing Cultural Competence in Clinical Psychology Work with BME Communities

Rashmi Shankar

Although the roots of clinical psychology lay in academic departments, the applied profession has evolved in response to social, economic and political forces (Hersch, 1969; Strickland, 1988). Clinical psychology practitioners nowadays therefore usually focus their efforts on alleviating human distress associated with disordered psychological functioning. This professional emphasis on improving the quality of life of children and adults, including those who were socially disadvantaged, has been maintained through various stages of its evolution (Kazarian & Evans, 1998). Through the application of theoretical knowledge in the areas of diagnosis, therapy and research, clinical psychologists have used their skills to 'help persons with behaviour disabilities and mental disorders to achieve better adjustment and self-expression' (Shakow, 1976, p. 559). Yet in spite of the expansion within the discipline (seen in the growth of subspecialities), it has been acknowledged internationally (Kazarian & Evans, 1998) that diverse ethnic groups are underrepresented among those who receive the services of clinical psychologists.

In Britain, where clinical psychologists work largely in health and social care settings, a number of official reports have documented the reduced access to psychological therapy for black and minority ethnic (BME) individuals (Department of Health, 2004) and the inadequate mental health service provision to these client groups (e.g. Department of Health, 1993). Inequalities in service use and the differences in outcomes are also acknowledged (Department of Health, 2003). This situation persists in spite of changes in legislation. For instance, the Race Relations Amendment Act (2000) places a duty on the public sector to prevent discrimination and to promote race equality. As corrective action, proposals and plans have been put forward (Department of Health, 2003, 2005) which are aimed at reforming the service experience and creating better outcomes for people from BME groups. Particular emphasis has been placed on developing a culturally competent workforce. However, the various terms used in this literature to impart the meaning of what may constitute such competencies (e.g. cultural 'awareness', 'sensitivity') seem not to be adequately explained. Authors have noted the tendency to focus on cultural knowledge or the descriptive characteristics of a group – e.g. religion, diet, language – while ignoring the structural inequalities that mark the lived experience of BME clients (Keating, 2007; Fernando, 2003). It is therefore important for clinical psychology practitioners to consider the various features that constitute culturally competent practice.

Updating a model of cultural competence in healthcare service delivery which was first proposed in 1991, Campinha-Bacote (2007) identified five constituent constructs: cultural awareness (an introspective focus on one's personal and professional biases, including awareness of inequalities in healthcare delivery); cultural knowledge (information on diverse worldviews); cultural encounter (face-to-face interactions); cultural desire (motivation to seek engagement with cultural awareness); and cultural skill or the ability to conduct a culturally appropriate assessment for the client's health problems. Others (e.g. Kemp & Rasbridge, 2004) have suggested a bifurcation into 'general' and 'specific' skills, where the former means an attitude of respect, openness and a willingness to learn skills related to working with diverse groups, while the latter skills focus on developing knowledge and communication related to diverse groups in the community. Bhui and Bhugra (2007) describe the term 'cultural capability' to include a focus on reflective practice and on new learning along with the competencies around specific tasks. Cross *et al.* (1989) presented a useful model of cultural competence which is elaborated upon in the final section of this chapter. In an influential report (Department of Health, 2003), a culturally capable service is recommended through workforce development, increased partnership working between the statutory and voluntary sectors, flexibility in adapting the service provision to diverse cultural norms and ensuring appropriate language access.

During the past decade, the author (a NHS consultant clinical psychologist) has developed and taught a module on issues of cultural competence as applied to clinical psychology practice with adult BME clients. The content of this training has been shaped by the questions and the stimulating discussions held with successive groups of participants (mainly clinical psychology trainees on the Oxford Doctoral Course and occasionally other professional groups). This valuable feedback served to highlight some of the topics that need to be considered in order to obtain an overview of the issues in this area. Partly guided by this, in the rest of this chapter the reader is introduced to certain contextual information about BME communities in Britain along with clinically relevant information. Since the meaning of certain terms may be unclear or unfamiliar to readers (for instance, race, culture and ethnicity can be used interchangeably) and the terms used to describe ethnicity may cause confusion (reported by many professionals), the next section lists some key definitions.

Definitions of Terms

a) *Black and minority ethnic (BME) people*: this term has been used to refer to all people who are of minority ethnic status in England (Department of Health, 2003). These individuals usually belong to groups who experience discrimination and social exclusion (e.g. people of Irish, African or Asian origin). These groups are heterogeneous with respect to context variables (e.g. social class, language, religion, ethnicity).

b) *'Race'*: although this term has been used to classify human beings on the basis of biological features, it has now been discredited scientifically. It has been shown that more than 80 per cent genetic variation exists between individuals *within* a group, rather than *between* members of different racial groups (see Zuckerman, 1998). Defined by Husband (1987) as a 'socially constructed categorisation which specifies rules for the identification of members' (p. 19), the term is more appropriately used to understand issues of power and discrimination in social relationships, for instance in the term 'race-relations.'

c) *Culture*: this term has stimulated much debate (see, for example, D'Andrade, 1984). Authors have emphasised the varied elements that constitute a learned system of meaning which can exist at physical (e.g. diet, dress), psychological (e.g. roles, values, beliefs) and social (e.g. institutions) levels for each individual. Culture is taken to mean the shared characteristics of any group or society such as language, social roles, dress codes, beliefs, family patterns, child-rearing practices, etc. that are passed on across generations. Fernando (2003) points out that rather than a closed system which can be defined clearly, culture is viewed as 'a flexible system of values and world-views that people live by and create and re-create continuously' (p. 11).

d) *Ethnicity*: often used interchangeably with culture, this term acknowledges 'the place of history, language and culture in the construction of subjectivity and identity' (Hall, 1992, p. 257). In this description, racial heritage is combined with cultural background and the importance of self-selection is recognised.

e) *Racism*: refers to the systematic application of prejudice in personal and institutional contexts. It can be understood as 'a means of domination, exploitation and enslavement at a personal, political and economic level' (Fernando, 1991 p. 28).

f) *Institutional racism*: refers to the reproduction of practices of power which discriminate against people on the ground of perceived race within institutions. Following the Stephen Lawrence case in the UK, the Macpherson Report (1999) defined this concept as: 'the collective failure of an organization to provide an appropriate and professional service to people because of their colour, culture or ethnic origin.' A recent example of institutional racism was reported by Strand (2008), who found that the expectation of low achievement could influence academic opportunity for black Caribbean pupils.

g) *Institutional religious intolerance*: describing negative attitudes on the basis of religion, this term was proposed by Mr Justice Keith who chaired an inquiry into the murder of Zahid Mubarek, a young Asian prisoner. (news.bbc.co.uk/1/hi/uk/5126614.stm).

h) *Descriptions of ethnic origin*: the discourse on social inequalities in mental health care has drawn attention to the need to collect data on ethnicity. For instance, in the NHS this data is now required to be collected routinely. The Census categories provide examples of the main ethnic groups in Britain. However, practitioners need to be mindful of the inherent diversity represented within these groups. Additionally, clients as well as international researchers may choose national categories to describe ethnicity. For example, people from India, Pakistan, Bangladesh, Sri Lanka, Bhutan, Nepal and Maldives might be described as 'South Asian' as these countries self-selected this description. www.saarc-sec.org/main.php

The Context

Although people from different ethnic communities have lived in Britain for many centuries (see Fryer, 1984; Husband, 1987), it was in 1991 that the Census first included a question on ethnicity. At the time, nearly 6 per cent of the population of England and Wales described themselves as belonging to an ethnic minority group. People of South Asian descent (mainly, India, Pakistan and Bangladesh) constituted half of this group and 30 per cent classified themselves as black (Commission for Racial Equality, 1999). The majority of these communities lived in urban centres, predominantly in London, the West Midlands, West Yorkshire and Greater Manchester. Chinese people seemed to be the most dispersed compared with the South Asian and Black groups. Numerous languages were represented among the members of these different ethnic communities. Punjabi, Urdu, Hindi, Gujarati, Bengali and Sylheti were used by the South Asian groups. Patois was spoken by some of the Caribbean groups and Cantonese was the most commonly spoken language among the Chinese community.

People from Ireland, Germany and Poland constituted a substantial part of the 'white' group that was born outside Britain.

The figures from the 2001 Census showed an increase in the ethnic population of England and Wales to about 9 per cent. This was partly due to the new category of 'mixed race'. For the first time, two areas in the country (London boroughs of Newham and Brent) recorded BME communities as being in the majority. In addition, with a third of the population described as Indian, Leicester was the city-wide authority with the largest proportion of a non-white group. An optional question on religion was asked for the first time. Christianity (71 per cent), Islam (3 per cent) and Hinduism (1.1 per cent) were the most frequently chosen responses. This result has to be seen against the fact that nearly 15 per cent recorded 'no religion'. Since the 2001 census, a substantial increase was also reported in the number of migrant workers coming to the UK, especially from the new eastern European EU member states: news.bbc.co.uk/2/shared/spl/hi/guides/457000/457021/html/nn5page1.stm.

Social Exclusion

Available evidence (e.g. the report of the Social Exclusion Unit: SEU, 2000) highlighted the complex issues related to social exclusion among minority ethnic groups. Compared with the general population, the people from these communities are more likely to live in poor housing in economically deprived areas, be unemployed, report poor health and be victims of crime. For instance, unemployment was more than double in BME communities (1998: 5.8 per cent white, BME: 13 per cent) and even higher in Pakistani and Bangladeshi people (20 and 23 per cent, respectively). People born in Ireland are twice as likely to be unemployed as the native-born and more likely to be involved in manual, unskilled and personal service employment (Bracken et al., 1998). The fourth National Survey of the Mental Health of Ethnic Minorities (Nazroo, 1997) emphasised the need to consider relationships between social variables such as ethnicity, migration, gender, class membership and marital status when making comparisons about the mental health status of individuals.

Psychological Distress and BME Groups

Based on hospital admission data, an overrepresentation of the schizophrenia diagnosis was reported for people born outside England and Wales, most often for people from the Caribbean, Africa and from South Asia (see Fernando, 1989). Several decades of research have been summarised (Department of Health, 1993) to show that in the case of the African-Caribbean groups, this diagnosis was used 3–6 times more often than the native-born. Compared with the incidence in Jamaica, that among British Caribbeans was significantly elevated. Rates of schizophrenia in second generation UK-born black people are reported to be higher than those for the first generation. Black people are more likely to be detained under the Mental Health Act (MHAC, 2005) and they are overrepresented in police admissions to psychiatric hospitals. They are also more likely to receive stronger forms of treatment. The higher reported rates for schizophrenia among the black in-patient groups seem at odds with the finding for similar rates for psychosis between white and Caribbean men in a community survey (Nazroo, 1997). Debates about the interpretation of the increased reports of schizophrenia have spanned over three decades. Explanations in the literature have referred to factors related to biology, selective migration, social exclusion, institutional racism, inaccurate diagnosis, stereotyped attitudes and professional perceptions of greater risk leading to more coercive clinical management (Fernando, 2003; Bhugra & Cochrane, 2001; Littlewood & Lipsedge, 1982).

A more inconsistent picture seems to emerge from the findings about mental health issues related to South Asian groups in the UK. Although there have been reports of more frequent diagnoses of schizophrenia for this group (e.g. Carpenter & Brockington, 1980) and higher hospital admissions (McGovern & Cope, 1991), the balance of evidence from in-patient studies (e.g. Cochrane, 1977), GP consultation rates (e.g. Gillam *et al.*, 1989) and community surveys (e.g. Nazroo, 1997; Cochrane & Stopes-Roe, 1981) suggests that the rates of psychiatric morbidity are similar to or lower than the native-born population. Reviewing quantitative studies to inquire into inequalities of mental health service use across ethnic groups, Bhui *et al.* (2003) found that of all ethnic groups South Asian patients were the least likely to be given a diagnosis for mental disorder. This could reflect difficulties in detection or miscommunications between the clients and their GPs (Ineichen, 1990). For instance, in situations where psychological complaints were expressed by Asian patients, this group received more physical diagnoses from GPs than their white counterparts (Wilson & MacCarthy, 1994). Reporting similar levels of anxiety and depression in a primary care sample, another study found that GPs were more likely to assign a psychiatric diagnosis to white English patients when compared with Punjabi Asians (Bhui *et al.*, 2001). Explanations for such discrepancies have been suggested in terms of different metaphors of distress (e.g. Krause, 1989) and the GP's own explanatory models of non-pathological presentations of subclinical distress (e.g. Bhui *et al.*, 2001). Interestingly, when the presence of a psychological disorder was recognised, the Asian groups were least likely to be referred to specialist care by GPs (Bhui *et al.*, 2003). It is suggested that aspects of their role (e.g. gate-keeping) and a reliance on physical idioms may affect GPs' estimation of the severity of common mental disorders (Bhui & Bhugra, 2007). The need for more systematic research in this area is further emphasised by the national finding of excess of suicides among South Asian women (Department of Health, 1993; Soni Raleigh, 1996).

The importance of looking beyond a dichotomy based on skin colour when considering the impact of social exclusion in Britain was acknowledged in a report following the 1991 Census which did not include a separate category for the classification of Irish ethnicity (Hickman & Walter, 1997). Irish people in Britain constituted the largest migrant minority in Western Europe (Bracken *et al.*, 1998). These authors have described the evidence of distress in this community, found in the high rates of psychiatric hospitalisation (twice as likely as the native-born) and in the predominance of Irish-born individuals in diagnostic categories such as depression and alcohol-related problems. Rates of schizophrenia were second to those for the African-Caribbean population, and an excess of mortality by suicide is reported in the literature (Harding & Balarajan, 1996; Neeleman *et al.*, 1997). According to an official report (Department of Health, 2003), there is concern that stereotyping, hostility, lack of patient satisfaction at the primary care level and inadequate information about services may act as barriers to some groups of Irish people (e.g. homeless men, Travellers). The change in the self-description categories in the 2001 Census to include an Irish category is seen as a positive step in addressing the health-related issues for this group (Harding & Balarajan, 2001).

Promoting Better Access to Services

During the past few decades the national and international published literature has reported on the need to promote more equitable access to mental health services (e.g. Flaskerud, 1986; Fernando, 2003). The stigma and shame associated with mental illness may keep potential users from accessing the mental health service networks. Therefore, it may be important for practitioners to consider issues related to information dissemination and to the local publicity of their services through community media. Certain practical considerations could also act as barriers. For instance, the service may not be located near the client's community, the hours of operation may be restrictive and assistance may be needed with transport and child care. The client may also need help with referral to agencies for social, economic, legal, immigration and medical problems. Encouraging and supporting user participation in the evaluation of services is essential for effective service planning. Many of these issues have been recommended as part of a culture-compatible approach to service delivery (Flaskerud, 1986).

Forging sustained working partnerships and engaging the community are approaches which have been endorsed in the UK government's policy agenda. According to a Maudsley discussion paper (MDP, 2000), the voluntary sector providers emerged as a response to the crisis in statutory provision for BME communities. Examples of community initiatives within the voluntary sector abound in the literature (Fernando, 2003; Lipsedge, 1993). In spite of the challenges posed by limited funding, marginalisation, poor management and diminished power to influence change, these projects have provided culture-congruent models of helping clients.

A useful exercise for practitioners aiming to become familiar with local needs can be to construct a demographic information profile for the population that is served by one's locality. This might include ethnic groups, housing, occupation, age, religion, and community languages. Getting acquainted with community local groups and community organisations can be a valuable step for statutory agencies. This can help joint working through which the deficits in service provision may be better identified.

Cultural Competence in Clinical Practice

In view of the issues raised in this chapter, one of the challenges for clinical psychology practitioners is how to develop clinical skills in the face of an evolving evidence base. Taking a critical look at clinical psychology service provision, Nadirshaw (1999) emphasised the need for changes to occur in the organisational structures that govern the operation of these services. Providing a systemic view of cultural competence, Cross *et al.* (1989) give a useful definition: 'cultural competence is a set of congruent behaviours, attitudes and policies that come together in a system, agency, or among professionals and enable that system, agency, or those professionals to work effectively in cross-cultural situations' (p. 28). In this monograph, six stages are described in the progression of a service from cultural destructiveness, incapacity, and blindness through to pre-competence, competence and finally to cultural proficiency. For the desired changes to occur within a service agency, the authors list actions that need to be adopted at the three levels of policy, service organisation and clinical practice. In order to arrive at a culturally competent formulation of a client's problems, the clinical psychology practitioner will be served well by this information base combined with the rich literature of clinical, cultural and cross-cultural psychology. Salient points that could guide the clinical psychologist to navigate through the tasks of an assessment session are:

- accessing appropriate language skills through interpreters;
- acknowledging the Eurocentric bias of Western professional models (e.g. Kleinman, 1987; Butcher *et al.*, 1998);
- addressing the reality of racism in clients' experiences (e.g. Keating, 2007);

- awareness of the influence of cross-cultural differences in social behaviour and communication (e.g. Sue & Sue, 1990);
- informing oneself about how the client's explanatory models may shape beliefs about psychological distress and about the resolution of this distress (e.g. Kaiser *et al.*, 1998);
- considering issues related to the client's ethnicity, socio-economic status, and social and/or gender role when arriving at psychological formulations;
- acquiring training to work with culturally sensitive professional models (e.g. Padesky & Greenberger, 1995; Laungani, 2004; Berry, 2006);
- exploring the role of religious/spiritual affiliations on the construction of core beliefs;
- addressing interpersonal and family issues in problem formulations (e.g. the role of negative expressed emotion).

Conclusion

Certain changes in UK legislation have sharpened the focus on the inequalities that exist in the delivery of mental health services to BME groups. In order to make services more equitable, changes are required both at the level of the individual practitioner and within the organisational environment. Drawing on the published literature, this chapter has sought to inform clinical psychology practitioners about the psychological service needs of BME groups and to stimulate thinking about the issues relevant to developing cultural competence in clinical psychology practice as applied to work with BME clients.

References

Berry, J. (2006). Stress perspectives on acculturation. In D. Sam & J. Berry (Eds.) *The Cambridge handbook of acculturation psychology* (pp. 43–57). Cambridge: Cambridge University Press.

Bhugra, D. & Cochrane, R. (2001). *Psychiatry in multicultural Britain*. London: Gaskell.

Bhui, K. & Bhugra, D. (2007). Ethnic inequalities and cultural capability framework in mental healthcare. In D. Bhugra & K. Bhui (Eds.) *Textbook of cultural psychiatry* (pp. 81–92). Cambridge: Cambridge University Press.

Bhui, K., Bhugra, D., Goldberg, D., Dunn, G. & Desai, M. (2001). Cultural influences on the prevalence of common mental disorder, general practitioners, assessments and help-seeking among Punjabi and English people visiting their general practitioner. *Psychological Medicine, 31*, 815–825.

Bhui, K., Stansfield, S., Hull, S., Priebe, S., Mole, F. & Feder, G. (2003). Ethnic variations in pathways to and use of specialist mental health services in the UK. Systematic review. *British Journal of Psychiatry, 182*, 105–116.

Bracken, P., Greenslade, L., Griffin, B. & Smyth, M. (1998). Mental health and ethnicity: An Irish dimension. *British Journal of Psychiatry, 172*, 103–105.

Butcher, J., Nezami, E. & Exner, J. (1998). Psychological assessment of people in diverse cultures. In S. Kazarian & D. Evans (Eds.) *Cultural clinical psychology* (pp. 61–105). Oxford: Oxford University Press.

Campinha-Bacote, J. (2007). The process of cultural competence in the delivery of healthcare services. Cincinnati, OH: Transcultural C.A.R.E Associates.

Commission for Racial Equality (1999). *Ethnic minorities in Britain*. London: Author.

Carpenter, L. & Brockington, I. (1980). A study of mental illness in Asians, West Indians and Africans living in Manchester. *British Journal of Psychiatry, 137,* 201–205.

Cochrane, R. (1977). Mental illness in immigrants in England and Wales: An analysis of mental hospital admissions, 1971. *Social Psychiatry, 12,* 23–35.

Cochrane, R. & Stopes-Roe, M. (1981). Psychological symptom levels in Indian immigrants to England – a comparison with native English. *Psychological Medicine, 11,* 319–327.

Cross, T., Bazron, B., Dennis, K. & Isaacs, M. (1989). *Towards a culturally competent system of care. A monograph on effective services for minority children who are severely emotionally disturbed*. Washington, DC: CASSP Technical Assistance Center, Georgetown University Child Development Center.

Department of Health (1993). Ethnicity and health. London: Author.

Department of Health (2003). Inside outside. London: Author.

Department of Health (2004). Organizing and delivering psychological therapies. London: Author.

Department of Health (2005). *Delivering race equality in mental health care*. London: Author.

D'Andrade, R. (1984). Cultural meaning systems. In R. Shweder & R. LeVine (Eds.) *Culture theory* (pp. 88–119). Cambridge: Cambridge University Press.

Fernando, S. (1989). *Race and culture in psychiatry*. London: Tavistock/Routledge.

Fernando, S. (1991). *Mental health, race and culture*. London: Macmillan-Mind.

Fernando, S. (2003). *Cultural diversity, mental health and psychiatry*. Hove: Brunner-Routledge.

Flaskerud, J. (1986). The effects of culture-compatible intervention on the utilization of mental health services by minority clients. *Community Mental Health Journal, 22,* 127–141.

Fryer, P. (1984). *Staying power: The history of black people in Britain*. London: Pluto Press.

Gillam, S., Jarman, B., White, P. & Law, R. (1989). Ethnic differences in consultation rates in urban general practice. *British Medical Journal, 299,* 953–957.

Hall, S. (1992). New ethnicities. In J. Donald & A. Rattansi (Eds.) *'Race', culture and difference* (pp. 246–262). London: Sage.

Harding, S. & Balarajan, R. (1996). Patterns of mortality in second generation Irish living in England and Wales: Longitudinal study. *British Medical Journal, 312,* 1389–1392.

Harding, S. & Balarajan, R. (2001). Mortality of third generation Irish people living in England and Wales: Longitudinal study. *British Medical Journal, 322,* 466–467.

Hersch, C. (1969). From mental health to social action: Clinical psychology in historical perspective. *American Psychologist, 24,* 909–916.

Hickman, M. & Walter, B. (1997). *Discrimination and the Irish community in Great Britain*. London: Commission for Racial Equality.

Husband, C. (1987). *'Race' in Britain: Continuity and change*. London: Hutchinson.

Ineichen, B. (1990). The mental health of Asians in Britain. *British Medical Journal, 300,* 1669–1670.

Kaiser, A., Katz, R. & Shaw, B. (1998). Cultural issues in the management of depression. In S. Kazarian & D. Evans (Eds.) *Cultural clinical psychology* (pp. 177–214). New York: Oxford University Press.

Kazarian, S. & Evans, D. (1998). *Cultural clinical psychology*. New York: Oxford University Press.

Keating, F. (2007). *African and Caribbean men and mental health*. Briefing paper. London: Race Equality Foundation.

Kemp, C. & Rasbridge, L. (2004). *Refugee and immigrant health*. Cambridge: Cambridge University Press.

Kleinman, A. (1987). Anthropology and psychiatry: The role of culture in cross-cultural research on illness. *British Journal of Psychiatry, 151,* 447–454.

Krause, I. (1989). Sinking heart: A Punjabi communication of distress. *Social Science and Medicine, 29,* 563–575.

Laungani, P. (2004). Asian perspectives in counselling and psychotherapy. Hove: Routledge.

Lipsedge, M. (1993). Mental health: Access to care for black and ethnic minority people. In A. Hopkins & V. Bahl (Eds.) *Access to health care for people from black and ethnic minorities* (pp. 169–183). London: Royal College Physicians.

Littlewood, R. & Lipsedge, M. (1982). *Aliens and alienists. Ethnic minorities and psychiatry.* Harmondsworth: Penguin.

Macpherson Report (1999). *The Stephen Lawrence Inquiry: Report of an inquiry by Sir William Macpherson of Cluny.* London: The Stationery Office.

McGovern, D. & Cope, R. (1991). Second generation Afro-Caribbeans and young whites with a first admission diagnosis of schizophrenia. *Social Psychiatry and Psychiatric Epidemiology, 26,* 95–99.

MDP (2000). *Specialist services for minority ethnic groups?* Maudsley Discussion Paper No. 8. London: Institute of Psychiatry, Maudsley Hospital.

MHAC (2005). *Count me in. Results of a national census of inpatients in mental health hospitals and facilities in England and Wales.* Nottingham: Mental Health Act Commission. CSIP. NIMHE Healthcare Commission.

Nadirshaw, Z. (1999). Clinical psychology. In K. Bhui & D. Olajide (Eds.) *Health service provision for a multi-cultural society* (pp. 156–168). Philadelphia: Saunders.

Nazroo, J. (1997). *Ethnicity and mental health*. London: Policy Studies Institute.

Neeleman, J., Mak, V. & Wessely, S. (1997). Suicide by age, ethnic group, coroners' verdicts and country of birth. *British Journal of Psychiatry, 171,* 463–467.

Padesky, C. & Greenberger, D. (1995). *Clinician's guide to mind over mood.* New York: Guilford Press.

SEU (2000). Minority ethnic issues in social exclusion and neighbourhood renewal. London: Social Exclusion Unit, Cabinet Office.

Shakow, D. (1976). What is clinical psychology? *American Psychologist, 29,* 553–560.

Soni Raleigh, V. (1996). Suicide patterns and trends in people of Indian subcontinent and Caribbean origin in England and Wales. *Ethnicity and Health, 1,* 55–63.

Strand, S. (2008). *Minority ethnic pupils in the longitudinal study of young people in England.* London: Department for Children, Schools and Families.

Strickland, B. (1988). Clinical psychology comes of age. *American Psychologist, 43,* 104–107.

Sue, D. & Sue, D. (1990). *Counselling the culturally different.* Chichester: John Wiley & Sons.

Wilson, M. & MacCarthy, B. (1994). GP consultation as a factor in the low rate of mental health service use by Asians. *Psychological Medicine, 24,* 113–119.

Zuckerman, M. (1998). Some dubious premises in research and theory on racial differences. In P. Organista, K. Chun & G. Marin (Eds.) *Readings in ethnic psychology* (pp. 59– 72). New York: Routledge.

21

Working with Personality Disorder

Damian Gardner

Overview and Scope of Chapter

This chapter begins with a discussion of the term 'personality disorder' before outlining why working with people who have significant difficulties related to personality function is likely to be relevant for every clinical psychologist. The core, special and reserved competencies required are then discussed along with more subtle but relevant attributes. This is followed by a review of some key tensions and themes commonly encountered. Finally, interventions that psychologists are likely to adopt with this client group are outlined in terms of assessment, formulation, treatment interventions, consultation, supervision and training, and service development, audit and research.

Issues of Definition

The full range of difficulties and varied presentations of individuals who meet general or specific diagnostic criteria for personality disorder can be both bewildering and overwhelming (*Diagnostic and Statistical Manual, Fourth Edition* (DSM-IV), American Psychiatric Association, 1994; *International Classification of Diseases 10th Edition* (ICD-10), World Health Organisation, 2006), even despite attempts by recently published textbooks or handbooks attempting to clarify the field (e.g. Oldham *et al.*, 2005; Livesley, 2001; Sperry, 2003; Magnavita, 2004). In day-to-day clinical practice in the UK, the diagnosis of personality disorder is often reserved for people with borderline/unstable personality disorder or antisocial personality disorder, and many NHS staff are unaware of the full range of personality disorder diagnoses. Similarly, key policy documents (National Institute for Mental Health in England, 2003a, 2003b) have referred broadly to 'personality disorder' but nevertheless focus on services for people with the borderline/unstable personality disorder pattern. This emphasis is doubtless a reflection of the particularly high levels of distress experienced by this specific group and the higher frequency with which this diagnosis is applied (Moran *et al.*, 2002), as well as reflecting the challenges services face in addressing this group's difficulties.

Definition and diagnosis are highly controversial and politicised and there are several serious objections to the term 'personality disorder' (Nehls, 1999; Ramon *et al.*, 2001). The label is stigmatising, globally descriptive of a person; also the label 'sticks' – even if the symptoms that led to the diagnosis disappear over time. In addition, the diagnosis has been associated with a great sense of hopelessness and helplessness on behalf of service providers, carrying connotations of incurability along with a legacy of prejudice and exclusion (Fallon, 2003; National Institute for Mental Health in England, 2003b).

Both scientifically and clinically, the criteria used for categorical diagnosis are deeply flawed, exhibiting 'excessive diagnostic co-occurrence, heterogeneity among persons with the same diagnosis, absence of a non-arbitrary boundary with normal functioning, and inadequate coverage of maladaptive functioning' (Widiger & Mullins-Sweatt, 2005, pp. 35–53). Psychiatric diagnostic categories do not map onto the dimensional model identified by personality research and there is little justification for a medical disease model in terms of an identified underlying physical pathology (Boyle, 2007). Giving the diagnosis does not in itself further understanding and, indeed, suggesting that people's difficulties can be understood as illness may militate against the search for self-understanding and psychological meaning. Even the term 'disorder' is of doubtful appropriateness; most people with personality disorder diagnoses actually have personality styles that are arguably overly rigid and too ordered, and even the most apparently chaotic and baffling personalities tend to reveal an underlying logic and coherence to a clinician who can collaborate in a painstaking exploration of thoughts, emotions, relationships and personal history. Finally, both day-to-day experience of contemporary services and systematic evidence from research make it clear that the application of the diagnosis is highly inconsistent, and varies with the biases of individual diagnosticians as well as being influenced by racial, ethnic and gender prejudice (Adler *et al.*, 1990; Widiger, 1998).

In contrast, there are some clinical psychologists who are quite comfortable with the use of the diagnosis, arguing that it is a purely descriptive label and an essential (or at least useful) aid to clear communication and research activity. Additionally, it can be argued that many clients are relieved to get a diagnosis, finding it not only a validation of their difficulties but sometimes a necessary passport to services. There is also no doubt that the use of the diagnostic label in a range of policy implementation guidance documents has led to service inclusion and improvement (e.g. National Institute for Mental Health in England, 2003a, 2003b).

Clinical psychologists need to be alert to the different arguments on both sides, aware of ethical and validity issues relating to diagnosis, and to be skilled in managing their use of diagnostic language. They also need to be aware that while personality disorder diagnoses may aid treatment planning and intervention, they can also be a barrier to constructing individualised and flexible formulations.

Ignoring the shortcomings and oppressiveness of these labels may be damaging, but so too can be the adoption of rigid or confrontational stances that may alienate colleagues, be perceived as naïve or self-righteous, and undermine the credibility of the clinical psychologist, thereby reducing influence or preventing collaborative working. Fortunately, differences and dilemmas around language can be turned into opportunities for dialogue and learning – especially if service users can be involved in the debate. Clarity over such questions is also essential to establishing rational referral systems for specialist services (Gardner, 2005).

Working with People Eligible for the Diagnosis

Recent policy guidance in the UK has led to the establishment of specialist teams and services commissioned to work with personality disorder (National Institute for Mental Health in England, 2003a, 2003b). Implementation of this guidance has been very varied and many different service models exist, including therapeutic communities, specialist therapy services and teams focusing on consultation and training. Only a small minority of clinical psychologists will be employed in specialist personality disorder services, but many working in other specialities or mainstream adult mental health will find that a significant percentage of their caseload will meet diagnostic criteria for personality disorder. Other specialities, such as addictions and forensic services, will have especially high prevalence rates (Moran *et al.*, 2002).

Competencies Required for Personality Disorder Work

Clinical psychologists may question whether they have the necessary skills for this work, especially early in their career. This can usefully be considered in terms of *core, special and reserved skills* (Division of Clinical Psychology, 2001). The *core* skills provided by clinical psychology training should be sufficient to equip the majority of practitioners, particularly the ability to attune and connect to people who have difficulties relating to others, while at the same time being able to retain a grounded and boundaried therapeutic stance. Many of the transferable skills of the profession, such as balancing structured empirically valid interventions with a reflective and collaborative therapeutic style, or communicating clearly in emotionally charged contexts, form the basic foundation for effective work.

A key finding emerging from the outcome literature is also the importance of *integrative treatments* or adapted forms of established therapies, such as cognitive analytic therapy (CAT; Ryle, 1997; Ryle & Glynkina, 2000), dialectical behavioural therapy (DBT; Linehan, 1993a; 1993b), schema-focused cognitive therapy (Young *et al.*, 2003) and therapeutic community treatments (Lees *et al.*, 1999; Chiesa & Fonagy, 2000). The integrative nature of these approaches gives them breadth and flexibility and allows the therapist to find a balance between maintaining structure and attending to process. This is highly relevant for clinical psychologists who are required to train in more than one form of therapy. Most clinical psychologists will thus find their generic therapeutic skills sufficient, so long as emphasis is placed upon the provision of a supportive working environment with regular quality clinical supervision and realistic expectations about caseload demands.

For some, however, personal interest and/or the demands of a particular job will lead them to seek to acquire further *special* skills such as advanced training in DBT or CAT. Alternatively, training in psychodynamic psychotherapeutic approaches that offer a framework for understanding and working with projective processes such as transference/countertransference, splitting and projective identification can be extremely beneficial. Specialist post-qualification training may be related to service development projects (see below), will add to the psychologist's skill base and are likely to increase personal motivation and job satisfaction.

Finally, there are *restricted* skills involving the use of psychometric assessments which are uniquely the preserve of applied psychologists and can on occasion be extremely helpful, particularly when needing to clarify complex or unusual presentations, and when integrated into a broader assessment and formulation process. In addition to routine outcome measures, this includes a range of general or specific assessments of personality function as well as assessment of mood, beliefs and, where appropriate, cognitive function. Key competencies here include far more than test administration, since engagement, integration of psychometry into a broader assessment and thoughtful summarising and feedback of findings may all require considerable care and attention.

Other relevant personal/professional qualities are similar to any clinically demanding area: a realistic and cautious sense of optimism, perseverance, ability to access good support outside work and a degree of resilience when faced with highly emotional or challenging clients. People with borderline personality adaptations often struggle with an overly professional or apparently disinterested manner in health professionals (Lord, 2007) and this work therefore requires an ability to be 'real' and make contact with clients. At the same time, staff must preserve sufficient professional distance and clear boundaries to contain therapy and to be able to think clearly when under intense emotional pressure.

Clinical psychologists need to be adept at making informed psychological decisions in the face of considerable challenges, notably the partial and at times contradictory evidence-based therapy outcomes (British Psychological Society, 2006; Binks *et al.*, 2007); demoralised, overwhelmed or even rejecting and hostile colleagues; and the uniquely powerful and often disturbing presentations of individual clients which at times ramify in complex and unpredictable ways through multiple service systems. Rising to these challenges requires an ability to think flexibly about relevant specialist research, to respond to the unique conditions of every individual client and to reflect always on wider service and systemic contexts.

Some more subtle 'competencies' may be identified as relevant to working with people eligible for borderline/unstable diagnoses. Constant exposure to attempted (and occasionally completed) suicide can be draining, even with good external supports. The value base of practitioners is important in this work and relevant to a range of therapeutic issues, such as managing boundaries and assumptions relating to blame and responsibility. It is also important not to be too unsettled by intense suffering that is impossible to relieve immediately. Mindfulness training, which is taught as part of

DBT but can be integrated with other therapies (Mace, 2007), offers one way of addressing these issues for the therapist. DBT also provides helpful guidance about recognising one's own limits (usually personal and not shared by all colleagues) and being open and clear about these with clients in order to preserve a working alliance in therapy (Linehan, 1993a, pp. 319–328).

When working with more challenging clients, good systems of supervision and case-consultation are essential. It is impossible to work effectively with this client group if there is unrealistic pressure over caseload size. It is also important to be able to rely on support from managers for positive risk taking since this provides the key to enabling clients to take on the exposure work required for therapeutic change.

Key Themes and Tensions

Some of the key tensions that can arise in this work are identified in Box 21.1. The challenge is to facilitate a useful solution that synthesises the valid perspectives of all involved. For example, a team wanting to exclude a very demanding and dependent client may be helped to identify that a more understanding and accepting (but boundaried) approach could lead to fewer demands on the team and an opportunity for everyone to learn and move on from a period of conflict. Linehan (1993a, pp. 199–220) has highlighted the value of dialectics as a useful approach to engaging with such tensions.

Constantly recurring themes are clarifying 'belonging' issues and identifying the most appropriate level of intervention (Box 21.2). Broadly speaking, the priorities raised by the questions in Box 21.2 are: achieving systemic clarity and containment; establishing an appropriate Care Programme Approach (CPA) process and risk assessment; and enabling formulation-based intervention goals and processes. Typically, these questions should be addressed sequentially (though this is not always feasible, especially if there are major risk or engagement issues involved). Answers to the questions may provide process information relevant to the formulation, sometimes

Box 21.1

- Maintaining structure vs. being flexible and process focused
- Accepting the client vs. pushing for change
- Making decisions/taking responsibility vs. providing reflective space/standing back
- Allowing for inpatient containment and safety vs. de-skilling, fostering dependency and avoiding risk
- Being professional and distanced vs. being 'real' and involved
- Advocating for the client vs. supporting carers or teams

Box 21.2

- Should this person be seen in the organisation?
- Are there urgent risk issues not being attended to while services process referrals or dispute boundaries?
- Which *part* of the organisation (service, geography) should be involved with this person and which individuals/professions should be involved?
- Is the person involved (or should they be) with other services?
- Is there appropriate communication and role-clarity between different professionals and services involved, and are there any symbolic re-enactments or concerning repetitive patterns being played out?
- Is there a proper personal history (including a genogram) and history of involvement of services?
- Have basic good practices been followed (such as carer assessments, written information on diagnosis or website recommendations, out-of-hours contact numbers provided etc.)?
- Is there a well-informed risk management plan that includes appropriate opportunities for exposure (i.e. positive risk taking)?
- Are intervention goals clear and agreed explicitly with the client?
- Has the intervention plan considered the pros and cons of trauma work or other activities that may increase emotion and/or impact on risk in potentially dangerous ways?
- Are the 'rules' or contracts around treatment, including what counts as dropping-out, and the basis for termination or discharge, sufficiently clear?

---

through the identification of powerful, dynamically symbolic processes (e.g. the determined and irrational rejection by services of a client who was severely neglected as a child, or the preponderance of domineering male professionals and a disempowered female care coordinator working with a woman who was multiply abused in childhood by men and unprotected by a frightened and unsupported mother).

Key Interventions and Roles

Assessment

The British Psychological Society (2006) has highlighted the value of psychological assessment and formulation in work with personality disordered clients. Psychological assessment brings structure into what may be an unstructured or even chaotic process. It also brings clarity and focus to complex presentations where confused or competing explanations (often a mixture of medical and 'folk psychology') have failed to achieve a convincing or useful understanding. As a rule of thumb, the greater the complexity of the client and the more entrenched the problems, then the more worthwhile the investment of time in an extended assessment, without necessarily committing to intervention. There is particular value in contracting with clients and colleagues to take the pressure off achieving change and instead to spend time on an extended assessment with an explicit 'no expectation of change' contract. Such an assessment may involve: summarising (sometimes very full) clinical files; meeting (potentially many times) with the client and others such as parents, partners, or key-workers; and using formal psychometric assessments such as the MCMI-III (Millon, 1997) or Young's Schema Questionnaire (Young & Brown, 1990). Psychometry is most helpful when clarity is needed about confusing presentations.

The British Psychological Society has rightly highlighted the benefits of formal, semi-structured interview assessments (British Psychological Society, 2006), although a more narrative assessment approach can also be helpful. Standard CPA assessment requires 'taking a history': this may be achieved most effectively by inviting the client to collaborate on 'telling and understanding their life-story'. The benefits of this are potentially increased engagement, subtle therapeutic changes, including cognitive restructuring, and the gathering of more accurate and complete information. Initial contracting around such an approach is crucial. Thought and explicit guidance may need to be given to the client about disclosure and trauma issues to make the process safe – for example by allowing blank sections in the story, and being clear that distressing events will not become the focus of trauma work without careful and clear agreement beforehand. Life story work may be combined with producing a genogram (McGoldrick & Gerson, 1989) or this could be done separately. Either way, a genogram invariably leads to insights for clients and professionals about the nature of both presenting symptoms and relationship conflicts.

A genogram can also add clarity when there are concurrent concerns about child protection and the ongoing threat posed by identified perpetrators of abuse. The majority of people diagnosed with borderline personality disorder have experienced significant childhood trauma, and it is not unusual for individual work to raise concerns elsewhere in the family and service systems. Child protection issues can never be ignored and a period of structured assessment offers a way of containing the process of evaluating risk and options, even when disclosure occurs during active intervention. Here psychologists need also to be familiar with local child protection procedures and whom to consult with when ethical dilemmas arise.

Time invested in a thorough assessment is considerable but the benefits invariably make this worthwhile. Many people with a personality disorder diagnosis have a story which is difficult to tell or unbearable to hear. Often users' stories are marked by trauma that has never been properly considered or reflected upon. Constant crises and chronic insecure attachments with services may be part of a just bearable existence, while ineffective coping strategies (such as self-harm or substance abuse) can provide a precarious safety in the present. However, these strategies may make it difficult or impossible for anyone to truly grasp the whole of the client's story and it is not unusual for the most familiar users of services also to be the people whose life stories and family relationships are least known.

Formulation

Formulation is critical (British Psychological Society, 2006; Johnstone & Dallos, 2006). The medical model is not an effective framework for helping people experiencing psychological distress as a result of their personality function any more than the diluted 'folk psychology' often found in the National Health Service.

In contrast, good psychological formulation provides meaning and in doing so allows for reflection – both by the client and others involved with them (Butler, 1998; British Psychological Society, 2006). This process is in itself therapeutic and provides a step towards reducing critical self-judgement and shame and interrupting patterns of impulsive behaviour.

Formulation can also enable staff to think more clearly and less judgementally, thus helping services to manage the process and content of their involvement with clients more effectively. Where multiple staff or services are involved, agreement on a formulation can enable everyone to make sense of their differing understandings and to resolve (or at least contain) potentially conflicting opinions. Ideally, this shared understanding can also include the client and key carers, producing, often for the first time, an integrated, non-judgemental and useful map of problems and suggesting ways to overcome these.

Clinical psychologists must consider how comprehensive to make their formulation and the most effective way of sharing it. When working with teams, a very comprehensive formulation can be a useful focus for consultation, allowing links to be made between history, personality function, psychological complaints (Bentall, 2007), relationships, and wider systemic and cultural factors. For clients this amount of information may be excessive, so partial and mini-formulations focusing on critical vicious circles, or promising areas for the first step towards change may be preferable. Generally, formulations should take account of both the inner world of the client and the links between this and patterns of relating (Gardner, 2006), particularly how problems or symptoms may have been survival strategies. Simultaneously, formulation can identify potentially more effective possibilities for the future (Nathan, 2006). The Sequential Diagrammatic Reformulation in CAT therapy (Ryle, 1997) offers a good example of this approach, but formulations using any psychological orientation can be adapted to achieve these aims.

Treatment interventions

A wide range of therapeutic intervention approaches may be helpful, but the appropriate level of intervention and the format of any direct work must be identified carefully (i.e. who, where, when, how often). The therapeutic relationship will be just one part of a more complex group of service relationships involving the client. Contracts, i.e. the psychological agreements about the purpose and process of intervention, need to be clear to the client and colleagues who may have differing or conflicting expectations of therapy. Pre-therapy work on clarifying expectations and building commitment is often essential and will save time later in reducing drop-out rates and non-attendance.

In the face of extreme hopelessness, eliciting a minimal commitment to explore options for building a more bearable life may be the most that can be achieved initially to engage clients. A stance of 'learning to live with and tolerate distress' is more realistic than a goal to reduce or eradicate emotional pain.

Clinical psychologists offering therapy should be cautious about adopting crisis intervention or more diffused care coordination duties that may undermine therapeutic boundaries and strain the therapeutic alliance. Where multiple roles are adopted, it is helpful to be very clear and explicit about this in setting up the psychological contract. In some settings, very formal agreements may be drawn up regarding the expectations of all parties, including the conditions under which people would be deemed to have dropped out of therapy.

A critical issue in psychological intervention with people with personality difficulties is whether to have a present or historical focus. Clients who struggle with emotional regulation may not be able to manage trauma work: the risks and consent issues associated with commencing such treatment are analogous to offering surgery to physically unhealthy or vulnerable patients. If it *is* felt advisable to work on trauma, then a clear assessment of support structures and coping techniques is required and robust crisis and contingency plans need to be in place. Prior assessment and teaching of emotional regulation and stabilisation techniques, such as the ability to self-soothe and ground oneself, may be critical (Linehan, 1993b). Ongoing thorough and systematic monitoring of self-harm and suicidality allows for an informed review of whether therapeutic work is being tolerated. Effective monitoring processes will depend upon establishing and maintaining collaborative relationships, and open communication between the client and key service providers.

Consultation, supervision and training

Consultation and supervision of complex cases in increasingly identified as an appropriate role for clinical psychologists (British Psychological Society, 2007). Formal consultation allows for an external perspective to be brought to situations that are difficult to understand for those more immediately involved. Consultation also enables an efficient use of scarce psychological resources, and enables both competency and confidence to be developed in consultees. Traditional 'referral-to-experts' processes can result in long-term systemic problems such as waiting lists and de-skilling of referrers, and there can be considerable benefits in offering 'consultation to referrer' as the point of access for referrals. This can have the further advantages of: preventing unnecessary exclusion from mainstream services; obviating multiple assessment; maintaining clients in a system rather than leaving them in the potentially dangerous interim position of awaiting assessment; and allowing for some of the systemic and case-management issues around the client (identified in Box 21.2 above) to be clarified and addressed with colleagues before considering direct work.

Having two consultants in partnership provides considerable advantages, especially when working with clients who potentially overwhelm service providers. Working from a psychodynamic model, this approach offers opportunities for holding and examining complex and intense transferences, and containing the powerful parallel processes that can occur around these clients.

Developing competencies and changing attitudes in staff working with people with personality disorder has been identified as a priority in policy guidance. Clinical psychologists have an important contribution to make to delivering this agenda. Training is most effective if focused on encouraging understanding and developing skills, through reflective discussion and experiential learning. Initial goals may be quite limited, for example to initiate a contained and thoughtful discussion about the challenges of working with this client group, and noting current aspects of good practice along with areas for review and development. Theoretical models are useful but need to be introduced with a degree of caution – a focus on key 'top tips' (keeping good boundaries, getting support, avoiding blame, etc.) may be better received. Sometimes training and consultation can be combined, for example by using the final session of a day training programme to draw up a draft formulation of a complex client well known to a team.

As with consultation, there are advantages to having two trainers present: dynamic processes in teaching can be significant in large groups, and powerful emotions may be felt and expressed. Explicit pre-established roles for trainers can help to manage this. Where possible, there are significant advantages in including service-user representatives in training, particularly with changing attitudes and challenging stereotypes and offering hope as to what may be achieved through collaborative engagement.

Service development, audit and research

Mental health trusts in the UK are now expected to provide specialist services for clients with the diagnosis of personality disorder. At the same time, NHS trusts are becoming more focused on evidence-based treatments, and specialist therapies such as DBT are becoming more commonly available within mainstream services. Pressure is also coming from the clients themselves, while social and political change has resulted in a more informed voice for clients with a greater sense of entitlement to effective therapies (National Institute for Mental Health in England, 2003a, 2003b; British Psychological Society, 2006, 2007). Clinical psychologists will continue to make a major contribution to such initiatives, often leading teams and identifying and implementing appropriate review and audit.

Having been relatively neglected for many years, the whole field of personality disorder is now receiving considerable attention by researchers at a national and international level. Well-implemented case series (Davidson & Tyrer, 1996), audits and qualitative methodologies (Jones, 2007) have as much to offer as highly powered quantitative studies, and are arguably more accessible to most practising clinicians.

Conclusion

Working with people eligible for a diagnosis of personality disorder is complex and challenging work. There is, however, a growing sense of optimism and a recognition that clinical psychologists can and should play a significant role in helping this client group. Working with people who have often not been helped (or who have been further damaged) by current mainstream approaches available in the health service can be hugely rewarding, both professionally and personally, whether working in a specialist service or as part of a broader role in mainstream services.

References

Adler, D.A., Drake, R.E. & Teague, G.B. (1990). Clinician's practices in personality assessment: Does gender influence the use of DSM-III Axis II? *Comprehensive Psychiatry, 31,* 125–133.

American Psychiatric Association (1994). *Diagnostic and statistical manual of mental disorders* (4th edn). Washington, DC: Author.

Bentall, R.P. (2007). Researching psychotic complaints. *The Psychologist, 20,* 293–295.

Binks, C.E., Fenton, M., McCarthy, L., Lee, T., Adams, C.E. & Duggan, C. (2007). Psychological therapies for people with borderline personality disorder. *Cochrane Database of Systemic Reviews, 4.* Retrieved 26 February 2009 from www.cochrane.org/reviews/en/ab005652.html

Boyle, M. (2007). The problem with diagnosis. *The Psychologist, 20,* 290–292.

British Psychological Society (2006). *Understanding personality disorder: A professional practice report by the British Psychological Society.* Leicester: Author.

British Psychological Society (2007). *New ways of working for applied psychologists in health and social care; the end of the beginning, summary report.* Leicester: Author.

Butler, G. (1998). Clinical formulation. In A.S. Bellack & M. Hersen (Eds.) *Comprehensive clinical psychology* (Vol. 6, pp. 1–24). Oxford: Pergamon.

Chiesa, M. & Fonagy, P. (2000). The Cassel personality disorder study: Methodology and treatment effects. *British Journal of Psychiatry, 176,* 485–491.

Davidson, K. & Tyrer, P. (1996). Cognitive therapy for antisocial and borderline personality disorders: Single cases study series. *British Journal of Clinical Psychology, 35,* 413–429.

Division of Clinical Psychology (2001). *Working in teams.* London: British Psychological Society.

Fallon, P. (2003). Travelling through the system: The lived experience of people with borderline personality disorder in contact with psychiatric services. *Journal of Psychiatric and Mental Health Nursing, 10,* 393–400.

Gardner, D. (2006). Getting it together: Integrative approaches to formulation. *Clinical Psychology Forum, 151,* 10–16.

Gardner, D. (2005). *Referral and consultation guidelines.* Unpublished Referral Guidelines for 'Number 63' Service. Available from the author.

Johnstone, L. & Dallos, R. (Eds.) (2006). *Formulation in psychology and psychotherapy: Making sense of people's problems.* London: Routledge.

Jones, J. (2007). *Service user representation & personality disorder: A qualitative investigation into the experience of service user representatives.* Thesis submitted in partial fulfilment of the degree of Doctor of Clinical Psychology, University of Oxford.

Lees, J., Manning, N. & Rawlings, B. (1999). *Therapeutic community effectiveness. A systemic review of therapeutic community treatment for people with personality disorder and mentally disordered offenders.* York: University of York (CRD report 17), NHS centre for reviews and dissemination.

Linehan, M.M. (1993a). *Cognitive-behavioural treatment of borderline personality disorder.* New York: Guilford Press.

Linehan, M.M. (1993b). *Skills training manual for treating borderline personality disorder*. New York: Guilford Press.

Livesley, W.J. (Ed.) (2001). *Handbook of personality disorders: Theory, research and treatment*. New York: Guilford Press.

Lord, S.A. (2007). Systemic work with clients with a diagnosis of borderline personality disorder. *Journal of Family Therapy, 29,* 203–221.

Mace, C. (2007). Mindfulness in psychotherapy: An introduction. *Advances in Psychiatric Treatment, 13,* 147–154.

Magnavita, J.L. (Ed.) (2004). *Handbook of personality disorders: Theory and practice*. Hoboken, NJ: Wiley.

McGoldrick, M. & Gerson, R. (1989). Genograms and the changing family life cycle. In B. Carter & M. McGoldrick (Eds.) *The changing family lifecycle: A framework for family therapy* (2nd edn, pp. 164–189). Boston: Allyn & Bacon.

Millon, T. (1997). *Millon Clinical Multiaxial Inventory-III manual* (2nd edn). Minneapolis, MN: National Computer Systems.

Moran, P., Jenkins, R., Tylee, A., Blizard, R. & Mann, A. (2002). The prevalence of personality disorder among UK primary care attenders. *Acta Psychiatrica Scandinavica, 102,* 52–57.

Nathan, J. (2006). Self-harm: A strategy for survival and nodal point of change. *Advances in psychiatric treatment, 12,* 327–329.

National Institute for Mental Health in England (2003a). *Breaking the cycles of rejection: The Personality Disorder Capability Framework*. London: NIMHE.

National Institute for Mental Health in England (2003b). *Personality disorder: No longer a diagnosis of exclusion. Policy implementation guidance for the development of services for people with personality disorder*. London: NIMHE.

Nehls, N. (1999). Borderline personality disorder: The voice of patients. *Research in Nursing and Health, 22,* 285–293.

Oldham, J. M., Skodol, A.E. & Bender, D.S. (Eds.) (2005). *Textbook of personality disorder*. Arlington, VA: American Psychiatric Association.

Ramon, S., Castillo, H. & Morant, N. (2001). Experiencing personality disorder: A participative research. *International Journal of Social Psychiatry, 47,* 1–15.

Ryle, A. (1997). *Cognitive analytic therapy and borderline personality disorder: The model and the method*. Chichester: Wiley.

Ryle, A. & Glynkina, K. (2000). Effectiveness of time limited cognitive analytic therapy of borderline personality disorder: Factors associated with outcome. *British Journal of Medical Psychology, 73,* 197–210.

Sperry, L. (2003). *Handbook of diagnosis and treatment of DSM-IV-TR personality disorders* (2nd edn). Hove: Brunner-Routledge.

Widiger, T.A. (1998). Invited essay: Sex biases in the diagnosis of personality disorder. *Journal of Personality Disorders, 12,* 95–118.

Widiger, T.A. & Mullins-Sweatt, S.N. (2005). Categorical and dimensional models of personality disorders. In J.O. Oldham, A.E. Skodal & D.S. Bender (Eds.) *Textbook of personality disorders* (pp. 35–53). Arlington, VA: American Psychiatric Association.

World Health Organisation (2006). *International statistical classification of diseases and related health problems* (10th rev.). Retrieved 26th February 2009 from www.who.int/classifications/apps/icd/icd10online/

Young, J.E. & Brown, G. (1990). *Young Scheme Questionnaire*. New York: Cognitive Therapy Center of New York.

Young, J.E., Klosko, J.S. & Weishaar, M.E. (2003). *Scheme therapy: A practitioner's guide*. New York: Guilford Press.

22

Systemic Therapy with Older People

Stephen Davies

Therapeutic work with older people is a growing area of interest for clinical psychological practice, as the demands for psychological therapy increase. However, the complexity of older people's lives demands more than an individually focused, empirically based response. Older people inhabit a complex social universe as they wrestle with the existential problem of maintaining autonomy in the face of increasing dependence. This chapter aims to explore the possibility of working systemically with older people, and also with the important people in their lives, This is significant because relationships are central to the psychological well-being of older people. This chapter will also argue that empirically based, individually focused psychological interventions have 'side effects' which a systemic approach can deal with in a more creative and effective way.

The Limitations of the Empirical Tradition for Psychological Work with Older People

Clinical psychology aspires to an empirical tradition, as does psychology as a discipline, partly in order to attain the same status for its findings and propositions as that attained by the natural sciences (Murdoch, 2007; Gallagher & Zahavi, 2008). While this may be a politically astute exercise, it may also come with significant drawbacks or 'side effects' which can be particularly visible in clinical work with older people. These are:

(i) The proximity effect. The empirical tradition can involve atomisation of the individual within their context. Causation can be seen as primarily linear (e.g. 'I don't like myself and I am depressed'). This focus can lead to assumptions that those factors most proximal to the individual, such as their thinking, are always the most important ones.

(ii)   The internalisation effect. With a focus on the individual, the search for causation and 'cure' may thus revolve around the state of the individual client, and the use of a 'tight', cause–effect model may mean that clinicians will look for internal causation for psychosocial phenomena first. Thus biological systems or cognitive products such as thinking patterns attain prominence rather than external factors such as kinship or social position factors.

(iii)   The agency effect. In so much that there is agreement empirically that a disorder is internally caused by some biological or psychological fault, then there is an assumption that this can be overcome by the individual internally (and individually) with external support. However, it is the individual's responsibility to effect this cure, or at least to assist in its outcome. In this way the absolute freedom of the individual to act without constraint is asserted. However, this is rarely the case with older people.

(iv)   The factual effect. There are assumed to be universal and immutable facts about the condition from which the individual suffers, which are the same across all individuals. The 'facts' of the condition rather than its experience by the person is what is seen as important for intervention. These facts are not to be discovered but already exist and should drive the direction of any psychological intervention.

The Current State of Systemic Work with Older People

Older people regularly tell researchers that their families are the most important psychological context in which their needs and worries are played out (Marriott, 2000; Nolan et al., 2001; Evans, 2004). Yet there is very little evidence that non-individual psychological therapy is widely used in older people's mental health services (Garner, 2003; Hepple, 2004). While there is some use of group work particularly in services for people with dementia, this tends to be rehabilitative in nature rather than primarily psychotherapeutic. The use of psychological approaches such as validation and reminiscence-based therapies is patchy in these services, both in terms of focus and availability. Yet there are convincing data that family-based or systemic interventions are necessary and useful (Clare & Woods, 2008). This chapter will present some of this evidence and its implications.

Before doing so, however, it should perhaps be noted that the lack of clarity about interventions is unsurprising, as any concept at all of psychological therapy for older people is relatively new. Several surveys of relevant literature have been conducted in recent years in England (Garner, 2003; Hepple, 2004) and Wales (Evans & Reynolds, 2006). These report low availability of specialised psychological therapy services. Hepple (2004) postulates that this slow development may be due to a combination of self-stigmatising ageism on the part of older people and their carers, the dominance of organic models of explanation for late life mental health conditions, and a need by society at large to deny death anxieties. A lack of agency for an older population is particularly important since 'old' is probably the most unwanted identity in capitalist society (Kaplan et al., 2000), hence the difficulty forming a coherent minority identity to drive political pressure to change this (Hepple, 2004).

The Nature of Systemic Work with Older People

The variety of psychological therapy that can be described as systemic can be distinguished both by type (e.g. structural, strategic, Milan systemic, narrative/social constructional, psychoeducational, behavioural (Asen, 2002)) and by context (e.g. family consultation, family group conferencing, individual, group- and family-based non-pharmacological treatment in dementia). This can lead to difficulty with tracking down a coherent body of literature, and the resultant lack of a clearly identifiable brand may also lead to lower uptake by practitioners. It is true that most family therapy work is systemic in nature (Marriott, 2000), although this does not mean that all systemic intervention is family based. Individualised and group approaches to systemic intervention also exist. Psychological work with older people often calls for non-standard therapeutic solutions, and systemic work with individuals, groups of individuals (e.g. people with dementia and the staff on a ward) or with couples or other alliances can provide these (Barnes *et al.*, 2000). What is important to the definition is that the psychological work is carried out with a systemic conceptualisation at its centre.

The basic assumption of this conceptualisation is that a mental health symptom is a cipher for imbalance in the system within which it exists. Thus, the symptom plays a central role in the homeostatic regulation of this system (Dallos & Stedmon, 2006). This is particularly important for late life symptoms where complex intergenerational (e.g. the need of an older person for care) and cross-societal (the need for a society to deny ageing and death) factors can lead to seriously unbalanced systems, which therefore sometimes require psychological attention. There is plenty of room for the use of psychological therapies for older people as there is so little current activity (Hepple, 2004; Davies, 2006). Unintentional or institutional ageism can be a particular problem when the service itself sets up and maintains systems which produce ageist outcomes. For example, collapsing the psychological therapy element of a specialist psychology service into a generic lifespan service may look like removing age discrimination but, without monitoring, it may prove to be institutionally ageist since resources are diverted to the demands of younger people. Older people themselves may also self-stigmatise in such situations, regarding themselves as less worthy of such interventions.

Highly individually based therapeutic approaches such as psychodynamic psychotherapy, cognitive behaviour therapy, cognitive analytic therapy and others are now being applied more consistently to the problems of late adulthood, most of which are similar to the psychological challenges faced earlier in life. Both policy (Hepple, 2004) and practice (Orbach, 1996) are now changing to allow older people access to a range of psychological therapies. However, this has been less successful with systemic therapy which is still often mainly associated with child and adolescent mental health services. The division of mental health services by age makes little sense pragmatically, as noted above, although it could also be seen as a defence against discrimination of resources (Davies, 2006). However, one of its negative 'side effects' is to isolate systemic services and expertise within children's services, which may then lead to a lack of confidence in and application of systemic work across the lifespan. Where this service coordination across the lifespan does exist, the cross-fertilisation of speciality-specific knowledge and systemic expertise can lead to wide applications of systemic practice, including features such as reflective teams.

Previously, the practice of any psychological therapy with people with dementia has tended to be avoided because of the presence of cognitive impairment. As a result, this group have tended to receive organically oriented interventions. However, Douglas *et al.* (2004) reviewed non-pharmacological treatments for people with dementia, and noted that these are now developing. The application of family and other modes of systemic work is increasing too as this group increasingly becomes re-conceptualised as being affected by systems in which they participate, and therefore as being open to systemic interventions (Smyer & Qualls, 1998). The acceptance of the importance of the psychosocial context in dementia is growing among professionals in this area, as is the idea that dementia is a relational disorder that affects others as much as the sufferer (Clare & Woods, 2008).

How can Systemic Therapy Be Useful for Older People's Psychological Problems?

'Events, dear boy, events'

The British Prime Minister Harold Macmillan's classic answer in the 1950s to an enquiry about what would divert a government from its legislative programme also rings true for the psychology of late life. Transitional life events are central to the experience of older adulthood. The myth that this is a time of serene calm and reflection is not generally true. Large adjustments in family and related systems such as friendship patterns, care environments and housing are much more the norm (Marriott, 2000). Systemic therapy approaches can assist older people with a conceptualisation which incorporates these factors. Systemic assumptions about the inevitability of change and adjustment to it can thereby be very helpful to older people and their families.

The usefulness of the underlying assumptions of systemic theory

The principles of therapist as co-participant not expert, the importance of language and its transformation through the therapeutic process, and the idea of a co-constructed sense of reality (Boston, 2000) can all assist older people. In a clinical setting where both clinician and client may have to deal with discrimination and marginalisation, these collaborative principles can aid in identifying significant influences. Thinking about rebalancing a system that is 'out of kilter' can be a more powerful way of restoring some degree of agency to an older person than passive reception of treatment. If one of the themes of later life is dealing with a reduction in ability and opportunity, individual therapy may unfortunately serve to concentrate on these disabilities rather than on opportunities for change in a constrained context.

Working against ageism

Systemic therapy takes issues of power and influence for granted (Dallos & Stedmon, 2006). Thus, issues such as ageism and the constraints that it can place on the older person are identified early in a systemic formulation. These can be then be addressed in the thinking of others in the system and in the older person themselves. For example, the ageist idea of older people not 'knowing their own minds' and being infantilised, can be usefully explored and challenged.

Formulation and intervention techniques

Dallos and Stedmon (2006) indicate that systemic formulation work involves problem exploration, progressive hypothesizing, belief elaboration and dynamic reformulation. The establishment of a developing, hypothesizing life narrative is close to the natural reminiscing and reflecting functions often undertaken by older people. Its familiarity may therefore be a useful advantage. Circular questioning, reframing and close attention to language can also help to build a shared narrative cooperatively (Vetere & Dallos, 2003).

The Practice of Systemic Therapy with Older People

In many ways this is no different from systemic work with any other group. It is sometimes complicated by the many non-standard situations that older people constantly find themselves in (an example might be an older person in hospital whom the staff want to move to a residential home, whose family preferred her dead husband, and whose child with whom she has the most conflicted relationship is the closest to her geographically). This may sometimes feel somewhat overwhelming for the new therapist, but the key advantage of doing family work with this group of people is the presence of the reflecting team. Therapists can themselves be sometimes distracted by their own thinking about later life and about the people who inhabit this phase of the life cycle, but the reflecting team should be able to take account of this and usefully comment in a trans-generational way.

Marriott (2000) rightly points out that there are specific events and issues for family therapy teams working with older people to consider. The more cohort-based events to be considered in a systemic family intervention involve decisions about permanent care (e.g. a care home), the mental health of carers, developmental life-cycle events such as loss, and change of important others (e.g. bereavement), elder abuse and family reactions to organic/physical impairment and illness. The families of older people are also required to deal with a lot of change, and a systemic intervention may help with this. Marriott (2000) points that family life-cycle issues of power (e.g. who decides on care), generativity (e.g. who will be here when I am gone), survivorship (e.g. I am the last man standing among my friends), loneliness, ageism and end of life ('making a good end') are crucial to assess and formulate in systemic interventions.

As with other age groups the evidence base for systemic work with older people is not well established. Asen (2002) indicates that there is reasonable evidence for systemic interventions in psychosis, depression, eating disorders, drug and alcohol problems, conduct disorder and marital distress. It would seem reasonable that these interventions would be valid for these types of problems across the lifespan. However, more research is needed to improve the evidence base generally for this approach, and specifically for older people.

Systemic consultation is a set of techniques which can also be used effectively in older people mental health contexts (Brown *et al.*, 2006). The use of a systemic understanding of a particular care or service environment can be useful in planning the strategic actions needed to rebalance the forces involved in such a system. For example, a GP's surgery that is being frequently contacted by a anxious older client can consider how to understand this process (recently bereaved, less family contact), what it does to them (the anger and distress left with them that causes them to 'tell the person off') and how it is maintained (unbalanced access to comfort and reassurance). Appropriate intervention at various levels may then follow.

Conclusion

The existential situation of older people highlights the limiting 'side effects' of the empirical approach within clinical psychology, and suggests the possibility of systemic therapy as a partner in assisting this client group. The needs of older people and their familiarity with narrative allow for the possibility of using systemic therapy, both in a family-based and consultative fashion. Perhaps most importantly, though, this approach to therapy may allow for an attenuation of the self-stigmatising ageism that can seriously impair the thinking and experience of the older person and their carers.

As a profession, clinical psychology has been slow to occupy the non-individually focused ground in psychological work with older people. The dominance of an organic focused model of understanding of the problems of older people, with its implicitly ageist assumptions about decline and disengagement, has made it difficult to consider an older person as still being connected to life. The systemic approach allows for this possibility and uses these crucial relationships with others as the vehicle of change to improve the psychological well-being of them and their carers.

References

Asen, E. (2002). Outcome research in family therapy. *Advances in Psychiatric Treatment, 8,* 230–238.

Barnes, G., Down, G. & McCann, D. (Eds.) (2000). *Systemic supervision: A portable guide for supervision training.* London: Jessica Kingsley.

Boston, P. (2000). Systemic family therapy and the influence of post-modernism. *Advances in Psychiatric treatment, 6,* 450–457.

Brown, D., Pryzwansky, W. & Schulte, A. (2006). *Psychological consultation and collaboration: Introduction to theory and practice* (6th edn). Boston: Pearson.

Clare, L. & Woods, R.T. (2008). *Handbook of clinical psychology of ageing* (2nd edn). Chichester: John Wiley & Sons.

Dallos, R. & Stedmon, J. (2006). Systemic formulation. In L. Johnstone & R. Dallos (Eds.) *Formulation in psychology and psychotherapy* (pp. 72–97). London: Routledge.

Davies, S. (2006). Not now dear: Ageism and mental health services for older people. *The Old Age Psychiatrist, 10,* 41.

Douglas, S., James, I. & Ballard, C. (2004). Non-pharmacological interventions in dementia. *Advances in Psychiatric Treatment, 10,* 171–179.

Evans, C. & Reynolds, P. (2006). Survey of the provision of psychological therapies for older people. *Psychiatric Bulletin, 30,* 10–13.

Evans, S. (2004). A survey of the provision of psychological treatments to older adults in the NHS. *Psychiatric Bulletin, 28,* 411–414.

Gallagher, S. & Zahavi, D. (2008). *The phenomenological mind: An introduction to philosophy of mind and cognitive science.* London: Routledge.

Garner, J. (2003). Psychotherapies and older adults. *Australian and New Zealand Journal of Psychiatry, 37*(5), 537–548.

Hepple, J. (2004). Psychotherapies with older people: An overview. *Advances in Psychiatric Treatment, 10,* 370–377.

Kaplan, G., Everson, S. & Lynch, J. (2000). The contribution of social and behavioural research to an understanding of the distribution of disease: A multilevel approach. In G. Kaplan (Ed.) *Promoting health: Intervention strategies from social and behavioural research* (pp. 4–22). New York: National Academy of Sciences Press.

Marriott, A. (2000). *Family therapy with older adults and their families.* Bicester: Winslow Press.

Murdoch, S. (2007). *IQ: The brilliant idea that failed.* Hoboken, NJ: Wiley.

Nolan, M., Keady, J. & Aveyard, E. (2001). Relationship-centred care: The next logical step. *British Journal of Nursing, 10*(12), 757.

Orbach, A. (1996). *Not too late: Psychotherapy and ageing.* London: Jessica Kingsley.

Smyer, M. & Qualls, S. (1998). *Aging and mental health.* New York: Blackwell.

Vetere, A. & Dallos, R. (2003). *Working systemically with families: Formulation, intervention and evaluation.* London: Karnac.

23

Working with Older People

Adrienne Little

What Do We Mean by 'Older'?

As people live longer, numbers of 'older' people are increasing; for example, by 2041 people over 60 will comprise 37 per cent of the UK population (Department of Health, 2005). This group is changing as well as growing. Successive cohorts are becoming older and more diverse, with increasing numbers of very old and black and minority ethnic (BME) people. They are also more psychologically minded than previous generations. Inevitably, these changes will impact on demand for psychology and psychological therapy services. Psychologists will clearly need the skills to meet these demands.

There is no absolute cut-off when 'old age' begins: 'To me old age is always 15 years older than I am' (Age Concern, 2006). Chronological age is an arbitrary construct. Social and biological age tap significant changes in physical well-being, cognitive ability, roles and relationships. These relate to chronological age but are not equivalent. For example, it has been conventional to retire at 60 or 65, but many retire younger or continue to work longer. We need to take account of these changes, not the numbers of candles on the cake.

Within Western cultures there are powerful but misleading stereotypes of old age. Many psychologists have limited contact with older people (less than half of people under 35 have a friend over 70) so will have little evidence to draw on to challenge these beliefs. Typically it is assumed that all old people are frail, forgetful, poor and facing overwhelming adversity. These stereotypes shape our beliefs about older people and impact on expectations and reactions. Unrealistic positive stereotypes (such as that age inevitably brings wisdom) may be equally misleading; old age is not all doom and gloom, although it does have a 'dark side' (Garland, 2005).

Old age spans a wide range of ages (from 60 to over 100) with enormous variability between people. The majority see themselves as fit and healthy, although disability and long-term illness do increase with age (World Health Organisation, 1999). While the incidence of dementia is age-related, only a minority at any age will have dementia. Many old people notice changes in memory or concentration. Studies examining cognitive changes with age, however, show inconsistent findings (Salthouse, 1991). Typically older samples score lower but have higher standard deviations than younger samples; this increased variability may be more robust than differences in means (Rabbitt, 1993, 1996). Likewise, while some older people subsist on inadequate pensions, others enjoy financial comfort. Old age is not a particularly adverse time. Older people are less likely to encounter some life events (redundancy, criminal prosecution, divorce) but more likely to encounter others (bereavement, death, ill health). Overall they score lower on life event inventories and appraise these as less stressful than younger people (Folkman *et al.*, 1987; Aldwin, 1990, 1991; Aldwin *et al.*, 1996).

Psychological Models

There are two influential models; both conceptualize aging as a dynamic process of adjustment and change.

Erikson's model is rooted in psychoanalytic developmental theory (Erikson, 1963). He identified eight developmental stages extending across the lifespan, with characteristic themes, or 'psychosocial crises', which the individual strives to resolve in order to develop a particular strength. As we age, we revisit earlier stages in order to resolve any unfinished crises from the perspective of our current stage. The developmental task for old age is to accept life and come to terms with any disappointments, thereby achieving 'ego integrity' and avoiding 'despair'. Key to this is the process of life review. This model was extended posthumously by Erikson's wife (Erikson, 1997), establishing a ninth stage characteristic of very old age. The task at this stage is to disengage from the world and develop a more spiritual perspective. This draws on the concept of 'gerotranscendence' described by Tornstam (1989, 1996) whereby the older person's meta-perspective shifts from concerns with the mundane to concerns with the universal. There is some evidence that life satisfaction ratings correlate with measures of resolution of earlier stages (Woods & Witte, 1981) and that very old age is related to increased spiritual activities (Dalby, 2006; Lowis & Brown, 2001). Clinically, Erikson's model is widely used, most obviously as the basis for life review therapy.

According to Baltes and Baltes' (1990) model, successful ageing involves adjustment to the challenges of social and biological age, fitting well within a positive psychology paradigm. They describe three strategies whereby the older person copes with restrictions imposed by age-related changes: 'selection' (i.e. prioritising), 'optimisation' (i.e. maximising capabilities) and compensation (i.e. using capabilities to offset any limitations). There is some evidence of a moderate relationship between life satisfaction and use of these strategies. This offers a useful model when working with clients facing realistic difficulties.

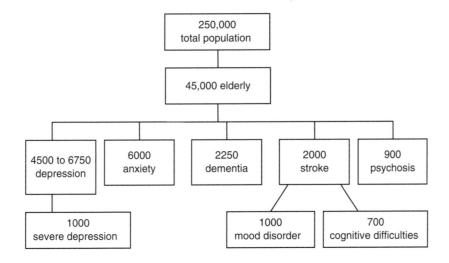

(Prevalence figures from Everybody's Business, Department of Health, 2005)

Figure 23.1 Psychological problems presented by older people in a 'typical' UK health district.

Overview of Psychological Problems

There is an extensive epidemiological literature (Livingston & Hinchcliffe, 1993). Figure 23.1 applies accepted prevalence figures to a typical UK health district population of 250,000.

Prevalence increases dramatically among service users: 40 per cent of older people attending their general practitioner (GP), 50 per cent of those in general hospital services and 60 per cent of care home residents show some mental health need.

None of these mental health problems are unique to older people. However, older patients are more likely to present with dementia and multiple, mental and/or physical health problems.

Models of Mental Health Services

The National Service Framework (NSF) for Older People (OP) (Department of Health, 2001) provides a UK framework for the development of services for older people with physical or mental health needs. This refers specifically to services in England, but there are broadly similar policy initiatives for other parts of the UK and elsewhere in the developed world. The NSF includes eight standards mapped onto four themes (Box 23.1). Standard 7 (Mental Health) refers to depression and dementia only. This policy has a strong psychological underpinning, with extensive reference to the need for psychology as a profession and for psychological approaches (Boddington, 2001; Lee *et al.*, 2002; Allen, 2006).

Box 23.1   The National Service Framework for Older People

Theme	Standard
1. Respecting the individual	1. Rooting out age discrimination
	2. Person-centred care
2. Intermediate care	3. Intermediate care
3. Evidence-based specialist care	4. General hospital services
	5. Stroke
	6. Falls
	7. Mental health
4. Health promotion	8. Promotion of health and active life in older age

---

Implementation of the NSF is spelt out in detail in subsequent UK policies, e.g. Everybody's Business (Department of Health, 2005), Securing Better Mental Health for Older Adults (Department of Health, 2005) and A New Ambition for Old Age (Department of Health, 2006). These identify target groups for health care: people with dementia, depression, physical illness and disability (stroke, falls and fear of falling, continence, pain, disability, palliative care) and health promotion. There are opportunities for psychological input across this spectrum.

A recurrent tension is whether services for older people should be mainstreamed (incorporated within general adult services) or specialist (Baty, 2006). Mainstream services may not recognise or respond to the particular needs of older people. Specialist services promote expertise and positive values, but may be less well resourced and potentially reinforce the view that older people are different. Current policy emphasises the need for both. Mainstream services should manage the majority of mild and moderate mental illness, supported by specialist services which also target severe or complex mental illness (including psychotic symptoms and early diagnosis of dementia). Models of specialist mental health services vary, defining their core business as any mental health need presented by someone over a certain age, or as specific needs such as dementia, or as needs developing *de novo* in old age, with variable age cut-offs.

Comorbidity requires the involvement of many agencies. Often older people receive care from a complex network of providers: primary and secondary, general health, mental health and social care systems. Recently independent and voluntary sectors have played an increasing role alongside statutory providers. Ideally this should be a coordinated, seamless package. In reality it can be a fragmented confusion. The aim of policy is to move towards joined-up working, with integrated services, partnership working and single assessment processes.

Psychology Services

Psychology services face two related challenges; access and availability.

Although older people present similar psychological needs as younger adults, they are least likely to receive mental health professional input (Landreville *et al.*, 2001) or clinical psychology (Harte, 2004). A recent survey of access to psychology and counselling services in Lambeth suggested that referral rates drop from 45 onwards (Sandford, 2006). There may be particular difficulties for black and minority ethnic elderly (Cinirella & Loewenthal, 1999) who face the 'triple jeopardy' of ageism, racism and inaccessible services (Norman, 1985). The under-utilisation of services may reflect a pervasive pessimism that older people do not benefit from psychological therapy, a legacy of Freud's assertion that as we approach 50, we become too rigid to change. Counter-therapeutic beliefs may be held by the older person, referrer or psychologist and act as barriers (Emery, 1981; Laidlaw *et al.*, 2003). Older people may perceive themselves as too old to change or adopt a medical rather than psychological model of their difficulties. As a consequence they may under-present or seek other services. When older people present with psychological needs, GPs may be reluctant to refer (Blanchard *et al.*, 1994; Weeple, 2004). Even if referred, therapists may react differently to older patients, perceiving them as less suitable (Settin, 1982). Lee *et al.* (2003a) found that while most clinical psychology trainees hold positive views of psychotherapy with older people, a significant minority hold very negative stereotypes.

Another factor determining access is availability of services. Boddington and Kirtley (2002) identified a national shortfall of clinical psychologists, with pockets of well-resourced services. The shortfall seems to reflect under-investment as well as historical recruitment difficulties (Scott & Bhutani, 1999). A recent survey of old age psychiatrists (Evans, 2004) suggested that the majority of psychological treatments offered within specialist mental health services is by non-psychologists.

Government policy emphasises the value of psychological perspectives and interventions with older people. In the UK, the National Institute for Health and Clinical Excellence (NICE) Guidelines for Depression (National Institute for Health and Clinical Excellence, 2004) and Dementia (National Institute for Health and Clinical Excellence, 2006) recommend psychological therapy for older people and their carers. Everybody's Business (Department of Health, 2005) states that psychological therapies should be considered routinely (including people with dementia): 'age is not an important factor in the choice of therapy, and need, not age, should determine access to therapies' (p.49). These are exciting opportunities for psychology, although sadly little money has followed the rhetoric.

Models and Competencies

PSIGE – Psychology Specialists Working with Older People (British Psychological Society, 2006) identifies 12 areas of capability required for work with older people (Box 23.2).

Box 23.2   PSIGE – Psychology Specialist Working with Older People, recommended capabilities for work with older people

Specific capabilities

- Recognise and address ageism
- Recognise and manage differences in age between psychologist and client
- Sensitive to culture specific expectations of ageing
- Aware of services available for older people

General capabilities

- Encourage autonomy, choice, well-being and motivation
- Recognise and minimise barriers to independence
- Communicate effectively
- Formulate complex presentations
- Apply scientist- and reflective- practitioner models
- Recognise and manage risk
- Work with other providers
- Recognise and manage boundary issues

Source: adapted from British Psychological Society Division of Clinical Psychology PSIGE (2006).

Some of these capabilities are specific to this client group, such as techniques (e.g. life review, care mapping, neuropsychological assessment), some relate to work with specific presenting problems (e.g. dementia, physical illness and disability), while other capabilities involve consolidating and adapting skills already learnt. Typically, older adult work offers opportunities to develop capabilities which can be transferred to other client groups (e.g. working with multi-agency care systems, complex formulations, and people with cognitive or sensory impairments). What must underpin this is reflective practice; a core element of work with older people is self-awareness, monitoring and reflecting on the personal impact of working with older people, and identifying and challenging any assumptions brought.

Evidence Base

There is a strong evidence base to challenge therapeutic pessimism and to establish 'the effectiveness of psychological interventions in the management of a wide range of mental and physical conditions in older people and their carers' (Department of Health,

Table 23.1 Meta-analyses of outcome studies of psychological therapies

Meta-analysis	Studies included	Number of studies
Scogin & McElreath (1994)	Psychosocial treatments for depression	17
Koder *et al.* (1996)	Psychological therapies for depression	18
Davies & Collerton (1997)	Psychological therapies for depression	17
Gatz *et al.* (1998)	Range of psychological therapies for various disorders (including depression, anxiety and dementia)	56
Arean & Cook (2002)	Psychological therapies and combined psychotherapy/pharmacology for depression	29

2005, p. 49). Evidence is strongest for interventions with dementia and depression. Other problems such as psychosis, substance abuse or anxiety are under-researched. This is reflected in the recommendations made by NICE, i.e. for cognitive behavioural therapy (CBT) with depression (Depression Guidelines); psychological therapy for anxiety and depression with people with dementia as well as for carers experiencing distress (Dementia Guidelines).

There are five recent meta-analyses of outcome studies of psychological therapies (Table 23.1).

Effect sizes (ESs) are good (for example, Scogin & McElreath, 1994, report a mean ES of 0.78 from 23 comparisons based on 765 patients with depression). Arean and Cook (2002) classified studies of interventions with depressed patients according to Chambless and Hollon's (1998) criteria. They report 'compelling' evidence for the value of CBT, problem solving therapy and combined interpersonal therapy (IPT) and anti-depressants; less strong evidence for stand-alone IPT, brief psychodynamic therapy and life review. Gatz *et al.* (1998) used the American Psychiatric Association Task Force criteria to evaluate outcomes in their more extensive review of psychological therapies for a range of disorders. The only interventions to meet the criteria of 'well-established' were behavioural and environmental interventions in dementia. Many met the criteria of 'probably efficacious', i.e. CBT, behaviour therapy and brief psychodynamic therapy in depression; life review; CBT for sleep disorders; memory and cognitive retraining with dementia; support groups for carers of people with dementia.

Engagement

As with any client group, engagement is fundamental. Older patients may be more reluctant to engage with psychology (Harte, 2004), although Clarke and Charlesworth

(2006) found that 75 per cent of older patients referred for psychological therapy opted in. Establishing and maintaining an effective therapeutic alliance is particularly challenging when working with clients from a different cohort and at a different developmental stage. Therapists may need to adapt standard therapeutic practices or adopt flexible boundaries; this may feel unsafe for established therapists let alone trainees (Kivnick & Kavka, 1999; Petford, 2006). The dynamic of the therapeutic relationship is different when seeing clients in their own homes (a common feature of work with older people) rather than in formal clinical settings.

To establish an effective working relationship, the psychologist must identify and address any potential blocks. These might include:

- communication difficulties (due to physical illness, cognitive or sensory impairments, language);
- the impact of age or cultural differences between psychologist and client;
- transference arising from any stage of life (so the therapist may be cast as child, grandchild, parent, spouse etc);
- countertransference such as responding to the client as a child to be nurtured, or as idealised authority figure;
- counter-therapeutic beliefs or misconceptions held by client or therapist;
- clients' lack of experience with psychological models of working (and lack of understanding of basic therapeutic ground rules);
- lack of informed consent (e.g. when the client has been referred by others).

Addressing these may take time. Dick *et al.* (1996) identify key tasks of the early phase of therapy as establishing rapport, socialising into the model and agreeing goals. They suggest this may require up to three sessions; many clients need longer. Therapists who do not appreciate the importance of this work may rush prematurely into active therapy. This will result in lack of progress and frustration.

Once engaged, older patients can be as or more motivated and attend more reliably, with DNA rates of up to half those of younger patients (McKenzie & Marks, 1997; Walker & Clarke, 2001; Harte, 2004), possibly because they are highly selected. Old age can be a good time to embark on psychological therapy. Older people have fewer external demands on their time and more opportunity to engage. They may be unable to tolerate psychotropic medication (because of coexisting physical health problems or drug–drug interactions). Therapy can fit well with the developmental challenges of later life (Kivnick & Kavka, 1999). Rokke and Scogin (1995) found that older depressed patients perceived psychological approaches as more credible and acceptable than medication compared with younger patients.

Formal Assessment

Work with older people provides an opportunity to develop skills in the formal assessment of mood, behaviour and cognition, including neuropsychological assessment.

There is a plethora of measures, some developed for older people, others taken from younger groups. These have been reviewed recently (Davies, 1996; Little & Doherty, 1996; Morris *et al.*, 2000; Clare, in press; Little, in press). Common issues include the validity and acceptability of measures and adequacy of norms. There is no gold-standard assessment protocol. Assessment raises ethical challenges: securing informed consent; working with clients who may not have capacity to consent (British Psychological Society, 2005; Twining, in press); providing honest, comprehensible and sensitive feedback of results; relaying distressing information such as diagnosis (Williams, 2002); negotiating the balance between professional responsibilities and therapeutic relationship should the neuropsychological assessment question fitness to continue driving (Major, 2007; Patience, 2007).

Psychological Therapies

NICE guidelines recommend CBT as treatment of choice for depression in older people (including those with dementia) and their carers (see Section 7). Useful resources include CBT specifically for older people (Laidlaw *et al.*, 2003), a recent review of the literature (Laidlaw, in press) and a bibliography (Kneebone, 2006). Older depressed patients show the distortions (Vezina & Bourque, 1984; Lam *et al.*, 1987) and memory biases (Fromholt *et al.*, 1995) characteristic of younger depressed patients. Evidence for psychological therapy comes principally from the work of Thompson and colleagues, who have designed and evaluated a structured, short-term (up to 20 sessions) package, targeting cognitive and behavioural changes with a range of CBT techniques (Gallagher & Thompson, 1981). They compared this to brief psychodynamic psychotherapy and behaviour therapy with a randomised double blind controlled trial including a two-year follow-up (Thompson *et al.*, 1987; Gallagher-Thompson *et al.*, 1990). All three treatment groups fared significantly better than waiting list controls and gains were maintained at follow-up. There was no evidence of differential improvement or maintenance between therapies. Further studies offer evidence for CBT protocol with specific groups of depressed older people, including carers (Gallagher-Thompson & Steffen, 1994), bereaved elderly (Florsheim & Gallagher-Thompson, 1990; Gantz *et al.*, 1992), suicidal patients (De Vries & Gallagher-Thompson, 1994), people with dementia (Thompson *et al.*, 1989), and patients with personality disorder (Coon, 1994; Dick & Gallagher-Thompson, 1996).

CBT has been less well studied with other disorders. Most evidence is drawn from case reports and uncontrolled case series, although Barrowclough *et al.* (2001) report a controlled trial of CBT with anxiety. Two studies (McKenzie & Marks, 1997; Walker & Clarke, 2001) compared the impact of CBT for older and younger patients presenting with various disorders (predominantly anxiety). There were no differences in outcome; both groups showed significant impact. However, both older groups were more cost-effective to treat, with significantly fewer DNAs.

Many depressed and anxious older patients will also present with physical illness and disabilities. These should not exclude people from treatment. It is easy to react hopelessly when confronted by often severe or untreatable conditions ('No wonder s/he is depressed') but CBT can be effective. Kemp *et al.* (1991/2) found that depressed older patients with severe or chronic physical illnesses responded as well to group CBT as healthy patients. Czirr and Gallagher (1983) and Rybarczyk *et al.* (1992) describe case studies using the Thompson *et al.* protocol with physically ill patients, focusing on helping patients view their depression as a reaction to physical illness, not an inevitable consequence. There are models for CBT interventions with specific groups such as fear of falling (Childs & Kneebone, 2002), post-fracture depression (Woodward, 2005) and post-stroke depression (Kneebone & Dunmore, 2000; Lincoln & Flanagan, 2003).

It may be necessary to adapt CBT to take account of coexisting physical morbidity, cognitive impairment or sensory difficulties. For example, Dick *et al.* (1996) describe ways of simplifying thought records. Older people may bring particular themes such as loss to therapy (Petford, 2006; Knight, 1996). However, therapy should be tailored to the needs of the individual patient, not the age group per se. For example, two studies illustrate very different approaches to formulation with older people. Laidlaw *et al.* (2004) describe the value of highly detailed conceptualisations; taking account of cohort beliefs, socio-cultural context, role transitions, physical health, family relationships, and providing a broad framework in which the conventional individual CBT conceptualisation is embedded. By contrast, Charlesworth and Reichelt (2004) describe how to keep conceptualisation simple, using mini-formulations which are particularly useful when working with clients who are cognitively impaired or less psychologically sophisticated.

Despite the emphasis given to CBT within NICE, it is not the only effective treatment with older people and may not be appropriate for a given patient. In clinical practice, as with any client group, clinician and patient need to select the therapeutic approach which fits best. CBT is the best researched, but other therapies are under-researched rather than proven ineffective. There is little compelling evidence to indicate that one therapy is better than another (e.g. Thompson *et al.*, 1987; Gallagher-Thompson *et al.*, 1990) and insufficient evidence to establish the differential effectiveness of psychological therapies and pharmacology (Gerson *et al.*, 1999). A reasonable working assumption is that an evidence base for an intervention with younger adults provides grounds for trying it with an older person, subject, of course, to careful monitoring and review of outcomes.

Examples of Specific Models and Interventions

As well as applying competencies acquired with other client groups, there are several specialist models and techniques.

Interventions for people with dementia and their carers

Practitioners' concerns over working with people with organic disorders such as stroke or dementia often stem from the belief that they will have nothing to offer. This sense

Table 23.2 Psychological interventions with dementia

Target problem	Examples of interventions
Adjustment to diagnosis	Individual and group psychotherapy (Yale, 1995; Cheston et al., 2003)
Emotional distress	• CBT (Teri & Gallagher-Thompson, 1991; James, 1999; James, 2001) • CBT with carers (Gallagher-Thompson & Steffen, 1994; Charlesworth, 2001; Walker, 2004)
Management of cognitive impairment	• Reality orientation and stimulation groups (Spector et al., 1998, 2003) • Memory training (De Vreese et al., 2001)
Management of challenging behaviour	• Functional analysis (Stokes, 1986a, b; Stokes, 1987a, b) • Bio-psychosocial analysis (Moniz-Cook & Bird, in press)

of impotence is unfounded. Psychological work here is much more than assessment. There are many opportunities for intervention (see Table 23.2 and Clare & Wood, in press).

Tom Kitwood's (1997) 'dialectical framework' of dementia has been highly influential, shaping the concept of person-centred care which is part of the NSF (OP). Kitwood describes dementia as not simply the unfolding of a biological disease process, but the interaction of multiple factors including neurological impairment, personality, life history, physical health and 'social psychology'. Social context can promote personhood (i.e. 'benign social psychology' such as providing safety and validation of experience) or undermine this (i.e. 'malignant social psychology' such as infantilising, labelling, or banishing). Typically, dementia attracts a malignant context which will compound neurological impairments (e.g. depriving the person of opportunities to do something will foster excess disability). Therapeutic dementia care builds a positive social psychology which goes some way towards mitigating impairment and maintaining personhood. Kitwood and Bredin (1992) developed a tool to analyse the care context (dementia care mapping). There is some evidence that person-centred care is beneficial, providing an effective alternative to narcoleptics for some clients with challenging behaviours (Fossey et al., 2006).

Reminiscence and life review

A key distinction is between reminiscence (recalling the past) and life review (coming to terms with past life). Reminiscence was developed as a recreational therapy; life review is a structured psychotherapy, consistent with the developmental task of old age to re-evaluate life and resolve conflicts (see above). Based upon earlier work by Butler (1963), Haight (1988, 1992; Haight et al., 1998) has developed and evaluated a protocol for life review therapy. Bohlmeijer et al. (2003) published a meta-analysis of controlled outcome studies of both life review (nine studies) and reminiscence

(13 studies). Both have significant impact on depressive symptoms, with an overall ES of 0.84. Life review seems more effective (ES 0.92 compared with 0.46) but this difference was not significant, and results varied widely. They concluded that the impact of life review is comparable to established treatments for depression such as antidepressants or CBT. However, studies have typically included mild depression only. Life review can be incorporated within CBT (Dick et al., 1996) or narrative therapy (e.g. Mills, 1997). It is important to use these approaches with caution. Reminiscence may have different functions and for some may be maladaptive, e.g. bitter rumination (Coleman, 2005; Cappeliez et al., 2005).

Working with bereavement and death

People face death at any age, but psychologists are most likely to encounter this amongst older people. Preparation for death is a key developmental task. This is a common source of concern for psychologists, who may feel apprehension at having to confront difficult and painful issues which may seem easier avoided (Knight, 1996). Research suggests that older people are less fearful about death than younger people; their concerns may relate more to how they will die (McKiernan, 1996). Older people cope well with bereavement, possibly better than younger people (Wortman & Silver, 1990). Earlier exposure to bereavement may develop a coping repertoire. However, bereavement is associated with increased risk of psychological and physical morbidity in all age groups. A range of interventions is available (Oyebode, in press), including guided mourning (Ramsay, 1977) and CBT (Florsheim & Gallagher-Thompson, 1990; Gantz et al., 1992). IPT has potential here but has not yet been evaluated with bereaved older patients.

Facing Challenges

The challenges of working with older people can provide excellent opportunities for learning and development, provided psychologists have the self-awareness and trust to bring these issues to supervision. It is important to remember that working with older people is enjoyable as well as challenging. Very few trainee psychologists (3 per cent), (Lee et al., 2003b) found nothing rewarding in their older adult training. Almost all identified rewards; the most frequently cited (by 40 per cent) was the sense of having made a positive contribution to someone's life: 'the same emotional rewards as working with any client group: being able to help' (p. 137).

References

Age Concern (2006). How ageist is Britain? London: Age Concern, England.
Aldwin, C. (1990). The Elders Life Stress Inventory: Egocentric and nonegocentric stress. In M.A.P. Stephens, S.E. Hobfall, J.H. Crowther & D.L. Tennenbaum (Eds.) Stress and coping in late life families (pp. 174–180). New York: Hemisphere.

Aldwin, C. (1991). Does age affect the stress and coping process? Implications of age differences in perceived control. *Journal of Gerontology: Psychological Sciences, 46*, 174–180.

Aldwin, C.M., Sutton, K.J., Chiara, G. & Spiro, A. (1996). Age differences in stress, coping and appraisal: Findings from the normative aging study. *Journal of Gerontology: Psychological Sciences, 51B*, 179–188.

Allen, C. (2006). New challenges, new possibilities and new solutions: The National Service Framework for Older People. *Clinical Psychology Forum, 161*, 11–14.

Arean, P.A. & Cook, B.L. (2002). Psychotherapy and combined psychotherapy/pharmacology for late life depression. *Society of Biological Psychiatry, 52*, 293–303.

Baltes, P.B. & Baltes, M.M. (1990). *Successful ageing: Perspectives from the behavioural sciences.* New York: Cambridge University Press.

Barrowclough, C., King, P., Colville, J., Russell, E., Burns, A. & Tarrier, N. (2001). A randomised trial of the effectiveness of cognitive-behavioural treatment and supportive counseling for anxiety symptoms in older adults. *Journal of Consulting and Clinical Psychology, 69*, 756–762.

Baty, F. (2006). Generalists and specialists in services for older people. *Clinical Psychology Forum, 161*, 29–32.

Blanchard, M.R., Waterreus, A. & Mann, A.H. (1994). The nature of depression among older people in Inner London, and the contact with primary care. *British Journal of Psychiatry, 164*, 396–402.

Boddington, S. (2001). National Service Framework – Older People. Summary and thoughts from a clinical psychologist's perspective. *PSIGE Newsletter, 77*, 5–11.

Boddington, S. & Kirtley, W. (2002). A survey of the availability of clinical psychology services for older people across the UK. *Clinical Psychology, 13*, 14–18.

Bohlmeijer, E., Smit, F. & Cuipers, P. (2003). Effects of reminiscence and life review on late-life depression: A meta-analysis. *International Journal of Geriatric Psychiatry, 18*, 1088–1094.

British Psychological Society Division of Clinical Psychology PSIGE (2006). Good practice guidelines for UK Clinical psychology training providers for the training and consolidation of clinical practice in relation to older people. Leicester: Author.

British Psychological Society Professional Practice Board (2005). *Assessment of capacity in adults: Interim guidance for psychologists.* Leicester: Author.

Butler, R.N. (1963). The life review: An interpretation of reminiscence in the aged. *Psychiatry, 26*, 65–76.

Cappeliez, P., O'Rourke, N. & Chaudhury, H. (2005). Functions of reminiscence and mental health in later life. *Aging and Mental Health, 9*, 295–301.

Chambless, D.L. & Hollon, S.D. (1998). Defining empirically supported therapies. *Journal of Consulting and Clinical Psychology, 66*, 7–18.

Charlesworth, G. (2001). Reflections on using cognitive therapy with depressed family caregivers of people with dementia. *PSIGE Newsletter, 78*, 26–30.

Charlesworth, G.M. & Reichelt, F.K. (2004). Keeping conceptualizations simple: Examples with family carers of people with dementia. *Behavioural and Cognitive Psychotherapy, 32*, 401–409.

Cheston, R., Jones, K. & Gilliard, J. (2003). Group psychotherapy and people with dementia. *Aging and Mental Health, 7*, 452–461.

Childs, L. & Kneebone, I. (2002). Falls, fear of falling and psychological management. *British Journal of Therapy and Rehabilitation, 6*, 225–231.

Cinirella, K.M. & Loewenthal, M. (1999). Religious and ethnic group influences on beliefs about mental illness. *British Journal of Medical Psychology, 72*, 505–524.

Clare, L. (in press). Neuropsychological assessment. In B. Woods & L. Clare (Eds.) *Handbook of the clinical psychology of ageing* (2nd edn). Chichester: Wiley.

Clare, L. & Woods, B. (in press). Interventions for people with cognitive impairment. In B. Woods & L. Clare (Eds.) *Handbook of the clinical psychology of ageing* (2nd edn). Chichester: Wiley.

Clarke, H. & Charlesworth, G. (2006). Is offering choice the preferred option? *Clinical Psychology Forum, 161,* 26–28.

Coleman, P.G. (2005). Uses of reminiscence: Functions and benefits. *Aging and Mental Health, 9,* 291–294.

Coon, D.W. (1994). Cognitive-behavioral interventions with avoidant personality: A single case study. *Journal of Cognitive Psychotherapy, 8,* 243–253.

Czirr, R. & Gallagher, D. (1983). Case report: Behavioral treatment of depression and somatic complaints in rheumatoid arthritis. *Clinical Gerontologist, 2,* 63–66.

Dalby, P. (2006). Is there a process of spiritual change or development associated with ageing? A critical review of research. *Aging and Mental Health, 10,* 4–12.

Davies, S. (1996). Neuropsychological assessment of the older person. In B. Woods (Ed.) *Handbook of the clinical psychology of ageing* (pp. 441–474). Chichester: Wiley.

Davies, C. & Collerton, D. (1997). Psychological therapies for depression with older adults: A qualitative review. *Journal of Mental Health, 6,* 335–344.

De Vries, H. & Gallagher-Thompson, D. (1994). Crises with geriatric patients. In F. Dattilio & A. Freeman (Eds.) *Cognitive-behavior therapy and crisis intervention* (pp. 200–218). New York: Guilford Press.

De Vreese, L., Neri, M., Fioravanti, M., Belloi, L. & Zanetti, O. (2001). Memory rehabilitation in Alzheimer's Disease: A review of progress. *International Journal of Geriatric Psychiatry, 16,* 794–809.

Department of Health (2001). *National Service Framework for Older People.* London: HMSO.

Department of Health (2005). *Everybody's business – integrating mental health services for older adults.* London: Author.

Department of Health (2005). *Securing better mental health for older adults.* London: Author.

Department of Health (2006). *A new ambition for old age: Next steps in implementing the National Service Framework for Older People.* London: Author.

Dick, L.P. & Gallagher-Thompson, D. (1996). Cognitive therapy to change the core beliefs of a distressed lonely caregiver. *Journal of Cognitive Psychotherapy, 9,* 215–227.

Dick, L.P., Gallagher-Thompson, D. & Thompson, L. (1996). Cognitive-behavioural therapy. In B. Woods (Ed.) *Handbook of the clinical psychology of ageing* (pp. 509–544). Chichester: Wiley.

Emery, G. (1981). Cognitive therapy with the elderly. In G. Emery, S.D. Hollon & R.C. Bedrosian (Eds.) *New directions in cognitive therapy* (pp. 84–98). New York: Guilford Press.

Erikson, E.H. (1963). *Childhood and society.* New York: W.W. Norton.

Erikson, J.M. (1997). *The life cycle completed: Extended version with new chapters on the ninth stage of development.* New York: W.W. Norton.

Evans, S. (2004). A survey of the provision of psychological treatments to older adults in the NHS. *Psychiatric Bulletin, 28,* 411–414.

Florsheim, M.J. & Gallagher-Thompson, D. (1990). Cognitive-behavioral treatment of atypical bereavement: A case study. *Clinical Gerontologist, 10,* 73–76.

Folkman, S., Lazarus, R.S., Pimley, S. & Novacek, J. (1987). Age differences in stress and coping processes. *Psychology and Aging, 2,* 171–184.

Fossey, J., Ballard, C.G., Juszczak, E., James, I.A., Alder, N., Jacoby, R. *et al.* (2006). Effect of enhanced psychosocial care on antipsychotic use in nursing home residents with severe dementia: Cluster randomised trial. *British Medical Journal, 332,* 756–758.

Fromholt, P., Larsen, P. & Larsen, S.F. (1995). Effects of late-onset depression and recovery on autobiographical memory. *Journal of Gerontology: Psychological Sciences, 50B,* 74–81.

Gallagher, D. & Thompson, L.W. (1981). *Depression in the elderly: A behavioral treatment manual.* Los Angeles: Ethel Percy Andrus Gerontology Center.

Gallagher-Thompson, D., Hanley-Peterson, P. & Thompson, L.W (1990). Maintenance of gains versus relapse following brief psychotherapy for depression. *Journal of Consulting and Clinical Psychology, 58,* 371–374.

Gallagher-Thompson, D. & Steffen, A. (1994). Comparative effects of cognitive-behavioral and brief psychodynamic psychotherapies for depressed family caregivers. *Journal of Consulting and Clinical Psychology, 62,* 543–549.

Gantz, F., Gallagher-Thompson, D. & Rodman, J. (1992). Cognitive-behavioral facilitation of inhibited grief, In A. Freeman & F. Dattilio (Eds.) *Comprehensive casebook of cognitive behavioral therapy* (pp. 359–379). London: Oxford University Press.

Garland, J. (2005). Facing up to ageing. *PSIGE Newsletter, 92,* 13–15.

Gatz, M., Fiske, A., Fox, L.S., Kaskie, B., Kasl-Godley, J.E., McCallum, T.J. *et al.* (1998). Empirically validated psychological treatments for older adults. *Journal of Mental Health and Ageing, 4,* 9–46.

Gerson, S., Belin, T.R., Kaufma, A., Mintz, J. & Jarvik, L. (1999). Pharmacological and psychological treatments for depressed older patients: A meta-analysis and overview of recent findings. *Harvard Review of Psychiatry, 7,* 1–28.

Haight, B.K. (1988). The therapeutic role of a structured life review process in homebound elderly subjects. *Journal of Gerontology, 43,* 40–44.

Haight, B.K. (1992). Long-term effects of a structured life review process in homebound elderly subjects. *Journal of Gerontology, 47,* 312–315.

Haight, B.K., Michel, Y. & Hendrix, S. (1998). Life review: Preventing despair in newly relocated nursing home residents: Short- and long-term effects. *International Journal of Aging and Human Development, 47,* 119–142.

Harte, C. (2004). An audit of clinical psychology referrals and provision for older adults in the Scottish borders. *PSIGE Newsletter, 87,* 36–41.

James, I.A. (1999). Using a cognitive rationale to conceptualise anxiety in people with dementia. *Behavioural and Cognitive Psychotherapy, 27,* 345–351.

James, I.A. (2001). Cognitive therapy formulations and interventions for treating distress in dementia. In C. Ballard, J. O'Brien, I. James & A. Swann (Eds.) *Management of behavioural and psychological symptoms in dementia* (pp. 143–167). Oxford: Oxford University Press.

Kemp, B.J., Cogiat, M. & Gill, C. (1991/1992). Effects of brief cognitive group psychotherapy in older persons with and without disabling illness. *Behaviour, Health and Ageing, 2,* 21–28.

Kitwood, T. (1997). *Dementia reconsidered.* Oxford: Oxford University Press.

Kitwood, T. & Bredin, K. (1992). A new approach to the evaluation of dementia care. *Journal of Advances in Health and Nursing Care, 1,* 41–60.

Kivnick, H.Q. & Kavka, A. (1999). It takes two: Therapeutic alliance with older clients. In M. Duffey (Ed.) *Handbook of counselling and psychotherapy with older adults* (pp. 125–143). Chichester: Wiley.

Kneebone, I. (2006). Behavioural and cognitive therapies with older people: A selected bibliography. *PSIGE Newsletter, 96,* 46–49.

Kneebone, I. & Dunmore, E. (2000). Psychological management of post-stroke depression. *British Journal of Clinical Psychology, 39,* 53–65.

Knight, B.G. (1996). Psychodynamic therapy with older adults: Lessons from scientific gerontology. In B. Woods (Ed.) *Handbook of the clinical psychology of ageing* (pp. 545–560). Chichester: Wiley.

Koder, D.A., Brodaty, H. & Anstey, K.J. (1996). Cognitive therapy for depression in the elderly. *International Journal of Geriatric Psychiatry, 13,* 79–99.

Laidlaw, K. (in press). CBT. In B. Woods & L. Clare (Eds.) *Handbook of the clinical psychology of ageing* (2nd edn). Chichester: Wiley.

Laidlaw, K., Thompson, L.W., Dick-Siskin, L. & Gallagher-Thompson, D. (2003). *Cognitive behaviour therapy with older people.* Chichester: Wiley.

Laidlaw, K., Thompson, L.W. & Gallagher-Thompson, D. (2004). Comprehensive conceptualization of cognitive behavior therapy for late life depression. *Behavioural and Cognitive Psychotherapy, 32,* 389–399.

Lam, D.H., Brewin, C.R., Woods, R.T. & Bebbington, P.E. (1987). Cognition and social adversity in the depressed elderly. *Journal of Abnormal Psychology, 96,* 23–26.

Landreville, P., Landry, J., Baillargeon, L., Guerette, A. & Matteau, E. (2001). Older adults acceptance of psychological and pharmacological treatments for depression. *Journal of Gerontology: Psychological Sciences, 50B,* 285–291.

Lee, T., Critchley-Robbins, S., Smyth, C., McDonagh, C. & Dooley, C. (2002). Implementing the National Service Framework for Older People: What can clinical psychologists do? *PSIGE Newsletter, 79,* 17–23.

Lee, T., Volans, P.J. & Gregory, N. (2003a). Attitudes towards psychotherapy with older people among clinical psychologists. *Aging and Mental Health, 7,* 133–141.

Lee, K., Volans, P.J. & Gregory, N. (2003b). Trainee clinical psychologists' views on recruitment to work with older people. *Aging and Society, 23,* 83–97.

Lincoln, N.B. & Flanagan, T. (2003). Cognitive behavioural psychotherapy for depression following stroke. *Stroke, 34,* 111–115.

Little, A. (in press). Assessment of functioning and behaviour. In B. Woods & L. Clare (Eds.) *Handbook of the clinical psychology of ageing* (2nd edn). Chichester: Wiley.

Little, A. & Doherty, B. (1996). Going beyond cognitive assessment: Assessment of adjustment, behaviour and the environment. In B. Woods (Ed.) *Handbook of the clinical psychology of ageing* (pp. 475–508). Chichester: Wiley.

Livingston, G. & Hinchcliffe, A.C. (1993). The epidemiology of psychiatric disorders in the elderly. *International Review of Psychiatry, 5,* 317–326.

Lowis, M. & Brown, C. (2001). Does evidence for Erickson's ninth stage of development inform us about appropriate psychological intervention in extreme old age? *PSIGE, 78,* 22–25.

Major, H. (2007). Dementia and driving: The DVLA position. *PSIGE, 98,* 9–15.

McKenzie, N. & Marks, I.M. (1997). Behavioural treatment of anxiety and other disorders in the elderly. *Primary Care Psychiatry, 3,* 21–24.

McKiernan, F. (1996). Bereavement and attitudes to death. In B. Woods (Ed.) *Handbook of the clinical psychology of ageing* (pp. 159–182). Chichester: Wiley.

Mills, M.A. (1997). Narrative identity and dementia: A study of emotion and narrative in older people with dementia. *Ageing and Society, 17,* 673–698.

Moniz-Cook, E. & Bird, M. (in press). In B. Woods & L. Clare (Eds.) *Handbook of the clinical psychology of ageing* (2nd edn). Chichester: Wiley.

Morris, R.G., Worsley, C. & Matthews, D. (2000). Neuropsychological assessment in older people: Old principles and new directions. *Advances in Psychiatric Treatment, 6,* 362–372.

National Institute for Health and Clinical Excellence (2004). Depression: Management of depression in primary and secondary care. Clinical Guideline 23. Retrieved 2004 from www.nice.org.uk/CG23

National Institute for Health and Clinical Excellence (2006). Dementia: Supporting people with dementia and their carers in health and social care. Clinical guideline 42. Retrieved 2006 from www.nice.org.uk/CG42

Norman, A. (1985). Triple jeopardy: Growing old in a second homeland. London: Centre for Policy on Ageing.

Oyebode, J. (in press). Death, dying and bereavement. In B. Woods & L. Clare (Eds.) *Handbook of the clinical psychology of ageing* (2nd edn). Chichester: Wiley.

Patience, L. (2007). Driving with dementia: In need of an A–Z. *PSIGE Newsletter, 97,* 28–30.

Petford, B. (2006). Supervising therapy with older clients. *PSIGE Newsletter, 94,* 36–38.

Rabbitt, P. (1993). Does it all go together when it goes? *Quarterly Journal of Experimental Psychology, 46,* 385–434.

Rabbitt, P. (1996). Speed of processing and ageing. In B. Woods (Ed.) *Handbook of the clinical psychology of ageing* (pp. 59–72). Chichester: Wiley.

Ramsay, R.W. (1977). Behavioural approaches to bereavement. *Behaviour, Research and Therapy, 15,* 131–155.

Rokke, P.D. & Scogin, F. (1995). Depression treatment preferences in younger and older adults. *Journal of Clinical Geropsychology, 1,* 243–257.

Rybarczyk, B., Gallagher-Thompson, D., Rodman, J., Zeiss, A., Gantz, F.E. & Yesavage, J. (1992). Applying cognitive behavioral psychotherapy to the chronically ill elderly: Treatment issues and case illustration. *International Psychogeriatrics, 4,* 127–140.

Salthouse, T.A. (1991). *Theoretical perspectives on cognitive aging.* Hillsdale, NJ: Lawrence Erlbaum.

Sandford, I. (2006). Review of primary care talking therapies. Report for Lambeth Primary Care Trust.

Scogin, F. & McElreath, L. (1994). Efficacy of psychosocial treatments for geriatric depression: A quantitative review. *Journal of Consulting and Clinical Psychology, 62,* 69–74.

Scott, A. & Bhutani, G. (1999). Career choices and attitudes to the older adult speciality. *Clinical Psychology Forum, 126,* 11–15.

Settin, J.M. (1982). Clinical judgement in geropsychology practice. *Psychotherapy: Theory, Research and Practice, 19,* 397–404.

Spector, A., Orrell, M. & Davies, S. (1998). *Reality orientation for dementia: A review of evidence for its effectiveness.* Oxford: Cochrane Library Issue 4.

Spector, A., Thorgrimsen, L., Woods, R., Royan, L., Davies, S., Butterworth, M. *et al.* (2003). Efficacy of an evidence-based cognitive stimulation programme for people with dementia. *British Journal of Psychiatry, 183,* 248–254.

Stokes, G. (1986a). *Shouting and screaming.* London: Winslow Press.

Stokes, G. (1986b). *Wandering.* London: Winslow Press.

Stokes, G. (1987a). *Aggression.* London: Winslow Press.

Stokes, G. (1987b). *Incontinence and inappropriate urinating.* London: Winslow Press.

Teri, L. & Gallagher-Thompson, D. (1991). Cognitive-behavioral interventions for treatment of depression in Alzheimer's patients. *Gerontologist, 31,* 413–416.

Thompson, L.W., Gallagher, D. & Breckenridge, J.S. (1987). Comparative effectiveness of psychotherapies for depressed elders. *Journal of Consulting and Clinical Psychology, 53,* 385–390.

Thompson, L.W., Wagner, B. & Zeiss, A. (1989). Cognitive-behavior therapy with early stage Alzheimer's patients. In E. Light & B. Lebowitz (Eds.) *Alzheimer's disease treatment and family stress* (pp. 383–397). NIMH: Us Government Printing Office: DHSS Publication No (ADM) 89–1569.

Tornstam, L. (1989). Gerotranscendence: A reformulation of disengagement theory. *Ageing, 1,* 55–63.

Tornstam, L. (1996). Gerotranscendence – a theory about maturing into old age. *Journal of Ageing and Identity, 1,* 37–50.

Twining, C. (in press). Capacity and consent. In B. Woods & L. Clare (Eds.) *Handbook of the clinical psychology of ageing* (2nd edn). Chichester: Wiley.

Vezina, J. & Bourque, P. (1984). The relationship between cognitive structure and symptoms of depression in the elderly. *Cognitive Therapy and Research, 8,* 29–36.

Walker, D.A. (2004). Cognitive behavioural therapy for depression in a person with Alzheimer's dementia. *Behavioural and Cognitive Psychotherapy, 32,* 495–500.

Walker, D.A. & Clarke, M. (2001). Cognitive behavioural psychotherapy: A comparison between younger and older adults in two inner city mental health teams. *Aging and Mental Health, 5,* 187–199.

Weeple, P. (2004). Management of psychological difficulties in later life: A survey of general practitioners. *PSIGE Newsletter, 87,* 42–49.

Williams, C. (2002). A description of pre-diagnostic counseling and disclosure of diagnosis in people assessed for dementia. *PSIGE, 81,* 36–39.

Woods, N. & Witte, K.L. (1981). Life satisfaction, fear of death, and ego identity in elderly adults. *Bulletin of the Psychonomic Society, 18,* 165–168.

Woodward, Y. (2005). A psychological intervention to prevent depression and anxiety, and maximize recovery following hip fracture surgery. *PSIGE Newsletter, 92,* 26–27.

World Health Organisation (1999). Ageing – exploding the myths. Geneva: Author.

Wortman, C.B. & Silver, R.C. (1990). Successful mastery of bereavement and widowhood: A life course perspective. In P.B. Baltes & M.M. Baltes (Eds.) *Successful aging: Perspectives from the behavioral sciences* (pp. 225–264). New York: Cambridge University Press.

Yale, R. (1995). *Developing support groups for individuals with early-stage Alzheimer's disease: Planning, implementation and evaluation.* Baltimore: Health Professionals Press.

4

Working with Special Populations

24

Post-Traumatic Stress Disorder following Childbirth and Pregnancy Loss

Antje Horsch

Introduction

Childbirth is a complex event that may lead to a variety of both negative and positive psychological responses in women and their partners. Frequently a welcome although physically and emotionally challenging event, in some cases it may lead to mental health problems, such as anxiety disorders, postnatal depression and postpartum psychosis (Brockington, 1996), particularly when women experience the process of labour as traumatic. This is more likely to be the case when women feel out of control during labour, when they have no confidence in the medical system and feel they are not receiving adequate support from medical staff, or when they experience obstetric complications, such as instrumental delivery or emergency Caesarean section (e.g., Ayers, 2004).

Although most pregnancies are carried to term, approximately 15 per cent of pregnant women will not, sadly, give birth to a healthy child but will lose their baby at the early stages of pregnancy (miscarriage) or later on (stillbirth) (Alberman, 1988). In most cases the loss is sudden and unexpected and women struggle to believe it has happened, as there is often no viable foetus to mourn. Women often feel as if a part of themselves has been lost, leading to feelings of emptiness, searching and incompleteness (Frost & Condon, 1996). Furthermore, women often lack appropriate social support because they may not have informed their social network about their pregnancy. In response to their loss, many women and their partners will experience normal bereavement reactions, such as acute sadness, loss of interest, anger, guilt (particularly when there is no medical explanation for the loss), distress, and preoccupation with the loss (Madden, 1994; Seibel & Graves, 1980). It has also been acknowledged that experiencing a pregnancy loss can have a detrimental effect on the couple's interpersonal and sexual relationships (Swanson, 2003).

Factors influencing the grieving process and the emotional outcome include timing of the loss (worse later in gestation), the importance and meaning of pregnancy (e.g. a first, wanted pregnancy near the end of the reproductive lifespan) and the difficulty in conceiving the pregnancy. More generally, the further the pregnancy has progressed, the stronger the sense of attachment and the greater the intensity of the grief reaction (Goldbach *et al.*, 1991); this process of mourning may take up to three years (Hughes & Riches, 2003). Over time, this reaction tends to decrease in severity and frequency, and the majority of women will come to terms with their loss. However, some women and their partners may develop mental health problems, such as anxiety, depression, and complicated grief (Brier, 2004; Geller *et al.*, 2001). Risk factors for the development of mental health problems include a history of psychiatric illness, childlessness, lack of social support or poor marital adjustment, prior pregnancy loss and ambivalence towards the foetus (Lok & Neugebauer, 2007).

Research has recently focused on post-traumatic stress disorder (PTSD) as a possible outcome of (traumatic) childbirth and following pregnancy loss, and efforts have been made to raise awareness as to its distinctiveness from other mental health problems, such as postnatal depression and complicated grief. Some limited research has been conducted on the nature of the trauma and its effects, and on ways of identifying psychological problems that result, or on the efficacy of possible treatments. It is apparent from the work now published that childbirth and loss in pregnancy can give rise to trauma sufficiently severe to be identified, and to warrant treatment, and this will be reviewed later in this chapter.

Understanding the psychological impact of pregnancy loss and traumatic birth is important in part because it can significantly influence the experience of subsequent pregnancies, with increased risk of maternal stress and its associated risks of intrauterine growth retardation, premature birth and low birth weight (Paarlberg *et al.*, 1999; Seng *et al.*, 2001; Levin & DeFrank, 1988). In subsequent pregnancies, parents have also shown elevated levels of anxiety (e.g. Cote-Arsenault, 2002), depression (e.g. Armstrong, 2002), attachment difficulties with the baby when born (e.g. Heller & Zeanah, 1999; Hughes *et al.*, 2001), and increased healthcare utilisation (e.g. Waterstone *et al.*, 2003). Postnatal post-traumatic stress disorder can lead to a fear of subsequent pregnancy (tokophobia), avoidance of sexual intercourse and avoidance of medical care to avoid being reminded of the pregnancy (Maker & Ogden, 2003; Bowles *et al.*, 2001). Furthermore, those with higher levels of symptoms at six weeks postnatally show an increased likelihood of deciding not to have further children (Czarnocka & Slade, 2000), and women after a traumatic birth who do embark on a subsequent pregnancy report delaying this longer than those without such an experience (Gottvall & Waldenstrom, 2002).

In this chapter, an attempt is made to summarise the current state of knowledge and understanding in relation to PTSD in this population. Firstly, diagnostic criteria of PTSD and its prevalence following childbirth and pregnancy loss will be discussed. Following this, specific issues in relation to the assessment and formulation of PTSD with this group will be raised, and the guidelines and evidence for treatment reviewed. The chapter concludes with implications for the psychological management of childbirth and pregnancy loss and points to the urgent need for further research and the involvement of clinical psychologists in specialist perinatal services to address PTSD and other mental health problems in this population.

Postnatal Post-Traumatic Stress Disorder

Traumatic childbirth or pregnancy loss may in some circumstances fulfil the description of a traumatic stressor according to the *Diagnostic and Statistical Manual for Psychiatric Disorders* (DSM-IV-TR; American Psychiatric Association, 2000), which defines a traumatic event as one that includes 'actual or threatened death or serious injury, or a threat to the physical integrity of self or others' (p. 427). In addition, the DSM-IV requires that the person's response at the time of the event involves intense feelings of horror, fear or helplessness. Leading up to a childbirth or pregnancy loss, there may be a concern that the unborn infant could die, and women might also perceive a threat to their own physical self (e.g. during labour or because of extreme blood loss in the case of placental abruption), which may lead to beliefs about lack of safety and a sense that health professionals were not able to prevent this or, in some cases, made the problem worse. Ayers and colleagues argue that 'women therefore have the combined problem of increased threat ("I could die at any time") coupled with a loss of confidence in health professionals ("they won't help me/save me")' (Ayers *et al.*, 2007, p. 182). Childbirth is qualitatively different from other traumatic stressors, since most women simultaneously perceive the birth of their baby as a positive outcome, even if they appraise the process of labour as traumatic (Ayers *et al.*, 2007). Furthermore, it is worth noting that some women may experience PTSD during pregnancy and after because of pre-existing symptoms connected with traumatic events prior to conception and unrelated to the context of pregnancy and childbirth, but this may still have a significant impact on the woman herself, her family and the (unborn) infant.

PTSD is an anxiety disorder characterised by symptoms of re-experiencing (e.g. intrusive memories, flashbacks, nightmares), avoidance of reminders of the event and numbing (e.g. restricted affect, estrangement from others), and increased arousal (e.g. increased startle response, sleep problems, irritability, hypervigilance). Anyone receiving such a diagnosis will have reported at least one re-experiencing symptom, three avoidance or numbing symptoms, and two symptoms of increased arousal, which must be present for more than one month post trauma and cause significant distress. If symptoms persist after three months, the disorder is regarded as chronic. It has been demonstrated that up to 60 per cent of individuals exposed to a traumatic event experience at least some PTSD symptoms in the immediate aftermath (Helzer *et al.*, 1987). Longitudinal studies in the general population have revealed that a substantial proportion of those who initially experience PTSD symptoms will eventually recover, and only a subgroup (about 30 per cent) will develop persistent PTSD (Breslau, 1998). In the general population, the rate of PTSD cases declines with increasing time since the trauma, with the recovery rate reaching a plateau between one and six years after the trauma (Kessler *et al.*, 1995).

Childbirth

Although approximately one-third of women appraise childbirth as traumatic, only one-tenth of these have traumatic stress responses in the initial weeks following childbirth, while between 1 and 6 per cent of them will develop PTSD (Ayers, 2004; Ayers & Pickering, 2001; Olde *et al.*, 2006; Czarnocka & Slade, 2000; Maggioni *et al.*, 2006; Adewuya *et al.*, 2006). In a longitudinal study by Söderquist and colleagues, 3 per cent of women reported PTSD at least once on self-report questionnaires, up to 11 months postpartum (Soederquist *et al.*, 2006). Women who experience PTSD symptoms are also likely to suffer from depression. Ayers (2004) reported that an increased risk of having post-traumatic stress following childbirth was associated with depression, severe fear of childbirth, 'pre'-traumatic stress, previous counselling related to pregnancy/childbirth, and self-reported previous psychological problems. To date, only one published study has measured PTSD during pregnancy and found that it was experienced by 8 per cent of women (Ayers & Pickering, 2001). Women may also develop PTSD symptoms after their baby was born prematurely. Following a premature birth, 26 per cent of mothers of low-risk babies and 41 per cent of high-risk babies reported PTSD when their child was 18 months old. This correlated with the child's behavioural problems, such as eating and sleeping (Pierrehumbert *et al.*, 2003).

Ayers (2004) proposed a model of vulnerability and risk factors for PTSD following childbirth, including prenatal vulnerability such as psychiatric history; delivery factors such as mode of delivery, care factors, pain control and social support, which may lead to the woman's appraisal of having experienced a traumatic birth. Further postnatal factors, such as coping style or additional stressors, may then determine whether the initial traumatic stress response develops into postnatal PTSD. Slade (2006) added another dimension to the conceptualisation of postnatal PTSD, which is currently under-researched, namely peritraumatic processing, such as dissociation and mental defeat.

Pregnancy loss

About 25 per cent of women will meet PTSD diagnosis one month after the loss of their foetus/unborn baby with a symptom severity that is similar to that of other traumatised populations (Engelhard *et al.*, 2001; Engelhard, 2002; Van Pampus *et al.*, 2004). Women reporting PTSD are also at an increased risk of developing depression. After four months, 7 per cent of these women will still meet criteria for PTSD diagnosis, which is significantly linked to gestational age at time of loss. One study interviewing women and their partners after pre-term and term pre-eclampsia found that PTSD symptom severity was not related to objective indicators of condition-severity, such as Caesarean section or length of hospital stay, but 61 per cent of PTSD symptoms were accounted for by psychological factors, such as peritraumatic dissociation, negative interpretations of symptoms and thought suppression. Turton and colleagues found PTSD prevalence rates of 29 per cent (lifetime) and 20 per cent (current) in a pregnant population subsequent to having experienced a stillbirth (24 weeks gestation or longer) (Turton *et al.*, 2001).

A few studies have recently tried to identify risk factors for PTSD following pregnancy loss. As in the general PTSD literature, PTSD is predicted by indicators of the severity of the stressor, such as gestational age (Engelhard *et al.*, 2001), which is related to parental bonding or the degree of exposure to blood and tissue (Engelhard, 2002). More recently, Engelhard and colleagues found that PTSD after miscarriage or stillbirth was significantly associated with higher maternal neuroticism, lower educational level and longer duration of gestation (Engelhard *et al.*, 2006). For women with a low educational level and a high score for neuroticism, the estimated risk of developing postnatal PTSD was 70 per cent. Furthermore, chronic PTSD symptoms after pregnancy loss was predicted by the degree of perceived threat and peritraumatic dissociation (predicted by prior low control over emotions, dissociative tendencies and low educational level) (Engelhard, 2002; Engelhard *et al.*, 2003).

Assessment and Formulation

Most commonly, women are identified as having mental health needs during a routine check for postnatal depression by the health visitor or general practitioner (GP). Alternatively, some women who have experienced a pregnancy loss may be routinely followed up by a bereavement midwife. However, in some cases postnatal PTSD will remain undiagnosed and will be treated as postnatal depression. The women who are eventually referred to a clinical psychologist often present with complex comorbid issues, such as postnatal depression, other anxiety disorders (most commonly obsessive-compulsive disorder (OCD) and panic disorder), complicated grief and substance misuse, which need to be carefully assessed and incorporated in the formulation. Women may also present with additional difficulties such as tokophobia, sexual avoidance and attachment difficulties with a baby born subsequent to a stillbirth.

The assessment involves taking a detailed account of the current presenting issues, how they developed, current maintaining factors and protective factors. Knowing about any previous mental health problems, the person's history and their view of their current difficulties is also important. For many women this may be their first contact with a mental health professional, which may raise fears of stigmatisation that also need to be addressed.

Assessment and engagement

Following their traumatic labour or pregnancy loss, women typically engage in a range of understandable but unhelpful behavioural (e.g. avoidance of reminders, such as hospitals/medical personnel) and cognitive strategies (e.g. suppression of intrusive thoughts/images) that are aimed at managing and reducing the distress caused by their PTSD symptoms. This may pose a challenge to any attempts to engage them in a detailed assessment or, indeed, treatment of their PTSD, as this involves having to think and talk about the traumatic experience. Psychoeducation about and normalisation of their PTSD symptoms as well as making sure the woman feels safe in the therapy room (no reminders that could trigger re-experiencing symptoms) and the establishment of a collaborative therapeutic relationship are helpful in engaging this client group.

When assessing for symptoms of PTSD, women need to be asked whether they experience any re-experiencing, avoidance/numbing or hyperarousal symptoms. Most commonly, the PTSD diagnosis is ascertained via administration of a structured clinical interview schedule, such as the Structured Clinical Interview for DSM-IV (SCID; First *et al.*, 1995) or the Clinician-Administered PTSD Scale (CAPS; Blake *et al.*, 1995). PTSD symptom self-report measures do not themselves provide a comprehensive diagnosis of the disorder but offer more detailed information about the severity and the frequency of specific PTSD symptoms. Examples are the Posttraumatic Diagnostic Scale (PDS; Foa *et al.*, 1999) and the Impact of Events Scale (IES; Horowitz *et al.*, 1979). However, none of these assessment tools has so far been validated in a perinatal population.

Differentiating PTSD from other mental health problems

It is not always easy to differentiate between symptoms of depression and PTSD, as many symptoms, such as lack of concentration or loss of interest and pleasure, overlap. However, at the heart of PTSD lie involuntary re-living experiences (intrusive thoughts, nightmares, flashbacks), whereas postnatal depression is more characterised by ruminative thoughts. Complicated grief also shares features with PTSD and major depressive disorder and, indeed, some authors have questioned the necessity of establishing complicated grief as a distinct disorder (Stroebe *et al.*, 2001). It is defined as present when, after the death of a significant other, two symptom clusters are present for at least six months: separation distress (yearning, searching, preoccupation with memories of the lost person and loneliness) and traumatic distress (e.g. efforts to avoid reminders of the loss, numbing, emptiness, shattered world view) (Prigerson *et al.*, 1997). PTSD most closely resembles complicated grief but there are important distinctions. PTSD diagnostic criteria do not include separation distress symptoms, avoidance symptoms are more complex and variable in traumatic grief and hypervigilance symptoms, which are common in PTSD, are often absent in traumatic grief (see Boelen *et al.*, 2006 for more detailed discussion).

Differentiating a grief reaction from clinical depression can be challenging because several symptoms overlap, such as sadness, sleep disturbance, tearfulness, guilt, anger, fatigue and poor concentration. However, significant feelings of worthlessness, suicidal ideation, early morning wakening and significant psychomotor retardation are more indicative of depression (Broquet, 1999).

Formulation

For the formulation of postnatal PTSD, the cognitive model proposed by Ehlers and Clark (2000) is very helpful. This suggests that a sense of current threat is produced by negative cognitive appraisals both during and after the traumatic event, in conjunction with a fragmented and poorly integrated traumatic memory that can be unintentionally triggered by situations resembling some aspect of the traumatic event. Unhelpful cognitive (e.g. thought suppression) and behavioural (e.g. avoidance of reminders) strategies aimed at controlling that sense of threat or the symptoms then maintain PTSD because they directly produce symptoms and/or prevent change in negative appraisals and in the nature of the trauma memory. When using this model as the basis for formulating a client's postnatal PTSD, careful assessment is needed of peri- and postnatal appraisals as well as cognitive and behavioural strategies (safety behaviours).

Another helpful model to draw on is the cognitive-behavioural conceptualisation of complicated grief developed by Boelen *et al.* (2006), describing three processes that are crucial in the development and maintenance of complicated grief: poor elaboration and integration of the separation with existing autobiographical knowledge; negative global beliefs and misinterpretations of grief reactions; and anxious and depressive avoidance strategies. To make sense of women's experiences of shame and guilt in relation to childbirth or pregnancy loss, and how this is linked to their PTSD, Lee and colleagues' cognitive model can be utilised (Lee *et al.*, 2001).

Case example

The following case example demonstrates the complexity of assessment and formulation in this field. Beryl, a mother of four, was referred to adult mental health services with 'severe depression' two years after she had experienced a stillbirth, although the initial assessment identified PTSD, depression, complicated grief and marital problems. One day before her due date, she had a placenta abruption, which led to a sudden onset of pain, excessive bleeding and a conviction that 'something is seriously wrong with me'; 'my baby is going to die'. When the ambulance came to take her into hospital, she was still hoping that the baby would survive. She then had a scan and was told that baby had died. Labour was induced and Beryl experienced strong and painful contractions, but no pain relief was given (she was not able to recall the reasons for this). Labour lasted 14 hours during which she felt that she was often left alone; she felt that no one had properly explained what was happening and remembered feeling utterly helpless. Beryl also described dissociative experiences during this time. She then spent three days in the mother and baby unit, where she would spend every day seeing, holding and dressing her stillborn infant and described the development of a strong bond with the infant. During this time she was still recovering from labour and described feelings of unreality, such as thinking that 'the baby was just asleep'. She tried to delay funeral arrangements for as long as possible ('just wanted to be with my baby') and afterwards went to the grave on a daily basis to 'talk to the baby'. After coming home from the hospital, she left the nursery unaltered, and never unpacked her hospital bag.

Some of Beryl's reliving symptoms were dissociative flashbacks triggered by using the bathroom (which is where the placenta abruption happened), ambulance sirens and her visits to the baby's grave; frequent nightmares and intrusive thoughts. She avoided going to the hospital, medical appointments, meeting other mothers with babies or pregnant women, physical examinations and physical intimacy, and described emotional numbing and feeling emotionally cut off from others, which made her feel guilty, particularly in relation to her children. Beryl also experienced arousal symptoms, such as increased irritability and lack of concentration. Cognitive appraisals about the event were 'It was my fault; I should have prevented the baby from dying' and about her symptoms, 'I'm going mad'. She also described frequent ruminations, such as 'Why did this happen?' Over time, her mood dropped further, she felt increasingly unable to cope with her other children and she felt under pressure by her husband who wanted another child, leading to marital tension.

Intervention

Research evidence

The National Institute for Health and Clinical Excellence (NICE) guideline on antenatal and postnatal mental health (Department of Health, 2007) makes specific recommendations on the identification, treatment and management of all mental health disorders in the perinatal population, and how other NICE guidance can be adapted for women who are pregnant, planning to become pregnant or are breastfeeding. It reports that there is no convincing evidence for drug treatment in any population with PTSD, and psychological treatments are therefore preferred. This means that trauma-focused cognitive behavioural therapy (CBT) or eye movement desensitisation and reprocessing (EMDR) should be offered to individuals with PTSD within three months of their trauma. Non-trauma-focused interventions, such as relaxation or non-directive therapy, should not be routinely offered within three months of the event. Furthermore, brief, single-session interventions (debriefing) that focus on the traumatic incident (e.g. traumatic birth) should not be offered routinely.

It is worth noting that the efficacy and acceptability of psychological treatments in the antenatal and postnatal period has not been widely researched, partly because of 'widely held but poorly substantiated beliefs that neither pregnancy nor the early postnatal period are times to make life changes and that psychological treatment may be harmful and should be avoided' (Department of Health, 2007, p. 125).

For women who have had traumatic births, most of the services (78 per cent) are midwife-led or obstetrician-led debriefing services, which typically consist of medical staff discussing the medical notes so that women gain a better understanding of what happened during labour (Ayers et al., 2006). Ayers and colleagues (2007) point out that although medical debriefing is not the same as psychological debriefing, in some ways it is similar in that it is usually one session only, which could actually increase distress and be counterproductive for some women. Indeed, studies investigating the efficacy of postnatal debriefing have found mixed results. Six randomised controlled trials found either that midwife-led debriefing reduces postnatal depression (Lavender & Walkinshaw, 1998) and PTSD (Gamble et al., 2005) or that it has no effect (Ryding et al., 2004; Kershaw et al., 2005; Priest et al., 2003; Small et al., 2000).

Cognitive behavioural therapy

Cognitive behavioural therapy for postnatal PTSD is based on the assumption that the factors described in the cognitive model need to be addressed in order to gain symptom relief (Ehlers & Clark, 2000). This includes the following changes:

a) the traumatic experience needs to be conceptually processed and integrated within the existing autobiographical memory;

b) unhelpful peri-and post-traumatic appraisals need to be identified and changed;
c) unhelpful behavioural and cognitive strategies need to be replaced by more helpful ones that facilitate adjustment.

Accordingly, treatment will most commonly consist of assessment and case conceptualisation; explaining the treatment rationale; psychoeducation and normalising of symptoms; facilitating integration of the fragmented traumatic memory into existing autobiographical memory, which includes reliving, identifying of hot spots, inserting new information into the traumatic memory; challenging unhelpful peri- and post-traumatic appraisals; and reducing unhelpful cognitive and behavioural strategies (for a more detailed description see Grey *et al.*, 2002; for case examples, see Ayers *et al.*, 2007).

As in other populations, some women with postnatal PTSD may present with predominantly primary emotions, such as fear, which is more responsive to exposure techniques, whereas other women may present with predominantly secondary emotions, such as shame or guilt, which responds better to cognitive reappraisal techniques (Ayers *et al.*, 2007).

Implications for the Psychological Management of Pregnancy and Birth

Service context

More than 90 per cent of women with perinatal mental health problems are currently treated in primary care (Department of Health, 2007). The remainder access specialist mental health services, including adult mental health services, liaison services, specialist perinatal services, and child and adolescent mental health services (CAMHS). Until now, the provision of mental health services to women antenatally and postnatally has been plagued by a lack of clear referral pathways, lack of prioritisation of these women in existing mental health services and a lack of expertise in relation to the special needs of this population. For example, a survey of primary care trusts (PCTs) in the UK showed that only 25 per cent had a fully developed and implemented policy for antenatal and postnatal mental health (Department of Health, 2007). Furthermore, of currently existing specialist perinatal teams, 20 per cent had no representation from psychiatrists or community psychiatric nurse (CPNs), 74 per cent had no clinical psychologist, and 79 per cent had no social worker. Over 30 per cent had limited or no access to prompt provision of specialist psychological treatments (Department of Health, 2007).

The recently published NICE guideline on antenatal and postnatal mental health (Department of Health, 2007) makes recommendations about the services required to support the delivery of the effective detection and treatment of most mental disorders during pregnancy and in the postnatal period in primary and secondary care. This has opened up new opportunities for clinical psychologists interested in this area. In particular, the guideline calls for the development of a 'specialist multidisci-plinary perinatal service in each locality, which provides direct services, consultation and advice to maternity services, other mental health services and community serv-ices' (p. 9). Clinical psychologists working within a specialist perinatal service would be well placed to liaise with and provide services to primary care services, adult mental health services, child and family services, obstetric services and the voluntary sector. The prioritisation of this population in existing primary and secondary care services is implied by the recommendation that women requiring psychological treatment should be seen within one month of initial assessment, and also by the recommenda-tion that women who present with symptoms of anxiety or depression that do not meet diagnostic criteria but do significantly interfere with personal and social func-tioning, and who have a history of anxiety or depression, should be offered brief (four to six sessions) of CBT or interpersonal psychotherapy (IPT). This in turn implies the need for more psychological therapists, including clinical psychologists. However, the Healthcare Commission (2008) found that only 55 per cent of trusts conducted all the mental health checks identified in NICE guidance for antenatal and postnatal mental health, and 42 per cent of trusts said that they did not have access to a special-ist mental health service, which clearly shows that service development in this area is still in its infancy.

Service implications

Given that the development of PTSD is triggered by cognitive appraisals of the event itself as well as the aftermath of the event, and that pre-existing traumatic experiences and beliefs contribute, managing the expectations of the labour process may be help-ful. Ayers *et al.* (2007) argued that health professionals need to ensure that when developing a birth plan with women, they explain that the outcome may not be as planned. Furthermore, in emergency situations that are not life threatening, health professionals should provide reassurance to women. Additionally, sensitive and supportive management of events during the labour process may contribute to the women's sense of control and positively influence the women's appraisal of these events. This includes giving the women as much information and choice as possible and being aware that even routine procedures during labour may make women highly anxious. Health professionals need to know that women are not only at risk of devel-oping postnatal PTSD because of their pregnancy loss or birth experience, but are still vulnerable in the postnatal period if they continue to experience problems with themselves and/or the baby (Ayers *et al.*, 2007). Women who have experienced a preg-nancy loss or traumatic birth but do not meet diagnostic criteria for PTSD may be vulnerable when they embark on a subsequent pregnancy and may therefore need more support.

The Birth Trauma Association (BTA), a charity in the UK founded in 2004, has been campaigning to raise awareness for the recognition of PTSD following childbirth, as many healthcare professional have been unaware of this condition. Another charity AIMS (Association for Improvements in the Maternity Services) has been campaigning for more than 40 years to raise awareness of (psychological) issues in relation to childbirth and to increase maternity choices aimed at empowering women.

Finally, it is well established that perceived social support can help prevent the development of PTSD. Therefore, women should be encouraged to make use of their social network, especially at this difficult time, and partners may also benefit from psychoeducation and normalisation of the women's (and/or their own) symptoms to provide support. Voluntary organisations, such as SANDS (Stillbirth and Neonatal Death Society), may help women to access support locally from other women with similar experiences.

Future Directions

Given the lack of research regarding the efficacy of different therapeutic treatments in this population, more research is urgently needed. This also includes a need to review and validate PTSD measures that can be used to screen women specifically in relation to postnatal PTSD. For example, Alder and colleagues adapted the diagnostic criteria to fit postnatal PTSD and suggest core questions for the detection of trauma symptoms (Alder *et al.*, 2006). Finally, the involvement is urgently needed of clinical psychologists in specialist perinatal mental health services, who are able to offer psychological interventions for postnatal PTSD, as well as consultation and training to medical, nursing and midwifery staff.

References

Adewuya, A.O., Ologun, Y.A. & Ibigbami, O.S. (2006). Post-traumatic stress disorder after childbirth in Nigerian women: Prevalence and risk factors. *BJOG: An International Journal of Obstetrics and Gynaecology, 113,* 284–288.

Alberman, E. (1988). The epidemiology of repeated abortion. In R.W. Beard & F. Sharp (Eds.) *Pregnancy loss: Mechanisms and treatment* (pp. 9–17). London: Springer Verlag.

Alder, J., Stadlmayr, W., Tschudin, S. & Bitzer, J. (2006). Post-traumatic symptoms after childbirth: What should we offer? *Journal of Psychosomatic Obstetrics and Gynecology, 27,* 107–112.

American Psychiatric Association (2000). *Diagnostic and statistical manual of mental disorders, 4th edition (DSM-IV-TR).* Washington, DC: Author.

Armstrong, D.S. (2002). Emotional distress and prenatal attachment in pregnancy after a perinatal loss. *Journal of Nursing Scholarship, 34,* 339–345.

Ayers, S. (2004). Delivery as a traumatic event: Prevalence, risk factors, and treatment for postnatal posttraumatic stress disorder. *Clinical Obstetrics and Gynecology, 47,* 552–567.

Ayers, S., Claypool, J. & Eagle, A. (2006). What happens after a difficult birth? Postnatal services for birth trauma in the UK. *British Journal of Midwifery, 14,* 157–161.

Ayers, S., McKenzie-McHarg, K. & Eagle, A. (2007). Cognitive behaviour therapy for postnatal posttraumatic stress disorder: Case studies. *Journal of Psychosomatic Obstetrics and Gynecology, 28,* 177–184.

Ayers, S. & Pickering, A.D. (2001). Do women get posttraumatic stress disorder as a result of childbirth? A prospective study of incidence. *Birth, 28,* 111–118.

Blake, D.D., Weathers, F.W., Nagy, L.M., Kaloupek, D.G., Gusman, F.D., Charney, D.S. *et al.* (1995). The development of a clinician-administered PTSD scale. *Journal of Traumatic Stress, 8,* 75–90.

Boelen, P.A., van den Hout, M.A. & van den Bout, J. (2006). A cognitive-behavioural conceptualization of complicated grief. *Clinical Psychology: Science and Practice, 13,* 109–128.

Bowles, S.V., James, L.C. & Solursh, D.S. (2001). Acute and posttraumatic stress disorder after spontaneous abortion. *American Family Physician, 61,* 1689–1696.

Breslau, N. (1998). Epidemiology of trauma and posttraumatic stress disorder. In R. Yehuda (Ed.) *Psychological trauma* (pp. 1–29). Washington, DC: American Psychiatric Press Inc.

Brier, N. (2004). Anxiety after miscarriage: A review of the empirical literature and implications for clinical practice. *Birth, 31,* 138–142.

Brockington, I.F. (1996). *Motherhood and mental health.* Oxford: Oxford University Press.

Broquet, K. (1999). Psychological reactions to pregnancy loss. *Primary Care Update in Obstetrics/ Gynecology, 6,* 12–16.

Cote-Arsenault, D. (2002). The influence of perinatal loss on anxiety in multigravidas. *Journal of Obstetric, Gynecologic, and Neonatal Nursing, 32,* 623–629.

Czarnocka, J. & Slade, P. (2000). Prevalence and predictors of posttraumatic stress symptoms following childbirth. *British Journal of Clinical Psychology, 39,* 35–51.

Department of Health (2007). Antenatal and postnatal mental health.

Ehlers, A. & Clark, D.M. (2000). A cognitive model of posttraumatic stress disorder. *Behaviour Research and Therapy, 38,* 319–345.

Engelhard, I.M. (2002). Miscarriage as a traumatic event. *Clinical Obstetrics & Gynecology, 47,* 547–551.

Engelhard, I.M., van den Hout, M.A. & Arntz, A. (2001). Posttraumatic stress disorder after pregnancy loss. *General Hospital Psychiatry, 23,* 62–66.

Engelhard, I.M., van den Hout, M.A., Kindt, M., Arntz, A. & Schouten, E. (2003). Peritraumatic dissociation and posttraumatic stress disorder after pregnancy loss: A prospective study. *Behaviour Research and Therapy, 41,* 67–78.

Engelhard, I.M., van den Hout, M.A. & Schouten, E.G.W. (2006). Neuroticism and low educational level predict the risk of posttraumatic stress disorder in women after miscarriage or stillbirth. *General Hospital Psychiatry, 28,* 414–417.

First, M.B., Spitzer, R.L., Gibbon, M. & Williams, J.B.W. (1995). *Structured Clinical Interview for DSM-IV Axis I Disorders – Patient Edition (SCID-I/P, Version 2.0).* New York: Biometrics Research Department of the New York State Psychiatric Institute.

Foa, E.B., Ehlers, A., Clark, D., Tolin, D.F. & Orsillo, S.M. (1999). The Posttraumatic Cognitions Inventory: Development and validation. *Psychological Assessment, 9,* 445–451.

Frost, M. & Condon, J.T. (1996). The psychological sequelae of miscarriage: A critical review of the literature. *Australian and New Zealand Journal of Psychiatry, 30,* 54–62.

Gamble, J., Creedy, D., Moyle, W., Webster, J., McAllister, M. & Dickson, P. (2005), Effectiveness of a counseling intervention after a traumatic childbirth: A randomized controlled trial. *Birth, 32,* 11–19.

Geller, P.A., Klier, C.M. & Neugebauer, R. (2001). Anxiety disorders following miscarriage. *Journal of Clinical Psychiatry, 62,* 432–438.

Goldbach, K.R.C., Dunn, D.S., Toedter, L.J. & Lasker, J.N. (1991). The effects of gestational age and gender on grief after pregnancy loss. *American Journal of Orthopsychiatry, 61,* 461–467.

Gottvall, K. & Waldenstrom, U. (2002). Does a traumatic birth experience have an impact on future reproduction? *British Journal of Obstetrics and Gynaecology, 109,* 254–260.

Grey, N., Young, K. & Holmes, E. (2002). Cognitive restructuring within reliving: A treatment for peritraumatic emotional 'hotspots' in posttraumatic stress disorder. *Behavioural and Cognitive Psychotherapy, 30,* 37–56.

Healthcare Commission (2008). Review of Maternity Services. Retrieved 14 February 2008 from (2007ratings.healthcarecommission.org.uk/newsandevents/news.cfm/cit_id/23628/widCall1/customWidgets.content_view_1/usecache/false).

Heller, S.S. & Zeanah, C.H. (1999). Attachment disturbances in infants born subsequent to perinatal loss: A pilot study. *Infant Mental Health Journal, 20,* 188–199.

Helzer, J.E., Robins, L.N. & McEvoy, L. (1987). Posttraumatic stress disorder in the general population: Findings of the Epidemiological Catchment Area Survey. *New England Journal of Medicine, 317,* 1630–1634.

Horowitz, M., Wilner, N. & Alvarez, W. (1979). Impact of Event Scale: A measure of subjective stress. *Psychosomatic Medicine, 41,* 209–218.

Hughes, P. & Riches, S. (2003). Psychological aspects of perinatal loss. *Current Opinion in Obstetrics and Gynecology, 15,* 107–111.

Hughes, P., Turton, P., Hopper, E., McCauley, G.A. & Fonagy, P. (2001). Disorganised attachment behaviour among infants born subsequent to stillbirth. *The Journal of Child Psychology and Psychiatry, 42,* 791–801.

Kershaw, K., Jolly, J., Bhabra, K. & Ford, J. (2005). Randomised controlled trial of community debriefing following operative delivery. *British Journal of Obstetrics and Gynaecology, 112,* 1504–1509.

Kessler, R.C., Sonnega, A., Bromet, E., Hughes, M. & Nelson, C.B. (1995). Posttraumatic stress disorder in the National Comorbidity Survey. *Archives of General Psychiatry, 52,* 1048–1060.

Lavender, T. & Walkinshaw, S.A. (1998). Can midwives reduce postpartum psychological morbidity? A randomised trial. *Birth, 25,* 215–219.

Lee, D.A., Scragg, P. & Turner, S. (2001). The role of shame and guilt in traumatic events: A clinical model of shame-based and guilt-based PTSD. *British Journal of Medical Psychology, 74,* 451–466.

Levin, J.S. & DeFrank, R.S. (1988). Maternal stress and pregnancy outcomes: A review of the psychosocial literature. *Journal of Psychosomatic Obstetrics and Gynecology, 9,* 3–16.

Lok, I.H. & Neugebauer, R. (2007). Psychological morbidity following miscarriage. *Best Practice and Research. Clinical Obstetrics and Gynaecology, 21,* 229–247.

Madden, M.E. (1994). The variety of emotional reactions to miscarriage. *Women Health, 21,* 85–104.

Maggioni, C., Margola, D. & Filippi, F. (2006). PTSD, risk factors, and expectations among women having a baby: A two-wave longitudinal study. *Journal of Psychosomatic Obstetrics and Gynaecology, 27,* 81–90.

Maker, C. & Ogden, J. (2003). The miscarriage experience: More than just a trigger to psychological morbidity? *Psychological Health, 18,* 403–415.

Olde, E., van der Hart, O., Kleber, R. & van Son, M. (2006). Posttraumatic stress following childbirth: A review. *Clinical Psychology Review, 26,* 1–16.

Paarlberg, K.M., Vingerhoets, A.J., Passchier, J., Dekker, G.A., Heinen, A.G. & van Geijn, H.P. (1999). Psychosocial predictors of low birthweight: A prospective study. *British Journal of Obstetrics and Gynaecology, 106,* 834–841.

Pierrehumbert, B., Nicole, A., Muller-Nix, C., Forcada-Guex, M. & Ansermet, F. (2003). Parental post-traumatic reactions after premature birth: implications for sleeping and eating problems in the infant. *Archives of Disease in Childhood. Fetal and Neonatal Edition, 88,* 400–404.

Priest, S.R., Henderson, J., Evans, S.F. & Hagan, R. (2003). Stress debriefing after childbirth: A randomised controlled trial. *Medical Journal of Australia, 178,* 542–545.

Prigerson, H.G., Bierhals, A.J., Kasl, S.V., Reynolds, C.F., Shear, M.K. & Day, N. (1997). Traumatic grief as a risk factor for mental and physical morbidity. *American Journal of Psychiatry, 154,* 616–623.

Ryding, E.L., Wiren, E., Johansson, G., Ceder, B. & Dahlstroem, A.M. (2004). Group counseling for mothers after emergency Cesarean section: A randomized controlled trial of intervention. *Birth, 31,* 247–253.

Seibel, M. & Graves, W.L. (1980). The psychological implications of spontaneous abortions. *Journal of Reproductive Medicine, 25,* 161–165.

Seng, J.S., Oakley, D.J., Sampselle, C.M., Killion, C., Graham-Bermann, S. & Liberzon, I. (2001). Posttraumatic stress disorder and pregnancy complications. *Obstetrics and Gynecology, 97,* 17–22.

Slade, P. (2006). Towards a conceptual framework for understanding post-traumatic stress symptoms following childbirth and implications for further research. *Journal of Psychosomatic Obstetrics and Gynecology, 27,* 99–105.

Small, R., Lumley, J., Donohue, L., Potter, A. & Waldenstrom, U. (2000). Randomised controlled trial of midwife led debriefing to reduce maternal depression after operative childbirth. *British Medical Journal, 321,* 1043–1047.

Söderquist J., Wijma B. & Wijma K. (2006). The longitudinal course of post-traumatic stress after childbirth. *Journal of Psychosomatic Obstetrics and Gynaecology, 27,* 113–9.

Stroebe, M., Schut, H. & Finkenhauer, C. (2001). The traumatisation of grief? A conceptual framework for understanding the trauma-bereavement interface. *Israeli Journal of Psychiatry and Related Sciences, 38,* 185–201.

Swanson, K.M. (2003). Miscarriage effects on couple's interpersonal and sexual relationships during the first year after loss: Women's perceptions. *Psychosomatic Medicine, 65,* 902–910.

Turton, P., Hughes, P., Evans, C.D.H. & Fainman, D. (2001). Incidence, correlates and predictors of posttraumatic stress disorder in the pregnancy after stillbirth. *British Journal of Psychiatry, 178,* 556–560.

Van Pampus, M.G., Wolf, H., Schultz, W.C.M., Neeleman, J. & Aarnoudse, J.G. (2004). Posttraumatic stress disorder following preeclampsia and HELLP syndrome. *Journal of Psychosomatic Obstetrics and Gynecology, 25,* 183–187.

Waterstone, M., Wolfe, C., Hooper, R. & Bewley, S. (2003). Postnatal morbidity after childbirth and severe obstetrical morbidity. *British Journal of Obstetrics and Gynaecology, 110,* 128–133.

25

Transition Services

Kobus Van Rensburg

Transition to adulthood is filled with many paradoxes: it is a time of independence and excitement, but also of uncertainty, confusion, and the taking on of new roles and responsibilities (Poa, 2006); it is a time when physical maturation brings peaks in 'strength, speed, and fitness', but also a time associated with mental health conditions such as depression, antisocial behaviour and substance misuse (Patton & Viner, 2007). In formal service terms, transition could be defined as 'a purposeful, planned process that addresses the medical, psychosocial and educational/vocational needs of adolescents and young adults with chronic physical and medical conditions as they move from child-centred to adult-oriented healthcare systems' (Blum *et al.* as cited in Department of Health, 2006).

Transition is therefore about crossing a threshold which, in the context of clinical services, predominantly means reaching a specific age, with services often having additional criteria for exclusion such as the absence of an identifiable mental illness, or intellectual functioning being above or below a cut-off point. Ideally the experience of transition should aim to be seamless, and there should be continuity of care and consistency, but this important period in a young person's life is in reality more often described as 'hurtling into a void', moving from a cohesive service to an uncoordinated one (Chamberlain & Kent, 2005), 'trapped in transition' (Poa, 2006), falling through the 'gap' (Social Exclusion Unit, 2005), and characterised by relationships (with clinicians) being 'severed' (Bailey *et al.*, 2003). Delays often exist in getting adult services established for young people with the most significant impairments, and they 'may end up in segregated, sometimes costly residential provision, due to the lack of alternative opportunities' (Department of Health, 2004).

Defining the Transition Period

The ON TRAC model (Paone *et al.*, 2006), used in a paediatric transplant clinic, provides an excellent description of the ultimate goal of transition services: 'for all adolescents to reach their attainable levels of independence, self-sufficiency, and self-worth while transferring safely and securely into adult healthcare services and adulthood'. However, variation exists in relation to the lower and upper ages as well as the duration of the transition period across a number of domains. For example, in the UK, some Child and Adolescent Mental Health Services (CAMHS) have historically used school-leaving age as a service boundary, implying that their support to young people was terminated at either 16 or 18 years of age. This made transition planning relatively uncomplicated as joint-working between child and adult mental health services could be initiated a year prior to the young person leaving school, which coincided with the time of leaving the children's service. However, a standard upper age limit of 18 years has now been introduced for all CAMHS, bringing with it the remit of supporting 16- to 18-year-olds who have already left school and who are presenting with concerns about further education, employment, accommodation, social support and other issues of adult life. The concept of 'early intervention' has also gained prominence in recent years, especially in the fields of psychosis (Department of Health, 2001a) and social exclusion (Social Exclusion Unit, 2005). The latter report highlights the relatively few examples of public services which address the needs of 16- to 25-year-olds to ensure an effective transition from youth to adult services.

For young people with a statement of special educational needs, transition planning in the UK starts at the age of 14, at the Year 9 Transition Review Meeting (Department for Education and Skills, 2001). This is also the time for adult social care services to take a proactive approach to transition planning in partnership with children's services, as well as for personal advisors from Connexions (UK public information, advice and support service) to start working with young people and their parents or carers, to ensure they access education, training and employment after 16. The upper age limit for this transition period is more difficult to specify; a service like Connexions, for example, normally remains involved until age 19, but could be extended to age 25 if the young adult has a learning difficulty or disability. For mental health clinicians working specifically with transitional issues, termination of support might not be linked with age, but rather with the resolution of significant issues.

Case example: A 17-year-old who has already left school and is presenting with depression might be offered: advice and support from Connexions about further education and career choices up to the age of 19; therapeutic input, focusing on the depression, from CAMHS up to the age of 18; and a period of joint-working between CAMHS and the Adult Mental Health Service (AMHS) up to the age of 18, following which the AMHS will remain involved until significant mental health issues are resolved.

The Challenge of Setting Up Transition Services

Good to excellent care in childhood unfortunately often contrasts with significant variability of care in adulthood for a range of clinical populations, e.g. those with chronic medical conditions, developmental conditions or other disabilities. In many instances no equivalent adult service is available, and specifically for young people with conditions such as attention deficit hyperactivity disorder (ADHD) there is often no readily identifiable service to support them once they leave children's services (Nutt *et al.*, 2007). A contrast often exists between needs and system status which prevents reform (Davis, 2003), and adult services may require major transformation to meet the needs of young people with serious mental health conditions during the transition period (Davis *et al.*, 2006).

So who initiates the change, and which service takes responsibility for ensuring adequate provision during this period of transition? Children's services have age-boundaries, and over-stretched adult services might simply not have the resources to focus on transitional issues to a satisfactory level. Furthermore, traditional views of developmental conditions such as ADHD, that individuals grow out of it by the time they reach adulthood, mean that relatively little research has been carried out in this field. More concerningly, a dearth of knowledge still exists in adult services concerning such developmental conditions. Rosenbaum and Stewart (2007) propose that part of the rethinking process should include a feed-forward of the best provision that exists in childhood services, so that clinicians working in children's services therefore need to take on training and consultancy roles for their colleagues based in adult services. Services need to examine their capacity to provide support during the transition period (Davis & Sondheimer, 2005) and local transition protocols need to be established to improve joint-working and easier access to services.

Where funding is secured, the establishment of a dedicated transition team could significantly improve the quality of service provision to young people and collaborative working between different services. Ideally such a team should have members from different professional backgrounds to enable it to provide a range of services, including transition planning, diagnostic assessments, treatment strategies, consultation and training. The establishment of transition services is supported by the Transition Champions Programme (Department of Health, 2006) which aims to identify champions at all levels – national, regional and individual. Through this, best practice could be disseminated more widely and gaps in service provision could be identified to promote development in policy and practice.

Transition Planning

Transition planning needs to be multidisciplinary and could potentially involve representatives from a range of services, including the child mental health, adult mental health, paediatric, social care, educational psychology, and where it exists, a dedicated transition service. Special needs coordinators and personal advisers are central to the planning process when wide-ranging needs are present. The transfer of all relevant health, psychosocial and educational information is vital to ensure a smooth transition and this could be enhanced by periods of joint-working to 'promote a collaborative approach' and 'facilitate continuity of care' (Kennedy *et al.*, 2007). The transition plan needs to promote autonomy (Bailey *et al.*, 2003) and should be a 'Life (not Illness) Plan' focusing on the future, even when the young person is living with a disability or a serious chronic illness (Olsen & Swigonski, 2004). Their wider needs and aspirations should be addressed alongside more immediate concerns, and where input from a range of services is required, a transition coordinator needs to be identified to integrate the support they receive (Betz & Redcay, 2005; Department of Health, 2006). Adequate systems and processes need to be in place to regularly monitor whether the transition plan is delivering the outcomes sought by the individual.

A person-centred approach: Person-centred planning is 'a process for continual listening and learning, focussing on what is important to someone now and in the future, and acting upon this in alliance with their family and friends; this listening is used to understand a person's capacities and choices' (Department of Health, 2002). Young people's voices need to be heard during transition planning to promote youth-focused service developments (Kennedy *et al.*, 2007). Interventions need to be individually tailored and should not just be a mere extension of what was received from children's services, or are about to be received from adult services (Vostanis, 2005). A person-centred approach is especially important when working with young people with a learning disability as some may take longer to process what is being said, they may use different ways of communicating their needs, or they may not understand everything being discussed (Grove & McIntosh, 2005).

Developmental and Other Childhood-Onset Chronic Conditions

Early detection, intervention and treatment are key national drivers in the UK (Department of Health, 2003, 2004), and clear targets exist for specific conditions such autistic spectrum conditions (Department of Health, 2001b). Young adults with an autistic spectrum condition such as Asperger's syndrome typically face significant challenges towards attaining independence. The presence of profound comprehension difficulties within a social context (e.g. literalness), differences in spoken language (e.g. repetitive use of language, the use of idiosyncratic words, or unintentionally coming across as blunt), difficulties dealing with abstract concepts, such as talking about the future or about emotions, and an absence of reciprocity in their language (Howlin, 1997) should compel clinicians to have comprehensive transition plans in place for these vulnerable members of society. Advocacy might be relevant throughout their life (Aman, 2005), but perhaps more than any other group, these individuals, who typically have a strong need for sameness of the environment (and therefore great difficulty coping with change), need clearly defined support packages during transition to adulthood.

Adult services are often unfamiliar with the subtleties of ADHD presentation in adulthood, and misdiagnosis and treatment are not uncommon (Asherson, 2005). ADHD may present differently during adolescence, e.g. hyperactivity features may be less noticeable; consequently the adolescent with predominantly inattentive features may easily be missed and could experience greater impairment than in childhood as the demands for independence increase (Carlson & Mann cited in Wolraich *et al.*, 2005).

Mannuzza *et al.* (1993) found that having ADHD placed children at a relative risk for educational or later employment disadvantage. Current guidance on managing ADHD during adolescence and adulthood, especially with regards to considering medication, relies heavily on the evidence base of childhood provision (Nutt *et al.*, 2007). Where awareness does exist in adult services, there may be reluctance to inaugurate the proven management procedures followed in children's services. This may be due to a lack of experience or few training/consultancy opportunities, but perhaps most significantly, it not being part of the clinician's basic training.

For a number of genetic conditions, e.g. cystic fibrosis, there is increasing life expectancy (Hagood *et al.*, 2005) but young people with neurological conditions such as cerebral palsy and muscular dystrophy, progressive neurodegenerative disorders, sensory impairments, acquired brain injury, spinal lesions, hydrocephalus or intractable epilepsy syndromes often receive no follow-up care once they leave children's services (Department of Health, 2006). More young people will therefore need support from adult services, which calls for the need to establish interdisciplinary care incorporating the views of service users and their families (Hagood *et al.*, 2005).

Mental Health and Transition

Young people with mental health difficulties often feel stigmatised and may experience numerous losses of 'identity, family, career choices, and educational and social standing' which disrupt transition to adulthood (Leavey, 2005). Vostanis's (2005) review of research findings showed that in addition to the high incidence of psychiatric disorders, young people approaching adulthood have high rates of mental health needs which may be related to life transitions. Aside from interventions for early psychosis, these needs were often not met as they fall between the remit of services, including that between mental health and social care services. Special consideration needs to be given to the mental health needs of young adults from ethnic minorities which might reflect their 'increasingly disadvantaged pathways into adulthood' (Gore & Aseltine, 2003) and to potential sex differences when considering the impact of contextual and contemporary variables on adolescent mental health (Gutman & Sameroff, 2004).

Outcomes of Transition

The outcome of this transition period varies between different groups of young people. For example:

- *Leaving care*: Tweddle's (2007) review of research findings indicates that young people leaving care are at much greater risk than their peers of experiencing mental health difficulties or coming into contact with the criminal justice system. Positive outcomes were associated with obtaining life skills and independent living training.

- *Offending behaviour*: Davis *et al.* (2004) suggested that patterns of offending behaviour indicates that intervention should occur prior to the age of 15, while Stouthamer-Loeber *et al.* (2004) found that being employed or in school promoted desistance from persistent serious delinquency during the transition to adulthood.
- *Disabilities*: Stewart *et al.*'s (2006) appraisal of literature that concerns the transition to adulthood for young people with disabilities identified a focus on skill development, environmental supports and taking an individualised approach as key factors for effective service delivery, but also highlighted the need for further research to address the complex issues of this transitional period. The support available to young people with disabilities is variable, and services may have difficulty coordinating their responses with other agencies and giving information at the right time (Department for Education and Skills, 2007).
- *Chronic or life-threatening disease*: Stam *et al.* (2006) found that young adults who grew up with cancer or with end-stage renal disease achieved significantly fewer milestones than their peers, but suggest that harm could be minimised by encouraging carers to stimulate social contacts and autonomy. Appropriate adult services need to be identified and provided with a 'comprehensive treatment history, problem list and monitoring plan' (Freyer & Kibrick-Lazear, 2006).
- Masten *et al.* (2004) found that success in developmental tasks during emerging and young adulthood was related to adaptive resources, which included 'planfulness/future motivation, autonomy, adult support, and coping skills'. They also argue that the transition period to adulthood provides a window of opportunity for changing the young person's life course.

Competencies Required

Working effectively with this group requires a range of competencies from clinical psychologists. For example:

- Different communication and consultation skills are needed from those required for work with children and adults. Clinicians should have adequate knowledge about generic health issues such as skin/weight concerns and sexuality (Department of Health, 2006).
- Since it is not uncommon for adolescents with a possible developmental condition to present undiagnosed, it is important for clinicians to have adequate knowledge about the diagnostic process and management of these conditions (Wolraich *et al.*, 2005).
- For those working in adult services, knowledge about the developmental tasks of adolescence could enhance young people's engagement of their new providers (Kennedy *et al.*, 2007). Adolescence is a period of brain maturation when regions which underlie cognitive functions such as attention and response inhibition (key ADHD features) undergo structural and functional reorganisation (Yurgelun-Todd, 2007). Further research is needed to identify the unique ADHD features of this developmental stage (Wolraich *et al.*, 2005).

- A holistic approach to transition planning is of paramount importance since, depending on the young person's condition or level of disability, transition may take place across a number of domains, e.g. health, education, employment, accommodation and social support (Department of Health, 2006). This is normally best addressed through multi-agency working, and sound organisational knowledge is therefore vital to ensure that attention is paid to all areas of the young person's life. This will be further enhanced by competent facilitation skills to promote successful person-centred planning (Department of Health, 2002).
- Consultancy and training, especially to providers of adult services, will be important roles for the clinician working in this field; this necessitates a thorough understanding of individual conditions and their evolution and consequences in adulthood (Department of Health, 2006).
- The provision of transition services is patchy and where it exists it tends to be under-resourced. Regular service evaluation is crucial for monitoring effectiveness and promoting expansion. This requires the clinician to liaise and consult with various agencies in order to influence the strategic planning and commissioning of services. Finally, there should also be ample opportunities to carry out research to contribute to the understanding of this emerging field.

Conclusions

A successful transition from childhood to adulthood involves a well-planned process rather than being a single event or transfer. Local transition protocols need to be in place to guarantee that all relevant services work together, and to ensure the young person's wishes are heard and needs are appropriately addressed. For the clinician working in this area, a range of competencies ranging from specialist knowledge and communication skills, to consultancy, training and research skills is essential to support young people in transition, and to contribute to the strategic planning and expansion of related services.

References

Aman, M.G. (2005). Treatment planning for patients with autism spectrum disorders. *The Journal of Clinical Psychiatry*, 66(Suppl. 10), 38–45.

Asherson, P. (2005). Assessment and treatment of attention deficit hyperactivity disorder in adults. *Expert review of Neurotherapeutics*, 5(4), 525–539.

Bailey, S., O'Connell, B. & Pearce, J. (2003). The transition from paediatric to adult health care services for young adults with a disability: An ethical perspective. *Australian Health Review*, 26(1), 64–69.

Betz, C.L. & Redcay, G. (2005). Dimensions of the transition service coordinator role. *Journal for Specialists in Pediatric Nursing*, 10(2), 49–59.

Chamberlain, M.A. & Kent, R.M. (2005). The needs of young people with disabilities in transition from paediatric to adult services. *Europa Medicophysica*, 41(2), 111–123.

Davis, M. (2003). Addressing the needs of youth in transition to adulthood. *Administration and Policy in Mental Health*, *30*(6), 495–509.

Davis, M., Banks, S., Fisher, W. & Grudzinskas, A. (2004). Longitudinal patterns of offending during the transition to adulthood in youth from the mental health system. *Journal of Behavioral Health Services and Research*, *31*(4), 351–366.

Davis, M., Geller, J.L. & Hunt, B. (2006). Within-state availability of transition-to-adulthood services for youths with serious mental health conditions. *Psychiatric Services*, *57*(11), 1594–1599

Davis, M. & Sondheimer, D.L. (2005). State child mental health efforts to support youth in transition to adulthood. *Journal of Behavioral Health Services and Research*, *32*(1), 27–42.

Department for Education and Skills (2001). *Special educational needs: Code of practice*. London: Author.

Department for Education and Skills (2007). *Aiming high for disabled children: Better support for families*. London: H.M. Treasury.

Department of Health (2001a). *The mental health policy implementation guide*. London: Author.

Department of Health (2001b). *Valuing people – people with learning disabilities and autistic spectrum disorders*. London: Author.

Department of Health (2002). *Valuing people: A new strategy for learning disability for the 21st century: planning with people towards person centred approaches – guidance for partnership boards*. London: Author.

Department of Health (2003). *Health inequalities: A programme for action*. London: Author.

Department of Health (2004). *National service framework for children, young people and maternity services: Every child matters*. London: Author.

Department of Health (2006). *Transition: Getting it right for young people*. London: Author.

Freyer, D.R. & Kibrick-Lazear, R. (2006). In sickness and in health: Transition of cancer-related care for older adolescents and young adults. *Cancer*, *107*(Suppl. 7), 1702–1709.

Gore, S. & Aseltine, R.H. Jr. (2003). Race and ethnic differences in depressed mood following the transition from high school. *Journal of Health and Social Behavior*, *44*(3), 370–389.

Grove, N. & McIntosh, B. (2005). *Communication for person-centred planning*. London: Foundation for People with Learning Disabilities.

Gutman, L.M. & Sameroff, A.J. (2004). Continuities in depression from adolescence to young adulthood: Contrasting ecological influences. *Development and Psychopathology*, *16*(4), 967–984.

Hagood, J.S., Lenker, C.V. & Thrasher, S. (2005). A course on the transition to adult care of patients with childhood-onset chronic illnesses. *Academic Medicine: Journal of the Association of American Colleges*, *80*(4), 352–355.

Howlin, P. (1997). *Autism: preparing for adulthood*. London: Routledge.

Kennedy, A., Sloman, F., Douglass, J.A. & Sawyer, S.M. (2007). Young people with chronic illness: The approach to transition. *Internal Medicine Journal*, *37*(8), 555–560.

Leavey, J.E. (2005). Youth experiences of living with mental health problems: Emergence, loss, adaptation and recovery (ELAR). *Canadian Journal of Community Mental Health*, *24*(2), 109–126.

Mannuzza, S., Klein, R.G., Bessler, A., Malloy, P. & LaPadula, M. (1993). Adult outcome of hyperactive boys: Educational achievement, occupational rank and psychiatric status. *Archives of General Psychiatry*, *50*(7), 565–576.

Masten, A.S., Burt, K.B., Roisman, G.I., Obradovi , J., Long, J.D. & Tellegen, A. (2004). Resources and resilience in the transition to adulthood: Continuity and change. *Development and Psychopathology*, *16*(4), 1071–1094.

Nutt, D.J., Fone, K., Asherson, P., Bramble, D., Hill, P., Matthews, K. *et al.* (2007). Evidence-based guidelines for management of attention-deficit/hyperactivity disorder in adolescents in transition to adult services and in adults: Recommendations from the British Association for Psychopharmacology. *Journal of Psychopharmacology, 21*(1), 10–41.

Olsen, D.G. & Swigonski, N.L. (2004). Transition to adulthood: The important role of the pediatrician. *Pediatrics, 113*(3 Pt 1), 159–162.

Paone, M.C., Wigle, M. & Saewyc, E. (2006). The ON TRAC model for transitional care of adolescents. *Progress in Transplantation, 16*(4), 291–302.

Patton, G.C. & Viner, R. (2007). Pubertal transitions in health. *Lancet, 31, 369*(9567), 1130–1139.

Poa, E. (2006). Trapped in transition: The complex young adult patient. *Bulletin of the Menninger Clinic, 70*(1), 29–52.

Rosenbaum, P. & Stewart, D. (2007). Perspectives on transitions: Rethinking services for children and youth with developmental disabilities. *Archives of Physical Medicine and Rehabilitation, 88*(8), 1080–1082.

Social Exclusion Unit (2005). *Improving services, improving lives.* London: Author.

Stam, H., Hartman, E.E., Deurloo, J.A., Groothoff, J. & Grootenhuis, M.A. (2006). Young adult patients with a history of pediatric disease: Impact on course of life and transition into adulthood. *The Journal of Adolescent Health, 39*(1), 4–13.

Stewart, D., Stavness, C., King, G., Antle, B. & Law, M. (2006). A critical appraisal of literature reviews about the transition to adulthood for youth with disabilities. *Physical and Occupational Therapy in Pediatrics, 26*(4), 5–24.

Stouthamer-Loeber, M., Wei, E., Loeber, R. & Masten, A.S. (2004). Desistance from persistent serious delinquency in the transition to adulthood. *Development and Psychopathology, 16*(4), 897–918.

Tweddle, A. (2007). Youth leaving care: How do they fare? *New Directions for Youth Development, 113,* 15–31, 9–10.

Vostanis, P. (2005). Patients as parents and young people approaching adulthood: How should we manage the interface between mental health services for young people and adults? *Current Opinion in Psychiatry, 18*(4), 449–454

Wolraich, M.L., Wibbelsman, C.J., Brown, T.E., Evans, S.W., Gotlieb, E.M., Knight, J.R. *et al.* (2005). Attention-deficit/hyperactivity disorder among adolescents: A review of the diagnosis, treatment, and clinical implications. *Pediatrics, 115*(6), 1734–1746.

Yurgelun-Todd, D. (2007). Emotional and cognitive changes during adolescence. *Current Opinion in Neurobiology, 17*(2), 251–257.

26

Eating Disorders

Myra Cooper and Rachel Woolrich

Eating disorders include anorexia nervosa (AN) and bulimia nervosa (BN) as well as binge eating disorder (BED) and eating disorder not otherwise specified (ED-NOS) (American Psychiatric Association, 2000). Patients may have problems with several behaviours, including difficulty maintaining a healthy weight, episodes of binge eating, and compensatory behaviours (e.g. self-induced vomiting after eating). Anxiety and depression are common, as are beliefs that weight and/or shape are important criteria for judging self-worth. The disturbances may result in significant medical complications.

AN is relatively uncommon, while BN has a prevalence of around 1–2 per cent in young women (Hoek, 2006). In clinical practice there is evidence that ED-NOS, which include BED, accounts for about 60 per cent of all cases (Fairburn & Bohn, 2005). There is debate about the validity of the diagnostic categories, in part due to the fact that many sufferers switch between them. A transdiagnostic approach has been suggested, in which their common elements receive greater emphasis (Fairburn *et al.*, 2003). However, others highlight the coherence of the categories (Keel *et al.*, 2004). BED is often associated with obesity and its relationship to the other eating disorders is not clear (Cooper, 2003). It probably accounts for a minority of clinical cases (Fairburn & Bohn, 2005), although prevalence in community samples is 1–2.5 per cent (Hay, 1998).

Eating disorders are most common in adolescent girls and young women, although not confined to these groups (Hoek, 2006). Patients are thus often dealing with adolescent and young people's developmental and social challenges (e.g. identity formation, peer relationships and the transition from home, school and the family to the wider world). Indeed, many eating disorder symptoms are known to be linked to these issues (Bruch, 1973). BED presents later, but its origins may lie in adolescence and childhood (Brody *et al.*, 1994). ED-NOS appears to have a similar course, history and presentation to AN and BN, and (excluding BED) presentation tends to either resemble AN or BN (Fairburn & Bohn, 2005). Thus, even in a transdiagnostic approach, different diagnoses may have utility.

Psychological treatment is the treatment of choice. For those with a binge eating or BN presentation this typically involves cognitive behaviour therapy (CBT) (National Institute for Health and Clinical Excellence, 2004). CBT is also used to treat those with AN, although family therapy is a useful option in very young patients (see review by Eisler, 2005). In many clinical settings treatment will be in individual or group format. Self-help treatments, including CBT, are available, and recommended for those with BN. These are useful either as a sole treatment for less severe disorders, or as guided self-help, where a trained therapist assists the patient with the programme (e.g. Schmidt *et al.*, 2007). A minority of patients, usually with AN, require intensive day or in-patient treatment, with individual and group activities, including supervised meals. NICE guidelines recommend that ED-NOS presentations should be treated according to the guidelines for AN or BN depending on the presentation and age of the patient. BED is an exception, in that while psychological treatment based on CBT is recommended, it is suggested that it is often most usefully delivered in primary care settings using self-help. Antidepressant medication also has a role in BN, particularly in a stepped care approach where self-help programmes have been unsuccessful (National Institute for Health and Clinical Excellence, 2004).

Services for eating disorders are patchy. Many patients are treated in general practice, particularly those with BN, and prescription of fluoxetine is common. If problems persist, patients are seen in general psychiatric clinics, or a specialist eating disorder service, if one is available. Specialist services offer individual psychological therapy, dietetic advice, psychiatric monitoring, family therapy, intensive group treatment and, for those at significant medical risk due to low weight, in-patient re-feeding programmes.

Clinical psychologists work in a number of roles across various settings. Typically they provide individual and family assessments, individual or group CBT. They often take a lead in the provision of clinical supervision and teaching of other professionals. They may also develop psychoeducational and therapeutic materials (e.g. Cooper *et al.*, 2000; Whitehead, 2007), or design and lead specialist services. It is important that they work closely with medical colleagues (typically GPs and/or in-patient teams) to monitor physical health and manage risk. Paucity of resources in statutory services means that prevention and early interventions are usually provided by non-statutory services.

Models and Competencies Used

Knowledge of cognitive behavioural models (Fairburn *et al.*, 1986; Garner & Bemis, 1982) is important. In practice, given that many patients do not respond adequately to standard CBT (see below), attention will need to be paid to interpersonal aspects and to core beliefs or schema (e.g. Cooper *et al.*, 2000; Waller *et al.*, 2007), and not only to overvaluation of weight and shape typically tackled in standard CBT. This involves schema-focused theory (Young *et al.*, 2003), attachment theory (Bowlby, 1969; Fonagy *et al.*, 2002), systemic theory (e.g. Minuchin *et al.*, 1978), and cognitive interpersonal models (Schmidt & Treasure, 2006). Treatment is likely to be longer term, especially for AN, than is typical of standard CBT for BN (e.g. Agras *et al.*, 2000).

Relationship skills are important when working with eating disorders, although in many instances the therapist–patient relationship is difficult. Patients often have issues with trust, and lack of empathy by therapists has been noted to be a problem (Geller et al., 2001). Patients may not appear keen to engage in psychological therapy, particularly when behaviour change rather than reflection is a focus, and excellent interpersonal and relationship skills are necessary to engage and motivate them.

A thorough and well-conducted assessment is important, particularly for planning treatment. Therapists may need to explicitly probe some areas since patients can be reluctant to report concerns due to shame (e.g. regarding quantities of food consumed). A detailed risk assessment, in relation to suicide, self-harm and physical complications, is important.

Standard CBT for BN uses a basic formulation template (Fairburn, 1996). Given that not all patients respond to this, and it is inappropriate for AN and other eating disorders, formulation is not necessarily straightforward. A thorough understanding of the cognitive, emotional, physiological and behavioural aspects of eating disorders and creativity are needed. Formulation may involve knowledge of developmental, attachment and systemic theory, as well as advanced cognitive/schema theory and its application to eating disorders (Cooper, 2005; Waller et al., 2007). Patients may need to be encouraged to 'own' the formulation, as the ego-syntonicity of some symptoms may make it difficult for them to see how what they value plays a role in their problems.

Re-feeding is an important focus in severe AN (Body Mass Index less than 14). It remains controversial whether patients are able to engage in psychological treatments at such low weights, due to compromised cognitive abilities. Psychological therapy is often offered alongside re-feeding programmes, but the latter have historically developed with physical health issues in mind, with little reference to psychological principles. A key challenge for a clinical psychologist is to integrate the two approaches.

When patients refuse treatment and present at severe physical risk (e.g. death through severe emaciation, electrolyte imbalance and cardiac failure through purging) or with a risk of self-harm, the Mental Health Act may be used. Clinical psychologists must be involved in this process while simultaneously trying to keep the patient engaged and motivated.

Self-awareness and reflection are important skills, not least because patients with eating disorders can trigger strong therapist reactions, often due to complex attachment experiences. When teams are involved, staff can easily divide into different groups with opposing views on treatment or what specific management plans to implement.

Understanding and knowledge of how to work effectively within a team is invaluable, as patients with eating disorders are often treated in a mental health team. It is crucial to work with the wider system when patients have day or in-patient care or when they need support with a chronic illness. It is also important to understand the socio cultural context, the role of peers, and the way in which these contribute to the maintenance of the disorder.

Work with eating disorders requires patience, ability to deal with numerous setbacks and false starts, and persistence. It is important to remain positive when faced (as often happens) with extreme hopelessness and depression, inexplicable self-harm or self-punishing behaviours. A judicious sense of humour also helps as, perhaps surprisingly, many patients retain an ability to see the funny side of things, including of their own thoughts and behaviour.

Engagement and Assessment

Even those who appear highly motivated inevitably have reservations about treatment when these are specifically enquired about (Cooper *et al.*, 2000; Geller *et al.*, 2001). The dropout rate from treatment is high in clinical practice (Mahon, 2000). Mahon (2000) notes that treatment options need to take greater account of this. Historically, few therapists have routinely addressed motivation and engagement. Geller (2002) has long deemed it vital to take a 'motivational stance' in the treatment of AN, and emphasises the value of encouraging patient motivation and engagement, which also forms an important part of a new, revised cognitive treatment for BN (Cooper *et al.*, 2008). Such work often makes use of the stages of change model (Prochaska & DiClemente, 1982), as well as motivational-style interviewing strategies (e.g. Cooper *et al.*, 2008). An example of motivational work is described in Example two below.

Evidence base

Treatment efficacy. Most research has focused on AN and BN. Treatment evaluation in particular has been primarily on BN and for CBT based on Fairburn and colleagues' model and therapy (Fairburn *et al.*, 1993). Several studies (e.g. Agras *et al.*, 2000) indicate that it can produce a good outcome. Nevertheless, at five-year follow-up, the outcome is less good, with around half still meeting criteria for an eating disorder (Fairburn *et al.*, 1995). BED also appears to respond to an adapted form of CBT for BN, at least in the short term (e.g. Telch *et al.*, 1990), but the outcome is less good at one year (Agras *et al.*, 1997). In contrast to BN, there have been few rigorous studies of CBT for AN. One study shows CBT to be helpful as part of the post hospitalisation care of those with AN (Pike *et al.*, 2003), but overall fewer than half those treated with CBT met criteria for a good outcome after treatment. Family therapy is helpful for young people with AN (Eisler, 2005), but at five-year follow-up, the effects of therapy were modest (Eisler *et al.* 1997). Other psychological therapies with modest effects in adults with AN include psychoanalytic psychotherapy and cognitive analytic therapy (Dare *et al.*, 2001).

Evidence for psychological models. The original theoretical constructs and predictions of cognitive behavioural theory (derived primarily from Garner & Bemis, 1982, and Fairburn *et al.*, 1986) are well supported (Cooper, 2005; Cooper, 1997). However, the finding that many people do not respond well to CBT has prompted exploration of missing ingredients and gaps in the models. As noted above, some revised cognitive models have been developed (Cooper *et al.*, 2004; Waller *et al.*, 2007). Termed second generation models (Cooper, 2005), they include additional constructs, and researchers have begun to explore the evidence for these. Second generation models draw on attachment and dynamic theories, which has sparked new interest in the role of emotional processing and early mother–infant relationships, as well as in the role of self and self-related processing, as represented, for example, in core beliefs (Beck *et al.*, 1990) and schema (Young *et al.*, 2003).

Examples of Specific Interventions by Clinical Psychologists

Example one – group CBT for BN – limiting binges. Working to limit binges is a step that integrates behavioural and cognitive elements. A functional analysis of bingeing behaviours with the group can elicit vulnerable situations and maintaining factors. This might include discussion of when binges happen, how people access binge food and what facilitates this, including relevant cognitions. The group may be encouraged to reflect on ways to interrupt the binge process using cognitive and behavioural strategies. This can generate ideas for patients to try at home, for example, changing shopping behaviours, storing food differently, using different flavours (e.g. peppermint) or markers (e.g. face washing) to stop eating. Patients can be asked to select specific ideas to test out the following week, and to make predictions about what they fear might happen, in order to test out important maintaining beliefs e.g. 'If I start eating then I will never stop' in the form of behavioural experiments (see Cooper, Whitehead & Boughton, 2004). Group discussion in particular can be both affirming and reduce shame.

    Example two – individual therapy for AN – motivational work to help patient to approach weight gain. Patients with AN are often fearful of engaging in therapy as they believe they will be 'forced' to gain weight. A helpful initial stance for the psychologist is a neutral position (assuming risks are appropriately managed), suggesting that they spend several sessions thinking about what they want to do in relation to their weight. Patients can find this liberating and it can allow them to engage more fully in the process. In addition to direct questions about what weight gain might mean to them, the psychologist can use other tools to elaborate the patient's thinking. For example, drawing a grid can help the patient consider the pros and cons of recovery (involving weight gain) and a continued life with the disorder. Patients can be encouraged to think about physical, psychological, interpersonal and educational/occupational domains. This can also be an opportunity to provide information (e.g. evidence regarding starvation sequelae). To facilitate reflection they can write letters to a friend, imagining it is in five years' time, both with and without the eating disorder (Serpell *et al.*, 1999). This helps identify their longer-term goals and how the eating disorder impacts on these. The meaning of having an eating disorder is then linked back to the formulation. At times, patients (and therapists) have to be prepared for the fact that they may not be ready to let go of their eating disorder.

Challenging Issues

One challenging issue is with whom responsibility lies for recovery. If therapists invest too much in taking responsibility for the patient's recovery, and hold all the anxiety regarding risk, the patient can distance themselves and take a passive role (Geller *et al.*, 2001). Therapists need to enable the patient to take responsibility for their recovery, assuming that the therapist is clear that the patient is informed about the risk and consequences of inaction.

Eating disorders can generate anxiety amongst professionals and families. Therapists may find themselves providing a containing role for others as well as for patients. Any involvement of family members may require careful negotiation with patients, within confidentiality boundaries, and regular supervision.

Many patients have dysfunctional attachment patterns which are enacted within the therapeutic relationship. While engaging with this group of patients can thus be challenging, patients may also find it difficult to disengage from their therapist/treatment, particularly if they have been in contact over many years. Patients are also (understandably) likely to attach differentially to individual team members and this will require reflection and discussion by all concerned.

In addition to the potential for teams to split around a patient, different elements of in-patient or day-patient treatment have the potential to 'split' the patient. It is an ongoing challenge for a psychologist to integrate the various facets of treatment e.g. group work, re-feeding, individual therapy and psychiatric monitoring. However, clinical psychologists are well placed to help teams take a psychologically coherent approach (e.g. by asking questions regarding the rationale behind treatment decisions and developing team formulations).

Sensitivity to cultural differences in eating and weight is important and clinical psychologists need to demonstrate an awareness of this. It can be challenging to disentangle motivations that are driven by the eating disorder and those which are idiosyncratic or culturally bound. Using the evidence base together with supervision and open reflection of dilemmas with the patient themselves are often helpful.

User and Carer Perspectives

Patients have noted that it is important to feel treated as an individual and not as 'another anorexic' and also that in-patient treatment can feel disconnected from real life, making discharge and post-treatment adjustment difficult (Offord *et al.*, 2006). Some patients report that treatment reinforces poor self-concept (Offord *et al.*, 2006). Engaging in recovery alongside other patients has been reported to be stressful and to elicit competitive drives, but peer relationships can also be supportive. Although most patients with eating disorders in the UK are young Caucasian women (National Institute for Clinical Excellence, 2004) it is important that services sensitively meet the needs of all patients.

Carer perspectives or experiences have begun to be explored in more detail recently (although mainly in relation to AN). Parents may have significant levels of distress connected to their child's eating disorder (Treasure *et al.*, 2001). Carers often feel it is extremely difficult to access services and report that they do not receive enough information or support (Haigh & Treasure, 2003). While most services aim to offer some carer support (e.g. a family and friends support group), in practice most carer support is provided by non-statutory agencies (e.g. B-EAT – the eating disorders charity (www.b-eat.org.uk)).

Research and Future Directions

While CBT models and treatment are promising they need more development, both for BN AN and the ED-NOS presentations. A good psychological model of AN (and AN-like presentations), and an accompanying evidence base, is particularly and urgently needed.

Second generation models show promise but need more work and development. Greater attention to engagement and motivation work, as well as broadening the focus beyond weight and shape and eating issues to consider self, attachment, interpersonal and (although not considered here) emotional processing, is needed. In intensive treatment a particularly important issue is how to make the different interventions psychologically coherent.

ED-NOS needs more work, but it is unclear how far diagnosis matters. Second generation theories have tended to focus on the key behaviours, with the idea that these exist on a continuum, and have suggested that it is more important to model these than allocate a diagnosis. However, different behaviours can occur for different reasons; for example, it is not clear that bingeing in BED is the same phenomena cognitively as in BN. A combination of diagnosis and identification of common processes may be most useful when planning treatment.

Identification of risk factors is important, not only to provide early intervention and to prevent eating disorders, but also to help prevent relapse. Currently, however, little of this work is undertaken by statutory services, despite the significance of eating disorders in public health terms. Carer support and help is relatively poor at present. As with prevention and early intervention, much of this is undertaken by voluntary services. Support for patients and carers whose relatives have chronic and severe problems is particularly lacking. Currently most clinical resources are directed at those in the severe and acute stages. However, psychologists are involved in research into the other areas, and a long-term aim might be that clinical work by psychologists extends to these as well.

References

Agras, W.S., Telch, C.F., Arnow, B., Eldredge, K. & Marnell, M. (1997). One year follow up of cognitive behavioural therapy for obese individuals with binge eating disorder. *Journal of Consulting and Clinical Psychology*, 65, 343–347.

Agras, W.S., Walsh, T., Fairburn, C.G., Wilson, G.T. & Kraemer, H.C. (2000). A multicentre comparison of cognitive behavioural therapy and interpersonal psychotherapy for bulimia nervosa. *Archives of General Psychiatry*, 57, 459–466.

American Psychiatric Association (2000). *Diagnostic and statistical manual IV, text revised.* New York: American Psychiatric Association.

Beck, A.T., Freeman, A. & Associates (1990). *Cognitive therapy of personality disorders.* New York: Guilford Press.

Bowlby, J. (1969). *Attachment and loss, vol. 1: Attachment.* New York: Basic Books.

Brody, M.L., Walsh, B.T. & Devlin, M.J. (1994). Binge eating disorder: reliability and validity of a new diagnostic category. *Journal of Consulting and Clinical Psychology, 62,* 381–386.

Bruch, H. (1973). *Eating disorders.* New York: Basic Books.

Cooper, M.J. (1997). Cognitive theory in anorexia nervosa and bulimia nervosa: A review. *Behavioural and Cognitive Psychotherapy, 25,* 113–145.

Cooper, M.J. (2003). *The psychology of bulimia nervosa: A cognitive perspective.* Oxford: Oxford University Press.

Cooper, M.J. (2005). Cognitive theory in anorexia nervosa and bulimia nervosa: progress, development and future directions. *Clinical Psychology Review, 25,* 511–531.

Cooper, M.J., Todd, G. & Wells, A. (2000). *A self-help cognitive therapy programme for bulimia nervosa.* London: Jessica Kingsley.

Cooper, M.J., Todd, G. & Wells, A. (2008). *Treating bulimia nervosa and binge eating: An integrated metacognitive and cognitive therapy manual.* London: Taylor & Francis.

Cooper, M.J., Wells, A. & Todd, G. (2004). A cognitive theory of bulimia nervosa. *British Journal of Clinical Psychology, 43,* 1–16.

Cooper, M.J., Whitehead, L. & Boughton, N. (2004). Eating disorders. In J. Bennett-Levy, G. Butler, M.J.V. Fennell, A. Hackmann, M. Mueller & D. Westbrook (Eds.) *Oxford guide to behavioural experiments* (pp. 267–286). Oxford: Oxford University Press.

Dare, C., Russell, G., Treasure, J. & Dodge, L. (2001). Psychological therapies for adults with anorexia nervosa. *British Journal of Psychiatry, 178,* 216–221.

Eisler, I. (2005). The empirical and theoretical base of family therapy and multiple family day therapy for adolescent anorexia nervosa. *Journal of Family Therapy, 27,* 104–131.

Eisler, I., Dare, C., Russell, G.F.. Szmukler, G., le Grange, D. & Dodge, E. (1997). Family and individual therapy in anorexia nervosa. A 5-year follow-up. *Archives of General Psychiatry, 54,* 1025–1030.

Fairburn, C.G. & Bohn, K. (2005). Eating disorder NOS (EDNOS): An example of the troublesome 'not otherwise specified (NOS) category' in DSM-IV. *Behaviour Research and Therapy, 43,* 691–701.

Fairburn, C.G., Cooper, P.J. & Cooper, Z. (1986). The clinical features and maintenance of bulimia nervosa. In K.D. Brownell & J.P. Foreyt (Eds.) *Physiology, psychology and treatment of the eating disorders* (pp. 389–404). New York: Basic Books.

Fairburn, C.G., Cooper, Z. & Shafran, R. (2003). Cognitive behaviour therapy for eating disorders: A transdiagnostic theory and treatment. *Behaviour Research and Therapy, 41,* 509–528.

Fairburn, C.G., Marcus, M.D. & Wilson, G.T. (1993). Cognitive-behavioral therapy for binge eating and bulimia nervosa: A comprehensive treatment manual. In C.G. Fairburn & G.T. Wilson (Eds.) *Binge eating: Nature, assessment and treatment* (pp. 361–404). New York: Guilford Press.

Fairburn, C.G., Norman, P.A., Welch, S.L., O'Connor, M.E., Doll, H.A. & Peveler, R.C. (1995). A prospective study of outcome in bulimia nervosa and the long term effects of three psychological treatments. *Archives of General Psychiatry, 52,* 304–312.

Fairburn, C.G.F. (1996). Eating disorders. In D.M. Clark & C.G. Fairburn (Eds.) *Science and practice of cognitive behaviour therapy* (pp. 389–404). Oxford: Oxford University Press.

Fonagy, P., Gergely, G., Jurist, E.L. & Target, M. (2002). *Affect regulation, mentalisation, and the development of the self*. New York: Other Press.

Garner, D.M. & Bemis, K.M. (1982). A cognitive–behavioural approach to anorexia nervosa. *Cognitive Therapy and Research, 6,* 123–150.

Geller, J. (2002) Estimating readiness to change in anorexia nervosa: Comparing clients, clinicians and research assessors. *International Journal of Eating Disorders, 31*(3), 251–260

Geller, J. Williams, K.D. & Srikameswaran, S. (2001). Clinician stance in the treatment of chronic eating disorders. *European Eating Disorders Review, 9,* 365–373.

Haigh, R. & Treasure, J. (2003). Investigating the needs of carers in the area of eating disorders: Development of the Carers Needs Assessment Measure (CaNAM). *European Eating Disorders Review, 11,* 125–141.

Hay P. (1998). The epidemiology of eating disorder behaviors: An Australian community-based survey. *International Journal of Eating Disorders, 23,* 371–382.

Hoek, H. (2006). Incidence, prevalence and mortality of anorexia nervosa and other eating disorders. *Current Opinion in Psychiatry, 19,* 389–394.

Keel, P.K., Fichter, M, Quadflieg, N., Bulik, C.M., Baxter, M.G., Thornton, L. *et al.* (2004). Application of a latent class analysis to empirically define eating disorder phenotypes. *Archives of General Psychiatry, 61,* 192–200.

Mahon, J. (2000). Dropping out from psychological treatment for eating disorders: What are the issues? *European Eating Disorders Review, 8,* 198–216.

Minuchin, S., Rosman, B.L. & Baker, L. (1978). *Psychosomatic families: Anorexia nervosa in context*. Cambridge, Massachussetts: Harvard University Press.

National Institute for Health and Clinical Excellence (2004). *Core interventions in the treatment and management of anorexia nervosa, bulimia nervosa and related eating disorders*. Leicester: The British Psychological Society. Also available online; retrieved 20 February 2009 from www.nice.org.uk

Offord, A., Turner, H. & Cooper, M.J. (2006). Adolescent inpatient treatment for anorexia nervosa: A qualitative study exploring young adults' retrospective views of treatment and discharge. *European Eating Disorders Review, 14,* 377–387.

Pike, K.M., Walsh, B.T., Vitousek, K., Wilson, G.T. & Bauer, J. (2003). Cognitive behavior therapy in the posthospitalisation treatment of anorexia nervosa. *American Journal of Psychiatry, 160,* 2046–2049.

Prochaska J.O. & DiClemente, C.C. (1982). Transtheoretical therapy: Towards an integrative model of change. *Psychotherapy Theory and Research Practice, 19,* 276–88.

Schmidt, U., Lee, S., Beecham, J., Perkins, S., Treasure, J., Yi, I. *et al.* (2007). A randomised controlled trial of family therapy and cognitive behaviour therapy guided self care for adolescents with bulimia nervosa and related disorders. *American Journal of Psychiatry, 164,* 591–598.

Schmidt, U. & Treasure, J. (2006). Anorexia nervosa: Valued and visible. A cognitive-interpersonal maintenance model and its implications for research and practice. *British Journal of Clinical Psychology, 45,* 343–366.

Serpell, L., Treasure, J., Teasdale, J. & Sullivan, V. (1999). Anorexia nervosa: Friend or foe? *International Journal of Eating Disorders, 25*(2), *177–186.*

Telch, C.F., Agras, W.S., Rossiter, E.M., Wilfley, D. & Kenardy, J. (1990). Group cognitive behavioural therapy for the nonpurging bulimic: An initial evaluation. *Journal of Consulting and Clinical Psychology*, *58*, 629–635.

Treasure, J., Murphy, T., Szmukler, T., Todd, G., Gavan, K. & Joyce, J. (2001). The experience of caregiving for severe mental illness: A comparison between anorexia nervosa and psychosis. *Social Psychiatry and Psychiatric Epidemiology*, *36, 343–347*.

Waller, G., Kennerley, H. & Ohanian, V. (2007). Schema focused cognitive behaviour therapy with the eating disorders. In L.P. Riso, P.T. duToit & J.E. Young (Eds.) *Cognitive schemas and core beliefs in psychiatric disorders: A scientist practitioner guide* (pp. 139–175). New York: American Psychological Association.

Whitehead, L. (2007) *Overcoming eating disorders*. Oxford: Oxford Cognitive Therapy Centre.

Young, J.E., Klosko, J.S. & Weisshaar, M.E. (2003). *Schema therapy: A practitioner's guide*. New York: Guilford Press.

27

Sexual Health

Cynthia A. Graham

Sexual health is an important part of physical and mental health. It is a key part of our identity as human beings together with the fundamental human rights to privacy, a family life and living free from discrimination. Essential elements of good sexual health are equitable relationships and sexual fulfilment with access to information and services to avoid the risk of unintended pregnancy, illness, or disease. (Department of Health, 2001, p. 5)

The above definition of sexual health, which is consistent with others put forward by the World Health Organisation (2002) and the US Surgeon General (US Department of Health and Human Services, 2001), highlights the close relationship between sexual health and both mental and physical health. It also emphasises that sexual health is much more than just the absence of disease or dysfunction; lack of information, risky sexual behaviour and gender inequality are just as often the cause of negative sexual health outcomes as infection or disease. Clinical psychologists, with their extensive training in research, theoretical models and cognitive behavioural interventions, should thus be well placed to make unique contributions to our understanding and management of sexual health problems.

This chapter will first provide an overview of the role and function of clinical psychologists in UK sexual health settings. Some of the key clinical issues that arise in this area and the most common approaches used to treat sexual health problems will be presented. Ethical and professional issues will be discussed, including the provision of sexuality teaching in clinical psychology training courses. The final section addresses research and possible future directions.

Sexual Health in the UK – the Role of Clinical Psychologists

Sexual health problems in the UK have grown in recent years. There is evidence of a rise in rates of sexually transmitted infection (STI) and an increase in high-risk sexual behaviour (Department of Health, 2001). Many STIs, including chlamydia and some genital wart infections, have serious and long-term effects on fertility and health. High rates of unintended pregnancy and abortion in the UK are a major public health concern. In 2001 the government put forward the first national strategy for sexual health and HIV (Department of Health, 2001). In this document, one of the four key elements of a comprehensive sexual health service identified was the inclusion of 'services that address psychological and sexual problems' (Department of Health, 2001, p. 22). Despite this, a recent survey carried out found that there was serious under-provision of clinical psychologists working in the field of sexual health (Faculty of HIV and Sexual Health, 2004). Moreover, there was great variation in the size, funding and commissioning of services in different areas of the UK.

Most clinical psychologists working in the area of sexual health are based in genitourinary (GUM) clinics and often work as part of multidisciplinary teams. Clinical psychology services within GUM clinics first appeared in the early 1980s, as part of the government and NHS response to the HIV/AIDS epidemic and the awareness that there are many psychological issues around the diagnosis and treatment of HIV. Psychological models such as the Theory of Reasoned Action (Ajzen & Fishbein, 1980) and the AIDS Risk-Reduction Model (Catania et al., 1990) have also provided a framework for much of the prevention and intervention research on HIV. However, clinical psychologists working in sexual health deal with many clinical issues beyond HIV, e.g. sexual problems, transgender, paraphilias (e.g. paedophilia), sexual violence. Direct clinical work encompasses assessment, treatment and intervention of primary and secondary psychological problems, and prevention of STI, HIV, and unplanned pregnancy. Indirect work includes research, services related to teaching and training of other health professionals, consultation, and service management and planning (British Psychological Society, 2002a).

Sexual Health – Areas of Psychological Need

Areas of psychological need can be broadly divided into two categories: (1) psychological problems arising secondary to a physical problem/condition, e.g. STIs, gynaecological problems or sexual trauma, and (2) primary psychological problems such as depression or anxiety that are associated with sexual health-related problems (British Psychological Society, 2002a). There is consistent evidence of high rates of psychological difficulties in GUM populations; in addition to HIV, conditions such as genital herpes and genital warts are often associated with adjustment, mood and relationship problems (Ciesla & Roberts, 2001; O'Carney et al., 1994). Other psychological problems that commonly present in GUM clinics include anxiety, self-harm behaviours and post-traumatic stress disorders. A wide range of short- and long-term psychological and sexual problems may occur following rape and sexual assault (Koss et al., 1991). Gynaecological problems such as pelvic pain (Fry et al., 1997) and abnormal smear test results (Richardson et al., 1997) often have psychological sequelae.

Many individuals attending GUM clinics do not, however, have any physical illness or infection but instead present with psychological issues relating to their behaviour or relationships, or to societal attitudes about their sexuality (Miller & Green, 2001). For example, rates of depression and distress are higher among men who have sex with men, regardless of HIV status (Mills *et al.*, 2005), which may be because of the discrimination/stress associated with being in a sexual minority group. Another client group that commonly present in GUM clinics are those who, despite being physically well and at low risk of HIV, have marked anxiety about HIV (the so-called 'worried well') (Miller, 1986); these individuals often seek repeated HIV testing and reassurance and therefore take up a disproportionate amount of clinic time.

Sexual Problems

In a UK national probability sample survey, persistent sexual problems (defined as lasting at least six months in the previous year) were reported by 15.6 per cent of women and 6.2 per cent of men (Mercer *et al.*, 2003). Lack of interest in sex (in women) and premature ejaculation (PE) (in men) were the most frequent complaints. A US national probability survey reported much higher prevalence figures; 43 per cent of women and 31 per cent of men were deemed to have a 'sexual dysfunction' (Laumann *et al.*, 1999) but distress associated with the sexual problem was not assessed in this study. Sexual difficulties are also a common presenting problem in sexual health/GUM settings and there is some evidence that services in the NHS often have difficulty finding the resources to provide psychosexual services (Faculty of HIV and Sexual Health, 2004).

Amongst clinical samples, the most common problems presented by men are erectile difficulties and PE. Erectile problems vary in severity and the difficulty may be in achieving an erection or in maintaining it long enough for satisfactory sexual intercourse. PE is essentially a problem when the man is unable to delay orgasm and ejaculation as he would wish; in severe cases, ejaculation occurs before vaginal penetration. In women, most surveys suggest that loss of sexual desire is the most common sexual problem reported (Mercer *et al.*, 2003; Laumann *et al.*, 1999). Difficulties reaching orgasm, particularly in younger women, are also fairly common; the problem may be situational, e.g. orgasm is possible with masturbation, but not during sexual activity with a partner, or may be 'global' and lifelong. Other sexual problems in women are pain during sexual intercourse (dyspareunia), and vaginismus, the recurrent or persistent involuntary spasm of the musculature of the outer third of the vagina, which makes intercourse difficult or impossible.

There is considerable overlap or comorbidity between sexual problems, particularly in women (Laumann *et al.*, 1999). Sexual problems are also often associated with primary psychological disorders. Depression and anxiety are typically associated with loss of sexual interest (Angst, 1998). Recent research suggests, however, that a minority of individuals experience a paradoxical pattern of increased sexual desire and/or activity during negative mood states, that may also be associated with sexual risk taking (Bancroft *et al.*, 2003; Lykins *et al.*, 2006).

A wide range of predictors of sexual dysfunction have been identified, including negative attitudes about sex, early experience of sexual abuse or trauma, low self-esteem, poor body image, and relationship difficulties (West *et al.*, 2004). Many physical illnesses and medications can also have adverse effects on sexual functioning (Bancroft, 2008).

Assessment

The ability to carry out comprehensive assessment and to develop complex problem formulations is an essential skill required of clinical psychologists working in sexual health settings. Psychologists should also be able to undertake a comprehensive risk assessment in HIV and sexual trauma, including both physical and mental health factors (British Psychological Society, 2006).

When taking a sexual history, it is important that clinicians are able to talk comfortably about sex with their clients. There is a need to understand lifespan aspects of sexual health and to be aware of how socio-cultural factors impact on individuals with sexual health/HIV problems, e.g. the effects of stigma and discrimination on those living with HIV. A wide variety of physical health conditions and medications can interfere with sexual functioning and it is essential that psychologists have some basic knowledge in this area. It is also important to be familiar with published guidelines about when physical examination and investigation are indicated and referral to specialist services may be necessary (e.g. in cases of erectile failure in men, and pain during sexual activity in women and men) (Bancroft, 2008). There are also now a number of standardised measures available to assess sexual functioning and satisfaction (for review, see Daker-White, 2002).

Interventions

A wide range of mental health problems may present in sexual health settings, and clinical psychologists utilise a broad array of psychological models and techniques in assessment and interventions. Interventions may be provided to individuals, couples or groups. In a recent survey of clinical psychologists working in sexual health settings (Faculty of HIV and Sexual Health, 2004), the predominant model used was cognitive behavioural (CBT) but the use of systemic models, psychodynamic approaches, counselling, and health behaviour models were also reported.

Behavioural treatment of sexual problems was pioneered by Masters and Johnson (1970) and later adapted, incorporating principles of psychoanalytic techniques (Kaplan, 1975) and CBT (Pridal & LoPiccolo, 2000; Hawton, 1985). Masters and Johnson's couple programme combines education, behavioural homework and cognitive reframing. The key elements of the approach are:

a) clearly defined tasks, which the couple are asked to attempt before the next therapy session;
b) those attempts, and any difficulties encountered, are examined in detail;

c) attitudes, feelings, and conflicts that make the tasks difficult to carry out are identified;

d) these are modified or resolved so that subsequent achievement of the tasks becomes possible;

e) the next tasks are set, and so on.

The tasks are mainly behavioural in nature and are chosen to facilitate the identification of relevant issues, but in some cases are sufficient in themselves to produce change. The behavioural programme is in three stages. In the first stage, the couple are asked to avoid any direct genital touching or stimulation and to focus on non-genital contact, alternating who initiates and who does the touching. These first, non-genital steps are effective in identifying important issues in the relationship, such as lack of trust or counterproductive stereotypical attitudes (e.g. once a man is aroused, he can't be expected not to have intercourse). Once this stage can be carried out satisfactorily, and related problematic issues dealt with, the programme moves on to the second stage, which allows genital touching to be combined with non-genital touching, with penile–vaginal intercourse still 'out of bounds'. In this second stage more intrapersonal problems, such as long-standing negative attitudes about sex, or the sequelae of earlier sexual trauma are likely to emerge. In the third stage, a gradual approach to vaginal–penile contact and insertion is undertaken. Here the issues most likely to arise are those related to performance anxiety and fear of pain. As the behavioural tasks reveal key issues that need to be resolved before moving on to the next stage, a variety of psychotherapeutic approaches, including CBT techniques, can be utilised (Graham & Bancroft, 2008).

The above approach is still widely used by sex therapists today; the main shortcoming has been inadequate outcome research on the efficacy of sex therapy (Graham & Bancroft, 2008). Although originally developed for use with heterosexual couples, the approach can be modified for use with individuals and with same-sex couples. The duration of sex therapy varies but 12 sessions over four to five months is typical.

There are also other specific behavioural techniques to deal with particular sexual problems such as premature ejaculation in men and orgasmic problems in women. For treatment of PE, relatively simple behavioural techniques, such as the 'stop-start' technique, where a man aims to stop sexual stimulation at a stage just short of the point of ejaculation, can be helpful. For orgasmic problems in women, guided masturbation (a gradual programme of self-touching) is generally the treatment of choice. In a 1997 review, Heiman and Meston (1997) concluded that behavioural techniques used to treat primary orgasmic problems in women and erectile disorders in men met established criteria for empirically validated treatments. However, for a number of other sexual problems, e.g. low sexual desire, dyspareunia (painful intercourse) in men and women, and delayed orgasm in men, there was inadequate support for the efficacy of any treatment. In the decade since this review, there have been a few controlled trials involving CBT for women with sexual pain disorders (Bergeron et al., 2001; Van Lankveld et al., 2006), and couples presenting with problems of low sexual desire (Trudel et al., 2001), all suggesting positive effects. There is a clear need for further outcome studies of psychological therapies.

In the past decade there has been a dramatic increase in medical assessment and pharmacological treatments, particularly for male sexual problems. The so-called Viagra revolution of the 1990s and the increase in other pharmacological treatments for sexual problems has led to concern that psychological methods of treatment would be rendered unnecessary (Rowland, 2007). However, a growing awareness of the limitations of pharmacological treatments administered on an individual basis has led to recognition that an integration of psychological and pharmacological methods, with emphasis on the couple, may be the most appropriate treatment model in most cases (Althof, 2006; Rosen, 2007). Moreover, as sexual problems are often secondary to other difficulties in the relationship or to mental health problems, psychological interventions are needed to address these problems.

Sexuality Teaching on Clinical Psychology Training Courses

A recent survey of sexuality teaching in UK clinical psychology courses (Shaw *et al.*, 2008) revealed that provision of teaching was patchy at best and there was little consistency across courses in the year of training and module that sexuality teaching was included. Post-qualification continuing professional development (CPD) on sexual health and HIV was also in very short supply, with only a few courses providing one-off workshops. Some of the reasons training courses gave for inadequate provision of sexuality teaching were difficulties finding psychologists with an adequate background/ experience who could provide this training, and problems fitting in this teaching into an already full curriculum. In my own experience, an additional problem is that many trainees perceive this area to be specialist despite the fact that sexual health issues and relationships are central to the lives of most of us and that sexuality issues may arise when working in any clinical setting or with any client group.

There are now guidelines available to assist training courses in planning and delivering teaching on sexual health. The Good Practice Guidelines for the Training and Consolidation of Clinical Psychology Practice in HIV/Sexual Health settings (British Psychological Society, 2006) sets out a list of minimum training competencies needed to work in sexual health/HIV settings. These competencies are related to the DCP accreditation standards for training courses (British Psychological Society, 2002b) and Agenda for Change Knowledge and Skills dimensions and levels (British Psychological Society, 2005). The Department of Health (2006) has issued core training standards for sexual orientation and also more generic quality standards for sexual health training (Department of Health, 2005). It is to be hoped that these detailed guidelines will be used to develop more comprehensive teaching on sexual health in UK training courses.

Ethical and Professional Issues

As sexuality is a sensitive topic for most people, psychologists working in this area need to be particularly mindful about issues related to confidentiality and disclosure. It is also crucial to be aware that stigma and discrimination often contribute to psychological problems, particularly in relation to HIV and within sexual minority groups.

Similarly, when assessing individuals or couples with sexual problems it is important to assure them that the information they provide will be treated as highly confidential. When assessing a couple, and seeing each partner separately, it is necessary to establish whether each individual agrees to any information not known by the other being shared during the joint sessions (e.g. details of previous sexual relationships). If a course of treatment or further assessment is offered, the individual or couple should be fully informed about what is involved before being asked to make their decision. Therapists also need to have an understanding of working with difference – cultural, sexual, age and disability (British Psychological Society, 2006). When working with an individual or a couple from a different culture from the therapist, there should be awareness, openness and discussion about contrasting values of cultural or religious origin. In this way differences can be negotiated, rather than have therapist values imposed.

Research and Future Directions

Clinical psychologists have an important role in conducting research on sexual health/ HIV and have already made valuable contributions in many areas. However, many gaps remain; in particular, there is an urgent need for outcome research on sex therapy, including studies that identify predictors of successful outcomes. There is clearly scope for further development of clinical psychology within sexual health/HIV services. Clinical psychology services should be made available in all sexual health and HIV settings, and it is important that clinical psychologists engage in indirect work such as consultation, training, and research as well as direct clinical work (British Psychological Society, 2002a). Lastly, there is a clear need to expand the teaching on sexual health provided to clinical psychology trainees.

References

Ajzen, I. & Fishbein, M. (1980). *Understanding attitudes and predicting social behavior*. Englewood Cliffs, NJ: Prentice-Hall.

Althof, S. (2006). Sexual therapy in the age of pharmacotherapy. *Annual Review of Sex Research, 17*, 116–131.

Angst, J. (1998). Sexual problems in healthy and depressed persons. *International Clinical Psychopharmacology, 13* (Suppl. 6), S1–4.

Bancroft, J. (2008, in press). *Human sexuality and its problems* (3rd edn). Oxford: Elsevier.

Bancroft, J., Janssen, E., Strong, D., Carnes, L., Vukadinovic, Z. & Long, J.S. (2003). The relation between mood and sexuality in heterosexual men. *Archives of Sexual Behavior, 32*, 217–230.

Bergeron, S., Binik, Y.M., Khalifé, S., Pagidas, K., Glazer, H.I., Meana, M. *et al.* (2001). A randomized comparison of group cognitive-behavioral therapy, surface electromyographic biofeedback, and vestibulectomy in the treatment of dyspareunia resulting from vulvar vestibulitis. *Pain, 91*, 297–306.

British Psychological Society (2002a). DCP Briefing Paper No. 17. *Clinical psychology services in HIV and sexual health.* Leicester: Author.

British Psychological Society (2002b). DCP TSG: *Criteria for the accreditation of postgraduate programmes in clinical psychology.* Leicester: Author.

British Psychological Society (2005). *BPS/Amicus family of psychology: Lifelong learning and the knowledge and skills framework for applied psychology.* Leicester: Author.

British Psychological Society (2006). *Good practice guidelines for the training and consolidation of clinical psychology practice in HIV/sexual health settings.* Leicester: Author.

Catania, J.A., Kegeles, S.M. & Coates, T.J. (1990). Towards an understanding of risk behavior: An AIDS Risk Reduction Model (ARRM). *Health Education and Behavior, 17,* 53–72.

Ciesla, J.A. & Roberts, J.E. (2001). Meta-analysis of the relationship between HIV infection and risk for depressive disorders. *American Journal of Psychiatry, 158,* 725–730.

Daker-White, G. (2002). Reliable and valid self-report outcome measures in sexual (dys)function: A systematic review. *Archives of Sexual Behavior, 31,* 197–209.

Department of Health (2001). *The national strategy for sexual health and HIV.* London: Author.

Department of Health (2005). *Recommended quality standards for sexual health training.* London: Author.

Department of Health (2006). *Core training standards for sexual orientation: Making National Health Services inclusive for LGB people.* London: Author.

Faculty of HIV and Sexual Health (2004). *Survey of clinical psychologists working in sexual health settings.* Leicester: British Psychological Society.

Fry, R.P., Crisp, A.J. & Beard, R.W. (1997). Sociopsychological factors in chronic pelvic pain. *Journal of Psychosomatic Research, 42,* 1–15.

Graham, C.A. & Bancroft, J. (2008, in press). The sexual dysfunctions. In M. Gelder, J. Lopez-Ibor, N. Andreasen & J. Geddes (Eds.) *New Oxford textbook of psychiatry* (2nd edn). Oxford: Oxford University Press.

Hawton, K. (1985). *Sex therapy: A practical guide.* Oxford: Oxford University Press.

Heiman, J.R. & Meston, C.M. (1997). Empirically validated treatment for sexual dysfunction. *Annual Review of Sex Research, 7,* 148–94.

Kaplan, H.S. (1975). *The new sex therapy.* London: Bailliere Tindall.

Koss, M.P., Koss, P.G. & Woodruff, W.J. (1991). Deleterious effects of criminal victimization on women's health and medical utilization. *Archives of International Medicine, 151,* 342–347.

Laumann, E.O., Paik, A. & Rosen, R.C. (1999). Sexual dysfunction in the United States. *Journal of the American Medical Association, 281,* 537–544.

Lykins, A., Janssen, E. & Graham, C.A. (2006). The relationship between negative mood and sexuality in heterosexual college women. *The Journal of Sex Research, 43,* 136–143.

Masters, W.H. & Johnson, V.E. (1970). *Human sexual inadequacy.* Boston: Little Brown.

Mercer, C.H., Fenton, K.A., Johnson, A.M., Wellings, K., Macdowall, W., McManus, S. *et al.* (2003). Sexual function problems and help seeking behaviour in Britain: National probability sample survey. *British Medical Journal, 327,* 426–427.

Miller, D. (1986). The worried well. In D. Miller, J. Weber & J. Green (Eds.) *The management of AIDS patients* (pp. 169–174). London: Macmillan Press.

Miller, D. & Green, J. (2001). The meaning of the psychology of sexual health. In D. Miller & J. Green (Eds.) *The psychology of sexual health* (pp. 3–7). Oxford: Blackwell Science.

Mills, T.C., Paul, J., Stall, R., Pollack, L., Canchola, J., Chang, Y.J. *et al.* (2005). Distress and depression in men who have sex with men: The Urban Men's Health Study. *American Journal of Psychiatry, 161,* 278–285.

O'Carney, O., Ross, E., Bunker, C., Ikkos, G. & Mindel, A. (1994). A prospective study of the psychological impact on patients with a first episode of genital herpes. *Genitourinary Medicine, 70,* 40–45.

Pridal, C.G. & LoPiccolo, J. (2000). Multielement treatment of desire disorders: Integration of cognitive, behavioural, and systemic therapy. In S.R. Leiblum & R.C. Rosen (Eds.) *Principles and practice of sex therapy* (3rd edn, pp.57–81). New York: Guilford Press.

Richardson, P.H., Doherty, I., Wolfe, C., Carman, N., Chamberlain, F., Holtom, R. *et al.* (1997). Evaluation of cognitive behavioural counselling for the distress associated with an abnormal cervical smear result. *British Journal of Health Psychology, 29,* 327–337.

Rosen R.C. (2007). Erectile dysfunction: Integration of medical and psychological approaches. In S.R. Leiblum (Ed.) *Principles and practice of sex therapy* (4th edn, pp. 277–312). New York: Guilford Press.

Rowland, D.L. (2007). Will medical solutions to sexual problems make sexological care and science obsolete? *Journal of Sex and Marital Therapy, 33,* 385–397.

Shaw, E., Butler, C. & Marriott, C. (2008, in press). *Sex and sexuality teaching in UK clinical psychology courses. Clinical Psychology Forum.*

Trudel, G., Marchand, A., Ravart, M., Aubin, S., Turgeon, L. & Fortier, P. (2001). The effect of a cognitive-behavioral group treatment program on hypoactive sexual desire in women. *Sexual and Relationship Therapy, 16,* 145–64.

US Department of Health and Human Services (2001). *The Surgeon General's call to action to promote sexual health and responsible sexual behavior.* Rockville, MD: Author.

Van Lankveld, J.D.M., ter Kuile, M.M., de Groot, H.E., Melles, R., Nefs, J. & Zandbergen, M. (2006). Cognitive-behavioral therapy for women with lifelong vaginismus: A randomized waiting-list controlled trial of efficacy. *Journal of Consulting and Clinical Psychology, 74,* 168–78.

West, S.L., Vinikoor, L.C. & Zolnoun, D. (2004). A systematic review of the literature on female sexual dysfunction: Prevalence and predictors. *Annual Review of Sex Research, 15,* 40–172.

World Health Organisation. (2002). *Gender and reproductive rights, glossary, sexual health.* Retrieved 20 October 2007 from www.who.int/reproductive-health/gender/glossary.html

Part III

Professional Practice

28

Supervision

Helen Beinart and Sue Clohessy

Introduction

Clinical supervision is the key part of the training of mental health professionals that contributes to the development of therapeutic competence and professional identity (Watkins, 1997). Indeed, Roth and Fonagy (2005) see it as an 'essential pre-requisite for the practice of psychotherapy' (p. 373). Clinical supervision forms a substantial part of the professional training of clinical psychologists and is seen as having an important quality control function both during and after training (Department of Health, 2001). In Britain, a minimum of 50 per cent of the three-year clinical psychology training must be spent in supervised clinical practice, the remainder being spent on academic work and research. (British Psychological Society (BPS), Division of Clinical Psychology (DCP), 2007). The current BPS minimum standard required for clinical supervision during clinical psychology training is one hour formal supervision and three hours informal contact per week. It will be of interest to see if this standard remains or is altered as the Health Professions Council (HPC) takes over the professional quality assurance and statutory registration of all applied psychologists in the next few years.

Post-qualification, clinical supervision is also seen as a necessary requirement for maintaining quality standards and is embedded in the professional practice guidelines of the Division of Clinical Psychology (British Psychological Society, 1995; Policy Guidelines on Supervision – British Psychological Society, 2003). All clinical psychologists, regardless of their seniority, are expected to have at least monthly clinical supervision. For more experienced practitioners this may take the form of peer or group supervision, whereas for those newly qualified or in training it will normally take the form of individual, one to one, meetings. The precise standards for other applied psychologists and health professionals may vary but it is generally accepted that formal supervision is essential to clinical governance and professional development. Professional registration with the HPC may well result in more consistency while still maintaining high quality standards in this important area.

Much has been written about clinical supervision in Britain in the form of practitioner guides (e.g. Scaife, 2001) and model development (e.g. Gilbert & Evans, 2000); however, until recently most of the supervision research has been conducted in the USA in the fields of counselling, counselling psychology and psychotherapy. The existing literature is clearly relevant and applicable but, due to differences in healthcare delivery systems, may not generalise easily. Nevertheless there is a growing body of research on clinical supervision in Britain which is beginning to investigate the supervision of clinical psychologists (Green, 1998; Milne & James, 1999, 2000; Beinart, 2002; Palomo, 2004; Frost, 2004; Clohessy, 2008).

What Is Clinical Supervision?

Supervision literally means to 'oversee', although there is a range of definitions in the literature (e.g. Bernard & Goodyear, 2004). Milne (2007) provides an operational definition: 'the formal provision, by approved supervisors, of a relationship-based education and training that is case-focused and which manages, supports, develops and evaluates the work of junior colleagues' (p. 440). The emphasis on the supervisory relationship, the educational endeavour, the importance of enhancing the service to clients by improving supervisee competence, and the evaluative and gate-keeping functions are all key elements of the definition of supervision. Holloway and Wolleat (1994) suggest that the goal of clinical supervision is to connect theory and practice. Supervisors thus need to have access to multiple knowledge bases, which may include clinical, ethical, theoretical, research, service, supervision as well as knowledge about supervisee needs (personal and training course related) and development. Competent supervisors understand the connections between these knowledge bases and apply them to both service and supervisee needs.

Supervision is thus among the most complex of all activities associated with the practice of clinical psychology. It is also one of the most difficult to research because of the multiple layers of professional activity involved. This complexity in understanding and defining supervision has been reflected in the research literature which will be discussed later. This chapter will explore clinical supervision in detail by discussing the functions and forms that supervision may take, theoretical models, the evidence base, and current best/effective practice, based on our understanding to date.

Numerous functions, tasks and modes of supervision have been identified in the literature, and vary according to a number of factors, including the professional role of supervisor and supervisee (e.g. qualified clinical psychologist and trainee clinical psychologist), level of experience of the supervisee, and the theoretical model used.

Functions of Supervision

Supervision serves a number of purposes. Inskipp and Proctor (1993) suggest the importance of formative, normative and restorative functions. Formative supervision focuses on the learning needs of the supervisee. The normative function of supervision refers to the ethical responsibility the supervisor has towards client welfare, and for those supervising trainees, there is an important gate-keeping role for the profession. The restorative function of supervision focuses on the emotional consequences of the clinical work for the supervisee. Holloway's Systems Approach to Supervision model (SAS) (Holloway, 1995) describes five functions of supervision. Monitoring/evaluation involves making judgements about a supervisee's performance and competence, and may involve formal evaluation procedures if the supervisee is in a training role. Monitoring the supervisee's conduct and ensuring ethical and competent practice has been suggested to be the most important task for the supervisor (Falender & Shafranske, 2004). Instructing/advising involves the supervisor providing information to the supervisee through suggestions and advice. Modelling professional behaviour and good practice is another important function of supervision, and consulting involves the supervisor exploring the opinions of the supervisee to encourage a problem-solving approach to clinical work. Finally, the supporting/sharing function of supervision involves the supervisor empathising, supporting, encouraging and constructively confronting the supervisee about important issues (Holloway, 1995).

Tasks of Supervision

Numerous tasks of supervision have also been identified. For example, Carroll (1996) suggests that there are seven tasks. Since supervision is relationship based, and (as will be discussed later) the supervisory relationship is vital for effective supervision to take place, an important first task is establishing the relationship. Additional tasks proposed by Carroll are those related to teaching and learning, counselling, monitoring and evaluation, and consultation and administration. Another important task is the development of the supervisory contract. This can be defined as an agreement between the supervisor and supervisee about 'the requirements of their agency contexts, timing and frequency of contacts with each other, supervisory role-relationships and the purpose and process of supervision' (Scaife, 2001, p. 52). The contracting process should be ongoing and regularly reviewed, in case supervisees' learning needs or supervisor circumstances change. Clarity about expectations and needs of the supervisee, supervisor and service context (and the training institution if the supervisee is still in training) is important (Scaife, 2001); clarity and rigour in contracting can help to promote good-quality supervisory relationships (Beinart, 2004; Lawton & Feltham, 2000).

   Holloway (1995) highlights five tasks in supervision. Learning and the development of skills in a number of areas are important, such as counselling skills (including establishment of therapeutic relationships); case conceptualisation/formulation (the links between theory and practice); professional role (including the ability to work ethically, develop appropriate professional relationships with colleagues, and participate in the supervisory relationship); emotional awareness (particularly of the emotional effects of the work carried out, and reactions to supervision); and finally self-evaluation (recognising one's own limitations and ongoing learning needs). Holloway suggests that the tasks and functions of supervision are interrelated. The interaction of deciding what to teach (task) and how to teach it (function) is described by Holloway as the process of supervision.

Modes of Supervision

There are a number of methods or modes that can be used in supervision to facilitate learning, and these again will be influenced by factors such as the supervisor's theoretical model and preferences (Scaife, 2001) as well as the learning needs of the supervisee. Observation of clinical work either through live supervision (for example using a one-way screen), or via recorded sessions, either video or audio-tapes, can be useful media for learning. However, Scaife (2001) notes that live observation can generate anxiety in supervisees and although recording sessions can be less intrusive, there are issues of consent and confidentiality to be considered. Reporting clinical material and session content is perhaps the most popular method used in supervision, although there may be limitations to relying completely on retrospective recall, as well as the possibility that important issues may not be raised in supervision because they are too sensitive (Scaife, 2001). A safe supervisory relationship seems important here. There is evidence to suggest that supervisees with unsatisfactory supervisory relationships are less likely to disclose, (Ladany *et al.*, 1996) which has important implications for the supervisor's role in safe-guarding the client and enhancing the professional competence of the supervisee. Finally, role-play provides an opportunity to practise or demonstrate particular skills within the safe setting of supervision (Scaife, 2001).

Models of Supervision

Models of supervision can be divided into two broad categories: those based on psychotherapy theories and those developed specifically for supervision. Early supervision models were direct extensions of psychotherapy theories. The earliest of these were based on psychodynamic theories, for example Ekstein and Wallerstein (1972). However, Bernard and Goodyear (2004) argue that while there are some similarities between supervision and therapy, there are substantial drawbacks to using therapy models for conceptualising supervision. As supervision differs from therapy, therapeutic models have proved too narrow to explain the complexity of supervision and have possibly restricted the evidence base by offering few directions for research and practice. Supervision is fundamentally an educational process which facilitates the learning of professional role (Scaife & Scaife, 2001; Holloway & Poulin, 1995). Models of adult learning, such as Kolb's Experiential Learning Model (1984), which stresses the importance of a learning cycle involving experience, experimentation, reflection and observation, and the application of theory or concepts, may be more helpful in understanding this process. Schön (1983) suggests that professional training draws on two different realms of knowledge: theory and research that forms the basis of an academic programme (technical knowledge); and knowledge derived from practitioner experience (reflective practice).

The recent growth of the therapy professions has led to an increasing emphasis on practitioner-led supervisor training, and much of the writing on supervision, particularly in the UK, reflects the realm of knowledge based on practitioner experience (e.g. Proctor, 1997; Scaife, 2001). The need for models to help train novice professionals has led to a shift from therapy-based models to the development of generic or supervision-specific models. The majority of therapeutic schools have developed their own supervision models and the reader is referred to Watkins (1997) for detailed discussion of therapy-specific models of supervision. The focus in this chapter is on the main transtheoretical or generic models that have been specifically developed to explain the complex phenomenon of supervision itself. These can be divided broadly into the developmental models (e.g. Stoltenberg *et al.*, 1998) and social role (or task and function) models (e.g. Bernard, 1979; Carroll, 1996). Recently, more integrative models have been developed which, although complex and hence challenging to test, provide more sophisticated accounts of supervision which attend both to the supervisory relationship and to the context in which supervision takes place (e.g. Holloway, 1995; Hawkins & Shohet, 2004).

Developmental models

Developmental models attempt to explain the complex transition from inexperienced supervisee to experienced clinician (Whiting *et al.*, 2001). Most developmental models share the fundamental assumptions that supervisees develop through a series of different stages on their journey towards competence and that supervisors need to adjust their supervisory style and approach to match the supervisee's level of development. For example, Stoltenberg *et al.* (1998) developed the Integrated Developmental Model (IDM) of supervision, which proposes three overriding structures (emotional and cognitive awareness of self and others, motivation, and autonomy) to monitor supervisee development across various aspects of clinical training and practice (intervention, assessment, client conceptualisation, individual differences, theoretical orientation, treatment goals and plans, and professional ethics). Each phase of development is characterised by particular learning needs. Level-one supervisees are described as anxious, highly motivated, self-focused and dependent on their supervisors for advice and guidance. Level-two supervisees have acquired sufficient skills and knowledge to focus less on themselves and to increase their focus on the client, however, motivation and autonomy vary. Level-three supervisees develop the ability to appropriately balance the client's perspective whilst maintaining self-awareness. Motivation stabilises as the supervisee begins to function relatively autonomously. In addition to addressing supervisee developmental needs, the IDM also identifies different tasks for supervisors at each development level. At level one the supervisor provides structure and encourages the early development of autonomy and appropriate risk taking. The supervisor's tasks include containing anxiety and providing a role model. At level two the supervisor provides less structure and encourages more autonomy. Tasks include clarifying trainee ambivalence, modelling and providing a more facilitative and less didactic focus. At level three the supervisor focuses more on personal/professional integration. The supervisor's task is to ensure consistency in performance across domains, identify any deficits, and work towards integration and refining a professional identity. Such developmental models are attractive as they appeal intuitively; however, there has been little longitudinal research to test their veracity. Nonetheless, there is some sound evidence for the need for direction and structure at an early phase of learning and increasing autonomy as supervisees mature (Borders, 1990).

Social role models

Several models of supervision include the tasks and functions (role) of the supervisor, for example Friedlander and Ward (1984), Williams (1995) and Carroll (1996). The most comprehensive of these models, the Discrimination Model, was developed by Bernard (1979) and developed in later texts (Bernard, 1997; Bernard & Goodyear, 2004). The Discrimination Model assumes flexibility on the part of the supervisor to respond to specific supervisee needs. There are two axes (roles and foci) within the model consisting of three basic supervisor roles (therapist, teacher and consultant) and three basic foci of supervision (process, conceptualisation and personalisation). Using this model there is thus a matrix of nine choices for supervisor intervention. Bernard (1997) describes the Discrimination model as a-theoretical and can be used across any model of therapy. At any one time the supervisor may take the role of therapist, teacher or consultant in order to support the development of process skills (therapy techniques such as engagement and interviewing), personalisation (managing the client's and therapist's feelings) and conceptualisation (theory–practice links involved in formulation). The emphasis between foci is likely to vary according to the theoretical orientation of the supervisor and the supervisee's level of development. For example, supervisors of beginning supervisees are likely to focus more on process skills such as interviewing whereas supervisors of more experienced supervisees are likely to focus on self-reflection (personalisation) and refining formulations (conceptualisation).

Integrative models

The Systems Approach to Supervision (SAS) model was developed as a dynamic model capable of assisting supervisors in a systematic assessment of supervisee learning needs, and supervision teaching interventions (Holloway & Neufeldt, 1995). Holloway's (1995) model builds on the social role models but sees the supervisory relationship as central and takes into account a range of contextual factors. The contextual factors include the client, the supervisee, the supervisor and the institution. It is proposed that the dimensions or components of the model (relationship, client, supervisee, supervisor, institution, tasks and function) are part of a dynamic process in that they mutually influence one another (hence, systems approach). The SAS model addresses the complexity of supervision and provides a map for analysing a particular episode of supervision in terms of: (a) the nature of the task; (b) the function the supervisor is performing; (c) the nature of the relationship; and (d) the contextual factors relevant to the process.

Holloway (1995) has identified three elements within the relationship: (a) the interpersonal structure of the relationship, including the dimensions of power and involvement; (b) three phases of the relationship (beginning, middle and terminating) referring to the development of the relationship specific to the participants; and (c) the supervisory contract which includes establishing a set of expectations regarding the tasks and functions of supervision (discussed in an earlier section).

According to Holloway's model, the supervisory relationship and the tasks and functions of supervision are also influenced by contextual factors related to the supervisor (experience, expectations, theoretical orientation, culture); the client (personal/cultural characteristics, identified problem, relationship); the supervisee (experience, theoretical orientation, learning style/needs, culture); and the institution (organisational structure and climate, professional ethics and standards). Much of this model is grounded in social influence theory which has some evidence base, but the complete model has not been tested partly due a lack of appropriate measures and complexity regarding outcomes.

The Process Model of Supervision developed by Hawkins and Shohet (2004) is another integrative model which combines relational and contextual factors as well as the tasks and functions of supervision. Sometimes known as the seven-eyed supervisor, the model presents seven possible foci during supervision. These include focus on: the client or content of a therapy session; therapeutic strategies or interventions; the therapeutic relationship or process; the therapist's emotional reactions or countertransference; the supervisory relationship and any parallels with the therapeutic relationship (parallel process); the impact on the supervisor or the supervisor's countertransference; and the overall organisational and social context (which may include professional ethics and codes). Hawkins and Shohet also emphasise contracting and educational, supportive and managerial tasks of the supervisor. This is a popular model within the UK but has had little empirical investigation.

As will be discussed in the next section, research in this area has been criticised because it is often not theory driven, hence there is limited support for the models of supervision discussed above. Aspects of some of the models have received some empirical support (for example, the need for structure early on in professional development, which loans some support to developmental models), but unfortunately there have been few longitudinal studies to fully test this. There is some agreement that supervisors take on different social roles during supervision depending on the task to be achieved, for example teaching when a new or unfamiliar technique is required by the supervisee. However, by far the strongest and growing evidence base lies with the importance of the supervisory relationship itself, and this will be discussed in more detail in a later section.

Evidence Base for the Effectiveness of Supervision

What constitutes effective supervision and how should this be assessed? The research literature on supervision is extensive, but has been criticised on methodological grounds (e.g. Ellis *et al.*, 1996). The reader is referred to reviews of the supervision literature for a full discussion of these issues (e.g. Ellis *et al.*, 1996; Holloway & Neufeldt, 1995; Spence *et al.*, 2001; Wheeler & Richards, 2007). In summary, these criticisms include small sample sizes, inadequate statistical power, lack of comparison groups (Ellis *et al.*, 1996), use of analogue situations and student trainees (which limits the generalisability of results), use of measures with poor reliability and validity, and reliance on single sources of outcome information (Spence *et al.*, 2001).

Nonetheless, Milne and James (2000) carried out a systematic review of the impact of supervision and consultancy (supervision to the supervisor). The focus of this review was on change processes in the 'educational pyramid' (i.e. from consultant to supervisor, supervisor to supervisee, and supervisee to clients). They found a number of studies that suggested the educational pyramid was beneficial to clients. Goal setting and the provision of feedback, modelling competence and giving clear instructions to supervisees were the dominant methods used in the studies reviewed, and were associated with benefits to supervisees. However, the majority of studies were from the learning disability field and thus may not be generalisable to other areas.

Effective supervision can be reflected in a number of ways such as positive client change (Ellis & Ladany, 1997), supervisees' developing skill, changes in behaviour in therapy (Wampold & Holloway, 1997), supervisee self-efficacy (Ladany *et al.*, 1999; Wheeler & Richards, 2007) or supervisee self-report on the quality and impact of supervision (Lehrman-Waterman & Ladany, 2001). However, attributing change in these areas to supervision, and effectively measuring such changes, is complex (Wampold & Holloway, 1997).

Client change

Few studies have looked at the impact of supervision on client outcome. Steinhelber *et al.* (1984) found that client attendance at therapy sessions was significantly related to the amount of supervision received, and that clients made significantly greater improvement when there was congruence between their therapist's theoretical orientation and that of the therapist's supervisor. Dodenhoff (1981) found that supervisors' use of direct instructions in supervision, such as giving an opinion, constructive feedback and providing information, was positively related to trainee effectiveness and client outcome as rated by the supervisor. However, supervisors' rating of client outcome differed from other ratings (e.g. that of the supervisee). In perhaps the most comprehensive supervision outcome study to date, Bambling and colleagues looked at the influence of clinical supervision on client working alliance and symptom reduction in the treatment of depression (Bambling *et al.*, 2006). Clients were randomly assigned to either a supervised or unsupervised therapist and received eight sessions of problem-solving treatment (Mynors-Wallis & Gath, 1997). Therapists in the supervised groups were randomly assigned to either eight sessions of alliance process-focused (with the emphasis on the therapists' sensitivity to the therapeutic relationship) or alliance skill-focused supervision (with an emphasis on the development of therapeutic skills thought to enhance the alliance). All therapists in the supervised groups had a pre-treatment meeting in which the supervision model was discussed, emphasising early alliance management and specific client characteristics and history. Results showed significant effects for both supervised groups. Clients had lower scores on the Beck Depression Inventory, were more satisfied with treatment, had higher scores on the Working Alliance Inventory (WAI) and were more likely to complete treatment than clients who had unsupervised therapists. Interestingly, there were no differences between alliance process- or alliance skill-focused supervision groups, so it is difficult to specify the mechanism by which supervision influenced treatment outcome. The authors also noted that the pre-treatment supervision meeting had an important impact: clients in the supervised groups had much higher WAI scores by the end of the first treatment session, and this remained consistent throughout treatment, making it difficult to separate out the impact of the pre-treatment supervision session from the regular supervision sessions. Further criticisms of the study include the possibility of positive expectancy and increased motivation of therapists receiving supervision, and that the principal researcher in the study conducted a proportion of the supervision in the study.

Development of supervisee competence and skill

A number of studies have looked at the impact of supervision on the competence and skill development of the supervisee. Worthen and McNeill (1996) found that supervision had an impact on conceptualisation and intervention skills. Raichelson *et al.* (1997) in their qualitative study on parallel process (the mirroring of the therapeutic relationship within the supervisory relationship) found that supervisees developed more self-awareness in their work with clients, particularly in discussion of transference and countertransference issues. Borders (1990) reviewed supervisees' perceptions of their own development, and found that they perceived themselves as applying their skills and knowledge more consistently as a result of supervision. Beck (1986) found that therapists who did not receive supervision following training in cognitive therapy showed a deterioration in skills compared with pre-training levels.

Supervisee self-report

There has been a great deal of research on what supervisees report that they value and need in supervision. Tracey *et al.* (1989) found that neophyte therapists preferred more direction and structure than more experienced therapists. However, in the face of a clinical crisis, more structured supervision was preferred across all experience levels. Trustworthiness of the supervisor has been identified as a quality rated highly by supervisees (e.g. Carey *et al.*, 1988). In a UK qualitative study of trainee clinical psychologists (Green 1998), characteristics such as special knowledge, credibility and integrity were identified by trainees as typifying influential supervisors. Green likened these characteristics to trustworthiness. Spence *et al.* (2001) summarised the research in this area, and highlighted characteristics such as empathy, enthusiasm, availability, flexibility, negotiating a supervision contract, focusing on specific examples of clinical activities and specific skills to be learned, and providing constructive feedback. In a study of UK clinical psychology trainees, effective aspects of supervision and supervisors were categorised as support, confidence, being respectful and valuing, including elements of monitoring and teaching, being attentive to practicalities, and having a dialogue about supervision (Hitchen *et al.*, 1997). Spence *et al.* (2001) summarised the literature on the qualities of supervision which are negatively regarded by supervisees. These include vague and unclear guidance or feedback, unrealistic goals, avoidance of challenging issues, being overly critical, inattentive and not respecting supervision boundaries.

Therapist self-efficacy

Self-efficacy (Bandura, 1977) refers to an individual's confidence and belief in their own ability, and has been demonstrated to influence how much people use a particular skill. Some researchers have highlighted this concept as a potential important outcome of supervision. Larson *et al.* (1992) found that use of role play in supervision was superior to reviewing videotapes of counselling skills in increasing supervisee self-efficacy. Efstation *et al.* (1990) in their development of the Supervisory Working Alliance Inventory found that rapport with supervisor, attractiveness of supervisor and task-centred supervision were significantly correlated with supervisee self-efficacy. Lehrman-Waterman and Ladany (2001) in developing the Evaluation Process within Supervision Inventory (EPSI) found that effective evaluation practices were associated with stronger perception of supervisor influence and self-efficacy.

The Supervisory Relationship

Although there have been difficulties in defining and measuring effective supervision in the literature, there has been increasing acknowledgement that the supervisory relationship (SR) is crucial to successful supervision (e.g. Ellis & Ladany, 1997; Beinart, 2004). It has been suggested that just as therapeutic outcome is closely related to the therapeutic relationship (e.g. Norcross, 2002), supervision outcome may also be related to the quality of the SR (Ladany *et al.*, 1999). According to some authors (e.g. Pistole & Watkins, 1995), the supervisory relationship has the potential to incorporate elements of other important relationships, and therefore can elicit attachment responses. Supervisors can function as a secure, safe base in the supervisory relationship from which supervisees can explore and develop their skills and professional identity. Pistole and Watkins (1995) suggest that an attachment bond can sometimes form between supervisor and supervisee, or elements of attachment relationships (such as safety and security) can be reflected within the SR. Attachment initially involves close monitoring and involvement of the supervisor in the SR, particularly at the beginning of the relationship. As the supervisee develops in skill and confidence, Pistole and Watkins (1995) suggest that they need less close involvement and monitoring in the SR. They suggest (similarly to the application of attachment theory in therapeutic relationships; Holmes, 1998) that supervisors can establish a secure supervisory base by being available and consistent, responsive, sensitive to needs and flexible, and in so doing can enhance the supervisee's learning. Watkins (1995) further suggests that most supervisees have attachment styles which are fundamentally secure in nature, even if there may be anxious, ambivalent or avoidant elements within those styles. However, sometimes insecure attachment processes can be triggered in the supervisory relationship despite the supervisors' best efforts at providing a safe and supportive environment. If the supervisee has a negative attachment style, this not only has implications for the SR, but potentially also for the supervisee's therapeutic relationships with clients. Neswald-McCalip (2001) described a number of supervisory scenarios in which attachment processes may operate. For example, she describes supervisees with secure attachment as having a working model of others as reliable and consistent, and as such they will be more likely to ask for help from their supervisor. Bennett and Vitale Saks (2006) suggest that those with secure attachments are able to ask for help, accept feedback and explore and reflect on new learning experiences. Neswald-McCalip also described scenarios with supervisees with anxious-resistant and anxious-avoidant attachment. Anxious-resistant attachment involves an internal working model of others as unreliable, which may mean that the supervisee is dependent on attachment figures and fearful when confronted with a crisis. Bennett and Vitale Saks suggest that these supervisees are unable to acknowledge their own competence and minimise their achievements. Neswald-McCalip emphasises the importance of the supervisor establishing clear boundaries and being available in these instances. In anxious-avoidant attachment, there is an internal working model of others as being unavailable when help is needed, and Neswald-McCalip suggests that these supervisees may behave autonomously in situations, whether or not they have the appropriate skills to manage. Bennett and Vitale Saks (2006) suggest that supervisees with this attachment style function too autonomously, deny the need for supervision and minimise their mistakes and insecurities.

Although a number of authors have focused on the attachment style of the supervisee, recent research suggests that it may be the supervisor's capacity for healthy attachment relationships which is important in the SR. For example, White and Queener (2003) investigated the individual characteristics of both supervisor and supervisee which predict the supervisory working alliance, in 67 US supervisory dyads. They found that the supervisor's ability to make adult attachments and social support was predictive of both the supervisor's and supervisee's perceptions of the working alliance. Interestingly, the supervisee's ability to make attachments and social support did not predict supervisor or supervisee perceptions of the working alliance at a significant level, although the authors reported that the effect sizes were large. It is important to note that there are limitations to this study in terms of generalisability. The authors also note that causal inferences cannot be made with regard to the ability to make attachments and access social support, and how the working alliance is perceived.

What constitutes a good supervisory relationship? Many of the characteristics of 'good supervision' reported by supervisees described above also describe qualities of the SR. A number of studies have looked at the characteristics of the SR in some detail. In a study of UK trainee and recently qualified clinical psychologists, Beinart (2002) found that satisfaction with supervision, rapport, and support discriminated between effective and ineffective SRs. A qualitative aspect of the study, using grounded theory analysis, found that qualities seen as 'necessary' for a safe framework within which the relationship could develop included 'boundaried, supportive, open, respectful and committed'. The presence of these qualities facilitated the process of the SR, which was then characterised as being sensitive to needs, collaborative, educative and evaluative. Palomo (2004) used Beinart's findings to develop a measure of the SR and identified that 'safe base', 'commitment' and 'structure' reflected the facilitative aspects of the relationship, while 'reflective education', 'role model' and 'formative feedback' reflected the educative and evaluative functions of supervision.

In a grounded theory study, Clohessy (2008) explored supervisors' perspectives on their SRs with trainee clinical psychologists and identified three categories as important in the quality of the relationship: contextual influences, the flow of supervision and core relational factors. Contextual influences on the development of the relationship included the team/service in which the SR took place, the presence of the training course, and the individual factors which the supervisor and trainee bring to the relationship (such as, for example, gender, ethnicity, prior experience of supervision). The flow of supervision reflects supervisor and trainee contributions to the process of supervision. Supervisor contributions were summarised as 'investing in the SR', and included ensuring a good beginning to the SR by planning ahead for the trainee, spending time together, establishing boundaries and expectations, encouraging learning and responding to individual needs. Trainee contributions to the flow of supervision were summarised as 'being open to learning' and included being enthusiastic and committed, adopting a proactive stance and being productive. The more open to learning the trainee appeared to be, the more the supervisor invested in the relationship. Finally, the core relational factors identified in the study were the interpersonal connection between the supervisor and trainee, the emotional tone or atmosphere of the relationship, and the degree of safety, trust, openness and honesty in the SR. The findings suggest a reciprocal relationship between these core relational factors and the flow of supervision. Although the best SRs described seemed to be characterised by positive characteristics in the three core categories identified, it seemed that SRs only needed to be 'good enough' to work effectively.

The research discussed above supports other findings in the field. Falender and Shafranske (2004), in their summary of the literature in this area, suggest that a good SR consists of facilitating attitudes, behaviours and practices including, for example, a sense of teamwork (Henderson *et al.*, 1999), empathy (Worthen & McNeill, 1996), approachability and attentiveness (Henderson *et al.*, 1999), encouragement of disclosures by supervisees (Ladany *et al.*, 1996), and supervisors' sensitivity to the developmental level of the supervisee (e.g. Magnuson *et al.*, 2000).

Effective Practice in Clinical Supervision

Having reviewed the extensive and somewhat confusing literature on the roles, modes, models and evidence base for clinical supervision, can we draw any conclusions which may contribute to good practice?

It is an exciting time in the development of this area, and we are beginning to see a confluence of practitioner knowledge and experience with a growing evidence base in the UK, to the extent that we can begin to make recommendations for best practice. Primarily, the establishment of a safe SR seems to be paramount and has been described by various authors as a safe base or a boundaried space. One of the ways of achieving a safe SR is by careful and clear contracting to allow the development of a relationship which supports 'collaboration for change' (Bordin, 1983). This should include a discussion about mutual expectations and responsibilities in supervision, as well as the content of learning, the expected outcomes or competencies, and how these will be evaluated. One of the ways of establishing and maintaining a strong SR is through overall modelling of ethical and respectful relationships with supervisee, clients and colleagues which is greatly enhanced by mutual observation.

The expectation of mutual, regular, honest, open feedback and constructive criticism also aids the process of supervision. Given the power dynamic inherent in the SR, it is the supervisor's responsibility to regularly invite and encourage feedback from the supervisee to ensure that their needs are being met. This is particularly pertinent in situations where cultural or gender issues may add to the inherent power imbalance. However, the supervisor also has a quality control function and has a responsibility to observe, directly or via recording, the supervisee's work and to provide detailed feedback, often best done through encouraging self-assessment and reflection (Falender & Shafranska, 2004). Providing support which encourages supervisee confidence and autonomy is important and needs to be tailored to the supervisee's learning needs. Supervisors also need to be available, adaptable and flexible in their supervision style, which should include openness and flexibility in approach and model. Collaborative thinking and building joint formulations which value the supervisee's and supervisor's knowledge and insights is important, as is playfulness with ideas and creativity (Beinart, 2004). Comfort with raising and discussing difficult issues, in a way which is safe and containing, allows both parties to learn from mistakes and work together to resolve the conflicts or miscommunications which inevitably occur in the majority of relationships. Overall, an atmosphere where both supervisor and supervisee are committed to and invested in the process of supervision and communicate this to one another is helpful, as is a commitment to ethical, values-based practice, which itself models both evidence-based and reflective practice, where both parties can mutually learn.

Conclusion

This chapter has provided the reader with an overview of the clinical supervision literature to date with an emphasis on clinical psychology in the UK. We have attempted to distil, from a range of sources, key theoretical models, as well as exploring some of the tasks and functions of supervision. We have discussed the complexity of outcomes in this area and provided some of the research relating to different types of outcomes which demonstrates both the complexity and infancy of the field. We have suggested that the quality of the supervisory relationship is key to good outcomes. Finally, we have identified themes for best practice and positively encourage practitioners and researchers to continue to develop this critical area of applied psychology.

References

Bambling, M., King, R., Raue, P., Schweitzer, R. & Lambert, W. (2006). Clinical supervision: Its influence on client-rated working alliance and client symptom reduction in the brief treatment of major depression. *Psychotherapy Research, 16*(3), 317–331.

Bandura, A. (1977). Self-efficacy: Toward a unifying theory of behavioural change. *Psychological Review, 84,* 191–215.

Beck, A.T. (1986). Cognitive therapy: A sign of retrogression or progress. *Behaviour Therapist, 9,* 2–3.

Beinart, H. (2002). *An exploration of the factors which predict the quality of the relationship in clinical supervision.* Unpublished D.Clin. Psych. dissertation, Open University/British Psychological Society.

Beinart, H. (2004). Models of supervision and the supervisory relationship and their evidence base. In I. Fleming & L. Steen (Eds.) *Supervision in clinical psychology* (pp. 36–50). Hove: Brunner Routledge.

Bennett, S. & Vitale Saks, L. (2006). A conceptual application of attachment theory and research to social work student–field instructor supervisory relationships. *Journal of Social Work Education, 42*(3), 669–682.

Bernard, J.M. (1979). Supervisor training: A discrimination model. *Counselor Education and Supervision, 19,* 60–68.

Bernard, J.M. (1997). The discrimination model. In C.E. Watkins (Ed.) *Handbook of psychotherapy supervision* (pp. 310–327). New York: Wiley.

Bernard, J.M. & Goodyear, R.K. (2004). *Fundamentals of clinical supervision* (3rd edn). Boston: Allyn & Bacon.

Borders, L.D. (1990). Developmental changes during supervisees' first practicum. *The Clinical Supervisor, 8,* 157–167.

Bordin, E.S. (1983). A working alliance model of supervision. *Counseling Psychologist, 11,* 35–42.

British Psychological Society (1995). *Professional practice guidelines.* Division of Clinical Psychology. Leicester: Author.

British Psychological Society (2003). *Policy guidelines on supervision in the practice of clinical psychology.* Division of Clinical Psychology. Leicester: Author.

British Psychological Society, Membership and Professional Training Board (2002 & 2007). *Criteria for the accreditation of postgraduate training programmes in clinical psychology.* Committee on Training in Clinical Psychology. Leicester: Author.

Carey, J.C., Williams, K.S. & Wells, M. (1988). Relationships between dimensions of supervisors' influence and counselor trainees' performance. *Counselor Education and Supervision, 28,* 130–139.

Carroll, M. (1996). *Counselling supervision: Theory, skills and practice.* London: Cassell.

Clohessy, S. (2008). *Supervisors' perspectives on their supervisory relationships: A qualitative study.* Unpublished PsyD thesis, University of Hull.

Department of Health (2001). *Placements in focus: Guidance for education in practice for health care professions.* London: English National Board for Nursing, Midwifery and Health Visiting and Department of Health Publications Section.

Dodenhoff, J. (1981). Interpersonal attraction and direct–indirect supervisor influence as predictors of counselor trainee effectiveness. *Journal of Counseling Psychology, 28,* 47–53.

Efstation, J.F., Patton, M.J. & Kardash, C.M. (1990). Measuring the working alliance in counselor supervision. *Journal of Counseling Psychology, 37,* 322–329.

Ekstein, R. & Wallerstein, R.S. (1972). *The teaching and learning of psychotherapy* (2nd edn). New York: International Universities Press.

Ellis, M.V. & Ladany, N. (1997). Inferences concerning supervisees and clients in clinical supervision: An integrative review. In C.E. Watkins (Ed.) *Handbook of psychotherapy supervision* (pp. 447–507). New York: Wiley.

Ellis, M.V., Ladany, N., Krengel, M. & Schult, D. (1996). Clinical supervision research from 1981 to 1993: A methodological critique. *Journal of Counselling Psychology, 43,* 35–50.

Falender, C. & Shafranske, E. (2004). *Clinical supervision: A competency-based approach.* Washington, DC: American Psychological Association.

Friedlander, M.L. & Ward, L.G. (1984). Development and validation of the Supervisory Styles Inventory. *Journal of Counseling Psychology, 31,* 541–557.

Frost, K. (2004). *A longitudinal exploration of the supervisory relationship: A qualitative study.* Unpublished D.Clin. Psych. dissertation, University of Oxford.

Gilbert, M.C. & Evans, K. (2000). *Psychotherapy supervision: An integrative relational approach to psychotherapy supervision.* Buckingham: Open University Press.

Green, D.R. (1998). *Investigating the core skills of clinical supervision: A qualitative analysis.* Unpublished D.Clin. Psych. dissertation, University of Leeds.

Hawkins, P. & Shohet, R. (2004). *Supervision in the helping professions.* Buckingham: Open University Press.

Henderson, C.E., Cawyer, C., Stringer, C.E. & Watkins, C.E. (1999). A comparison of student and supervisor perceptions of effective practicum supervision. *Clinical Supervisor, 18*(1), 47–74.

Hitchen, J., Gurney-Smith, B. & King, C. (1997). 'Perspectives on supervision. Opening the dialogue': A workshop for supervisors run by trainees. *Clinical Psychology Forum, 109,* 21–25.

Holloway, E.L. (1995). *Clinical supervision: A systems approach.* Thousand Oaks, CA: Sage.

Holloway, E.L. & Neufeldt, S.A. (1995). Supervision: Its contribution to treatment efficacy. *Journal of Consulting and Clinical Psychology, 63,* 207–213.

Holloway, E.L. & Poulin, K. (1995). Discourse in supervision. In J. Siegfried (Ed.) *Therapeutic and everyday discourse on behaviour change: Towards a microanalysis in psychotherapy process research* (pp. 245–273). New York: Ablex.

Holloway, E.L. & Wolleat, P.L. (1994). Supervision: The pragmatics of empowerment. *Journal of Education and Psychological Consultation, 5,* 23–43.

Holmes, J. (1998). *John Bowlby and attachment theory.* London: Routledge.

Inskipp, F. & Proctor, B (1993). *The art, craft and tasks of counselling supervision, Part 1. Making the most of supervision.* Twickenham: Cascade publications.

Kolb, D. (1984). Experiential learning: *Experience as the source of learning and development.* Englewood Cliffs, NJ: Prentice-Hall.

Ladany, N., Ellis, M.V. & Friedlander, M.L. (1999). The supervisory working alliance, trainee self-efficacy and satisfaction. *Journal of Counseling and Development, 77,* 447–455.

Ladany, N., Hill C., Corbett, M. & Nutt, E. (1996). Nature, extent and importance of what psychotherapy trainees do not disclose to their supervisors. *Journal of Counseling Psychology, 43,* 10–24.

Larson, L.M., Suzuki, L.A., Gillespie, K.N., Potenza, M.T., Bechtel, M.A. & Toulouse, A.L (1992). Development and validation of the counseling self-estimate inventory. *Journal of Counseling Psychology, 39,* 105–120.

Lawton, B. & Feltham, C. (2000). *Taking supervision forward: Enquiries and trends in counselling and Psychotherapy.* London: Sage.

Lehrman-Waterman, D. & Ladany, N. (2001). Development and validation of the evaluation process within supervision inventory. *Journal of Counseling Psychology, 48,* 2, 168–177.

Magnuson, S., Wilcoxon, S.E. & Norem, K. (2000). A profile of lousy supervision: Experienced counselors' perspectives. *Counselor Education and Supervision, 39*(3), 189–203.

Milne, D. (2007). An empirical definition of clinical supervision. *British Journal of Clinical Psychology, 46*(4), 437–447.

Milne, D.L. & James, I. (1999). Evidence-based clinical supervision: Review and guidelines. *Clinical Psychology Forum, 133,* 32–36.

Milne, D.L. & James, I. (2000). A systematic review of effective cognitive-behavioural supervision. *British Journal of Clinical Psychology, 39,* 111–127.

Mynors-Wallis, L. & Gath, D. (1997). Predictors of treatment outcome for major depression in primary care. *Psychological Medicine, 27,* 731–736.

Neswald-McCalip, R. (2001). Development of the secure counselor: Case examples supporting Pistole & Watkins's (1995) discussion of attachment theory in counseling supervision. *Counselor Education and Supervision, 41*(1), 18–27.

Norcross, J.C. (Ed.) (2002). *Psychotherapy relationships that work. Therapist contributions and responsiveness to patients.* Oxford: Oxford University Press.

Palomo, M.(2004). *Development and validation of a questionnaire measure of the supervisory relationship (SRQ).* Unpublished D. Clin. Psych. dissertation, University of Oxford.

Pistole, M.C. & Watkins, C.E. (1995). Attachment theory, counseling process, and supervision. *The Counseling Psychologist, 23*(3), 457–478.

Proctor, B. (1997). Contracting in supervision. In C. Sills (Ed.) *Contracts in counselling* (pp. 190–206). London: Sage.

Raichelson, S.H., Herron, W, Primavera, L.H. & Ramirez, S.M. (1997). Incidence and effects of parallel process in psychotherapy. *The Clinical Supervisor, 15*(2), 37–48.

Roth, A. & Fonagy, P. (2005). *What works for whom: A critical review of psychotherapy research.* New York: Guilford Press.

Scaife, J. (2001). *Supervision in the mental health professions: A practitioner's guide.* Hove: Brunner-Routledge.

Scaife, J. & Scaife, J. (2001). Supervision and learning. In *Supervision in the mental health professions: A practitioner's guide* (pp. 30–51). Hove: Brunner-Routledge.

Schön, D.A. (1983). *The reflective practitioner: How professionals think in action.* New York: Basic Books.

Spence, S.H., Wilson, J., Kavanagh, D., Strong, J. & Worrall, L. (2001). Clinical supervision in four mental health professions: A review of the evidence. *Behaviour Change, 18*(3), 135–155.

Steinhelber, J., Patterson, V., Cliffe, K. & LeGoullon, M. (1984). An investigation of some relationships between psychotherapy supervision and patient change. *Journal of Clinical Psychology, 40*(3), 1346–1353.

Stoltenberg, C., McNeill, B. & Delworth, U. (1998). *IDM supervision: An integrated developmental model for supervising counselors and therapists.* San Francisco: Jossey-Bass.

Tracey, T.J., Ellikson, J.L. & Sherry, D. (1989). Reactance in relation to different supervisory environments and counsellor development. *Journal of Counseling Psychology, 36,* 336–344.

Wampold, B. & Holloway, E. (1997). Methodology, design and evaluation in psychotherapy supervision research. In C.E. Watkins (Ed.) *Handbook of psychotherapy supervision* (pp. 11–30). New York: Wiley.

Watkins, C.E. (1995). Pathological attachment styles in psychotherapy supervision. *Psychotherapy, 32*(2), 333–340.

Watkins, C.E. (Ed.) (1997). *Handbook of psychotherapy supervision*. New York: Wiley.

Wheeler, S. & Richards, K. (2007). The impact of clinical supervision on counsellors and therapists, their practice and their clients: A systematic review of the literature. *Counselling and Psychotherapy Research*, *7*, 54–65.

White, V.E. & Queener, J. (2003). Supervisor and supervisee attachments and social provisions related to the supervisory working alliance. *Counselor Education and Supervision*, *42*, 203–218.

Whiting, P.P., Bradley, L.J. & Planny, K.J. (2001). Supervision-based developmental models of counselor supervision. In L.J. Bradley & N. Ladany (Eds.) *Counselor supervision: Principles, process and practice* (pp. 125–146). Philadelphia: Brunner-Routledge.

Williams, A. (1995). *Visual and active supervision: Roles, focus, technique*. New York: W.W. Norton.

Worthen, V. & McNeill, B.W. (1996). A phenomenological investigation of 'good' supervision events. *Journal of Counseling Psychology*, *43*, 25–34.

29

Clinical Psychology as a Profession

Development, Organisation and Dilemmas

Graham Turpin and Susan Llewelyn

Introduction

This chapter will identify some of the key issues that have faced, and are facing, the profession of clinical psychology, both historically and currently. The chapter largely concerns the UK, including its devolved legislatures, and in particular the National Health Service (NHS), which has recently celebrated its 60th anniversary. The past 60 years is also the duration over which the profession of clinical psychology has developed in the UK, which has in many respects mirrored the NHS's form and structure. Indeed, it is probably realistic to say that where clinical psychology in the UK positions itself in the future will be determined in large part by organisational and political decisions regarding the future of the NHS and the rest of the public sector. This link to socially funded provision will not pertain so closely in other parts of the world, although public sector funding is likely to be significant in most legislatures and, as such, it is hoped that aspects of this chapter may also apply more widely. The discussion will open with a brief historical review of policy initiatives associated with service organisation and developments in clinical psychology training and workforce, extracting some of the key issues with which the profession has struggled over the years. This will be followed by an overview of the current policy landscape of the NHS where the key challenges facing the profession in the present and future will be identified, and by a consideration of how the profession and the British Psychological Society (BPS)'s Division of Clinical Psychology (DCP) in particular has positioned itself in order to meet these challenges. Finally, some possible future challenges and directions will be identified.

One preliminary observation at least from the UK experience is the seemingly constant change which has characterised both the profession and its organisational backdrop. Anyone who has worked as a psychologist within Britain's NHS during the past three to four decades can attest to the impact of continuous reorganisation. The 1970s saw the emergence of the profession of clinical psychology based around district services, to be followed in the 1980s by the demise of district and regional health authorities and the move to local service provision and autonomy in the form of general practitioner (GP) fund-holding and NHS trusts, and the consequent fragmentation of many district psychology services. Following this in the 1990s there was increased central control and command in the form of the national service frameworks, prioritised targets and implementation plans, which then gave way in the new century to local health communities, foundation trusts and practice-based commissioning. The impact of all these macro-organisational changes, together with other external drivers, on the development of the profession of clinical psychology, and how these professional and policy initiatives filter down to the jobs and roles of practising psychologists, will constitute some of the issues that this chapter seeks to explore.

Sixty Years of Clinical Psychology

The beginnings

How do you date a profession? Is it from the establishment of its first training course, or the first professional to be awarded a national honour, or perhaps the first to be disciplined by a regulatory body? Irrespective of the criterion, clinical psychology is relatively young. As noted in Chapter 1, applied psychology within the UK originally developed from child services and education prior to the Second World War, and then, as a consequence of the number of psychological casualties of the war suffering from trauma and brain damage, many academic psychologists were drawn into applied practice within the newly formed NHS. For clinical psychology, these forays into the real world took the form of psychologists employing their assessment and psychometric skills, usually working for psychiatrists within the old long-stay mental hospitals. Assessments were directed at cognitive and intellectual functioning, including intelligence, diagnostic and personality testing, together with attempts at rehabilitation, education and retraining.

A significant step was the establishment of a diploma in clinical psychology at the Institute of Psychiatry by Monte Shapiro, which lasted 13 months, and consisted of almost 300 hours of teaching, of which 96 were for testing, 60 for statistics, 43 for personality and clinical seminars, 22 for adult psychiatry, and 20 for child psychiatry and education (Shapiro, 1955). Psychological interventions or psychotherapy *per se* did not specifically feature within the curriculum. There was also provision for students to undertake a further 2 years of research training in order to achieve a PhD. Many of those who did so went on to establish post-graduate clinical psychology training courses at major universities throughout the UK, some of the earliest being Birmingham, Edinburgh, Leeds and Manchester. By 1960 there were 500 clinical psychologists employed within the NHS; some trained within the university sector whereas others were psychological technicians trained under supervision within the NHS. About this time the BPS also started to establish formal requirements for education and training.

The Trethowan Report

From the 1960s onwards the profession slowly expanded into a number of different clinical specialities, primarily associated with child and adult mental health services. During this time, psychology as an academic discipline received growing attention, with psychologists such as Eysenck promoting psychology both as a popular science and as a potential source of interventions (Eysenck, 1953, 1960) that could rival both psychiatry and psychotherapy in clinical effectiveness. Its presence as an emerging applied discipline also began to gain recognition, such that the Department of Health commissioned a review of psychology services (Trethowan, 1977), representing a watershed in the profession's development and parallel existence within the NHS. The Trethowan Report recognised the potential benefits of psychology to the health service generally, but suggested that it could not realise its potential due a major shortfall in workforce supply or 'manpower' (sic). In 1973 there were only 585 psychologists in post, and Trethowan calculated that a conservative estimate of need for a local district health authority would be for around 1 psychologist per 30 to 60 thousand of the population. The report also predicted a target of 1,100 psychologists in post by the end of the decade. This would require a doubling of the profession in two years, which was partly to be obtained by creating more psychology assistant posts. (Doubling the workforce and the size of the psychology graduate population are themes that would recur on a number of future occasions.) Another major focus was that many client groups had no access whatsoever to psychological services: this included people with learning disability, older people and sometimes children. Rather than seeing psychology develop in a piecemeal fashion, with psychologists working opportunistically into different services largely under the control of local psychiatrists, Trethowan suggested the establishment of local district psychology services, based upon a recognised career and salary structure.

Manpower planning – MAS and MPAG Reports

Following Trethowan, there was a decade of gradual expansion whereby local district psychology services and a range of different specialisms were introduced, together with a recognised career structure. However, although training had been expanding with the establishment of new MSc university courses, together with the development of in-service diploma training courses now accredited by the BPS, overall training numbers were insufficient to achieve the targets set for expansion. Two major reviews of the profession were therefore conducted at the end of the 1980s. The first was an independent review (Management Advisory Service, 1989) conducted by Mowbray, an occupational psychologist, which examined the role of clinical psychology services within the NHS and made three important observations. First, psychological provision was not the unique responsibility of clinical psychologists within the NHS and any future policy surrounding the delivery of psychological services would also need to factor in other healthcare professionals. Second, psychological interventions could be delivered across a range of levels, from general healthcare practice, whereby staff should be informed by psychological principles, to specific protocol-based techniques taught by psychologists and delivered by non-psychologists, to the provision of individualised interventions based on the application of psychological theory and expertise by qualified psychologists. These were referred to as MAS levels 1 to 3 and have been highly influential in helping to define psychologists' roles both within and outside the profession. Mowbray's final observation was that clinical psychology was no longer the single business of psychiatry, and that clinical psychology had much to offer health care generally; in particular to physical health and long-term chronic conditions.

The second report, the MPAG report (Manpower Planning Advisory Group, 1990), examined 'manpower planning' (sic) which might underpin the implementation of such recommendations. This first real attempt at workforce planning revealed staff shortages across the board and particularly in areas such as learning disabilities and services for older people. Moreover, the report estimated that the demand would grow exponentially across ensuing decades. Although real expansion didn't really reveal itself until a decade later in 2000, the case for this had now been firmly established.

Meeting health service demand

There were several reasons as to why the recommended expansion didn't happen immediately. First, there was a change of government and NHS policy such that many district psychology services were fragmented by the introduction of more autonomous NHS trusts, so that many psychologists contributed individually to services, and were often managed by non-psychologists. This in turn impacted negatively on service organisation and coherence, resulting in diffuse management and accountability structures, together with a downturn in the supply of clinical supervisors to oversee clinical psychology training provision on placement. Second, major changes were taking place within NHS education and training generally, and specifically within clinical psychology. The BPS accreditation criteria had been revised in 1989 and required trainees to obtain three years' clinical experience on clinical placements in at least services for adults, children, people with learning disabilities and older people, reflecting the greater range of interventions and clients identified in the MAS report. At the same time there was convergence of the three-year in-service NHS training courses and the two-year University courses. This followed yet another NHS reorganisation which saw the demise of the large regional health authorities which had organised the in-service training courses and a policy shift whereby all NHS education and training was fully economically costed and moved into Higher Education. The taught practitioner doctoral qualification emerged following recognition that award of a masters degree for a three-year training programme was inconsistent with masters awards in other subjects. Loosely based on the Psy.D programmes developed in the USA, this rapidly became accepted as the norm, such that by 1995 all UK courses became clinical doctorates with enhanced research training requirements.

Not all of these changes were necessarily welcomed by services or commissioners of training, since although newly qualified psychologists were better prepared for more extended roles across a wider number of client groups, the duration and costs of training had been increased by around 50 per cent. This remains a somewhat contested issue (see below). Nevertheless, a joint Department of Health/BPS options appraisal then recommended greater investment within clinical psychology training which saw more than a doubling of training places from around 200 to over 500 places in the next decade (British Psychological Society, 1997, 1996). This expansion process continued with the introduction of more effective and robust workforce planning mechanisms within the NHS, which has resulted in around 600 places being commissioned in 2008.

Clinical Psychology in the Present

Psychologists today inhabit a professional context that has been shaped by the gradually growing influence within the NHS and society in general of both psychological thinking and scientifically based psychological research. There is now general consensus that NHS interventions and practice must be based on good evidence, that services should be subject to clinical governance and be as socially inclusive as possible, and that the views of the service user, family or carer should be considered in clinical decision making (Department of Health, 1999). All of these developments are entirely consistent with the practices and values of most psychologists, and at least some of them have been directly supported by psychological research and thinking. This does not mean, however, that most services are as yet psychologically well informed or resourced, if only because of low numbers of psychologists. Some services, particularly those for older people, physically and learning disabled people, children and those with chronic conditions, employ relatively few psychologists, while others remain medically dominated (British Psychological Society/Department of Health, 2005). There is still an enormous amount to do in being able to influence the ways in which the NHS operates, to ensure that the psychological perspective is embedded in health care. Nonetheless, the rhetoric regarding the need for evidence-based practice, for socially inclusive practice, for good quality research in health care, and for user and carer involvement provides a potentially good environment for the influence of clinical psychologists in services. Having said that, some of the old dilemmas can still be found in the present, and these will now be outlined.

Professional identities

The profession is still struggling with its identity and how it is understood or compared with other professions. As outlined above and elsewhere (Hall *et al.*, 2003), there has been a shift from psychometrician to therapist to consultant or leader, who is able to intervene across a variety of different levels, contexts and therapeutic modalities. A key role has also been that of researcher, who is able to contribute both in the evaluation of services and in the development of novel approaches to treatment or understanding of clinical problems. Interestingly, the Department of Health (DoH) have treated psychologists variably at different times as synonymous with medical staff, clinical scientists and allied health professions. It is noteworthy, and worrying, that the recent Darzi report on the NHS workforce has failed to locate psychology within any of these groups (Darzi, 2008). Simultaneously there has been a process of differentiation within applied psychology in the UK, including the development of counselling, health, sports and exercise, and coaching psychologists, raising the question as to how applied psychologists can be distinguished. This question has been tackled by the BPS, albeit with little consequence, through various projects including National Vocational Standards (Skills for Health, 2006) and National Occupational Standards (ENTO, 2007). The issue of unique competency has come to the fore again due to the statutory regulation of applied psychologists by the Health Professions Council (HPC). The BPS's professional accreditation process has always played a key part in defining identity (see Chapter 2), so it is not yet clear what the impact of HPC regulation will be on developing or diminishing clinical psychology's sense of its own particular uniqueness, and how (or if) the different branches of applied psychology will maintain their own separate identities.

As clinical psychology has developed as a profession, the goodness of fit within a more closely managed NHS has sometimes caused some discomfort. The breadth of role, extending from therapist to researcher, through to organisational consultant, working with clients across the age range and with both physical and psychological health needs, together with an ability to draw on a range of different psychological and psychotherapeutic models, ought to be seen as a unique strength. However, there is also the danger that in comparison with other professions who have perhaps more narrow and specific job roles, with accompanying trainings and accreditations, psychologists can be seen as 'Jacks (and Jills) of all trades and masters of none'. Moreover, the prevalent workforce model within the NHS is currently not to recruit or plan by profession, but to specify the clinical competences, or skills mix, of staff required to deliver a particular care pathway designed to meet the individual needs of patients or service users (National Institute for Mental Health in England & Sainsbury Centre for Mental Health, 2004). This service philosophy is best illustrated by the New Ways of Working projects (New Ways of Working, 2005, 2007a, 2007b; Department of Health, 2007a) as well as initiatives around Improving Access to Psychological Therapies (IAPT) (Department of Health, 2007b; Turpin et al., 2006; Care Services Improvement Partnership, 2007), discussed further below, which have specified therapeutic competencies associated with psychotherapy for adults of working age, and more specifically with cognitive behaviour therapy (CBT) (Department of Health, 2004b, 2007c; Roth & Pilling, 2007). A key requirement for the profession and also individual clinical psychologists, therefore, is to evidence which competences are reliably, routinely and, perhaps, uniquely delivered by clinical psychologists. Aspirational claims to competence by different professional groups no longer fit with a healthcare system that demands both evidenced practice (Sackett et al., 2000) and adherence to clinical guidelines (for example, National Institute for Health and Clinical Excellence, 2004a, 2004b), nor one where professions are regulated according to general standards of proficiency, such as through the HPC.

Capacity issues: demand and supply

While workforce numbers have obviously exceeded Trethowan's targets, and have in fact followed an exponential growth curve as estimated by MPAG, there are still insufficient clinical psychologists within the workforce. Annual recommendations to the strategic health authorities for training commissions have emphasised annual year-on-year increases of around 15 per cent. The reasons for this are continuing issues of vacancies and unfilled NHS posts, together with the recognition that many current DoH policy areas of service improvement also identify the need for additional psychological input. A series of workforce reports specific to applied psychology have been published (for example, Lavender & Paxton, 2004) together with accounts of other workforce models around the recent IAPT initiative (Turpin et al., 2006), all of which conclude that the demand for psychological services will always outstrip the government's investment in training An associated issue relates to the diversity of the workforce (Turpin & Fensom, 2004; Williams et al., 2006) and the ability of the NHS to field a psychology workforce which is able to engage meaningfully with the diversity within the UK's numerous communities.

Affordability, career grades and skill mix

The advent of a new century has also seen the introduction of a new salary structure for the NHS: Agenda for Change (Department of Health, 2004c). This model of remuneration means that rather than the individual (that is, their own qualifications, experience, competences) being assessed and rewarded, it is the post and the requirements of the job that are evaluated using a standardised assessment tool, supported by the Knowledge and Skills Framework (Department of Health, 2004d). This tool assesses the task difficulty and requirements of a particular job, throughout the NHS and across all professions, workers and levels of responsibility (except medical and dental staff), using a common set of dimensions and scales. Agenda for Change had a number of significant impacts, the most obvious one being that, with the exception of medical and dental staff, salaries within the NHS are transparent and can be read from one occupational group to the next. This raises questions about value for money and added value, when job roles based on a particular set of competencies (for example, a CBT therapist) are delivered by a range of professional groups (Skills for Health, 2006).

   Clinical psychology training is one of the few NHS training pathways outside medicine whereby trainees are employed, not bursaried. Hence Agenda for Change has also impacted on training, with pay increases for trainees and some NHS training staff. If comparisons are made between psychologists and undergraduate nurses or allied health professions, clinical psychology appears disproportionately costly. However, if retention both during training and following graduation is taken into account, then, in terms of the costs per retained year in the NHS, psychologists emerge as one of the most cost-efficient professional groups. Moreover, comparison with the costs of undergraduate and post-registration medical training up to the level of consultant also demonstrates good value for money (Lavender & Willis, 2007).

Despite such rational arguments in support of both training costs and the added value of qualified consultant psychologists, issues of affordability and cost containment (especially for newly and financially independent foundation trusts) mean that career and salary structures for psychologists are coming under closer scrutiny. One 'solution' has been redundancy, job re-grading, and reappointing/restructuring to lower, more economical grades. Such an approach, however, raises issues about suitable levels of experience and responsibility, including capacity to supervise within services. Moreover, the New Ways of Working for Applied Psychology reports (for example, Lavender & Hope, 2007) stress the leadership functions of psychologists and their ability to lead teams, and to use their skills to promote effective teamwork within the NHS and social care. This emphasis on leadership (and research skills) results partly from a recognition of the NHS's need to supplement or replace consultant psychiatrists (who are both costly and often hard to recruit and retain) but also from a recognition of the potential of psychologists to contribute as key players in the delivery of services. Clinical psychology is increasingly being thought of as a good source of thoughtful, able, user-focused and creative people, who can make a real difference to how services are delivered (see also Chapter 30 for further discussion of this issue).

A second approach, also consistent with New Ways of Working, concerns skills mix, both within the profession and also across all services delivering psychological therapies (Department of Health, 2007a). Within the profession, as in the 1970s, there is a debate about whether to establish a second tier of delivery by graduate psychologists working under the supervision of chartered clinical psychologists (originally suggested by Trethowan). Currently the large workforce of psychology assistants receives little formal training and has rather piecemeal and insecure posts and career prospects. Various proposals have been made about recognising them as a formal and budgeted component of the psychology workforce, with access to agreed frameworks of training and supervision. An alternative model is to create a psychology practitioner level between the untrained assistant and the chartered clinical psychologists, or clinical assistants. The various pros and cons of each these approaches have been discussed widely within the profession, and some models have been implemented, for example in Scotland and the north of England. If these models are developed further, a major challenge for the regulator (HPC) will be differentiation of two levels of psychology practitioner, and how the public will be able to distinguish between their different roles and competencies.

Future Challenges

Reading the future is hazardous, but it is nonetheless needed for effective strategic planning. A good place to start may be articulation of current challenges and strengths, which appear to have significant implications for the profession, and may offer a pointer to future opportunities for growth and influence.

Improving access to psychological therapy

Until very recently, psychological services have been patchy, with most people who have psychological needs being offered either medical care or no services at all (Layard, 2005). Yet equitable and timely access to evidence-based psychological therapies has the potential to improve radically the lives of many people: alleviating distress both in individuals and families, promoting well-being and understanding of mental health problems, reducing stigma, and supporting people in work or return to work. Although a limited number of counselling, psychotherapy and clinical psychology services have been available through the NHS for at least the past five decades, it is only relatively recently that these services have started to attract much attention (Parry, 2000). There are many reasons why access is now regarded as a priority, including demonstrated effectiveness through the publication of NICE guidelines (National Institute for Health and Clinical Excellence, 2004a, 2004b), patient choice in wanting greater access to talking therapies (Department of Health, 2001, 2004a, 2004b; Rankin, 2005; Sainsbury Centre for Mental Health, 2006), and recognition of socioeconomic benefits on individuals' well-being and the nation's wealth in the form of impact on disability and welfare benefits (Layard, 2005, 2006; Layard *et al.*, 2007). The relative costs of mental well-being and ill health on productivity in work and 'presentee-ism' have also been emphasised (Sainsbury Centre for Mental Health, 2007; Black Report, 2008) as exceeding the overall costs of disability and benefits.

As a consequence, in 2007 the UK government announced a major investment in the Improving Access to Psychological Therapies Programme (IAPT) of £30m in the first year, £100m in the second year and culminating in £170m in 2010/11 (Department of Health, 2007c). These IAPT services are provided by a range of professions, together with professionally non-aligned staff, particularly from the voluntary sector, and are located across a range of primary and secondary care services. They involve NHS and third sector providers, although it seems unlikely that any single model of service delivery will satisfy either the individual requirements of local health communities or their commissioners. Although such a plurality of providers might raise concerns about possible service fragmentation, these services will be commissioned through a strengthened NHS commissioning process as envisaged by the DoH World Class Commissioning (Department of Health, 2008). This will throw up particular challenges for psychology and psychological therapy services, since many are located within secondary care, whereas the focus of IAPT has been through primary care commissioning.

Another concern is that the focus of the new services (to provide CBT for anxiety and depression for adults of working age) is narrow given the context of the psychological needs of the population. Plans do exist, however, to extend these services across the lifespan in primary care, and to provide systemic, psychodynamic and other evidence-based therapeutic services. It will also be vital to provide easily accessible services to the many millions of people with chronic and comorbid healthcare conditions, those with learning or physical disabilities, and people within the forensic services. Clinical psychologists may be particularly well suited to work in this way with services in secondary or tertiary care, as well as to promote the values and principles of social inclusion.

Finally, concerns have been expressed about the feasibility of services being able to deliver effective psychological interventions using staff with relatively short training periods, using only one main theoretical model, and with a huge range of presenting issues (for example, John & Vetere, 2008; Gilbert, 2008; Holford, 2008). The success of this initiative will be very closely monitored. (See also Chapter 19.)

Career frameworks

Another challenge is for psychologists to regard the provision of psychological therapies as a multi-professional agenda and one that they do not own by right, but have to earn through clinical leadership, and by adding value. Currently there is no unified career framework for psychological therapists. Despite the impact of Agenda for Change and the current implementation of the Knowledge and Skills Framework (KSF), different psychological therapist practitioners are still represented by different job profiles, which tend to reflect their professional roles (e.g. nurse, psychologist), together with their specific job role within the workplace. Although the final outcome of Agenda for Change is not yet fully known, there are clear inconsistencies in banding between and within different psychotherapy practitioners. There are also a number of new groups of staff contributing to the delivery of psychological therapy services, including graduate workers, primary care mental health workers (PCMHWs) and self-help support workers whose role and future career pathways within the NHS is as yet unclear. The success of the PCMHWs has been limited by there being no clear career progression other than applying for clinical psychology training (Harkness *et al.*, 2005). Given the range of competencies and roles (i.e. expert therapist and supervisor to graduate worker) within the psychological therapies workforce, arguably it would be helpful for another clear career framework to be developed around the delivery of psychological therapies. This would obviously have an impact on the profession of clinical psychology.

NHS reforms, new roles and added value of applied psychology

If it is accepted that a range of professions can contribute to the delivery of psychological therapies, and that there may be a range of levels of intervention which can contribute to a psychological therapies service (for example, as part of a stepped care model; Bower & Gilbody, 2005), the issue of competition between psychology and other professions and the need to demonstrate value for money becomes even more important. The solution is probably the one which has provided the unique selling point of the profession in the past: that is, the capacity to work with a range of clients, using a range of psychological approaches, and at different organisational levels, and with well-developed research and audit skills. It will also be crucial for the profession to promote the additional contributions, beyond just offering therapy, that clinical psychologists can make to the delivery of psychological therapy services. This includes the ability to offer comprehensive assessments, question existing models, remain open to alternative ways of formulating both clinical and organisational assumptions, and provide both clinical and research supervision, training and consultation.

Service innovation

The new century has witnessed the proliferation of alternative forms of service provision, including the increasing importance of the voluntary sector, and ongoing attempts to integrate social and health care. Clinical psychologists have therefore had to adapt to, participate in, and lead new forms of service organisation and delivery. Important initiatives have included the emphasis on carer and service user input, increasing access for disadvantaged groups, and the recognition of the diverse nature of society, demanding a responsive range of services within an increasingly competitive workplace. How this is best to be achieved is hotly debated across the profession. Indeed, the DCP has recently reported on how clinical psychologists can market their services and unique contributions more effectively to commissioners (Division of Clinical Psychology, 2008). Other future challenges are likely to include the changing demographic profile of society, the importance of ever-changing healthcare technologies, and the growing psychological sophistication of healthcare users. Choosing the most appropriate form of delivery within which to offer clinical psychology services will demand the ability of clinical psychologists to use their range of competencies to the full, not least those of leadership and service evaluation.

Conclusion

Within 60 years, clinical psychology has had a major influence on the delivery of health care in the UK. Much of the research and policy development underlying the expansion of access to psychological therapies and services has been originated or conducted by clinical psychologists, the majority of whom work and practise within the NHS. These achievements are recognised internationally (DeAngelis, 2008) and should help consolidate the profession's confidence in moving forward to face and overcome the future challenges inherent in the delivery of psychological health care within the UK. To succeed, the profession needs to maintain its focus on evidence-based practice, to be able to innovate using knowledge gained from psychological science, to reflect on professional roles and functions, and to respect the needs of service users and the communities in which they live.

References

Black Report (2008). Practical implications. *Occupational Health*, 18 March.

Bower, P. & Gilbody, S. (2005). Stepped care in psychological therapies: Access, effectiveness and efficiency. National literature review. *British Journal of Psychiatry, 186,* 1–17.

British Psychological Society (1996). *Clinical psychology training: Meeting Health Service demand.* Leicester: Author.

British Psychological Society (1997). *Guidance for purchasers of clinical psychology training.* Leicester: Author.

British Psychological Society/Department of Health (2005). *English survey of applied psychologists in health and social care and in the probation and prison service*. Leicester: British Psychological Society.

Care Services Improvement Partnership (2007). *Good practice guide on the contribution of applied psychologists to improving access for psychological therapies*. Leicester: British Psychological Society.

Darzi Report (2008). *High quality care for all*. London: Department of Health.

DeAngelis, T. (2008). When do meds make the difference? *APA Monitor on Psychology, 39,* 48–51.

Department of Health (1999). *National service framework for mental Health: Modern standards and service models*. HSC 1999/223. London: Author.

Department of Health (2001). *Treatment choice in psychological therapies and counselling*. London: Author.

Department of Health (2004a). *The national service framework for mental health: Five years on*. London: Author.

Department of Health (2004b). *Organising and delivering psychological therapies*. London: Author.

Department of Health (2004c). *Agenda for Change*. Retrieved July 2008 from www.dh.gov.uk/en/ Managingyourorganisation/Humanresourcesandtraining/Modernisingpay/Agendaforchange/ index.htm

Department of Health (2004d). *Knowledge and skills framework*. London: Author.

Department of Health (2007a). *Mental health: New ways of working for everyone*. London: Author.

Department of Health (2007b). *Commissioning a brighter future: Improving access to psychological therapies. Positive practice guide*. London: Author.

Department of Health (2007c). *Johnson announces £170 million boost to mental health therapies*. Press release. London: Author. Retrieved October 2007 from www.gnn.gov.uk/environment/full Detail.asp?ReleaseID=321341&NewsAreaID=2&NavigatedFromDepartment=False

Department of Health (2008). *World class commissioning*. Retrieved November 2008 from www. dh.gov.uk/en/Policyandguidance/Organisationpolicy/Commissioning/Worldclasscommissioning/ index.htm

Division of Clinical Psychology (2008). Marketing Strategy. Leicester: British Psychological Society.

ENTO (2007). *National occupational standards for counselling*. Leicester: British Psychological Society.

Eysenck, H. (1953). *Uses and abuses of psychology*. Harmondsworth: Penguin.

Eysenck, H. (1960). *Behaviour therapy and the neuroses*. Oxford: Pergamon.

Gilbert, P. (2008). Improving access to psychological therapy: The Doncaster demonstration site organisational model: Commentary. *Clinical Psychology Forum, 181,* 17–21.

Hall, J., Lavender, T. & Llewelyn, S. (2003). A history of clinical psychology in Britain: Some impressions and reflections. *History and Philosophy of Psychology, 4,* 32–48.

Harkness, E., Bower, P., Gask, L. & Sibbald, B. (2005). Improving primary care mental health: Survey of evaluation of an innovative workforce development in England. *Primary Care Mental Health, 3,* 253–260.

Holford, E. (2008). Improving access to psychological therapy: The Doncaster demonstration site organisational model: Commentary. *Clinical Psychology Forum, 181,* 22–24.

John, M. & Vetere, A. (2008). It's important, and it's only one way of helping, and one way only. *Clinical Psychology Forum, 181,* 25–27.

Lavender, T. & Hope, R. (2007). *New ways of working for applied psychologists in health and social care: The end of the beginning.* Leicester: British Psychological Society.

Lavender, T. & Paxton, R. (2004). *Estimating the applied psychology demand in adult mental health.* Leicester: British Psychological Society.

Lavender, A. & Willis, R. (2007). Training and staff retention: National issues and findings from the South Thames clinical psychology training programme. *Clinical Psychology Forum, 180,* 38–45.

Layard, R. (2005). *The depression report: A new deal for depression and anxiety disorders.* London: London School of Economics Centre for Economic Performance and Mental Health Policy.

Layard, R. (2006). The case for psychological treatment centres. *British Medical Journal, 332,* 1030–1032.

Layard, R., Clark, D., Knapp, M. & Mayraz, G. (2007). Cost–benefit analysis of psychological therapy. *National Institute Economic Review, 202,* 90–98.

Management Advisory Service (1989). *Review of clinical psychology services and staffing.* London: Author.

Manpower Planning Advisory Group (1990). *Clinical psychology project report.* Cheltenham: Author.

National Institute for Health and Clinical Excellence (NICE) (2004a). *Clinical guideline 23: Depression: management of depression in primary and secondary care.* London: Author.

National Institute for Health and Clinical Excellence (NICE) (2004b). *Clinical guideline 22: Anxiety: management of anxiety (panic disorder, with or without agoraphobia, and generalised anxiety disorder) in adults in primary, secondary and community care.* London: Author.

National Institute for Mental Health in England & Sainsbury Centre for Mental Health (2004). *The ten shared capabilities: A framework for the whole of the mental health services.* London: Department of Health.

New Ways of Working in Mental Health (2005). *New ways of working for psychiatrists: Final report but not the end of the story!* London: Department of Health.

New Ways of Working in Mental Health (2007a). *Mental health: New ways of working for everyone.* London: Department of Health.

New Ways of Working in Mental Health (2007b). *New ways of working for applied psychologists in health and social care: The end of the beginning.* London: Department of Health.

Parry, G. (2000). Evidence based psychotherapy: Special case or special pleading? *Evidence Based Mental Health, 3,* 35–37.

Rankin, J. (2005). *Mental health in the mainstream: A good choice for mental health.* London: Institute of Public Policy Research.

Roth, A. & Pilling, S. (2007). *The competencies required to deliver effective cognitive and behavioural therapy for people with depression and anxiety disorders.* Leicester: British Psychological Society.

Sackett, D.L., Straus, S.E., Richardson, S.W., Rosenberg, W. & Haynes, R.B. (2000). *Evidence-based medicine: How to practise and teach EBM* (2nd edn). Edinburgh: Churchill Livingstone.

Sainsbury Centre for Mental Health (2006). *Choice in mental health.* Briefing Paper 31. London: Sainsbury's Centre.

Sainsbury Centre for Mental Health (2007). *Mental health at work: Developing the business case.* Policy Paper 8. London: Author.

Shapiro, M. (1955). Training of clinical psychologists. *Bulletin of the British Psychological Society, 34,* 9–19.

Skills for Health (2006). *Career framework for health: Validation process*. London: Author.

Trethowan, W.H. (1977). *The role of the clinical psychologist in health services*. London: HMSO.

Turpin, G. & Fensom, P. (2004). *Widening access within undergraduate psychology education and its implications for professional psychology*. Leicester: British Psychological Society.

Turpin, G., Hope, R., Duffy, R., Fossey, M. & Seward, J. (2006). Improving access to psychological therapies: Implications for the mental health workforce. *Journal of Mental Health Workforce Development, 1*, 12–21.

Williams, P.E., Turpin, G. & Hardy, G. (2006). Clinical psychology service provision and ethnic diversity within the UK: A review of the literature. *Clinical Psychology and Psychotherapy, 13*, 324–338.

30

Leadership, Teamwork and Consultancy in Clinical Psychology

Susan Llewelyn and Andrew Cuthbertson

This chapter introduces the role and activities of clinical psychologists working as leaders, team-workers and consultants. These aspects of clinical psychology practice are steadily gaining prominence, as clinical psychologists both choose, and are encouraged, to provide psychological resources within health and social care by working indirectly or in multidisciplinary teams, or as leaders. As argued elsewhere in this book, clinical psychology is still a small profession, so it risks lacking the political, numerical or cultural power to make a fundamental difference to health and social care for the vast majority of users of services, simply by implementing routine one-to-one clinical practice, no matter how high its quality. In the UK for instance, the NHS workforce is around 1.3 million, of whom only around 6000 are qualified clinical psychologists, meaning that the chances of any one patient ever meeting a clinical psychologist are very small indeed. So, to ensure that psychological perspectives inform health care more widely, psychologists need to work differently, and this chapter suggests some ways in which this may be achieved. First, leadership will be discussed, and then the particular role of psychologists in teams will be considered, concluding with a brief overview of consultancy approaches.

Leadership

What is leadership?

The term 'leadership' rapidly conjures up images of political figures such as Winston Churchill, Nelson Mandela or Ghandi, and quite reasonably most clinical psychologists do not consider that they could possibly emulate such figures, even if they wanted to do so. It is important, therefore, to see that leadership in health and social care contexts is something rather different, and that although leaders are people who are influential and often respected, they are not necessarily orators, demagogues or powerful public speakers who can persuade people into or out of challenging situations or beliefs. In fact, there are many ways of being a leader, and many contemporary theories of leadership emphasise the ability to work collaboratively with others, enabling them to achieve a shared valued objective (Kouzes & Posner, 2003). This is far more applicable to the healthcare context than a 'great man' (sic) theory which might be more familiar from the world of politics or international relations.

The literature on leadership is replete with definitions of the concept. The current collaborative emphasis informs the definition proposed by Yuki (2002), who defines leadership as 'the process of influencing others to understand and agree about what needs to be done and how it can be done effectively, and the process of facilitating individual and collective efforts to accomplish the shared objectives'. In contrast to the 'great man' concept, this view sees leadership as a process of influencing and facilitating, which is likely to be reasonably congruent with the approach of many clinical psychologists when working with teams or members of other professional disciplines. Likewise, according to Senge (1993), leadership 'is about tapping energy to create … it energises … and spawns higher levels of performance', which again sounds like the aspirations of many effective clinical psychologists when working with colleagues or trainees. A further, similar point made by Yuki (op. cit.) is that leadership is the business of 'influencing others to understand and agree about what needs to be done and how it can be done effectively'.

There have, however, been expressions of caution when considering the wide range of definitions available. Grint (2005), for example, notes '[d]espite over half a century of research into leadership, we appear to be no nearer a consensus as to its basic meaning, let alone whether it can be taught or its moral effects measured and predicted' (pp. 14–15). However, if, as Grint suggests, we accept that the concept of leadership is 'essentially contested', this gives us the freedom to 'consider how [any area of dispute] affects the way leadership is perceived, enacted, recruited and supported' in organisations, and thereby how such organisations 'promote individuals on the basis of one particular interpretation of leadership' (p. 17). This opens up opportunities for psychologists to provide leadership in helping organisations to re-evaluate and reconstruct their established ways of doing business, be that at a whole-system or subsystem level.

Given these points, leadership can be understood as being consistent with many of the competencies which characterise our profession rather than being an alien concept performed by others, with special inborn or claimed gifts. It can also be thought of as having three separate but linked dimensions. The first is a *creative* dimension, whereby a personal leadership style helps people make constructive sense out of their social worlds and any challenges they may encounter. The second is a *political* dimension concerned with valuing possible lines of action in specific contexts. The third is a *performative* dimension whereby individuals perform roles within organisations where leadership is defined and recognised in particular ways. Combining these dimensions, a psychologist who is taking a *creative* leadership role might encourage team members to respond constructively to a proposed reduction in funding or to a clinical crisis; taking a *political* stance, the psychologist might decide how best to argue for resources for a new service or to introduce a new treatment approach; while on the *performative* dimension, they might take appropriate actions to obtain these resources or facilitate the change of clinical direction.

Another example of how all these dimensions might be used simultaneously would be strategic planning undertaken by a senior psychologist aimed at enabling junior staff, including non-psychologists, to extend their therapeutic competencies in novel organisational or clinical environments. This could be achieved by deploying the psychological competencies of assessment and formulation with staff, demonstrating how psychological approaches can be applied, thereby broadening the psychological-mindedness of the workforce. In this way clinical psychologists can show leadership in a range of situations, including clinical team meetings, departmental meetings or community interventions, as well as in formal managerial settings. As pointed out by Russell (2001), this does not mean having 'too many chiefs', hampering inter-professional working, but is rather about influencing the delivery of health and social care in a psychologically informed direction.

Even in the early stages of their career, psychologists can, should and probably already do (although they may not label it as such) provide leadership. As part of the New Ways of Working initiative carried out by the British Psychological Society in association with the Department of Health in 2007 (British Psychological Society, 2007a), a profile of leadership qualities across the career ladder was developed, demonstrating how psychologists can act as leaders at all levels of their working lives. This document suggests that there are at least three types of leadership, namely strategic leadership, professional leadership and clinical leadership. The last of these is characterised as 'facilitating evidenced-based practice and improved patient outcomes through local care' (Millward & Bryan, 2005), and is thus the bread-and-butter work of most psychologists in teams. Necessary competencies include analytic thinking and interpersonal skills, plus 'knowing how to use the right styles in each situation' (Moiden, 2002), as well as being able to draw on the theories and knowledge of psychology as an academic and applied discipline, and to communicate these effectively to others.

Having said this, in practice most clinical psychologists begin to think seriously about themselves as possible leaders when they undertake more senior roles, as professional and strategic leaders, after several years of clinical practice. It is perhaps helpful here to distinguish management and leadership. In brief, current conceptions of these two domains suggest that managers reproduce and maintain existing systems, by following existing paths; they tend to focus on current demands, structures and processes, promote order and solve problems. By contrast, leaders innovate and develop services, challenge existing functions and set the direction, tending to focus on people, possibilities and potential; they motivate others to work towards a chosen direction and will often take risks, inspiring trust in followers (Clark, 2002). Leaders are inspired by values, whereas managers are motivated to meet targets. It is important to note that, in practice, these roles often coexist, and that leaders also establish and run structures, solve problems and address difficult issues while at the same time delegating where appropriate, and empowering others.

What do leaders in clinical psychology actually do?

Current mainstream conceptualisations of leadership draw primarily on the *transformational leader* model, which points to the interpersonal and influencing skills of leaders (Bennis, 1998; Denis *et al.*, 2000). This suggests that effective leadership involves psychological skills, including flexibility and responsiveness to circumstances, as well as the ability to engage and motivate others (Clegg, 2000; Outhwaite, 2003). Another current model is *authentic leadership*, which suggests that 'effective leaders operate by making the most of the qualities they already possess. They utilise their strengths and understand their weaknesses. Authentic leadership involves introspection and heightened self-awareness' (British Psychological Society, 2007a, p. 44). This model implies that leaders should have good judgement about themselves, others and the future. Appraisal of the environment is key, and a high level of organisational astuteness is crucial in practice: 'Leaders need to help others to see the big picture with the underlying trends, forces, and potential surprises. They need to think systemically and be able to foresee how internal and external factors might benefit or destroy the organisation. Patience and persistence is needed to decipher and analyse large amounts of complicated and sometimes contradictory information' (British Psychological Society, 2007a, p. 46). Effective leaders must have 'political' skills (that is, the ability to understand how decisions are made, an appreciation of hierarchies, sensitivities and conflict, and how to influence organisations), and to operate confidently, from an informed position, in their particular health or social care organisation.

Most psychologists are probably not initially attracted to the career because of the opportunity to develop and apply 'political' skills. Nonetheless, in order to develop services within modern health and social care, psychologists need to develop a degree of organisational competence. There are alternative ways of approaching the consideration of politics within organisations, and it is often a lack of clarity about which form is being referred to that deters psychologists from being involved in organisational leadership. Frequently, organisational politics is viewed from the perspective of how individuals can get things done their own way. This is a version of '*power in action*, worked out through the use of techniques of influence and other (more or less extreme) tactics' (Buchanan & Badham, 1999, p. 11, italics added). In this way, organisations are environments where individuals undertake political manoeuvres in order to achieve their own desired goals. In contrast, however, organisations can be viewed as systems, with embedded political structures and processes, in which it is possible to specify legitimate political choices that are open to individuals. This *political theory* approach (Heywood, 2004) provides a framework where psychologists (and others) can use their power over others legitimately and on the basis of recognised authority.

Psychologists as leaders need to become aware of the steps by which legitimate political competence and power can be achieved. Box 30.1 provides a simplified list of what this involves. Developing these skills takes time, effort and thought, and may be best developed through observation, discussion, mentoring and supervision from other more experienced leaders. The profession has until recently been rather slow to encourage the systematic development of leadership (although there are some notable

Box 30.1

- Identify the significant power holders in the system
- Understand their position in relation to your own, particularly with regard to your own legitimacy
- Work out how your plans or vision fits in with their position
- Anticipate problems in introducing your ideas
- Work out how your ideas can be developed to help the power holders also to deliver your objectives as well as their own
- Find allies and create networks
- Plan your tactics carefully, and also have contingency plans for when these do not work
- Consider sustainability

exceptions), possibly confusing it with authoritarian or managerial power in action. In recent years, however, leadership has been recognised as a key competence alongside other more obvious clinical competencies, and has also recently been included as a training requirement for UK pre-qualification doctorate programmes (British Psychological Society, 2007b).

Most contemporary models of leadership, especially in health and social care contexts, highlight the importance of vision and values (for example, the NHS Leadership Quality Framework; NHS Institute for Innovation and Improvement, 2003). Although obvious, it is always worth emphasising this point: if leaders do not know where they are going, the enterprise is effectively directionless, and can only react non-strategically to events. Most models agree that the leader must have some vision or goal, some aim or direction where they are headed, which provides a steer for action, and for evaluation. This normally also entails a drive for improvement and a willingness to tolerate constant challenge. Leaders are often described as optimistic and as having a positive outlook, which in turn motivates others to act positively. Like not having a clear vision, if a leader is not optimistic, it is hard for an organisation to keep going in the face of setbacks. An additional important component here is the creation and management of meaning (Gabriel, 1999; Gabriel *et al.*, 2000). Leaders help others to understand what is going on around them and what the implications and choices are, again suggesting that the skills involved parallel those of psychological therapists working clinically with patients. There seems no good reason why such skills should not also be applied systemically to benefit the wider healthcare organisation and its staff.

Although not based on psychological research, effective leaders are often thought to have high levels of emotional intelligence (Goleman, 2001; Goleman *et al.*, 2002), that is, the ability to work well with others. Despite its origins outside academic psychology, there is some preliminary evidence for its utility in predicting effective leadership, and it 'makes sense' to many non-psychologists. Its components are said to include high levels of social skill and an orientation to others, hence the ability to empower others to reach higher levels of performance. For example, the emotionally intelligent leader is one who encourages a junior colleague to attempt more challenging tasks, understanding both their anxieties and their aspirations. Other components include social competence, such as awareness of the reactions, competencies, motives and limitations of others; relationship management skills; and empathy. Yet again there is a striking resemblance to the skills of the competent therapist.

The context of leadership

One important limitation of many historical models of leadership is the emphasis on the centrality of the leader figure, and the assumption that leadership exists in a social vacuum, irrespective of context. Instead, some more recent writers have distinguished between *leaders* and *leadership* and to conceptualise leadership as a behaviour which may occur in a specific context, thus acknowledging the limits of the power that any single individual may hold. This approach calls attention to the importance of followers or collaborators, and to the interactive context within which the leader is working, hence to the importance of leaders having the support of social networks and teams (Hickey, 2008). This in turn points to the need for psychologists to develop interpersonal, group working and communication skills in the organisational context. Indeed, West (2005) sees leadership as a process of dispersed influence, thus making leadership and team work processes inextricable. Furthermore, Western (2008) argues that 'the dynamic [between leadership and followership] is not unidirectional in either direction' but 'symbiotically interdependent' (p. 55). Indeed, West (2005) refers to three key tasks of the leader: first, to create the conditions that enable the team to do its job; second, to build and maintain the team as a performing unit; and third, to coach and support the team to success.

In all these respects, therefore, leaders have to be good at understanding and managing others, which again is a quintessentially psychological task. This goes beyond persuasion or influence of individuals; instead it implies establishing a culture which enables and promotes certain ways of proceeding. Much research on team functioning suggests that how team leaders get members to 'go the extra mile' has little to do with the personality or charisma of individual leaders but rather 'in the higher order relationships between leaders and followers … an emergent social identity in which leaders and followers are creatively united' and thus changing 'me' and 'you' into 'us' (Haslam & Platow, 2001). Knowing how teams work can contribute very significantly to the enterprise of promoting psychological perspectives in health care, hence a key component of effective leadership is the ability to understand and lead teams. This then forms the next section of this chapter.

Teamwork

Understanding teamwork is important for clinical psychologists for three main reasons. First, working with other groups of staff is essential in all forms of modern health and social care. Increasing specialisation demands good communication and collaboration so that high-quality care can be delivered by the most appropriate team member, usually in conjunction with other forms of care delivered by other disciplines (Borrill *et al.*, 2000). Many cases of poor clinical care are either caused by or linked with poor communication (Department of Health, 2001). Staff morale is also linked to effective team-working, which is another significant contributor to the long-term effective delivery of care. As specialists in human behaviour and experience, psychologists should have a role in encouraging and promoting effective team functioning.

The second reason that understanding teamwork is important for the profession is that psychologists must work within teams, partly because of the relative scarcity of psychologists, but also because of the specialist skills that they can contribute, based on the high level of their pre-qualification training and the wide range of models that they can call upon. Yet their role or value in teams is not guaranteed or even certain because of this; no one is going to promote or even listen to psychologists just because they are psychologists. As Lavender and Allcock (2006) suggest, the lack of clarity about lines of authority for clinical psychologists working within medically dominated, hierarchical systems, and the different, non-medical academic foundation of the discipline, mean that each psychologist has to demonstrate anew how they can be useful, and in what way they can contribute collaboratively. This implies that they need to be constantly aware of the priorities and needs of others, and to work flexibly and responsively, if their contribution is going to be effective or even heard. Most healthcare organisations are profoundly hierarchical, with clear power differences between groups, so awareness of and competence in negotiation skills is essential. This is especially true if psychologists attempt to influence multidisciplinary teams, or to develop strategic leadership at an organisational level, rather then end up marginalised.

The third reason, again because of numbers, is that psychologists often have to work indirectly, supporting and directing others in the delivery of psychologically informed care, whether this be staff or relatives and carers. Previous chapters of this book have provided many examples of how this has been done effectively in a range of medical, clinical and community settings, so only theoretical points will be introduced here, using general principles drawn from social psychology. A full discussion of determinants of team performance is outside the scope of this chapter, but many significant issues are included in the following section.

Group dynamics and team working in health care contexts: an overview

At a general level, there is reasonable consensus about what characterises effective team working in the workplace, although the absence of implementation of this knowledge is also apparent in the pervasiveness of team conflict and staff unhappiness within health service contexts (Borrill *et al.*, 2000). Sadly, numerous examples exist of groups of staff who are mutually intolerant, whose dislike or distrust of each other causes significant problems for patient care. Likewise, some staff groups feel undervalued and unheard. Many of the features of both healthy and unhealthy group dynamics which recur within healthcare team working can be linked to conformity pressures, and inter- or intra-group conflict, well known to social and organisational psychologists (for example, van Knippenberg & Schippers, 2007). Conformity results from our essentially social nature, which means we are influenced by the example, behaviour and opinions of others. This can lead to both positive effects as teams inspire high standards of work, but also to a loss of creativity when the potentially important views of dissidents or the less powerful are not heard. For example, medically led teams may ignore the insights of non-medical members, disregarding the perspectives or potential input of minority or non-medical colleagues even when they may possess key information or competencies. As repeatedly shown, inter- and intra-group conflict results from our wish to belong and to develop a valued identity, but also leads to a rejection of others and stereotyping of difference. Awareness of these issues should empower psychologists in determining what to suggest in order to improve functioning, as well as to ensure that a psychological perspective is heard. Establishing structures which encourage participation by all levels of staff, and good communication, can help to mitigate some of these unhelpful dynamics, which consume unhelpful amounts of team time and energy (Homan *et al.*, 2007).

At a more focused level, the BPS's Working Psychologically in Teams report (British Psychological Society, 2007c) included a thorough review of effective team working, which is intended as a resource for psychologists in a range of work environments. This review suggested that as well as having a robust leadership structure, healthy teams are characterised by having:

- *Clear and achievable objectives*, so that each member knows what they are supposed to be doing. Surprising numbers of teams work without defining objectives, or the establishment of measures and criteria whereby they will assess the success of their activities. Psychologists in teams may be able to add significantly to team performance by helping to introduce robust audit or assessment systems, for example.
- *Differentiated, diverse and clear roles.* Teams work best with some degree of specialisation so that each member can deliver what they are good at or trained for. Our human tendency to prefer people who share our own values and characteristics can lead to teams being made up of similar people, which can in turn lead to stagnation or even 'group think'. Alternatively, highly heterogeneous teams can lead to dysfunctional levels of conflict within the team. Psychologists may be able to help teams by calling attention to the need for diversity while being clear about individual roles and functions, and the need for integration.
- *Collective sense of identity, a need to work together to meet shared objectives.* Communication is central here, whereby individuals can be encouraged to participate in decision making and action as well as building personal networks, which also contributes to team integration and stability.
- *The leader having sufficient control and access to resources* to allow the team to achieve its objectives. This usually implicates the application of 'political' skills as described in Box 30.1.

- *Communication structures and processes*, enabling team members to 'debate, disagree and develop ideas together' (British Psychological Society, 2007c). For this to be successful, the number of team members should ideally not exceed around eight, although of course in many health and social care settings the numbers routinely exceed this. There is therefore a crucial need for regular consultation, especially if the contribution of less senior members is to be given sufficient consideration.
- *A chance to review and reflect*. Demand levels often preclude this, but teams work best when they have some time to question and revise their procedures in the light of evidence and experience (West, 2005). Here psychologists' familiarity with the skills of reflective practice, supervision, and research or audit are all highly relevant.

In summary, teamwork is crucial in most forms of health and social care delivery, and in the promotion of psychological perspective in health and social care. Clinical psychologists may well be in a position to promote effective teams functioning through proper exercise of a variety of competencies, and in particular by drawing on their understanding of team dynamics. This is central to effective leadership, but also to the routine work of competent clinical psychologists in most working environments.

Consultancy

One of the best ways of promoting psychological approaches and thinking in teams is through consultancy. When clinical psychologists act as consultants, they must be able to understand and formulate using indirectly obtained information, and to respond so as to promote effective intervention or action carried out by others. Organisational consultancy in general has a long history, with particular expansion in the past twenty years (Kipping & Saint-Martin, 2005; Kitay & Wright, 2004). There are many definitions of consultancy, but Øvretveit *et al.* (1992) provide a suitably comprehensive overview:

> [consultancy is] a process involving a consultant who is invited to help a consultee with a work related issue. The consultee can be an individual, group or organisation which enters into a *negotiated contract* with the consultant agreeing the boundaries of time, place and focus of consultancy work. The consultant uses his or her skills, knowledge and feelings in an attempt to understand the processes involved, sharing his or her observations to help the consultee fulfil a specific task. The responsibility for fulfilling the task lies with the consultee, whereas the responsibility for deepening the understanding of the processes lies with the consultant, who may use a variety of methods to achieve it.

This definition is important in several respects but emphasises, in particular, the highly boundaried nature of the process. This requires anyone engaging in consultancy to be clear from the start of the work what is required and how this will be achieved. Indeed, Kitay and Wright (2004) emphasise the importance of being clear about the nature of boundaries within the organisation as this significantly affects the relationship between consultant and consultee.

From a more systemic point of view, Huffington and Brunning (1994) suggest that consultants can help clients address difficulties by collaborative exploration, aiming to resolve issues by conceptualising and sharing the meaning which the inability to solve problems has for the larger organisation. In this respect, the role of the psychologist here may be to help the team or service understand and accept a variety of perspectives and hence grow in capacity by being able to use these diverse perspectives as solutions to the problems faced.

A distinction must be made between *internal* and *external* consultancy. Essentially, the difference lies in the employee status of the consultant, with the *external* consultant being brought in either in a private capacity, or as someone employed by an external or specialist organisation. The *internal* consultant is 'a person from another department or another area of the organisation who offers expert advice' (Heary & Noon, 2001, p. 177). In general, clinical psychologists are likely to act as internal, rather than external, consultants. Their remit is usually to enable a team or group to develop novel solutions to problems that have become intractable. Alternatively, consultants may be employed as a source of novel perspectives, and to act to galvanise new approaches in an organisation. There has been a significant increase in the use of consultants in the commercial sphere, and the public sector is no different, with little quantification of the benefits of using them (Lapsley & Oldfield, 2001). Indeed, it has been argued that their use can become something of an 'addiction' (Kipping & Saint-Martin, 2005), or can function as a way of cutting costs. However, the main value of engaging consultants appears to be in the promotion of change where there is significant resistance, often said to be a particular characteristic of the public sector (Lapsley & Oldfield, 2001).

Critical to this process is the relationship of trust which must be established before consultees can contemplate the risks involved in change. A recent survey of consultees (Handley *et al.*, 2006) identified six characteristics of consultants which they felt enhanced the relationship:

- a commitment to and passion for the task;
- flexibility;
- a willingness to challenge the client and be challenged;
- openness and integrity;
- the ability to gain respect of the client's staff;
- an understanding of the client's business.

As with leadership, it is probably helpful to see consultancy as an activity not dissimilar from other types of clinical work. A number of models can be used to underpin the process, including the systemic, psychodynamic and mentoring models. Lake (2008) describes a consultancy model based on an integration of many familiar models, including cognitive behavioural therapy (CBT), cognitive analytic therapy (CAT) and attachment theory, which he and colleagues use in mental health teams to develop formulations of people who present significant challenges to a team. The consultancy meeting, which lasts approximately one and a half hours, is attended by a range of professional staff, and does not seek solutions, but encourages the development of an understanding of how present difficulties or symptoms may have evolved, as well as of how the team's own responses may inadvertently repeat or reinforce dysfunctional patterns. Lake's model incorporates developmental issues, the cultural context and any biosocial issues, and aims to raise psychological awareness as well as to enable more effective team working. Lake points out that such an approach requires the active support of influential members of the team, and works best if it is actively requested by the team. Space for the meeting also needs to be protected. This form of consultancy aims to empower the team to work more effectively, by drawing on both the psychologist's formulation skills and on his or her ability to facilitate the development of others. Using this model, Lake *et al.* (2008) urge psychologists to be aware of the potential pitfalls of consultancy, such as positioning oneself as the 'expert', or confusing consultancy and supervision. They also stress the point made earlier about the need for a clear contract, especially if the consultancy is provided to a team of which one is a member.

Stages in the consultancy process

We suggest that any psychologist considering undertaking consultancy work should consider the following stages of the consultancy process, based on the work of the Organisational Development consultancy model (Gallos, 2006; Schien, 1999).

1. Negotiating entry/establishing a clear contract; in particular, who is the client and what are the expected outcomes? Establish clearly the responsibility of the consultant and of the client. Consider what resources are available and the power dynamics within the organisation.
2. Analysing the problem, hypothesising, data gathering.
3. Problem formulation: this is a collaborative process with the client, and feedback should be sought throughout.
4. Assessing resources: this is particularly important where there is resistance to change. Assessment and evaluation of the resources that people bring to their work situation are critical and relate directly to the discussion of 'political' competence in the leadership section above. Valuing the contribution of those involved is also highly important here.
5. Planning, implementing, maybe reframing, helping the client to think differently, developing a joint understanding.
6. Evaluation of the outcomes and reflection on the process.
7. Exiting from the system that was being consulted into; this should have been specified in the initial contract, with any changes being explicitly agreed during the process of consultation.

There are now increasing numbers of psychologists from other non-clinical specialist areas (occupational and health, for example) working within health services, and it may be that the role of psychologist as consultant will expand in the future. This will be based on increasing experience of, and acceptance of, the insights that can be provided by thinking more organisationally (or systemically), as well as individualistically. It fact, in many care groups where vulnerable clients are looked after (for example, those with learning disabilities or older people), consultation is already a widely used mode of intervention (see, for example, a number of chapters in this book).

Conclusion

Modern health and social care acutely needs psychological input, in a wide range of contexts, using a variety of forms of delivery. Clinical psychologists must therefore develop the competencies not only to provide effective interventions indirectly as well as directly, but also to argue effectively for the importance of psychologically informed care, and for the resources enabling this to happen. This requires good leadership at strategic, professional and clinical levels. Much health care is delivered in teams and groups, which are vital, but in many instances may be dysfunctional, negatively impacting patient or client care and the working lives of healthcare staff. An understanding of group functioning, and how to influence this, is therefore another key skill for psychologists. All of these issues mean that leadership, team-working skills and consultancy are increasingly being seen as crucial competencies. This chapter has argued that these skills are consistent with existing clinical competencies and values. It remains a challenge for the future, however, to ensure that effective leadership is developed at all levels, and that future generations of clinical psychologists continue to deliver and promote the values and achievements of the discipline, in the interests of all of our clients and colleagues. It will be critical for our profession not to shy away from involvement at these levels, since there is now an increasing recognition of the importance of what we can contribute to the welfare of clients, and to the wider heath and social care system.

References

Bennis, W. (1998). *On becoming a leader*. Reading, MA: Addison-Wesley.

Borrill, C., West, M., Shapiro, D. & Rees, A. (2000). Team working and effectiveness in health care. *British Journal of Health Care Management, 6*, 364–371.

British Psychological Society (2007a). *Organising, managing and leading psychological services*. Leicester: Author.

British Psychological Society (2007b). *Criteria for the accreditation of postgraduate training programmes in clinical psychology*. Membership and Professional Training Board, Committee on Training in Clinical Psychology. Leicester: Author.

British Psychological Society (2007c). *Working psychologically in teams*. Leicester: Author.

Buchanan, D.A. & Badham, R.J. (1999). *Power, politics, and organizational change: Winning the turf game*. London: Sage.

Clark, J. (2002). Clinical management and leadership – an international perspective. *HSMC Newsletter, 8*(3).

Clegg, A. (2000). Leadership: Improving the quality of patient care. *Nursing Standard, 14*, 43–45.

Denis, J., Langley, A. & Pineault, M. (2000). Becoming a leader in a complex organisation. *Journal of Management Studies, 37*(8), 1063–1099.

Department of Health (2001). *Shifting the Balance of Power within the NHS.* London: The Stationary Office.

Gabriel, Y. (Ed.) (1999). *Organisations in depth: The psychoanalysis of organisations.* London: Sage.

Gabriel, Y., Fineman, S. & Sims. D. (2000). *Organising and organisations* (2nd edn). London: Sage.

Gallos, J.V. (2006). *Organisational development.* San Francisco: Jossey-Bass.

Goleman, D. (2001). What makes a leader? In J. Henry (Ed.) *Creative management* (2nd edn, pp. 125–139). London: Sage.

Goleman, D., Boyatzis, R.E. & McKee, A. (2002). *The new leaders: Transforming the art of leadership into the science of results.* London: Little Brown.

Grint, K. (2005). *Leadership: Limits and possibilities.* Basingstoke: Palgrave Macmillan.

Handley, K., Sturdy, A., Clark, T. & Fincham, R. (2006). The type of relationship clients really want with their consultancies. *People Management, 12*(10), 52–52.

Haslam, S.A. & Platow, M.J. (2001). The link between leadership and followership. *Personality and Social Psychology Bulletin, 27,* 1469–1479.

Heary, E. & Noon, M. (2001). Internal consultancy. In *Dictionary of human resource management* (p. 177). Oxford: Oxford University Press.

Heywood, A. (2004). *Political theory: An introduction* (3rd edn). Basingstoke: Palgrave Macmillan.

Hickey, E. (2008). Leaders, followers and resistance to service change. *DCP Forum,* 15–18.

Homan, A.C., van Knippenberg, D., Van Kleef, G.A. & de Dreu, C. (2007). Bridging faultlines by valuing diversity: Diversity beliefs, information elaborations and performance in diverse work groups. *Journal of Applied Psychology, 92,* 1189–1199.

Huffington, C. & Brunning, H. (1994). *Internal consultancy in the public sector: Case studies.* London: Karnac.

Kipping, M. & Saint-Martin, D. (2005). Between regulation, promotion and consumption: Government and management consultancy in Britain. *Business History, 47*(3), 449–465.

Kitay, J. & Wright, C. (2004). Take the money and run? Organisational boundaries and consultants' roles. *Service Industries Journal, 24*(3), 1–18.

Kouzes, J. & Posner, B. (2003). *The leadership challenge.* San Francisco: Jossey-Bass.

Lake, N. (2008). Developing skills in consultation: 1 and 2, *Clinical Psychology Forum, 186,* 13–24.

Lake, N., Solts, B. & Preedy, K. (2008). Developing skills in consultation: 4. *Clinical Psychology Forum, 186,* 29–33.

Lapsley, I. & Oldfield, R. (2001). Transforming the public sector: Management consultants as agents of change. *European Accounting Review, 10*(3), 523–543.

Lavender, T. & Allcock, S. (2006). Working with others. In J. Hall & S. Llewelyn (Eds.) *What is clinical psychology?* (pp. 297–312). Oxford: Oxford University Press.

Millward, L. & Bryan, K. (2005). Clinical leadership in health care: A position statement. *Leadership in Health Services, 18,* 13–25.

Moiden, N. (2002). Evolution of leadership in nursing. *Nursing Management, 9,* 24–28.

NHS Institute for Innovation and Improvement (2003). *Leadership quality framework.* Retrieved June 2004 from www.nhs.leadershipquality.nhs.uk

Outhwaite, S. (2003). The importance of leadership in the development of an integrated team. *Journal of Nursing Management, 11,* 371–376.

Øvretveit, J., Brunning, H. & Huffington, C. (1992). Adapt or decay: Why clinical psychologists must develop the consulting role. *Clinical Psychology Forum, 46,* 27–29.

Russell, R. (2001). Too many chiefs (or can we all be leaders?). *British Medical Journal,* 17 December.

Schien, E.H. (1999). *Process consultation revisited: Building the helping relationship.* Reading, MA: Addison Wesley.

Senge, P.M. (1993). *The fifth discipline: Art and practice of the learning organisation.* New York: Random House Business.

van Knippenberg, D. & Schippers, M.C. (2007). Work group diversity. *Annual Review of Psychology, 58,* 515–541

West, M. (2005). *Effective teamwork.* Oxford: Blackwell/British Psychological Society.

Western, S. (2008.). *Leadership: A critical text.* London: Sage.

Yuki, G. (2002). *Leadership in Organisations* (5th edn). Englewood Cliffs, NJ: Prentice Hall.

31

Community Approaches, Social Inclusion and User Involvement

Annie Mitchell and Rachel Purtell

Treatment and therapy play a modest role in the face of the challenges and deprivations experienced by those who live on the edge, or are excluded from mainstream society. In order to thrive, everyone needs fair access to socially valued resources, including a decent income and housing, meaningful relationships and occupation, and liberation from restrictions, stigma and prejudice (Bentall, 2004; Department for International Development, 2005; Mitchell & Cormack, 1998). In the UK, following a series of public enquiries into the functioning of the National Health Service (NHS) (notably the Bristol Royal Infirmary Inquiry; Department of Health, 2002), there has been a culture shift towards involving and empowering patients and service users as active partners and decision makers both in their own care and in broader planning, organisation and care delivery (Coulter, 2002). There is an increased emphasis on prevention, promoting mental health and well-being through social inclusion (Department of Health, 2007a). In this chapter we explore how psychologists and people who use services can work in partnership for social change.

Involvement operates at different levels: in individual care, and more systemically, in community development, service delivery, planning, research and training. In this chapter we will focus on more systemic levels of involvement and draw on our experience to illustrate how this may work in practice. The authors of this chapter worked together to develop a research programme in the UK, Folk.us, funded in 2000 by the South West Regional Strategic Health Authority and latterly by the Department of Health, to promote service user and carer influence over health and social care research in South West England (Baxter *et al.*, 2001; Purtell *et al.*, 2003). One of the authors, Rachel Purtell, is Programme Coordinator; having completed her MA in Disability Studies by distance learning, and worked for Surrey Users' Network. Without a traditional academic background, she is experienced at challenging the expert model. Her experience developed through growing up with rare medical conditions. It was often apparent that she had far more knowledge about her condition than the alleged experts, yet the experts themselves often seemed to have difficulty acknowledging this. As a young person, Rachel's experience of psychologists was also not positive. They seemed preoccupied with asking apparently meaningless and irrelevant questions to inform preconceived decisions about schooling. Through her MA Rachel gained an understanding of the social model of disability, differentiating impairment from disability, and understanding the importance of communal experience of oppression encountered by disabled people. The other author, Annie Mitchell, is influenced both by her upbringing in the north east of England where solidarity was a basic value, and also by her training in developmental psychology and community clinical psychology and subsequent work in child services and healthcare settings. The authors find that working effectively together comes through shared values, appreciating different skills, trusting each other to be competent, trying not to be defensive, superior or competitive, while not avoiding confrontation. Instead, we find that our work has been enhanced by arguing points through until a shared understanding is reached, and solution found (or, sometimes, recognising irreconcilable differences). We believe our approach mirrors the experience of others who work in partnership: power sharing requires us to be open, mutually respectful and ready to acknowledge, appreciate and work with difference. We hope to demonstrate this in this chapter.

Why Should Psychologists Promote Involvement and Social Inclusion?

Reaching those most in need

Extensive epidemiological evidence shows that living conditions and social circumstances determine much of our health and well-being (Davey Smith, 2003; Meltzer *et al.*, 2003). Deep social inequalities underpin massive inequalities in health and mental health. Unequal access to resources (money, status, privilege, relationships and influence) is associated with increased suffering and ill-health (Sayer, 2005; Social Exclusion Unit, 2004; Wilkinson, 1996, 2005). Access to resources tends to be determined by people's socially ascribed position, such as age, gender, race, ethnicity, class and disability (Pilgrim, 1997; Social Exclusion Unit, 2004; Williams & Watson, 1988). Those who are young, old, homeless, immigrants and asylum seekers, prisoners, from deprived or lower social classes, disabled, or with chronic ill health are amongst those who experience greatest poverty, disadvantage and discrimination and poorest physical and psychological well-being.

Social inclusion means ensuring that everyone can participate fully in the life of their community so that they can flourish and realise their potential. Comprehensive social inclusion entails challenging the systematic exclusion of those who are discriminated against on the basis of their social identity (Department for International Development, 2005). If we are serious about preventing distress and promoting well-being, psychologists have a responsibility to contribute skills and knowledge to collective efforts to redress the balance towards greater social justice.

Involvement has been defined from a policy perspective in the UK as a process of placing equal value on the expertise that all people – be they users or professionals – contribute (Sutcliffe, 2007). Various policy developments towards involvement and partnership with clients, service users, carers and citizens are, however, driven by differing value bases.

On the one hand, there is a consumerist emphasis on improving quality and marketing of services, emphasising choice and individual responsibility. Consumerist approaches are well embedded in NHS and social care policy, both at an individual care level (as seen, for example, in self-care and shared decision-making initiatives such as the Expert Patient Programme (Department of Health, 2006) and Choice Matters (Department of Health, 2007b) and also at the collective level of service development and regulation as demonstrated in Standards for Better Health (Department of Health, 2007c). The vision here is of a system of public engagement in which patients and service users become active participants in their own care.

On the other hand, more radically, the democratic human rights and empowerment agenda promotes progressive social change. Involvement from the perspective of the service user movement concerns social activism and collectivism. It recognises exclusion, oppression and abuse in a society that systematically favours those who are already advantaged, and works both within social groupings and in partnership across social divisions to promote structural change.

Value-based practice

Recognition of these differing value bases underpinning involvement requires us to critically question and examine the value base of our practice. The National Institute for Mental Health in England, for example, have developed a national Framework of Values for Mental Health (Woodbridge & Fulford, 2004), recognising the complexity and potential incompatibility of the values espoused by professionals and community members and suggesting that the values of individual service users and their communities should not only be the starting point but also the key determinant for all actions in mental health work. There is a tension here for traditionally trained clinical psychologists who are exhorted to espouse the core value of evidence-based practice, which, while perhaps at best tempered by critical reflection, still remains the bedrock of the role of the psychologist as scientist-practitioner. Values-based practice is intended to redress the balance between the (apparently) neutral and objective values of scientist-practitioners (often experienced by service users as distant, paternalistic and over-protective; see Coulter, 2002) towards a greater emphasis on shared humanity, cultural meaning and context-determined practice (Woodbridge & Fulford, 2004).

In the UK, service user values underpinned the recent development of the Ten Essential Shared Capabilities: A Framework for the Whole of the Mental Health Workforce (Department of Health, 2004). This promotes working in partnership; respecting diversity, practising ethically, challenging inequality, promoting recovery, identifying people's needs and strengths, providing user-centred care, promoting safety and positive risk taking, and personal development and learning. The framework has been expanded to specify capabilities needed for socially inclusive practice across child, adult mental health and disability services (Department of Health, 2007a). There is a shift in emphasis from victim models, protection and risk aversion towards appreciating and working with people's strengths, both individually and within their wider communities, in services that are flexible and enabling rather than rigid, prescriptive and protectionist.

Where Is the Psychology in This?

Challenging social inequalities and promoting involvement has hitherto remained largely peripheral to psychological theory as well as practice, especially in Britain (Burton *et al.*, 2007). Psychological ideas are largely drawn from (and support) a modern culture of Western individualism, in which people are seen as atomised individuals, or, at their most relational, as partners in attachment and family relationships, independent of the powerful web of cultural, social, economic and political forces which influences us all. The current emphasis on good practice guidelines and evidence-based practice (National Institute for Health and Clinical Excellence, 2005; Roth & Fonagy, 2004) assumes expert-based knowledge framed within medical model therapeutic assumptions, which allows relatively little room for creative and shared approaches that take into account the complexity of people's social circumstances. Fortunately there has, however, been a thoughtful and critical set of voices from both psychology and the service user movement, encouraging us to shift our gaze and actions outwards to external sources of power, influence and support, so as to act in solidarity with people working to empower themselves and others in our divided world. There are theoretical approaches, from psychology and beyond, to underpin involvement and inclusion work.

Critical community psychology emphasises the significance of the environment in determining human functioning at micro-, meso- and macro-levels (Bronfenbrenner, 1979), and in particular the role of social support or social capital and social power (Orford, 1992, 2008), with a critical awareness of the hidden nature of power and vested interests (Smail, 2005). Burton (2007) argues that the value of community psychology is to act as a laboratory of social relations, which, if appropriately focused and connected to relevant struggles and movements, could help point to better ways of organising society. The social model of disability (Barnes *et al.*, 1999; Campbell & Oliver, 1986) focuses on the societal nature of the restrictions and limitations on people's lives: society is seen as erecting barriers that prevent disabled people from participating in everyday activities and restrict their opportunities. Within this framework the burden of blame and responsibility usually placed on the victims of circumstance is lifted, and the challenge becomes a shared social responsibility to shift attitudes, enable access and change institutions.

Key values for community psychologists include working inclusively, devolving professional power, taking a universalist perspective on people's experiences and focusing on strengths (Bostock & Diamond, 2005). Positive psychology challenges the preoccupation of psychologists with pathology and victimhood, and instead, focuses on people's resilience and resourcefulness. According to its leading proponents positive psychology is 'a science of positive subjective experiences, positive individual traits, and positive institutions [which is concerned to identify] the factors that allow individuals, communities, and societies to flourish' (Seligman & Csikszentmihalyi, 2000, p. 5). Although it tends to promote an overly individualistic stance, and does not engage with notions of power or critical challenge, positive psychology provides a constructive counterbalance to vulnerability models.

Central to critical community psychology thinking is the relational nature of human life and development. We are embedded in a world of relationships and social connections that are critically important to our sense of ourselves and our well-being. Social psychology, and in particular social identity theory, is useful in considering how to break down prejudices between people from different social groups (Tajfel & Turner, 1986). Recent work (Hewstone *et al.*, 2005) indicates that optimal conditions for constructive contact between members of different social groups includes providing a safe environment and encouraging perspective taking, along with ensuring that participants retain awareness of their own and others' group membership.

Psychologists do not have to limit themselves to psychological theory and evidence to inform their work: involvement and inclusion liberates us to draw from other disciplines. Knowledge from sociology, anthropology, development studies and political science, as well as literature, the arts and first-person accounts can all help to widen our perspectives.

Examples of Partnership Work between Psychologists and Community Members

Current moves towards new roles and new ways of working provide opportunities to extend the scope of practice towards more inclusive work at all levels. Examples include assessment of people's access to power (Hagan & Smail, 1997); understanding the role of social inequalities in formulations of aetiology and maintenance of distress (Miller & McClelland, 2006); providing transformational consultation, supervision and leadership that challenges traditional power hierarchies (Bostock & Diamond, 2005; Patel, 2004); supporting collective social action (Holland, 1994); and promoting recovery-based models that value people's own lived experiences and draw on their strengths (Care Services Improvement Partnership and Royal College of Psychiatrists and Social Care Institute for Excellence, 2007). In the next section, three different types of partnership work are outlined to indicate the range of current approaches in which psychologists are involved.

Expert Patients' Programme – and an alternative

The Expert Patients' Programme (Department of Health, 2006), a mainstream approach to partnership work, is a lay-led, group-based programme for people living with long-term conditions (including diabetes, heart disease and stroke). The programme, based on the notion of self-efficacy (Bandura, 1977), was developed by the psychologist Kate Lorig at Stanford University during the late 1980s. The focus is on cognitive symptom management and self-care, encouraging people to take active control of their condition, increase confidence and improve quality of life. Internal evaluation indicates significant success in minimising the impact of common symptoms (including pain and depression) on everyday life, and in reducing the frequency of primary and secondary healthcare appointments.

While the programme intends to empower individual patients, it is a consumerist approach and not a radical programme designed to challenge broader structural and economic inequalities. It could be argued that it is aimed more at reducing NHS costs and improving efficiency than at real empowerment (though these aims are not necessarily mutually exclusive). There remains a concern (Taylor & Bury, 2007) that enhancing awareness of cognitive factors may draw attention away from the social determinants and contexts of health. A further criticism is that the programme may privilege the knowledge of some patients over that of others, and does not fit with the preferences or practical circumstances of all patients (Newbould et al., 2006). Despite the concerns of some service users, it may ironically be too radical for more conventional practitioners: there are indications that some professionals are reluctant to support the programme, perhaps because they are threatened by the term 'expert patient' (McIver, 1999).

The expert patient approach requires people to change their beliefs and behaviours. Ward (2004), reflecting on pain management groups, observed that patients' suffering is as much to do with difficulties with employment, access to benefits and social isolation as with the physical experience, thoughts and beliefs about the pain itself. In response to this, in partnership with patients, Ward set up links with benefits and return to work advisers and provided information about pain patients' particular requirements; provided training for fitness instructors at local sports centres on the specific needs of those with chronic pain; ran workshops with local Job Centres and Careers Advice Centres; and designed leaflets for patients to help them negotiate employment and benefit regulations. Formal evaluation is under way; informal feedback indicates that people feel more socially empowered, less fearful of approaching statutory agencies, are reintegrating into previously enjoyed activities and taking active steps to return to work.

User involvement in training

The second approach involves users in the education of staff. The National Service Framework for Mental Health proposed that 'service users … should be involved in planning, providing and evaluating education and training' (Department of Health, 1999, p. 109). This can happen both at the level of professional training and as part of wider preventative efforts to reduce discrimination and prejudice.

At the University of Exeter, for example, a Service User and Carer Advisory Group grew out of a short-term piece of consultative work for the Doctorate in Clinical Psychology (Curle & Mitchell, 2004). Changes that resulted include curriculum and placement developments to increase awareness of contextual influences in practice and enhance cultural competence, user and carer involvement in selection and in membership of the Programme Management Committee. The decision to continue after the initial consultation was reached because members felt that they had been heard and their views acted upon and because everyone (programme staff included) felt refreshed and encouraged by mutual support. Formal and informal feedback indicates that trainees highly value user and carer input and that teaching by users and carers is amongst the most influential teaching they receive, making a positive impact on personal values and motivation in relation to becoming a practitioner.

User and carer involvement in training is becoming standard practice across professional groups. *A Guide to Good Practice in User and Carer Involvement in Training* for the Division of Clinical Psychology has recently been published (Hayward & Riddell, 2008). This refers to the policy framework for involvement in training, giving examples from other professions and noting that work is needed to identify the indicators of success and to evaluate the outcomes and impact of this work.

Examples of service users working with psychologists to deliver training to reduce mental health discrimination include user-led training on mental health issues for prison staff, recognising that prisoners are (almost by definition) the most socially excluded of groups, with levels of mental health difficulties substantially greater than the general population (Shepherd, 2007). Another example of educational intervention delivered by a mental health service user (with a clinical psychology trainee) was found to reduce negative and stereotypical attitudes and increase sophistication of young people's understanding of psychosocial causes of mental health difficulties, as well as to increase their stated readiness to act inclusively (Harper & Sholl, 2007).

Assisting, enabling and contributing to collective action in response to social need

The third example involves the provision of support for those involved in community action. Notions of involvement and participation have been critically examined, seeing the risk of a new tyranny on professionals' terms (Cooke & Kothari, 2001). For example, participative action research with community activists in housing estates in areas of high material and economic deprivation in Manchester revealed practical and emotional exhaustion for people working alongside (and challenging) professional systems. There are huge pressures, with no colleagues to share the load, no specified working hours, no development activities, training, supervision or support, and usually no pay (Kagan, 2006; Kagan *et al.*, 2005).

Clinical psychologists could use their knowledge and skills to support the collective actions of community members. In Northumberland, for example, psychology from a public health perspective contributed to local actions to promote financial literacy in people experiencing debt and low income (Bostock & Lavelle, 2007). In Great Yarmouth, clinical psychologists engaged in qualitative research with migrant workers, refugees and asylum seekers, which led to arts-based anti-stigma work and education to promote women's rights. In Devon, clinical psychology trainees worked with people with learning difficulties to identify their own research issues, resulting in participative work together with a local drama group to reduce bullying by school children (Thorne & White, 2005) and with residents with mental health problems in a rural village to empower one another through group work and sustainable community projects (Howard *et al.*, 2005).

Latin American liberation social psychology, extending the work of Freire (1972), Martín-Baró (1996) and Montero (1996), in the context of repression, civil war, aftermath of dictatorships and extreme poverty, sees social liberation as a process originating in the interaction between external catalytic agents (which could, for example, be psychologists) and members of the oppressed groups themselves (Burton & Kagan, 2005). Psychologists become a resource for the community, offering expertise in investigation, understanding of processes such as leadership and group dynamics, and systemic knowledge. Burton and Kagan cite the work of ILAS (Latin American Institute of Mental Health and Human Rights) in working with the aftermath of political violence and trauma, using traditional ceremony in making suffering a social shared experience ('de-privatisation'), linking with people's existential meanings and enabling active social roles with political and legal action to redress injustices. In this work, psychotherapeutic psychology, social psychology, local tradition and political action come together in an attempt to transform, rather than simply ameliorate, people's oppressed and excluded social conditions.

What Competencies Do Clinical Psychologists Need to Promote Involvement and Social Inclusion?

We highlight three particular competencies needed for partnership work: facilitation, networking and critical reflection.

Facilitation means working in a way that draws people together constructively and proactively. A good facilitator attends to the 'bit before the beginning' – ensuring clarity of purposes and intentions and linkage with wider systems; providing safe accessible spaces in which people can work harmoniously; enabling people to articulate hopes and fears; ensuring that all involved listen and have a voice; helping to set clear agendas and negotiate shared expectations, ground rules and boundaries; clarifying and sharing responsibilities; providing structure and tools for a range of communication styles and abilities; avoiding becoming too central in the work; looking for ways to allow differences to be explored and avoiding false consensus; helping to clarify decisions and actions; networking with others to ensure that actions are taken; attending to the 'bit after the end' – making sure that power differentials in the wider system are taken into account so that suitable links are made to sustain the work.

Networking means building strong links and connections between people and available resources and services. A good networker invests time and effort in exploring what is going on in their community and is proactive in putting people in touch with one another. They know how to access sources of funding, advice and information, understand different roles and contributions of statutory, voluntary and independent agencies, and know where informal and formal support can be accessed, thereby actively contributing as a resource for others and building links with strategic allies.

Critical reflection means constantly evaluating whose interests are being served – and responding by shifting activity towards greater promotion of the interests of those who are most disadvantaged. A critically reflective practitioner considers their own cultural, professional and personal background, explores implications of power differences, takes nothing for granted, is open to questioning and exploring their own knowledge, assumptions and values, acknowledges weaknesses, vulnerabilities and mistakes (as well as strengths), appreciates uncertainty, complexity and difference, and makes connections between intentions, actions, reflections and outcomes.

User-Centred Tips for Good Practice in Public Involvement

1. *Be practical*: Consider ways to make involvement feasible within people's life circumstances. Consider the best timings for different people depending on their life stages and responsibilities; choose accessible and neutral venues; consider people's out of pocket expenses and needs for carers, translators and disability access.
2. *Be honest and realistic*: Ensure a realistic chance that the involvement may make a difference, or may change attitudes and expectations (i.e. not tokenistic). Keep in mind whose interests should be served by the involvement. Acknowledge constraints of time, money and potential for influence. Recognise potential social and emotional costs of partnership for all involved. Give people the chance to consider the impact of involvement on their lives and relationships, trying to make it possible for people to join and withdraw without guilt or exhaustion.
3. *Be thoughtful about your own impact*: Consider what messages your own behaviour, presentation, use of language and cultural and professional assumptions convey.
4. Don't assume that you know what the outcome will be: Be ready to be surprised!
5. *Be aware of your own anxieties but don't let anxiety push you into being controlling*: You don't have to know the answers in advance, nor to have everything sorted and clear from the start. When problems are presented you can work together to find shared solutions.
6. *Be ready to share your own life experiences*: Share on equal terms, but only when relevant and helpful.
7. *Be sociable*: Build in some relaxed social time. Consider the possibility that people may want to remain friends and colleagues with you afterwards.
8. *Be flexible*: Use a range of methods and be aware that tools and people involved may change as the process evolves. Consider a variety of approaches, both informal and formal. Go to where the people are. Don't assume involvement requires endless meetings – consider conversations, focus groups, citizens' juries, surveys, questionnaires, email discussions, participatory appraisal, action research, drama workshops and other creative activities.
9. *Close the loop*: Always feed back what has and hasn't happened. People are sympathetic when ideas and suggestions cannot be implemented, if the reasons are

clarified. Conversely, they feel cynical or exploited when nothing happens without explanation, or when changes are made without acknowledgement of where they originated.

10. *Think of involvement as organically evolving*: Reflect and review at transition points in the process of involvement. The 'bits before the beginning and after the end' are perhaps the most important. Think about how, and where, involvement might be sustained, both for individuals and for the system, and where the next involvement might begin.

Conclusion

We hope that this chapter will encourage clinical psychologists to consider potential roles beyond therapeutic work with clients, seeking ways to contribute knowledge and skills to collaborative efforts towards more just and equitable social conditions. Despite policy directives urging us towards partnership work, it can be difficult to justify working in more preventive and empowering ways in an NHS climate that seems to be becoming ever more bureaucratised and risk averse. By its very nature, inclusive practice challenges the status quo, and therefore risks being marginalised and sabotaged. This work requires initiative, creativity and innovation and is hard to evaluate using the research methodologies currently favoured for practice guidelines. Nevertheless, it is our experience that trainee clinical psychologists join the NHS in the hope of working in the sorts of inclusive and value-based ways proposed in this chapter. Our shared task is to retain the inclusive values, aspirations and mutual trust that inspire professionals, service users, carers and community members to work together in true partnership towards a fairer world and improved well-being for all.

References

Bandura, A. (1977). Self-efficacy: Toward a unifying theory of behavioral change. *Psychological Review, 84*(2), 191–215.

Barnes, C., Mercer, G. & Shakespeare, T. (1999). *Exploring disability: A sociological introduction* Cambridge: Polity.

Baxter, L., Thorne, L. & Mitchell, A. (2001). *Small voices, big noises. Lay involvement in health research; lessons from other fields*. Exeter: Washington Singer Press.

Bentall, R.P. (2004). *Madness explained: Psychosis and human nature*. London: Penguin.

Bostock, J. & Diamond, B. (2005). The value of community psychology: Critical reflections from the NHS. *Clinical Psychology Forum, 153*, 23–25.

Bostock, J. & Lavelle, M. (2007). *Working with service users to promote financial and emotional well-being*. Paper presented at the Social inclusion seminar.

Bronfenbrenner, U. (1979). *The ecology of human development: Experiments by nature and design*. Cambridge, MA: Harvard University Press.

Burton, M. (2007). *A global context for psychology*. Paper presented at the UK Community Psychology discussion group on community psychology in a global context.

Burton, M., Boyle, S., Harris, C. & Kagan, C. (2007). Community psychology in Britain. In S. Reich, I. Reimer, L. Prilleltnensky & M. Montero (Eds.) *International community psychology* (pp. 219–237). New York: Kluwer Academic Press.

Burton, M. & Kagan, C. (2005). Liberation social psychology: Learning from Latin America. *Journal of Community and Applied Social Psychology*, 15(1), 63–78.

Campbell, J. & Oliver, M. (1986). *Disability politics*. London: Routledge.

Care Services Improvement Partnership and Royal College of Psychiatrists and Social Care Institute for Excellence (2007). *A common purpose; recovery in future mental health services*. Leeds and London: Social Care Institute for Excellence.

Cooke, B. & Kothari, U. (Eds.) (2001). *Participation: The new tyranny?* London: Zed Books.

Coulter, A. (2002). *The autonomous patient: Ending paternalism in medical care*. Norwich: The Stationery Office.

Curle, C. & Mitchell, A. (2004). Hand in hand: User and carer involvement in clinical psychology training. *Clinical Psychology*, 33, 12–15.

Davey Smith, G. (Ed.) (2003). *Health inequalities*. Bristol: Policy Press.

Department of Health (1999). *National service framework for mental health*. Leeds: Author.

Department of Health (2002). *Learning from Bristol: The Department of Health's response to the Report of the Public Inquiry into children's heart surgery at the Bristol Royal Infirmary 1984–1995*. London: The Stationery Office.

Department of Health (2004). *The ten essential shared capabilities: A framework for the whole of the mental health workforce*. London: Author.

Department of Health (2006). *Expert Patients Programme*. Retrieved 28 February 2009 from www.dh.gov.uk/en/Aboutus/MinistersandDepartmentLeaders/ChiefMedicalOfficer/ProgressOnPolicy/ProgressBrowsableDocument/DH_4102757

Department of Health (2007a). *Capabilities for inclusive practice*. London: Author.

Department of Health (2007b). *Choice matters 2007–08: Putting patients in control*. London: Author.

Department of Health (2007c). *Standards for better health*. Retrieved 28 February 2009 from www.dh.gov.uk/en/publicationsandstatistics/publications/publicationspolicyandguidance/dh_4086665

Department for International Development (2005). *Reducing poverty by tackling social exclusion*. London: Author.

Freire, P. (1972). *Pedagogy of the oppressed*. Harmondsworth: Penguin.

Hagan, T. & Smail, D. (1997). Power-mapping 1. Background and basic methodology. *Journal of Community and Applied Social Psychology*, 7, 257–267.

Harper, D. & Sholl, C. (2007). *Working with young people to challenge discrimination against mental health service users: A psycho-social approach*. London: Unpublished paper presented at the British Psychological Society Social Inclusion Seminar.

Hayward, M. & Riddell, B. (2008). *Good practice guide. Service user and carer involvement within clinical psychology training*. Leicester: Division of Clinical Psychology, British Psychological Society.

Hewstone, M., Cairns, E., Voci, A., Paolini, S., McLernon, F., Crisp, R. *et al.* (2005). Intergroup contact in a divided society; challenging segregation in Northern Ireland. In D. Abrams, M.A. Hogg & J.M. Marques (Eds.) *The social psychology of inclusion and exclusion* (ch. 12, pp. 265–292). Hove: Psychology Press.

Holland, S. (1994). From social abuse to social action: A neighbourhood psychotherapy and social action project for women. In J. Ussher & P. Nicholson (Eds.) *Gender issues in clinical psychology* (ch. 3, pp. 68–77). London: Routledge.

Howard, N., Meadow, G., Meadows, S., Parcell, D., Parcell, R., Wooding, G. *et al.* (2005). Greenroots: Attempting to build a sustainable community. *Clinical Psychology Forum, 153,* 39–43.

Kagan, C. (2006). *Making a difference. Participation and well-being.* Sheffield: New Start Publishing.

Kagan, C., Castile, S. & Stewart, A. (2005). Participation: Are some more equal than others? *Clinical Psychology Forum, 153,* 30–34.

Martín-Baró, I. (1996). Towards a liberation psychology. In S. Aron & S. Corne (Eds.) *Writings for a liberation psychology* (pp. 17–32). New York: Harvard University Press.

McIver, S. (1999). Expert patients. So you think you know it all? *The Health Service Journal, 109* (5672), 22–23.

Meltzer, D., Jenkins, R. & Fryers, T. (2003). *Social inequalities and the distribution of the common mental disorders.* Hove: Psychology Press.

Miller, J. & McClelland, L. (2006). Social inequalities formulation: Mad, bad and dangerous to know. In L. Johnstone & R. Dallos (Eds.) *Formulation in psychology and psychotherapy* (ch. 6, pp. 126–153). Hove: Routledge.

Mitchell, A. & Cormack, M. (1998). *The therapeutic relationship in complementary health care.* Edinburgh: Churchill Livingstone.

Montero, M. (1996). Parallel lives: Community psychology in Latin America and the United States. *American Journal of Community Psychology, 24,* 589–606.

National Institute for Health and Clinical Excellence (2005). *A guide to NICE.* London: Author.

Newbould, J., Taylor, D. & Bury, M. (2006). Lay-led self-management in chronic illness: A review of the evidence. *Chronic Illness, 2*(4), 249–261.

Orford, J. (1992). *Community psychology theory and practice.* Chichester: Wiley.

Orford, J. (2008). *Community psychology: Challenges, controversies and emerging consensus.* Chichester: Wiley-Blackwell.

Patel, N. (2004). Difference and power in supervision: The case of culture and racism. In I. Fleming & L. Steen (Eds.) *Supervision and clinical psychology* (pp. 108–134). Hove: Brunner-Routledge.

Pilgrim, D. (1997). *Psychotherapy and society.* London: Sage.

Purtell, R., Baxter, B. & Mitchell, A. (2003). Doing research together: The Forum for Collaboration with Users in Research (Folk.us) at Exeter University. In R. Shulamit (Ed.) *Users researching health and social care: An empowering agenda?* (ch 11, pp. 133–141). Birmingham: Venture Press.

Roth, A. & Fonagy, P. (2004). *What works for whom: A critical review of psychotherapy research* (2nd edn). New York: Guilford Press.

Sayer, A. (2005). *The moral significance of class.* Cambridge: Cambridge University Press.

Seligman, M.E.P. & Csikszentmihalyi, M. (2000). Positive psychology: An introduction. *American Psychologist, 55*(1), 5–14.

Shepherd, D. (2007). *Prisoners.* Paper presented at the British Psychological Society Social Inclusion Seminar.

Smail, D. (2005). *Power, interest and psychology: Elements of a social materialist understanding of distress.* Ross-on-Wye: PCCS Books.

Social Exclusion Unit (2004). *Mental health and social exclusion* London: Office of the Deputy Prime Minister.

Sutcliffe, V. (2007). *Building capacity and capability to involve: A report from the Patient and Public Involvement Learning and Development Project.* Taunton: NHS South West.

Tajfel, H. & Turner, J.C. (1986). The social identity theory of intergroup behaviour. In S. Worchel & W. Auston (Eds.) *Psychology of intergroup relations* (pp. 7–24). Chicago: Nelson-Hall.

Taylor, D. & Bury, M. (2007). Chronic illness, expert patients and care transition. *Sociology of Health and Illness*, 29(1), 27–45.

Thorne, L. & White, C. (2005). Working together to find out about bullying of people with learning difficulties. *Clinical Psychology Forum*, 153, 35–38.

Ward, C. (2004). Critical community psychology in practice – examples from a chronic pain service. *Health Psychology Update*, 13(1), 37–39.

Wilkinson, R. (1996). *Unhealthy societies*. London: Routledge.

Wilkinson, R. (2005). *The impact of inequality*. London: Routledge.

Williams, J. & Watson, G. (1988). Sexual inequality, family life and family therapy. In E. Street & W. Dryden (Eds.) *Family therapy in Britain* (pp. 29–44). Maidenhead: Open University Press.

Woodbridge, K. & Fulford, K.W. (2004). *Whose values? A workbook for values-based practice in mental health care*. London: Sainsbury Centre for Mental Health.

Afterword

Integration, Conclusions and Future Developments

Helen Beinart, Paul Kennedy and Susan Llewelyn

This book has presented the key features that underpin the practice of clinical psychology, which we hope will make a significant contribution by describing clearly the core elements associated with the practice of our profession. In Chapter 1, we discussed the conceptual models of how people are understood and some of the key qualities of clinical psychologists, as well as providing an introduction to training, clinical services and to the book itself. Chapter 2 discusses competency-based approaches and describes both meta-competencies and specific competencies, placing technical skills firmly within an ethical values base which is both respectful and collaborative. Chapter 3 explores the scientist-practitioner model underpinning the profession and highlights the links between theory, research and professional practice, as well as examining the integration of reflective practice and the sometimes uncomfortable gap between what we need to know in practice, and current theory and research. Chapter 4 describes the importance of high quality research and evaluation and describes the range of research methods available, both qualitative and quantitative. It introduces the concept of research as a 'state of mind' and proposes that this approach is one of the unique features of the profession. Throughout these early chapters we argue the importance of each element of the profession, and rather than privileging one aspect, we believe it is the integration of all the key features – effective interpersonal skills, reflective, ethical practice, clinical competence, a sound theoretical and research base and the ability to select and apply these skills to solve clinical, theoretical or research problems – that is unique to clinical psychology.

The middle section of this book provides examples of high quality and innovative practice across the lifespan, and the chapter authors ably demonstrate the breadth and depth of clinical applications and integrative practice. The list is not meant to be exhaustive but is indicative of the quality and range of service contributions from practitioners.

The final section demonstrates some of the broader professional roles such as clinical supervision, leadership and teamwork, user-led community approaches, and organisational issues for the profession within the National Health Service (NHS). Again, all of these broader roles reflect the theory, evidence base and professional, reflective practice issues that make up the core of the profession. A virtuous cycle of best practice is created via the emphasis placed upon both the importance of personal and professional development for the practitioner and the maintenance of a personally curious stance informed by critical thinking, while simultaneously holding user issues central to the endeavour. This also includes awareness that evidence-based practice is embedded in values-based practice and that, in order to facilitate psychological change in any context, partnership and ethics are crucial.

Frequently, however, there are good reasons to use approaches that are not supported by 'best evidence', where the evidence base is currently being constructed or where there is very limited theory and evidence to guide practice. Under these circumstances, it may be most appropriate to develop a tailor-made approach and to encourage feedback in order to evaluate whether it meets a user's need, and indeed may contribute to the beginning of a new model which can then be evaluated in turn. This is an example of how practice-based evidence can lead to evidence-based practice, and requires willingness, creativity and partnership between users, practitioners, service managers and commissioners. This is also part of the growing social responsibility of the profession, as we engage with social inclusion and socio-political issues in order to find ways to support the most vulnerable in society. We also need to encourage our new and fledgling professionals to make the most of their comprehensive training, and to provide service contexts which support innovative developments in all spheres: clinical (in the broadest sense), theoretical, research and personal/professional.

Finally, this book provides a wide range of pointers to the future of clinical psychology, and the strategic direction that it should take. The innovative services described in earlier chapters are testaments to the creativity of the profession and its capacity to develop new and improved ways of responding effectively to the needs of the service users. Examples include the promotion of bibliotherapy (Chapter 18), the delivery of culturally sensitive services (Chapter 20); early intervention for people with psychosis (Chapter 17); consultancy for personality disorder services (Chapter 21); interventions for children in care (Chapter 7); therapeutic work with older people (Chapters 22 and 23); intensive interaction for severely disabled people (Chapter 15); and many more.

There is no shortage of need for clinical psychology services. What is clearly required is better articulation and promotion of what clinical psychologists can do. This will require skilled professional leadership, supported by high quality research and evidence regarding the effectiveness of psychological interventions. It will also involve careful analysis of provision in the public sector and, as always, sensitive team working with colleagues, other professional groups, service users, carers and families. For our future, we need to promote and develop partnerships between practitioners and researchers, between commissioners and service managers and finally between clinicians and service users. These partnerships need to be proactive, transparent and based on mutual respect and inclusivity, thereby characterising our profession at its best.

Index